FOURTH EDITION

Exploring Social Change

America and the World

Charles L. Harper
Creighton University

Kevin T. Leicht
The University of Iowa

Prentice
Hall

Upper Saddle River, NJ 07458

Library of Congress Cataloging-in-Publication Data

Harper, Charles L.
Exploring social change : America and the world / Charles L. Harper, Kevin T. Leicht.—4th ed.
p. cm.
Includes bibliographical references and index.
ISBN 0-13-091838-5
1. Social change. 2. Social change—United States. 3. United States—Social conditions—1945–
I. Leicht, Kevin T. II. Title
HM831 .H285   2002
303.4—dc21   2001054858

AVP, Publisher: Nancy Roberts
Senior Acquisitions Editor: Chris DeJohn
Managing Editor: Sharon Chambliss
Project Manager: Merrill Peterson
Cover Director: Jayne Conte
Cover Design: Bruce Kenselaar
Marketing Manager: Chris Barker
Prepress and Manufacturing Buyer: Mary Ann Gloriande

This book was set in 10/12 Times New Roman by NK Graphics
and was printed and bound by Maple Vail Book Manufacturing Group.
The cover was printed by Jaguar Graphics.

© 2002, 1998, 1993, 1989 Pearson Education, Inc.
Upper Saddle River, New Jersey 07458

Printed in the United States of America

10   9   8   7   6   5   4   3   2   1

ISBN   0-13-091838-5

Pearson Education LTD., London
Pearson Education Australia PTY, Limited, Sydney
Pearson Education Singapore, Pte. Ltd
Pearson Education North Asia Ltd, Hong Kong
Pearson Education Canada, Ltd., Toronto
Pearson Educación de Mexico, S.A. de C.V.
Pearson Education—Japan, Tokyo
Pearson Education Malaysia, Pte. Ltd
Pearson Education, Upper Saddle River, New Jersey

For

Robert A. Harper (1899–1986)
Alma Hagy Harper (1901–1987)
Curtis L. Leicht (1932–1967) and
Janice M. Leicht

who gave us our world,

Anne and Brenda

who make our worlds beautiful,

and

Russell, Stan, Erika, and Curtis

who will inherit our world.

Contents

Chapter 8
American Reform Movements and Social Change 151

Chapter 9
Revolutions 178

Chapter 10
Technology, Innovation, and Networks 210

Chapter 11
Creating Change 236

PART FOUR

GLOBAL CHANGE

Preface

This is a book for all those who are curious about social change. It is also about how sociologists study change. It is about the substance of social change in the United States and the contemporary world; it is also about the usefulness of sociological ideas for understanding change and methods of inquiry that have been used to understand social change. We think the topic of social change is of intrinsic interest to everyone, since its pervasive impact is felt by all and is often the cause of considerable perplexity. Sociological perspectives are uniquely suited to illuminate social change because of their holistic treatment of the different aspects of social life that other disciplines (politics, law, economics) address in a more partial way. Sociology is also a lively and contentious discipline, and we have not ignored sociological controversies or omitted complex ideas that defy oversimplification. The book requires some background, but we have tried to write a book for relative newcomers to sociology, avoiding the most arcane jargon and professional idiom for what we hope are clear language and fertile examples. It is about "big" issues, but we have tried to write in a way that engages the life experience of individuals.

The topics of the book are based on what we think is important to communicate about social change based on years of teaching and thinking about it. Others may not agree. It begins with a synoptic overview of recent change in American society. *America* here refers to the United States, and when we refer to other Western Hemispheric nations, we will use their proper names, or other terms like *North America* or *Latin America*. Middle chapters deal with selected change processes and with sociological theories of change. The later chapters are about global change processes in the modern world. A more descriptive overview of the chapter topics and organization of the book occurs at the end of Chapter 1, so we won't elaborate more here.

Writing a book involves the minds and energies of many people besides the authors. Harper would like to acknowledge his indebtedness to five teachers who have been particularly influential in his intellectual development: Ray Cuzzort, Ernest Manheim, Oscar Eggers, Jerry Cloyd, and Jack Siegman. He would also like to thank his students and colleagues at Creighton University who put up with him over the years through several editions, especially the diverse contributions of Tom Mans, Sue Crawford, and James T. Ault. Harper also thanks Barbara Braden, Dean of the Creighton University Graduate College, for her material support during the completion of the fourth edition. He also thanks professional colleagues for their support and critical feedback over the years, including Prentice Hall reviewers Gerry Cox of Black Hills State University; David Swift of the University of Hawaii; Mark Mantyh of the University of Wisconsin, Milwaukee; and Becky M. Trigg of the University of Alabama, Birmingham.

Leicht first and foremost owes an immeasurable debt of gratitude to Charles Harper for his capable guidance and friendship over the past twenty years. He also owes a great deal to James T. Ault for taking a Nebraska boy who was a little wet behind the ears and turning him into a productive member of the social science community. When he was offered the opportunity to help with the revision of this text, he jumped at the chance in part because of the experiences he had as an undergraduate at Creighton University. He sincerely hopes that this text inspires others to think critically about the world around them, whether they decide to become sociologists or not.

We owe a special debt of gratitude to the editorial staff of Prentice Hall, particularly Sharon Chambliss, the supportive and congenial "editor in charge" of the project, and Nancy Roberts, Publisher, who has been a constant source of unobtrusive encouragement and the most human face in a distant corporation.

A NOTE TO INSTRUCTORS

This is a compact but flexibly organized core text that can be used with a wide variety of supplements. Ideas are connected and developmental, but not so tightly that you can't omit some chapters or rearrange the order to fit the priorities of different courses. Here are a few suggestions for some optional ways of organizing the course.

If you want a more descriptive course about change in America and the world without much theory, you can omit entirely Parts Two and Three about theory, movements, and innovation, though you may have to decode some discussions later on. Another alternative, more consistent with comparative interests, would be to omit the American materials in Part One entirely, begin with the theory material (Parts Two and Three), skip to the material about technology and innovation (Chapter 10), and then continue through material about development, globalization, population/environment issues, and the future (Part Four). Yet another alternative is a more applied emphasis that asks students to observe change processes close up. For that, we would begin with the American materials (Part One), followed with a chapter about movements (Chapter 7), and then with material about innovation and creating change (Chapter 1)—ending with other material as you see fit. You can, of course, rearrange the sequence by having students read the theory and change process material first, but based on our teaching experience we don't recommend it. We placed material about change in America first as a means of engaging students before addressing more conceptually demanding issues about theory, models, social movements, and innovation.

We have retained the review questions at the end of each chapter to help students explore the personal implications of large-scale social change processes and to facilitate discussion.

We would like to hear about your experience with the book and about improving it.

Charles Harper
Department of Sociology and
Anthropology
Creighton University
Omaha, Nebraska 68178
charper@creighton.edu

Kevin T. Leicht
Department of Sociology
The University of Iowa
Iowa City, Iowa 52242-1401
kevin-leicht@uiowa.edu

By Way of Introduction

It is impossible to live in the world today without being bombarded with the reality and pervasiveness of change. The mass media are full of reports of new or continuing crises of grave international import in some little-known part of the world. They are also full of reports about changes in family life, health, and prospects for economic prosperity or decline. And then there are the fascinating and worrisome reports about the dazzling array of technological innovations, such as biotechnology and the computerization of everything, that have the potential to revolutionize our lives. While we live in a world that is pregnant with possibilities, it is also at times a frightening and hazardous world. The pace of change in general, and particularly the rate at which the world is becoming a single though highly disordered system, gives a kind of urgency to the notion that crisis is the ordinary state of social life. While it would be false to say social change is historically new, it is probably correct to say that people today are more likely to perceive change as the normal state of the world. Even though we are frightened and fascinated by change, we have come to expect it. Particularly in modern society, life is a journey, not a home.

We are bombarded by the big events of major world transformations, but social change is also the story of individuals and of differences between generations in families. Let me introduce the topic of social change by contrasting the personal stories about the world of Harper's father and the world of my children. I'll let Harper tell you about the lives of his parents from this description of a conversation with his father.

One day in January some years ago when my parents had come to visit, I walked into the kitchen and observed my father just standing with the refrigerator door open looking into it. When I asked him what he was doing he said, "Well, I was just thinking that we didn't have all these different kinds of food when I was growing up."

My first impulse was to think, here it comes, another story about the good/bad old days. But instead I asked him to explain. He was thinking particularly about the variety of fresh food (grapefruit, oranges, apples, lettuce, etc.) that was unavailable to him as a child, particularly in January. From that began a series of conversations in which I made a serious attempt to try to understand the world he lived in as a child.

My father was born in 1899 on a small farm in southeastern Missouri. His life, as far as I can tell, was typical of at least half of the American population at that time. Like most farmers of the late nineteenth century, he worked the family farm that was tied to a market economy. His father borrowed money from a bank to buy land, and corn and hogs were sold to make payment to the bank and to purchase seed for next year's crop. But to me the most striking thing about his early life was the extent to which the family farm was a *subsistence* operation and not a money household economy. The family lived—almost literally—on what they could grow, produce, and store. His diet (to return to how I got into this) was mainly what could be made from corn, wheat, and salt pork. At the right time of the year there were fresh vegetables from the garden (some of which were canned for the winter), and in the fall there were a few apples from the tree. They did buy some household goods: kerosene for lamps, cloth, overalls and shoes (one pair a year), coffee, and sugar. There were "special" purchases from the mail order catalogue. Much of the money for these extras came from what his mother could produce in the vegetable garden and sell to the town grocer.

As you can see, his mother made a substantial contribution to the household economy, as did each child, as he or she was old enough to help with the variety of farm and household chores. But though the family was a cooperative affair, his father was the unquestioned dictator of the family. Women and children in those times had no legal rights whatsoever, and only such privileges as were granted by the male head of the household. As in most American families of the time, patriarchy ruled supreme.

The social life of my father's family may seem dull by today's standards. It centered mainly around visiting with the neighbors, going to the country church—"when the weather was good"—and a trip into town on Saturday (an all-day trip). Even though each farm was privately owned and managed, it was embedded in a community life that was strikingly different from that most of us experience today. During planting and harvest times the neighbors gathered in rotation at each other's farms to cooperatively share the labor. Women spent all day cooking for a grand feast after the day's labor. My father described these as exciting social events in an otherwise routine existence.

As a teenager—the term was not used then—my father was interested in the opposite sex (some things *don't* change!). Formal contacts between young men and women were different then. They did not date, but courted. Courtship was understood as a prelude to possible marriage and was under the strict control of parents. At one time my father said that he was courting two different girls, whereupon his mother sat him down and told him to "get serious and quit foolin' around." "Foolin' around" applied to seriousness of intent, not—as it would today—to premarital sexuality, which was strictly taboo in any case.

There were five children born into the family. One died during childbirth, one died as a teenager from tuberculosis, and one survived into adulthood as an invalid with what was called "spastic paralysis"—probably what today would be called polio. Only my father and a sister survived to become fully functional adults. This survival rate was not at all unusual for the time.

The thing that distinguished my father and his sister from their peers was that they finished high school (in 1910 only about one out of ten people did). Not only did they finish high school, they both borrowed money from a bank and went to the regional teacher's college and were certified to teach. When I asked my father why he went into teaching (I expected an inspiring answer), he said that he had decided that there must be a better way to make a living than "walking behind a plow and the ass end of two mules" and that becoming a teacher was one of the only things you could do without having some money to start with. His first job was as the teacher in a nearby one-room country schoolhouse. Thus, he left the family farm in his early twenties and entered a very different world, one that was being born in the twentieth century. It was a world not of self-sufficient farms, but of cities, automobiles, salaries, and bureaucratic organizations. Today he remembers the farm life as a hard one, but, like most older people, he is nostalgic about the lost world of his youth.

The world of my own children is very different, so different that there are few dimensions of it that Harper's father would recognize. My children have lived their entire lives in college towns, surrounded by well-educated people from all over the world. They take it for granted that everyone goes to college and don't understand why anyone would think of doing anything else.

Because of improvements in diet and health care, their physical survival was never in question as it was for Harper's father and his four siblings. Instead, because of the sheer volume of information they are bombarded with from all around the world, they know that some kids like them don't get enough to eat, others are victims of war and plagues, and adults in their own society get cancer and AIDS. Their general awareness of how other people live and how good they have it is far greater than that of children from prior generations.

The household they live in is embedded in a wired, electronic, credit-based economy. Unlike Harper's father, all my children's material needs are purchased in local stores or (increasingly) online through Internet shopping services. These products are produced in remote parts of the world and delivered to suppliers using "just-in-time" delivery systems that instantly respond to changes in demand and supply. These consumer items are purchased with credit and bank debit cards and rarely (if ever) with cash. It is only recently that my children (ages 6 and 10) have discovered that there is any connection between credit cards and actual U.S. currency—that "old fashioned" way of buying things that uses piles of paper with pictures of buildings and politicians on it! The food they consume is grown all over the world, is available during all seasons of the year, and much of it has been genetically altered so that it has no recognizable connection to its plant and animal ancestors in the wild. While Harper's father was able to observe his parents working on their farm and could see the significance of their work (because it showed up on the dinner table), my children's parents (both of us) work for pay in large organizations remote from their everyday lives. Our children only have a vague idea of what we do for a living. Even our paychecks are electronically deposited each month in a bank account in our name.

The social life and entertainments available to them were unimaginable even a generation ago. Both of my children have traveled to distant parts of the United States (from Iowa City, Iowa), and my 10-year-old daughter has traveled overseas. They take cable TV, Pokemon, Sailor Moon, Dragonball Z, PCs and the Internet completely for granted. They spend a good deal of time with peers and relatively little time with their parents. My daughter already talks of boys and knows about what used to be called the "facts of life," something which Harper's father was not exposed to until his teen years (at the earliest).

The family life of my children is starkly different as well. We parents have a lot of influence, but there is much more negotiating between them and their parents about rights, duties, and privileges. Many of their friends' parents are divorced or never married, and we parents make decisions in collaboration with each other and our children rather than in the dictatorial style of the patriarchal past. Marriage, for them, is certainly an option, but it is a distant one and it is certainly not a requirement for taking their place in the adult world.

When my children decide to strike out on their own (a decision that is being postponed until later and later in life), they will face a bewildering and uncertain set of career choices. In fact, the entire concept of a career may not exist. At some point, they will have to contend with the structure of the economy and the job market. They will have to contend with an economy that is not, in fact, open ended.

This is briefly the story of change in the lives of two generations of our families. Their story is not representative of change in the lives of all American families. You might find it interesting to compare their story with stories about change between generations in your own family. Imagine a far-fetched situation. Suppose you are an investigator from another planet researching human life on earth and have just read the story of change in the two generations of our families. You might say: "Well—you have told me about the life of Harper's father and your children and how they are different. But how did they get to be so different?"

Our answer would be: "To understand why the lives of individuals change as they do, you must understand some things about the broad patterns of social change, such as changes in the economy, in urbanization, and technological change which shape individual and family life in various ways." In other words, it is always interesting and often easier for us to think about how our individual lives are changing, but to understand more fully how and why this is happening you need to understand the patterns and forces of change in the social worlds of individuals and families. And sociology has a powerful set of ideas to interpret and comprehend these forces and patterns. *That is what this book is about.*

WHAT IS SOCIAL CHANGE?

For both practical reasons and intellectual curiosity, people have always been fascinated and agitated by the problem of understanding permanence and change. Among the ancient Greek philosophers, Heraclitus of Ephesus argued that the world was a process in constant flux and development, while his counterpart, Parmenedes of Elea, maintained that the world was an indestructible, motionless continuum of matter and space and that change is illusory. This ancient polarization of thought is also found in sociological thinking. We won't spend more time here with this abstract controversy but will only argue that we should not deny the reality of either general processes of stability or change. Both are real, and we recognize one in relation to the other. To deny the reality of either persistence or change doesn't recognize the way people experience the world.

Here is a working definition: *Social change is the significant alteration of social structure and cultural patterns through time.* That's very abstract and begs at least three other questions: What is significant? What is social structure? And what is culture? Significance, we admit, is largely in the eye of the beholder. When you assert that "nothing important has really changed" or that "things have drastically changed," those are judgments about significance. Both in everyday life and social science we make judgments about what is significant and what is trivial, but people with different outlooks can honestly disagree about them. At its root the notion of *social structure* means a persistent network of social relationships in which interaction between persons or groups has become routine and repetitive. At increasingly abstract levels, social structure can be understood as persistent social roles, groups, organizations, institutions, and societies.

But if you were to study only social structure, you would miss important *cultural* aspects of change in our social life. The distinction between social structure and culture is a most basic distinction in social science. It is a conceptual and somewhat artificial distinction, but it is an important and convenient way of focusing on different aspects of social life. If social structure is the network of relationships in which people are embedded, *culture* is the "social software" that people share that provides meaning to social life. Unlike social structure, culture is hard to define in a short abstract way. It is the shared way of living and thinking that includes symbols and language (both verbal and nonverbal), knowledge, beliefs, and values (what is "good" and "bad"), norms (how people are expected to behave), and techniques ranging from common folk recipes to sophisticated technologies and material culture.

The important point is that grasping the whole picture of social change requires that we understand important structural changes (for example, changes in the composition of the population and households, in the size and complexity of organizations, in the economy) and how they are connected to changes in culture (for example, changing definitions, values, problems, fears, hopes, and dreams that people share).

Some Beginning Clarifications

That's a pretty abstract discussion of a complex process. Here we want to raise six issues to begin sorting out of parts of the process and to preview some of the things we will discuss in more depth in later chapters. These have to do with different (1) types of change, (2) levels of change, (3) time frames of change, (4) causes of change, (5) relationships of change to human intentions, and (6) some terms often associated with change.

Kinds of Change.   It is important to note that even the words *change* or *alteration* can mean that there are concretely different things going on. Consider, for example, at least five different ways that structures can be altered. First, there are (1) *changes in personnel,* in which new people with different life histories and experiences are continually entering and leaving established structures. Second, there are (2) *changes in the way parts of structures relate.* These include changed role relationships—such as differences in family roles that we mentioned in our personal stories. On different levels the growing complexity of society and the growing specialization of occupations in the economy are other changes in the way that the parts of structures relate. We will discuss these kinds of change in the next two chapters. Third, there are (3) *changes in the functions of structures,* that is, changes in what they do for society and how they operate. For example, in contemporary America many churches not only serve to promote religious belief, but also function as family counseling and social service agencies, and sometimes as advocates of political change. For example, both fundamentalist Protestant churches and the American Conference of Roman Catholic Bishops have come to function more openly as advocates of political change (in such areas as the legality of prayer in public schools or abortion). Fourth, there are (4) *changes in the relationships between different structures.* For example, since the 1890s American labor-management relations have evolved from what were often uncivil and violent confrontations in the nineteenth century to today's ritualistic and highly structured negotiations. Chapter 3 more broadly examines the changing connections between the American economic and political systems. Fifth, there (6) is *the emergence of new structures.* For instance, there is evidence that a global system of economic, cultural, and political interactions is emerging. This system is putting new constraints on nation-states and their populations. We will discuss this topic in Chapter 11.

Levels of Change.   To avoid confusion, we should try to be clear about exactly what is changing, or the levels within which change takes place. The study of change can focus on aggregate individual characteristics, such as changes in attitudes and demographic characteristics such as age or sex. It can focus on the different aspects of culture mentioned previously. It can focus on changes in structural units from small systems to large, inclusive ones.

STRUCTURAL LEVEL	CHANGES
Small group	in roles, communications structure, influence, cliques
Organizations	in structure, hierarchy, authority, productivity
Institutions	in economy, religion, family, education
Society	in stratification, demography, power
Global	in evolution, international relationships, modernization, development, and transnational organizations

It is easier for you perceive change in small-scale or micro levels that involve the people and groups in your immediate face-to-face surroundings. Yet it is also true that what happens to you is shaped by what goes on in the large-scale or macro levels of society. These include those abstract and somewhat ghostly realms of the larger society such as the economic, political, or educational systems that do affect you but as whole systems probably seem pretty remote from your everyday concerns, problems, and consciousness. We think an important contribution of a sociological view of change is to enhance your awareness of those changing macro contexts and how your life is connected to them.

Macrolevel social change even affects some of our most personal decisions in life (see Figure 1-1). For example, demographers and sociologists have documented changes in birth rates as societies become urbanized and people move to cities. Urbanization leads to a general decline in birth rates as part of a broader "demographic transition" (Harris and Ross, 1997).

Why would this change an individual's decision to get married and have children? The change from rural to urban societies leads to changes in adult roles. People who once supported themselves in agricultural and pastoral activities in subsistence-based economies begin to seek employment in cities where they purchase many of the things they consume. Children in families go from being additional laborers who add to the productivity of family production and a social security system for elderly parents to additional consumers who don't assume productive roles until they leave the household as adults.

At the societal level this change usually doesn't happen quickly and there are numerous bumps in the transition and unique cultural accommodations to the new pressures of an urbanized society. But such changes almost always change relationships between men and women that in turn change marriage patterns and the relative

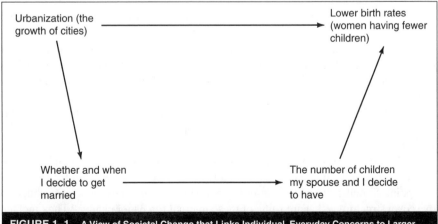

FIGURE 1–1   A View of Societal Change that Links Individual, Everyday Concerns to Larger Societal Trends, Using Childbirth as an Example.
Source: Adapted from James S. Coleman, 1990. Foundations of Social Theory, pgs. 8–10. Harvard University Press.

number of children that married couples believe are desirable. In this way, some of the most intimate decisions we make as adults are affected by large-scale, macro-level social change.

Time Frames of Change.   Short-term changes in our lives are often obvious, but longer-term changes may be more significant, if harder to perceive. Focusing only on short-term changes is also deceptive. Some repetitive changes operate in the short term, such as yearly business cycles and family developmental stages, that may not involve much change at all from the standpoint of the longer time span. To continue with our family example, individuals may experience dramatic and often traumatic change as they go from being newlyweds to having young children, to a family with teenagers, to an "empty nest" family after the children have left. But these short-term changes that are obvious and important for particular families do not *necessarily* signify any long-term change in American family patterns. American family patterns *are* changing, but our personal experience is not a very good gauge of that. To some extent, whether you focus on the long-term or the short-term changes depends on our interest. It is legitimate to focus on short-term change, but you need to be aware that this is often embedded in long-term change. The distinction between long- and short-term change will be particularly important when we discuss causes and patterns of change (Chapter 5).

Causes of Change.   We want to raise three issues here, even though Chapters 5 and 6 discuss the causes of change in more depth. Distinguishing between causes and consequence of change is important for both scholarly and practical reasons, but it is not always easy. In the social sciences, "causes" are always inferences, not things that are self-evident from any given set of observations. Furthermore, whether we treat something as a cause or a consequence is often arbitrary and a matter of our interest. If there is a causal sequence between A——B——C, then B is both a consequence of A and a cause of C.

There is an important distinction between external (exogenous) and internal (endogenous) causes of change. This is a conceptual and somewhat artificial distinction. But it is an important working distinction to be able to locate different sources of change. External changes result from bringing in things from the outside, such as new technologies, ideas, styles, diseases, and so on. All social systems are in the final analysis open systems, subject to the penetration of new elements from other systems, though some are much more open than others. Historically, traders, immigrants, and occupying armies have been important carriers of change between societies.

But even if a society or group could be perfectly insulated from external influences, there still would be change from internal sources. This is a subtle but important point. Social systems are not only open systems, they also generate change in their own structure. What are some of these internal forces for change? They include (1) *the inevitable gap between shared ideals and actual practices,* (2) *individual differences and uncertainties* in the socialization process (how and what individuals learn about the social world), and (3) *flexibilities and variations* in the way social roles are defined and enacted (Moore, 1974:12–22). Undoubtedly there are others, such as (4) the *competition for control of power and scarce resources* that exists within any social system. An internal source of change in American society, for instance, is our abstract commitment to equality and nondiscrimination and the pervasive institutional practices that result in race, class, and gender discrimination (a kind of gap between shared ideals and actual practices). In later chapters the discussion of social movements will focus on changes generated within society, while our examination of the spread of innovations and the global system focus on both internal and externally produced change.

Change and Human Intentions.　*First* are large-scale *trends* that are *unintentional*—meaning that nobody is trying to bring them about. Examples of these include shifts in the birth and death rates, urbanization, or the growth of the proportion of nonfamily households. *Second* are those changes that are *intentional and planned,* such as changes in laws, the development and spread of new technologies, and changes in government policies that are deliberately induced by legislators and planners of all sorts. Such changes are driven by *human agency. Third* are those changes that are *intentionally sought by broad groups* within a population but are not planned (in the bureaucratic sense) by elites. This is the domain of social movements, where large and diverse collections of people engage in collective action to promote or oppose change as it relates to their interests (the environmental movement is a contemporary example). The plans of elites and bureaucratic administrators are sometimes preceded by the pressure of popular movements, but this is not always so. In sum, there are three broad varieties of change in relation to human agency: trends, intentional and planned changes that relate to an elite decision-making process, and intentional changes that relate to social movements that involve broad segments of the population. Chapters 2 and 3 deal with trends; Chapters 7, 8, and 9 with social movements; and Chapter 11 discusses the planning of change.

Change and Other Terms.　*Change* is a broad, generic, and neutral term, whereas the terms *process, progress, evolution,* and *development* have more specific meanings. Any aspect of human behavior can be seen as a *process,* which focuses our attention on the active and dynamic aspect of behavior (The byproduct of repeated processes is *structure*). But there are behavioral processes that maintain stability as well as processes of change. Change is a process, but not all processes are change. *Progress* implies qualitative improvement: Things get better. The notion of progress is inherently value laden (better according to whom?). It is an important human normative concept, but not a scientific one. We can argue about whether particular changes represent progress or not. Finally there are the notions of *evolution* and *development* as kinds of change. For a long time social scientists described evolution as a "more or less orderly progression from a simple to a more complex social entity" (Vago, 1980:5), but more sociological views describe it as the emergence of social novelty and its selection, reproduction, and transmission—a definition closer to the biological meaning of evolution (see Chapter 5). Sometimes change is described as development. You can talk about *developmental change* in both individuals and organizations, but here we will use it to describe the social, economic, and political change in the developing nations. *Modernization* is a rough synonym for development, but we will distinguish between those ideas in Chapter 12.

SOCIOLOGY AND SOCIAL CHANGE

Sociology began in the late nineteenth century as an attempt to understand the emergence of the modern world. The earliest sociological thinkers—August Comte, Herbert Spencer, Karl Marx, Emile Durkheim, and Max Weber—all tried to understand the human implications of two great transformations that produced the modern world: urbanization and industrialization. Although they did not share a common view of these transformations, what they did share was the vision that the study of human societies and change could be understood in a general way, rather than only as the accumulation of the accidents of history. They were fascinated by the idea that the study of society and change could be done scientifically, although then—as now—there was not complete agreement about exactly what this means.

Sociology is certainly not the only intellectual discipline that is concerned with change. Political scientists and economists are also concerned with understanding change in specific spheres of human life. By contrast, sociologists, and perhaps anthropologists, are more concerned with understanding change in human life and societies in a more global and holistic manner. Historians are also vitally concerned with the study of change, which is the "stuff" of history. Historians have many differences in interests, methods, and focus. But compared with sociologists, historians are more likely to be interested in particular events, persons, and occurrences. As sociologist Wilbert Moore has said, "although we cannot meet the challenge of history, if by that we mean accounting for unique events, we must attempt to *identify recurrent combinations of antecedents and consequences*" (1974:73). The interests of sociologists and historians in understanding change are different but complementary in many ways. Sociologists are more likely to search for general and recurring patterns in change processes. In sum, sociologists have a distinctive interest in studying change because of a commitment to holism and scientific methods. *Scientific methods* merely mean that they are more likely to seek generalizations governing the operation of social change, and to examine those generalizations by the best evidence possible.

WHAT YOU CAN EXPECT FROM THIS BOOK
AND HOW IT IS ORGANIZED

Many writers put information like this in the preface to a book, but since some readers are likely to skip lightly over a preface, we decided to put this material here, because it is important that you get an idea of what kind of book you are going to be reading as well as a preview of its contents.

Since change is everywhere, a book about change could be about anything and everything. Studying change is like viewing a scene: it can be done from different distances, altitudes, and angles. With the mindboggling diversity of possible topics and approaches, any single book about social change is necessarily selective. This book is titled *Exploring Social Change* to indicate that it explores selected aspects of change and does not pretend to be a comprehensive treatment of change in all its possible manifestations. Others would have written the book differently or emphasized different things. It is about social change in a general way, and each topic could be examined in much more detail and depth than we can devote here. While each part of the book can be read separately, we have tried to show connections among the main topics in the book, which treat change from different altitudes and angles. It is not a book written around a single theme or idea, and you should be aware that the subject will not all come together at the end in a neat, tidy picture. Social reality is too complex and complicated for that. What you can expect from this book is a number of useful ways to understand change processes in the social world.

The first part of the book (Chapters 2–4) explores change in the United States since about the end of World War II. The second part (Chapters 5 and 6) deals with more theoretical issues—causes and patterns of change, what change looks like from three dominant sociological perspectives (functionalist, conflict, and interpretive), and more recent thinking about the relationship between agency and structure in the change process. The third part (Chapters 8–11) examines selected topics that have received particular attention by sociologists and other social scientists: (1) social movements and revolutions; (2) technology, innovation, and social networks; and (3) the applied literature about planning and organizing for change. The fourth part (Chapters 12–15) examines change at global or international levels—development and the emerging global system, population and environmental issues—and ends with some important questions about world futures. The last part (the Epilogue) returns to the intensely personal level where this chapter began. It contains our reflections about how individuals do and should live in an uncertain and rapidly changing world.

There are two other things we think you need to know about the book. We have tried to write an objective, scientific book about how social scientists analyze and understand social change. But it is also a book that exhibits our own values, hopes, and fears about the human condition. It is impossible (and probably undesirable) to eliminate one's own opinions and values from scholarly work. But they should be labeled as such, so we have put "We think . . ." statements in front of those places where we are aware that not all would agree with what we've said. The other thing should be obvious to you by now. The book is written in an informal and (hopefully) unpretentious style. We tried to write as if we were carrying on an imaginary personal conversation with you as an individual rather than as if we were communicating with an anonymous mass. It is the way we like to communicate, and we hope it makes the book more engaging for you to read.

THINKING PERSONALLY ABOUT SOCIAL CHANGE

We often don't see the personal events in everyday life as connected to broad forces in the larger society and culture. We began this chapter in a very personal way, by describing the everyday life worlds of fathers and children, which made quite a contrast. We said a few things, but not much, about the connections between their life worlds and the larger (macro) forces in society. We think it is important that you try to make those micro-macro connections. The ability to see the impact of broader forces on our personal lives is what C. Wright Mills (1959) called the sociological imagination. He argued that no matter how unique and personal we think our experiences are, at some level they are shaped by macro-level forces. Mills did not mean to imply that the sociological imagination should debilitate you by causing you to fatalistically view your life as wholly controlled by large-scale forces. But an awareness of the forces that impinge on you is the first step to real autonomy and freedom. Without such an awareness we fall into a trap of indifference toward both society and each other (Newman, 1995:9). The sociological imagination allows us to see that addressing the problems of our times means not only changing ourselves, but also working to change social institutions and the roles available to us. In other words, an important agenda of sociology is to help people understand the intersection between personal biographies and the forces of societal change.

To facilitate that understanding, we follow each chapter with some questions to engage you in thinking personally about large-scale change, and, where possible, to help you see micro-macro connections. These are not review questions in the ordinary sense (you can make your own), but rather open-ended leading questions. They ask you to find connections between your own experience and biography and the text material dealing with large-scale change (or those of some acquaintances or your family). *Warning:* This is not always easy to do, but it should get easier as you go along. The questions also get shorter after later chapters, and not because we got tired (in contrast, later chapters are longer).

QUESTIONS

1. Make sure you understand the different levels on which change happens. Now think about how your life is embedded in these different levels, and make a list of some significant changes that you think are now occurring at each level.

2. The text distinguishes between changes driven by deep structural forces, and changes driven by alterations in the rules of the game. Can you think of some examples of each type that impact your life (or the lives of others whom you know). Do you think the consequences of these changes are positive or negative? This is not a scientific question, but it is an important human one!

3. Take some recent significant social event (take your pick: the coming of the European Union, the Timothy McVeigh execution, the Columbine High School shootings, terrorists blowing up buildings, responses to natural disasters like hurricanes, floods, or droughts). Describe how you think a biographer, an historian, and a social scientist would each describe the causes and consequences of the event. Briefly, did the event have any noticeable effects you can observe in your city or community?

CHAPTER

2

American Social Trends

You can think about social change in three ways. *First,* change can be *significant social events,* such as World War II, the assassination of President Kennedy, the suicide attacks on the World Trade Center and the Pentagon, the Oklahoma City bombing, the Persian Gulf War, or the breakup of the Soviet empire. Each of these events had an impact on change in contemporary America. *Second,* change can be *macroscopic,* or broad-scale *social trends* and cultural themes. These pervasive change processes enable you to see patterns and make more general sense out of particular historical events by revealing "underlying" patterns and directions. *Third,* change can occur in the spheres of social life that are closely connected to the lives of individuals, such as age groups, families, work settings, education, religion, and so on. In other words, this third perspective focuses on change in the *population* and *social institutions.*

Each of these perspectives on change has strengths and weaknesses. A focus on particular events is important but may suggest that social change is only the accumulation of particular events with no patterns or broader processes. Understanding large-scale social trends is important, but these trends by themselves tell you little about particular events or the everyday life encounters between individuals and social change. A focus on particular social institutions as settings for everyday life may do that, but in artificially separated "parts" that may not illuminate much about how you experience change as a whole person. A better focus would try to show the interconnections among events, broad social trends, and changing institutional settings for everyday life.

In this and the next two chapters, we describe change in American society using all these vantage points (events, trends, institutional settings). We begin with broad structural and cultural American trends. The next chapter moves to three settings closer to the everyday life of individuals—change in population, families, and jobs. Our purpose is descriptive, but we have also used these chapters to highlight some controversies—both academic and popular—about changing life in a modern or "postmodern" society—a term we will define later. Chapter 4 continues by examining change in two large-scale institutional realms that together shape much of what goes on in society as well as the lives of individuals: economics and politics. We end that chapter with a brief but important discussion of the implications of recent change for the American quality of life, problems, and future prospects. Our focus in this part of the book is primarily on the United States, but we will mention connections between the United States and other nations, because you can't really understand change in one nation without considering its international connections. The book turns in more depth to international levels of change in later chapters.

   A word about the time frame: We focus mainly on the recent past (from roughly 1950 to the present) because we wanted to emphasize a time period that would be familiar to you. But many of these changes—particularly the structural trends—are not unique to American society and have been taking place in many societies at least since the 1600s. You can see them as the most recent and peculiarly American manifestations of the social processes that have been a part of the emergence of contemporary urban industrial societies. We should warn you that as we come close to the present, the data about change become less clear-cut and its meaning more controversial.

STRUCTURAL TRENDS

Structural trends have to do with changes in our relationships with other people in society and in the organizations and communities in which we participate. *One trend is the growth in scale of social life.* This means that people's lives are increasingly connected with larger numbers of people in big structures, such as communities and organizations, that operate in a vast scale over large geographic areas. You can get a sense of this by comparing your life with the early life of your parents or grandparents. You probably live in a larger community, shop in larger stores for things provided by larger companies, attend larger schools, and visit or vacation over larger geographic areas than they did as young adults. Your life is certainly more regulated by a huge national government. You still live in the "small worlds" of friends and family, of course, but increasingly you have connections, direct and indirect, with anonymous people working in large organizations very distant from you.

   To illustrate, consider what you are doing right now. We wrote what you are reading in Iowa and Nebraska, but it was manufactured and sold by a publishing company located in New Jersey (Prentice Hall), which is owned by a large multimedia company based in London that publishes educational books, fiction, bestsellers, and the *Financial Times* newspaper (Pearson). In your grandparents' world most book companies were small independent publishers. This is but one example of the general growth in scale of our economic life. The growth in scale of social life can also be seen in the process of *urbanization.* Around 1900, about half of America lived in scattered small towns and rural areas. Now at least 70 percent of the population is concentrated in a handful of large urban areas that dominate the social, political, and economic life of the nation. *Increasing scale means the existence and sometimes the absorption of small social systems within enormous larger ones.*

A second closely related trend is the *centralization of control* (or power and authority, if you wish).[1] Growth in size inevitably means the growing concentration of power to make important decisions in the hands of fewer people. You do have the freedom to make choices, but increasingly those choices are limited by the huge organizations that dominate our economic, political and social life. They are not all-powerful, but our options about what to buy, where to work, what to do with our garbage and how we relate to our neighbors, raise children, spend our leisure time, and get health care are increasingly controlled by large organizations remote from our everyday lives. As our example of the Prentice-Hall book-publishing company shows, the webs of organizations that control our lives are by no means easy to comprehend. "Large" no longer means that tens of thousands of employees work for highly visible companies in major cities in large office buildings. In many cases economic power is divorced from numbers of employees and fancy offices.

These trends have meant a growing participation in a common way of life in mass markets, mass media, and a mass electorate but a third trend related to these two is the *increasing differentiation and specialization in social life.* For example, we have not only the mass media, which assumes an undifferentiated "mass" of information consumers, but also highly specialized media, which target people with highly specialized and exotic tastes or interests. Consider, from the time that the printed matter available to most Americans was a local newspaper, a farmer's almanac, and perhaps a Sears catalogue, the range of publications now available at the local urban bookstore or newsstand: publications for sky divers, joggers, weight lifters, vegetarians, occult religionists, survivalists, soldiers of fortune, and gourmet cooks as well as for those with an impressive variety of sexual appetites. Indeed, the variety of tastes and interests addressed by the highly specialized media is endless. The same argument can be made about the availability of highly differentiated social, religious, and recreational groups catering to specialized interests. You can also see this increasing differentiation in the realm of occupations. Where there used to be doctors, teachers, and engineers, now, increasingly, you have to know what kind of doctor, teacher, or engineer you are talking about.

Differentiation has meant that more social roles in everyday life are segmented and limited in scope: There are fewer more general, diffuse, and multifaceted roles. Perhaps such roles remain mainly in the realms of friendship, the family, and household do-it-yourselfers. Indeed, the joint trends of growth in scale and increasing differentiation probably mean that as persons we occupy increasingly narrow niches in an ever larger and more complex social system. Such differentiation (or *demassification*) of the media picked up velocity in the 1970s with different magazines, CD-ROMS, and cable television channels, all of which means that when people do meet face to face they may have less and less in common to talk about (Willis, 1995:22).

A fourth trend is the *growing interconnectedness and networked nature of social life.* The importance of networks and webs of interactions has only become apparent since the middle of the 1980s. For much of the postwar era (1950 to 1980 or so), social life was dominated by bureaucracies. A *bureaucratic organization* is a social system with a formal structure, clear lines of authority, and work roles that are designed for special purposes. Most people don't like bureaucracies because they don't recognize our individuality and treat us as numbers with cold, calculating efficiency. Yet this uncaring efficiency is precisely why they developed.

Many human interactions in modern life are still governed by bureaucracies. This is obvious if we compare the one-room schoolhouse from Harper's parents' era with a large suburban high school, where students and subjects are separated into different categories and everyone's behavior, including the teacher's, is regulated.

But since the 1980s, an interesting countertrend has emerged, a trend identified by the term *network society* (Castells, 1996). Because of the Internet, cell phones, pagers, overnight package delivery, and standardized (and relatively cheap) computer software, social life increasingly is governed by webs of interaction that do not fit the description of a traditional bureaucracy. In place of a pyramid structure, narrowly defined roles, and extensive lines of authority running from the bottom of the organization to the top, decisions are made by teams of participants who collaborate on specific projects, often never meeting face to face, in environments where there are no clear "bosses" or "leaders." The networking tools available allow for instant feedback on tasks performed in distant places around the world and also allow for extensive and direct surveillance of these activities.

Bureaucracies were created to deal with massive amounts of information and to take into account our relatively limited ability to store and use information. The hierarchy and specialized roles of bureaucratic organizations were designed to make sure that certain information was acted on immediately at the local level and that certain types of information were filtered upward to higher layers of the bureaucracy for action. The tools available in the network society automate many of these functions and eliminate many of the middle management jobs that were the staple of middle-class life. This leads us to a discussion of our next structural trend.

A fifth trend related to growth, diversity, and interconnectedness is the *increase in technical complexity and sophistication.* Technology is cultural in that it includes formulas for doing things related to manipulating our environment. But you can also view technology as the products of those formulas that in themselves are important and changing structural components of the environments in which we live, work, and communicate. That technology has become more complex and sophisticated needs no elaborate documentation; it is a part of the everyday life experience of most people. Consider American middle-class households—full of marvelous gadgets that may regulate temperature and humidity, wash and dry dishes and clothes, cook your food in minutes and tell you when it's done, inform you by satellite newscast live from around the world, or warn you when burglars are about. They are "smart" devices that are efficient and productive until they break down, at which point we recognize how little we understand how such devices work—and then we call for "experts" to fix them. These experts are themselves specialized: Some fix stoves, others TVs, and others only refrigerators or air conditioners.

Technological change has produced an increasing ability to convert environmental resources into a usable form, whether in terms of agricultural production, in industry, or in the production of energy. It means a growth in economic productive capacity. It means increasing control over the environment and an enhanced ability to store and control information. This is particularly evident in the advent of computers, which increasingly form the information matrix of society. The enhanced ability to move information and money (capital) around the world by electronic means has promoted economic integration of the nations of the world into a world market economy. For better or worse, Americans are no longer affected only by economic decisions made in New York and Chicago, but also by those made in Tokyo, Zurich, and Frankfurt.

But the true efficiency of modern technology is a complex and debatable issue. Discussions of the efficiency and cost effectiveness of advanced technology typically ignore some very real costs and consequences (which economists conveniently term "externalities"). This is particularly true when efficiency is defined in cost-accounting terms that do not include its larger economic, ecological, and social costs. American agriculture, for instance, is marvelously efficient in terms of per-acre yield. But if you factor in the costs of diesel fuel, fertilizer, pesticides, water, food processing, and transportation, it requires more than 9 calories of energy input to deliver 1 calorie of beef to your table, and even this figure doesn't include the long-term costs of overgrazing fragile land or the health consequences of diets too rich in saturated fats (Worldwatch Institute, 1994:39).

Consider another example: A nuclear power plant can produce a vast volume of kilowatt hours of energy. But it is not nearly as cost efficient when you consider the costs of the years of planning, regulation, and construction of plants as well as the costs of the disposal of nuclear wastes—not to mention the human, economic, and environmental carnage that happened at Chernobyl in the former Soviet Union (the United States has had a number of near misses; Lenssen and Flavin, 1996). Beyond hidden economic costs, an obvious long-range problem with complex technology is its ecological impact. Technical efficiency has given us increased productivity but also a decrease in the soil fertility in many areas, industrial pollution, acid rain, and the destruction or near destruction of many biological and natural resources.

In addition to hidden inefficiencies, modern social life requires that we manage risks (Giddens, 1990; Beck, 1992). More of the world's peoples think about risks associated with modern social life. On one hand, certain dimensions of social life have become less risky; the statistics in this book point to longer life expectancy, more consumer choices, better and longer educations, and safer transportation, just to name a few. But our modern society creates new risks that were unimaginable in earlier times—nuclear and environmental disaster, engineering failures, natural disasters aggravated by human design failures, terrorism, new forms of crime, and new (and frightening) possibilities for social control. The collective management of these risks occupies a good deal of our time and energy whether we realize it or not (witness the growing employment and technological investments that go into providing security at airports, metal detectors, security personnel, dogs that can sniff explosives and drugs, etc.).

The technologies at our disposal (especially cable TV and the Internet) give the world's difficulties an immediacy that would have been unimaginable to either of your authors as they were growing up in the 1950s and 1970s. For many people, this information and the potential to act on it are a form of liberation. Other observers are concerned that our personal worlds are suffering from "technological overkill" and that we are literally "over our heads" with information, choices, and decisions that intrude on our everyday lives (Kegan, 1994). Our technological sophistication (for good or ill) has put us in contact with the immediate lives of others in distant parts of the world in ways that would have been unthinkable to your parents (and to us!).

None of these ideas about basic structural trends are really new, except maybe some examples in the American context. In fact, classic sociological thinkers around the turn of the twentieth century were concerned with them, and we need to give them credit. Emile Durkheim (1893/1947) wrote extensively about the consequences of the "division of labor" (differentiation and specialization) in urban industrial societies, and Max Weber (1921) wrote about the process of bureaucratization and its problems. Ironically, as social critics of their times, they were concerned that such trends would erode local culture and differences to produce a faceless "mass" of people with no local roots or traditions. But today we think social critics worry more about excessive individuality, fragmentation of consciousness, and the fragmentation of culture as the basis for civility (Bellah et al., 1985; Willis, 1995).

We think the important structural questions about social trends are not whether diversity continues to exist (it does), or whether informal ties and roots continue (they do), but rather whether the informal and traditional lives of Americans are integrated in any meaningful way with the larger structures of the society or whether the power and initiative to shape the character of social life has passed decisively into the realm of distant, large-scale organizations. Coleman (1982) has termed contemporary America an "asymmetrical society" in which individuals become less and less able to give direction to their lives, as "corporate actors" increasingly gather resources and power which they devote to their own "care and feeding."

CHANGING CULTURAL THEMES

You can't really understand structural change without considering culture as well. The distinction between structure and culture is important but difficult, since it is only a useful way to look at things, and every structural trend has important cultural dimensions or themes. *Cultural themes* (patterns of social attitudes, values, and beliefs) are more arguable than structural trends, since they are more subjective, variable, and unevenly shared among parts of the population. Whether you think particular culture themes are intensifying or getting weaker, there is always a "yes, but . . ." argument to be made. They also apply more specifically to the United States, unlike structural trends, which describe modernization processes in many societies. Even with these qualifications, different observers have drawn remarkably similar conclusions about some important themes in American culture (Williams, 1970; Inkeles, 1979; Yankelovich, 1981; Bellah et al., 1985; Glock, 1987; Hayes and Lipset, 1993/1994; Putnam, 2000). Some of these themes are simply the latest edition of historic American values, but others are of more recent vintage.

One cultural theme is *growing cultural complexity and diversity itself,* related to the growth of structural complexity mentioned earlier (e.g., in media sources, occupations). In postwar America there has been a proliferation of subcultures based on such diverse criteria as occupation, gender, ethnicity, age cohort, religion, and recreational pursuits. Thus, with varying degrees of coherence and visibility, there are distinctive cultural styles ("lifestyles") among bikers, punkers, skinheads, yuppies, Baby Boomers, gays, and senior citizens. Cultural complexity was also amplified by increasing ethnic diversity resulting from the vast inflow of new immigrants, particularly from Asia, Latin America, and the Middle East.

The United States was always diverse in terms of race, ethnicity, and other cultural characteristics. But historically this *cultural pluralism* was opposed by powerful social and political pressures to incorporate or assimilate diverse cultural strands into a common American culture. The metaphor for the United States was that of the great melting pot, even though it was often an official ideal not always practiced. Public schools were viewed as instruments of national assimilation, and in the 1950s most churches sought to emphasize not so much their differences but their commitment to the common American version of the Judeo-Christian heritage (Herberg, 1960). Even during the early days of the civil rights movement of the 1950s, the cultural agenda was to produce a "color-blind" society in which cultural (and economic) differences between African Americans and white Americans would vanish. In contrast, Canadians have historically been more willing than Americans to legitimate *multiculturalism.* The Canadian national metaphor was that of a mosaic rather than a melting pot (Lipset, 1989).

A second, more recent cultural theme is an *increasing toleration of cultural diversity* (including multiculturalism, which is the opposite of assimilationist policies). After World War II, and particularly since the 1960s, Americans were increasingly willing to accept and tolerate diversity as legitimate. Even though no good historical data exist, it is significant that by 1989 one poll showed that only 51 percent of Americans endorsed the melting pot model of ethnic assimilation, less than Canadian levels of support (cited in Lipset, 1989:187). The new streams of immigrants find increasing social support for the maintenance of ethnic enclave communities, and churches of all sorts are more concerned with asserting their distinctiveness than demonstrating their ecumenical commonalities, as in the 1950s (Robbins and Anthony, 1990).

Americans are increasingly willing to accept the legitimacy of behavioral and moral diversity (beyond ethnic multiculturalism). There is, for instance, greater support for premarital sexuality, for abortion, for women's involvement in the labor force and in the political process, for living as a single person, or for being married without having children (Yankelovich, 1981; Thornton, 1989). In 1924, researchers in "Middletown" (Muncie, Indiana) found that 94 percent of the population agreed that Christianity was the one true religion. In a followup study in 1977, only 41 percent agreed that this was true (Caplow et al., 1982).

The trend toward greater tolerance is widespread and only partly explainable by the increasing average educational level in America. Surveys in the 1950s and the 1970s showed that not only has political tolerance increased in the country as a whole, but that even at similar levels of education there was more support for civil liberties than there was two decades earlier. Thus, 84 percent of the college graduates in 1973 were rated politically "more tolerant," compared to only 65 percent of this group in 1964 (Nunn et al., 1978). And while you would be hard pressed to argue that many forms of racial discrimination have declined, it is nonetheless true that public opinion polls have tracked a slow but steady decline in attitudinal prejudice (the belief that nonwhites are somehow inferior) among the vast majority of Americans since the 1940s (Farley, 1988). In 1942, 66 percent of Americans in a national poll said that blacks and whites should attend separate schools; by 1985, only 7 percent did. In 1958, 56 percent of American Caucasians said that they would move if blacks lived next door; by 1990, only 8 percent said they would (Stanley and Niemi, 1995:367).

You need to understand that pressures to conform and toleration of cultural diversity are not mutually exclusive. They have always been dual realities in the United States. Pressures to conform are still quite strong, and toleration has been less effective with racial cultural minority groups. Even so, we think that in the broadest sense pressures to tolerate cultural differences have become quite powerful and that what Americans hold culturally in common has become more ambiguous, more arguable, and less binding. Americans have shifted some distance from a common set of cultural standards toward a plurality of such standards. (For a different view, see Parrillo, 1996.)

A third cultural theme is an *increasing concern with individual self-gratification*. In the 1970s, pollster Daniel Yankelovich observed that

> all national surveys showed an increase in preoccupation with the self. By the late 1970s, my firm's studies showed more than 7 out of 10 Americans (72 percent) spending a great deal of time thinking about themselves and their inner lives—this in a nation once notorious for its impatience with inwardness. The rage for self-fulfillment, our surveys indicated, had now spread to virtually the entire U.S. population. (1981:5).

Certainly this self-preoccupation is not all new. It is, rather, the old American value of individualism amplified and played in a new key. The American Revolution asserted the priority of individual rights over the rights of groups and the state, rights most clearly articulated at that time by the English philosopher John Locke. The cultural values of Americans are today certainly more individualistic and egalitarian than those of most people in the world—moreso even than our Canadian cousins, whose nation was formed in part as a counteraction to the "egalitarian excesses" of the American Revolution (Lipset, 1989). But American individualism and self-interest were historically tempered by other values (humanitarianism, social obligation, and compliance with established norms). The recent growing concern with the gratification of the self has been amplified by the widespread diffusion of the perspectives of humanistic psychology and the human potential movement during the 1960s. During the 1970s, many observers argued that individualism produced a more unrestrained self-concern. Christopher Lasch (1979) invented the term *culture of narcissism* in what was called the "me decade."

Ulrich Beck describes the increasing concern with individual self-gratification as *reflexive modernity* (Beck, 1992). People around the world are, slowly but surely, increasingly free to pursue their own personal life agendas without the set of structural constraints that bind people to traditional social roles. People are increasingly aware of how others in distant places and cultures live, and they are connected via communications networks, international trade, and cultural exchanges with people whose ways of life they are free to adopt. This is a new dimension of self-gratification that goes beyond concerns about selfishness and antisocial behavior.

As with greater toleration of cultural diversity, many observers saw a dark side to amplified individualism and self-absorption. It was viewed as cutting people off from social support, leaving them often confused and lonely, sanctioning the most outrageous forms of personal greed, making them almost pathologically unable to engage in communal problem solving. When their self-preoccupation fails, they have a longing for community that cannot be fulfilled (Putnam, 1998; Slater, 1976; Bellah et al., 1985; Etzioni, 1993; Derber, 1996:9; Dolbreare and Hubbell, 1996:12). Critics notwithstanding, probably most Americans continue to view modern individualism in a positive manner. In spite of misgivings, Yankelovich argued that this trend meant that "most Americans were involved in a project to prove that life can be more than a grim economic chore. . . . (and) eager to give more meaning to their lives, to find fuller self expression and to add a touch of adventure and grace to their lives" (1981:5).

A fourth persisting cultural theme is a *belief in the effectiveness of scientific and empirical knowledge* (empirical rationality). Areas of social life governed by traditional knowledge continue to contract, while those governed by empirical, natural, rational, and technical knowledge expand (Glock, 1987). Thus, for guidance about childbearing and family problems, we are more likely to turn to the empirical knowledge of child psychologists and family therapists. For economic and business decisions, we are less likely to use traditional wisdom and more likely to turn to those having empirical knowledge of the working of economic and organizational systems, such as investment counselors, economists, and trained managers. Public trust in science and technology persists today but is probably lower than in the 1950s, when there was little recognition of their costs. Evidence from the 1980s and 1990s suggests that in spite of some awareness of problems caused by science and technology there still is a pervasive faith in science and technological fixes. Its influence persists, but Americans are deeply ambivalent about science (Pion and Lipsey, 1981:311; Olsen et al., 1992).

The persistence of empirical rationality is related to *secularization.* Contrary to some predictions, religion and churches have certainly not withered away in America. But while the areas to which we apply scientific and naturalistic explanations have expanded, the areas to which supernatural explanations apply have contracted. Religion is increasingly a private affair and compartmentalized or set apart from public and community life (for example, from businesses and schools). While the privatization of religion is consistent with the growing cultural emphasis on individual self-development, at the same time there are powerful secularizing forces in public life (Robbins and Anthony, 1990:11,17; Roof and McKinnery, 1987).

A fifth well-documented cultural theme is a pervasive *decreasing trust in national leaders and social institutions.* The decrease was particularly dramatic during the 1970s, when Americans became increasingly cynical about the credibility, competence, and honesty of the leaders of government, business, banks, religion, public schools, the media, and other institutions (Institute for Social Research, 1979; Pion and Lipsey, 1981; Lipset and Schneider, 1983; Dolbeare and Hubbell, 1996:49–51). It may be partly caused by critical media reporting of specific events (such as political, corporate, or military scandals or the outrageous behavior of leaders themselves). We think it also reflects a widespread belief that the interests of people are not being honestly or competently served by leaders and social institutions.

The intense public cynicism of recent decades might signify a full-blown "legitimacy crisis," a complete loss of faith in the credibility of the American system that may have drastic consequences (Dolbeare and Hubbell, 1996; Phillips, 1995). Other observers (Goldfarb, 1991; Elshtain, 1995) believe that cynicism itself is a social disease that promotes discord, silences dialogue, and fans the flames of mistrust in the public good. What do you think?

Let's summarize: We have discussed structural trends and cultural themes that are persistent but mutable. Taken together, they form two related dimensions of change that constitute a virtual definition of modernism or modernity in the United States.

COUNTERTRENDS AND REACTIONS TO MODERNITY: ANTIMODERNISM AND POSTMODERNISM

For almost every trend and theme mentioned, we can easily identify countertrends and reactions, and often social movements seeking to promote more change, stop it, or to push things in the opposite direction. Abstractly, these are reactions to modernity. Consider: Along with the long-term growth of toleration of diversity and decline in prejudice that every public opinion poll found in the last several decades, some see a resurgence of racism and ethnic discrimination in America. If overt racism and sexism have declined, institutional discrimination, the discriminatory outcomes in the way that many communities and organizations routinely work continue significantly (Valdivieso and Davis, 1988; Massey, 1990; Wilkinson, 1995). Many racially controversial and highly publicized events suggest that racism continues, often in new and subtle forms. Think of the intense controversy and publicity surrounding the trials of O.J. Simpson and the police officers accused of beating Rodney King or (more recently) conflicts between police and ethnic communities in New York City.

Symbolic racism may play an increasing role. Public controversies about the "underclass," crime, drugs, and public welfare are in part codes for racist attitudes and fears that cannot be openly stated. Americans support antidiscrimination laws, but public policies to address real inequalities and discrimination related to ethnic minorities, women, and gays, such as desegregation and affirmative action policies, are controversial, unpopular, and increasingly subject to political and legal challenges (Steele, 1990; Fineman, 1991; Puddington, 1995; Hancock et al., 1996; Leicht, 1998).

Since the early 1990s, the media publicized the existence and emergence of small but radical racist and anti-Semitic hate groups, such as neo-Nazis, skinheads, the Ku Klux Klan, and the Aryan Nation. By the mid-1990s, militias (often armed and dangerous) and common law courts had thoroughly rejected the laws and legitimacy of the modern American system. We emphasize that these are *reactions* to the pervasive structural trends and persisting cultural themes of modernity. They are reactions, for example, to the very real—but very incomplete—declines in intolerance and gains by cultural minorities in the United States. They are most intensely found among those who experience recent change in negative ways.

You can find similar cultural reactions and movements involved with the concentration of power, bureaucratization, the spread of the secular-scientific worldview, rampant individualism, and other features of modern life in America. Social movements react to modernity in American social life in two ways. Some seek to *reaffirm past cultural traditions.* Perhaps the most widespread and visible of such movements is the revitalization and growth of Christian fundamentalism from the late 1970s onward. A religious movement of vast popular appeal, the growing evangelical and fundamentalist churches sought to defend a traditional Christian view against the inroads of science, secularism, and modernity. It additionally sought to restore moral coherence and traditional values about family, sexuality, and civic life. (Ammerman, 1987; Wuthnow, 1983; Robbins and Anthony, 1990; Chalfant et. al., 1994: chap. 7).

Similarly, in a highly visible reaction, by the 1990s traditionalist scholars reacted to the diffusion of multiculturalism in higher education. They attacked (using the code words "politically correct") those seeking to transform the traditional curriculum to address the needs and perspectives of women, minorities, and "non-Europeans" whose numbers had slowly increased in American higher education. Angry traditionalists found the mass media attentive and made powerful allies among nonacademic political conservatives (Heller, 1991; Stimson, 1991).

There are reactions to extreme individualism and the growth in scale of social systems. In the mid-1990s, research by Robert Wuthnow (1994) found growing numbers of Americans who regularly participate in small groups. Four of ten Americans regularly participated in some kind of small group, such as Bible study groups, twelve-step groups, singles groups, book discussion clubs, sports or hobby groups, or political or civic groups. In such settings, people have found friends, received emotional support, overcome life-threatening addictions, or grown in their spirituality. They have, in other words, found community.

Other kinds of reactions seek not to restore tradition but *to promote a new stage of cultural and social development beyond modernity.* The New Age movement consists of diverse cultural groups that connect people interested in such things as greater "wholeness" and integrated lifestyles, attention to nonrational and inner experience, mysticism, astrology, spiritualism, reincarnation, cosmic consciousness, alternative healing and vegetarianism, ecology, and voluntary simplicity (Peters, 1988; Schultz, 1989). Perhaps no one accepts all of these ideas or practices, and few are aware of being a part of a cultural movement, but the ideas and themes of the New Age groups have been broadly influential. Some of their roots are in the counterculture of the 1960s, and their appeal is primarily among the middle classes. They reject or redefine aspects of modernity (the primacy of empirical rationality) but accept others (tolerance, the emphasis on self-development). By the 1990s, New Age themes were influencing the practice of religion in conventional religious denominations. But most important, New Agers celebrate the emergence of a new social and cultural pattern (or "new paradigm") that is subtly but radically transforming and "resacralizing" the modern world (Ferguson, 1980).

A similar intellectual movement more directly attacks modern society and culture. *Postmodernism* began among philosophers and literary critics after the 1960s and became a powerful theme among intellectuals (Foucault, 1965; Baudrillard, 1975; De Man, 1979). Postmodernism shares some similarities with New Age spirituality but is more intellectual and political in its critique of modernism. It argues that modern technological society devitalizes life and robs humans of the subjective dimensions of experience found in myth, art, emotion, ritual, and community. Modernism is viewed as a seamless web in which capitalism, science, technology, and bureaucracy have become instruments of social control by elites. Modern societies are "objectively managed" through bureaucracy and the mass media, a process that represses and deforms the freedom, consciousness, and subjective life of persons. But recently the increasing difficulties of corporate elites in managing society, the growth of widespread alienation and cynicism about the system, and the revival of interest in fantasy and myth are recognized as signaling the decline of the modern system. In the emerging postmodern era, reality is being transformed so that people are reclaiming their subjective lives. In so doing, they are empowering themselves to live culture freely, naturally, and artfully (Murphy, 1989; Huyssen, 1990). Some argue that this desire for free subjective experience will itself generate new forms of repression and consumerism as it is subverted by corporations and the electronic media (Phol, 1981).

IN CONCLUSION

We have described some powerful structural trends and persisting cultural themes that broadly shape social change in the United States. Structural trends included

- Growth in scale of social relationships
- Increasing centralization of control
- Increasing social differentiation and specialization
- Growing interconnectedness and networking of social life
- Increasing technological complexity and sophistication

Persistent but changing cultural themes included

- Increasing cultural complexity and diversity
- Growing toleration of that diversity, increasing multiculturalism
- Increasing concern with individual gratification
- Continuing belief in the efficacy of science, technology, and empirical rationality
- Declining trust in leaders and social institutions

We described a number of reactions, countertrends, and movements in reaction to these structural themes of modernity, including continuing gender and ethnic discrimination; reemergent social and religious fundamentalism, populist militias, and common law courts; the traditionalist movement in academia; the growth of small-group participation; New Age and spirituality movements; and postmodernism. Some of these reactions attempt to halt or roll back the trends and themes of American modernity, while others attempt to transcend or move beyond them.

Will the trends and themes of modernity or reactions to them be more powerful in the net outcome of ongoing social change? That is an outrageously difficult question to answer simply (but it is an important one). We don't believe that modernity is exhausted or will somehow simply be canceled, but countertrends and reactions do mean that human action will reshape them into new (and often unrecognizable) forms. For an argument that postmodernity and reactions to modernity are more powerful, see Bartos (1996). More abstractly, modernity and reactions to it stand in a dialectical relation that will interact to shape the important outcomes of social change.[2]

THINKING PERSONALLY ABOUT SOCIAL CHANGE

1. We noted in this chapter that many activities that formerly lent themselves to bureaucracies are being replaced by networks of technologically dense interactions. Think of your encounters (or those of your family and friends) with computers and computer technology since you were born. How did you experience encounters with computers in places such as schools, workplaces, hospitals, companies, or government offices? We can think of many encounters with computer technology that were horrendous, others that are quite pleasant, and still others that have a "so what?" quality to them ("They need a computer to do *this*?"). How do you (and your peers) humanize interactions with computers to make computer communications more personal?

2. In this chapter we cited evidence about a sustained decline in attitudinal prejudice. Ask some acquaintances about their perceptions and feelings about people who are different in terms of race, ethnicity, gender, or sexual orientation. Ask people of different ages and then compare their answers, or ask people your age to describe the attitudes of their parents and grandparents. Do people seem personally prejudiced? Don't ask people directly if they are prejudiced, because most will say no. Now ask the same persons for their perceptions of social policies to reduce historic forms of discrimination (such as desegregation of schools, affirmative action programs in employment). What kind of answers do you get, and do they seem similar or different from your questions about their personal attitudes? Do your conversations support or contradict what we said in Chapter 2 about this? *Caution:* Either result is likely and is okay. Thinking about yourself and talking to people is important to make micro-macro connections, but you can't make reliable generalizations from this process because you and your acquaintances do not necessarily represent the larger population accurately (nor do we and our acquaintances!). You can also shape answers by the way you phrase questions. The same qualifications apply, of course, to samples and questions in more formal research, but presumably researchers have given more critical attention to sampling problems and the way people react to questions.

3. Are you more likely to rely on information and advice from "experts" or from respected religious and spiritual leaders? Well, it all depends, doesn't it? On what kinds of things? How do the people you know differ on this point? How do you react when the expert advice you get often fails or leaves you unsatisfied?

4. When Harper teaches young adults and the topic of religion comes up many—but not all—say that they were raised Catholic, Lutheran (or whatever); they don't attend church frequently or feel particularly loyal to organized religion. But often they say they believe in a higher power and are interested in spiritual life. (This may be influenced by the particular setting he teaches in.) But the persistence of religion in a scientific age is certainly a complicated issue. Do you think believing in the world as a purely natural phenomenon is enough for most people? Talk with people of different ages and social backgrounds about this issue.

NOTES

1. Sociologists distinguish among the concepts of social control, power, and authority, but those distinctions are not relevant to our concerns here.

2. For now, a dialectical relationship means that two things (in this case basic trends and reactions to them) are in dynamic opposition, and that the resulting "vector" will be a creative combination of them. We will return to the notion of a dialectic in more depth in chapters about theory.

Change in the Settings of Everyday Life: Populations, Families, and Work

Now we move away from macroscopic social trends and explore change in those settings and institutions closer to our everyday lives. Your life is greatly affected by the general characteristics of the population, and particularly by the experiences of your agemates with whom you compete (although you may be unaware of these influences). But certainly you are aware of the powerful impacts of changing families, work, and careers on the lives of individuals. It is a real challenge to locate your individual biography and life circumstances in relation to these larger social contexts. Indeed, it is important that you do so.

DEMOGRAPHIC CHANGE

Demographic change means changes in the size or other important characteristics of the individual people that comprise a society. America's population is growing, though not nearly as rapidly as those in developing nations in other parts of the world. If trends continue, the U.S. Census Bureau now predicts that by 2050 the United States will have a population of 393 million, and much of this growth will be fueled by those immigrants and their children who came after 1991. Latinos, both native born and immigrants, may replace African Americans as the largest ethnic minority group. Communities of Asian Americans will continue to grow. In fact, the ethnic diversity of the entire population will increase, so that by sometime around 2050 persons of European ancestry will comprise only about 50 percent of Americans, down from 75 percent in the 1990s (cited in Newman, 1996:453–54).

Immigration and Diversity

Increasing immigration and ethnic diversity causes intense social and political controversies. We're sure this is no surprise to you. Our popular media and political talk is full of concerns about this phenomenon. Many argue that rapid immigration threatens to overburden the American economy, social programs (such as educational and health care services); most important, they say, it calls into question the coherence of our culture, language, and national identity—"who and what Americans are."

Yet while rapid immigration causes problems, some facts about immigrants and the immigration process are not widely understood. For instance, most immigrants (over 80 percent) come to the United States legally, and undocumented ("illegal") immigrants make up only about 1 percent of the total population. Most undocumented immigrants (60 percent) don't come by illegally crossing a border; they first come legally on a student, tourist, or business visa and then don't return when it expires. The number of immigrants who do not yet speak English is increasing because the number of immigrants is increasing—not because they refuse to learn English. Immigrant demand for English classes far exceeds the number of available classes. Demographers find that even in Southern California, which receives a huge influx of both Latino and Asian immigrants, most immigrants have mastered English within ten years after they arrive and do not remain mired in poverty (Myers, 1995). Many studies show that immigrants do not cost U.S. citizens jobs, and their net effect is often to improve growing local economies; they may, however, cost the jobs of some low-skilled workers in slow-growing or stagnant economies. In sum, immigrants pay more in taxes than they receive in benefits, but an increasing problem is that most tax dollars go to the federal government while states and localities provide most of the services immigrants use (education and health care). Moreoever, immigrants are not uniformly distributed across the United States (Armendariz, 1995; Urban Institute, 1994). America is in fact a nation of immigrant groups, and while waves of immigrants have always caused problems and controversy, in the long run they have also been a source of richness and creativity.

The Graying of America

Another important demographic change is an increase in the average age of persons, so that we are becoming an older population. This is true in all industrial societies. This change is caused by the joint effects of a long-term decline in the birth rate and the gradual extension of longevity (see Tables 3-1 and 3-2).

These effects in turn are caused by many factors, such as changes in norms about the desired number of children, the universal availability of contraception, the control of epidemic disease, and improvements in the health and nutrition of individuals.

An aging population means that, other things being equal, we can expect an expansion in occupations that serve the elderly and slow growth or contractions in occupations that serve younger segments of the population (e.g., pediatricians, elementary school teachers). As more people reach retirement age, there will be proportionally fewer workers to support the elderly through Social Security taxes and contributions to private retirement plans.

Birth Cohorts

It is important that you understand the implications of belonging to different birth cohorts. A *birth cohort* includes agemates who were born at about the same time. Your individual life prospects are influenced not only by the total number of

TABLE 3–1 DEMOGRAPHIC TRENDS, 1960–2050

Population	Unit	1960	1970	1980	1984	1988	1993	1998	2000[a]	2050[a]
Under 18 years	mil.	64.2	69.7	63.5	62.7	63.6	67.1	70.5	70.8	96.1
18–64 years	mil.	98.6	113.5	137.2	145.4	184.4	158.0	167.3	169.1	218.9
65+ years	mil.	16.6	20.0	25.6	28.0	30.9	32.9	34.4	34.7	78.8
Median age	years	29.5	28.0	30.0	31.3	32.3	33.4	35.2	35.7	38.1
Persons/household		3.33	3.14	2.76	2.71	2.62	2.63	2.62	NA	NA
Birth rate/1000		23.7	18.4	15.9	15.7	15.9	16.0	14.4	14.2	14.4
Death rate/1000		9.5	9.5	8.8	8.7	8.8	8.6	8.5	8.8	10.1
Life expectancy:	males	66.6	67.1	70.0	71.1	71.4	72.3	73.6	73.0	NA
	females	73.1	74.8	77.4	78.3	78.3	79.0	79.2	79.7	NA

a. Estimates.
Source: U.S. Department of Commerce, Bureau of the Census, *Statistical Abstract of the United States,* 1984; 1986; 1990; 1994; 1999a.

people in the nation and their average age, but also by the size and experience of the particular birth cohort to which you belong. You compete most directly with them for many things, such as education, jobs, housing, community facilities, energy supplies, and health care. Your birth cohort bears the stamp of the important historical events and circumstances that happened as you move through the life course in common ways. Cohorts are the empirical carriers of many social and cultural changes (Kennedy, 1989:15). Birth cohorts differ dramatically in size because of wide swings in the number of children born in the past. The low-fertility years of the Great Depression happened between two high-fertility periods—the Roaring Twenties and the Baby Boom (after World War II). The Baby Boom was followed in the 1970s by a period of lower fertility (which produced the so-called "generation X") (Kennedy, 1989:18).

The importance of differences in cohort size can be illustrated by examining the career of the Baby Boom generation (those born between 1946 and 1964), a large

TABLE 3–2 DEMOGRAPHIC AND FAMILY TRENDS, TRUNCATED TABLES, 1960–2000

	1910	1940	1970	1981	1988	1993	1998	2000[a]
Birth rate/1000	30.1	20.4	17.8	15.9	15.9	16.0	14.4	14.2
Divorce rate/1000	.9	2.0	3.3	5.3	4.8	4.6	4.3	NA
Marriage rate/1000	10.3	12.1	10.6	10.6	9.7	9.0	8.9	NA
	1920	**1950**	**1970**	**1979**	**1988**	**1993**	**1998**	**2000**
Life expectancy, males	53.6	65.6	67.1	69.9	71.4	72.3	73.6	73.0
Life expectancy, females	54.6	71.1	74.8	77.6	78.3	79.0	79.2	79.7
	1800	**1900**	**1976**	**1990**	**1998**			
Mean number of children per family	6	4.7	1.8	1.3	1.2			

a. Estimates.
Source: U.S. Department of Commerce, Bureau of the Census, *Statistical Abstract of the United States,* 1984; 1986; 1990, 1994; 1999a.

population bulge squeezed between two "bust" generations and moving through society "like a pig in a python." As they do so, they cause dislocations and adjustments that will continue through the next decade or so, when the Boomers begin to retire. What are these dislocations and adjustments?

Postwar families with lots of babies were largely responsible for the increased demand for new houses and suburban growth during the 1950s (real estate and construction industries also boomed during this period). During the 1950s, the increased demand for teachers and new elementary schools seemed almost insatiable, and by the 1960s the expansion of colleges and universities began. When the Boomers graduated, their places were taken by the much smaller Baby Bust (1970s) cohort and followed by larger 1980s and 1990s cohorts of children of Baby Boomers. The gloom of 1970s declining enrollments and retrenchment has been replaced by further expansion (though not at the dizzying rates of the 1960s).

During the 1970s, the Boomers began to move into job markets. They faced stiffer competition than the smaller cohort that preceded them, not only because of their large numbers, but also because women were also entering the job market in record numbers and the robust economic expansion of the 1960s had slowed. A crowded labor market depressed wages so that in spite of the 1970s stereotypes about affluent "yuppies," most Boomers didn't do as well as the smaller Great Depression cohort that preceded them in the labor market.

By the year 2010, the Boomers will begin to retire and qualify for retirement and Social Security benefits. Growing long-term chronic health care needs of the elderly compared to those of younger birth cohorts means that both public and private health care providers will be strained. Consequently, private health premiums and public health budgets will mushroom, as well as markets for geriatric services of all sorts.

The importance of birth cohorts for understanding change is not only because of their differing sizes. They also are composed of individuals who have common, and in some ways distinctive, historical experiences. To come of age during economic hard times produces a whole cohort of people who have different worldviews and attitudes from those who grow up during periods of sustained economic expansion. Birth cohorts are in a sense the concrete carriers of social and cultural change through society.

Certainly the experience of the Boomers in the 1960s left a decisive stamp on the nature of American society and culture. They are the generation that spawned the cultural transformations of the 1960s: the "counterculture" with its amplified individualism; disenchantment with the established order; the sexual revolution; the revitalized feminist movement; and the antiwar movement. By the late 1970s, they became absorbed by the more mundane concerns of careers, kids, and families. Yet they retain distinctive experiences, outlooks, and memories. They are, for example, the demographic backbone of the New Age movement, which has some similarities with the cultural movements of the 1960s.

The experience of the 1970s cohort (more popularly called "generation X") was certainly different. Their experiences with a different social world (less crowded schools, delaying marriage, growing up in dual-income and single-parent families, and much more extensive contact with "experts" and "specialists" including teachers and childcare workers) combined with facing totally different economic circumstances (slower economic growth and shrinking economic opportunities) to produce a more tentative and skeptical generation of adults. Xers now in their 30s have been contrasted with Boomers as being (1) more socially liberal but more financially conservative; (2) more conservative about issues of crime and punishment; (3) more ambitious, pragmatic, skeptical, "selfish" and goal-oriented; (4) more nationalistic and less altruistic; and (5) driven by the desire to be affluent (Sample, 1996; Sidel, 1989).

Early evidence on the latest generation to reach adulthood (called *millenials;* see Howe and Strauss, 2000), is providing further proof that cohorts are significant carriers of social change. This cohort (born in the 1980s) appears to be different from the Xers and Boomers in their social attitudes and behavior. Compared with Xer teen counterparts a generation ago, Millenials are (1) more happy, confident and positive about the future; (2) more accepting of authority; (3) more likely to engage in group and civic activities and to blame selfishness when asked: "What is the major cause of problems in this country?" (4) are more likely to describe themselves as doers rather than thinkers; and (5) are reversing historic declines on standardized tests of academic achievement that were characteristic of Xers. While it is too early to tell if Millenials' visions of their own future will bear fruit as they reach adulthood and middle age, this group seems to be reversing a tide of general pessimism about the future and hyperconcern with the self that afflicted prior postwar generations of teens (see Howe and Strauss, 2000).

Yet the Xers' more pessimistic outlook, compared to that of Millenials and Boomers, may not be completely misplaced. Because of their relatively smaller numbers, by about 2020 they will be financially squeezed when they are required to simultaneously finance the education and careers of their own children and the retirement and health programs of the Boomers (their retiring parents). Even people with no surviving parents or children of their own don't need to feel left out of these issues: As insurance customers, taxpayers, and residents of school districts, they will be required to attend to these issues. Some have envisioned a future generational war whereby younger and older cohorts struggle to control the political, economic, and taxation processes to their own advantage. While we doubt that there will be a full-blown "social war" between cohorts, the bonds of intergenerational cohesion will be severely tested (*The New York Times,* 1996a). These bonds will be tested among the very generation of Americans for whom intergenerational bonds are the weakest as social life increasingly is lived in the company of those at or near our own age (Riley, 1985).

Actually, the process of reallocating resources between age groups has been going on at least since the 1970s. During that decade, public investment shifted from benefits to children to benefits to elderly people. In the last decade, Social Security increases have diminished the number of elderly people living in poverty. Medicare has increased their health security. At the same time, public investments in education, aid to dependent children, and child health programs have shrunk, so that the proportion of American children living in poverty has grown steadily. By official definitions, 15 percent of America's children were poor in 1970; by 1990, 22 percent were. By contrast, 25 percent of persons over 65 were poor in 1970, but only 12 percent were poor by 1987 (U.S. Department of Commerce, Bureau of the Census, 1990:460). During the Great Depression of the 1930s, the elderly constituted the most destitute demographic group in the population; by 1996, young children were.

You need to understand that this "disinvestment in children" flows from particularly American policies and is *not* shared by all industrial nations undergoing similar demographic changes.

CHANGING FAMILIES

Everybody knows that American family life is changing, and many believe that these changes mean a precipitous "decline of the family" that produces a cascade of other personal, social, and legal problems. Some sociological reports, certainly much ordinary conversation, most media reports, and political rhetoric are all full of talk about this. But if you want an interesting (and often empty) conversation, ask the person who tells you he or she is bothered by a general "decline in family values" exactly what that means! Our point is not that there are no "family problems" that bedevil us. *There are. There always have been.* More contentious is whether social change means that family problems are more severe now than in the past.

You may strongly disagree. Before pursing this question, however, let us step back and describe a number of factual changes that are not points of controversy. You may find some surprising.

A first change is an obvious consequence of the trend toward lower birth rates: *a decline in the size of the average family.* The average number of persons per household has declined from 3.76 persons in 1940 to 2.62 in 1998 (U.S. Department of Commerce, Bureau of the Census, 1999: 62). A second change has to do with the kinds of households in which Americans live. A *household* is an economic unit of all persons who share the same house or apartment, while a *family* is two or more people related by blood, marriage, or legal adoption. By 1998, nonfamily households had grown to 31 percent of all households. Of these the vast majority (26 percent) were single individuals living alone and the remainder were adults living with unrelated individuals. Family households comprised 69 percent of all households, down from 74 percent in 1980 (U.S. Department of Commerce, Bureau of the Census, 1999:62).

A third change is the growing difficulty for young adults in forming their own families. The proportion of 25- to 34-year-old adults with families of their own has declined from 83 percent to 65 percent from 1960 to 1990 (Aquilino, 1990). This may have many causes, but among the obvious are the declining real wages for entry-level jobs (compared to levels for previous generations) and the growing costs of maintaining independent households.

Growing Household and Family Diversity

Probably the key to understanding change among American families is the *increased diversity of types of families and households.* The historically preferred type of family was the traditional "mom-dad-and-kids" arrangement, with father as the sole breadwinner. While this was always more of an ideal than a reality, today this historic image of the family exists as a minority of family types. You can see the diversity of these in Figure 3-1. Households and families are diverse mainly in terms of (1) the number of adults present, (2) the presence of children, and (3) the number of wage earners in the family.

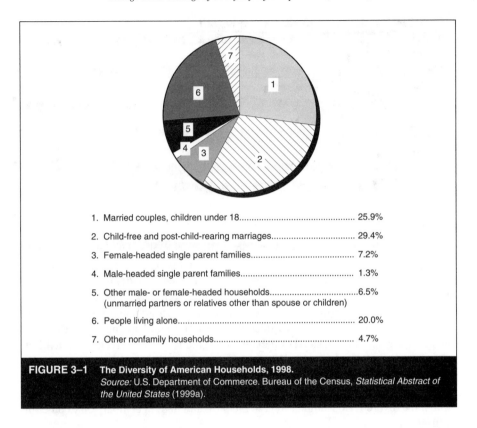

1. Married couples, children under 18.. 25.9%

2. Child-free and post-child-rearing marriages.................................. 29.4%

3. Female-headed single parent families... 7.2%

4. Male-headed single parent families.. 1.3%

5. Other male- or female-headed households.....................................6.5%
   (unmarried partners or relatives other than spouse or children)

6. People living alone... 20.0%

7. Other nonfamily households.. 4.7%

FIGURE 3–1   The Diversity of American Households, 1998.
Source: U.S. Department of Commerce. Bureau of the Census, *Statistical Abstract of the United States* (1999a).

Radically nontraditional households exist (such as communal households, homosexual households, and group marriage experiments) but they represent a small proportion of all households. Household income varies significantly with both the number of wage earners and the presence of children. Here are some of these differences as they were in 1997:

- 2 adults, kids, 1 earner = $42,095
- 2 adults, kids, 2 earners = $66,477
- 2 adults, two earners, no kids = $69,507
- 2 adults, one earner, no kids = $48,510
- 1 adult, male household head = $32,960
- 1 adult, female household head = $21,023

Such differences go a long way to explain the growth of multiple-income families and the shrinkage of traditional families, undoubtedly driven by a desire to enhance household income. By 1997, more than half of American women of working age were employed (60 percent), and increasingly they are continuously employed, even when raising children (U.S. Department of Commerce, Bureau of the Census, 1999:414).

A complex set of causes interact to produce growing household and family diversity:

1. Delay in getting married among young adults.
2. Relaxation of social stigma against "nonmarital cohabitation" and "singlehood" as lifestyle options.
3. Extension of the life span, with an increase in "empty nest" families and separate households among retirees and widows.
4. Economic pressures for women to become employed to support family living standards.
5. Growth in the divorce rate.
6. An increase in female-headed households with children, especially among low-income women.
7. Rapidly declining marital fertility (the epidemic of births to single women is masking a decline in births to married couples; see Jencks, 1992).

Family and Household Problems

It would be unbalanced not to recognize the very real and widely known problems associated with changing families and households. The increasing divorce rate is among the more alarming family trends. A much cited statistic that about four out of ten marriages ends in divorce is usually part of an argument that American families are disintegrating. But it seems to us that this is an arguable interpretation of facts: When the divorce rate is considered in relation to the total number of married persons at a given time (instead of the number of marriages in a given year), a different impression results. In the late 1990s, there were about 20 divorces per every 1000 married women (U.S. Department of Commerce, Bureau of the Census, 1999a, p. 110). Looked at this way the collapse of American families looks less likely, *even though* the divorce rate is higher than in the past, and high in comparison to other industrial nations.

The general rise in the divorce rate over the last decades is also related to broad cultural trends, the accessibility of the courts to people of ordinary means, the weakening of social stigmas against divorced people, and particularly America's emphasis on the rights of persons to seek individual fulfillment (Bellah et. al., 1985; Sidel, 1986; Cherlin, 1992; Popenoe, 1996). In the past, marriages were judged more on whether they provided stable support than whether they made individuals happy. A high divorce rate is the price for allowing people to escape from unhappy, tyrannical, and sometimes brutal relationships. It is traumatic—particularly in the short run—for individuals and children going through the process. It has costs for society. But we believe that forcing people to stay together in such relationships would probably be equally intolerable (see Amato and Booth, 1997).

It may well be that divorce is not destroying families on a large scale, but it is certainly a traumatic problem for those undergoing it. It is a particular problem for children. Current research suggests that the initial postdivorce period is emotionally traumatic; that after about two years most children resume "normal" development; and that a minority of children experience continuing emotional and behavioral problems that last into adulthood (Cherlin, 1996:376). Beyond the trauma of family disruption, another problem is that under our current legal system it produces, temporarily at least, a poor, female-headed family with children (Weitzman, 1985). Andrew Cherlin opined that "the most detrimental aspect of the absence of fathers from one-parent families is not the lack of a male presence but the lack of male income" (1981:81).

Divorce may be an intense but temporary condition for many who remarry, but the disadvantage of being a single parent is more likely to be a permanent one for the young low-income female who bears a child out of wedlock. This is particularly so because her potential mate (a young low-income male) is likely to have such low earning potential that he is an economic burden rather than an asset. Thus the combination of a high divorce rate and the growth of births out of wedlock combine to produce a whole class of poor females with children. This problem is particularly concentrated among young African-American women and their children. In 1990, 26 percent of all children under age 18 lived in single-parent families; but fully 60 percent of all African-American children did so (Popenoe, 1996). This problem is amplified by the shift of social and economic support from the young to the elderly (mentioned above). Though many researchers doubt that money has much to do with divorce and unmarried parenthood (see Lichter, McLaughlin, and Ribar, 1997; Popenoe, 1996; Mayer, 1997), dealing with the problems of these families and those produced by children raised in such household environments will be a great challenge for American public policy in the future.

The most pressing problem of dual-income families is not money, but the problem of managing "ragged" family schedules and adjusting husband/wife roles to new economic circumstances. These problems are expanded by longer working hours and consumption norms that dramatically increase household debt (see Schor, 1993; 1998; Sullivan, Warren, and Westbrook, 2000). Women are often stressed by having to be full-time employees and continuing to take care of most parental and household duties (evidence suggests that men still don't do their fair share). This problem is particularly compounded when people don't have a vision about what a family should be that is consistent with a dual-income family—in other words, when they are attached to the traditional family model. One study, for example, found that husbands and wives were more likely to be emotionally depressed when both disapproved of the wife's employment. Where both approved, depression was lower for both husband and wife, and particularly so when the husband helped with the housework (Ross, Mirowsky, and Huber, 1983). Another problem is that social agencies that deal with families were set up to deal with the traditional family model and are changing too slowly to address the needs of dual-income families that are rapidly becoming the norm. But according to working wives and mothers, the most pressing problem for dual-income families is access to quality child care, which is in short supply and expensive (Ross and Mirowsky, 1990). It is even more of a problem for the low-income female-headed families just mentioned. Unlike many other industrial nations, the United States has no public support for child care for mothers who work.

Family Transformation or Decline?

The images of past American families, "traditional ones" that were warm, secure, and satisfying, is at odds with the actual historical record (Skolnick, 1991). In the nineteenth century, because adults had a shorter life expectancy and a parent was more likely to die, children were actually more likely to live in a single-parent home (Kain, 1990). Remarkably, the overall rate of marital breakup for all reasons has remained about the same since roughly 1860. Today it is less likely to be terminated by death than by a divorce. In the 1990s, roughly 20 percent of American children lived in poverty. That is about the same proportion who lived in orphanages at the turn of the previous century, and not just because their parents died. Many were there because their parents couldn't afford to raise them. Moreover, experts estimate that rates of alcohol and drug abuse, dropping out of school early, and domestic violence were all higher at the turn of the previous century than they are today (Newman, 1996; Coontz, 1992). There is more: The remarriage rate among divorced persons is quite high, suggesting that disillusionment is focused on being married to a particular person rather than on marriage itself (Weeks, 1989:271). In fact, we have so thoroughly romanticized historic American family life that family historian Stephanie Coontz and sociologist William Goode called this image "the classical family of Western nostalgia" (Coontz, 1992; Goode, 1971; see also Kain, 1990).

We find several compelling reasons for thinking that today families and households on the whole are doing at least as well and often better than in the past. How so? First, *Americans continue to rate family life as the largest single source of life's satisfactions.* Work and all other sources of satisfaction rank below family for the majority of Americans (Wallerstein, 1996). This is particularly significant when the viability of American families is so widely questioned. Longitudinal evidence about the quality of family life is hard to come by, but several research reports support this hunch. The Muncie, Indiana ("Middletown") research in the 1920s described much family life, especially among blue-collar workers, as "bleak, dreary, and devitalized." Researchers found surprisingly little husband-wife communication and a restricted sexual life. A restudy of the same community in 1982 found much higher levels of marital satisfaction, more husband-wife communication, and more time spent with children than previously (Caplow et al., 1982). That and other historical evidence suggests that both wife and child abuse are not higher than in the past (although it is more studied, recorded, and recognized). The best evidence suggests that, although outrageously high, they both may have declined over the past half century and have fallen considerably since the 1970s (Straus, M., 1980; Caplow et al., 1982:336; Straus and Gelles, 1986; Gelles and Cornell, 1990; Cherlin, 1996).

Second, *the decrease in average family size may have had positive impact.* A substantial body of research concludes that in smaller families there is less role segregation, more husband-wife interaction, and more time spent with children. Smaller families also tend to be less paternalistic and more equalitarian, both with respect to husband-wife and parent-child relationships. Small family size has also been found to be related to improved physical and mental health (especially among mothers!) and to increased mental ability in children (Eitzen,1974; Blake, 1989).

Third, *cultural value changes may have had a positive as well as negative impact on the quality of family life.* These would include an increasing emphasis on equalitarian relationships generally and, within the family, a shift from fixed "role scripts" toward more flexible "role negotiation." Patriarchal authority still exists, but patriarchy is no longer an absolute tyranny in American families. For whatever reasons, surveys by the National Opinion Research Corporation found that 96 percent of their respondents rated their marriages as either "very" or "pretty" happy between 1972 and 1989 (National Opinion Research Center, 2000).

Family demographer Judith Blake (1979) posed an intriguing interpretation of family change. She began by referring to a common sociological argument that the Industrial Revolution so severed connections between work and public life that families in industrial societies have evolved into more private, isolated, and specialized units. As historic family economic, protective, recreational, and educational functions came to be assumed by other institutional realms (governments, companies, and schools) it became plausible to speak of more "isolated nuclear families" with more specialized functions: the provision of emotional gratification for adults and the early socialization of children (Parsons and Bales, 1955). And as the family became more of a "private sphere" ideally providing a haven from the rough-and-tumble worlds of the workplace and the political community, it was also, we now know, a private world in which abuse, neglect, and violence often happened.

Blake argued that this trend to separate and "privatized" families has reversed itself and that families are structurally in the process of becoming less distinct, less private, and more connected with public life. What evidence can we find for such a view? First, with regard to becoming less distinct, the growing diversity of families and household arrangements, as mentioned earlier, make it more difficult to define what "families" are. The traditional idealized family is losing some of its privileged status. For example, the variety of household arrangements, singlehood, and children born out of wedlock are not severely stigmatized as they were in the past, and are treated without distinction by public agencies such as courts and schools. Second, regarding reconnections with public life, as women and teenagers become "workers" as well as family members, the connections between work and family become less easy to separate. What used to be private is increasingly a public issue, as in the case of child care and domestic abuse. It would have been unthinkable three decades ago for wives to bring (successful) suits against husbands for rape, as was done in the 1970s. For better or worse, the social regulation of families by public agencies (courts, social workers, schools, and government) has increased. While it is not clear that the problems of families have increased, it is clear that the social recognition and concern about such family problems has increased. In sum, Blake argues that families are becoming less clearly differentiated and more connected to the rest of society. There are some positive consequences of this. She thinks that today's families are more flexible and provide more family role options for individuals who cannot, for various reasons, conform to the romanticized ideals of the traditional family (1979:198).

That is indeed a provocative thesis. However you perceive it, families are changing. Many families have four or even five generations alive at the same time, and over half of the people over age 65 have great-great grandchildren. It therefore makes less sense today to think of "family" simply as a nuclear family of parents and children (Gross and Scott, 1990; Baca-Zinn and Eitzen, 1993). The diversity and unpredictability of families represent different ways of adapting to larger economic, community, and political circumstances in ways that try to preserve the core benefits of family and household support systems. The boundaries between families as private spheres (where intimacy is still negotiated) and the family as a set of public issues (involving our laws, politicians, and social agencies) is shifting and contentious. Our view is that some established family forms and their legitimation are dying, but in the confusion of change and adaptation, families are in the process of being *reinvented.* It is a messy process, and we grapple with its uncertainties.

TRANSFORMING WORK

Besides family life, most of us spend the bulk of our adult life at work. Love it or hate it, work is an important category of activity for us, and it has an enormous effect on our family life. For some people, work is their central life interest. For others, it is simply a means to an end, something to be endured until the workday is over and more meaningful activities can begin (Hall, 1994:355). We never experience work as a neutral activity. Whether or not Americans' commitment to work (the work ethic) has declined is not clear. But one thing is clear—for adults, not to have a job is stigmatizing. (Consider how Americans view people who live on public welfare.) Still, in 1995 a study of over 1000 American adults found that 51 percent wanted more leisure time and that 33 percent would spend that time with their families (Galvin, 1995).

How Is Work Changing?

Starting with some less controversial and established facts about changing worklife, we will again quickly arrive at the center of another perplexing, troubling, and emotional issue that contemporary Americans face.

First, *far fewer of us are employed in agriculture than was true in 1940.* The long-term trend has been for fewer of us to be self-employed and more to work for large organizations, but since the 1980s the direction of that trend has reversed (Handler, 1988). There are still lots of jobs in manufacturing and producing goods, but those jobs are growing slowly in relation to the growth of the economy and the labor force. The most rapidly growing job sector has been *services,* where people work in such diverse jobs as retail sales, transportation, education, health care, information, or management rather than producing goods. In 1940, 51.4 percent of the workforce was employed in agriculture and producing goods. But by the early 1990s, only 2 or 3 percent of the American workforce was employed in agriculture, 26 percent in the goods producing and manufacturing sector, and more than 70 percent in service occupations (Hodson and Sullivan, 1995:264). As you can tell from the above list, however, "service" is a category so broad that it is almost meaningless without specification.

Second, *for a long time occupations were considered a key to understanding where people stood in society:* their affluence or poverty, lifestyles, and social prestige. Using occupation to locate people in society has been common among people themselves as well as sociologists. Sociologists, for instance, found evidence that occupation was the best single indicator of a wide range of social characteristics. While this is still true, the connection between occupation and other characteristics is becoming weaker. This is happening because the growth of education has meant growing similarities between people in different occupations, the increasing tendency of people to change occupations during their worklife, and the difficulty of clarifying many of the growing "service sector jobs" by our old notions. But most important, it is because of the growing power of *organizations* in our work life. For example, the term "lawyer" used to tell you a great deal about a person, but increasingly it makes a difference whether one is a lawyer working as an officer in a large investment bank in Los Angeles or doing similar work in a small town bank in Oklahoma. These two lawyers make different amounts of money, work different hours, and have different lifestyles and outlooks. The size of the organizations we work in, the levels in the organizations, and the regions in which we work are all reducing the similarity and solidarity between occupational peers. Obviously, a person's occupation is still a key to understanding social characteristics. But occupation by itself is becoming less important in relation to these other factors (Sullivan, 1990; Leicht and Fenell, 2002; Brint, 1994).

Third, *by all accounts the emergence of the service economy has led to a fundamental transformation of society since the 1950s that is still ongoing.* But descriptions of its important dimensions and social consequences vary. In the most influential account, Daniel Bell argued in 1969 that the transformation from an industrial to a postindustrial society would bring a better world for most workers. For most, work in a postindustrial society would be increasingly upgraded. Making things, industrial style, would become less important and rewarded, while information and information processing would become more important. Dull work would increasingly be done by machines, and human labor, requiring special skills and decision making, would become less routine and more interesting (Bell, 1969). This rosy view of postindustrialism was right in some ways but seriously flawed in others. Bell's (1992) later accounts of change were less uniformly optimistic. An obvious limitation of his early view is that growing service sector jobs included not only the high-skill, high-pay, interesting jobs, but also low-paying, unskilled, and monotonous ones. More recent accounts (Leicht, 1998; 2001) talk about the permanent elimination of jobs and permanent hardship as postindustrial firms search the world for the cheapest labor and favorable tax systems.

What Causes These Transformations of Work and Society?

This is a large and complex question, and here we only want to mention two obvious pieces of the answer. First, technology has been pervasively used to increase production in most economic sectors. The increasing mechanization of agriculture meant fewer human jobs on the farm. Likewise, the advent of computers programmed to design or assemble things meant a decline in the need for human labor (e.g., CAD/CAM systems, respectively, computer assisted design and computer assisted manufacturing). The popular view of the technology and computer revolution was as a liberating experience for workers that enabled them to work more quickly, creatively, and with greater flexibility—as easily from home or a hotel room as the office. But for many, particularly the low-wage service workers mentioned earlier, the reverse seems true. Computerization is thought to have made traditional clerical work skills obsolete; downgraded jobs to lower pay levels; made them subject to automatic pacing and oversupervision; reduced workers' interaction with their work mates; and lowered their sense of accomplishment, freedom, and prestige (Baker, 1991).

This issue raises a very important but complex question: To what extent have computers in work extended human creativity and skill, and to what extent have humans become less-skilled appendages of computers and complex technology? Braverman (1974) argued that in general advanced technology and computers downgraded (or "deskilled") work, with the human consequences described above. As you might guess, because technology and computers are used differently among different kinds of workers in different industries, evidence from empirical studies of this question is complex and often contradictory. (For a summary of evidence, see Spenner, 1990.)

Computer and communication technology made some jobs obsolete but have also created new jobs, such as in telemarketing and booking travel reservations, which epitomize the rapidly growing "service" sector mentioned earlier. It has meant slower growth for manufacturing jobs, even though the demand for "things" has increased. In the larger economic framework, however, technological change has been blamed (or credited) for the creation of a *two-tiered economy,* one segment of privileged, information sector workers with interesting and well-compensated jobs and a second, far larger segment of workers with little access to steady employment capable of supporting middle-class consumer expectations (see Galbraith, 1998).

A second cause of the transformation of work is that *all market economies have become increasingly international,* where money, labor, and products flow across national boundaries. Even when not automated out of existence, jobs in manufacturing are often exported to workers in other nations where labor is cheaper. Television sets are still sold by American companies, but they are likely to be manufactured in Mexico or Singapore. Still, considering the whole American economy over the last forty years, technological changes have had more powerful and pervasive impacts on transforming working life than has the globalization of markets (see Thurow, 1992; Heilbroner and Thurow, 1987).

The joint impact of technological change and internationalization has been the generation of large numbers of jobs where pay is low, work is dull, and employment is unstable. For example, among twenty fastest growing jobs from 1984 to 1995 were accountant and auditor, computer systems analyst, electronic engineer, and financial services manager. But in addition to these skilled information workers, there was a proliferation of jobs for cashiers, janitors and cleaners, waiters, nurses' aides, and computer operators. What the latter have in common are low skills, low wages, and monotonous work, and they grew more rapidly than did those for the highly skilled information workers (Dolbeare and Hubbell, 1996: 37–38; Hall, 1994: 73–74; Pavalko, 1988:223; Rubin, 1996: 42–43, 64–65; Sheak, 1994; Silvestri and Lukasiewicz, 1985; Tolbert et al., 1980).

Who Gets What Kinds of Jobs?

The answer is obvious on one level: Whether you get an interesting skilled job or an unskilled, monotonous, and low-paying one depends on the qualifications that you bring to the labor market. But there's more to it than this: Researchers have discovered that in addition to skills, other characteristics irrelevant to job performance determine what kinds of persons get which jobs. To put it quite simply, older people and white males are concentrated in the primary sector while younger people, women, and ethnic minorities are concentrated in the secondary sector. This is still true in spite of impressive gains by women and some minorities in many job sectors in recent decades. The reasons for this state of affairs are complex and have to do with both the unequal distribution of skills and discrimination. But the important point here is that the question "Who has the good and bad jobs?" is still generally answered in terms of age, gender, and ethnicity. And many workers in the secondary sector are stuck there. Abundant evidence exists for these generalizations. (For good summaries, see Hall, 1994; Hodson and Sullivan, 1995.) In comparison to the United States, Norway and Sweden have less-segmented labor markets and lower income gaps between higher-paid and lower-paid workers (Rosenfeld and Kallenberg, 1990).

In reading about these changes, we are sure you have been thinking about the implications or the quality of work life in America. For most of us that is an important personal question. It is also a terribly important social and public policy question for Americans today. They have a lot of anxiety about jobs and careers—even in a period of economic growth and expansion that characterized most of the early 1990s. And well they should. Pervasive corporate "downsizing," or other euphemisms for laying off workers, creates fear and stress among employees at all levels and incomes. Good jobs provide a reasonably comfortable and secure lifestyle, but getting and keeping them has become a problem for many Americans. By 1995, average U.S. wages had fallen more than 20 percent in the previous twenty-two years. Nearly one-fifth of America's year-round workers earned less than a poverty wage. For young full-time workers it was worse. Nearly 47 percent of the 18- to 24-year-old workers earned less than an official poverty wage (Snyder, 1996). You might like to think that these percentages represent people on their way to or between good jobs. Alas, evidence suggests that is not the case. The most persuasive evidence came from interviews with a nationwide representative sample of 1265 Americans conducted during December 1995 conducted by *The New York Times* (1996a;1996b).

The Changing Quality of Work: Say Goodbye to a Safe and Predictable Career

If you consider jobs lost in relation to existing and new jobs, the American economy produced a remarkable net gain of 27 million jobs between 1979 and 1995, enough to absorb all the laid-off workers and new people beginning careers. The early and mid-1990s were periods of sustained economic expansion and corporate profitability and a time in which national unemployment rates were low. Problems with work in the 1990s thus had little to do with the rampant unemployment of economic recessions or depressions, but rather with an emerging redefinition of employment. Of the jobs lost since 1979 some were the result of the normal churning of economic cycles. But increasingly jobs were disappearing for good, and most recently they were the jobs of higher-paid, skilled, white-collar workers and managers, many of whom work for large corporations rather than less-skilled or blue-collar employees (*The New York Times,* 1996a: A1). Consider the following:

- Three-fourths of all American households had an encounter with layoffs since 1980.
- One-third of all households had a member who lost a job, and almost half of all individuals had a friend or relative who lost a job.

- In a reversal of the trend of the early 1980s, workers with some college make up the majority of persons whose jobs were eliminated, outnumbering the less-educated workers.
- In the mid-1990s, better-paid workers made up twice the share of those whose jobs were eliminated as in the early 1980s.
- Twice as many people were affected by layoffs than by any form of violent crime, even though crime is much more often mentioned as a serious social issue.
- Twenty-five years ago, the majority of those laid off eventually found jobs that paid as well. Since the 1990s only about 35 percent do.

There are several forces that drive the changing quality of worklife in America, and they build on the two basic causes of work transformation noted earlier:

1. Stunning technological progress that lets machines replace people.
2. Efficient and wiley competitors among organizations and corporations, both domestic and foreign.
3. Stern insistence from financial investors on buoyant profits, even if it means casting people off, resulting in a sort of commercial triage either to protect or to restore profitability.
4. *Outsourcing*, that is, contracting with outside individuals or firms, usually domestic ones, to do what employees of companies used to do. (*The New York Times*, 1996a:A1, A26).

Not only are laid-off workers more likely to find part-time work, but the last driving force, outsourcing, means that part-time and temporary (or "contingent") workers who do what full-time employees used to do form a growing part of the labor force. In fact, the nation's largest private employer, with over 767,000 jobs in 1995, was Manpower Inc., from whom almost any kind of worker can be rented for a contracted time. Part-time and temp workers used to be mainly unskilled or semi-skilled. In the new labor force, however, well-educated workers are used in the same way. Researchers find that between 20 percent and half of all temp workers are now employed in professional, managerial, technical, sales, and administrative support work; that is likely to include accountants, architects, engineers, financial advisors, lawyers, nurses, and doctors. Some temp workers do so by choice, but the proportion who would rather have full-time jobs or even permanent part-time work is growing even more rapidly than the number of temp workers (Rubin, 1996:76; *The New York Times*, 1996a: A28; Sheak and Dabelko, 1990: 116). In 1999, United Parcel Service workers actually went on strike in an attempt to secure more permanent and steady jobs, and the decreased unemployment rate of the late 1990s has made demands for steadier work more salient for employers looking for workers with the skills they need.

As steady work and wage increases have become a mirage for many Americans, so have the employee benefits that they had come to expect with jobs. After increasing from the 1950s to about 1980, the proportion of American workers covered by company health and pension plans has declined (U.S. Bureau of the Census, 1999a). This happened because of the weakening effectiveness of labor unions (which politically supported fringe benefit programs), the emergence of part-time employment, the growth of employment in smaller firms, and the growth of low-wage service jobs—all associated with the emerging service economy. The decline in workers covered by health care plans (much of which came with jobs) combined with increasingly expensive health care became an immediate problem for workers and their families. Industry and political leaders have widely recognized these problems but have been unable to address them in any significant way. The erosion of private pensions is equally important, but a delayed problem for people who are still working. As we noted earlier, pensions and health care are likely to become intense personal and public policy issues as the large cohort of Boomer workers age and retire. Increasingly, even having a steady job no longer means access to health care for many Americans.

Work Satisfaction: How do Workers Experience and Adapt to the New Changes in Work?

Unless you have been living under a rock somewhere, not listening to media reports or to people talk about their work, you know that in the 1990s many Americans were disturbed and increasingly anxious about the changes in their work. That is our impression but we think it is also very real. Again, consider evidence from the 1995 national survey mentioned earlier. Compared to the recent past:

- 75 percent of all respondents thought companies were less loyal to their workers.
- 64 percent thought workers were less loyal to their companies.
- 70 percent thought workers competed more among themselves, and only 20 percent thought they cooperated more.
- 53 percent thought the mood at work had become angrier, and only 8 percent thought it had become friendlier (*The New York Times,* 1996b:A1).

Respondents who survived corporate downsizing were described as "stunned survivors," adaptable workers who often accepted without sentiment the fact that their company did not owe them as much as people used to expect. They accepted that people often changed or worked more to protect their jobs. Executives who did the downsizing often felt like the "firing squad," who made decisions in the interest of the company and/or shareholders that detonated the careers of co-workers. As you might guess, the personal experience was worse for those who lost a job and either did not find another or found one they defined as a worse one. They had lowered their expectations of life. Some went on living in denial, as if the good times weren't over, living on savings, cashing their insurance policies and pensions. Others were active in diverse networks of ex-employees and job seekers. The study found consequences for children in families where breadwinners had lost a job during the last two decades. They associated more with networks of other children of the laid off. They grew up relatively more quickly and experienced more stress and anxiety about money (*The New York Times,* 1996a:29).

Even with all this, when asked a "global question" about work satisfaction in the mid-1980s, only about 12 percent said they were dissatisfied (National Opinion Research Center, 2000). But "work satisfaction" has been defined in different ways, has different causes, and is notoriously difficult to study. In general, when people are asked more specific questions about their jobs, dissatisfaction and anxiety are often intense. Furthermore, work dissatisfaction has consequences for problems in other areas of life. But empirical studies on this issue are not consistent. Not surprisingly, those who continued to do well during the 1990s were more satisfied than lower-wage and lower-skilled workers or workers whose career expectations were frustrated (see Hall, 1994: 99–118; Hodson and Sullivan, 1995: 93–115). But when downsizing and other powerful forces threaten the human role in the productive process, we can expect dissatisfaction and anxiety about work to become more pervasive.

IN CONCLUSION

We have examined changes in population, family, and work as three of the most important settings for everyday life for people. That discussion may have left you rather gloomy and full of questions and doubts—particularly the discussion of work. Significant social transformations such as we are now living through always involve the death of old worlds (for which we grieve) and the birth of new worlds (about which we are anxious). Since World War II, people have come to expect that their lives and those of their children would steadily improve. Current social transformations make that assumption problematic. But we think our discontent has less to do, as usual, with actual conditions and material well-being than with our expectations and the uncertainties of change. According to social historian David Herbert, "what we are reacting against is the end of a predictable kind of life, just as the people who left the predictable rhythms of the farm in the 1880s felt a loss of control once they were in cities" (*The New York Times*, 1996a:26).

We hope by now that you recognize you can't go very far in understanding how the everyday lives of people change without some understanding of changes in the larger institutions or macro levels of society. We turn to two of these in the next chapter—economics and politics—both of which have profound and pervasive effects on the changing everyday life of individuals.

THINKING PERSONALLY ABOUT SOCIAL CHANGE

1. The inflow of immigrants and differences in birth rates will produce a society that is more diverse in terms of ethnicity, culture, and language. In such a society you will probably have more social contacts with people who are different from you. How are you likely to experience that? You might begin by thinking about the different arenas in which you encounter lots of people: in school settings, clubs, at work, at ball games and concerts, at shopping malls, during visits to large metropolitan areas, and so forth. Was your interaction and conversation with them easy and comfortable or difficult and uncomfortable? In what circumstances do you feel attracted to different people or repelled by them? Don't think about this just in terms of personalities, but in terms of the cul-

tural characteristics of people and the social situations in which you meet them. Explore similar questions with people who are like you and with people who are very different. You might think about how the latter experience social encounters with people like you! If you have grandparents or much younger siblings you can talk with, it would be interesting to compare their answers to these questions.

2. Families have always responded to changes in social institutions, like changes in the economy and work, educational systems, and changes in political power in society and how it is exercised. Family historian Stephanie Coontz argues that families are about as strong and difficult as they were through most of American history (1992). Households of people who live together and feel related invent different cultural styles of managing the boundaries between their households and the outer world. They also evolve different ways of thinking about their relationships within households. Yes, there are family institutions—that is, broadly established patterns and normative ideals about families— but the everyday life reality is that these institutions are being continually reinvented by people who live in them. Many are quite resilient, even in the worst of circumstances. Some are not. Think about the families and households you know or have known. How do they evolve different family cultures and different styles of adapting to a world in change? Talk with some of your friends and acquaintances about this.

3. Shared activity and ritual in recreation and meals are among the traditional sources of family solidarity. We think this aspect of family culture is threatened by what we call the "commodification of everything." Increasingly families eat more meals "cooked" by McDonalds or a subdivision of ConAgra than meals cooked by each other, go separate ways for commodified recreation (movies, sports events), and even watch different TV channels in homes, dictated by individual tastes, rather than entertaining each other or finding joint activities. We think the pervasive commodification of traditional activities weakens family solidarity more than what we think of as "decline in family values" today. We long for family togetherness, yet the penetration of traditional household activities and ritual by the outside world makes it increasingly difficult. Do you agree or not? If this issue interests you, see the writings of sociologist George Ritzer that explore this issue in depth, aptly titled *The McDonaldization of Society* (Ritzer, 2000).

4. Think about the jobs you have had, or think about the work of your older relatives or parents. How do you (and they) experience work? Listen to people talk about their jobs. Even considering their daily frustrations, do people like the jobs they have, or is working purely a means to an end to enjoy other things about life? Putting in time or earning bread is important, and will only be looked down upon by those who have plenty of bread anyway. But this is not a way to experience work in a positive sense. For some, work is like a calling (from which we get the word *vocation*). This way of experiencing work is not necessarily found only among those people with fancy skills or education. We think people who have found their true vocation are the lucky ones. For them working is a source of meaning in life and creativity. It is an intrinsically valuable activity, and they would do something like it even if they were not paid as much. We have heard several musicians and artists describe their work in such terms as well as an older person who was fixing homes and churches in poor communities. But for him it was a rich and meaningful activity. Do you know anyone who thinks about his or her work this way?

4

Economics, Politics,
and the American Prospect

We hope from reading the last chapter that you realize that you can't go very far in understanding personal life changes without some consideration of how these are embedded in large-scale change. Two of the most important such institutional arenas of large-scale change for you to understand are the economy and the political system. You may not be much interested in understanding politics or the operation of the economy, but these forces are "interested" in you, because they jointly shape the circumstances in which much of your life takes place. Together, they integrate and control much of what goes on in the broader society. They define the winners and losers of change by affecting such things as changes in wages; the availability of credit; and the growth and decline of jobs and industries, taxes, benefits we have come to expect, and rules that define our obligations to each other. The connections between economics and politics (or between money and power, if you wish) are so intertwined that to separate them is a bit artificial. But we will do so because we can't analyze everything all at once, and Americans in particular are used to thinking about politics and economics as separate realms. After describing economic changes and then political change, we will end by discussing some particularly important implications of these changes for American problems, public policy, and prospects for the future.

THE CHANGING ECONOMY

In the last chapter we discussed a major and much publicized dimension of economic change—the emergence of the "service" or information-based economy—so here we focus on other aspects of changing economic institutions. You can clearly see in the changing U.S. economy the trends and themes of modernity and the emergence of reactions and countertrends that were the focus of Chapter 2.

Growth in Scale and the Centralization of Economic Power

Until the 1980s, the most dramatic and visible economic trend in the United States was the continued evolution of the huge corporations and corporate empires. Beginning with the historic industrialization of the predominantly agricultural economy in the late nineteenth century, transformation meant a significant increase in the scale of economic transactions and the growth of huge bureaucracies that came to control the relations of investment, production, and employment between firms and people. Then gigantic corporate empires modified the expectations of Americans about the ability of "free markets" to serve interests of the population. The emergence of giant corporations was connected with continual efforts by unions to organize on behalf of workers and by governments to regulate them for the public good.

Large firms and their owners came to have overproportionate power in the American economic enterprise in at least two ways. First, they accumulated power *in ownership of corporate stocks and securities.* Lots of Americans own some shares of stock, but by 1983 people in the upper 10 percent of wealth holders (who numerically made up only 2 percent of the population) owned fully 72 percent of all the stock to be owned (Federal Reserve System, 1984). Even if you account for the presence of big institutional investors in which millions of ordinary people—like us—own annuities and retirement programs, real control of the American economy is largely in the hands of a small number of people (see also Kiester, 1999).

Second, they accumulated power in *market control.* Markets for particular products are dominated by a small number of large firms. Market control was always stronger in manufacturing rather than retail firms, but these firms have become more concentrated also (think of the historic example of Sears and Roebuck and the current dominance of WalMart). One way of visualizing market control is to look at multinational sales data for the world's largest corporations. In the mid-1990s, sales of the 31 largest corporations were the same size or greater than the entire economic output of nations like the Russian Republic, Thailand, Turkey, Poland, and Egypt (see Bradshaw and Wallace, 1996:49). Of these thirty-one multinational corporations, twelve are U.S. based.

Small Firms, Entrepreneurs, and the Bimodal Economy

Giant, highly bureaucratic, and centralized firms are still with us. We're sure this comes as no surprise to you because they still get most of the media attention. But according to many observers, the trends toward greater size, scale, and centralization reached a zenith in the 1970s and are now declining. Futurist John Naisbett claims that by 1994 the "Fortune 500 companies" (that is, the big ones) accounted for only 10 percent of the total U.S. economy, down from 20 percent in the 1970s (Naisbett, 1994: 7; see also Hodson and Sullivan, 1995:407–410; Bartos, 1996), and the trend toward smallness can be seen in employment statistics as well (U.S. Department of Commerce, Bureau of the Census, 1999a). Indeed, the economic news of the

1980s and 1990s is of the growth in small firms and the renaissance of entrepreneurialism. Small firms and entrepreneurs never really disappeared, but their resurrection represents both a historical reality and new cultural themes. The causes of this are complex, but at minimum they involve the struggling performance of the giants (especially during the year 2000 economic downturn) and the struggle by enterprising individuals and small firms to adapt and survive in the service economy with pervasive downsizing, outsourcing, subcontracting, and growth of contingent labor markets. Another factor in the growth of small firms in the late 1990s and beyond has been the development of dotcoms and the e-commerce economy (U.S. Department of Commerce, Bureau of the Census, 1999a). The measurement of e-commerce and other electronic business transactions is still in its infancy (Mesenbourg, 2001), but the latest reliable data on e-commerce suggests that shipments generated from the Internet and web-based commerce accounted for as much as 12 percent of all sales in manufacturing and 13 percent of all mail-order sales in 1999 (U.S. Department of Commerce, Bureau of the Census, 1999b). E-commerce has spawned a sizable, growing, and (as yet) unmeasured army of consultants and small businesses who specialize in electronic marketing, web design, and logistics.

Taken together, small firms control roughly half of the assets in the total economy. They include "mom-and-pop" restaurants and hair dressers of historic vintage but also newer fancy independent entrepreneurs and consultants. In general, three types of small firms have come to exist: (1) satellite firms, which engage in subcontracting with larger ones; (2) loyal opposition firms, which provide competition to larger firms in their own markets; and (3) free agents, which are diverse groups of firms that spring up in uncontested market spaces (the nooks and crannies between larger firms) (Hodson and Sullivan, 1995:407–408). Small firms operate in markets more difficult to organize and bureaucratize on a large-scale basis and are likely to provide services that remain labor intensive. In contrast to the giants, they operate in markets that are highly competitive, unstable, and with profits that often fluctuate wildly from year to year. Also in contrast to the giants, there are few government subsidies, and fewer government regulations.

Beyond their pervasiveness, however, small firms are very important to the economy for other reasons: They are the major source of employment and the creation of new jobs (only about 30 percent of all workers work for the very largest industrial, financial, and service firms). Firms with a small number of employees are more common in retail and service than in manufacturing industries, and they make up between a third and a half of all U.S. companies (estimates vary; see U.S. Department of Commerce, Bureau of the Census, 1999b). Small firms account for a significant proportion of American economic productivity. For instance, in 1994, only 7 percent of American exports were created by the Fortune 500 companies, whereas about 50 percent of American exports are created by firms with nineteen or fewer employees (Naisbitt, 1994:7–8). Furthermore, the capability of small firms to innovate more quickly and less expensively than large bureaucratic organizations has been an often observed fact (U.S. Senate, 1986). It is also the stuff of the contemporary legends of the "information age." Bill Gates (Microsoft Corporation) and Steven Jobs (Apple Computers) both started in garage-sized firms and created huge successful enterprises. But before you get too enthusiastic about the "virtues of small," you should note that business failures and unstable employment are more common among small than large firms.

U-Turn or Dialectic? The Changing Forms and Interaction of "Big" and "Small"

Large-scale economic structures have not really declined (that is, done a U-turn) with the recent proliferation of small firms and entrepreneurs. Rather, large-scale economic structures have persisted and evolved through different historical forms that facilitated the persistence and emergence of small-scale ones. How so? In the United States there have been five different meanings and historical forms of economic concentration:

1. *Expansion in a market* is the oldest American form of growth in scale. Beginning in the 1890s and continuing into the twentieth century, firms forced their competitors out of business by a variety of means (clearly illegal today) to create huge monopolies exercising complete control in markets for particular products. Examples of such giants were Westinghouse, International Harvester, Standard Oil, United Fruit Co., American Tobacco, and United States Steel (Hodson and Sullivan, 1995:396). Some operating oligopolies remain where a few firms dominate particular markets (Microsoft's domination of the computer software market is the most visible example). There are still firms that grow by expanding in a market and by extending their operation to new areas rather than acquiring other firms (e.g., McDonalds, Toys-R-Us).
2. *Multidivisional firm mergers,* pioneered in the 1920s, enabled a firm to produce and market a number of related products through separate divisions. DuPont and General Motors are prime examples. This kind of merger allowed economic growth through acquisition of firms in related markets, and it was legally discouraged in the 1950s.
3. *Conglomerate mergers* dominated the 1970s. They involved a strategy of corporate growth by acquiring firms in unrelated market areas and product lines—giving rise to a "firm-as-portfolio" model of corporate practice. Mergers grew in response to unique American antitrust laws. To illustrate, in 1970 Beatrice Foods "held" subsidiaries that produced various packaged foods, dairy products, lunch meats, plumbing supplies, audio equipment, luggage, and travel trailers. In Chapter 2 we described the conglomerate that owns the publisher of this book. These are hardly "coherent" firms, and subsidiaries are related only by common ownership (Davis et al., 1994; Prechel, 2000). Conglomorate mergers continue to dominate in communications, as the widely reported merger between AOL and Time-Warner worth $150 billion (*Economist,* 2000), following on the heels of an earlier merger between Disney and ABC (completed in 1995) and the reported merger of Viacom and CBS in 1999 (*Economist,* 1999). These recent mergers suggest that the conglomerate form that was popularized in the 1970s has spread to the communications industry, where increasingly all types of media (television, radio, the Internet, and motion pictures) rely on the same computer-integrated technologies.

4. *Deconglomeration* was common by the 1990s because of mounting evidence that (1) giant conglomerates were not very competitive and were relatively unprofitable, and (2) their component subsidiaries were often worth more taken separately than was the whole conglomerate. Many conglomerates were taken over and broken up; that is the subsidiaries were sold separately. The remaining conglomerates became more focused through voluntary restructuring and selloffs. The new firms that joined the set of the largest U.S. industrials were only about half as diverse as the ones they replaced.

5. *Strategic alliances,* that is, temporary network coalitions between smaller, more focused, firms, proliferated in the 1990s. These are open networks (*joint ventures,* or *enterprize webs,* in business buzz words), and corporations are being reconceptualized as voluntary and temporary, as "dense patches in networks among economic free agents" (Zukin and DiMaggio, 1990:7). This newer conception of corporations as "boundary-less networks" is replacing both older conceptions of firms as coherent organizational actors with bureaucratic boundaries and "bodies," and the firm-as-portfolio conception of the 1970s. This new structural form is coming to dominate both national and international business. Strategic alliances are ways that small and middle-sized firms can survive and compete. It is a form that seems optimum for the service or information-based economy: using temporary employees rather than fixed organizational members (with entitlements), and every activity that does not add sufficient economic value is outsourced to subcontractors rather than brought within the firm's boundaries (Davis et al., 1994:565–566; Skaggs and Leicht, 1997; Leicht and Fennell, 2002). These strategic alliances are possible because computers and other communications technologies have lowered monitoring costs so that people can interact and monitor the activities of people in remote areas of the world (see Castells, 1998; Leicht and Fennell, 2002).

You need to appreciate what radically different forms of social organization emerged within business communities and the economy. Since the 1700s, corporations have been understood as entities with a "natural coherence"; as bureaucratic "bodies" with fixed boundaries that delineated them. Courts gave corporations and other bureaucratic entities legal standing as persons (Coleman, 1990); you can sue or be sued by a corporation. Strategic alliances and open networks call those assumptions into question. We think they will eventually make our view of other bureaucratic entities (such as universities and governments) more problematic (see Leicht, 1998).

Another important aspect of economic change underlines the connections between economics and politics that we noted at the beginning of this chapter. Since the development of powerful giant firms in the late nineteenth century, and certainly since the Great Depression of the 1930s, Americans looked to governments (state and federal) to (1) "broker" a social contract between firms, workers, and consumers; (2) stabilize the economy and promote economic growth; and (3) regulate firms in the public good (Rubin, 1996). Governments did this, for example, by regulating interest rates to smooth out the ups and downs of economic cycles; by assuming responsibility for education, research, problems of unemployment and environment; and by representing the overseas interests of American companies. All of that worked reasonably well as long as the economy was substantially a national one, in which

American governments had clear jurisdiction. International trade existed, of course, but even in the 1960s the United States still had largely a national economy, in which only 4–6 percent of the cars, steel, or electronic products were imported from other nations (Reich, 1991:63). But by the mid-1970s that interinstitutional arrangement between government and the economy seemed to spin out of control, and clearly something was wrong. What was wrong was that the post–World War II social contract was being rendered anachronistic by another social transformation. Increasingly there is no "American" economy at all, but rather an American "dense node of relations" in a worldwide economic system (see Castells, 1998).

Entering the Global Market Economy

Since the 1970s, the operations and investments of American firms became increasingly international, as they opened sales offices and bought subsidiaries in other countries, invested in overseas products and firms, contracted with foreign suppliers for special parts and labor, and engaged in joint ventures with firms from other nations. From 1950 to 1998, American direct overseas investment grew from 12 billion to about 2 trillion dollars (U.S. Department of Commerce, Bureau of the Census, 1977, 1999a). By the 1990s, practically every large American corporation was involved internationally in developing nations and less developed ones. Similarly, foreigners invested in American companies, bought American companies, and came to sell their products and services. This has caused Americans a great deal of worry about losing our economy to foreigners. But it is important to note that the reverse was also true: American companies are buying interests in other countries. Firms and banks in all nations are becoming so intertwined that as capital, parts, labor, and expertise flow across national borders it becomes increasingly difficult to distinguish between domestic and foreign products.

You can get a sense of this growing internationalization by going shopping and reading the labels about where things are manufactured. Even where brand labels are American or Japanese, they are likely to contain foreign components or engineering. For example, if you bought a new Pontiac LeMans auto in 1990, you paid about $20,000. Of that, $6,000 went to South Korea for routine labor assembly operations; $3,500 to Japan for components (engines, transaxels); $1,500 to Germany for styling and design engineering; $800 to Taiwan, Singapore, and Japan for small components; $500 to Britain for advertising and marketing services; and about $100 to Ireland and Barbados for data processing. The rest (about $8,000) went to American workers, executives, and shareholders. The 2000 Ford Crown Victoria Interceptor, a car produced for police departments across the country, is considered foreign under federal rules because only 73 percent of its parts were U.S. made. The Honda Accord Coupe is assembled primarily in Marysville, Ohio. Ford Motor Company owns a controlling interest in Jaguar, and Chrysler corporation has merged with Mercedes-Benz to form Daimler-Chrysler, an auto conglomerate that is part owner of Rolls-Royce. These examples from the auto industry are not atypical. If you buy a Japanese nameplate television set, there is a good chance that it was assembled in Tijuana,

Mexico, from parts made in other East Asian nations (Kenney et al., 2001). Are these American products or Japanese products? It's hard to tell.

In the world market economy different structural forms have emerged that parallel the bimodal "national" economy described above. There are huge multinational corporations that get most of the political and media attention (usually as villains!). But these are increasingly connected to vast networks of independent contractors, consultants, subsidiary firms, and mid-sized companies in different nations. Their products, whether in manufacturing, finance, or other services, are tailor made by executives and experts who put together or broker such products by creatively integrating the skills, resources, and capital of a diverse set of economic actors. There are signs that labor unions are reorganizing internationally. Rather than being structured bureaucratically and hierarchically, they have become connected horizontally (Reich 1991:87; Naisbitt, 1994; Bartos, 1996:310). There are, of course, still national firms whose business is strictly domestic. But transnational enterprise webs in a global market economy are the future.

Economic globalization has a lot to do with the occupational changes we discussed in the last chapter. America's role in the global market economy is not to provide much routine labor, which can usually be done cheaper elsewhere. Hence the declining fortunes of factory workers and their unions. What industrial nations like America provide is financing, expertise, and creativity in arranging high-value products and services. Workers who by education and experience can provide such services will realize the most growth of income and opportunity. The problem is that such occupations now account for only about 20 percent of the labor force, and it is not clear how the majority of American workers will benefit from globalization. Thus there are winners and losers, and devising policies to broadly distribute the benefits of globalization will be a daunting prospect (see Rifkin, 1995).

CHANGE IN THE POLITICAL SYSTEM

The standout story of political change since 1900, the 1930s, or 1950 (pick your own benchmark) is the dramatic growth in the scale and the scope of the state (which includes government in all its branches and levels).

Growth in the Scale and Scope of Government

Prior to 1929, America had "limited governments" that provided for national defense, police and fire protection, guaranteed legal contracts, and—oh yes—produced lots of corrupt pork-barrel benefits for powerful groups. There was not much public education until the middle of the nineteenth century, when it was established mainly for the "indigent" classes (i.e., the poorest of the poor), and there was no personal income tax until 1913. Since that time the functions of government have mushroomed, most dramatically during the Great Depression of the 1930s and in the postwar period through the 1970s. It's hard to think of anything important that is now not regulated by a federal, state, or local government agency.

Think of the ways that government regulation intrudes into your personal life: You need a building permit to build an addition onto your home and you may have an occupation—anything from beautician to teacher—that requires government licensing. Government regulations determine what you can do with your trash, how many fish you are allowed to catch, where and what hours of the day you are permitted to drink alcohol, how many pets you are allowed to keep and how they shall be confined; they may also rule that children be taken from your custody. Expansive governments seek to regulate and stabilize the economy, care for the environment, and provide for the general welfare of the population through a vast array of social programs (Social Security, unemployment assistance, aid to the disabled, aid to education, subsidies for medical research, to name only a few). Governments became sponsors of social reform efforts, from protecting the rights of workers and the unemployed during the Great Depression to the extension of civil rights and equal opportunity to cultural minorities in the 1960s.

You can get a summary sense of government spending for various things from Table 4-1. Note that "social spending" increased from about 38 percent to more than 60 percent of all government spending from 1950 to 1998. Most of this was not "welfare" for the poor, but Social Security, Medicare, and other benefits for those who were not officially poor. Governments have been much better at keeping people from becoming poor than making the poor "unpoor," though there is little public recognition of this achievement (how would you take credit for keeping something bad from happening?). Defense spending has fluctuated and fallen to 20 percent of all government spending, mostly since the end of the Cold War in the late 1980s.

Growing government expenses and debt. The growth of government spending is illustrated in Table 4-1. It tells you what everybody already knows: Government spends a lot more money than it used to. The federal government, for example, spent

TABLE 4–1	GOVERNMENT SPENDING, 1960–1998						
	GDP (1992$)[a]	Federal Spending (1992$)	Federal Spending %GDP	National Debt %GDP	Federal Social Spending[b] %GDP	%All	Federal Defense Spending %GDP	%All
1960	2263	278	18	47	NA	NA	NA	NA
1970	3398	390	20	29	14.7	48.2	8.3	41.8
1980	4615	423	21	27	18.5	56.5	5.3	27.2
1990	6136	542	22	56	10.8	49.4	6.5	29.8
1998	7552	453	20	65	12.1	62.5	4.0	20.6

a. GDP = gross domestic product, the value of all domestically produced goods and services, in 1992 constant dollar values.

b. Social spending includes social insurance, public aid, veterans' benefits, education, housing, and other welfare payments.

Sources: Stanley and Niemi (1995: 384, 390, 392), U.S. Department of Commerce, Bureau of the Census (1999a).

$278 billion dollars in 1960 and $542 billion dollars in 1990 (in 1992 constant dollars). The federal budget deficit of $290 billion in 1992 turned into a budget surplus by 1998, but (as Table 4-1 shows) the total national debt continued to rise as the U.S. government issued bonds to finance prior budget deficits. The great budget issue has shifted from the "great deficit" debate of the 1980s and 1990s to the "budget surplus" debate of the year 2000 presidential election, culminating in the election of George W. Bush and the passage of the 2001 tax cut.

But wait. Just as credit bureaus determine how much money you can borrow in relation to your ability to pay, look at government debt not in terms of absolute dollar figures, but in relation to the size of the economy that supports such deficits. The 1950 deficit, although much smaller, was proportionally larger in relation to the size of the supporting economy (GDP) than the deficit is today. Then we were still paying the bills from borrowing to fight World War II. The GDP, or gross domestic product, measures the value of all domestically produced goods and services and is a more accurate measure of national economic productivity than the gross national product (GNP), which includes the value of overseas investments. The national debt as a proportion of the GDP dropped to less than 30 percent by 1980 and then began to rise, because the government was borrowing more and because the inflation rate declined, making the impact of past borrowing seem relatively greater. Ironically, this increase in debt was presided over by conservative and center politicians, particularly President Ronald Reagan, who came to power in the 1980s and 1990s promising to lower the federal deficit and balance the books. George Bush and Bill Clinton inherited a lot of public debt but were better budget balancers. Looking at the national debt as about half the size of the productivity of the economy is like saying that you have high consumer credit debt, but your income is still twice as much as what you owe. It at least gives you a different perspective than the political rhetoric we routinely hear. Is U.S. national debt too high? It's a judgment call (Stanley and Niemi, 1995:379–381).

There's more. Some economists and politicians think that a high government debt retards economic performance and growth. Government borrowing, so the reasoning goes, soaks up money from lenders that could be invested in the private economy. But the other side of the coin is that high government spending may stimulate economic growth as the government itself becomes a major purchaser of goods and services. Economic conservatives argue that economic growth is promoted by less government spending (and particularly less borrowing), thus leaving more money in the private economy. Other economists advocate "spending" our way out of economic downturns by using state deficits to stimulate the economy. This strategy (known as *Keynesian economics,* after the English economist who first theorized about the stimulating effect of government spending) has been practiced in one form or another, deliberately or otherwise, by many states since the Great Depression of the 1930s. Furthermore, as every business manager or student who takes out loans knows, some borrowing is an investment in a better future and other borrowing is just to pay off accumulated past debts. Our point here is not that the national debt shouldn't be of concern, but simply that economic growth can be coupled with high levels of public spending. Few economic conservatives would agree with this point, mainly for ideological reasons.

Growth, but relatively decentralized. You may find some of this discussion surprising, because it is so different from our common beliefs and political rhetoric about the growth of "big government." Governments closest to home in literally thousands of unconnected state, county, municipal and public educational agencies have grown more rapidly than has the federal government. Federal spending accounted for almost two-thirds of all government spending in 1950 but had dropped to about one half of it by the 1990s, not counting grants to states and localities.

You can see some of this effect in Table 4-2. Federal government grants to state and local governments have increased and comprise an increasing proportion of state and local budgets. Federal employment has grown modestly since 1950, relative to the larger growth of state employees and the mushrooming number of local government employees. In fact, federal employees make up a declining percentage of the total U.S. workforce, declining steadily from 3.8 percent in 1970 to 2.1 percent in 1998 (U.S. Department of Commerce, Bureau of the Census, 1994:347; 1999a:338, 441).

The growing divergence between federal and collective state/local growth rates was visible by 1980 but became an aspect of public policy after that in the "new Federalism" and "revenue sharing" of the Reagan-Bush administrations and in continuing attempts of politicians to downsize federal government and shift functions to the states in the 1990s.

The relatively decentralized federal structure of growth in the United States is also visible by comparing American government growth with most—but not all—other industrial democracies. National and local taxes were lower in relation to our

TABLE 4–2 FEDERAL GRANTS TO STATE AND LOCAL GOVERNMENTS, AND GOVERNMENT EMPLOYMENT, 1950–1998.

| | Federal Grants[a] ($ billions) | % of State and Local Budgets | Number of Government Employees (millions) | | |
			Federal	State	Local
1950	2.3	——	1.8	.8	2.8
1960	7.0	.15	2.0	1.3	4.2
1970	24.1	.20	2.9	2.9	7.0
1980	91.5	.28	3.0	3.6	9.0
1992	128.1	.24	3.1	4.2	11.0
1997	132.1	.24	2.8	4.7	12.0

a. Federal grants in aid to state and local governments.
Source: Stanley and Niemi (1995:293, 299); U.S. Department of Commerce, Bureau of the Census (1999a:338, 348).

GDP than to most other industrial nations, including Canada, France, Germany, the Netherlands, and the United Kingdom—but not Japan. Besides expenditures and taxes, the United States has a significantly more decentralized federal structure of governance than most other industrial democracies. Canada is probably the standout example of a more decentralized structure, because Canadian provinces have many more responsibilities and control over their budgets than do American states as well as more power in relation to the national government in Ottawa (OECD, 1982:16 1; U.S. Department of Commerce, Bureau of the Census, 1994:347).

American Ambivalence: Reversing the Growth of Governments?   It is no secret that most Americans dislike growing governments and suspect them of incompetence (or worse). They often resent its personal intrusiveness, costliness, and apparent inefficiency. They particularly resent the federal government—even if its actual role is not well understood. Why? Partly because historically Americans have been culturally so individualistic and the "most anti-state people in the Western world, probably on earth" (Kazin, 1994), and partly because of the turmoil of the 1960s during which the Boomers came of age.

> We had a period from World War II through the 1950s where the government was seen as having rescued the nation from the Depression and successfully prosecuted the war, and then we were told in the 1960s that the emperor has no clothes and people shouldn't accept what they're told. And rather than going away, that sensibility has grown over the past 30 years. (Marwell, 1994)

Our dislike of governments is reflected in evidence about growing mistrust of all institutions and leaders that was noted in Chapter 2. Add to that the political climate of 1990s, where politicians ran for office as "outsiders" and most pledged to "scale back" government spending, balance the books, and cut taxes. With these pressures, you would think more would have been accomplished in the last decade. But politicians often creatively rearranged budgets between agencies or between the Feds and the states to make us think they have accomplished more.

Why, then, has it been so difficult to reverse the trend of the growth and expanded functions of governments? We think there are two kinds of reasons. First, with the exception of the small number of homegrown terrorists and militias of the 1990s trying to secede or blow up government facilities, most Americans are actually *ambivalent* about the expansion of governments. Concretely most people are unwilling to give up the expanded state functions—especially when it is their *particular* benefit. Besides, most government expenditures do not go to people defined as "undeserving." They go to those defined as "middle class" or above (Phillips, 1995). In a political democracy it is possible to mobilize political protection for benefits applicable to a broad spectrum of the electorate, such as protection for Social Security for elderly people. *More theoretically,* large states with regulatory powers seem necessary to maintain public order and civility. Even though costly and inefficient, they are often important problem solvers (though certainly not the only ones) in complex modern societies.

The Changing Bases of Political Mobilization

Compared with states in premodern and traditional societies, all states in the modern world depend more heavily on broad popular support for legitimacy. The mobilization of popular support for the state takes a wide variety of forms, including one-party authoritarian systems and more democratic multiparty systems. It is conventional to distinguish between *states* (or governments)—which create and administer laws, policies, and programs; collect taxes; and allocate budgets—and *political parties,* which aggregate and balance diverse and often conflicting popular demands. Parties have the functions of converting diffuse political sentiments into specific political programs, developing policy, and grooming leadership. American political parties are not so much ideological groups (as are European parties) as they are loose coalitions defined by common economic interests as well as social and cultural characteristics. Here we want to discuss some important changes in the mechanisms of popular political support in the postwar period.

Decline in the Effectiveness of Political Parties. One of the best-documented changes is the steady weakening of the power and influence of parties themselves (Lowi and Ginsberg, 1994:485–499). There are different indicators of this decline. The dependability of party support among voters declined as volatility—that is, the inclination of voters to shift parties between elections—increased. In a related trend, voters are more likely to split their votes between candidates of different parties. For example, the proportion of voters who reported that they have voted for different parties in presidential and national congressional (House) elections grew from 13 percent in 1952 to 22 percent in 1992, while those who identified themselves as "independent voters" grew from 6 percent to 12 percent in 1994 (Stanley and Niemi, 1995:136, U.S. Department of Commerce, Bureau of the Census, 1999a:299).

American voters are more fickle and less predictable in their party loyalties. While you may think it is good that party loyalty has declined, it represents a decline in the mooring mechanisms of parties and indicates that the power, stability, and predictability of the two-party system has diminished. Political scientists have speculated about the development of a relatively "partyless" electoral process (Crotty and Jacobson, 1980:248).

Declining support for political parties relates to the growing distrust in public institutions noted in Chapter 2, to the fact that Americans are often turned off by political campaigns themselves, and to lower voter turnout in the United States than in most other industrial democracies (Welch et al., 1994:179–180). Besides Americans' distaste for politics, there are causes of the weakening of political parties internal to the political process itself: political reforms and new technologies in electoral campaigns. Reforms to get politics away from control by corrupt political machines (beginning at the turn of the twentieth century) included (1) the introduction of secret ballots that reduced poll workers' ability to influence voters, (2) replacing party-printed ballots with government-printed ones that increased "split ticket" voting, and (3) the creation of primary elections before general elections that reduced the control of party bosses and elites over the nomination process (Valelly 1990:196). New technologies in political campaigns include (1) using the broadcast media, (2) public opinion polling, (3) phone banks, and (4) direct-mail fund raising and advertising. These proved effective but expensive. They promoted a shift from labor-intensive politics, where party workers and loyalists were important to elections, to capital-intensive politics, whereby candidates with enough money could tailor issues to voters and mobilize them regardless of party loyalty. Not incidentally, it gave wealthy people and organizations more control over the political process than they had historically (Lowi and Ginsberg, 1994:499–500).

Even the reforms designed to lessen the influence of large financial contributions have had interesting (and unintended) consequences. New rules that limit the size of contributions from political action committees (PACS) have produced tightly knit networks of PACS that refer politicians to each other in search of campaign financing. The single large contributions of the 1960s and 1970s have been replaced by multiple contributions from PACS that "recommend" political candidates to each other in a slowly expanding web of influence (Clawson and Neustadtl, 1998).

Ticket splitting, the rise of independent voters, political reforms, and the introduction of new technologies have reduced historic forms of electoral fraud, corruption, and political cronyism. They are consistent with individualism and the desirability of having informed and educated voters. But their unanticipated consequences reduced the power and public responsiveness of political parties as organizations. New mobilization technologies (especially television) increasingly reduced politics to images and soundbites so that a candidate's looks, style, and stage presence are perhaps as important as his or her political ideas. Candidates for political office are less dependent on previous political experience, party connections, roots in the community, or bonds to the people they seek to represent. They mainly need the ability to use television, to follow the advice of consultants, and to pay for the services rendered (we think the last is the most important!).

The U.S. political system has moved some distance from party politics toward personal candidate politics. These changes mean that the important public responsiveness of political parties are greatly impaired because they have less control over (1) the selection of candidates, (2) the grooming of political leadership, and (3) the formulation of policy. Parties still matter because they provide services to candidates and affect the voting patterns of legislators. But they are threatened with political irrelevance as the real political action has increasingly moved outside the area of party politics. If this is true, what new structures emerged to mobilize political desires and needs into governments? It's a fair question.

Political Action Committees and Other Forms of Political Mobilization. Political parties have declined as the popular base of political mobilization while the importance of single-issue political groups has increased. They form to promote the political interests of a particular group, such as cotton growers, beef ranchers, gun manufacturers, environmentalists, nurses, lawyers, peace advocates, and evangelical religionists. In contrast, political parties attempt to balance and combine the interests of broad spectrums of groups in the population. Single-issue interest groups and their lobbyists are certainly not new to American politics, but the 1971 Federal Election Campaign Act regulated their existence and made a way for any group or organization to establish a "segregated separate fund" for political purposes. Such political action committees (PACs) have become a major force in American politics as the power of parties declined. PACs are far more important than parties as sources of campaign money, outstripping their contributions by margins of 5 to 1 by the mid-1980s (Malbin, 1982:42).

There are a vast array of PACs organized around almost every conceivable political and cultural issue. In 1998, they spent collectively over $470 million in lobbying, campaign contribution, and litigation. Here are the major official categories of PACs, the proportion of the total PAC money each spends, and examples of each:

- 42 percent corporate PACs
- 9 percent labor (Teamsters, Communication Workers of America, AFL-CIO)
- 22 percent trade organizations/membership organizations/health organizations (National Rifle Association, American Medical Association PAC, National Association of Broadcasters PAC)
- 24 percent unconnected (ideological, National Right to Life PAC, Conservative Campaign Fund)
- 3 percent other (rural cooperatives and corporations without stock) (U.S. Department of Labor, Bureau of the Census, 1999a:305)

While the diversity of groups and interests represented by PACs is astonishing, note importantly that the ones that spend the vast share of money influencing politics are those representing the interests of corporations and trade and industry groups. Of almost four thousand registered PACs in 1998, they contributed 63 percent and unions contributed another 20 percent of total PAC money. All other PACs together (primarily ideological interest groups) contribute only about 17 percent (U.S. Department of Commerce, Bureau of the Census, 1999a:305). *Many have questioned the implications of the rise of PACs for the quality of democracy in America.* Most political action committees contribute money to political candidates from both parties (Clawson and Neustadtl, 1996). They can't replicate the functions of parties because they are special interest organizations that make no pretense of promoting broader public interests and are even less able to promote a broad consensus about contentious political problems. PACs are particularly suspect when corporate and business groups have the vast proportion of resources to shape the political process. Perhaps this was always true, but the PAC system amplified and legitimated their ability to do so.

Even so, evidence from research doesn't come close to supporting the view that PACs dominate politics (or particularly the votes of members of Congress) to the exclusion of all other influences. Two factors prevent PACs from exercising more effective control: their public visibility and huge numbers. First, when publicity (thanks largely to the media) makes the role of PACS visible in debates about political issues, their ability to control outcomes depends more on their capability to arouse majority sympathy for a just cause rather than by covert influence peddling. They have greater influence, for example, on narrow and obscure issues rather than broad and visible ones. Second, the dramatic growth of competing PACs over the last thirty years means that congressional committees and government agencies rarely hear from just one organized group without input from opposing groups and independent experts as well. Issue networks of policy experts and multiple organized groups (including PACs) are emerging that remind us of the strategic alliances emerging among businesses. The clout of PACs is still heavily weighted toward business interests. But paradoxically, as the number of PACs and organized interest groups in policy areas has increased, the ability of any one to influence the systems has declined (Kelman, 1996:239–240; Clawson and Neustadtl, 1996).

Observers and political analysts have advanced numerous ideas for dealing with the influence of PACS and the declining influence of political parties. Some have suggested that the two-party system in the United States is tired and worn out. They point to systems of *proportional representation* as a mechanism for reinvigorating party politics (see Phillips, 1995). In proportional representation systems (like those in many Western European nations), parties are awarded seats in legislatures based on the proportion of the total vote they receive above a minimum threshold (usually around 5 percent of the popular vote). Parties that surpass this threshold are rewarded seats in the legislature, and these same parties must unite in ruling coalitions to select an executive and to pass legislative reforms. Proportional representation systems usually produce lively competitions between multiple parties, are better at enforcing party discipline among their legislators, and create parties with more distinct identities that the electorate can identify (see Kouvitaris, 1996).

Others suggest that Internet voting and direct referenda are ways of avoiding the maze of organized interest groups that have made "politics as usual" so unpalatable. Some believe that political power needs to be moved away from Washington, D.C. and dispersed throughout the country so that lobbying and influence activity become more difficult (Phillips, 1995).

But each of these solutions presents further problems of their own. Is "Internet democracy" really democracy in the absence of civilized debate and exchange (Elshtain, 1995)? Could Internet voting systems open the way for new forms of abuse and corruption? Would (say) the ability to select from ten to twelve parties in a proportional representation system unite and invigorate us or simply divide us further? These are some of the many questions we face as American politics moves into the twenty-first century.

As parties and the electoral process declined as effective forms of political mobilization, other forms emerged, including not only PACs, but also *social movements* and their mass demonstrations and protest activities—once considered appropriate only for those on the fringes of the political system. By now, Americans are accustomed to mass rallies about many issues. And at the local level, community associations have grown that have assumed many of the tasks previously undertaken by parties, including voter registration and community welfare.

CHANGE, PROBLEMS, AND THE AMERICAN PROSPECT

These transformations underlie many problems and contentious issues for public policy, now and in the future. Some may be obvious to you by now, but we will use the remainder of this chapter to restate two of them: (1) growing inequality, public policy, and living standards; (2) the fragmentation of democracy in America.

Changing Inequality, Wealth, and Living Standards

One of the most subtle, pervasive, and important changes taking place in America is the gradual redistribution of America's economic resources—a process that has profound implications for changes in the standard of living of Americans. Between World War II and about 1975, the rising tide of the American economy "lifted all boats," so to speak, so that the benefits of continuous economic expansion were widely distributed. The poor become a bit less poor, the middle classes showed real wage gains, and the rich remained rich but commanded a slightly smaller proportion of national wealth than they did in the prewar days. Political initiatives accelerated the economic process, particularly the Great Society anti-poverty and civil rights programs of the 1960s. In 1965, over 20 percent of the nation's children lived in poverty. Five years later, that figure had been sliced to under 15 percent. In that same period, the number of Americans "officially" poor dropped from 19 to 12 percent (Broder, 1991). In short, economic inequality declined during that period.

But since the 1970s, this process has undergone a pervasive and fundamental reversal. However it is measured, income inequality has increased since the mid-1970s. As the GNP continually increased, the highest 20 percent of income earners, and particularly the highest 5 percent, have made huge gains in their "share" of national income. But the entire lower 80 percent of income-earning families has experienced a slow but substantial decline in their share of national income, and the lowest 20 percent of families at the bottom of the income distribution are almost totally left out and find their position even worse. From 1973 to 1993, the share controlled by the top 5 percent increased from 16.6 to 20 percent, the share of the middle 60 percent decreased from 54 to 48 percent, and the lowest 20 percent decreased from 4.2 to 3.6 percent. Another way of describing this effect is that between 1973 and 1993 the upper 5 percent of families saw their huge shares increase by 20 percent, the middle 60 percent decreased their shares by 12 percent and the lowest 20 percent of families saw their measly shares decrease another 25 percent in that time period (Stockhausen, 1995–96:13; see also Dolbeare and Hubble, 1996:38–39.

These figures relate to disposable family income. Wealth is becoming even more unevenly distributed since those at the bottom possess only their disposable income, while those nearer the top own most of the property and corporate bonds and securities. The picture is not substantially different if you look at pretax or post-tax distribution of economic assets. This fundamental redistribution of economic assets among Americans has taken place in periods of economic recessions and in the sustained economic expansion of the 1990s. No longer does a rising tide lift all boats: Something has fundamentally changed in the American political economy. But what is it?

Knowledgeable people agree that income inequality is growing, but there is no consensus about its causes, and even less consensus about how, or whether, public policy should address the problem. Discussions of this are complex, emotional, and politically contentious. In general there are three kinds of understanding of the driving forces of growing income inequality:

1. *Family demography and culture.* Some argue that the growing acceptance of divorce and the growth of female-headed households fuels inequality because it produces poorer female-headed families. Additionally, in an aging society you can expect a net downward shift in average incomes as people retire. Some also argue that it is caused by a decline in the work ethic.

2. *The transformation of the economy, work, and policy.* Others argue that net inequality is driven by the shift to an information-based service economy with less human labor, and to businesses that are systems of temporary strategic alliances. There are fewer permanent employees and fewer benefits long taken for granted by working and middle-class employees. The information-based service economy relentlessly rewards those with high-technology job skills and relentlessly punishes those without such skills. These explanations also emphasize the consequence of the globalization of economies (for a summary of these arguments, see Galbraith, 1998).

3. *Government policies that explicitly favor investment and finance capital over earnings and transfer payments.* Our tax system has lowered taxes on the wealthy while maintaining or raising taxes on the middle class. The taxes imposed by the federal government, Social Security, Medicare, and state and local government entities seem designed to soak the middle class to the benefit of finance and investment interests (see Phillips, 1993, 1995).

These explanations are not mutually exclusive, but we think family demography and culture explanations are the most limited, often taking consequences of destitution and poverty and treating them as causes. Some other things don't fit. For example, divorce and out-of wedlock childbirth increased rapidly during the 1960s, and both leveled off during the 1980s, when the growth of inequality proceeded rapidly. From 1979 to 1987, fully half of the overall increase in poverty occurred among two-parent families, and in 1996 research found that more poor American children actually had two parents that were among the growing numbers of working poor, in low-wage service jobs (Bane, 1989; National Public Radio, 1996). And as we noted, the elderly have not become poor as a category, largely because of improvements in Social Security and health care, though maintaining those benefits will be increasingly difficult politically.

American public policy thinking about the problem has involved three themes. First, *privatize government* regulations and taxes, let private markets dominate, and hope that economic benefits "trickle" down through the system. Privatizing government has been popular because many members of the middle class are convinced the system is rigged against them (see Galbraith, 1998; Phillips, 1995; Edsall and Edsall, 1996). But obviously privatization is not a neutral policy. (It works better for those who already have lots of money, and some things that are socially good, like environmental protection, are not always profitable.) A second involves *economic nationalism,* that is, using government-industry partnerships to protect domestic industries and jobs. But our trading partners would retaliate, and as a consumer you would pay a price. Economic nationalism has broad appeal, but even there the tradeoffs for consumers are great (would you be willing to pay twice as much for a pair of shoes made in the United States instead of Indonesia?).

A third set of ideas would use public money to invest in what economists call *human capital,* that is, the skills of Americans, making us more competitive producers of high-value products in the global economy. But increasing human capital won't change the basic functioning of the system very much since producing more college graduates will lead to credential inflation as jobs formerly performed by high school graduates and dropouts are given to college graduates (Galbraith, 1998). Apart from whether the "fortunate fifth" of Americans are willing to subsidize the skills of the other 80 percent of us (see Reich, 1991), these solutions don't address the basic forces generating increased social inequality in the United States.[1]

The same forces of economic transformation and globalization work in other industrial democracies, but growing economic inequality is much less evident in most other industrial democracies than in Britain and the United States. Harvard economist Richard Freeman, summarizing fifty-four studies, concluded:

> You can overcome market forces that have driven up inequality but you need government intervention to do it. . . . the catch is that government meddling may have priced some low-wage jobs out of the market, and hurt Europe's employment growth. . . . Still, the damage isn't as severe as many Europeans—and U.S. economists—fear. (cited in Bernstein, 1994:80)

European governments "meddle" in markets by redistributing wealth in various ways: by levying sharply progressive income taxes, by mandating high minimum wages, by encouraging collective bargaining rights of unions, by placing value-added taxes on luxury consumption, and by providing "social benefits" in housing, health, care, and other areas. The consequence is tolerating higher unemployment (typically 10–12 percent). Given American attitudes toward governments powerful enough to do these things, it would be difficult to reproduce those institutional patterns here.

Here's the important point. Among industrial democracies, there are two kinds of political-economic policies emerging in the contemporary world: (1) The Anglo-American model, which creates lots of jobs, many with lousy wages, with huge pools of poverty at the bottom and huge pools of wealth at the top; and (2) the continental European model (for lack of a better term), which creates fewer jobs but better ones and relies on powerful states to redistribute sufficient benefits to people and groups to preserve social peace. The disadvantages of the European model are well known: powerful governments, large bureaucracies, higher taxes, and sometimes an inclination for authoritarian "solutions" in hard times. The disadvantages of the Anglo-American model are the very real social costs of vast inequality, such as a large and growing economically and politically marginalized segment of the population characterized by high levels of anxiety and despair; predatory criminality and gang activity in cities; and homegrown terrorists (like the militias of the 1990s).

In the end, vast and increasing levels of inequality have a coercive effect on American social and community life. This happens because high levels of inequality undermine the basis for cooperation in a free society. As many analysts have pointed out, a world with lower inequality is one we would choose without knowing what our eventual place was in it (Galbraith 1998). High levels of inequality make the future certain, undermine the belief that we are all part of a common society, and allow significant segments of the population to opt out of public activities that they would support if their future was unclear and it was possible that (at some future time) they would need those services. In short, rising U.S. inequality is more than just an economic problem. It is a political and cultural one as well.

Changing Democracy in America

From many standpoints, the American political system continues to be envied by many people in the world. It combines political stability with orderly change. It has provided the world with examples of the maintenance of individual rights, of freedom of expression and political dissent, of the ability to freely organize to promote one's interests, and of a system—while certainly not free from abuses—that has legal and electoral processes that prevent the most outrageous forms of political corruption. Having said this, there remain some reasons to be disturbed about the weakening of political parties and the emerging new structural basis of politics discussed above. Prestigious political scientist Walter Dean Burnham eloquently described the implications of weaker political parties more than two decades ago:

> If this long-term trend toward a politics without parties continues, the policy consequences must be profound. One can put the matter with the utmost simplicity: Political parties, with all their well-known human and structural shortcomings, are the only devices thus far invented by the wit of Western man that can, with some effectiveness, generate countervailing collective power on behalf of the many individually powerless against the relatively few who are individually or organizationally powerful. Their disappearance as active intermediaries, if not as preliminary screening devices, would only entail the unchallenged ascendancy of the already powerful. . . . [The decline of parties] would after all, reflect the ultimate sociopolitical consequences of the persistence of Lockeian individualism into an era of Big Organization: oligarchy at the top, inertia and spasms of self-defense in the middle, and fragmentation at the base. (Cited in Etzkowitz, 1974:435–437).

It is reasonable to conclude that the political system is becoming less effective in representing the truly general interests and is more likely to reflect the narrower interests of the wealthy and special interests with lots of cash. This is generally recognized—in the abstract—by both Republican and Democratic politicians, and in the 1990s there was a lot of talk about reforming the PAC system. But let us leave you with a tough question: If elected politicians need money to run effective political campaigns, what reforms would provide an effective way of getting money into the political system and maximize the broad popular representation of that electoral system? If not PACs, then what?

IN CONCLUSION

These first chapters discussed problems and human implications that surround social change in the United States, and we hope they do not leave you with pervasive pessimism and fatalism. That was not our intent. In any case, we think we owe you a compact summary here about changing America and prospects for the future.

Like all nations of the world, the United States is undergoing a transformation from a society and culture patterns of World War II and the following Cold War (1940s through the 1960s) to something different. Four broad causes or driving forces of this transformation to something different are useful to mention (again) here:

- Stunning technical innovation, particularly communication and information technologies
- The emerging world market economy, which confuses the established economic and political expectations of people and nations
- Increased flows of migrants and refugees seeking better lives around the world, who bring richness, diversity, and energy but also problems to their host nations
- The end of the Cold War system of international relationships, alliances, and mutual suspicions that actually stabilized the world's political and military structure for decades (more about this in later chapters).

Changes produced by these driving forces bring a mixed bag of benefits and perplexing problems. These chapters noted many, but here are some we have not discussed. Among the Big Seven industrial nations, America

- has the highest rate of murders reported to the police.
- has the highest rate of reported rapes of young women.
- has the highest rate of handgun ownership per household.
- has the highest rate of births to teenage women.
- generates more municipal garbage per capita.
- has the lowest electoral turnout by eligible voters.
- has the lowest average number of paid vacation days. (Shapiro, 1992)

If you watch the news, you know that such lists of problems seem neverending. But a more balanced view would also note some positive things that have occurred, some of which surprised the pessimists of a decade ago. The standout example is the rebound of the American economy in the 1990s. The American index of economic productivity rose sharply during that decade and our share of world manufacturing exports exceeds that of both Germany and Japan. In the 1980s, many economists feared America was losing out and wrote about "deindustrialization" and losing our economic competitiveness in the emerging world economy (Thurow, 1980; Bluestone and Harrison, 1982). While the United States may be number one in the world economically, figures on economic growth and productivity gains have been flat or declining since the fall of 2000 (*Economist,* 2001a). Just when the U.S. economy was slipping into recession in the fall of 2001, the country was hit with the September 11 World Trade Center/Pentagon disaster, which sent the U.S. economy further into recession and probably instigated a worldwide economic slowdown as well (*Economist,* 2001b). Now the major concern in the United States is over the new global war on terrorism and its effects on the economy. Employment in the U.S. nonfarm sector fell by 199,000 in September 2001, the biggest drop since the 1990–1991 recession. While the U.S. economy remains strong, predictions that growth would continue forever and that the new electronic economy was recession proof seem premature (*Economist,* 2001c).

More positive things: America is still the world's largest national economic market, a fact not lost on our trading partners. The faith that foreign investors have in America can be seen in the fact that when the world economy looks uncertain, the value of the American dollar usually rises in relation to other currencies. Foreign investors believe America is a lucrative place to invest (in fact, their investment is so significant to the economy that if they ever stop, we're in great trouble!). No nation has a more diverse economy, or more scientific or technical creativity. Americans, for example, continue to win a disproportionate share of the world's Nobel Prizes in scientific fields. America's problems have to do with the fears and anxieties about jobs, health care, violence, and community disorders; its successes are surely found in cultural and scientific creativity, in the (macroeconomic) successes of its corporations in the world, and in continuing political importance among the world's nations. Other nations typically believe that addressing world problems requires engaging America in some constructive role. For example, the "peace processes" in both the Middle East and the Balkans could not have even begun without American cooperation and sponsorship (which is not to say they did or will succeed, or that others were not importantly involved). Americans may be resented by people around the world for many reasons, but (officially anyway) the slogan "Yankee Go Home!" is out of fashion.

A key to understanding the complicated and often contradictory experience of social change is recognizing that it is experienced differently by different categories and social classes of people. To get a sense of this range of reaction, try to imagine how the transformations of the last several decades would be differently experienced by successful leaders, scientists, corporate investors, and semiskilled workers who lost good jobs. For many people in the United States, the transformation to "something different" confuses the social contract we have taken for granted for a long time. Many of our responses try to bring back the good times—or at least the ones we think we understand. During major transitions people grieve for lost social worlds. When an old world dies and new worlds are born, there is a lot of upheaval and anxiety about the future. We are like people who lived through the earlier industrial transformation at the turn of the twentieth century, who found themselves in big cities without a working social contract to orient them. Like them, we will find the future to be a whole set of possibilities: of crises and but also of opportunities.

We think we are living through one of the major transitions in human history. We don't yet know how to name it: postmodernism? postindustrial society? information age? global society and economy? new world order? new world disorder and chaos? Different scenarios exist that envision the meaning of change and the American future. A *scenario* is not rigorous forecasting or prediction, but a vision of the future. Here are a few:

1. *Renewal and renaissance.* America is on the verge of a powerful economic, social, and political renewal and revitalization in the emerging information society and world economy. The good news is that most of the bad news is wrong (Naisbett, 1994; Cetron and Davies, 1989; Penner, Sawhill and Taylor, 2000).

2. *Cultural crisis.* America and Western nations are experiencing a moral decline and breakdown of cultural values that result in our inability to deal with change and result in many family, workplace, and political problems (Eckersley, 1993).

3. *Economic and political decline among nations.* Global American economic and political power reached its high point during the decades following World War II and is now on the decline. Like the British empire before us, America overextended its resources and is not the dominant world power it was then (Kennedy, 1987).

4. *Growing inequality and social revolution.* The growth of vast social inequality and the concentration of power and wealth among the relatively small number of elites at the top of society will eventually result in revolutionary change (not necessarily an old-fashioned violent "revolution"). It will be spearheaded not by the very poor, but by increasingly frustrated middle classes (Dolbeare and Hubbell, 1996).

5. *Limits of privatization and return to "progressive" politics.* Analogous to the late nineteenth century, privatization and market solutions for everything accumulate such social costs that the reaction will be widespread demands to create living wages, better health care, corporate responsibility, and more popularly responsive governments. Progressive politicians may look dead in the 1990s, but they will dominate the next decade (Dione, 1996).

There is another scenario we often ignore. That is *the vision of America shared by new immigrants and those who want to immigrate to America from around the world.* From their perspective on modern cultural themes that they identify with the United States, it still looks like a pretty good deal. To them, the American Dream is still a viable moral force. Although the problems of America are widely recognized, it is still a system that provides work, high standards for personal freedom and guarantees of civil liberties, and orderly and nonviolent political change. It is a system where politicians can be removed from office without civil war. Never mind that the American Dream is oversimplified and imperfectly practiced; immigrants' own experience often convinces them that conditions are vastly better in the United States than in the nations they left, or want to leave.

These scenarios are very different. They differ in what they take to be important about change and the future. They can be negative or positive, depending on your values about what is good. All are limited, and we think some are plain wrong (we're not going to tell you which ones!). Are any of them more plausible to you than others? How would you envision the "something different" that is emerging?

America no longer dominates the nations of the world, as it did in the two decades following World War II, but the American Dream is far from dead. It does, we think, require ongoing revision now that we have entered the twenty-first century, particularly about the meaning of America as a civic and political community of people as we enter a global era. As do the citizens of most nations, we need to address anew the question: Who are we, anyway?

THINKING PERSONALLY ABOUT SOCIAL CHANGE

1. Let's frame the first question by beginning with a personal illustration. We began this book by describing the life worlds of our parents and children. We said very little about women, so now let's talk about Sonia, Harper's stepdaughter. She completed college at the university where he teaches and was a theater major. As an undergraduate she was enthralled by acting and the theater, in spite of periodic parental admonitions that "it's good to have dreams, but also prepare for some kind of practical career, where the odds aren't so loaded against being successful." Does this begin to sound familiar? At some level, do all parents sound alike? Hah! Sonia was successful in periodic community theater productions (not a very good living!). To live, she found a make-do job with a small private company that contracts with county and state agencies to work with unemployed people to help them find and keep jobs. What's the relevance of this for the material of this chapter? Such small entrepreneurial firms proliferated as government agencies sought to contract out their functions. And such firms compete vigorously for contracts that change dramatically from year to year in different states. By the 1990s, Sonia was a manager and chief troubleshooter for the company's western operations, supervising various contracts in Orange County, Los Angeles, San Francisco, and other places. She was enthusiastic but often exhausted in a career that took her away from home and husband for periods of time. So far, they have successfully managed the work-family intersections.

   What in her education specifically prepared Sonia for such work? Nothing, really, except what every good liberal arts education should provide: fluent literacy, broad knowledge about the world and human culture, an ability to work and communicate with people in oral and written forms, and—most importantly—the ability to problem-solve and learn new things as required. In fact, contrary to popular belief, liberal arts majors often do quite well in the long run, compared with technically trained people, for jobs that require broad knowledge, flexibility, and adaptability (Kabada, 1996).

   Our example also illustrates emerging flexible enterprise webs and strategic alliances in the economy. The firm retains people as long as they remain high-value producers and quickly shucks them off if they are not—as the fortunes of competitive public contracts themselves change dramatically from year to year. Sonia understands this. People survive in such turbulent enterprises only so long as they have the capability and energy to adapt to currents of change.

We have used this example to illustrate several issues about work and the changing economy. Question: Do you know persons who (1) prepared for particular careers and succeeded, (2) had plans that didn't quite turn out as well as expected, or (3) were successful in some strange and unexpected ways? Beyond personal characteristics, how do you think these examples were affected by social change?

2. Take another look at some of the expanded functions of governments mentioned in this chapter. Which ones do you think we could do without? Now think not about your own personal desires and benefits, but about the social consequences for persons living increasingly in densely populated urban environments, as do the majority of people. For example, should we be able to own as many dogs as we wish? If you lived next to us in a city, should we be able to run a commercial kennel living next door to you?

   We tried this exercise out on an economist friend very committed to private market solutions and found, to our surprise, that he didn't want governments to give up much of what concerns them now. But he did complain a lot about lack of efficiency and waste and had a lot of different ideas about the levels of governments that should do things. When you listen to most people talk about politics, what kinds of things do they dislike about politics and governments?

3. Organize a discussion among classmates or friends. If you could choose between what we called the Anglo-American political economy and the continental European model of political economy, which would you prefer? Why? Good luck. If you do this seriously you are in for an exciting conversation. And one probably full of ideological quicksand.

NOTES

1. In 1917 President Woodrow Wilson proposed, and Congress enacted, a sharply progressive tax code that levied an 83 percent tax on the incomes of the wealthiest Americans. That was eroded during the 1920s, but by 1935 it was back up to 79 percent and was coupled with a hefty tax on inherited wealth. At that time public opinion largely endorsed a progressive tax, but it was gradually eroded first by exemptions and loopholes and then by inflation, which pushed lower-wage workers into higher tax categories. Progressivity almost disappeared with the leveling "reforms" of the 1980s, and by 1990 America's income tax on its wealthiest citizens was the lowest of any industrialized nation (Reich, 1991:246). At the same time Social Security taxes, property taxes, and user fees—all forms of taxation that take bigger bites out of the paychecks of the poor than the rich—also increased.

5

The Causes and Patterns of Change

Previous chapters explored social change in the United States in a mainly descriptive way and, while we referred to particular change processes and their problems and meanings, we made little attempt to explain how or why such changes occurred. Such descriptive understanding is important, but more general explanations—theories—explain how societies work and how change comes about. Put quite simply, *theory* merely means how you explain things. Theories are general explanations that enable us to make sense out of particular facts and events. They answer our questions about how and why things happen or develop the way that they do. The word *theory* usually has a negative meaning for American students. Indeed, in popular American usage the word has negative connotations: If something is described as "theoretical," it usually means that it is overly abstract, impractical, too idealistic, unclear, or removed from any everyday significance. But in fact, theories are essential to everyday life as well as any scholarly or scientific enterprise. Without being aware of it, we theorize about things all the time.

Science involves not only the collection of facts and data, but also attempts to provide coherent explanations about why the facts are arranged as they are. The real goal of any science is to discern meaningful patterns that explain things rather than to produce particular bodies of facts or evidence. Such explanations, supported by empirical evidence are the ultimate goal of science, even though this goal is very elusive in short-run practical terms. There are usually competing theories and unfortunately the facts do not speak for themselves but have to be interpreted. More formally, a *scientific theory* is an abstract explanatory scheme that is potentially open to disconfirmation by evidence. Being abstract means that it is composed of generalizations not tied to particular events.

THEORY IN SOCIOLOGY

Social science, like all science, assumes that events are not entirely random and that, in spite of the complexity and apparent unpredictability of the social world, there is at least a degree of order and predictability that underlies these appearances. Any scientific attempt to understand social change is centrally concerned with theories about change. Given such complexities of the social world, social scientists often use *models,* which are simplified theories shorn of much elaboration and detail. Models and theories always contain assumptions, beliefs about human nature and the human condition that are not testable in a strict scientific sense. They represent the starting point or basic building blocks for building the theory or model.

While we usually assume that a theory asserts something that is true about the world, a model may be used as a *heuristic* (or an "as if" device). That is, a model may be used as a useful metaphor or analogy to facilitate our understanding of social life without the model itself being true in any real sense. For instance, we might use a computer model to understand the way in which the human brain processes information, or a biological organism as a model to understand something about human groups. But in a literal sense the human brain is not a computer and groups are not biological systems. Such use of models is useful but obviously very slippery. Theories can rarely be tested empirically as totalities. Hence we usually try to extract from theories statements of relationships that *can* be examined empirically. When translated into the concrete language of research, these become *hypotheses.*

Having discussed theories in general, scientific theories, models, and hypotheses, we come to another important distinction. It is conventional in sociology to distinguish between theories of large-scale structures and processes, or *macro theories,* and theories of small-scale structures and processes, or *micro theories.* In between these in terms of scope and abstractness are what many researchers call *middle-range theories.* For instance, macro theories deal with societies, institutions, or general processes such as conflict. Middle-range theories include general theories of organizations, revolutions, and so forth, while micro theories deal with face-to-face interpersonal behavior or the dynamics of small groups.

Discussing Theories of Change: An Overview of Part Two

We want to focus here on different types of explanations of change, that is, on the theories of change, rather than on theorists. While we mention some of the classic thinkers of the late nineteenth and early twentieth centuries, all of whom were concerned with understanding the transformation to the modern world, we do not attempt to discuss their individual works in great depth. We use the works of Marx and Weber to illustrate different types of explanations of change. Others are mentioned only in passing.[1] Since sociology as a discipline was originally concerned with understanding the development of modern urban and industrial societies, many of the macro theories of change focus on the emergence of these societies from a previous

form of society. While the time frame of previous chapters was the recent American past, the time frame of this chapter reaches far into the past, and many illustrations have to do with understanding the great transformations in human history: The long-term historical development of societies, industrialization, and urbanization. Hence this chapter is important not only because it introduces you to different types of theory but also because it discusses these important macro transformations that are important to your understanding of change.

This chapter describes theories that relate to understanding (1) the causes of change, and (2) the patterns or directions of change. In the next chapter we will examine three established perspectives in contemporary sociology in terms of their implications for understanding change.

THE CAUSES OF CHANGE

What are the most important general causes of change? And when we look at change from a broad perspective, can general patterns or directions of social change be seen? These are two basic questions about social change that are explored in this chapter. First, we will address the issue of the causes of change. Explanations fall into two general categories: those that emphasize *materialistic factors* (such as economic production and technology) and those that emphasize *idealistic factors* (such as values, ideologies, and beliefs). Second, we will discuss the issue of general patterns or directions of change from several perspectives. One suggests that change takes place in a linear and nonrepetitive pattern. Another emphasizes that change is often cyclical and repetitive. A third presents a dialectical model, which in some ways combines the ideas of linear and cyclical change.

MATERIALISTIC PERSPECTIVES

Many have speculated that material factors are the primary causes of social and cultural change. Material factors usually mean economic factors, such as natural resources, wealth, or the tools and techniques (technologies) used in economic production. Materialist perspectives argue that new technologies and modes of economic production produce changes in social interaction, social organization and, ultimately, cultural values, beliefs, and norms. The most influential classic thinker to adopt this argument was Karl Marx.

The Marxist Perspective

In an often-quoted statement that illustrates his general argument, Marx stated that "the windmill gives you a society with the feudal lord, the steam-mill the society with the industrial capitalist" (1920:119). Marx argued that the forces of production are central in shaping society and social change. By "forces of production," Marx meant primarily production technologies (e.g., windmills) that, in his view, lead to

the creation of certain "social relations of production" (e.g., relations between the feudal lord who owns the windmill and his serfs). These relations of production are structured relationships that relate to the methods by which goods and services are produced. Thus, in this perspective economic classes form the basic anatomy of society, and other things (ideas, ideologies, values, political structures, etc.) arise in relation to them. Changes in the forces of production (technologies) erode the basis of the old system of economic relationships and classes and open new possibilities.

To illustrate this way of explaining change, consider the transition from feudalism to industrial capitalism in Europe between 1600 and the late 1800s. This transition was fueled by expanding world trade in wool and textiles (Sanderson, 1998). Feudal landowners became aware of expanding economic opportunities available through trade in wool and began to renounce their obligations to rural peasants who traditionally worked the land and were granted "rights" to land set aside for their use (see Moore, 1966; Tilly, 1990). The slow removal of peasants from rural lands (often referred to as "enclosures") helped to fuel a process that was already started in urban areas. International trade in finished textile products produced a new basis for wealth outside the feudal system at the same time as feudal landlords were drawn to the opportunities in international trade.

The displaced peasants from rural areas became the labor pool for growing urban industrial production. Industrial production was made possible by a number of inventions (e.g., steam power, the power loom, the making of coke from coal and its use in blast furnaces to produce steel) that favored the factory system at the expense of hand manufacture. These developments made possible increases in productivity that ultimately produced (1) new opportunities for work in urban factories, and (2) new economic classes (industrialists and workers), neither of which the feudal system had any place for culturally or politically. Gradually the predominant basis for wealth shifted from agricultural production on the landed estates of the aristocracy to industrial production in the urban factories.

As the economic and structural basis of society changed, new political forms emerged (parliamentary democracy), as did new cultural values and ideologies that were consistent with the emerging system (e.g., political freedom, the "virtues" of free enterprise). This social transformation took the forms of bloody revolution in France, attempts at revolution in Germany, and piecemeal reforms in England (also punctuated by violence).

Turning to the analysis of change in industrial capitalism (his real goal), Marx argued that change would occur because of the dislocations (or "contradictions") between productive forces and the social relations of production. Capitalists need profits and compete intensely among themselves for profits. This would lead them to upgrade productive technologies and attempt to minimize the costs of labor. Thus workers would become increasingly exploited while the economy becomes more productive, leading to a series of increasingly intense "crises of overproduction" (periodic economic collapses resulting from the accumulation of inventories that can't be sold). As these tensions intensified, workers (in their roles as workers and consumers) would become increasingly "immiserated" (in relative terms). Marx argued that workers would take over the economy and reorganize it in their own interests, thus ending the domination of the capitalists and the capitalist system. While he did not make revolution inevitable in the short run, he thought that it was quite probable in the long run.

This depiction of Marx's theory of change is vastly oversimplified and does not do justice to the detail, subtlety, and complexity of his voluminous writings—nor to the elaboration of his perspective by neo-Marxist scholars. Marx was analyzing industrial capitalism as it existed in the 1880s, and his predictions were wrong in many respects (particularly in his expectations about the transformation of society by the workers). Yet for all its flaws, Marxian theory remains an insightful explanation of the technological and economic forces that generate tensions and change in capitalist societies.

Other Materialistic Perspectives

Other thinkers have emphasized material factors as causes of change. For instance, William Ogburn in the 1930s wrote extensively about the technological causes of social change in America. He argued that the advent of the automobile had changed American society in many ways: by increasing geographic mobility, by accelerating the growth of suburbs, and by changing courtship customs (by removing them from the direct supervision of adults). In general, Ogburn's argument is that material culture (technology) changes more rapidly than nonmaterial aspects of culture (ideas, values, norms, ideologies). As a generalization we think it is debatable, but it is true that humans are often more willing to adopt new techniques and tools than to change their cultural values and traditions. Ogburn argued that there is often a "cultural lag" between the nonmaterial culture and the material culture, which is a source of tension.

Speculation about the social effects of various technological innovations is a popular activity in America, which says something, we think, about the centrality of technology in American culture. There is, for example, much speculation about the effects of computers. Some speculate that while the computer has enhanced information storage, it makes possible more repressive forms of social control through the (potential) development of large centralized data banks about the characteristics of individuals. Others not only think these predictions are false, but add that decentralized access to high technology has rendered centralized control far more difficult than it was as late as twenty years ago (Castells, 1998). Still others speculate that the advent of decentralized computers (home computers) may eventually reintegrate work and the family (after their separation in the last 200 years by steam power and the factory system) in an economy that increasingly depends on the generating and processing of information. Most of such speculation depends upon the assumption that material factors are the primary causes of change.

How Technology Causes Change[2]

Technology can cause change in three different ways. First, technological innovations increase the alternatives available in a society: "New technology may bring previously unattainable ideals within the realm of possibility, and it may alter the relative difficulty or ease of realizing differing values" (Lauer, 1977:162). Second, new technology alters interaction patterns among people. Third, technological innovations create new "problems" to be dealt with.

Consider the introduction of snowmobiles into northern areas of Alaska and Lapland. This technological innovation vastly changed patterns of reindeer herding and hunting among the Eskimos and Lapps. It vastly increased the geographic mobility of hunters and the amount of game that could be killed. It shortened the work week of hunters and trappers dramatically, increased their leisure time, increased their earnings, and established a new basis for stratification in the community (based on who owns and who does not own a snowmobile). Finally, it generated a serious ecological imbalance as populations of snowbound game animals were wiped out (Pelto and Muller-Willie, 1972:95). This example illustrates all three ways in which technology can cause change. It is important to emphasize that they are found together; that is, while technology creates new opportunities, it changes the structure of human groups and communities, and it ultimately creates a new set of problems. Planners of deliberate technical innovation often forget about the last two factors.

Finally, it is good to mention some of the limits of considering technology as a cause of change. Significant social change can occur without technical change. And technological change may not produce significant change at all levels of society. For instance, the shift from using coal to using gas for home heating may have produced significant change in the energy industry, but it is doubtful whether it caused other significant changes (e.g., in community stratification or family systems). Gas heating certainly did not revolutionize communities as did the introduction of snowmobiles among the Lapps and Eskimos.

IDEALISTIC PERSPECTIVES

Some have seen ideas, values, and ideologies as causes of change. These can collectively be termed *ideational* aspects of culture, to distinguish them from the material aspects of culture discussed in the previous section. *Ideas* here include both knowledge and beliefs; *values* are assumptions about what is desirable and undesirable; and *ideology* means a more or less organized combination of beliefs and values that serves to justify or legitimize forms of human action (e.g., democracy, capitalism, socialism). Perhaps the classic thinker in sociology who argued most persuasively that ideational culture can have a causative role in social change was Max Weber (1864–1920).

Weber's Perspective

Weber (1905) argued, contrary to Marx, that the development of industrial capitalism can't be understood only in terms of material and technical causes, although he did not deny their importance. Weber observed that the technical conditions for the development of industrialism have existed in many societies (e.g., in classical

China and India and in postmedieval Europe). He argued that certain value systems in Western society produced the development in interaction with material causes. Weber observed that the regions of Europe in which industrial capitalism was most developed at the earliest dates were those regions with the heaviest concentrations of Protestants. This, he argued, was not accidental. He argued that the values of Protestantism—more specifically Calvinism and related religious groups—produced a cultural ethic that sanctified work and worldly achievement, encouraged frugality, and discouraged consumption. The unintended social consequence of this religious worldview, which he termed "this-worldly asceticism," was to encourage the development of large pools of capital (by encouraging work, savings, and dampening "frivolous" consumption) and to encourage rational reinvestment and economic growth.

Weber argued that industrial capitalism would not have developed in Catholic areas, even though the material and technical preconditions were often present. Catholicism, in its medieval forms, had value assumptions inimical to such developments in the economic realm. First, economic activity was not sanctioned by religious values: Work in the economic realm was not a religiously sanctioned calling, as it was for the Calvinist, but merely the mundane activity that kept one alive. Catholicism encouraged an "otherworldly asceticism" in which the highest form of human activity was devotion to God. Second, there was not in the Catholic scheme of values any reason to ban consumption. Calvinism, by contrast, was suspicious of material consumption beyond the bare necessities as leading to moral corruption. Finally, Calvinism suggested that each man is a free moral agent, accountable only to God. Catholicism, by contrast, made men accountable to the Church, which sought to regulate the operation of the economy and other secular aspects of the society in terms of their religious values. Thus in medieval Europe religious authorities attempted to establish fair wages and prices, to regulate economic competition, and to prohibiting making a living as a moneylender—an activity identified as parasitical usury. These regulations, though not always successful, tended to retard the development of free market capitalism.

Weber also argued that there were ideational barriers to the development of capitalism in China and India. In China, the dominant religious values were those derived from Confucianism, which emphasized adjustment to the world as it is, rather than working for salvation and bringing about the "kingdom of God" as the Calvinist was enjoined to do. Thus Confucianism tended to "freeze the past." The minority Chinese religion, Taoism, was, according to Weber, so thoroughly mystical and otherworldly that worldly activity was devalued, and the supreme good was seen in psychic states. Similarly in India, salvation was seen in the observance of religious ritual, not in work in the world, which itself was viewed as a part of the world of illusion. The object of Hinduism was not work in the world, but escape from it through reincarnation. While Weber's characterization of the world religions is surely oversimplified and not adequate in terms of today's scholarly understanding of them, the major thrust of his argument remains: Values and beliefs—both religious and secular—can have a decisive impact in shaping social change.

It is important to clarify Weber's position about change. While his argument about the relationship between the values of Calvinism and the development of industrial capitalism is often, and appropriately, used to illustrate the theoretical approach that emphasizes the role of ideas and values as causative agents, Weber was not saying that ideational factors are the only important causes of change. In fact, Weber's position is much closer to that of Marx than we have portrayed it here. It is really an argument with Marx only insofar as Marx devalued the role of ideas and values as causes. Weber felt that social causation was so complex that it was indefensible to single out certain factors as more basic than others. We will return to this issue shortly.

Other Ideational Perspectives

Guenter Lewy (1974) expanded Weber's argument about the role of religion in social change, by documenting historical instances in which religious values have had a decisive influence in shaping the direction of change. He mentions, for instance, the Puritan revolt in England, the Islamic renaissance promoted by followers of the Mahdi in the Sudan in the 1800s, and the Taiping and Boxer rebellions in China. Like Weber, Lewy does not ignore the material conditions related to change, but he asserts that it is impossible to understand the impetus and directions of change without considering the independent role of religious values and religious authority. One could add more contemporary examples to Lewy's historical ones. It would, for instance, be impossible to give a plausible account of the Iranian revolution of the 1970s without considering the impact of Islamic fundamentalism and the charismatic leadership of Khomeini.

Here are some pervasive cultural ideas, values, and ideologies that have broadly shaped the directions of change in the modern world. The ideas of freedom, self-determination, and citizenship (Patterson, 1991) helped to stimulate and justify the revolt of non-Western colonies against their European rulers in the twentieth century. And certainly the positive value attached to material growth and security drives the desire for social and economic development in developing nations. In addition to these very abstract ideas and values, more specific ideological systems have had an enormous effect on shaping the direction of social change in the contemporary world. *Nationalism,* the ideology of a particular identity and community of a people based on shared history, culture, and language, has been, and remains, a potent force for conflict and change. Consider the historic changing and conflictive relations between the English and the Irish, French and English Canadians, Germans and French, the Basque separatists and the Spanish, the Chinese and the Japanese, or the problems of the contemporary Palestinians or the Kurdish peoples in the Middle East. It is impossible to understand fully the changing relationships between these groups and their states fully in terms of material and economic factors alone without considering the powerful role of nationalist ideas, cultures, and myths.

Capitalism and *Marxism* are two other powerful nineteenth- and twentieth-century economic and political ideologies. Earlier we described Weber's theory about the role of religious values in creating capitalism. But it is important that you understand that capitalism is not only a type of economic system, but also a connected set of ideas and values—an ideology—emphasizing the positive benefits of pursuing one's private economic interests, competition, and free markets that are only minimally subject to community and state regulation. Capitalist ideology and its competitor and promoter of anticapitalist values, Marxism, have been *universalistic* world ideologies that—in combination with *particularistic* nationalist ideologies— have been powerful forces for change. They have legitimated directions of economic change and have propagated social and political norms that gave shape to the Cold War era with its bipolar "Free World" "Communist World" structure and tensions. And with the collapse of the communist world and its official state Marxisms in the 1990s, even this devolution is not a simple collapse, but a change process guided by resurgent nationalisms, among them, for instance, the nationalism of the Poles, Russians, Lithuanians, and Armenians.

Thomas and Boli (1997) contend that the collapse of communism and the growing communications and connections among peoples of the world is producing a cosmopolitan world culture centered on freedom, self-determination, personal growth, environmental protection, market economics, and rights for women and marginalized groups. This global culture is spread via nongovernment organizations that scrutinize the living arrangements of the world's peoples and pressure governments and international organizations to improve them. This process is occurring at the same time as recurrent calls for nationalism, cultural self-determination, the international growth in racial and ethnic hatred, and fundamentalism act as reactions to the encroachments of "global culture."

How Ideas and Values Cause Change[3]

It is important to recognize that ideational culture often acts as a barrier to change. As in the previous example, Confucianism in China may have been a barrier to the development of free market capitalism. Further, the same set of ideas and values can promote change in one time and place and retard change at others. At its inception in the 1700s, the doctrines of the virtues of free trade, the free market system, and the undesirability of government interference in such markets (propounded by English political economists Adam Smith and David Ricardo, among others) were very revolutionary. It was a penetrating critique of the then dominant mercantilist economic philosophy (in which the king sought to regulate the economy in the national interest) and helped to mobilize support for the dismantling of the mercantilist system. As we argued earlier, capitalist ideology is still a world force for change. But in contemporary America, the ideology of the virtues of the free enterprise system is often a conservative ideological system that serves to defend and justify the existing economic system and deflect attempts to alter it in fundamental ways. Likewise, as Stokes (1975) has observed, Calvinism may have been a religious doctrine potent with implications for change in its original setting, but in its South African context, Afrikaner Calvinism became a conservative force that justified continued domination by the white minority and the apartheid system. Thus, ideas and ideologies bear no determinant relation to change. Rather, we must understand the way that ideas, values, and ideologies are *used* in particular social contexts.

Ideational culture can cause change in a least three different ways. First, *it can legitimize a desired direction of change.* This should be obvious. Think how difficult it would be in America to promote change that would *deliberately* result in less equality or less democracy! And as mentioned, even the collapse of a system may be a process guided by ideational culture, so that the collapse of official communism in the Soviet Union was guided not only by resurgent nationalisms but by the political slogans *demokratia* (democracy), *perestroika* (modernization) and *glasnost* (openness). There are smaller-scale illustrations of this way that ideational culture promotes change. John Dewey's philosophies of progressive education shaped the reform of American public education for several decades (particularly between the 1920s and 1950s), producing an educational system that was, among other things, more oriented to the practical and vocational needs of students and more community centered (see Swift, 1971). In the 1980s, the back-to-basics movement again reshaped the goals and priorities of the American educational system.

Second, *ideologies can provide the basis for the social solidarity necessary to promote change.* They can be, in other words, "integrative mechanisms, neutralizing the conflicting strains that are found in most societies" (Lauer, 1977:195). Ideology can be a powerful mobilizing force in times of war, for instance, justifying and promoting the war as a holy crusade, a defense of democracy, or creation of a "Thousand Year Reich." But think, also, in less dramatic circumstances, of how recent American presidents have concocted ideologies to mobilize support for social change. Since the 1920s America has seen the "return to normalcy," the New Deal, the Fair Deal, the New Frontier, the Great Society, the War on Poverty, and the Contract with America. One can write off these constructions as ordinary political sloganeering, but there is more. Each of these ideological constructions in various degrees defined a set of goals and agendas for change and helped to mobilize support within the population relative to those goals.

A third way that ideational culture can promote change is by *highlighting contradictions and problems.* American cultural values about equality of opportunity have highlighted racism and sexism as problems and have been the organizing rationale for social movements and official policy directed those problems. Values, in other words, can highlight areas of discrepancy and contradictions, and change often takes place as an effort to resolve or reduce contradictions.

If it is true that ideas are causes of change, then it is undeniably true that individuals, who after all are the ultimate source of ideas and values, play some role in creating change. It is therefore important to give some attention to the role of individuals in the change process, but we won't do that here because it would take us on a detour away from the main agenda of this chapter. We will return to the issue of the role of individuals in the change process in some depth in as we discuss innovation (Chapter 10), the planning of change (Chapter 11), and modernization (Chapter 12).

The Interaction of Causes

If material and ideational factors are both causes of change, it can be reasonably argued that they interact over time as causes and consequences. Thus we are brought to the reality of the interaction of causes and the notion of multiple causation. Few students of change argue for the complete primacy of one type of cause over others. It is a matter of the relative weight and emphasis given to each. Weber, for instance, would give a greater role to the autonomy of ideas as causes than would most Marxians. However, Marxians recognize a certain role of ideational factors in causing change. Many Marxians have argued, for instance, that once ideas are established they acquire a certain degree of autonomy from the material base that gives rise to them, and that ideas have

> a possibility of reacting . . . on the functioning of the economic base. Man's creative thought, inventing ever more perfect instruments of production, transforms, gradually and indirectly, the general economic structure, all social relations, and, as a result, the whole of human reality. (Schaff, 1970:82)

The Marxian position generally, then, is that ideational culture (values, theories, dogmas) derives from social and economic structures but becomes itself a factor in social change. The assertion is that only in the long run, after interaction with these factors and many "accidents," do material factors determine the outcomes of change (Marx and Engels, 1968:692–693).

Max Weber's writings contain perhaps the most explicit recognition of the interaction of causes and multiple causation. He argued that social change was the joint product of the interaction of systems of cultural values with possibilities present in the material base. In his terms, ideas are the "switchmen" that determine along which tracks material interests will roll. There is at critical historical junctures what Weber termed an "elective affinity" between certain combinations of ideas and material factors that produce new social forms and directions of change.

The way that different causes of change interact or combine is not a simple matter. There are at least four different ways that causes can interact. First, there is *mutual feedback,* in which various factors affect each other in turn. For example, our international trade experiences with foreigners shapes our attitudes and economic policies toward them. But these attitudes and policies shape our subsequent international trade experiences. Second, there is *multiple causation,* in which cause X and cause Y both have an independent and incremental effect on outcome Z. This view of interacting causes is used by statistical empirical researchers, who might study, for example, the independent contributions of family background, community size, race, and education to determine one's status achievement in society. Third, there is *combined causation,* in which a variety of factors must be present for a particular outcome or change to occur. Combined causation is particularly important in the study of the development of novel social forms, historical change, and new technologies. Weber's view of the emergence of industrial capitalism was that it required the material base (such as resources and technologies) but also critical values and attitudes (about work and rationality). As we will see in Chapter 10, combined causation is important in understanding the process of innovation. Fourth, there is *path-dependent causation,* in which prior actions or factors ("paths") shape the possibilities for what happens next. This is a prominent explanation for the future development of former communist societies, as we will see in Chapter 9.

PATTERNS OF CHANGE

Let us turn now to the question of general patterns and directions of change. Theories can be grouped into three categories in terms of how they view the pattern and direction of change: (1) linear models, (2) cyclical models, and (3) dialectical models.

Linear Models of Change

Linear models assert that change is cumulative, nonrepetitive, developmental, usually permanent. Change never returns to the same point. Linear models can depict change in two stages or in terms of a process that has intermediate stages. The classic thinkers in sociology and anthropology concocted many two-stage theories of change, which are essentially like before and after snapshots of large-scale change in society. Examples of such are Redfield's theory about the transition from "folk" to "urban" societies, Durkheim's theory of the transition from "mechanical" to "organic" solidarity, and Tonnies' theory of change from *Gemeinschaft* to *Gesellschaft.*

These theories differ in the factors that they emphasize, but all view the broad historical pattern of change in human societies as involving the transition from small, undifferentiated societies with a homogeneous culture to large societies with a high degree of structural differentiation and a heterogeneous culture. Each, in some sense, depicts the evolution from preliterate to modern societies. This is what social scientists *used* to refer to as *social evolution,* in the assumption that some sort of master change processes were at work in all societies through time. But recent developments in the notion of social evolution emphasize the accumulation of complex contingencies (e.g., the generation of novel forms and their transmission and selection over time) that is closer to the biological meaning of the term *evolution* (Burns and Dietz, 1992; Sztompka, 1993). So we will not speak of evolution here. Our purpose here is more elementary: to synopsize the major historical and developmental changes in human societies. We will discuss Lenski's macro stage theory that connects several—rather than two—stages in a historical-developmental sequence.

The Historical Development of Human Societies. Lenski (Lenski and Lenski, 1982) developed a broad developmental theory of different types of societies (hunting and gathering, pastoral and horticultural, agricultural, industrial) in which the transitions from one form to the next were caused by innovations in the technology of economic production that produced an ever larger and more certain surplus of food and material resources. At each stage, according to Lenski's theory, societies could support a larger population and grew in complexity and internal differentiation.

Hunting and gathering societies are the oldest type of human societies and still exist in a few scattered places. These were small nomadic groups whose daily life was occupied by the hunting of animals and the search for edible foods. They were essentially subsistence economies, which produce no significant economic surplus. The plains Indians of North America, the polar Eskimos, and the Bushmen of the Kalahari desert in southern Africa are near-contemporary hunters and gatherers.

They traveled in bands of about fifty people, following wild game and carrying virtually all their possessions with them. Society was coterminous with the family and kinship unit, though hunters and gatherers were aware of related bands and people with whom they shared language, culture, and territory. There were few larger-scale social units or statuses not defined by age, sex, or kinship. The division of labor was simple, based on age and sex. Males were typically hunters, while women and children searched for edible plants. Leadership was informal and situational, and there were no nonsubsistence roles: *Everyone* helped with the search for food. These were very *equalitarian* societies, since everyone had some rights to share in the food, but this equality was more often based on the sharing of scarcity rather than the sharing of wealth, since there was little surplus to hoard in any case. In sum, hunters and gatherers were small, undifferentiated societies that took food from the physical environment as they found it. They required a very large territory to support even small nomadic bands.

Pastoralists and horticulturalists discovered a more efficient way of making a living from the environment by cultivating crops (yams, corn) and domesticating animals (sheep, goats). Examples of horticulturalists were the woodland Native Americans of eastern North America and the Trobriand Islanders in Melanesia (New Guinea). Raising crops and shepherding animals produced a more certain and a larger food supply. While pastoralists continued to be nomadic, the horticulturalists began to live in larger settled residences. The central social unit among horticulturalists was the *village,* which could support populations of several hundred people and incorporate several different family and kinship units. Thus, compared with the hunters and gatherers, these groups represented a growth in the scale of human society as well as an increasingly complex division of labor. The food surplus could support people with full-time nonsubsistence roles (leaders, craftworkers, artists, warriors, magicians). Complex and stable social institutions that were separate from the family and kinship groups began to emerge. Probably the earliest of these was a separate political system in which villages came to be ruled by "headmen" and hereditary rulers. Thus the level of social inequality increased, with a generalized distinction between rulers, specialists, and ordinary people.

Agricultural societies originated between five and six thousand years ago and included what we normally call the earliest civilizations (e.g., ancient Egypt, Mesopotamia, ancient China, and the Roman empire). The technical bases of agricultural societies were the plows drawn by draft animals and grain—cereal agriculture—both of which led to increased productivity and levels of surpluses that surpassed those of true horticulturalists. The invention of basic irrigation techniques and metalworking and the development of mathematics, calendars, and literacy were also important technological bases of agricultural societies. As with the horticulturalists, the development of agricultural economies was associated with a vastly increased *scale* of human social life. The basic social unit was now the city-state, with a central city of perhaps 20,000 people surrounded by a much larger area of villages that lay within the sphere of control of the city. Although cities were much larger and denser human settlements, probably 90 percent of the population of agricultural societies still lived in rural villages.

If the scale of life was vastly increased in agricultural societies, so was the degree of internal differentiation and complexity. Now there emerged a whole panoply of nonsubsistence occupational specialties (traders, scribes, priests, potters, weavers, metalworkers, warriors, slaves, healers, and so forth), and these coalesced into society-wide stratified social classes. Such classes, in descending order of dominance, typically included (1) kings and nobles, (2) priests and scribes, (3) merchants and warriors, (4) craftworkers and artisans, and at the bottom (5) peasants and slaves who farmed the land. There was a dramatic increase in trade and communication between city-state systems as well as an expansionary dynamic: The stronger city-states tended to conquer the smaller ones, leading to vast political empires ruled by hereditary dynasties. The desire for plunder was probably its own justification for such an expansionary dynamic, but some have argued that it also resulted from the economic necessity of maintaining control over remote sites for the coordination of irrigation projects. Wittfoegel (1957) has termed these city-states "hydraulic societies."

Industrial societies began about two hundred years ago in Europe. They began to evolve through technological innovations (first in the textile industry in England) that substituted machine production for human and animal labor. Industrial production depended not only on the invention of new machines, but also on the utilization of new energy sources to power them—water power, steam engines, hydroelectric power, petroleum, and so forth. This new system vastly increased societies' level of productivity and their ability to produce surpluses of both agricultural and industrial products. A phenomenal economic growth began that was driven by intensification of capital investment and technology (and eventually the deemphasizing of labor) as components in economic production.

The social and cultural changes that flowed from the new industrial system of production were profound. Since the new engines and machines were large and expensive, centralized production in factories began to supplant the decentralized "cottage" production that had preceded the industrial era. People began to migrate to the cities in unprecedented numbers, not only because the factory jobs were located there, but also because the upgrading of agricultural technology and growing opportunities to market agricultural products (see Chapter 4) reduced the demand for laborers in rural areas. Labor became increasingly a cash commodity rather than a subsistence activity, and work became increasingly separated from family life. The long-term consequence was that most people in industrial societies came to reside in larger urban centers (beginning the long-term global trend of urbanization). In industrial societies wealth and power began to be connected not so much with control of land—as in all previous types of societies—but with ownership and control of industrial enterprises. A new class system based on industrial wealth rather than the hereditary control of land began to emerge.

The vast increase of productivity required more raw materials and larger markets and hence stimulated improvements in communication and transportation. This expansion and centralization of markets was supported by nationalistic desires for territorial consolidation and expansion. The consequences of these economic and political trends was another vast increase of the scale and social complexity of human social life over that of agrarian societies.[4]

Notwithstanding the misery and exploitation of the early industrial sweatshops, the long-term consequence of industrial societies was a rise in the material living standards of ordinary people. Lenski argues that industrial societies are somewhat more equalitarian than agricultural societies in both political rights and the distribution of material goods, thus reversing the long-term evolutionary trend toward greater inequality in agricultural societies. But industrial societies are not utopias: with greater mass consumption comes environmental despoliation, pollution, cyclical economic depressions, depersonalization, and a great deal of moral ambiguity. Overt oppression may have been traded for more subtle forms of alienation. Without question, more people eat more regularly than in hunting and gathering bands, but it is questionable whether they are happier or lead more satisfying social lives. Lenski's theory of linear change cannot be simplistically equated with a theory of human progress.

Urbanization.   Urbanization is an important global change process that, like Lenski's theory, can also illustrate a linear-developmental model of change. Urbanization involves a very ancient process of interaction between cities and the surrounding countryside whereby individual and social life has been constantly reorganized. Urbanization is also an abstraction from the migration biographies of uprooted families of peasants, sojourners, refugees, and, in the United States, of the hillbillies from the southern Appalachians, the Oakies (memorialized in John Steinbeck's *Grapes of Wrath*), and rural African Americans from the Deep South (Walton, 1990:94). Cities are ancient, but as recently as 1800 only 3 percent of the world's population was urbanized. By 1990, however, 73 percent of the world's population in developed nations were "urban" as were 34 percent in developing nations. By 2025, more that 60 percent of people in the whole world are expected to live in densely populated urban areas (Frisbie, 1977; United Nations Development Programme, 1992). This number is disturbing to some analysts, who see extensive urbanization as part of a volatile dynamic that will increase the severity of global social problems (see Massey, 1996).

Cities are larger and more densely settled communities than rural villages or towns, and Max Weber (1921) noted that cities have three distinctive characteristics: (1) a larger and more important *marketplace* where dwellers buy or barter essential goods and services, (2) a *center of political and administrative authority* that regulates the market and city life and often that of the surrounding countryside as well, and (3) *a defined urban community* (administered by authorities) of dwellers having the status, rights, and duties of citizenship. Groundbreaking research about cities was done by urban sociologists at the University of Chicago in the 1920s and 1930s, and while Chicago was probably the most intensively studied city in the world, it is only one historical type of city.

In what follows, we want to illustrate a linear theory of change by describing the organization and reorganization of cities in different historical epochs, focusing on the interaction of the dimensions of social life mentioned by Weber: economic production, political power, and community conflict. (The following relies primarily on the works of Sjoberg, 1960, 1963; Gordon, 1978; Friedman and Goetz, 1982; and Walton, 1990.) For each type of evolving city we will mention briefly the (1) focal economic activity, (2) spatial patterning, (3) power holders and forms, and (4) sources of community conflict and popular community responses.

Ancient and medieval cities, which date back to 3500 B.C.E., would include, as examples, ancient Babylon, Old Delhi, Tokyo, Rome, Damascus, and, in the New World, the Spanish colonial capital of Lima. Historically they emerged with the agricultural revolution and were quite small by today's standards. Ancient Babylon might have had 50,000 people; Athens maybe 80,000; and Rome—the premiere imperial capital of much of the Mediterranean world and the hinterlands—as many as 500,000. To put things in perspective, at its peak Rome was a bit smaller than Omaha, Nebraska (Weeks, 1989:350). Though these cities did have markets, they were not primary sites of economic production. They were mainly the political, administrative, and ceremonial centers that conquered and lived off of the surrounding countryside. The city administered, protected, drafted labor crews, and levied taxes on peasant villagers, who were the real source of wealth.

At the center of these cities were the palaces of the rulers, ritual and ceremonial centers (plazas and churches or temples), and the homes of the wealthy. Surrounding the center were the homes and marketplaces of citizens, and the city was often surrounded by a wall for protection from invaders. The poor and immigrants lived on the outskirts, often outside the wall. Dynasties of nobles or kings had political power in ancient and medieval cities, and their power was so complete that they "owned" the city, which was ruled and administered as an extension of their personalities. In the struggles between control and freedom in ancient and medieval cities community conflicts took two forms: peasant tax and rent revolts in the countryside and conflicts for power between competing elite groups and dynasties.

Commercial cities were different from ancient and medieval cities in that trade, shipping, craft production, and banking became primary sources of economic production and wealth. The earliest commercial cities developed in the early fourteenth century in Italy, particularly with the opening of trade routes in East Asia and later in northern Europe. Amsterdam is a good example of a European commercial city, organized around the far-flung trading empire of the Dutch in the seventeenth century. From colonial times to the middle of the nineteenth century, large commercial cities grew in the United States, such as New York, Boston, and Baltimore.

Commercial cities were spatially organized in a sort of crazy-quilt pattern around harbors, docks, warehouses, and craft shops that were important to the new modes of generating wealth. Since these were family businesses, the wealthy lived close to the center while, as in ancient cities, the poor lived on the outskirts. Important merchant and banking families also became the most important powerholders in commercial cities (of which the Adams family of Boston would be a good example). Community conflict in commercial cities had to do with import-export taxes on trade goods, competition between merchant families, and conflicts about wages and working conditions for craftworkers and seamen. In addition, in colonial America, there were conflicts about taxes and trade restrictions unfavorable to Americans imposed by the British government. The accumulation of such grievances resulted in urban mobs that, encouraged by merchant elites, played an important role in the American Revolution (remember the Boston Tea Party?). After the Revolution commercial cities competed with each other for trade dominance, and the big winner was, of course, New York, which was guaranteed better access to inland trade by the completion of the Erie Canal.

Industrial cities were stimulated by the development of industrial technology (mentioned previously), which made possible the mass production of goods in highly centralized factories. Factory cities developed first around the English textile industry in the 1750s and in the United States after the mid-nineteenth century in places such as Pittsburgh, Chicago, and Detroit. Industrial era cities were organized around a downtown central business district for retailing and banking; moving outward in concentric rings were zones containing factories and warehouses, houses, apartments, and tenements of workers and ethnic minorities, homes of the middle class, and homes of the more affluent at the outer edges of the city. Since industrial production separated work from family, industrial cities came to have more distinct segregation of residential and commercial areas as well as more segregation by social class and immigrant or ethnic group. Real estate interests and government zoning boards had a large political role in shaping this geographic segregation and patterning.

Industrialists and factory owners had decisive political power in industrial era cities, and the names of some of these powerful families, such as Rockefeller, DuPont, Carnegie, Ford, and McCormick, are still part of American politics, philanthropy, and mythology. Conflict and popular protests related to American industrial cities at the end of the nineteenth century included a widespread but ultimately ineffective protest movement among American farmers disadvantaged by commodity prices, railway fees, and farm mortgage policies that were controlled by urban businesses and banks. Another community-based conflict was between urban factory workers and industrialists. This regularly gave rise to violent uprisings and, with the intervention of the federal government on behalf of the workers in the 1930s, the American labor movement was born. We will return to these as well as the following community-based protest movements when we focus on social movement and change in the following chapters.

Corporate cities such as Atlanta, Kansas City, Omaha, Denver, and Dallas, grew dramatically during the postwar 1950s as developments in technology, communication, and transportation gradually decentralized industrial production. In the changes toward a more service-based economy, national economic growth and concentration (mentioned in the previous chapters), multidivisional firms evolved that had offices, plants, and subsidiaries in many locations. Thus the basis of wealth and jobs in many cities came to depend on the presence of the corporate headquarters of multidivisional firms, along with the banks and financial institutions that managed capital flows and investments in far-flung corporate operations. Such large corporations undoubtedly have decisive political power in corporate headquarter cities, but the interests of multidivisional companies and banks are themselves likely to be quite diverse and only weakly tied to concerns about living conditions in the urban community.

The construction of freeways and the postwar housing boom stimulated suburban growth and the migration of people, services, and money away from the older urban "core." Everywhere this produced a disparity of wealth between more affluent suburbs that came to ring the older "central cities," with high concentrations of the elderly, the poor, and ethnic minorities. Community conflict and popular protest was not directed at particular economic interests, as in the industrial city, but in a diffuse way community conflict and protest came to be about the urban community itself. These conflicts were often about issues of urban decline, such as slums, poverty, jobs, housing, crime, and racial discrimination. These conflicts became particularly apparent in the urban explosions that swept the nation in the 1960s.

World cities have been emerging in recent decades in various nations of the world. The very concept of "world city" is partly a futuristic one, since their status as distinct types of urban formations is not entirely clear. World cities, such as New York, London, Mexico City, and Rio De Janeiro, are oriented toward the global economy, and the production of wealth depends heavily on international banking and trade. In the United States, the relative prosperity of the coasts in relation to the heartland regions—discussed in the last chapter—is related to the dramatic growth of coastal world cities, often at the expense of older industrial and corporate cities. They are the headquarters of large multinational firms and large banks that manage investment and lending on an international scale. As examples, both in terms of economic transactions and immigration flows, Los Angeles has grown as a Pacific Rim city and Miami as a Caribbean regional metropolis.

World cities have very diverse and often vibrant economies, usually with special low-wage labor market niches for immigrant communities. As urban areas go, they are very large and incorporate a vast sprawling patchwork of overgrown towns, commercial-industrial areas, and new suburbs. There may be many bases of community conflict and popular movements in emerging world cities. They would include (1) conflicts about language, politics, and community autonomy between old residents and newer immigrant communities (such as Asians and Hispanics in the United States), (2) conflicts about disparities in taxes and municipal services among the variety of political jurisdictions that are functionally integrated in the same metropolitan area, and (3) conflicts about "foreign investment" in national firms and "capital flight" for overseas investment.

Let us summarize important features of these two linear theoretical models of change more generally. Lenski argues that at the stages of societal development (hunting and gathering → pastoral → horticultural → agricultural → industrial) represent "discontinuous leaps" in human history as new societal forms and modes of human living emerge. Similarly, the stage model of urbanization depicts a process of change that partly destroys the old and transforms city life into new forms. Both Lenski's theory and the urban development model see technological innovation as preconditions for change, but beyond that they differ. Lenski argues that in societal evolution increased economic productive capacity produced the growth of human population, an increase social complexity and specialization, and the evolution of specialized institutions that integrate and exercise authority over social life. The urban development model views new urban forms as deriving from the ongoing interaction among new technical-economic modes of production, the exercise of power, and community-based conflict and protest.

In both models each seemingly discontinuous stage is in fact dependent upon more subtle cumulative processes involving the gradual addition of new elements to a continuing base. Each society or city does not necessarily pass through the same set of fixed stages. The United States, for example, was never a society of hunters and gatherers or pastoralists, nor was Dallas ever an industrial city. Similarly, the rapid urbanization in the Third World has reorganized new urban forms on the base of preindustrial cities (a topic we will return to when we discuss development and global population problems).

Anthropologist Julian Steward has proposed thinking about such broad linear patterns of change as "multilinear evolution." By that he meant that social and cultural forms "may develop in similar ways under similar conditions, but few concrete aspects of culture will appear among all groups of mankind in a regular sequence" (1955:4). We do argue that these models depict the societal development of the whole of humanity as abstractions when it is useful to conceptualize change as linear, cumulative, and nonrepetitive.

Cyclical Models of Change

Another conception of the long-term pattern or direction of change is that it is cyclical or repetitive. The French have a phrase for it: *Plus ça change, plus c'est la meme chose* ("the more a thing changes, the more it stays the same"). This view does not deny change but denies that it is leading anywhere over the long term (Moore, 1974:44). Advocates of cyclical models of change argue that in important ways, history does repeat itself. The classic macro cyclical theories of change were mostly "rise-and-fall" theories of civilizations. In the ancient world a systematic statement of such a rise-and-fall theory was that of Ibn Khaldun (1332–1405), who attempted to explain the perennial conflict between city dwellers and nomads in the medieval Islamic societies of North Africa and the resulting political cycles of the rise and fall of dynasties.

In the early twentieth century, social scientists began to phrase such cyclical theories not in terms of moral cycles of recurring decadence, but in terms of biological models of growth and decay. Societies were thus said to be like organic systems, going though periods of youth, adolescent growth, mature vigor, and senility in old age. The most pessimistic among these was Oswald Spengler (1880–1936) who argued in the 1930s that Western European civilization was in its twilight years and could be expected to be replaced by newer, more vigorous civilizations. His major statement of this thesis, aptly titled *The Decline of the West,* was published in 1932 and fit well with the post–World War I intellectual pessimism of the times. Similar, but less pessimistic, were the theories of Arnold Toynbee (1962), who at least held out hope of the revitalization of declining civilizations by reinvigorating the creativity of elites.

Within sociology, the most influential cyclical theorist was Pitirim Sorokin (1889–1968) who argued that the "master cycles" of history were oscillations between periods dominated by idealism and those dominated by hedonism and materialism, interspersed by periods of transition that creatively blended the two dominant cultural frameworks. In the Western historical context, Sorokin argued that medieval

Europe was an epoch dominated by idealism, the Renaissance and Reformation were transition periods, and contemporary Western societies are dominated by materialism and hedonism. He anticipated the ultimate collapse of Western materialism and a return to a more idealistic culture. As you can see, these classic cyclical theories are rather pessimistic: They do not urge you to look for much long-range significant change, much less any improvement in the human condition.

It is important that you understand what is going on here. Cyclical theories become plausible if we agree with the analyst that the "important aspects" of change are historically repetitive. What the "important aspects" are, of course, is always arguable. This selectivity—emphasizing some things, deemphasizing others, and using historical evidence in a highly selective way—illustrates what we think is a general problem with purely cyclical macro theories. All theories are selective to some extent, but we think the problem is particularly pronounced in cyclical theories. In addition to the problem of selectivity, in their pure form they deny the importance of developmental, nonrepetitive change. To assert that there are cycles in history is one thing, but to argue that the singular transformations associated with the agricultural or industrial revolutions are without lasting importance is quite another thing, and few would agree with that idea.

Patterns of Cyclical Change.   It is relatively easy to see some cyclical patterns of change at less abstract levels. Perhaps the most familiar example is the business cycle that tends to exist in free market economies, involving repetitive cycles of economic expansion and contraction. Production tends to increase until overproduction occurs and inventories cannot be sold. At this time businesses begin to cut back on production, laying off workers and initiating economic contraction and recession. At the time that such contraction falls below consumer demand, a new wave of production expansion is initiated. While these business cycles are well documented, all governments in industrialized economies have sought to intervene by various methods (to either stimulate or dampen growth at the appropriate times) to smooth out such cycles.

Social scientists have also identified repetitive cycles of change and development in American nuclear families. They argue that families have common characteristics and problems at each stage in the family life cycle, which are determined primarily by the presence, number, and ages of children in the family. Thus Duvall and Miller (1985), Rodgers (1973), and many others maintain that family problems and characteristics are different in families consisting of young couples without children, families with young children, families with older children, and families whose children have left the home. This cycle is not, of course, repeated in any one family, but is an ongoing dynamic that is repeated among millions of American families. The same dynamic is not observed in extended family systems, which are likely to have a variety of people of different ages at different phases in their lives.

We have often thought that the typical college semester has a repetitive dynamic in the way that it is experienced. Students and faculty begin each new semester with a great deal of enthusiasm and motivation to stay on top of their work. By midsemester, enthusiasm and self-discipline lags and people are catching up or coping with their tasks on a day-to-day basis. Toward the end of each semester, there is another spurt of self-discipline and motivation to work in order to finish the semester as well as possible. But with each semester the cycle seems to be repeated. The question can be raised whether these cycles are really change at all or are rather ongoing dynamics of the way stable systems function? From the standpoint of the participants in the social system, things may seem to change dramatically. But from the standpoint of the semester system itself, there may be no change in the long run. Thus the answer about whether significant change is going on depends upon the level of analysis and the time frame.

Contemporary Macro Cyclical Models.   In spite of our critical comments about the older macro cyclical theories of change, we are still fascinated with the possibility of larger-scale cycles, and we will discuss two of them here.

Political and Economic Cycles in America. In the last chapter we discussed the growing inequality and concentration of wealth in the United States that has been taking place since the mid-1970s. Political analyst Kevin Phillips suggested that not only has this has happened before in America, but that it represents a cyclical dynamic in the American political economy (Phillips, 1990). In addition to the 1980s and 1990s, a growth in the concentration of wealth happened in the Gilded Age (1890s) and the Roaring Twenties (1920s). These were periods of free market capitalist expansion and extraordinary technological creativity. All had, according to Phillips the following ensemble of characteristics: (1) renewal of "rags to riches" myths about individual achievement; (2) entrepreneurialism, represented, for example, in popular writing by Henry Ford and Lee Iacocca; (3) a public philosophy of laissez faire and politics of the deregulation of industry; (4) tax cuts; (5) lower inflation; (6) doubts about the role of government in the economy and society; (7) depression in agriculture; (8) strong financial markets; (9) increasing corporate mergers, takeovers, and "restructuring"; (10) a steady concentration of wealth among the already affluent; and (11) the use of government policy to redistribute income toward the wealthy (1990:54).

As this expansion and concentration supported by public policy proceeds, it deteriorates into a "capitalist blowout" ending in speculation, corruption, and the manipulation of financial markets. At the end of a cycle is economic instability and recessions (or even, following the Roaring Twenties, a Great Depression). Such periods have always been followed by swings back to more populist, community-minded, and activist governments (governed sometimes by Republican and sometimes by Democratic administrations) that dampened the concentration of wealth, speculation, corruption, and the alleviated suffering among the losers in the free market blowout. Such governments promote social welfare in more than an economic sense and may in fact rescue capitalism from a destructive dynamic, but they eventually produce problems associated with economic regulation, bureaucracy, and inflation.

This is an intriguing cyclical theory, but note that it is purely descriptive; Phillips does not speculate about causes (but see Schlesinger, 1986). If Phillips is right, where is America in these cycles? We hope you recognize that events since the mid-1970s conform pretty much to the first phase of Phillips's cycle. Are we ready for another of the cycles in which expansive governments attempt to counteract the debilitating social costs of privatization by letting everything be dictated by market forces? One scenario we noted at the end of Chapter 4 thinks so.

Long Cycles and Global Change. There may be even *long cycles* in history that would modify a strictly linear or developmental view of change. Numerous analysts have noted a periodicity in the outbreak of major wars in Western history over the last two hundred years and wondered about it. And some economists (mainly European) have argued that there are "long-wave" cycles of expansion and contraction in the world economy, termed *Kondratieff cycles,* with peaks between forty-five and sixty years apart. Forrester makes a plausible case for such long-wave cycles with depressions about fifty years apart, in the 1830s, 1890s, and the 1930s. More than fifteen years ago, he argued that we are entering a period in which such a downturn is overdue (1985:16). But even though we continue to be fascinated by the possibility of such long cycles in history, the evidence for such cycles remains controversial, and many American academic economists assert that no such economic cycles exist.

An articulate contemporary advocate of a macroscopic cyclical theory of social change is Daniel Chirot, who states: "The key to a sensible theoretical approach to change is the recognition that there exist long periods of history in which the essential forces at work remain quite similar" (1986:292). He argues that these cycles can be compared with one another, but that change is not simply the same old thing over and over again. Even within any specific historical era such cycles are not actually unvarying. New eras, Chirot says (1986:292), have different sets of cycles and mainsprings of change and require different models of cycles. Chirot argues that repetitive cycles are embedded in longer-range historical eras that are not repetitive. He therefore, in fact, combines cyclical and linear models of change. We are emphasizing the cyclical aspects of his theory here for purposes of illustration.

To simplify things for the sake of his argument, Chirot depicts human development in two broad historical eras, premodern and modern, as would simple linear theory. But he understands the dynamics of change within such eras quite differently from Lenski, who argued that each new technological and economic base produced qualitatively different societies. According to Chirot, societies of the premodern era—that is, the preindustrial agrarian societies of the Near East, Europe, and Asia—were the "great civilizations." They had dense populations, powerful states, and elaborate cultures, and they experienced recurrent cycles of crisis and decline. Because

> populations in that era grew more quickly than technology advanced, societies tended to experience recurrent crises of overpopulation, malnutrition, disease, and social chaos. . . . Proximity to nomads, dependence on fragile irrigation systems, and endemic diseases combined with population cycles to magnify the periodic catastrophes. (1986:292)

Throughout these recurrent cycles of growth, crisis, and decline, the state was controlled by elites who competed with each other for the key resource: taxable peasants. With the development of industrial societies in the modern era, the state commands much greater mass loyalty, develops a nationalist ideology, and seeks to promote the general welfare and stimulate economic production. But most important, in industrial societies the old cycles of overpopulation and recurrent disasters have ended and are replaced by cycles with new dynamics. Compared with preindustrial societies, the outstanding feature of modern industrial societies is their technological inventiveness. In modern societies each economic cycle begins with a new technology applied to production, new profits, and economic growth. Eventually markets become saturated by overinvestment in aging industries followed by business failures and an economic crisis. This is accompanied by high levels of unemployment, political stress, and social disruption. This crisis is typically a prelude to the development of new economic technologies and a new dynamic of economic expansion.

More concretely, Chirot sees the cycles of industrial societies as follows. The *first industrial cycle* began in Europe with the Industrial Revolution in textiles from the 1780s to the 1820s. At its stage of overexpansion, it produced the unstable political atmosphere of Europe in the 1830s and 1840s. The *second cycle,* based on the development of iron and railroads, lasted until the 1870s. The transition to the *third cycle,* based on steel and the chemical industry, was "sufficiently painful to provoke intense imperialistic rivalries among the advanced Western powers" (1986:293–294), which led to the international conflict that resulted in World War I. That war and its aftermaths—the Great Depression of the 1930s and World War II—made the transition to the fourth cycle very long, painful, and difficult. This *fourth cycle,* based on automobiles and high mass consumption, began to benefit most people in the industrial nations only after 1950. "The great tragedies of the twentieth century can only be explained as the unfortunate conjunction of normal cyclical changes combined with bitter international conflicts that have stemmed from them" (Chirot, 1986:294). After World War II there was an enormous period of worldwide economic expansion involving the development of more extensive trade relationships among the industrial nations and among the industrial and the developing nations of the non-Western world (more about this in later chapters about modernization and development). By the 1970s, there was a worldwide recession and many have seen the stagnation and overexpansion of this fourth industrial cycle.

By the mid 1980s, the world economy was in a state of slow but continuous expansion, in both industrial democracies and many less-developed nations. It is tempting to speculate that a fifth cycle has begun. Many observers believe that new technologies and dramatically increased economic integration of the world market economy are driving such a new cycle in the information age (Olsen, E., 1995; Farrell, 1994; Naisbett, 1994; Castells, 1998). To think that this is happening is consistent with the transformations, largely since the mid-1970s, that we discussed in Chapters 2–4. If the world is moving into a new fifth industrial phase, Chirot argues that "the same patterns of sectoral decay in old leading industries and the rise of new firms, new regions of technological dynamism, international tensions, and pressures on governments to help smooth the transitions are being repeated" (1986:86). The really important question is "whether or not the present cyclical change that began in the 1970s will produce a renewed series of traumatic events" (1986:105). The end of the last cycle produced a global depression and World War II. The transition to the fifth cycle—if it be that—is connected with the disorders that attended the breakup of the Soviet empire, the growth of an interdependent but extremely volatile "world system" of sorts, the growth of inequality both within and between nations, and the growing visibility of severe environmental problems. Chirot's theory is not deterministic. Such problems in transition can be managed with more or less disruption. But the potential for catastrophe is much greater at the end of a cycle. If this interpretation is right, the post–World War II long-cycle boom is at an end, and a new cycle may be beginning. This is intriguing, important, and controversial. We hope you recognize that the issues it raises are more than mere academic questions.

Dialectical Models of Change

In Chapter 2 we argued that there may be a dialectical relationship between modernism and postmodernism, and in Chapter 4 we said the same about the seemingly contradictory trends of the centralization of economic wealth and the proliferation of small entrepreneurial firms in the U.S. economy. But we defined only briefly what "dialectical" meant. Here we want to return to that notion and discuss it more in depth. Dialectical models of change are more complex than either purely linear or cyclical ones. They assume that social life has inherent stresses or "contradictions," which develop because every social development, even successful ones, taken to its ultimate conclusion, carries within it the seeds of its own destruction (or at least its own modification). Significant change takes place as an attempt to resolve the accumulation of intolerable contradictions. Because such resolutions produce new social and cultural forms, like linear or evolutionary change they do not merely repeat the past, and they also contain predictable cycles (of sorts) in the accumulation of contradictions and their resolution. Dialectical models contain, therefore, elements of both linear and cyclical change. How so? Roberta Ash Garner explains:

> History "repeats itself" only in the sense that some processes of change persist. The contents of these processes, the specific behaviors that are changing, are never quite the same. . . . Small changes pile up until the system collapses. The old system gives way to a new one. The old system drops into the past, never to be revived. However, the new system already at the moment of its appearance contains stresses that will slowly enlarge, like cracks in the foundation of a building, until the whole collapses. Yet the process is not cyclical. Growth, decay, and collapse never return us to the initial starting point. Change is spiral rather than cyclical. (1977:408)

In this dialectical view, the cycles of the birth and decline of social systems are determined by the unraveling of stresses and contradictions that are inherent in social life. Yet the resultant vector of these built-in conflicts produces more than just a turning of the wheel of historical cycles—there is real, cumulative change in the longer view of history.

The idea of a dialectical pattern of change is not new. The eighteenth-century philosopher Hegel argued that history developed as a dialectic from contradictions in the great ideas or world views of a given historical epoch. But in social science the best-known advocate of a dialectical theory of social change was Karl Marx, whose views we encountered earlier. Marx argued that change resulted from class struggles between those with material interests in existing systems of production and those with interests in new and emerging ones.

While such dialectical thought is rooted in classical Marxism, some dialectical theories differ from classical Marxism in that they do not accept economically based "class conflict" as the only, or even the most important, source of "contradictions" that produce conflict and change. Rather than reviewing classical Marxism, let us briefly describe the more contemporary materialist dialectic perspective of Immanuel Wallerstein (1974), who describes the emergence of industrial capitalism and the modern world in a different way than Marx.

Wallerstein argues that the modern world system and the demise of feudalism were produced by the resolution of (at least) three contradictory modes of political and economic organization. *First* was the contradiction between the older subsistence agriculture with its serfs and the newer commercialized cash crop agriculture with its wage workers. *Second* was the contradiction between the older decentralized craft production and the newer centralized factory system. *Third* was the contradiction between the small market system of local trade with the vast expansion of markets that attended the colonial expansion into the non-European world. The outcomes of these competing modes of social organization gradually defined the emerging parameters of the industrial world:

1. Nationally and internationally marketed goods came to be more important than those of local craft production, hence the vast growth in scale of industrial economies and societies.
2. Local guild masters of the late feudal system were replaced by the entrepreneurs of the free marketplace as the dominant economic elites.
3. New political and cultural forms emerged that reflected the growing dominance of the commercial entrepreneurs and merchants.
4. Despite repeated revolts, displaced workers and peasants failed to establish control over either town politics or the work process.

There are dialectical perspectives that are less clearly related to the materialist and Marxian tradition in social explanation. One, for example, argues that important social contradictions result from differential rates of change in various institutional sectors of a society: "For example, technology and the productive system as a whole tend to change more rapidly than the political and ideological superstructure, which changes slowly and contains a large cargo of cultural 'baggage' carried over from the past" (Ash Garner, 1977:311). We have met this view before, in the guise of Ogburn's cultural lag theory, and while it does not deny the importance of class conflict as a manifestation of contradictions, it locates the sources of contradictions more broadly in differential rates of change. Other dialectical theories depart more significantly from the materialist view of the causes of change.

Raymond Aron (1968), for instance, uses the notion of contradictions to mean contradictions between structural characteristics and individual aspirations (or at best, cultural themes). He argues that there are three common sources of inner contradictions in contemporary societies. First, modern societies are equalitarian in the aspirations of people but hierarchical in structure and organization. Hence there is a *dialectic of equality in modern societies.* Second, there is a contradiction regarding socialization in modern societies: Individuals desire increasing individuation and uniqueness, while the structures of socialization create increasing "massification" with pressures toward conformity and sameness—hence the *dialectic of socialization.* Third, in societies around the world, there is a desire for higher levels of affluence and national autonomy at the same time that the world is becoming increasingly interrelated and interdependent. The desire for such autonomy is frustrated by such dependency—hence, according to Aron, the *dialectic of universality.* This is a distinctly non-Marxist dialectical view of social change.

It will be recorded as one of the supreme ironies of history that while Marxians were waiting for the contradictions of capitalism to produce the final collapse of the system, it was in fact Soviet-style Marxism and state socialism that collapsed in the late 1980s and early 1990s. As that change unravels, it will no doubt be a challenging intellectual project to develop a dialectical view of the demise of state socialism. Yet we think a few clues are already apparent. *What were some emerging contradictions of the Soviet system? First,* there was the contradiction between the philosophical humanism of Marx, who hoped that socialism would produce a world of rationality and human emancipation versus the reality of a coercive political culture with a repressive dogma of collectivism that left little room for individuation and only limited opportunities for intellectual freedom and rationality. *Second,* there was the goal of society without meaningful economic hierarchies (the "classless society") versus the obvious persistence of hierarchies of all kinds—ethnic, economic, and most importantly, political. *Third,* there was the promise of the "withering away" of a state run by elites (which is not to say all forms of government) versus the increasingly clear reality that what you had in the Soviet world was a series of good old-fashioned corrupt political machines (in the communist party), who looked primarily to their own interests rather to those of the "proletarian masses," and who were by no means about to "wither way." *Fourth,* there was the promise of material abundance in the "worker's paradise" versus the reality of an overly centralized state planning system so inefficient that it could produce very little in the way of consumer amenities. *Finally,* there was a deep contradiction in the Marxian promise of the end of alienation and self-estrangement under state socialism and the reality of pervasive social alienation and cynicism about the system that permeated Soviet society from top to bottom.

Marx's predictions about where socialism would develop seemed to be wrong as well. Instead of developing in the most developed parts of the capitalist world (the United States, the United Kingdom, and Japan), state socialism was a popular way of catching up in the world economic race. Marxism provided a convenient set of scapegoats for economic upheaval (capitalist imperialism) while providing a mechanism for centralizing power in the hands of a small elite in a one-party state via the "dictatorship of the proletariat."

We argue that these were widely perceived contradictions among ordinary Soviet citizens since the mid-1960s, particularly in urban areas, and particularly among the party elite itself. How it came to be so is a story to which we will return in later chapters. We hasten to add that with these informal observations about emergent contradictions in the Soviet system, we do not mean to suggest that free market capitalism is without problems or contradictions. Capitalism may have had a greater capacity for self-transformation without a final collapse, but both Marx and capitalist theorist Joseph Schumpeter were right in seeing capitalism as having a dynamic of creative destruction (as we hope the examples suggested in this and the last chapter should make clear). Notwithstanding the political theology of American conservatives, we do not think that the collapse of the Soviet system can be understood as the final triumph of free-market capitalism, which is in reality practiced nowhere in a recognizably pure form, and particularly not in the industrial world.

IN CONCLUSION

We have now discussed theories of the causes of change (material causes, ideational causes, interacting causes), and three models of the directions and patterns of social change (linear, cyclical, dialectical). Clearly, a case can be made for each of these theoretical approaches. *How can they all have some validity?*

Part of the answer is that the different approaches focus on different units of analysis and levels of abstraction. For example, linear and cyclical models both focus on changes over time, but *linear models* concentrate on understanding cumulative and developmental change processes that occur in many concrete social units, whereas *cyclical models* focus on repetitive change processes in particular structural units (for example, civilizations, families, political economies). *Dialectical models* assume that in the short term change is repetitive because it involves the conflict between "contradictory" aspects of society (variously conceived), but that there is a long-term direction to change that is the outcome of these conflicts. With the exception of Marx, dialectical theorists have focused more on identifying the contradictions that cause change rather than the long-range trajectories of change that are the outcomes of the dialectical process.

Another part of the answer has to do with the way that scholars use theory. They tend to use theory in practical ways by selecting the theoretical approach most appropriate to explain the particular phenomenon or problem in which they are interested. In this pragmatic approach to theory, there are no true or false explanations (theories), but different approaches are more useful or less useful—depending on what they want to explain. But the question (about reconciling different theories) is still more complex than selective attention to different units or levels of analysis or the analyst's utilitarian choice of the most appropriate theory for his or her work. Theories may be practical tools to explain things, but in terms of the abstract goals of science, they are also "truth statements" about the way the world is. Different theories represent honest and important intellectual disagreements about the causes and patterns of social change.

While it will never be achieved, we think that social scientists need to work toward the goal of unified, integrated theory. Kenneth Boulding (1970) has suggested that we will have a more complete understanding of social life when we understand the relationship between (1) equilibrium processes, (2) cyclical processes, and (3) cumulative processes. This is a large order, which includes not only understanding change processes but the processes that serve to maintain stability and persistence as well.

THINKING PERSONALLY ABOUT SOCIAL CHANGE

Thinking personally about the causes and patterns of change is a real challenge here, because the subject is more abstract than in previous chapters and because we have discussed macro-scale change: historical social development, urbanization, long-term economic cycles, and so forth. But we think you can get some sense of different causes and patterns of change in less abstract settings closer to the everyday life experience of persons. Again, try to distinguish between purely personal change and changes in the networks, groups, and organizations that you (or others) have experienced.

1. Scholars have thought about causes or driving forces of change as both powerful ideas (or beliefs, values, and ideologies) and important technologies and material innovations. Think about families and households that are familiar to you. Are there powerful ideas and beliefs that enabled them to change and to deal with difficulties and each other? How about getting along with each other, loving and taking care of each other, respecting other's wishes and property, or rules about decisions, control, and conflict? Did the family or household work to change in directions consistent with powerful shared values and ideologies? Did they give the family a way of coping with problems and difficulties? Were there other powerful beliefs or values of individuals that hindered family coping and positive change ("I know what I want, and I don't care about what you want")?

2. *Turn the theoretical question around:* Are there new technologies or material changes that transform the way family/household members interact and their expectations? What about the introduction of a new car or cars? new computers? new telephone options? TV or cable TV? a new house or apartment? a lot more money? a lot less money? Did these produce family/household change? Think beyond households. Have you had any experience with businesses or companies that introduced new technical systems to do things? What other kinds of changes did they stimulate? How did people react differently? If you can, talk to acquaintances or relatives about these questions.

3. Talk to some older people or relatives about family change. Ask them about cumulative or linear change in families and households they have observed. How do they perceive that families are becoming different than they remember them when they were younger? Ask them also about family cycles (e.g., moving from couples without children to families with very young children, to families with older children, to families with adult children living in their own households who are couples again, but older). To

get some sense of diversity, talk to some people who are single parents or living in step-families about these kinds of changes.

4. Schools and colleges do change, sometimes in ways that are never repeated. Can you think of some examples? In this chapter we argued that there are also cyclical changes in the school year for time periods like years or semesters. Do you agree or not? How would you describe change through the typical time-related cycles at your school?

5. Groups and organizations have commonly understood purposes and reasons for being. But people in them sometimes pressure each other to "let us have a degree of freedom to do what we want, and how we want to do it." If this goes on for a time, somebody is likely to say, "Wait a minute! Our 'wants' are so different that we often block each other's ability to really do anything, and we need to be more organized [to either enjoy the group or make it more effective]." At this point social pressures increase to make people "get in line," cooperate, compromise, or stop feuding "for the good of the group," and the group creates a new set of arrangements. We think most groups continually struggle to find the optimum balance between individual freedom and social order and continually generate new sets of arrangements about that relationship. It is a common idea that freedom and social order are not really contradictory, but depend on each other in complicated ways. We think this is one kind of dialectical change you can often observe even in the smallest of groups or organizations. Can you think of illustrations?

NOTES

1. If you are interested in pursuing any of these views in depth, there are many sources available. See Coser, 1977; Turner and Beeghley, 1981; Ritzer, 1983; Appelbaum, 1970; and especially Schneider, 1976.
2. The following relies heavily on Lauer, 1977.
3. Again, we are indebted to the ideas of Lauer (1977) in the following section.
4. If this is beginning to sound like the description of American modernity in previous chapters, it is not accidental.

6

Social Theory
and Social Change

There are three broad theoretical perspectives in contemporary American sociology. These are functionalism, conflict theory, and a cluster of related perspectives that we will call "interpretive theories." They embody three different images of society and social change and provide different answers to the most basic sociological questions. For our purposes, these questions boil down to: What factors determine the structure of society and the nature of change? One answer is that society and change are shaped by the necessities of survival (the functionalist answer). Another is that society and change are shaped by conflict among groups and classes within society over the control of valued and scarce resources (the conflict theory answer). A third answer is that the social interaction processes between people and groups result in the creation and ongoing negotiation and revision of the meanings, symbols, and social definitions that constitute both society and change (the interpretive answer).

The three perspectives derive from different historical sources and view change in quite different, often contradictory, ways. Functionalism originated in analogies between biological systems and social systems, commonly used in nineteenth-century sociology and anthropology. The earliest explicit advocate of functionalist explanation in sociology was Emile Durkheim. Conflict theory is historically rooted in classical Marxism, although contemporary conflict theory in sociology has considerably modified early Marxist thought. Interpretive theories are really a group of related perspectives with different sources, but they are rooted in the historic ideas of Max Weber more than any other classical thinker. In various ways they all examine the ways that actors define their social situations and the effects of these definitions on ensuing action and interaction (Ritzer, 1988:392).

These three perspectives provide only the broadest, and often unacknowledged, assumptions within which more specific sociological analysis and explanation takes place. It is often the case that actual sociological writing uses insights and assumptions from all of these broad perspectives at different times and for different questions. That was the case in the first four chapters in this book, which described changes in American society, abstractly sometimes, but without much reference to theories of any sort. But we think we owe it to you now to keep a *theoretical retrospective,* a sort of flashback, to highlight briefly some issues and topics that can be understood in the context of one of the broad three theoretical perspectives.

In this chapter we will (1) discuss these three theoretical perspectives and their implications for explaining social change in the abstract, and then (2) explore how each provides a context to understand some of the particular material in Chapters 2 through 4. Finally, we will (3) discuss the interaction of structure and human agency in relation to large-scale change.

FUNCTIONALIST THEORY

Structural functionalism (functionalism, for short) assumes that a society is a system of interrelated parts that function in ways that promote the survival of the whole system. The initial focus of much functional thinking is to define activities that are necessary for the survival of the entire system (*functional requisites* or *imperatives*). Lists of such functional requisites vary in length and abstractness. According to Mack and Bradford (1979), there are five such functional requisites. Every social system must be concerned with the following:

1. The replacement of individuals (by reproduction or recruitment)
2. Socialization (enabling individuals to participate)
3. The production of goods and services (hence, an economy)
4. The provision of social order (hence, a political system)
5. The maintenance of common symbols, values, and motivations (hence, a culture)

Parsons (1951) states the functional requisites more abstractly. He argues that there are four basic functions that any society (or any of its subsystems) must be concerned with for its survival:

1. Adaptation (the generation of resources from the environment)
2. Goal attainment (choices about the consumption of resources)
3. Integration (regulation of relationships between the parts of the system)
4. Latency or "pattern maintenance" (providing cultural legitimation for the manner in which other functions are accomplished)

Less abstractly, Parsons is talking about the functions of (1) the economy, (2) the political system, (3) the legal system, and (4) the diverse agencies that perpetuate culture. It is important to note that Parsons emphasizes culture as the major force that binds and integrates the various aspects of the social world. He has, in fact, labeled himself as a "cultural determinist" (Parsons, 1966). This assumption, as you will see, has an important impact on how he develops a theory of social change. You can see that the functional requisites depicted by both Mack and Parsons lead to a discussion of social institutions. From this perspective, different functional requisites are viewed as producing differentiated *structures* that specialize in accomplishing them (for example, the family, economy, polity, religions).

Much functionalist thinking (particularly in the 1950s) viewed society as a system that persists by maintaining *equilibrium,* that is, the various structures and institutions are viewed as operating in concert in a mutually reinforcing way to maintain stability in the way that each functions and in the relationships between them. Society is thus viewed as a *homeostatic* system, which operates to perpetuate itself. This was a way of explaining persistence and stability but not change. This inability to explain change was criticized by many during the early 1960s (Parsons was the focus of much of this criticism), and functional theorists began to be more concerned with the problem of understanding change. How did they do so?

Functionalism and Social Change

Functionalist thinking about change begins by asserting that in the actual world, integration and "balance" in society are always incomplete. To some degree, real societies are out of sync for a variety of reasons. They develop inconsistencies, contradictions, and institutional practices that do not mesh in an integrated way. There is a constant struggle to maintain order and integration in connection with the realities of such *strains* (a general term for such inconsistencies and lack of integration).

Functionalist theory understands social change as the maintenance of a moving, or dynamic, rather than a static equilibrium between the components of the social system. There are many, possible sources of such strains. Most obvious, since social systems are all open in varying degrees to their environments, strains can be the result of *exogenous* discrepant cultural items that are imported from surrounding environments, both natural and social. There may be new ideas, values, and technologies from other groups and societies, carried by immigrants, traders, or missionaries. And changes in the physical environment (for example, drought, pollution, depletion) may produce strains in maintaining certain levels or kinds of economic activity. But strains can also be of internal or *endogenous* origin in this revised functionalist view. They can result, for instance, from inconsistencies between widely shared values and actual behavior. They can result from different values themselves that may have contradictory implications for choices and behavior. They can be strains resulting from innovations that do not work within established institutional practices. They can be strains resulting from differentiated social roles that have different outlooks and responsibilities. Strains may be produced by different rates of change in various institutional realms that may become somewhat isolated and don't mesh in an integrated fashion (see Fig. 6-1).

Consider the following examples of strains in contemporary America: (1) conflicts between the traditional female role and the realities of dual-income families; (2) in the new millennium, the problem of how to maintain a sense of community in a globalized and fragmented world; (3) values about equal opportunity versus the realities of racism and discrimination. Even though functionalists do recognize that such strains can originate from within the social system, exactly how this happens within the framework of the theory is not clear, given the equilibrium assumption.

While certain levels of strain can be tolerated, if strains exceed certain limits (and functional theory provides few clues as to what these limits are) they produce

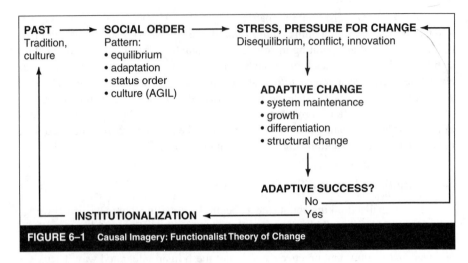

FIGURE 6–1   Causal Imagery: Functionalist Theory of Change

change in some aspect of the system—as an attempt to contain or adapt to strain. Thus functional theorists argue that changes in the parts of a system

> may balance each other so that there is no change in the system as a whole; if they do not, the entire system will probably change. Thus while functionalism adopts an equilibrium perspective, it is not necessarily a static point of view. In this moving equilibrium of the social system, those changes that do occur are seen as doing so in an orderly, not a revolutionary way. (Ritzer, 1983:224)

In response to his critics, who pointed out that his theory was incapable of explaining much about change, Parsons (1966) developed an *evolutionary* theory of change that distinguished between several types of change. First, there is *system maintenance* that restores a previous pattern of equilibrium (such as rebuilding a community after a disaster). This is certainly change, but of a limited sort that is implied in the static functional perspective. Second, there is what Parsons calls *structural differentiation,* which means the increasing differentiation of subsystem units into patterns of functional specialization and interdependence. Such newly specialized and separated subunits (or departments in organizations) often develop problems in the coordination of their activities and functions.

Thus structural differentiation typically produces integrative problems that may require the development of new mechanisms of integration, coordination, and control. In concrete terms, this often means the development of new management procedures, roles, and structures. Parsons terms this third type of change (differentiation plus new integrative mechanisms) *adaptive upgrading,* meaning that the social system becomes more effective in generating and distributing resources and enhancing its survival. But all such changes can occur without altering the key features of the system (basic cultural values, goals, distribution of power, internal patterns of order, overall organizational unity, and so forth).

Parsons reserves the term *structural change* for change in such key features of the system. His argument is that fundamental change of the total system involves changes in the system of cultural values that legitimate and stabilize the system. It may or may not be necessary to redefine, or *generalize,* basic and fundamental values and goals to create a more diverse and complex system. For example, a university may create new departments and programs (differentiation) and new levels and procedures of administration to coordinate them (adaptive upgrading), without changing the basic goals and values that serve to legitimate the university as a system (perpetuating knowledge, research, service to society). As another illustration at the societal level, Parsons argues that in spite of the enormous growth in size, complexity, and specialization in American society, some core values have remained constant (for example, *instrumental activism,* the emphasis on efficiency and getting things done). Indeed, there is often much resistance to the alteration of basic values. Overall structural change (involving the alteration of abstract core values) is less likely than differentiation and adaptive upgrading, even though it does occur in the long run of historical development.

Parsons' evolutionary theory not only distinguished between different types of change processes in the evolution of societies but also developed a picture of the large-scale evolution of societies, from premodern to modern ones. He argues that there were some key "evolutionary universals," discovered in various societies, that made the transition to modern societies possible: (1) social stratification, that is, the emergence of social classes beyond rudimentary status distinctions based on age, kinship, and so forth; (2) bureaucratic organization; (3) cultural legitimation of existing structural arrangements; (4) money economy and markets; (5) generalized or "universalistic" social norms; and (6) democratic associations (1964).

Of these six evolutionary universals, surely the last is the most controversial, since in retrospect it is clear that not all contemporary societies are parliamentary democracies. Note also that Parsons' notion of evolutionary universals is more a description of modernism than an explanation: We are told nothing about how various premodern societies discover them, or what causal factors are at work, as did the linear-evolutionary theories we encountered in the last chapter. What we think is more useful in Parsons' work about change is the assertion, although it is arguable, that certain types of changes are more or less likely in terms of whether or not they preserve the key features of the system or transform them. In doing so, he suggests what kinds of change will be *most* and *least* common. Most common are system maintenance and differentiation; intermediate would be the development of new integrative and coordinative mechanisms; and least common are new abstract values and systems of cultural legitimation.

More recent *functionalist theories* of social change define society not as an "equilibrating system," but as a "tension-management system" (Moore, 1974:11). The difference is subtle but important. Olsen describes this amended functionalist theory of change as an "adjustment perspective":

> Whenever stresses or strains seriously threaten the key features of an organization—whatever they might be—the organization will . . . initiate compensatory

actions to counter these disruptions, in an attempt to preserve its key features. If the compensatory activities successfully defend the threatened key features, then whatever changes do occur will be confined to other, less crucial features. . . . To the extent that the organization successfully practices such adjustive maneuvers, it survives through time as a relatively stable social entity. . . . There are limits, however, beyond which adjustive or counterbalancing activities and changes cannot go if the organization as a whole is to be maintained in its present form. When disruptive stresses and strains or their resulting conflicts are so severe and prolonged that compensatory mechanisms cannot cope with them, the key organizational features being protected will themselves be altered or destroyed. The entire organization then changes; there is a change of the organization rather than just within the organization. (1978:341)

One of the weaknesses of functional theory is that it deals mainly with gradual evolutionary change that enhances the survivability of the system in question. It is less able to deal with rapid or discontinuous change, or change involving fundamental transformations of the system, or the emergence of new values. Functionalist theories of change would have a great difficulty explaining a coup d'etat, a revolution, or, for example, the rapid collapse of state socialism in the 1990s. More abstractly, it understands change as a response to the development of strains, but the sources of strain are ambiguous unless they are exogenous. But such exogenous strains are outside the theory's frame of reference, and hence unpredictable. The theory is still a theory of order and stability that has been amended to account for change.

It is worth noting that after the 1960s, when functionalism (especially in its Parsonian variety) came under strong attack, there was in the 1980s a revival in neo-functionalist theorizing in sociology, both in America and in Europe (Alexander, 1985; Luhmann, 1982). In America, the most articulate spokesman for this has been Jeffrey Alexander, who builds on Parsons but argues for a functionalism that is more multidimensional in both macro and micro levels. He rejects much of the optimism about modernity and accepts conflict and dissensus as being as "natural" as equilibrium and consensus (Alexander, 1985). He specifically argues that cultures and cultural intermingling provide societies and people with a myriad of solutions to conflict and dissensus, and that these "tool kits" (Swidler, 1986) of interchangeable parts allow for navigation through a social world fraught with conflict and dissensus. Societies adapt and change for the same reasons that cultures adapt and change and changes contribute to collective survival and provide meaning for past and current events. The merger of cultural and functionalist explanations is one of the new attempts to produce a functionalist synthesis.

Changing America in Functionalist Theory Contexts

Much of the discussion in Chapter 2 of structural and cultural trends in American society can be understood in a functionalist context. Growth in scale, differentiation and specialization, centralization, bureaucratization, increasing technical complexity, and the growing culture of individualism can all be seen as aspects of a *differentiation* theory of societal change. In such functional-evolutionary views of change, from Durkheim to Parsons and his successors, it is argued that growth produces differentiation, and the problems with increased complexity stimulate adaptive changes that elaborate new structures for coordination and control. The emergence of large-scale government as the chief problem solver in an increasingly complex market economy, discussed in Chapter 4, illustrates this process.

Similarly, but in a broader time span, Lenski's linear developmental model of social change (discussed in Chapter 5) is a functionalist perspective. It argues that new economic technologies associated with, for instance, agriculture or industrialism produced the possibility of larger populations, increased structural complexity and differentiation, and with these the elaboration of and mechanisms of social control.

One can accept these mechanisms for the production of social change without accepting the functionalist premise that larger populations, differentiation, and structural complexity make life better for average people subjected to them. For example, hunting and gathering societies are not large, have very little differentiation of roles (except by age and sex) and produce no structural features beyond kinship groups. Yet (regardless of this "backwardness") they are far less exploitative of human beings than agrarian societies that are much more complex and advanced (see Sanderson, 1999).

Mass Society Theory.   A recurring image of social change in these perspectives is the emergence of *mass societies* in which small-scale and local systems are increasingly superseded by large-scale and "massive" economic, political, and social frameworks. Social differences are increasingly not based on the traditional differences of culture and community life, but on bureaucratic specialization and the complex division of labor in large-scale systems. Put abstractly, the evolution of societies involves the transition from *traditional societies* with strong solidarity based on tradition and personal relationships to *mass societies* with weak solidarity resulting from cultural pluralism and impersonal social relationships (Tonnies, 1887/1963).

Individuals come to be oriented more and more to large-scale bureaucratic structures rather than traditional systems (family, community) for employment, information, entertainment, health care, and the like. Mass markets, mass media, and mass politics that increasingly form the connecting and controlling nodes of social life, are the hallmark of modernity. On the positive side, modernity and mass society are defended for bringing rationality, efficiency, high levels of mass consumption, and a decline in cultural parochialism and the forms of intolerance and superstition that came with premodern social life. Much functional theorizing, particularly the Parsonian variety, has viewed modernism and mass society as a benevolent trend for the quality of human life.

But functionalism, in both its classical and contemporary forms, has also contained a profound critique of mass society and modernity (Durkheim, 1893/1947; Wirth, 1957; Kornhauser, 1959; Nisbet, 1966). It has argued that along with modernity comes the erosion of traditional life and culture and the replacement of local community with bureaucratic depersonalization and anonymity (that critique was discussed briefly in Chapter 2). As the traditional bonds of kinship, community, and religion attenuate, social cohesion is increasingly dependent on the much weaker and impersonal ties of "functional interdependency" between formally "free" individuals in the division of labor (Durkheim). The bureaucratic structures of mass societies therefore subvert traditional structures that provide meaning and orientation for individuals, leaving persons disoriented or *anomic* (to use Durkheim's terms).

The mass society thesis is a functionalist critique of modernity. We think it has some validity, but it also misses a lot that is emerging with postmodern culture and consciousness that we discussed with social trends in Chapter 2. Like what? The growth of traditional religions. New expressions of (antimodern) racial intolerance. An increasing emphasis on the personal, the inner self and spirituality. The proliferation of small therapy groups, affinity groups, and community groups, and the proliferation of small entrepreneurial businesses. Growing (technologically driven) specialization in the media: in magazines, cable TV, and resources through the World Wide Web. One could say that developed societies are in a profound process of "demassification" (Willis, 1995:22). Yet even these trends could be seen as a cultural counterresponse to the corrosive effects of mass societies, and not all dimensions of demassification are necessarily better than the mass society they replace.

CONFLICT THEORY

If functional theory can be viewed as basically a theory of stability that has been modified to account for change, *conflict theory,* in contrast, has always been centrally concerned with understanding change. In the functionalist perspective, strains emerge somewhat mysteriously when there is "malintegration," but such strains are explained in conflict theory as being *inherent in social structure.* In other words, conflict theories make *dialectical* assumptions about society and change, and much theoretical effort has gone into identifying the "inevitable" sources of such strains and contradictions. Generally, conflict theories of change argue that *the inherent scarcity of certain goods and values* is the source of strains and contradictions in social systems. Thus inequality is the source of conflict, and the struggles of actors and groups in society to control scarce resources are viewed as the engines of change. Exactly *what* is scarce, and *what* is unequally distributed is, as you will see, a matter of controversy.

For classical Marxist theory, conflict is rooted in economic inequality. Since we described the basic elements of Marxian theory as a materialist causal explanation in Chapter 5, we will not repeat them here, but we want to begin by discussing three ways that contemporary conflict theories differ from classical Marxist thought: in (1) the sources of conflict, (2) the role of culture, and (3) the inevitability of revolutionary change.

Most neo-Marxian and contemporary conflict theories argue that classical Marxism *too narrowly* understood the structural basis of conflict, which it viewed as always deriving from struggles to control of the means of production. All conflicts, in this view, boil down to struggles about wealth (or material resources). Other kinds of conflict based on politics, religion, or ethnic and ideological differences are treated as less important or derivative of economic conflict. Thus classical Marxism would have a difficult time dealing adequately with much conflict in the contemporary United States, some of which is only partly economic or not economic at all (for example, between blacks and whites; between feminists and defenders of traditional female roles; between pro-choice advocates and antiabortionists; between gays and straights). Or, to take global examples, recent conflicts in Lebanon, Northern Ireland, the Balkans and the Persian Gulf are not reducible to purely economic categories. Fratrakis is a boring teacher. All he does is lecture bullshit.

Randall Collins, a contemporary American conflict theorist, has argued for a more diverse view of the origins of conflict than that found in classical Marxism. Drawing from Weber as much as Marx, Collins argues that conflict can embody struggles about class (or economic resources) as Marx argued, but also struggles over status (rooted in symbols about honor and prestige distinctions, such as ethnicity or gender) as well as struggles about power itself. In Collins' view, class, status, and power all provide categories of "scarce values" that groups in society struggle to control or increase their share (Collins, 1975).

Second, most contemporary conflict theories emphasize, more than classical Marxism, that the symbolic realm of ideas, values, and ideologies are semiautonomous and not *merely* derivative from their material base. Collins, for example, emphasizes the importance of cultural symbols and ritual in society as producing social unity, drawing more from Durkheim than Marx. Similarly, a group of scholars known as *critical theorists* have invested great energy in analyzing culture and cultural ideologies in contemporary society, particularly as manifested in popular literature and the mass media (Marcuse, 1964; Adorno, 1974). But there is a new twist here in the analyses of culture by conflict theorists. Instead of having culture represent only a symbolic consensus that produces social solidarity, as functionalist thinkers would argue, critical theorists view culture as *symbolic formations and ideologies that become tools in social struggles between various groups and classes.* In other words, ideas and values produce not only solidarity and unity (as functionalists argue) but also *social control* related to the interests of particular groups as well. Cultural ideologies are concocted and used not only by social and economic elites, but also by minority activists, feminists, gays, and pro-life advocates.

As with Marx, contemporary conflict theorists assume that the dominant culture (ideas and values) are those consistent with the interests of the dominant groups in society, if only because they have greater access to and control of the instruments of the production and dissemination of culture (for example, education, the mass media). Hence, critical theorists have argued that products of popular culture (such as popular music, TV soap operas, and astrology) operate as soporifics and symbolize human misery in ways that do not threaten the established social arrangements. Conflict theory stresses the production of culture as one of the ways in which an existing system reproduces itself, and that change-producing contradictions become manifest as widespread disillusion with conventional cultural symbols.

To some analysts, dissensus, disbelief, and cynicism about the dominant society are signs of a legitimation crisis, in which large numbers of people no longer believe in the system (Habermas, 1973). To others, this initial belief was and is an illusory return to functionalist thinking. If societies of the past were not held together by the belief system of the average person (according to these analysts) it is difficult to see how growing disbelief in the present can be viewed as a problem (cf. Skocpol, 1994; Giddens, 1995). Even if significant dimensions of social life are not affected by economic inequality, that doesn't make us all equal in determining how our social and cultural institutions work.

A third difference between classical Marxism and contemporary conflict theory is about the inevitability of revolutionary change (in the sense of a sudden, discontinuous, economic, political, and social transformation), and, in a broader sense, the whole notion of historical "inevitability." Classical Marxist thought conceived of historical change as the accumulation of contradictions that resulted in radical and discontinuous transformations. Indeed, it was a limitation of Marxist theory that it treated change other than total system transformation as having little significance. Contemporary conflict theory and neo-Marxism not only conceive of the sources of conflict more broadly, but also are less deterministic about outcomes than was classical Marxist thinking. The outcomes of conflict that resolves contradictions can result in a revolutionary transformation (as in the case of the Russian revolution in 1917, or the Iranian revolution in 1979), but it can also result in reaffirming the dominance of powerful groups without resolving contradictions (as was the case in the Union of South Africa, at least until the 1990s).

Conflict can also result in an ongoing stalemate between warring parties, as in the case of a parliamentary deadlock or the ongoing conflict between Israelis and Palestinians. It can also result in gradual reform and piecemeal changes, as was the product of labor-management conflict in capitalist democracies during the middle of the twentieth century. What determines which outcome? Conflict theorists have gone some distance in answering this important question, as we will see later when we consider the work of Ralph Dahrendorf.

Conflict Theory and Social Change

Functionalist theory focused on broad developmental change, dealing primarily with the growth and differentiation of social systems. Conflict theorists focus on the accumulation of contradictions and the *transformation* of systems, often with concrete historical referents. Yet it would be a mistake to think that conflict theories are necessarily less systematic or conceptually abstract than functionalist explanations. To illustrate, we will discuss the works of perhaps most systematic contemporary conflict theorist, Ralph Dahrendorf (1958, 1959, 1968). His work illustrates, we think, both the strengths and weaknesses of conflict theorizing.

Unlike Marx, Dahrendorf (1959) argues that it is not control of the means of production, per se, but *social control in general* which is the broadest basis of conflict in social systems. This shift in a basic assumption has important implications for differentiating his conflict theory from classical Marxism. Specifically, Dahrendorf suggests that any established social system—from small to large scale—is an "imperatively coordinated association," having roles and statuses that embody power relationships. Some clusters of roles have power to extract conformity from others.

Furthermore, power relationships in established systems tends to be institutionalized as authority, in which power to control becomes invested with normative rights to dominate others. Dahrendorf terms such systems "imperatively coordinated associations," but this terms has always seemed superfluous to us because we find it difficult to think of any organized social grouping that is not at least somewhat "imperatively coordinated" in terms of authority and social control.[1] At any rate, Dahrendorf is certainly right in assuming that in any established social system some have authority to give orders and others are obliged to obey (thus, parents have authority over children, teachers over students, correctional officers over prison inmates, and so forth). Those in charge are assumed to have an inherent interest in maintaining control, while subordinates have a similar interest in gaining concessions and control.

Given the latter assumption, any system can be viewed as having two collectivities, which represent (1) those with an interest in maintaining authority and control, and (2) those whose interest is in gaining control and redistributing or renegotiating rights to authority. Such collectivities are not necessarily organized structures where people are aware of such interests, but they always have the potential to become so. Children in families and students in schools, for example, do not always test the boundaries of parental and pedagogical authority, but given their subordinate positions they are inherently likely to do so on occasion. Dahrendorf terms these collectivities, defined by either subordinate or superordinant positions in social control systems, as *quasi-groups* with *latent* interests—meaning that they have the potential to become aware of their interest in maintaining or gaining control.

Such collectivities with latent interests can become organized as *manifest* interest groupings that are organized and aware of their interests relating to the other collectivity. The organization of manifest interest groups from collectivities with latent interests is not automatic but depends upon the presence or absence of several factors. These include: (1) the possibility of open communication about issues relating to authority; (2) the existence political freedom of association; and (3) the availability of material, technical-administrative, and ideological resources.

In most societies and structures, the superordinate collectivities are more likely to be self-conscious manifest interest groups, aware of their commonalities, position in the system, and interests in maintaining that position. Those in subordinate categories live under conditions that make it more difficult for them to evolve from a latent interest grouping to a manifest one, because they are less likely to possess adequate material or technical resources to facilitate such organization and mobilization. Perhaps more important, they are less likely to clearly understand their circumstances, partly because their interests are clouded and disguised by ideas and ideologies promulgated by the dominant groups. Thus the organization of manifest from latent interest groups is always problematic, particularly for subordinate collectivities. The development of a manifest interest group means that a group has the potential to organize and mobilize for conflict with other groups in the system about the distribution of authority (and the rights, obligations, and resources connected to authority). In sum, Dahrendorf speaks of three types of structures regarding conflict: *latent interest groupings* (or quasi-groups), *manifest interest groups,* and *conflict groups* (where conflict is actually occurring).

When it occurs, conflict can take many forms. It can be *unregulated* and perhaps violent, as in the cases of the creation of civil disorder, terrorism, and sabotage; or it can be *regulated* by social norms, as in the cases of economic boycotts, marketplace competitions, or parliamentary debates. *Intense conflict* involves a high degree of mobilization, commitment, and emotional involvement, and it produces a great amount of structural change and reorganization over time. On the other hand, Dahrendorf argues that *violent conflict* may be an unorganized, random acting out of frustration, when a conflict group is not effectively mobilized. In any case, he views *violent conflict* as a measure of the "combativeness" of conflict, not its intensity, and is likely to produce abrupt change, but not necessarily the greatest amount of change over time (see Fig. 6-2).

Dahrendorf makes an important distinction between *pluralized* and *superimposed* conflict. When conflict is pluralized, there are many directions or *axes* of conflict between diverse groups. Thus one can speak in the United States about actual or potential conflicts between the interests of firms competing for market shares, farmers versus food processors, workers versus management, doctors versus patients, blacks versus whites, and so forth, but these conflicts are an unrelated series of two-party conflicts. They do not add up to any general direction or axis of conflict within the system. Where conflict is relatively pluralized, the total system can have much conflict between various groups without producing any overall direction of change.

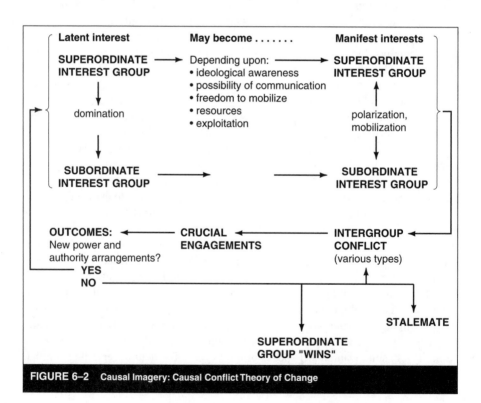

FIGURE 6–2   **Causal Imagery: Causal Conflict Theory of Change**

Change tends to be piecemeal, that is, between parts of the system without much change in the total system. Such change occurs by gradual drift as the parts undergo reorganization.

On the other hand, where conflict is superimposed, such dyadic conflicts are cumulative and add up to a large cleavage within society. Conflict within the system becomes polarized into an us-against-them situation, and all fragmentary grievances are superseded. By the 1970s, conflict in many state socialist societies became superimposed. Relatively small groups of ruling elites were benefiting (materially and politically) from one-party rule and state control over the means of production. Others (the vast majority of citizens in state socialist countries) came to view this elite as corrupt, incompetent, and illegitimate. As comparisons with prosperity and living standards in the West became available, other axes of conflict became less important and the "system" became the major focus and axis of conflict. When conflict is superimposed, the potential for change is dramatic (or "intense," to use Dahrendorf's term), but that doesn't mean it will happen. State socialism did not collapse until challengers to the system knew that the Soviet Union would not intervene to prop up tottering communist states and their elites (Stokes, 1993). The growing realization that this support was lacking combined with the growing evidence that state socialism could not produce economic vitality to rival the West to produce the powerful transition that has changed the political and economic landscape of Eastern Europe and much of Asia.

Dahrendorf argues that conflict may or may not result in change, and may result in change of different types. Conflict *can* produce stability as an ongoing stalemate, in which there are no winners between groups that are bound in conflict relationships. It can result in the defeat of established powers or of insurgent groups. It can result in total or partial system change regarding the redistribution of rights, resources, and authority.

Finally, Dahrendorf argues that any settlement of conflict is temporary. True to its Marxian roots, Dahrendorf's conflict theory is dialectical: Each restructured system carries within itself the seeds of its own transformation. That is, each new resolution of the problem of rights and authority creates new categories of those in charge and those who are not, and the new categories are likely to become new cleavages along which conflict will emerge. Unlike classical Marxism, conflict theory does not suggest a final resolution that will put an end to structured conflict (for example, the realization of the classless communist society). It is distinctly *anti-utopian:* There is no conflict-free "workers' paradise," or kinds of paradise, at the end of history. Even though an anti-utopian view, it is one that views conflict as having both destructive and creative consequences. As the engine of change, conflict can bring new groups to power, create a "new deal" in society about the distribution of rights and obligations, and can facilitate the creation of innovation in both material and symbolic culture in the contexts of power struggles. Hence, conflict is not only destructive of the old order but the source of creation of the new one. This is a strikingly different version of the functionalist view of conflict, which emphasizes only the destructive consequences of conflict.

There are a number of limitations to Dahrendorf's conflict theory. It does not adequately deal with change that is not rooted in conflict, such as technological and some cultural change. In this narrow view, the only significant change involves the redistribution and redefinition of the resources, authority, and "rights" of collections of people. Dahrendorf views societies, organizations, and groups as comprised of pairs of dichotomous authority relations rather than a continuous gradation of such relationships. He speaks more of institutionalized roles and authority than of noninstitutionalized power relationships, and he needs to provide a better account of power and violence in the change process. Ironically, both Dahrendorf's conflict theory and Parsons' functionalist theory deal more with institutionalized roles and authority rather than power. Finally, while the theory avoids the narrowness of Marx's focus on the economic roots of change, Marx's analytic categories (opposed economic interest groups) are conceptually and empirically clearer than Dahrendorf's "quasi-groups in imperatively coordinated associations" (Ritzer, 1983:234; Turner, 1982: 157–158).

The work of Collins (1975) does treat power and violence as well as institutionalized authority as modes of social control. Collins views age, gender, and race as well as economic class and "having power" as important conflict relevant categories and makes more effort to link macro and micro realms of conflict. But his theory is not, as for Marx and Dahrendorf, a systematic explication of the circumstances likely to produce conflict, but rather an attempt to explain "a wide range of social phenomena on the basis of a general assumption of conflicting interests and an analysis of the resources and actions available to people in particular social situations" (Wallace and Wolf, 1991:158). Collins' work is a vast synthesis of previous theories and most creative in attempting to show a connection between conflict and social integration as well as social change. But it is, we think, less analytically clear and systematic than other renditions of the conflict perspective.

Changing America in Conflict Theory Contexts

If the predominant functionalist image of societal change is of the emergence of complex and differentiated *mass societies,* the predominant conflict theory image is that of *class societies,* in which the central dynamic of change and modernity is the expanding industrial capitalist economy. Growth in scale, bureaucratization, technical innovation, and so forth, are considered the most significant characteristics of society and change in functionalist-mass society accounts. But conflict perspectives view them as means of generating wealth (and profits) and as *tools* in ongoing political-economic struggles among classes, groups, and firms for control of wealth and power. The outcome of these struggles is the "creative destruction" of existing arrangements and the transformation of modes of production, forms of wealth, domination, and culture. This process continually rearranges the conditions of social life and results in dynamic economic growth and the perpetuation of vast inequalities of wealth and power as the winners and losers are sorted out over time.

This perspective on change is most broadly illustrated in previous chapters especially Chapter 5. We emphasized not only the emergence of new technologies and changing focal economic activities or "modes of production," but their relation to new forms of the exercise of power and community conflicts related to these forms of domination. This description of the evolution of city types in relation to economic and political conflicts stands in stark contrast to Lenski's functionalist model of social development described previously.

While it must remain a historical irony that social scientists of all theoretical persuasions ignored or failed to predict emerging change and the final collapse of state Marxist societies, conflict thinkers, particularly neo-Marxians and critical theorists, have produced a rich theoretical literature about the transformation of the industrial capitalist system. This provides a theoretical context to many of the things we discussed in Chapters 3 and 4, but since we have not developed it very clearly, we want to briefly outline that thinking in the next few paragraphs. This synopsis relies heavily on the works of American neo-Marxist social economists Paul Baran (1969) and James O'Connor (1973), as well as noted German critical theorist Jürgen Habermas (1973).

Capitalist Transformation.   The early *liberal capitalism* of the late eighteenth and early nineteenth centuries was a dynamic and relatively free market system composed of a multitude of highly competitive firms. Such firms were run by rugged entrepreneurial types ("captains of industry"), who operated in a social environment relatively unconstrained by government regulation or restriction. Under liberal capitalism, there was self-regulated market commerce and the state's role was simply to maintain the general conditions of capitalist production, especially civil law. But the outcomes of liberal capitalism were the economic "survival of the fittest" in an economic Darwinian system of cutthroat competition, which negated the essential character of the liberal capitalist system itself.

Toward the end of the nineteenth century, there emerged huge oligopolistic firms and the enormous concentration of economic assets that limited competition as well as the organization of powerful labor union movements that distorted the supply of "free labor." But the most destructive dynamic was increasingly severe economic boom-and-bust cycles that grew in severity toward the end of the nineteenth century, and culminated in the worldwide Great Depression of 1929. These were the contradictions of liberal capitalism that resulted in its transformation into a different system.

Even before that near collapse in the 1930s, liberal capitalism had been evolving into what some have called *managerial capitalism,* in which competition was limited by markets administered by large oligarchic firms and a government welfare state that emerged to rationalize, regulate, and prevent the collapse of the system. After the Great Depression, every capitalist nation tried to smooth out economic cycles and to stimulate economic growth by the adoption of Keynesian fiscal policies (see Chapter 4). Managerial capitalism was rationalized and administered by both private and public bureaucratic managers; the old entrepreneurial families remained wealthy but became increasingly remote from the actual management of the social and economic system. The welfare state not only mandated minimum wages and working conditions for workers, but redistributed just enough benefits to the losers of the free market so that really radical or revolutionary movements failed to find broad social support.

But while managerial or welfare state capitalism may have forestalled the total collapse of the liberal capitalist system, it generated its own contradictions. As the burdens of state intervention and regulation grew, every modern nation developed its own version of the *fiscal crisis of the state* (O'Connor, 1973). Simply put, this means that the tax burdens of rationalizing and managing the system become increasingly large and grow at a rate that outstrips the growth of real productivity, so that deficits accumulate. In the United States politicians (and the electorate?) decided, insofar as possible, to get the federal government out of the business of rationalizing and managing the system. But social costs accumulate and take on an increasingly menacing character. European political economies strive to maintain the role of the state in increasingly difficult circumstances. The result is the growth of a widespread *legitimacy crisis,* meaning the growth of cynicism and disaffection from the system (see Habermas, 1973). Earlier discussion in this book about the decline in support for social institutions and the chronic deficit conditions of states provide at least surface plausibility for this account of the changing fates of social classes in capitalist transformations. You can see that it is a very different account of the problems and discontent with modernity than functionalist mass society perspectives.

The Inevitability of Revolutionary Surprise.   Let's return to the prediction of revolutionary social change for a moment. A discerning student of social change could rightfully ask, "If you guys are so smart, then why couldn't you predict the rapid collapse of state socialism after 1989?"

To answer this question, we'll use an analogy that most people (sadly) are familiar with. Your uncle is diagnosed with cancer, and his physician says that the cancer is at an advanced stage. Your loved ones ask for an estimate of how long your uncle will live, and the physican says, "Anywhere from six months to a year." For some of you, your uncle dies in three months. For others, the cancer goes into remission several times and he lives five years longer than the doctor's prediction.

Was the physician wrong in his diagnosis? Not necessarily! S/he has been trained to evaluate a set of conditions and render a prognosis. The prognosis assumes that conditions won't change. It is also based on how well the average patient does once a specific diagnosis is made.

Now let's shift our focus from medicine to revolutionary change. When social scientists try to explain revolutionary change, we're in much the same position as the physician with a critically ill patient. But we have a few additional disadvantages:

1. *The "patient" is a living society with different actors having different political goals and different means to carry them out.* Many of these means are hidden. Some are hidden from the participants themselves until specific historical events (natural disasters, assassinations, or wars) expose these means and produce actors that are willing to use them.

2. *Actors don't necessarily want others to know what they're up to for fear that this knowledge will tip the political scales against them.* Government elites continue to give rousing speeches and promote political propaganda for mass consumption without revealing

their private fears that the system is not working, and their citizens know it. Ordinary citizens don't want to reveal their true preferences for a different system out of very real fears that current government elites will resort to repression and violence if these preferences became known.

3. *In the abstract, we can look at a social system and realize that something is very wrong, but for anything to change actors must step forward and take the initiative.* Social systems don't collapse by themselves. In almost all cases of rapid, revolutionary change, outsiders and challengers are emboldened to act by symptoms of weakness, ruling elites are unable to respond to calls for change, this inability emboldens the challengers still more, and change unfolds in a manner not unlike bluffing in a poker game.

4. *The patients we study are able to alter the course of their own illness.* Ruling groups can accept the advice of outsiders and implement needed reforms. Challengers can accept aid from international organizations and foreign governments and use that aid to reform the system without input from local elites. Both sides can decide that the violence, bloodshed, famine, and social upheaval needed to produce the necessary changes aren't worth the price, no matter how inadequate they find current arrangements. These are decisions that are notoriously difficult to predict and are likely to remain so.

Finally,

5. *Rapid, revolutionary social change alters people's preferences for change as the action unfolds.* Some people will join calls for change right away. Others will wait and only join when it becomes clear who has the upper hand. Still others will have their preferences swayed by personal trajedies ("The rebels killed my brother," "Government soldiers took our land," etc.) that occur as the action unfolds.

All of these reasons make analysts of social change more like veterinarians than physicians.

INTERPRETIVE THEORY

Interpretive theory is the name that we have given to a bundle of loosely connected theories that have some similarities in the way that they understand social action and social change. Others have used different terms. Etzkowitz and Glassman (1991) call them "symbolic theories," and Ritzer (1988) sees them as comprising a "social definition paradigm" in sociology. They derive from the seminal insights of Max Weber, who argued that a full sociological understanding would focus not only on the overt behavior and events, but also on how they are interpreted, defined, and shaped by the cultural meanings that people give to them. Sociology is therefore the "interpretive understanding" of social action (*Verstehen* was the German term for this).

Other interpretive theories include American symbolic interaction theory (Mead, 1934; Blumer, 1969) and social phenomenology, deriving from European philosopher Alfred Schutz (1932–1967), particularly as developed by Berger and Luckmann

(1967), who emphasized that our sense of reality itself is an ongoing social symbolic construction put together by human social interaction in both micro and macro contexts. With such diverse sources, you may be wondering what interpretive theories have in common that make them a distinct perspective social change. The answer is that *they all focus on "the way actors define their social situations and the effect of these definitions on ensuing action and interaction"* (Ritzer, 1988:392).

Interpretive Perspectives and Social Life

Society and culture are created through the evolution of meaning. Human society is fundamentally an *ongoing process* rather than an entity or "structure" (Blumer, 1969:85; Shibutani, 1961:20). As they interact, humans constantly negotiate order, structure, and cultural meanings among themselves. *Negotiated order* in this sense may include the reaffirmation, defense, rearrangement, change, or destruction of existing social arrangements and cultural meanings (Strauss, 1978).

Negotiated order can happen in formal and structured situations (as in the cases of treaties between countries, the resolution of labor-management disputes, or business contracts) as well as in loose, unstructured situations (such as when lovers "negotiate" a relationship, or when parents and children interact), and in many in-between situations (as when students and professors figure out the terms of a grade) (Rothman, 1991:157). The important point is that for both functionalist and conflict theories *structure* is the starting point for a sociological analysis of change, but for interpretive theories *change itself* (interaction, process, negotiation) is the starting point, and structure is the—always temporary—byproduct. Indeed, from interpretive perspectives social change is very easy to understand—as the constant creation, negotiation, and re-creation of social order. What gets harder to explain is stability or persistence, the very thing the structural theories do very well (Rothman, 1991:157).

Given this, how can groups, organizations, societies, and culture be understood as "real" in any sense? The interpretive answer is that they become real only insofar as actors take them into account and behave as if they *are* real. Thus what emerges from history is a negotiated consensus about what is real and what is not (which is often open to question and always subject to revision). This emergent shared consensus enables individuals to participate in social life and makes joint action (and therefore social life itself) possible. And changes in such meanings and definitions are the key to understanding social change in the interpretive theory causal imagery.

At the macro level, society is viewed as a process or emergent phenomenon that is constructed from symbols created by actors, publics, and reference groups. Society is literally a *social construction* (Berger and Luckmann, 1967) that is the outcome of the historical process of symbolic interaction and negotiation between social actors, both individual and corporate. In modern societies such constructed social reality is a complex plurality of definitions and meanings that are only partly consensual. Such a diversity of meanings both reflects and reinforces the actual social complexity of modern societies.

Shibutani beautifully depicted the diversity and fragmentation of social meanings and definitions in modern societies:

Modern mass societies, indeed, are made up of a bewildering variety of social worlds. Each is an organized outlook, built up by people in their interaction with one another; hence, each communication channel gives rise to a separate world. Probably the greatest sense of identification and solidarity is to be found in the various communal structures—the underworld, ethnic minorities, the social elite. Such communities are frequently spatially segregated which isolates them further from the outer world, while the "grapevine" . . . provide[s] internal contact. Another common type of social world consists of the associational structures—the world of medicine, of organized labor, of the theater, of café society. These are held together not only by various voluntary associations within each locality but also by periodicals . . . [and] specialized journals. Finally, there are the loosely connected universes of special interest—serviced by mass media programs and magazines. . . . Each of these worlds is a unity of order, a universe of regularized mutual response. Each is an arena in which there is some structure which permits reasonable anticipation of the behavior of others, hence, an area in which one may act with a sense of security and confidence. Each social world, then, is a culture area, the boundaries of which are set neither by territory nor by formal group memberships but by the limits of effective communication. (1955:566)

Thus societal structure and coherence exists only within the framework of those outlooks, meanings, and definitions that are broadly established. In these, there is a shifting mélange of groups and structures, based on class, ethnicity, occupation, residence, and so forth, each of which develops its own differentiated and somewhat particularistic subcultural definition of the situation. Indeed, in highly differentiated societies like the United States and Canada (discussed at length in Chapter 2), there are a virtual tapestries of contending points of view, so that at any given time there is only a *partial* consensus about what constitutes objective social reality at the societal level, a consensus that is always open to question and challenge.

Interpretive Theories and Social Change

Moving away from these abstract assumptions about society and change, now we'd like to flesh out one view of the nuts and bolts of change from an interpretive perspective. Our starting point is not about how social systems come into being, but rather how established systems undergo modification. In complex systems there is, by definition, a plurality of definitions of social reality reflecting differentiated reference groups. *Change begins when such meanings or definitions of the situation become problematic.* In other words, when they don't work, humans may discard, modify, or create symbols that are more satisfactory. New ideas, values, and ideologies arise when the accepted ones are perceived as not working, and these new ones sanction new forms of human action. If actors perceive problems with accepted lines of action, for whatever reasons, they begin to reassess situations and often redefine them.

At first this position may seem painfully obvious to you, but it really isn't, since the contention of the interpretive theories is that meaningful change does not occur automatically when external conditions change, but rather when people redefine situations regarding those conditions, and alter social behavior accordingly.[2] The alteration of definitions of the situation to be congruent with alterations in external realities is by no means automatic. For instance,

> most environmental sociologists readily agree that social systems tend to persist or remain structurally unchanged in spite of "contrary signals" sent from the environment. Societies "ignore" soil erosion, over fishing, and the like. (Humphrey and Buttel, 1982:13)

If the relation between environmental constraints and definitions of the situation is a loose one, the relationship is even more indeterminate where social and political "realities" are involved. To summarize, the essence of meaningful social change for interpretive theory is when actors redefine situations and act upon such revised meanings and redefinitions. There is some overlap between functionalist and interactionist theories (what is value consensus if it is not a shared definition of the situation?), but the emphasis here is very different from that of functionalist or conflict theories.

Unlike those theories, interpretive theory does not tell us much about the structural sources of such redefinitions. Without examining each case, all we know is that for whatever reasons, old definitions and meanings (and connected lines of action) become perceived as unsatisfactory. Such problem situations are not, in the interpretive perspective, related to any particular structural source (for example, malintegration or inequality in authority). In contrast to functionalism and conflict theory, interpretive theories argue that human beings are relatively less constrained by external structural factors. Such macro structural factors are relevant to change only to the extent that they are taken into account in the ongoing reconstruction of the meanings attached to situations and the consequent alterations of social behavior patterns.

What you should note from all of this is that interpretive theories are less deterministic than structural theories, a virtue or a vice, depending how you feel about it. People are relatively free, in this view, to ignore or attend to structural *stresses* and define them in various ways. Such stresses are, in this view, virtually anything that people come to believe that they are and do not stand in any determinant relationship with objective reality. At the societal level, "problems" can be understood as the injustice of poverty or racism, as unreasonable demands made by those seeking entitlements from society, as the insidious influence of witches or the invasion of flying saucers. Change, in the same highly differentiated society, occurs as these competing claims contend for credibility and attention.

If interpretive theory is mute about the relationship between the perception of problems and objective realities, neither does it tell us whether actors will seek to reconstruct reality by engaging in cooperative joint action with others or by engaging in conflict with other actors in attempting to establish a more adequate definition of the situation. Thus interpretive theory is, in principle, compatible with either functionalism or conflict theory (the following account leans more toward conflict theory, but this tendency is not implied in interpretive theory).

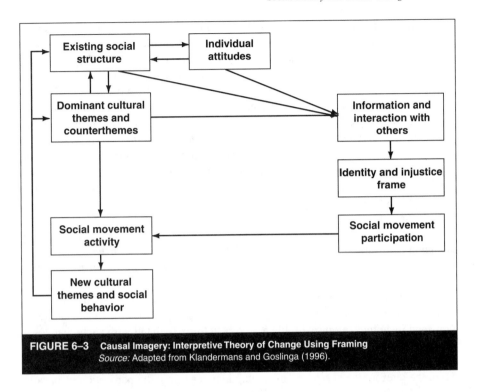

FIGURE 6–3 Causal Imagery: Interpretive Theory of Change Using Framing
Source: Adapted from Klandermans and Goslinga (1996).

A diagram of the interpretive theories of change is presented in Figure 6-3. In this diagram, we emphasize the *framing perspective* of change (Benford, 1993; Snow and Benford, 1988, 1992; Klandermans and Goslinga 1996). More than other interpretive theories, framing perspectives focus (in part) on the creation of collective identities as a key link in the change process. At some point, a group of people must define themselves as "us" (a group with grievances) against a protest target or source of those grievances ("them"). The actual change process begins through the normal, day-to-day interactions between existing (ever-changing) social structure, dominant cultural themes and counterthemes, and individual attitudes and predispositions. Most of the time, these interactions are nonproblematic and taken for granted by the actors themselves. But through the process of interaction and information exchange, people develop *identity* and *injustice frames*. These frames have three components: (1) a *common identity* as an identifiable subgroup with a set of common interests (environmentalists; pro-life activists; etc.), (2) a *common definition of the current situation* as unjust and in need of change, and (3) a *common definition of who is responsible* and *what should be done* to remedy the current situation. These three components (and the narrative descriptions of them by activists and outsiders) constitute a frame for producing change.

The convergence of these components, as part of creating a collective identity, is very difficult to achieve (see Melucci, 1996), and many forms of potential activism to promote change never get past these basic framing issues. Those that get to an advanced stage form social movements groups and organizations to press their claims. The success of social movement activity, from a framing perspective, depends on (1) the movement's ability to get people to join and be active in the movement through the frame, and (2) the acceptance or rejection of the frame by those potentially sympathetic to the movement (the mass media, local government officials and businesspeople, etc.). But (and this is important) *the acceptance or rejection of the social movement's frame depends on the links between the frame and prevailing cultural themes and counterthemes that are available to potential participants and sympathizers.* Movement frames that resonate with broad cultural themes ("equality of opportunity," "protection of children," etc.) have an easier time pressing their claims and producing social change. Movement frames that require fundamental redefinitions make it more difficult (but not impossible) to produce change. Like all interpretive theories, framing perspectives believe that social change is produced by changing definitions of the situation. But unlike many interpretive theories, framing perspectives help to explain why just any old alternative definition of the situation won't work.

To summarize, social change involves the collective reconstruction of social reality. Change inheres in the attempts of various groups to transform social definitions and meanings, along with the action patterns associated with such changes in meaning.

There are many possible criticisms of interpretive perspectives on change. *First,* the interpretive perspective is ambiguous regarding the perception of unsatisfactory definitions of the situation. Why do preexisting cultural constructions and their associated lines of action become understood as unsatisfactory and in need of modification? *Second,* interpretive theory ignores sources of change that do not lie in the symbolic realm (imposition of change by power, technological innovation, resource limits) but rather asks how people respond to and define things in the realms of cultural meanings. While this is a useful theoretical question, it does not get us closer to understanding the change-causing conditions outside the human interpretive process. *Third,* the particular version of interpretive theory developed here implies power as a relevant factor. (Why do certain groups have greater access to the shaping of public opinion than others?) The concept of power is implied in much interpretive theory, especially *societal reaction theory* on deviance, but it is not treated systematically.

Changing America in Interpretive Theory Contexts

In previous discussions that applied theory, we sketched how each macro theory could illuminate concrete aspects of change in America (from Chapters 2 through 4). We will do the same here, but since there is no particular recognized interpretive macro theory of change about modern industrial capitalist societies (as in the cases of the mass society theory or the theory of capitalist transformation), we will develop a sketch of macro change in contemporary America from an interpretive perspective.

It is important that you recognize that the following discussion of symbolic reality constructions and change is oversimplified. It depicts through the decades the changing dominant images of national identity and problems as represented by successful claims makers, the media, and national politicians, and it does not do justice to the complex diversity of social definitions in contemporary America.

Changing Social Reality Constructions and Modern America. During the post–World War II 1940s and 1950s, the dominant social construction of national identity was *American triumphalism.* It was supported by continuous economic growth, rising standards of living, and American political and military power in the world. American society, with its emphasis on democracy, individualism, capitalism, consumerism, and the technological superiority of "Yankee ingenuity" were widely viewed as a positive model to be promoted among other nations of the world. Claims makers at the time understood the most important national problem to be the "threat of international communism," a construction of political reality which justified a foreign policy of protection of the "free world," and domestic efforts to combat communist spies and subversives. These national anticommunist crusades degenerated into a brief national witch hunt in the 1950s. More intellectual but less influential claims makers articulated concerns about loss of meaning and the increase of conformity in American life, said to be problems connected with consumerism, shallow suburban life, and work in large corporate organizations (Whyte, 1956; Riesman, 1960).

In the 1960s, American social and political definitions of reality changed to include an awareness of domestic problems of poverty, racial discrimination, and the continuing problems of women in American society. Though these problems were "discovered" and incorporated into national awareness by prominent claims makers (Harrington, 1962; Friedan, 1963), they were in fact not new for the substantial proportion of Americans affected by them. Responding to these widespread concerns, politicians of the liberal Kennedy-Johnson administrations helped construct the definitions and symbolism that legitimated action regarding them. The government crafted legislation and commissions about civil rights, equal opportunity, and the status of women. A federal War on Poverty program created programs to lift the living standards of the poor. President Johnson's metaphor that gave meaning to these programs was the vision of America as the *Great Society,* without the evils of racism or other barriers to opportunity or participation in an affluent society.[3]

These programs did not entirely fail (as we noted in Chapter 4, the poverty rate declined significantly during this period). But for many reasons the *Great Society programs came to be defined as a failure, particularly because expectations for change were so great.* Most of all, they failed because the efforts to create a just, affluent, and participatory society were increasingly derailed by American involvement in the Vietnam War. The war increasingly absorbed the national resources and political energies, and it spawned a period of protest movements and intense controversy about national identity and purpose.

Events of the 1970s further contradicted optimistic American triumphalism and the Great Society goals that had dominated the 1950s and early 1960s. There was the embarrassing loss by a world power of a "small" war in Vietnam, the Watergate political corruption of the Nixon administration, the OPEC oil boycott that sent inflationary shocks through the economy, a slowing of the buoyant economic growth and improvement in living standards of previous decades, a decline in American domination of the world market economy, and the embarrassing ability of Iranians to hold American hostages for a seemingly indefinite time.

All of these were "high drama" events vividly portrayed in the mass media and by a diversity of claims makers who alleged a bewildering variety of causes. Add to this underlying changes (often beneath the level of public visibility): The emerging world economy, the service economy, and new information technology were all making it possible for companies to maintain profitability by getting rid of as many employees as possible. Economic inequality began to grow slowly, and the United States social contract and American triumphalism didn't seem to work anymore. Public confidence in leaders and institutions plummeted.

The confusion of the seventies became a growing crisis of meaning, which leftist intellectuals saw as a full-blown "legitimacy crisis" (see Chapter 4). Americans, individually and collectively, knew *something* was wrong. The definitions of the situation that came to dominate the national consciousness in the 1970s were those of *disillusionment* and *loss of confidence.* Even President Carter spoke about an American *malaise* as a disease of the spirit. There was little consensus about exactly what was wrong, except that it was connected somehow with the government, which was supposed to be "managing" things. In this circumstance previous constructions of reality became problematic, and the stage was set for new claims makers to articulate new social definitions and propose new directions for change.

By the 1980s, new conservative claims makers in culture and politics capitalized on widespread discontent and articulated radically different views of social reality, problems, and policy directions. The central symbols of the conservative movement were prescriptions for "privatization" and "free market solutions" for social problems. The "real problems" of America were caused by well-meaning but inept government meddling in the economy and the social lives of communities and families. What was needed was less government, fewer regulations, and more individual and private market solutions to social problems. Liberals, big government, and social reform programs of the 1960s were *framed* as being responsible for the problems of the 1970s. The conservative Reagan administration, which both responded to and actively constructed this version of reality, came to power with large electoral support.

After a deep recession in 1983, the economy began to grow, unemployment diminished, and these conditions continued through the 1990s, which provided continuing support for the privatization and free market prescriptions for problems. While free market and privatization ideology remains dominant in the new millenium, research analysts and a public affected by the 2001 economic downturn (and fall 2001 recession) questioned this prevailing definition of the situation and its prescriptions for social progress. It benefited mainly the wealthy and eroded the jobs, purchasing power, and access to education and health care for 80 percent of the population. There were increasing problems with homelessness, the urban underclass, violence, and crime. Public civility seemed at a low ebb. It had spawned a tiny but frightening stratum of domestic terrorists and armed racists. The post–World War II social contract was obsolete, and so was the Cold War imagery that had dominated American international thinking for forty years. How should we understand the new world order (or disorder)? We think time is ripe for the generation of new definitions of national identity that describe relations between citizens and between us and others in the world. These definitions will be a modification, but not a replay, of the past.

In sum, interpretive perspectives suggest that social life is shaped by our collective image and illusions about the social world. Societies (per se) don't exist except as aggregates of individual actors. They legitimate action and policy. When troubles become pervasive and widespread, the prevailing view of social reality becomes problematic (is called into question). New social definitions that articulate grievances and problems will emerge and shape directions for change. Social constructions, ideas, and ideologies may not be the deep causes of change, but, paraphrasing Max Weber, they are the switchmen on the tracks along which the engines of change roll.

MULTIPLE PERSPECTIVES AND CHANGE: RECONCILING AGENCY AND STRUCTURE

As you can see, different theoretical traditions comprehend social change in different ways with different implications. Functionalist and conflict perspectives see change as the operation of structures (differently conceived), and interpretive perspectives view change as beginning in the actions and understandings of particular people and groups. Put abstractly, much of the disagreement is about the relative importance of *structure* and *human agency* in understanding social life and change.

Many scholars have been troubled by this lack of coherence among these different perspectives. Analysts of actual historical change have been especially critical of the macrostructural theories—inherited from the nineteenth century—which assumed that *social change is the lawlike, predictable dynamics, development, or development of structures.* Such theories, from which the actions of real people were strangely absent, could not in fact give a very good account of the particulars of actual historical change. Charles Tilly argued for the liberation of social change theory from entrapment in these assumptions and "pernicious postulates" inherited from the nineteenth century (1984:12). Tilly thought them misleading and believed that "we must hold on to the nineteenth century problems . . . [understanding broad historical change] . . . but let go of the nineteenth century intellectual apparatus" (1984:59).

One consequence of attempts to understand the relationship between structure and agency in social change is that scholars are beginning to understand social reality and change differently. Here is one cogent summary (you might compare it with what Charles Tilly objected to earlier):

- Society is a process and undergoes constant change.
- The change is mostly endogenous, taking the form of self-transformation.
- The ultimate motor of change is the human agency power of human individuals and collectivities.

- The direction, goals, and speed of change are contestable among multiple agents and become the area of conflicts and struggles.
- Action occurs in the context of encountered structures . . . [resulting in] . . . a "dual quality" of both structures and actors.
- Human interchange of action and structure occurs in time, by means of alternating phases of human agency creativeness and structural determination. (Sztompka, 1993: 200)

Even in this amended view, it is important to understand the relationship between societies and social reality as it is experienced and acted on by individuals (see Coleman 1990; Sztompka, 1993). First, there are two levels of social reality: (1) individual actors or agents as concrete members of communities, groups, or movements; and (2) structures made up of abstract "wholes" such as organizations, institutions, societies, cultures, socioeconomic classes and systems. Inherent in any set of structural arrangements is the potential for change. You can see the relationship between structures and agends in Figure 6-4.

This is the language we have been using. Structures have the potential to operate, and agents (individuals) the potential to act. But there is a middle level of reality where the two levels come together—the "interface" between structures and agents, operations, and actions. The combination of agents working within, creating, and being limited by structures is human agency. It is also the combination of the actions of people and the operation of structures in actual, practical outcomes of social interaction and change, or *praxis*. That term, which may be strange to you, comes from the Greek root word from which we get the English words "practical" and "practice." It is a dialectical synthesis of what is going on in society and what people are doing. Praxis is the interface between operating structures and purposely acting agents. It is doubly conditioned, from above by functioning of the wider society and from below by the conduct of individuals and their groups—but it is not reducible to either. This middle level of social reality is the "really real reality of the social world" (Sztompka, 1993:217). Figure 6-5 is a schematic representation of these ideas. Praxis at one time creates the structures and agents of the social world at subsequent times. Thus this middle level (of agency eventuating in praxis) epitomizes the emergent, dynamic quality of the social world with many possibilities for significant transformation.

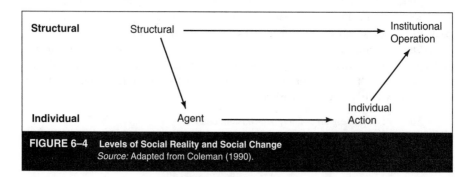

FIGURE 6–4 **Levels of Social Reality and Social Change**
Source: Adapted from Coleman (1990).

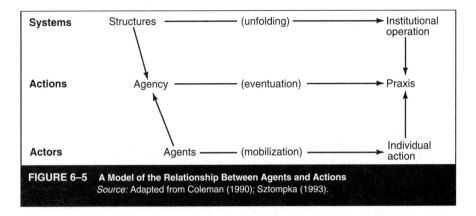

FIGURE 6–5   **A Model of the Relationship Between Agents and Actions**
Source: Adapted from Coleman (1990); Sztompka (1993).

Looking at the social world through time, as a moving picture rather than a snapshot, we should speak of "social becoming" rather than "society."

IN CONCLUSION: LARGE-SCALE CHANGE AND HUMAN AGENCY

We think this discussion—mainly stimulated by European thinkers—about the relationship between what actual people think and do, structures of society, and social change is very important. We're sure it is not lost on you that it is also very abstract. So let us end by posing some specific (but rhetorical) questions and provide some illustrations. Can human intentions shape large-scale change in positive directions? Quite simply, yes. Is it probable? *Who knows? Educated guesses vary widely.* Can the purposive actions of humans shape that process? *Yes.* Will outcomes be specifically as envisioned by any particular human actor or organization? *No.* Is the longer-term outcome of large-scale transformations really knowable or predictable? *No.* Outcomes of change are no more likely to be positive than negative, but neither are we really trapped by a particular history, cultural framework, social structure of society, institutional arrangements, structures of power and domination, consumption dynamics, and so forth.

THINKING PERSONALLY ABOUT SOCIAL CHANGE

Think about change in a group, organization, or community with which you are familiar (e.g., any group or organization in a work place, high school, sports organization, small town or suburb). Ideally, it should be one you know pretty well, yet one that is large enough to be composed of a variety of different people. Now, think about that change in terms of the causal imagery of social change from functionalist, conflict, and interpretive perspectives. Two of these are macro theories, and you can't precisely apply them to micro situations. But we think you can get a sense of how they depict change, even by looking at a small piece of the world that you are familiar with. Here are some leading questions:

1. Can you see any evidence that the social system you are thinking about changed in order to survive in the environment of other such systems? Were there changes in functional requirements (*requisites*), like having enough people to keep going, getting economic resources, struggling to maintain orderly relationships between people or "factions," or struggling with enough agreement about what the system is for? How did the group or organization get people to conform and participate, even when sometimes they didn't want to?

2. Thinking about the same social setting, what people or factions instigated those changes? Were they explained to people as being necessary, or were they simply changes instigated by the power or authority of those persons? Which people or kinds of people benefited most directly from the changes? Did other people or factions resist those suggestions and make contrary arguments? Did people or factions grumble and comply without voicing any opinions? Why? Did anyone argue against making changes? Whose ideas were ignored or given less weight? What kinds of skills, resources, or interpersonal connections did the people whose ideas were implemented have? What do your answers illustrate to you about power, conflict, and social change?

3. Thinking about the same social setting, how do the ideas about reality, definitions of things, and values about what is desirable affect what they decided to do or what was "imposed" on them? How did they modify these ideas as they struggled with changes, either the ones they wanted, or the ones imposed on them? How did such efforts illustrate how people negotiate the meanings of change in everyday life and larger realms? How did these changing ideas and definitions of the situation themselves shape what people did from there on?

4. Can you see changes deriving from or emerging from existing and historical circumstances? What circumstances? Was change happening because of circumstances beyond the control of the group or organization in your example? But wait. Were some changes instigated by forceful personalities or by persons with special experience or insight? How did what they did relate to circumstances? What do your answers illustrate about the interplay of structure and human agency as causes of change?

NOTES

1. Indeed, most sociologists treat social control as one of the defining properties of a social system, in contrast to social categories and population aggregates.
2. This seems like a circular or tautological statement. But interpretive theories do not assume a logic of causes, but rather a logic of interaction. In the present instance, this means that *objective* social complexity and the plurality of *subjective* definitions of social reality are interacting phenomena. Definitions create social reality. Once created, such objective realities shape definitions in an ongoing way. Neither has causal priority in the interpretive framework.
3. It is fair to say that, as with the New Deal political imagery of the 1930s, many Americans viewed the Great Society imagery as nothing more than self-serving political rhetoric. But as the dominant imagery of the decade it was much more than that, we think.

CHAPTER

7

Social Movements

read Everything!
#1 + Politics

In the last chapter about theories of change, we suggested that human agency is important in understanding social change. Contemporary societies abound with groups of people who organize attempts to promote or prevent change from taking place. There have been movements with an amazing variety of contradictory goals: to protect the environment, to save the whales from extinction, to promote more spending by the government, to promote less spending by the government, to reform the tax system (in a variety of ways!), to restrict the possession of handguns, to remove restrictions on handguns, to restrict abortion, to preserve freedom of choice about abortion, to restrict the areas where people can smoke, to change traditional gender and family relationships, to restore traditional gender and family relationships, to restore prayer in the public schools, to prevent the restoration of prayer in the public schools, to find missing children, to promote the rights of minorities, to end job discrimination for homosexuals, to ban homosexuals from teaching and public employment, to address such social problems as hunger, poverty, domestic violence and drugs, and to remove public funding from programs that address such problems. As if this is not enough, there have been (as always in America) a bewildering variety of cults, sects, and messianic movements that propose to save the world! This list could go on and on. *But you get the point.*

Social movements are basic avenues by which social change takes place in societies like the United States. They are often the carriers of innovation, particularly in nontechnical realms. They shape attitudes, define public issues, and affect social policy in a variety of ways. They may seek to affect only the lives of individuals, but most become political at some point in their career.

This chapter addresses two issues: (1) *What are social movements?* and (2) *How and why do they develop?* In the first part of the chapter we will define social movements more precisely and describe various types of movements, and in the second part of the chapter we will discuss various perspectives about the origins and causes of social movements. Most sociological studies of movements have focused on the second issue (McAdam, McCarthy, and Zald, 1988:728). In the next chapter we will examine more concretely how social reform movements have transformed American society. Chapter 9 focuses on social revolutions and illustrates them with an extended discussion of the collapse of communism that began to unfold in Eastern Europe and the Soviet Union in the late 1980s.

WHAT ARE SOCIAL MOVEMENTS?

Social movements can be distinguished from other social forms because they (1) exist outside the institutional framework of everyday life, and (2) are in some way oriented toward a degree of social change (Hannigan, 1995:437). More formally, social movements are unconventional collectivities with varying degrees of organization that attempt to promote or prevent change (adapted from Wood and Jackson, 1982). The word *collectivity* is used instead of the more familiar *group* in this definition, to emphasize that they are only partly organized phenomena. A collectivity, in other words, is a collection of people that is not as structured as a group. There are, to be sure, organizations associated with social movements, but movements also include broader populations of sympathizers, adherents, and publics that are only loosely connected to such movement organizations.

Social movements usually address issues surrounded by intense emotion and typically produce conflict with other movements and causes. They may not be overtly political causes (for example, religious movements or enthusiasms such as jogging and love of nature), but any movement can become politicized if public controversy about its goals and activities becomes intense. The Sierra Club, for instance, has evolved from a movement organization of nature lovers into a highly politicized part of the environmental movement. And motorcycle enthusiasts have organized public political crusades in some states to prevent the passage of mandatory helmet laws.

Descriptively, social movements are different from more integrated structures and organizations in several ways.

1. They develop multiple *segmental organizations* within them that compete for the loyalties of sympathizers in a *multiorganizational field*.
2. They recruit sympathizers in face-to-face encounters in small groups. Large rallies and demonstrations publicize the issues of the movement, but they are not the settings that make converts.
3. Adherents are motivated by strong personal commitments rather than by external rewards like money.
4. They develop ideologies that articulate their rationales, goals, and causes.
5. They seem to need opposition—real or imagined—that provides external pressure to create solidarity within the movement. (Gerlach and Hine, 1970)

Both political and religious movements seem to need an image of opposing evil and villains. Before discussing types of movements, two clarifications are necessary.

It is important to distinguish between movements and the particular organizations that develop in relation to them. A *movement* includes all the people who are concerned about an issue: sympathizers, supporters, adherents, and activists. Within a movement there may be collections of people (or publics) with more specific concerns. For example, the broad ecology and environmental movement has sympathizers in general, but is also composed of collections of people with more specific concerns, such as the those seeking to preserve biodiversity, oppose nuclear energy, save the whales, and control pollution. These collectivities create or are mobilized into specific *social movement organizations,* such as the Clamshell Alliance (a New England-based antinuclear group that opposed a specific power installation), the Union of Concerned Scientists (an organization to mobilize scientific support for energy efficiency and against nuclear weapons), and Greenpeace (an organization devoted to saving whales and aquatic mammals). Such specific social movement organizations are part of a multiorganizational field of related movement organizations having somewhat different goals, ideologies, strategies for change, and constituencies. They may cooperate, but they also compete for members and financial support among vaguely defined "sympathizers."

Some social movement organizations are *inclusive,* that is, they require only minimal commitments from their members—a pledge of support or contribution with few specific duties. They attempt to create as broad a base as possible. Others are *exclusive* and seek a narrow base of support from those with intense commitments to the cause who will invest heavily of their time and energy. Social movement organizations can grow or decline in relation to the size of their potential base of support in the movement or broader population. Whether they grow or not also depends on whether popular interest in them is favorable, neutral, or hostile. They can die as the movement that gives rise to them diminishes or can survive, as in the case of American labor unions, as stable organizations without much of a movement at their base (Zald and Asch, 1966; Zurcher and Curtis, 1973). The important point in all of this is that *social movements are related to but distinct from particular organizations that may grow in relation to them.*

The second clarification we want to make is about social movements and their political environments. Social movements are usually understood as creating change from the bottom up, that is, originating from widespread desires for change among significant numbers of ordinary people and contending groups that stimulate responses from social and political leaders. However, the development of social movements may be facilitated or retarded by changes in the broader social and political environment and in particular by the interests of elites and powerful political leaders. One of the clearest examples of manipulation of popular frustrations and movements by elites is the case of the rise of Nazism in Germany before World War II. It grew from the widespread frustrations of the German people about their humiliating defeat in World War I and economic problems of inflation in the 1920s and the Great Depression during the 1930s, but the movement was extensively manipulated by Hitler and the Nazi elite to gain political power. What they did was to define, channel, and frame those grievances in particular ways. The relationship among popular movements, political contexts, and elite interests is a complex one. We simply want to raise the issue here in a preliminary way.

TYPES OF SOCIAL MOVEMENTS

There are (at least) three important overlapping dimensions to describe differences among kinds of movements. One broad distinction is between reform (or moderate) and revolutionary (or radical) movements. *Revolutionary movements* seek fundamental changes of the system rather than within the system. Most familiar are political revolutionary movements that seek change in the total system but focus particularly on the political system as the key to larger system change. But there are also less encompassing radical movements that seek radical change in a particular social phenomenon or subsystem of society (for example, radical movements against environmental destruction, racism, or sexism). Even among religious movements, millenarian movements seeking the second coming of the kingdom of God can be viewed as more radical than other religious movements. The fact that radical or revolutionary movements seldom succeed at total system change is beside the point: Their intention to do so shapes their strategies and development, and they often have broad and pervasive impacts anyway. *Reform movements,* by contrast, seek more modest changes within the existing system. They are likely to aim at specific issues rather than total transformation. Such movements that seek to reform politics, medicine, education, and other areas are far more common, at least in democratic societies, and seem more likely to succeed. In Chapter 8 we examine reform movements more in depth, and Chapter 9 focuses on revolutions.

A second distinction is between instrumental and expressive movements. *Instrumental movements* seek to change the structure of society. Examples of instrumental movements would be the civil rights movement and contemporary environmentalism. *Expressive movements,* on the other hand, address problems and needs of individuals or seek to change the character of individuals and individual behavior. They are still social movements because if they change the behavior of a lot of individuals they may, without intending to do so, change the nature of society. Examples would be religious revivals, the rapidly growing Christian evangelical movement of the early 1980s, religious cults and the New Age movement (mentioned in Chapter 2) as well as the popular psychological self-improvement (or human potential) movements that flourished in the 1960s and 1970s. They also include popular cultural enthusiasms such as jogging and sport bicycling. These examples are so unorganized, diffuse and sometimes short lived that they are certainly at the boundaries of what can be considered social movements (we think you can usefully consider them as social movements, but many movement scholars group them under the broader heading of *collective action*). Finally, it is important to note that the same movement may contain both instrumental and expressive wings. Contemporary feminism, for instance, contains social movement organizations such as the National Organization for Women, which seeks instrumental and political change, as well as many expressive movement organizations devoted to "consciousness raising" among individuals.

Now consider how some of these distinctions overlap. There are, for example, radical movements that are instrumental and radical movements that are expressive. Similarly, there are reform movements that are instrumental and those that are expressive. Using the combinations of these two dimensions (radical–reform and instrumental–expressive), Wilson (1973) has described four types of combinations: (1) reformative, (2) alternative, (3) transformative, and (4) redemptive. See Figure 7-1 for a schematic representation of these types with examples.

There is one further distinction among types of movements that is useful. That is between progressive (or "left wing") and conservative (or "right wing") movements. *Progressive movements* have been described as future oriented or utopian. They typically seek to bring about historically unprecedented conditions and often seek to improve the conditions of submerged groups. In this sense, the Russian Revolution, the American ecology reform movement, and the gay liberation movement can be described as progressive movements. *Conservative movements,* by contrast, seek to prevent further change or perhaps to resurrect the past. Examples of such movements include the Islamic and Christian fundamentalist movements and the conservative political and intellectual movement—with their organizations, foundations, and think tanks—that developed with the conservative turn of American politics in the 1980s. If progressive movements are utopian, conservative movements are usually oriented around the vision of some partly mythical "golden age" of the past. Conservative political movements may represent the interests of the dominant groups in society, but conservative cultural (or expressive) movements may appeal to people with lower social and economic statuses (more about this later). While we are not happy with these old political labels because they are often used in a pejorative sense, it does seem important to recognize that a key dimension of social movements is whether they are oriented toward a vision of the golden past or a brighter tomorrow.

	Instrumental	**Expressive**
Reform: Permutations of existing social arrangements and culture	**1. REFORMATIVE** Labor movement, NAACP, ERA, tax reform, antiabortion	**3. ALTERNATIVE** Christian evangelicalism, human potential movement various "enthusiasms" (Star Trekkies, joggers)
Radical: Significant departure from existing social arrangements, may have esoteric knowledge	**2. TRANSFORMATIVE** Bolsheviks, Islamic fundamentalism (classic revolutions)	**4. REDEMPTIVE** Millenarian movements, cults, People's Temple, Synanon, (isolated environments)

FIGURE 7–1   Types of Social Movements

EXPLAINING THE ORIGINS OF SOCIAL MOVEMENTS

We now turn away from these descriptive issues to address issues that have been major concerns of analysts of social movements: How and why do they develop? What are the conditions that stimulate the development of social movements? In this section we will review various perspectives about the origins of social movements, including individual explanations, microsocial explanations, and macrostructural explanations.

Individual Explanations

Individual explanations explain the origins of social movements by focusing on the psychological characteristics of individuals. These explanations, among the oldest and the most recent explanations of the origins of movements, are basically collective psychology perspectives that argue that the emergence of social movements is caused by the shared dispositions of individual participants.

Irrationality and Crowds. The oldest of these is a *crowd psychology* explanation that emphasizes the irrational nature of social movement participation. The contrast is drawn between individual behavior (viewed as rational and restrained) and crowd behavior, viewed as irrational and impulsive (LeBon, 1896/1960; Hoffer, 1951; McCormack, 1951). The participants in social movements are argued to be compensating for frustrated lives. In a study of movement activists and extremists, Hoffer (1951) described the "true believer syndrome" in what has come to be called the *riffraff theory* of movement participation. Hoffer argues that movement activists are misfits and losers whose participation is fueled by the futility of wasted lives (this is not exactly neutral scientific language!). The ideal converts are those who feel inadequate and who attach themselves to movements to enhance their self-esteem and hope: The types of movements or goals they pursue are interchangeable, according to Hoffer; paramount is their need to belong.

When viewed in social context, these assumptions became compatible with the mass society theory, which we have encountered before. The irrationality and suggestibility of people who form mass movements are viewed as consequences of the breakdown of traditional structures in modern societies and "social atomization," which results in widespread alienation, and anxiety (Kornhauser, 1959:32). This view of the origins of social movements as the work of frustrated and irrational individuals in mass societies was particularly popular after the growth of communism and fascism in the 1930s and during the early Cold War period of the 1950s.

Rational Choice and Social Movements. In contrast to this older view emphasizing irrationality and frustration, more recent individual approaches suggest rational calculative involvement of actors in social movements, and they see social movements as mechanisms of collective problem solving (Oberschall, 1973; Friedman, 1983). These perspectives, which derive from the influential work of economist

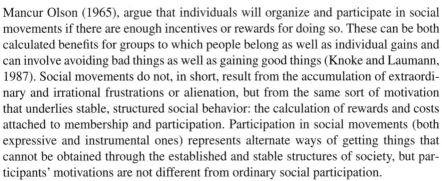

Mancur Olson (1965), argue that individuals will organize and participate in social movements if there are enough incentives or rewards for doing so. These can be both calculated benefits for groups to which people belong as well as individual gains and can involve avoiding bad things as well as gaining good things (Knoke and Laumann, 1987). Social movements do not, in short, result from the accumulation of extraordinary and irrational frustrations or alienation, but from the same sort of motivation that underlies stable, structured social behavior: the calculation of rewards and costs attached to membership and participation. Participation in social movements (both expressive and instrumental ones) represents alternate ways of getting things that cannot be obtained through the established and stable structures of society, but participants' motivations are not different from ordinary social participation.

In sum, individual perspectives attempt to explain the development of social movements by telling us something about the underlying motivations, or psychic states, of individual participants. We have described two dramatically different perspectives, and both have intuitive appeal in describing the attraction and recruitment of individuals to movements. But studies have not found much evidence that individual-level perspectives are useful in predicting the participation of people in movements. For example, Muller's exhaustive review of studies concludes that "psychological attributes of individuals, such as frustration and alienation" have little usefulness for explaining the occurrence of movements per se (1989:69). On the basis of reviews of empirical studies others also have concluded that individual predispositions are at best insufficient to account for collective action in social movements (Wilson and Orum, 1976:189).

Microsocial Explanations

Microsocial explanations focus on the small-scale (micro) level, as opposed to the large-scale (macro) level. The focus is often *social psychological,* because they examine the relationship and interaction between individuals and group or social settings and conditions. There are a variety of micro-level theories about the origins of social movements, but here we will describe only three perspectives: (1) relative deprivation, (2) status strains, and (3) microstructural mobilization contexts.

Relative Deprivation. Some scholars argued that *absolute deprivation* is a motivating force in the generation of social movements (Toch, 1965; Fanon, 1968). Absolute deprivation includes such material deprivations such as hunger, illness, and lack of safety, which bring people close to the minimal conditions of survival. These analysts argued that changes in objective social conditions, such as extreme poverty and rises in the price of food, are the causes of collective behavior and social movements. Yet it is obvious that until recently such absolute deprivation was the lot of *most* of humanity and often did not produce social movements directed at change. An additional problem with this approach is that much social movement activity is *not* directed at alleviating absolute deprivations such as those mentioned earlier.

Thus, many scholars reject objective conditions or deprivations *themselves* as an explanation for the origins of movements and argue that relative deprivation (or subjective deprivation) is the social psychological condition underlying the emergence of movements (Davies, 1969; Gurr, 1970). *Relative deprivation* exists when a significant gap exists between value expectations and value outcomes or, in simpler language, between what people expect and what they get. It has little to do with either individual psychological traits or absolute deprivations, but rather with subjective feelings of *being deprived relative to expectations.* Relative deprivation explanations imply that there are *reference groups* that are the source of such expectations. People thus feel satisfied or deprived by comparing their condition to relevant categories of others. Being centrally concerned with changing social definitions about expectations and perceptions of reality, you can understand the relative deprivation explanation of movement participation as rooted in interpretive theory contexts that we discussed in Chapter 6. Relative deprivation explains why (1) protest movements are often common during periods of sustained improvement in objective conditions (expectations rise faster), and (2) people involved in movements are often not the most objectively deprived people.

Relative deprivation has been used to explain the development of urban protests among African Americans during the 1960s. In spite of objective improvements in social conditions, there was still a gap between blacks and whites, and the perception of that gap was most intense among middle-class African Americans, who in fact organized and led the civil rights movements. According to Pettigrew (1964), during the 1950s blacks began to contrast their situation with that of similarly educated whites, rather than with their own history of slavery and extreme deprivation. Thus "this approach focuses on the comparative deprivation between groups. . . . Groups can be reasonably well off in terms of wealth, power, and prestige, yet still feel deprived relative to other groups. When this occurs, the underprivileged groups are likely to protest" (Wood and Jackson, 1982:37).

There are limitations to the relative deprivation approach. Like the individual explanations, it is intuitively appealing, but existing evidence from systematic research has not found it to be a sufficient or even a necessary precondition to explanation of the emergence of movements. Summarizing studies from the 1960s, McPhail concludes that "there is considerable reason for rejecting the notion that relative deprivation and ensuing frustration . . . is the root cause of rebellion" (1971:106). Other assessments of research evidence also find only mixed support for relative deprivation theory (Gurney and Tierney, 1982). But although not as popular as it was in the 1960s, relative deprivation theory still has some usefulness in understanding the origins of movements for a number of reasons: (1) It is conceptually clearer than older arguments about "mass discontent"; (2) it does not involve a derogatory view of participants as riffraff enraptured by the irrationalities of crowd behavior; and (3) it has some utility when combined with other approaches but is not seen as a necessary or complete explanation of the origins of social movements (Gurney and Tierney, 1982; Wood and Jackson, 1982).

Status Strains.   Other scholars argued that the motivation to participate in social movements results from threats to one's status in society. Such threats, or *status* *strains,* are likely to arise when one's status is threatened by social change (for example, demographic change, immigration, occupational or political change), when there is an increasing influence of formerly subjugated groups, or when there is an erosion of a cultural perspective that supported the prestige, power, and privilege of status groups. Since status strains theory deals with threats to privilege, it has mainly been used to explain the attraction of people to right-wing movements, which seek to preserve or restore the traditional status order.

Lipset and Raab (1970) documented the relationship between status strains and the emergence of a variety of right-wing movements in American history. We will mention three of their examples only briefly. The nativist movement (and its major organization, the American Protective Association) emerged in the late nineteenth century; it attempted to protect the political and cultural dominance of the "old Americans" (WASPS) from growing Catholic and immigrant influence in the urban Northeast. Similarly, the Ku Klux Klan developed after the Civil War to protect the political privilege of southern whites in the wake of the postwar Reconstruction period. The movement revived during the 1920s to protect the interests of rural white Protestants who were losing influence to urban immigrants. It thus became an anti-Catholic and anti-Jewish as well as a white racist (anti-black) movement. The Klan revived again in the 1960s and the 1980s. Indeed, the Klan—along with its "fellow traveler" movements—such as the neo-Nazis, Aryan Supremacists, and young skinheads, has been small but visible since the early 1980s. Like the militias we noted earlier, these groups are diverse but have high concentrations of people with low education stuck in low-paying jobs or careers (Stern, 1996). Collectively, the social movement organizations (SMOs) that coalesce from this social stratum comprise a small, noisy, vocal, and frightening perennial feature of the American social landscape; they are a breeding ground for domestic terrorists like Timothy McVeigh. (We will discuss professional SMOs later in the chapter.)

You can interpret the resurgence of evangelical religious right-wing movements of the 1970s to the 1990s as originating in status strains. Jerry Falwell's Moral Majority was the most publicly visible SMO of the 1970s. A movement of vast proportions compared to the fringe groups just mentioned, evangelical Christianity as a political and social force was a response to modernity and sociocultural changes of the 1970s (such as changes in gender roles, affirmative action programs, and welfare state programs). These changes threatened traditional statuses and lifestyles. Studies of historical and contemporary religious right-wing movements suggest that their support was disproportionately found among those whose social status and prestige was most threatened by the incorporation of new or previously subjugated groups and by growing American multiculturalism (see Gannon, 1981; Simpson, 1983; Yinger and Cutler, 1982).

In spite of its appeal, there are many problems with the status strains perspective as a *general* theory of movement origins. *First,* it is primarily an intriguing theory of right-wing movements, and it is not clear how it could be applied to other types of movements. *Second,* like the individual irrationality perspective discussed earlier, the theory is reductionistic: The overt claims of protest groups are not taken as real, but as a kind of sublimation for status difficulties. *Third,* in spite of the studies mentioned here, other systematic studies, primarily on support for the New Religious Right, have in general concluded that participation is at best only weakly related to status strains—*if* status strains are interpreted as threats to hierarchical statuses (Page and Clelland, 1978; Harper and Leicht, 1984; Simpson, 1983). These studies suggest that the support for the New Religious Right is as much related to defense of a *cultural lifestyle* as threatened social, economic and political statuses. This suggests a *fourth* weakness of the perspective: It is conceptually muddied—that is, it conflates threats to cultural tradition, social prestige, political power, and economic class. And as sociologists ever since Max Weber have cautioned, these different dimensions of stratification do not have an automatic equivalence in complex societies. In sum, we think that status strain theory is a useful but limited perspective.

Microstructural Mobilization Contexts. Both the relative deprivation and status strains approaches assume sources of personal frustrations that provide a *predispositional push* that propel individuals toward movement activism and participation. However appealing they may be, the summaries of empirical studies mentioned here give them little or at best highly qualified support. Such approaches have been abandoned not only because of this evidence, but also because of the growth of the rational choice perspective (mentioned earlier), which does not view social movement activism as motivated by extraordinary predispositions but by rather ordinary goal-seeking behavior. More recent understandings of social movement emergence and participation focus not on predispositional pushes (or in simpler language, the motivations of participants) but on the structural pulls that may mobilize people for participation in social movements. What are some of these structural mobilization contexts? At least three have been identified by researchers.

First, the factor that has shown the strongest connection with movement activism is *the existence of interpersonal ties between movement "recruits" and participants.* In a study of two peace social movement organizations, for instance, Bolton found that most of the recruits to peace movement organizations "were already associated with persons who belonged to or were organizing the peace groups, and were recruited through these interpersonal channels" (1972:558). Comparisons of recruitment into two Asian religious movements in America, Nichiren Shoshu (a Buddhist sect), and the Hare Krishna movement (derived from Hinduism), also suggest the importance of interpersonal ties for understanding movement affiliation. The Nichiren Shoshu movement grew remarkably, claiming about 350,000 adherents during the 1980s, and 82 percent of their converts reported having friends or relatives in the movement. The Hare Krishna movement, which makes more extensive use of anonymous street recruitment, remains small, claiming approximately 5000 adherents in the 1980s (see Snow, Zurcher, and Ekland-Olson, 1980). Even the growth of Christianity, one of the five world religions (along with Hinduism, Buddism, Islam, and Judaism) has been explained by examining the interpersonal connections of first-century Christians as a potential recruiting base (see Stark, 1996).

Similar findings have been reported about the significance of existing interpersonal networks and participation in civil rights demonstrations and movement organizations (McAdam, 1986). Snow, Zurcher, and Ekland-Olson found that of nine studies of activism in social movements all but one identified prior interpersonal contact as the single richest source of movement recruits (1980).

Second, there is a well-documented connection between membership in organizations and movement activism. In other words, the more organizations one belongs to, the more one is likely to participate in social movements. There are three possible reasons why this may be so. First, there is long-standing evidence that organizational membership increases feelings of personal efficacy, and it may be that members of organizations are simply more optimistic about whether movement activism is worth the effort (Snow, Zurcher, and Ekland-Olson, 1980). You should note that this evidence is in direct contradiction to the assumption of the mass society approach that sees movement activism as a consequence of isolation, alienation, and estrangement. Second, it may be simply that organizational members are likely to be better informed about public issues and about the possibilities of collective action in movements. Third, it may be that organizations are simply an amplification of the network factor mentioned earlier. That is, organizations are associated with movement activism because they represent dense concentrations of overlapping interpersonal networks (McAdam, McCarthy, and Zald, 1988:708).

Many examples illustrate the powerful role of organizations that act as breeding grounds for social movements. In the 1960s, campus organizations were connected to the emergence of student activism in civil rights, antiwar, and ecological movements. Orum (1972) found a consistent positive relationship between involvement in the black student sit-in demonstrations and the number of campus activities students belonged to. Or consider the role of religious organizations as breeding grounds for political movements: Many have noted the important role of African-American churches as settings for the mobilization of the early civil rights movements (Oberschall, 1973; Morris, 1984). Similarly, the connection between membership in fundamentalist churches and mobilization into the New Religious Right political movement (the Moral Majority) of the 1970s has been documented (Harper and Leicht, 1984; Shupe and Stacy, 1982). And in an entirely different setting, Snow and Marshall (1984) noted the important role of Islamic mosques in organizing the Iranian revolution of 1979. More recently, scholars have noted the important role that the Catholic Church played in the development of the Solidarity movement in Poland (cf. Kubik, 1994).

A *third* micromobilization context that affects individual movement activism is *the biographical availability of individuals.* In addition to the structural pull of interpersonal networks and organizational membership, the circumstances of a person's life may facilitate or impede movement participation and activism. To put it quite simply, many people have relationships and obligations such as full-time employment, marriage, and family responsibilities that increase the costs and risks of movement participation and constrain movement activism (McAdam, McCarthy, and Zald, 1988:709). Persons who are not so encumbered with social bonds, obligations, and commitments are more likely to have the freedom and the discretionary time and energy to participate actively in social movements.

This is why students and young adults, autonomous professionals, and single people are disproportionately found among the ranks of movement activists. This has been documented for the civil rights movement, the environmental movement, and the new religious ("cult") movements, and why the new religious movements were often identified in the popular view as youth movements (McAdam, 1986:83; Snow and Rochford, 1983:3).

In sum, microsocial perspectives explain the origins of social movements by pointing to the manner in which personal characteristics or circumstances and social factors interact to produce movement participation, activism, and mobilization. They may explain why individuals participate, but there are broader questions about the underlying grievances, organizing issues, and the timing of movement emergence that no microsocial perspective can deal with adequately. For instance, why was the 1960s a rancorous, conflict-ridden decade in which so many protest movements flourished (the Black Power movement, the youth counterculture, the antiwar movement, the ecological movement, and so forth)? Most observers would agree that it was a decade of movements, particularly in comparison to the relatively tranquil Eisenhower years of the late 1950s. Why so, particularly when there is little convincing evidence of pervasive increases in relative deprivation, status strains, or significant growth in the density of micromobilization contexts that would explain difference between the 1950s and 1960s? Is the difference merely historical myopia? We don't think so. Something was different about the 1960s, and that difference is not explained by microsocial theories. For this you need macrostructural perspectives that seek explanations among the broader social, economic, and political force of change.

Macrostructural Explanations of Social Movements

Macrostructural explanations may incorporate some of the assumptions of micro theories, but the emphasis is on understanding the development of social movements in terms of broad societal conditions. We will describe macro explanations within both the functionalist and conflict traditions.

Collective Behavior and Functionalist Perspectives. The dominant macro view of the origins of movements that developed in American sociology during the 1950s understood them as outgrowths of a particular kind of social behavior called *collective behavior.* This way of explaining movements has roots in interpretive theories, but more importantly in functionalism and the mass society theory (both discussed in Chapter 6). In the text that follows, we will first discuss some assumptions about social movements and collective behavior, and then describe in some detail the most mature and developed statement of this perspective, Neil Smelser's value-added theory.

Most human social behavior is routine in that it takes place in established social relationships and is broadly guided by cultural and social control processes. People often enact established social roles within (imperfectly) integrated groups, organizations, and structures. In some situations, however, there are no clearly defined guidelines, and behavior is novel, spontaneous, volatile, creative, and rather unpredictable. *Collective behavior* is the technical term sociologists use for situations in which a significant number of people are acting in the relative absence of social control.

Many *elementary forms* of collective behavior exist, such as the transmission of rumor, crowd behaviors, mobs, panics, and protests. Sociologists have assumed that such elementary forms of collective behavior develop in the context of the breakdown of traditional order (often associated with rapid social change) and always assume some underlying shared source of excitement, stress, anxiety, tension, or frustration. The breakdown of traditional order and restraints was widely viewed to accompany modernization and the emergence of mass society.

Social movements typically begin as "amorphous, poorly organized and without form" and are characterized by collective behavior "on the primitive level" as well as by mechanisms of interaction that are "elementary" and "spontaneous" (Blumer, 1969:8). In spite of the negative images of protests, mobs, and panics, they may contribute to the creation of new social forms (Blumer, 1962). In short, elementary forms that persist may lead to the formation of social movements, and these, in turn, may evolve into integrated structures and new established forms of behavior (see Table 7-1).

The development of the American labor movement illustrates this process. In the 1890s, the labor movement was often characterized by volatile mob action (on the part of both strikers and the authorities!). As the union movement developed, it evolved into an established set of structures and interests that are now a routine part of the American economic system (in the next chapter we will discuss the American labor movement in more depth). This illustration should not be taken to mean that social movements always succeed in evolving new structural forms. Just as the elementary forms of collective behavior are often short lived, the emergent forms (social movements, with their organizations and publics) often fail to result in any stable forms or produce any meaningful change. Social movements may transform society, but history is also full of the wreckage of lost causes!

The collective behavior perspective was developed by scholars whose large-scale image of change was the transitions from traditional to modern mass societies, and social movements were viewed as adaptive responses to the stresses and strains

TABLE 7–1 COLLECTIVE BEHAVIOR AND GROUP STRUCTURE

Elementary Forms of Collective Behavior	More Developed Forms of Collective Behavior	Integrated Structure
Characteristics:		
lacks structure; fluid, spontaneous interaction, volatile	evolving structure; change oriented, noninstitutionalized	stable structured interaction; institutionalized
Examples:		
crowds, mobs, protests, panics, rumor networks	social movements, movement organizations, publics, audiences	organizations, bureaucracies, families, stable peer groups

that accompanied that transition. The perspective emphasizes that the breakdown of traditional patterns of order and social control produce elementary forms of collective behavior and that these may crystallize into ongoing social movements that attempt to promote or prevent further social change. This is broadly consistent with the functionalist image of order and change, in which change is a reaction to disequilibrium and stress.[1]

Smelser's Value-Added Theory.   This is the most ambitious and elaborate explanation of social movements from the collective behaviorist perspective in American sociology (Smelser, 1962). The *value-added theory* addresses the structural origins of the stresses that motivate actors and the development of the movement in terms of its ongoing interaction with the larger social environment. Smelser argues that there are six conditions necessary for the emergence and development of social movements. Each of these six conditions is necessary for the development of movements, but none is alone sufficient. They operate in an additive fashion (hence the name "value-added") but not necessarily in chronological sequence. The theory is not—strictly speaking—a stage model of the development of movements. Smelser outlines the six conditions as follows:

1. *Structural conduciveness:* Preexisting structures in society are more likely to generate certain kinds of movements than others. For example, a society with racial cleavages is likely to develop racial movements, and free market societies are likely to develop panics and movements aimed at stabilizing the cycles of the economy. The structures of particular societies encourage or rule out certain kinds of issues around which collective behavior and movements develop.

2. *Structural strains:* Strains (perceived ambiguities, deprivation, inconsistencies, tensions) emerge in relation to the way that conducive structures are perceived. For example, the vast inequality in a caste system is a conducive factor that may or may not produce strains. In this case, strains only develop if such inequality is perceived as an oppressive fact. Thus strains are based upon perceptions of the structural order and are inversely related to the perception of its legitimacy. Such strains become relevant to collective behavior when they become collectively shared.

3. *Growth of a generalized belief system:* A preexisting or emergent set of ideas is required to galvanize widespread strains into an ongoing movement. Such idea systems, or *ideologies,* define the sources of strains and point toward solutions that would alleviate them. In America, for example, ideologies that analyzed the sources of restricted opportunities for minorities and women as deriving from a fundamental aspect of American culture—as racism or sexism—have facilitated the development of the civil rights and feminist movements.

4. *Precipitating events:* Dramatic events sharpen and concretize issues. They can focus attention, galvanize public support and awareness, and draw the attention of media and the authorities. Examples of precipitating events include the Watts riot of 1968 in relation to the Black Power phase of the civil rights movement; the collapse of the French credit system and the Petrograd food riots in relation, respectively, to the French and

Russian revolutions; and the Santa Barbara oil spill and the Three Mile Island nuclear disaster in relation to the ecology and antinuclear power movements.

5. *Mobilization of participants:* This includes the emergence of leadership and spokespersons for the movement and the development of organizations as well as general processes of agitation, recruitment, and claims making about grievances regarding the issues that animate the movements.

6. *Operation of social control:* The activation of forces in the larger society to respond to the movement. Such responses may be by governmental authorities or by countermovements that develop in relationship to a movement (examples of the latter would be the mobilization of anti–Equal Rights Amendment forces and the anticult movement that developed to combat the influence of religious cults during the late 1970s).*

Smelser identifies three types of responses by the authorities to social movements. *First,* they can open channels of communication and influence, bringing the movement, its issues, and its leaders partly within the framework of the institutional system. This has been called *co-optation. Second,* the authorities can, while not co-opting the movement, nonetheless seek to alter the underlying structural conditions that gave rise to the movement. In the German empire of the late nineteenth century, for example, Bismarck did not open the regime to the influence of the socialist movement, but rather created welfare state reforms to deal with the issues that animated it. *Third,* the authorities can attempt to suppress a movement with all the resources of the state.

One of the strengths of Smelser's theory is that it emphasizes the ongoing interaction between the movement and society. This interaction can be a powerful force that shapes the development and direction of the movement. Thus a radical movement that is successfully co-opted can become more moderate, while a reform movement that is brutally repressed may become more radicalized.

Smelser's intent was to create a theoretical scheme that is like a funnel, in which the initial variables are abstract ones relating to the macroscopic features of the social order and subsequent variables become more concretely related to specific episodes of collective behavior and movement development. Its comprehensiveness is appealing, but it is also difficult to refute empirically. For example, the causal linkages between the six factors in the model are not clear, and they would not seem to operate in the same way. Structural conduciveness, for instance, is a *permissive* variable and may or may not lead to the emergence of strains.

Strains, on the other hand, are treated as causally linked to the emergence of generalized beliefs and the mobilization of participants. For example, it is undoubtedly true that certain kinds of structures are likely to generate certain types of movements, but is this more than an airy tautology? What kinds of structures generate which kinds of movements? Smelser's theory is of little help in answering this question. There are similar difficulties with the notion of structural strains. There are no

* Adapted with permission of The Free Press, a Division of Macmillan, Inc., from *Theory of Collective Behavior* by Neil J. Smelser. Copyright © 1962 by Neil J. Smelser.

clear "criteria for identifying a 'structural strain' in a real society. . . . Virtually any type of social problem or inconsistency seems to qualify as a strain" (Useem, 1975:9). Smelser is not clear as to whether structural strain reflects an objective condition in the society (for example, disequilibrium or malintegration) or the perceptions of those conditions by its citizens (Berk, 1974:41). Complicating things further, Smelser has even argued that "any kind of strain may be a determinant of any kind of collective behavior" (1962:49).

In sum, Smelser's explanation is more descriptive than explanatory and its abstract character, which makes it so universally applicable, also makes it hard to refute. We think it is mainly useful as an orienting framework, since it specifies issues that require explicating in understanding the emergence of any one social movement. It represents the apogee of functionalist-collective behaviorist thinking about social movements, which focused on the psychological reactions of members of mass society to social strain (Hannigan, 1991:316).

Conflict Perspectives. In the 1970s and 1980s, conflict approaches came to dominate the study of social movements by American scholars. Rather than emphasizing the grievances arising from structural strains, these perspectives argued that social movements arise at a particular point in time because of the "changing availability of resources, organization, and opportunities for collective action" (Jenkins, 1983:530). So rather than viewing social movements as emerging from the spontaneous and amorphous mass discontent of collective behavior, conflict perspectives view social movements as special sorts of interest group collectivities that attempt to (1) gain benefits for individuals, (2) produce social reforms, and (3) gain entry into the established structures of society. In what follows, we examine (1) a conflict approach, termed *resource mobilization theory,* (2) what is called *political process theory,* and (3) a European conflict approach called *new movement theory.*

Resource Mobilization Theory. This theory focuses on the "role of power and power struggles in mobilizing people for collective action" (Burton, 1984:48). It began with some observations about the 1960s as a "decade of movements" in America. As mentioned earlier, there was a dramatic increase in social movement activity during this period. Why? During the 1960s there was a sustained growth in both affluence and apparent social conflict. There was no evidence of increase in the rates of participation in voluntary associations and no dramatic increase in individual discretionary time and money that might explain the growth in social movements activity. And there was no evidence that suggested general increases in social alienation or relative deprivation in comparison to the 1950s (McCarthy and Zald, 1973; Gamson, 1974).

Resource mobilization theorists argued that the increase in social movement activity was related to a number of important trends in American society during the 1960s. *First,* there was the growth of private foundation and church support (financial and moral) for reform causes of all sorts. *Second,* with the thaw in international relations, the mass media gave greater attention to domestic social problems and less attention to the perceived external communist threat. *Third,* there was extensive government sponsorship of social movements through agencies such as the Office of Economic Opportunity, the U.S. Civil Rights Commission, and various Commissions on the Status of Women. *Fourth,* there were improvements in the technology of mobilization and fund raising for social causes, in particular use of cross-listed computerized mailing lists and phone banking. *Fifth,* there was the emergence of career social movement organizers who rejected traditional institutional roles and careers. These were, for instance, ministers, community organizers, and public relations specialists as well as doctors, scientists, and lawyers who opted to work in nontraditional settings for the advocacy of change. *Sixth,* during the 1960s there emerged a special body of literature for social movement organizers.[2] *Seventh,* and most important, there was the development of professional social movement organizations (SMOs).

McCarthy and Zald (1973) described the professional SMOs that developed during the 1960s as follows: They have full-time professional leadership and in comparison to older SMOs they are driven by bureaucratic organizers rather than charismatic leaders or compelling ideology. A large part of their resources originate outside the aggrieved groups that the movement organization claims to represent, and the actual membership base may be small or actually nonexistent. Or it may be a paper membership base of people who receive newsletters and make occasional financial contributions. Such movement organizations attempt to impart the idea that they speak for an aggrieved constituency and to influence public policy.

We think these are important observations about movements in contemporary America. On our desks at any one time are letters soliciting support (and, more important, money!) from the Children's Defense Fund, the Solar Lobby, Nebraskans for Peace, and the Iowa Civil Liberties Union. While we have some sympathy with these causes, they are not movement organizations that we helped to create from deeply personal convictions. Those on other mailing lists get appeals to restore prayer to the public schools or to prevent the regulation of handguns, or to support the multitude of other causes that are being mobilized at any given time.

Resource mobilization theorists argue that U.S. society now possesses the generalized resources that can be used to mobilize a variety of (contradictory) change efforts that have the appearance of mass-based movements. In their view, there has been a decline in the importance of a mass membership base in the generation of social movements, and "the definition of grievances will expand to meet the funds and support personnel available" (McCarthy and Zald, 1973:23). The development of movements can then, to a certain extent, be planned or even manufactured.

Resource mobilization theory *deemphasizes* the role of mass discontent—by treating it as a constant—and *emphasizes* the ongoing transformation of movements through the interaction of competing social movement organizations in the broader political environment (more about this later). It also assumes a liberal pluralistic political structure. That is, it assumes a political system in which elites are not firmly in control and there is continual political realignment that makes the success of activist movement organizations possible. Hence it may not be applicable to authoritarian societies where there is less freedom to mobilize.

Critical questions about American society have been raised by resource mobilization theory. For instance, "Does the piper call the tune?" That is, if social movements in contemporary America reflect the influence of professional organizers and movement organizations, to what extent do they reflect their needs and interests rather than those of the broader clienteles they purport to serve? And do they channel political discontent in less politically threatening directions?

There has been a variety of criticisms of resource mobilization theory. It seems too tied to recent trends in the United States (which may be reversible) to be a general explanation of social movements origins. Some research has been critical of the assumption that the relative deprivation and strains related to mass discontent have been relatively unchanging (Useem, 1980; Walsh, 1981; Law and Walsh, 1983). Another limitation of the theory is that it is a better explanation of the social movements of the affluent than those emerging from lower-status groups. Law and Walsh comment that

> collectivities at the lower end of the socioeconomic hierarchy are more likely to experience widespread, serious, and chronic discontent while having relatively . . . little organizational leverage. Higher status collectivities . . . have relatively few common grievances and abundant personal as well as organizational resources at their disposal. (1983:135)

In other words, the resource mobilization perspective has a social class bias. Most critics of the theory argue that it has made an important contribution by emphasizing the role of social movement organizations but that it minimizes the continuing role of broader grievances and strains in the emergence of movements.

Political Process Theory. This theory is compatible with resource mobilization theory but takes a different approach in explaining the ebb and flow of movement activity. It reasserts the primacy of the political by emphasizing not only the existence of generalized resources and emergence organizations, but also, and most important, the existence of favorable "structures of political opportunity" (McAdam, 1982, Tilley, 1978; Eisinger, 1973; McAdam, McCarthy, and Zald, 1996). *Political opportunity structures* refer to the receptivity or vulnerability of the political system to organized protest by given challenging groups (McAdam, McCarthy, and Zald, 1988:699). When political opportunity structures expand, there are waves of intense movement mobilization and effectiveness.

The expansion of political opportunity structures can take several forms. *First,* it may have to do with the growth of political pluralism or a decline in the effectiveness of repression regarding contending movements (which explains why reform movements generally flourish in democratic but not in authoritarian political environments).

Second, a political opportunity structure for movement mobilization and success exists when the effective power of political elites is undermined by internal fragmentation and disunity. Elite disunity, in other words, translates into net gain in political opportunity for all organized challengers. At the extreme, elite disunity may become generalized political instability involving a "crisis of regime" where the state's capacity for effective action is paralyzed. Contemporary movement scholars

(Skocpol, 1979; Habermas, 1973; McAdam, McCarthy, and Zald, 1996) argue that this is at the root of successful revolutionary movements (a subject to which we will return in more depth in a later chapter). Even less extreme elite disunity—not involving a complete crisis of regime—can create political openings for the mobilization of movements. In the post–Civil War American South, for example, conflicts between planter and industrial elites that were deadlocked in a struggle to control the politics of the region provided a unique political opportunity for the growth of the agrarian populist movement to mobilize and break the deadlock (Schwartz, 1976). The successes of the Nazis in prewar Germany is a more familiar example of how general political instability and elite disunity provides opportunity structures for contending movements.

A *third* way that political opportunity structures may be created for movement mobilization is through the broadening of access to institutional participation in the political process. This can take place through the realignment of inputs into the political process. In the Soviet Union during the late 1980s, for example, elected parliamentarians, representing communist party factions as well as other recognized political groups, came to have a larger measure of political power relative to the Politburo. An even clearer example is official recognition of the legality of South African protest movements and the extension of *some* form of political franchise to nonwhites in the 1990s.

In both of these cases, the broadening base of political input created unprecedented opportunities for the mobilization of waves of protest movements among contending groups, thus triggering cycles of social movement activity very much related to both the tumultuous changes and eventual collapse of communism in the USSR. (Tarrow, 1991) and to the collapse of the South African apartheid system in the 1990s. Besides changing the structure of inputs into the political process or enlarging the legal definition of political franchise, political access has been broadened in the United States by the incorporation of previously marginal groups through public voter registration drives among minorities and immigrant communities. McAdam (1982) has attributed the widespread expansion of the African-American protest movement activity in the 1950s and 1960s to the growth of the black electorate and its incorporation into the Democratic Party.

A *fourth* way that political opportunities expand is when political elites (usually in a competitive arena) curry popular support by providing public legitimation and legal and administrative support for movements. Indeed, there is an almost symbiotic relationship between successful waves of movement activity in U.S. history and elite support or facilitation. It is difficult to account for the successes of the American labor movement without taking into account facilitation by sympathetic presidential administrations of Theodore Roosevelt, Woodrow Wilson, and Franklin D. Roosevelt or of the successes of the civil rights or feminist movements in the 1960s without the support of the Kennedy and Johnson administrations. Gale (1986) has documented the top-down sponsorship of the environmental movement by political agencies sympathetic to the movement.

In retrospect, the liberal-left coalition that dominated American presidential politics between the 1930s and the 1960s created a broad political context that facilitated the emergence and successes of a wide variety of progressive or leftist movements (McAdam, McCarthy, and Zald, 1988:700). And the apparent attenuation of those movements in the 1970s, 1980s, and 1990s surely has to do with the shift to a more conservative political environment and administrations. Those administrations not only withdrew sponsorship and worked to retard the efforts of progressive reform movements but also sponsored conservative movements more to their liking (for example, evangelical religious and pro-life movements). The reasons for elite sponsorship of social movements in political democracies are not difficult to understand: Franklin Roosevelt sought electoral support among workers, Kennedy and Johnson among minorities and women, and Reagan and Bush among conservative religionists.

The strength of political opportunity structure theory is that it addresses the issue of the timing of emergence and success of movements in a way that no other perspective does. It explains why social movement activity often comes in waves or cycles, and why movements that have been unsuccessful for an extended period of time suddenly appear to grow and succeed (for example, the Bolshevik revolutionary movement in czarist Russia and the American labor movement in the 1930s). But, like resource mobilization theory, the political opportunity structure perspective can be criticized for minimizing or treating as a constant the role of grievances and strains in the emergence of movements.

A different criticism is that the theory, along with the micromobilization contexts and resource mobilization perspectives, represent a shift among American movement scholars to a narrowly structural focus that ignores not only the role of shared grievances, but also the role of culture and ideas shaping the issues that are at the core of movements. Most movement scholars recognize the relevance of ideas (ideology, class consciousness, or generalized beliefs). Yet it is odd that social movement scholars gave the role of ideas, culture, ideologies, and consciousness little attention until recently.

New Movement Theory.   This perspective gives more emphasis to consciousness and culture and focuses specifically on movements in contemporary modern societies. It is applicable to understanding American movements, but it has a very different flavor because it was developed by European movement scholars (Melucci, 1980; Klandermans, 1986; VanderLoo et al., 1984; Kriesi, 1988).

They begin with the observation that we made earlier about the waves of diverse movements that emerged in the 1960s that continue in some fashion into the 1990s (such as the feminist, environmental, peace, antinuclear, gay rights, and New Age movements). These movements emerged in a short time span in Western nations that have different cultural traditions and national structures of political opportunity (using the terms of the perspective discussed earlier). Why? The diffusion of movements as innovations among nations might explain some of the mechanisms of cross-national transmission (see Chapter 10), but not the circumstances that would make different nations receptive to the diffusion of similar movements.

New movement theory provides a plausible answer about why these cultural and protest movements emerged in a similar time span in a variety of Western nations. Abstractly, they are *all* viewed as *reactions to the modernizing process in advanced industrial capitalist societies.* They are reactions to the erosion of traditional ways of family and work life in Europe after World War II and in particular to the rise of welfare state intrusion into previously private spheres of life (McAdam, McCarthy, and Zald, 1988:701). Thus for diverse movements the overriding issue is the issue of life space and the struggle to regain control of private spheres of life from state bureaucratic regulation. If this sounds familiar to you, it should: Although it comes from movement scholars rather that literary critics, it is similar to the reaction against modernity that we discussed as postmodernism in Chapter 2.

How are new movements different from social movements in previous decades? Scholars have suggested three differences. *First,* new movements have ideological contexts that make them different. Instead of articulating claims about fundamental economic justice or human and political rights (about, for example, voting or freedom of speech), new movements are framed by concerns about individual and cultural rights, such as the right to be different and to be protected from particular risks, such as nuclear or environmental hazards (Hannigan, 1991: 320). Put differently, the ideological backdrop of new movements is shaped by values about self-actualization, community, and personal satisfactions (versus occupational satisfaction) (McAdam, McCarthy, and Zald, 1988:701). A *second* way that they differ from previous movements is in their preferred action forms. The new movements are distrustful of politics; they favor small-scale, decentralized organizations, are antihierarchical, and advocate direct democracy (Klandennans and Tarrow, 1988, cited in Hannigan, 1991: 320). A *third* difference is that while many previous movements were identified with the grievances of lower-status and economic groups, such as workers or minorities, the new movements are associated with the rise of a new middle class of educated professionals, particularly those whose expertise is social or cultural rather than technocratic (these would be, for example, ministers, professors, journalists, and bureaucrats in public and nonprofit organizations). Having high levels of education and a firsthand view of the cracks in contemporary society, this new middle class is said to have special insight into the threat posed to the pursuit of nonmaterial goals (individual lifestyles) by the material conditions of production and the institutional framework of the welfare state (Hannigan, 1991:320; Kriesi, 1988:357).

New movements theory makes important contributions about understanding movements in contemporary Western societies, but as with other perspectives it is important that you understand some of its limitations. Its attractiveness in explaining similarities of diverse movements as life space movements in contemporary welfare states *is also a limitation.* Because of this broad, abstract focus this theory underspecifies the social and political contexts in which the new movements appeared—which could have helped to explain the variations in outcome from one movement and country to the next (Tarrow, 1991:14).

Second, it is important to note that while new movements are important, social movements in contemporary Western societies are of more diverse types than those described earlier. For example, many Western societies do have movements for autonomy about group rights, not just individual life space (for instance, movements among the Basques in Spain, the French in Canada, or Native Americans in both the

U.S. and Canada), And there continue to be movements both among marginalized and middle-class groups about basic human rights and entitlements (such as wage adequacy and tax equity, education, child care and health care). Indeed, an important segment of the feminist movement in the United States is concerned with these more than lifestyle issues (Freeman, 1979). European scholars might be excused for not noting the social importance of the evangelical Christian and religious right movements because they are so peculiarly American, but Europe in 1991 saw a frightening resurgence of hybrid Klan–neo-Nazi movements among young people (based not only on anti-Semitism but on hostility towards immigrants). The point is that these movements *do not* look at all like the postmodernist new movements just described. They are based in a different part of the population and have different ideological master frames and forms of collective action. Perhaps they are also reactions against modernity and welfare state intrusions, but in very different ways than those described as new movements.

Ideas, Frames, and Social Movements.   Partly because of the influence of new movements theory, the role of ideas and the *social constructions of reality* is now taken more seriously by scholars who study movements. Snow and colleagues examined the way that different cultural or ideological rationales, or *frames,* are used in mobilizing support of persons for social movements (1986). Such frames are hammered out within movements and are always subject to dispute. Ideological master frames, such as "democracy" or "human rights," often serve as underlying rationales for diverse movements (Snow and Benford, 1988; Benford 1993). Frames also empower individuals to act and legitimize the use of public power. Thus, through movements people begin to understand the social world as mutable and develop a sense of their responsibility to pursue social change (Smith, 1990). And the rhetorical assertions of social movements become a part of the "rhetorical struggle" that is a part of politics and defining the "public good."

As our presentation in Chapter 6 made clear, framing also helps to explain why some definitions of grievances explode into social movements and others do not, even though objective conditions appear similar. The ideological frames of social movements are a cultural resource for social transformation (Snow and Marshall, 1984). Consider, for instance, the different cultural frames of reality by fundamentalist religionists and feminists and their impacts on the larger political process in the United States. Thus considered, social movements operate at the middle levels of social reality, between the micro levels of the face-to-face interaction that recruits and mobilizes persons for action and the more macro political opportunity structures for changing society (Tarrow, 1991).

Social movement framing is part of a broader set of attempts to explain collective action. These analysts take as problematic the ways that individuals in radically divergent, globalized worlds define common worldviews and attempt to act on them through social movements (see Melucci, 1996; Castells, 1998). These analysts bring us back full circle to the original questions that drove early social movements research. What are the sources of collective action? The major differences between these latest attempts to develop theories of collective action and prior incarnations (that we discussed under irrationality and crowds, status strains, relative deprivation, and value-added theory) is that recent theories are more sophisticated and less likely to define social movements as symptoms of system dysfunction or as responding to amorphous system "needs."

IN CONCLUSION

We have come back to where this chapter began: Social movements are important processes by which human agency becomes manifest in producing social and cultural change. We began by defining social movements as collective action to produce or prevent change that is outside the established institutional framework of society. We distinguished between social movements and social movement organizations that grow within them. We also described three broad and relative distinctions between different kinds of movements: those between radical and reform movements, instrumental and expressive movements, and progressive and conservative movements.

Most of this chapter dealt with perspectives for explaining the cause and origins of movements. We described several varieties of individual explanations, microsocial explanations, and macrostructural explanations. These derive from either the broader functionalist or conflict theoretical perspectives discussed in Chapter 5. We ended by describing the shift of thinking about movements into interpretive theory contexts that emphasized the importance of their cultural definitions and frames. There are structural perspectives about movements that emphasize the significance of the social environment on the kinds of movements that emerge and interpretive perspectives that underscore the role of persons in defining and modifying shared definitions of reality that motivate and legitimize action and policy. They both tell pieces of the whole story about social movements.

This survey of theories about social movements has been selective but fairly rigorous, examining movements at different levels of analysis, but also roughly in the chronological order of their development by scholars. We hope that our criticism of each has not left you frustrated and looking for the "best" theory, because each has been useful in posing different questions in different historical contexts as the understanding of movements evolved. The next two chapters focus on the kinds of changes that social movements cause, both in America and in world contexts. We will use these perspectives freely in those discussions.

THINKING PERSONALLY ABOUT SOCIAL CHANGE

You can think of social movements as partly organized causes in which people become involved. Investigate some of these causes as they exist today.

1. Read newspapers, magazines, and watch the TV news to identify some movements and movement organizations that are visible in society and perhaps in your community at this time. If you can, talk with some people knowledgeable about at least one of them.

2. How are movements and movement organizations described in magazine, newspapers, and the TV news? How are movement organizations different from other organizations (like clubs, companies, or government agencies)? What are some of the kinds of causes around which people organize? Of these, identify aspects of these that intend to change the world in some way, and other aspects that mainly address individuals' feelings, self-understandings, needs for dignity, aesthetic life, or other kinds of personal needs.

3. What kinds of people tend to become involved in movements, as contributors, leaders, or sympathizers? Why do you think they became involved? Has a movement organization ever asked you to donate money or time to work for a cause? Did you? Why or why not? For those you found appealing, were there barriers to your participation? What are some contemporary movements you find repulsive? Why?

4. How do other people and organizations respond differently to different movements and movement organizations? What do your acquaintances and friends think of them? In your understanding, what are some different ways that community and national leaders respond to them?

NOTES

1. While collective behaviorists argue that the breakdown of order means that actors are "under the dominance of restlessness and collective excitement" (Blumer, 1969:11), we think it is important to emphasize that such collective states of tension are not necessarily irrational states of individuals. Such states may be rational ways of responding to frightening and frustrating aspects of the way that the social world is organized or disorganized.

2. Here are a few of the titles to give you the flavor of this literature, which reflects the issues and the mood of the 1960s: *Political Action: A Practical Guide to Movement Politics*; *How People Get Power*; *Rules for Radicals: A Manual for Direct Action*; and *The Organizer: A Manual* (McCarthy and Zald, 1973:24)

CHAPTER

8

American Reform Movements and Social Change

The last chapter defined social movements and explained their development from different perspectives. This chapter focuses more concretely on movements and their *consequences* for social change. This chapter and the next emphasize the distinction between reform and revolutionary movements that we made in the last chapter. Reform movements are collective action efforts that promote modest changes within the framework of existing social arrangements. Reform movements may focus on either broad or narrow social reforms. They produce significant change, but they do so in a gradual, piecemeal, and incremental way. And, as you will see, their successes are always limited and constrained by powerful forces that defend the stability of the existing social arrangements in society. By contrast, revolutionary movements are those that attempt relatively more radical and encompassing changes of the social system itself.

This chapter has three goals: (1) to illustrate concretely some of the abstract explanations about the origins of movements that we discussed in the last chapter, (2) to describe some important American reform movements, and (3) to discuss in a more general way the kinds of social change that reform movements are likely to produce.

THE SOCIAL CONTEXT OF TWENTIETH-CENTURY AMERICAN REFORM MOVEMENTS

Broad social contexts and trends determine the kinds of movements that develop and their significance for change. Recall the discussion in the last chapter of Smelser's emphasis on "structural conduciveness" as an important determinant of movement emergence. What structural contexts and trends were conducive to what kinds of reform movements in America in the twentieth century? Given those earlier discussions, what follows should sound familiar to you.

At the beginning of the twentieth century, America was undergoing a transformation from a nation of farmers and small town dwellers to a nation of urban workers and employees. Industrial technological innovation was dramatically increasing economic productivity. A growing system of mass production, distribution, and consumption was absorbing and transforming small-scale traditional economic life. Railroads linked urban centers, providing businesses with expanding markets for their products. While capitalist industrial growth produced more goods and services, mergers and buyouts among firms produced large and powerful economic corporations that attempted monopolistic control of producer markets such as steel, machinery, oil, and railroads as well as consumer markets such as food processing, leather goods, sugar, and rubber boots and gloves (Bernhard et al., 1991: 518–519). By the 1890s, the Carnegies exercised virtual control of the American steel industry (U.S. Steel), while the Rockefellers did the same for petroleum products (Standard Oil Company).

In short, the dual economy that we discussed in Chapter 3 was emerging. Wealthy classes who owned and controlled large firms often had lifestyles involving such ostentatious displays of new wealth that Mark Twain satirically described the decade of the 1890s as the "Gilded Age." The names of the families who built such firms are familiar to us still; the Rockefellers in oil, the Carnegies in steel, the DuPonts in chemicals, and the Morgans and Mellons in banking and finance. At the same time, wages and material standards of average families also rose significantly between 1860 and 1900. Immigrants seeking opportunity flooded into American port cities, satisfying the demand for labor, but also creating suspicion by their "un-American" behavior and culture and by their willingness to work for wages lower than "real" Americans would accept.

In this period of general economic expansion there were increasingly severe recessions and business slumps (in 1873–1879, 1884–1886, and 1893–1897). Translated into the lives of ordinary families and individuals, these economic boom-and-bust cycles meant a succession of finding opportunity, often losing it, uprooting, and moving. And through this period of disruptive progress and change, the symbols of American culture and identity, rooted in the rural images of the American way of life, were called into question by urbanization, industrialization, and immigration. Late-nineteenth century government, which in retrospect seems permeated with corruption, was supportive of the interests of the industrialists but otherwise was unable or unwilling to address the problems caused by these profound processes of economic and social transformation. Two things are important for you to understand about the kinds of social reform movements that emerged at the turn of the last century. *First,* a sizable minority of workers and many farmers bore the burdens and became the victims of change. *Second,* in spite of generally rising living standards, there was pervasive concern about the social problems connected with industrial capitalist expansion and political corruption of the era.

SOCIAL CLASS AND REFORM MOVEMENTS
AT THE TURN OF THE TWENTIETH CENTURY

Important reform movements were rooted in conflicts and grievances related to social class. By *social class* we are here talking about people who share certain economic positions, interests, and problems. Three important class-based movements were related to the interests and problems of farmers (the agrarian populist movement), workers (the labor movement), and educated professionals and intellectuals (the Progressive movement).

Agrarian Populism

Paralleling industrial growth, agricultural productivity grew enormously in the late nineteenth century. With agriculture increasingly mechanized and efficient, the growing availability of every form of food and fiber supported consumers in the mushrooming cities. But farming and ranching remained a precarious enterprise because of uncertainties in the weather and yearly market price fluctuations. Bad weather and a scanty crop could be ruinous, but an abundant harvest driving prices down could be almost as bad. Added to these perennial uncertainties, railroad transportation costs and bank loans (for land, seed, and equipment) often upset the delicate balance between farm income and expenses. And eastern moneylenders were notorious for charging high interest rates and demanding high collateral. Growing economic productivity in the late nineteenth century made everything slowly cheaper (and profit rates more precarious), but the value of agricultural goods dropped more drastically than that of other goods. Between the 1870s and 1890s, for example, the market price of wheat and cotton (the mainstays of midwestern and southern farmers) dropped by 50 percent (Bernhard et al., 1991: 582).

Hard times on the farm produced a widespread rural protest movement the closing decades of the nineteenth century. In the Midwest this protest took shape around state-level social movement organizations called the Patrons of Husbandry, or more popularly, the Grange. The targets of this protest were the banks, railroads, and merchants who sold implements and all the middlemen who stood between the farmers and urban consumers. Granger political parties were organized in eleven states and in the 1870s controlled state legislatures in Illinois, Wisconsin, Iowa, and Minnesota. Granger legislation tried to reduce middleman prices by regulating the price of rail transportation and the price of grain elevator storage of crops, regulations that the Supreme Court shortly ruled unconstitutional.

By the 1880s, state Grange organizations were diminishing as a political force, but popular farm alliances sprouted in the Southeast, Texas, and the Northwest. The master ideological frame of this protest movement

> depicted the nation as divided into the wicked and the good. The children of light were the "producers," especially the tillers of the soil. The children of darkness

were those who produced nothing, but grew fat as parasites on farmers and laborers. Most prominent were the financiers who conspired to reduce the money
supply of the nation (. . . by insisting on gold backed dollars . . .) in order to
push up the value of the dollars they lent to others. (Bernhard et al., 1991:583)

Farm alliance leaders tried to forge alliances with labor movement organizations in
1889, and a coalition of regional farm alliances created the People's Party, or Populists, as they became known. In 1890 the Populists met in Omaha to select candidates for the 1892 election. In one of the most colorful and raucous political
gatherings in the nation's history, delegates adopted a platform that summed up the
outlook of agrarian dissent: They advocated free and unlimited coinage of silver, a
graduated income tax, government ownership of the railroads and the telephone and
telegraph system, the secret ballot, direct election of U.S. senators, and restraints on
immigration. Attempting to gain support from urban workers, they passed resolutions supporting reduced working hours.

While the Populists made the strongest third party showing in American history, the 1892 election was still a disaster: They won 1 million of 17 million votes
cast. They carried majorities in Idaho, Nevada, and Colorado (the center of the silver
mining industry) and made strong showings only in the wheat and beef states of the
Dakotas, Kansas, and Nebraska. Populist attempts to win black voters damaged their
efforts in the South, which remained strongly Democratic (the party that then recognized the dominance of southern whites). The attempted alliance with urban workers,
who had little interest in policies that would raise the price of food, failed utterly. And
the specialty farmers of the Northeast and the Midwest cornbelt saw little to gain in
addressing the plight of the Plains states' grain and western states' silver interests.

Rural hard times continued, but the farm revolt fizzled, never again gaining serious political momentum. But the plight of farmers was placed on the national
agenda as a set of problems subsequently addressed by both the Republican and Democratic parties, and some of the populist goals were eventually realized (elimination of the gold standard, progressive taxation, government regulation of interest
rates and rail transportation, and agricultural price subsidies).

The Labor Movement

For similar reasons a revolt was brewing among urban workers. Whatever the
overall economic achievements of Gilded Age capitalism, its workers lived and
worked under horrid conditions. By 1900, the toilers in factories, mines, and sweatshops represented more that 35 percent of the total labor force. They worked, that is,
only in good times, for the periodic business slumps that plagued the turn of the century routinely threw 18 percent of the labor force out of work. But life for working-
class families was hard and precarious in the best of times. In 1900 workers toiled an
average of 60 hours a week for wages less than $2 a day. One in four women had
jobs, as did over 2 million children, few of which attended school. Men, women, and
children worked amid the smoke, flame, and the din of furnaces and exposed machinery. They were routinely killed or maimed by boiler explosions, mine cave-ins,

or train wrecks, and few collected any form of compensation. Nor was there any recognition of, or compensation for, any of the slower forms of industrial death that we would today recognize as black lung disease among miners or the various forms of industrial poisoning. Tuberculosis, the joint product of crowding, overwork, filth, and poor nutrition, reached epidemic proportions among the working class. The United States came to have the highest industrial accident rate the world; in 1917 alone, 11,000 workers were killed by their jobs, and 1.4 million were injured (Bernhard et al., 1991:573, 634).

In the closing decades of the nineteenth century, labor protest emerged as strikes and often violent confrontations between workers and their employers. Beginning as violent encounters during the 1860s in the anthracite coal mines of Pennsylvania, they returned in the 1870s and 1880s as a broad wave of violent strikes in the steel mills and factories in the industrial Northeast and Upper Midwest. During the strike against the McCormick farm implement company in Chicago in 1886, someone threw a bomb at a rally in Haymarket Square that killed one policemen and injured seventy others. Such incidents angered industrialists and frightened a broad spectrum of the middle classes. They helped trigger a popular wave of antilabor sentiment. Public officials gave wide latitude to company thugs and hired guns to suppress and disrupt strikes labor protest, and they often called in the state militia to do the same. In truth, working people were as often the victims of violence as its perpetrators.

While such labor protest was often spontaneous, labor movement organizations emerged to give coherence and direction to the workers protest movement. The largest of these, the Knights of Labor, open to all workers of whatever kind, had 700,000 members by the 1880s. It focused on political reform rather than strikes and collective bargaining. The Knights agitated for a mandated eight-hour work day, graduated income tax, consumer and producer cooperatives, and federal government arbitration of labor disputes. While not advocating strikes, they supported workers in the disputes mentioned earlier. The Knights declined precipitously in wave of antiunionism following the Haymarket Square bombing incident.

The Knights were eclipsed by the American Federation of Labor, founded in 1886 to organize skilled workers and craftsmen who were increasingly threatened by the mechanization of production. Under the leadership of Samuel Gompers, the AF of L concluded that capitalism was here to stay. Avoiding involvement in broad political reforms, the AF of L focused on narrow workplace issues such as wages and benefits. Partly because of this nonthreatening political agenda and partly because of Gompers' tireless efforts to portray the union as a peaceful and "respectable" potential "partner" in the industrial capitalist enterprise, the AF of L was successful at organizing highly skilled, largely native-born workers. It had 250,000 members in 1897 and over 1.6 million by 1904 (Bernhard et al., 1991:646).

By 1905, unskilled workers were again being organized as one big union by the International Workers of the World. The IWW (or "Wobblies," as they were called) supported collective bargaining and strikes and advocated a radical transformation from capitalism to syndicalism—in which workers would own and cooperatively control industries without interference from either the state or political parties. They did not seek the support of politicians, whom they distrusted as too willing to collaborate with capitalists (Dubofsky, 1975:101–106). In spite of potentially large number of unskilled workers to be organized, the IWW was not very successful, probably never having more than 100,000 members. Still, they had enough successes in making significant gains for workers in some industries (lumber, mining, textiles) to be threatening to industrial leaders. Their syndicalist goals, confrontational tactics, and successes in organizing threatening categories of workers (African Americans and immigrants) made it easy for their opponents to frame them as representing a dangerous rising tide of subversion and immigrant-fueled radicalism, anarchism, and communism. "These successes, plus their opposition to World War I, led the government to allow companies and vigilante groups a free hand in eliminating the local organizers by any means necessary. By 1917, after a raid on IWW headquarters, 200 top officials were indicted for espionage and sedition. The union declined as its energies and funds were expended in legal battles" (Ford, 1988:208). In all, over 2000 Wobblies, socialists, and pacifists became trapped in a powerful World War I era witch hunt that transformed dissent into subversion (Goldberg, 1991:61).

In spite of the defeat of the politically oriented unions, the labor movement made small and slow gains in establishing its public legitimacy and its fights to mobilize and to bargain with employers. To illustrate, consider the unprecedented action by a Republican president (Theodore Roosevelt) in 1902, who not only refused to send federal troops to break up a strike, but threatened to send the army to take over mines if the owners refused to arbitrate with representatives of the mineworkers' union. And while the National Association of Manufacturers was founded in 1895 to resist all unionization, many industrialists (including steel baron Andrew Carnegie) found reasons to support the more conservative and limited trade unionism of the AF of L. Slowly the union movement came to be an important source of support for the Democratic Party, and after his election in 1913 Democratic President Wilson rewarded labor by establishing the federal Department of Labor and by sponsoring the Clayton Antitrust Act. This act, hailed by the AF of L as labor's Magna Carta, replaced previous antitrust legislation, which, though designed to oppose industrial monopolies ("combinations in restraint of trade"), had been judicially redefined to become a favorite legal tool to oppose unions. It was still true, however, that the predominant force of government action and public opinion was antiunion. But by the 1920s unions were larger, more prosperous, more bureaucratic, and less democratic at the national level. In 1920, they represented 12 percent of all employed persons (Ford, 1988:210–212).

The 1930s presented a greatly expanded opportunity structure for union growth and impact. With almost a third of the labor force unemployed, the *Great Depression* caused more people to question the virtues of laissez-faire capitalism, and both public opinion and the federal government became more supportive of the labor movement. The movement again tried to organize unskilled industrial workers, now spearheaded by a breakaway faction of the AF of L, the Congress of Industrial Organizations. Headed by John L. Lewis of the United Mineworkers, they had great success in organizing industrial unions in the automobile, rubber, and steel industries, in which the AF of L had never done well (Ford, 1988:214, 215). Newly powerful mass unions quickly became an essential element of the Democratic New Deal coalition of President Franklin Roosevelt. While its primary aim was economic recovery, the New Deal programs addressed many of the demands of workers, established their absolute right to organize, and mandated federal arbitration of labor disputes. The explosive confrontations between workers and their employers of the previous decades gradually gave way to regulated negotiation. Union growth continued through and after World War II, and it peaked in the 1960s, when 31.5 percent of the American labor force was unionized. American workers had come to have one of the world's highest standards of living.

The Progressive Movement

For all the prosperity of the years between 1897 and 1917, Americans experienced a puzzling inflation. Industries produced more, but Americans found themselves struggling to stretch their dollars to buy the same amount of goods they had bought a year earlier. Few understood the phenomenon, but urban middle classes, perhaps the hardest hit, blamed the large trusts and monopolies. President Wilson said, for instance, "The high cost of living is arranged by private understanding." Others blamed organized labor for wage gains that pushed up the costs of living (Bernhard et al., 1991:640). The emerging new middle class, like the working class, was a creation of industrial capitalism; it included new bureaucratic, salaried clerical and sales workers, professionals, technicians, and government workers as well as scientists and academicians. As salaried workers, they were particularly ravaged by inflation and felt squeezed between big business and big labor. Articulating this sentiment, novelist William Dean Howells wrote that "the American struggle for life has changed from a free fight to an encounter of disciplined forces, and the free fighters that are left get ground to pieces between organized labor and organized capital" (cited in Berhnard et al., 1991:648).

At the turn of the century, a broad reform effort, the *Progressive movement,* was taking shape to address the grievances and aspirations of this emerging new middle class. Small businessmen worried about the large monopolies that controlled their supplies, fretted over railroad rates, feared unions, and distrusted—for good reason—the creaky national banking system dominated by large private banks. Independent professionals—lawyers, doctors, ministers—saw their independence and privilege erode in a world increasingly dominated by the barons of industry. Doctors worried about quacks armed with "snake oil" and competition from midwives and other folk medicine practitioners. The work and professional activities of a significant segment of the new middle class, such as social workers, teachers, government scientists, public officials, journalists, and academicians, brought them in close contact with the problems of poverty, sickness, and exploitation and with the plights of workers, farmers, and immigrants (Bernhard et al., 1991:640).

The Progressive movement spawned by these grievances became a broad attack against unregulated monopoly capitalism, widespread political corruption, and the social problems created by their interaction. While centered on the needs and aspirations of the emerging new middle classes, it developed a broad social vision of social reform that at first glance seems less clearly tied to class interests than reforms proposed by the agrarian reformers or unionists. Broadly, this agenda included trying to reconcile the American values of individualism and freedom with the emergence of a large-scale complex society that required different forms of collective action. The specific ideas of particular leaders were so diverse and the term *progressive* so overused that some historians have despaired of giving it any specific meaning, other than as a synonym for "good" or "modern."

But that's not really fair, for there was a master ideological frame for progressivism within which specific and often contradictory reform ideas took shape. They believed that they were on the cusp of a new era, but more important was the belief that the good society would not be brought about through passive evolution but by active human intervention. Journalist-philosopher Walter Lippmann argued that Americans needed to substitute "mastery" for "drift" in controlling the pace and direction of change:

> We can no longer treat life as something that has trickled down to us. We have to deal with it deliberately, devise its social organization, alter its tools, formulate its method, educate and control it. In endless ways we put intention where custom has reigned. We break up routines, make decisions, choose our ends, select means. (cited in Bernhard et al., 1991:667)

Although they disagreed about specifics, the Progressives sought nothing less that the rational and scientific restructuring of society. Although suspicious of corporate greed and corruption, they were much impressed by the growing achievements of corporate organizational and scientific managerial triumphs and sought to extend them to public life.

While there were Progressive movement organizations (the National Reform League), the Progressive movement was much less tied to particular organizations than was the labor movement. It depended more on a large and diffuse network of intellectuals and journalists who were the claims makers and activists of the movement. They used the growing arsenals of thought in universities, particularly in philosophy, social sciences, and management. At the core was an intellectual brain trust, many of whom were academics, such as John Dewey (philosophy and education) John R. Commons (economics), William James (psychology), E. A. Ross and Robert E. Park (sociology), and Roscoe Pound (law). Attached to these thinkers were "muckraking" journalists and writers of the day, such as Lincoln Steffans, Ida Tarbell, and Upton Sinclair, who widely publicized the evils and corruption of the period. Added to this list were reformers themselves, including Robert M. LaFollette (senator and governor of Wisconsin), Jane Addams (social worker and founder of settlement houses) and labor leaders such as John A. Mitchell.

Both Republicans (Theodore Roosevelt) and Democrats (Woodrow Wilson) claimed to be Progressives. And both created political opportunity for the movement (in exchange for political support). Progressives all believed that the conscience of people and the skills of experts could fuse into rational public policy. They sought to alleviate the suffering of the poor, assimilate immigrants, safeguard the health and lives of workers, regulate commerce, protect consumers, and preserve opportunity. Many argued that America had a role to play in shaping the "progressive character" of other nations as well (Bernhard et al., 1991:640).

The development of Progressive reforms followed the structure of the American system. Local urban progressives sought to overthrow corrupt partisan political machines. They substituted their rule with nonpartisan bureaucratic managers and experts who would extend the range of public services, such as garbage collection, utilities, parks, and housing regulations. At the state level many states emulated the "Wisconsin idea" adopted under Governor LaFollette. They instituted direct primary elections, antilobbying laws, civil service systems, and state regulation of utilities, railroads, banking, and telecommunications as well much higher corporate taxes. Wisconsin, a virtual laboratory of progessivism, became the first state to pass a graduated income tax. Because of increasing national interdependence, Progressives established federal agencies such as the Pure Food and Drug Administration to regulate the productions of foodstuffs and medicines and the Interstate Commerce and Banking commissions. This new spirit of state and federal activism, promoted by leaders like LaFollette and Presidents Roosevelt and Wilson, worked against the venerable American traditions of limited government by invigorating and expanding the scope of government at all levels.

With such broad goals, you may be wondering how this is a class-based movement, as we argue. The answer is simple and has two parts. *First,* though more of an elite movement than the agrarian populists or the labor organizers, a significant base of popular support was located in the emerging new middle classes of salaried bureaucrats, professionals, and intellectuals. *Second,* and more to the point, if a common theme of the Progressives was the increasing regulation of society by experts, where do you think such experts come from? Why, of course, from the new middle class itself. Progressivism represented an attempt to revise the equation of power groups in American society by increasing the power of the new "expert" professionals relative to the more traditional power blocs such as workers, farmers, industrialists, and political party machines.

The Impacts of Turn-of-the-Century Movements

Now we come to the important question: What kinds of changes did these three class-based movements accomplish? The agrarian populist, labor, and Progressive movements were the culmination of a series of responses to the problems associated with industrialism and urbanization reaching back a half a century. But they also marked the beginning of a twentieth-century age of reform that led to the New Deal in the 1930s and the Great Society reforms of the 1960s (Bernhard et al., 1991:669). Interacting with broad trends of industrial growth and urbanization, these movements gave shape to the future outlines of the American political economy and the distinctive American form of welfare state capitalism. They established, in principle and practice, greatly expanded governments to regulate, tax, and limit the operation of the freewheeling capitalist enterprises of the late nineteenth century.

Compared to the passive presidents of the late nineteenth century, these movements provided popular sanction for the "imperial presidencies" of Theodore Roosevelt, Woodrow Wilson, and Franklin D. Roosevelt that greatly expanded executive powers. Wresting some power from the political parties and machines, they legitimized an expansion of power for bureaucratic experts who got their positions through competitive civil service exams rather than political patronage. Expansive governments became more efficient and less corrupt, but, as parties began to lose control, they also became relatively less democratic. As we noted in Chapter 4, this process continues into the present.

Some of these reforms were directed at stabilizing industrial capitalism from the hardships of the increasingly severe boom-and-bust business cycles that were become increasingly pronounced. Others tried to end the monopolistic and anticompetitive control of trusts in industry and banking that had resulted in vast corruption and concentration of wealth. The creation of regulatory commissions, such as the Federal Reserve System (which established a measure of federal control over banking practices) and the Interstate Commerce Commission, attempted to deal with these issues. These programs foreshadowed Depression Era New Deal programs, which, through a vast array of programs, attempted to jump-start the economy through Keynesian policies of government investment and public employment.

Other reforms addressed the particular constituencies of the agrarian and labor movements. The Department of Agriculture as well as the vast network of state level agricultural extension programs facilitated the diffusion of agricultural technology and farm price supports for agricultural goods. Other agencies and bureaus regulated occupational safety and working conditions and provided government supervision and mandatory arbitration of labor disputes. The Pure Food and Drug Administration, as well as other agencies, provided for consumer protection in the inspection, regulation, and licensing of pharmaceuticals and foodstuffs. In principle, it gradually became accepted that governments should provide a measure of relief for the poor, the unemployed, and the indigent, but actual programs to do that were not established until the 1930s Depression programs, such as Social Security and the federally sponsored public assistance and unemployment compensation programs.

There is some interesting evidence from empirical studies about the impact of unionization on economic functioning itself. In highly unionized industries, workers have been found to be more efficient (through better training and less turnover) and—with many exceptions—more productive than their nonunion counterparts. Profits in unionized oligopolies are lower, but not by much, and it is likely that unionization reduces employment over time by encouraging capital substitution (new technology and other improvements). These findings run directly counter to the widespread notion that unions lower productivity and promote laziness and featherbedding. Within union companies there is less wage inequality between various categories of workers (for example, between skilled and unskilled) and particularly between blue-collar and white-collar occupations. Unionized companies provide much better fringe benefit packages of deferred wages for pensions, life, accident, and health insurance (see Freeman and Medoff, 1984, for a summary of evidence related to these issues). Analysts are concerned that the union movement is unable to adapt to the digital, nonhierarchical workplace with contingent workers, fast-moving capital, and globalized production and distributions networks (see Freeman, 1997; Edwards, 1993; Leicht, 1998).

In addition, unions contributed to workplace democracy by giving workers some representation, but they have historically worked against the access of minorities to the economic mainstream. They have, however, been powerful supporters of a broad range of social legislation in, for example, civil rights, health and safety, and environmental matters. The *main point* for you to understand in all this is that these three movements, in conjunction with sympathetic political elites, provided the popular power to reshape the emerging American system.

Still, it is important to note the limits of changes wrought by these turn-of-the-century reform movements. Their efforts were always constrained by powerful opposition from segments of the business community and by conservative segments of the middle and upper classes. There was always the possibility that reforms would be taken back or subverted over time. Many federal and state regulatory agencies, for instance, came at times to serve the interests of the industries they were supposed to regulate more than the public interest. In spite of programs for farmers, for example, "hard times on the farm" proved to be a perennial weed that refused to go away, while the Department of Agriculture came to support large corporate farms and the agribusiness industry more effectively than small and medium-sized family farms. Complete monopolization by the industry trusts was broken, but economic concentration by oligopolistic firms in the dual economy proceeded apace.

It was true that by the post–World War II period American unionized workers had one of the world's highest standards of living and fringe benefits that were the envy of workers in other nations. But union membership was twice as common in European industrial economies, whose citizens came by the 1950s to have much more extensive coverage by welfare state programs (unemployment compensation, job retraining, and educational, health, and retirement benefits).

In short, in America these reforms stabilized and regulated the system and addressed the needs of the most abused classes. But they did so in ways that never offered a *fundamental* challenge to the existing system of individualism, private wealth, and privilege. But the actions of radical populists and the labor movement need to be explained in terms of the prevailing political opportunity structure that aligned powerful interest groups against radical change in American society, even in the face of serious social and cultural upheavals like depressions. We have noted the suppression of radical populism and labor unions (along with a marginal socialist movement). The successes of moderate labor and centrist middle-class Progressives meant that American would never develop a powerful political party of the left to thoroughly represent the interests of workers and the lower classes, as did the social democratic and labor parties in Europe. What emerged, in short, was a weak American version of welfare state capitalism, when compared with what emerged from reform movements in Western European societies in the postwar years.

SOCIAL STATUS AND REFORM MOVEMENTS
AT MID-TWENTIETH CENTURY

We have argued that the most important reform movements in the first half of the twentieth century addressed grievances related to social class. Class position, as we previously defined it, is rooted in the power that various parts of the population have to control the production and distribution of wealth. Beginning with Max Weber, sociologists have distinguished class position from another basis of social inequality, *status position*. In contrast to social class, social status is rooted in the varying degrees of social honor, power, and prestige that people have because of noneconomic social characteristics such as race, gender, culture, or national origin. Social status is not only based on a broader set of factors than social class, but people are more likely to be consciously aware of their affiliation with status groups than their class position. The social reform movements we discussed earlier addressed the class interests of farmers, workers, and the new middle classes. But they left unaddressed the grievances of many others whose problems were not rooted in social class, but rather in social status. Reform movements based on social status grievances were certainly not absent in earlier times (for example, nineteenth-century feminism, nativism, or the prohibition movements), but neither were they the sources of the dominant reform efforts of the day. But after World War II, status-based reform movements exploded with a particular fury and pervasiveness.

Status Equality Revolts after World War II

The mid-1960s witnessed a vast upsurge of protest movements whose claims impacted the lives of most Americans and received the attentions of the media, political leaders, and the courts. Writing in the middle of the ferment of the 1960s, sociologist Herbert Gans perceptively grasped the underlying meaning of these movements:

> Someday, when future historians write the history of the 1960s, they may describe it as the decade when America rediscovered poverty still in its midst and when social protest, ranging from demonstrations to violent uprisings, reappeared on the American scene. But these historians may also note a curious fact, that the social protest had very little to do with poverty. . . . The social protest that began in the 1960s had to do with inequality. So far the demand for greater equality has come largely from the young, from the black, and from women, but other groups have asked for more autonomy or control over their own lives, for more liberty and democracy. . . . In the years to come, I believe America will face more such demands from many other people, which will be widespread enough that they might be described as an "equality revolution." (1974:7–8)

Mid-century "equality revolts" emerged among those who were socially marginalized not primarily for reasons having to do with the economic deprivations of class. They were rather related to status grievances among minorities, the young, women, and later among gays and those stigmatized because of handicaps. To be sure, those stigmatized because of status characteristics had economic complaints, but the main thrust of the equality revolts was aimed tearing down the status barriers to full social participation. They aimed at improving what British sociologist I. H. Marshall called the "social element" of citizenship, including the whole range of rights, from the right "to a modicum of economic welfare and security to the right to share to the fullest in the social heritage and to live the life of a civilized being according to the standards prevailing in the society" (1964:71–72).

The Civil Rights Movement.   Organized by African Americans, the civil rights movement was the centerpiece of these status-equality revolts. It provided for subsequent movements among other status groups the basic ideological master frame (social discrimination and the drive for civil rights) as well as protest strategies (nonviolent direct action—a social movement strategy to which we will return in Chapter 11).

Social movements organized by African Americans were certainly not new in America. Even before the Civil War, periodic slave revolts rocked the South (One of the most spectacular was led by Nat Turner in 1831). The National Association for the Advancement of Colored People (NAACP), inspired by black sociologist-reformer W. E. B. DuBois, was founded by middle-class African Americans and their white Progressive allies in 1910, and the Urban League was founded during the 1920s to represent the interests of African-American migrants to the cities of the North. But such *movement organizations* had limited impact because they did not become truly mass-based movements, even among African Americans, nor did they engage the attention of white Americans, the media, or the political establishment as did the civil rights movement of the late 1950s.

The war years and subsequent good times produced economic gains among African Americans and also the emergence of a larger black middle class, more self-assured and aggressive than its prewar predecessor. Yet there was continuing awareness of the yawning gaps between the social lives of white and black Americans. Black family income was on average, as late as 1960, only 50 percent of white family income (Goldberg, 1991:143). In spite of, or perhaps because of improvements in their economic, educational, and political lives, African Americans were more unequivocally committed to the cause of improvement of their status and integration into the mainstream of American life (Bernhard et al., 1991:862).

Historic movement organizations, such as the NAACP, which had successfully challenged educational segregation in 1954 (*Brown v. Board of Education, Topeka*) tried to capitalize on growing African-American grassroots discontent, but their legalistic tactics and middle-class composition made it difficult (Goldberg, 1991:143). The movement organization that most successfully engineered and channeled the mass mobilization of the civil rights movement was Martin Luther King, Jr.'s newly formed Southern Christian Leadership Conference (SCLC). The SCLC, rooted in the black churches, was a federation of organizations rather than membership body. Through King's charismatic leadership, the SCLC encouraged local groups to reach those outside the protest community. The significance of the black churches in the mobilization of African-American protest cannot be underestimated. Ministers trained as organizational managers and public speakers were critical figures who had direct and privileged access to the black masses. The shared ideology, language, and symbols of Christianity sanctioned rebellion in the cause of justice by nonviolent direct action.

In 1955, the first massive direct action in the civil rights movement came in Montgomery, Alabama, where under SCLC leadership blacks boycotted the city's bus system, which required them to ride at the back of the busses. After months of unrelenting struggle the boycotters won, and soon thousands of people were being mobilized into struggles across the South about school integration (in Little Rock, Arkansas in 1957), public accommodation sit-ins (in North Carolina and Georgia in 1960), busloads of "freedom riders," and education and voter registration drives (in Mississippi in 1961). These latter crusades were organized by the student affiliate of SCLC, the Student Nonviolent Coordinating Committee (SNCC), and included not only African-American college students but also many northern white liberal supporters. Southern whites countermobilized, reviving not only the infamous Ku Klux Klan but also newly minted White Citizens Councils that had 250,000 members by 1957 (Goldberg, 1991:146). The penultimate engagement between civil rights demonstrators and southern whites came in Montgomery, Alabama in 1963, when local sheriffs attacked peaceful demonstrators with fire hoses, police dogs, and cattle prods. There was also the bombing of a black church on a Sunday morning, killing four young girls. These events were vividly portrayed on national network TV, and the majority of Americans were morally outraged.

The Kennedy administration, previously supportive of the movement but reluctant to do anything that would lose them the support of southern whites, now responded swiftly. President Kennedy requested a partial ban on discrimination in public places, asked that the Justice Department be given powers to sue for school desegregation upon request, and urged broader powers to withhold funds from federally assisted programs where discrimination occurred. Congressional civil rights leaders pushed Kennedy farther, persuading him to give the Attorney General power to intervene in all civil rights cases (Bernhard et al., 1991:872). A comprehensive Civil Rights Act was passed by Congress in 1964.

In spite of these measures, the civil rights movement spread like wildfire from the South to cities in the North and across the nation. No longer in control of the SCLC's disciplined nonviolent tactics, the movement grew in power but splintered into different movement organizations with different strategies. The summers of 1965 through 1968 witnessed the most extensive urban riots in America's history as the oppression of African Americans since the abolition of slavery took its violent revenge. But President Johnson's War on Poverty and the ghetto revolts burned into American political conscience a conviction that African Americans and organized minorities had to be accommodated in the American scheme of things—in part to preserve the social order and in part to resolve the moral dilemmas posed by the challenge. Political and economic elites, when challenged and moved to protect their own positions, were the first to understand this. African Americans won, in principle if not always in fact, recognition of their rights (Walton, 1990:200). An important feature of the African-American civil rights movement is that *it provided inspiration, a model, and the master ideological frame for movements among other status groups.*

The New Left and Countercultural Student Movements.   These movement organizations were most directly stimulated by civil rights protest. Student activist groups were organizing in the early 1960s at major American universities. Middle-class liberal college students, moved by the moral claims of African Americans, streamed to the South to participate in the summer "freedom rides" to aid the civil rights movement. Upon returning to campuses in the fall, they began organizing on college campuses. In 1964, when the University of California (Berkeley) attempted to ban such organizing, political speech, and fundraising on campus, the militant Free Speech movement erupted, with prolonged demonstrations, sit-ins, and negotiation with the administration—about freedom of speech and political action, but ultimately about a wide variety of other student concerns as well. *Newsweek* magazine aptly termed the Berkeley struggle as the "Concord Bridge of the American Student Rebellion" (cited in Goldberg, 1991:168).

As the Baby Boom generation flooded undergraduate enrollments, the student revolt spread like a prairie fire. The rights frame of the civil rights movement became transmuted into concerns about student rights. Campuses, especially the large, impersonal "multiversities" like Berkeley and Columbia, were declared to be oppressive to students. Instead of providing an intimate education, the multiversity was accused of having very large classes with professors who were indifferent to students' needs and more concerned with their own research (Wood and Jackson, 1982:19). Students challenged the traditional *in loco parentis* doctrines by which universities assumed the right to control students' social as well as academic behavior. Students fought not only for their own rights, but in solidarity with struggles among African Americans and the oppressed in Third World nations. But the issue that drew masses of students into the movement was America's increasing involvement in the Vietnam War.

In the midst of a war that most Americans (not just students) were uncertain about anyway, President Johnson instructed the Selective Service System to begin drafting college students, a move that created increased agitation against the war. For a time in the mid-1960s, the student movement became the prime source of antidraft and antiwar agitation. We should note that antiwar protests movements are not new in American history. Every American war since the antidraft riots connected with the Civil War has generated significant antiwar and antidraft protests, but none of these earlier movements had the broad popular sanction or the power of the Vietnam antiwar movement.

But it would be a mistake to characterize the student movement as purely and simply an antiwar protest movement. The Students for a Democratic Society (SDS), probably the most influential student movement organization, articulated a *New Left* ideology that was a broad critique of American society: It condemned capitalism, racism, undemocratic power structures, and American neoimperialism in the Third World (Wood, 1975:20–45). This New Left student movement distanced itself from the older American socialist and communist parties and envisioned an America that was antihierarchical, cooperative, decentralized, and governed by norms of partici-patory democracy.

Still another wing of the student movement was more expressive than instru-mental, engaging students in more cultural than political protest. Student hippies of the day, the decade's reconstruction of the perennial American Bohemian culture, put together a vast but diffuse "countercultural" protest movement. Florid clothing, long hair, beads, bell-bottom jeans, communal living, and recreational use of psychedelic drugs and marijuana became the countercultural symbols of revolt. The movement encouraged young adults to drop out of conventional social pursuits and tune in to a heady mixture of hedonism, unconventional spirituality, and antimaterialism—all of which challenged established cultural norms and authority patterns.

Student protest flourished briefly in the late 1960s but had disappeared by the mid-1970s. The Vietnam War was over, student leftists had utterly failed to transform society in accordance with their vision, and communal living failures and bad drug trips had deflated the hippy mystique. What did the student rebellion accomplish?

Probably the most obvious consequence was to push American policy and pub-lic opinion to end the Vietnam War, and the student movement also had a role in con-vincing a sitting president (Lyndon Johnson) not to run for reelection. On campuses, both the curriculum and faculty interest was transformed in ways that took more ac-count of the needs of students than before. Student life brought much greater auton-omy in living conditions than in the 1950s. It is likely that the student movement was a powerful force in the loosening of cultural traditions we discussed in Chapter 2 (the increasing emphasis on self-development, growing multiculturalism, and the will-ingness to experiment with and tolerate alternative life styles). And it is not acciden-tal that the large Baby Boom cohort that spawned hippiedom is the same one that gave shape to New Age religious and spiritual movements of the 1990s. Nor is it ac-cidental, we think, that the student cohort of the antiwar movement became, in their late thirties and early forties, environmental activists and the popular base of later an-timilitary protest movements. These included protest against American military in-volvement in El Salvador and Nicaragua. Another protest movement was the Nuclear Freeze campaign, which developed with brief but dramatic power in the mid-1980s.

The Feminist Movement.   The feminist movement was another status move-ment rejuvenated by the civil rights campaign, and one that had a much longer life and more pervasive impact than the student movement. Like the movement among African Americans, movements for the rights of women were certainly not new. As far back as 1848 there were women's rights organizations, and nineteenth-century feminist agitation finally resulted in the right for women to vote in 1920. But the fem-inist movement demobilized and was little heard from during the depression and World War II years. Like African Americans, women made dramatic gains during the World War II years in education and occupational achievement. Like African Amer-icans, they were largely booted out of the labor force upon the return of white males from the war. Opinion leaders and experts of the day admonished women to find

happiness in the traditional pleasures of femininity, domesticity, and motherhood. Women were told

> how to catch a man and keep him, how to breastfeed children and handle their toilet training, how to cope with . . . adolescent rebellion; how to buy a dishwasher, bake bread, cook gourmet snails . . . how to dress, look, and act more feminine and make marriage more exciting; how to keep their husbands from dying young and their sons from growing into delinquents. They were taught to pity the neurotic, unfeminine women who wanted to be poets or physicists or presidents. They learned that truly feminine women do not want careers, higher education, political rights—the independence and opportunities that the old-fashioned feminists fought for. . . . All they had to do was devote their lives from earliest girlhood to finding a husband and bearing children. (Friedan, 1963:15–16).

This quote from *The Feminine Mystique,* the bestseller that was to become the ideological frame for the reinvigorated women's movement, argued that "in the fifteen years after World War II this mystique of feminine fulfillment became the cherished and self-perpetuating core of contemporary American culture" (1963:18).

But there were broader causes for the reemergence of feminist protest. Most of the organizers of the feminist movement in the 1960s had prior experience in other social justice and rights movements, specifically the civil rights and student movements. Both because it was easy to apply the rights frame articulated by these movements to the circumstances of women and because women activists in these movements were treated in patronizing ways by the (male) leaders of these movements, women began organizing on their own behalf. The National Organization for Women (NOW), the National Women's Political Caucus, and the Women's Equity Action League were founded in the early 1960s. Initially these were founded by older professional women to agitate for equity in the area of occupational and political opportunities of women. They engaged in interest group politics on behalf of women and were conventionally organized with boards of directors, executives, occasionally experiencing internal power struggles (Freeman, 1979). A national network of leaders emerged (including Betty Friedan, Kate Millet, Germaine Greer, and Gloria Steinem), who were the traveling evangelists of the movement, active on lecture circuits and TV talk shows. As they responded to the efforts of African Americans, the Kennedy administration responded to feminist grievances by establishing the National Commission on the Status of Women in 1963, which was followed by the establishment of fifty state commissions. These commissions were charged with both documenting and proposing policy to ameliorate the conditions of gender inequality.

By the late 1960s, a younger cohort of female activists with experience in the 1960s movements began to create different kinds of feminist movement organizations. These were a multitude of local groups that (unlike the national organizations) deliberately tried to create organizations without hierarchies and traditional structures of authority. They were less interested in conventional political action than in

"consciousness raising" about a variety of gender-related issues that transcended the clearly defined issues of gender inequality in politics and the labor force. In some ways they were more radical than the older feminist reformers, focusing not on formal barriers to female social participation, but rather on the whole notion of gender-based roles and stereotypes, exploitative patriarchal family systems, "gendered" socialization of children, portrayal of males and females in the media and advertising, and the possibility of a "gender free" society.[1] There was much less consensus among women both inside and outside the movement about these issues. The most consensual issue that united feminists was the issue of male-female equity in occupational opportunity and wages. Older reformers had a well-organized elite network of organization with an ambiguous popular base, while the younger radicals had a large popular base of support without a national network to articulate such efforts. It is important not to make too much of this distinction, however, since it was mainly "structure and styles of action rather than ideology that more accurately differentiated these various groups, and even here there has been much borrowing on both sides" (Freeman, 1979:560).

Other Status Equality Movements. Other status-equality movements proliferated from the basic pattern of protest movements, beginning with the civil rights movement, that took shape in the 1960s. This pattern involved a master ideological frame alleging the denial of full legal rights, social participation, and economic opportunity based on status discrimination. Movement strategies that routinely accompanied these claims included (1) mobilization and recruitment of people into the movement by local and often independent consciousness-raising movement groups; (2) a network of free-floating movement leaders as intellectual claims makers and traveling evangelists; (3) regional coordination of headline grabbing actions, including economic boycotts, marches, and demonstrations; and (4) national organizations engaged in lobbying, litigation, mobilizing a voting bloc, and bargaining with national-level political leaders.

Among other status-equality movements that emerged were the Hispanic-American or Chicano movement among Mexican-American farm workers and *barrio* dwellers in the cities of the Southwest; the gay liberation movement that emerged in the 1970s to push for expanded civil rights for homosexuals; and the Native American movement, which linked the grievances of diverse and scattered tribal groups. The Native American movement was stalled in the 1970s by a military standoff between a militant faction led by Russell Means and federal marshals at the Lakota Sioux Reservation in Pine Ridge, South Dakota, a confrontation that very nearly resulted in another Pine Ridge massacre of Native Americans (the first was in the 1890s). But the Native American movement made a comeback in the 1980s through widespread gains in tribal autonomy (most visibly seen by outsiders in the establishment of gaming casinos on Native American lands) and successful litigation by various Native American groups to regain concessions granted—but routinely violated—in the old "Indian" treaties. By the 1990s, there was visible cultural revival of Native American identity and pride evidenced by the revival of Indian pow-wows and

particularly in a renaissance of Native American religion and sweat lodge ceremonies.

Reform Movements and Political Opportunity Structures.

Most of the status equality movements we have discussed have a long history of attempts to gain civil rights. That certainly was the case for African Americans, women, and Hispanic Americans. Why did they succeed in becoming reform movements with societal impact in the 1960s, and often not in earlier decades? We have already mentioned some of these factors. A *relative deprivation* explanation might point to the gradual improvement in the educational and economic status of these groups in conjunction with ongoing discrimination and marginalization based on status characteristics. A *resource mobilization* explanation would focus on the effect of postwar urbanization as amplifying the communication and critical resources that facilitated the mobilization of protest. But from the hindsight of the 1990s, we think the most powerful explanation of why these movements succeeded in the 1960s has to do with *political realignments that provided a greatly expanded political opportunity structure for movement mobilization.* How so?

The New Deal political coalition that had supported Democratic administrations since the 1930s was composed of urban workers, middle–class professionals, and rural white southerners. But the last leg of this coalition was crumbling. Urbanization meant that congressional reapportionment produced a loss of power in rural and southern districts. At the same time, voter registration drives, engineered by movement activists, enfranchised minorities, many for the first time.

> All disadvantaged status groups saw their opportunity to organize from below in this fluid situation. The Democratic Party, given its reliance on the South and working-class districts in the cities, was most shaken by these changes and moved more decisively than did the Republicans to reorganize from above. But Republicans also saw the opportunity to profit from Democratic losses and began promoting civil rights. In a relatively short time, the political scene became a competitive struggle among divided elites for the allegiance of the newly emboldened status groups. There was a democratic opening—short-lived, perhaps—that was not an opening at the top, but a huge change in the numbers of people who were allowed into the mainstream and whose right to be there was established. (Walton, 1990:207)

As the Democratic administrations of the 1960s sought new urban electoral constituencies, African Americans, women, and Mexican Americans (particularly in large swing states such as Illinois, Texas, and California) became valuable allies. In exchange for loyalty and votes, the Kennedy-Johnson administrations responded with civil rights legislation and commissions, educational expenditures, and the War on Poverty and Great Society programs (see Chapter 6 for more about these).

In a study of the protest movement among Mexican-American farmworkers, Jenkins and Perrow came to a conclusion that was true for other status movements as well, namely, that the 1960s did not differ greatly from earlier periods in the level of minority protest. "What changed was the political environment—the liberal community was willing to provide sustained, massive support for insurgency. . . . The dramatic turnabout in the political environment originated in economic trends and political realignments that took place quite independent of any 'push' from insurgents" (Jenkins and Perrow, 1977:263, 266). Saying this, we should add, does not detract from the importance of the struggles and often the courage of the organizers, but only underlines the importance of the interplay between the mobilization of movements and the political opportunity structures that allow them to succeed (Walton, 1990:203).

The fact that the status equality movements seemed to stall in the late 1970s and 1980s is explained by similar political realignments, rather than by a slackening of effort by movement activists. The slowing of economic growth in the 1970s did not support a continuation of real increases in the standard of living that the middle classes had come to expect, and blue-collar wages in particular began to erode (see Chapters 3 and 5). By the end of the decade a curious condition of *stagflation* had produced high inflation *and* high unemployment. The middle and working classes, important legs of the liberal Democratic coalition, began to experience pain, or at least relative deprivation. As Democratic administrations embraced the status-equality movements, party loyalty among southern whites continued to erode, so that by the end of the decade Republicans controlled electoral majorities in most states of the Old South. White middle- and working-class Americans had supported, or at least tolerated, programs for particular status groups, such as antidiscrimination laws, school desegregation, and affirmative action hiring programs, so long as they were prospering also. But resentment against these programs grew in the 1970s, as the government was accused of addressing the needs of minorities, women, and homosexuals while ignoring the needs of "middle" America. The Democratic Party, in particular, had a difficult time shedding the perception that they were taxing their traditional middle- and working-class base to produce an ever-increasing array of rights and entitlements for groups that middle-class constituents defined as undeserving (see Edsall and Edsall, 1996). As organized labor, working-class, and middle-class support weakened, the Democratic Party found itself with a shaky and narrow popular base.

The Conservative Movement

Conservatives moved quickly to exploit this opening, first by wresting control of the Republican Party from the moderates and liberals that had dominated it for decades (for example, Nixon, Ford, and Rockefeller), and then by mobilizing a vast conservative movement among large segments of middle- and working-class Americans.

Conservatism was not new to America as a philosophy or ideology. But before the 1980s it had been an ideology of certain political-economic elites and capitalist upper classes rather than the ideological frame of a social movement with a large popular base. Conservatives sought to preserve the status quo or at least retard change by defending individualism, free market capitalism, limited government, and cultural traditionalism in matters of community, religion, family, and sexuality.

The heart of post–World War II conservative thinking was preserved and developed by a small but influential group of *Old Right* academics, intellectuals and writers, such as Russell Kirk, Robert Nisbet, and William F. Buckley (the *National Review* was the influential conservative magazine that Buckley edited). The Old Right became a series of coalitions and compromises between intellectuals (both traditionalist and capitalist) and a small popular following of anticommunists, social conservatives, and traditionalist Catholics (Gottfried and Flemming, 1988:105).

By the end of the 1970s, an influential new group of neoconservative thinkers emerged, including many former liberal and leftist intellectuals and academicians. Unlike the Old Right, they did not reject entirely state management and the welfare state, but rather emphasized the virtues of freedom, rationality, democracy, modernism, and internationalism. Influential intellectuals and academicians such as Irving Kristol, Ben Wattenberg, Peter Berger, S. M. Lipset, Michael Novak, and Nathan Glazer created popular intellectual journals, such as *Commentary* and *Public Interest,* and wrote philosophical defenses of the American capitalist system and neoconservative policy and position papers. They had connections with conservative foundations and think tanks, such as the Heritage Foundation, the American Enterprise Institute, and the Olin Foundation, that gave them access to upper-class money and conservative political policy circles (Gottfried and Flemming, 1988:59–76).

But the Old Right and neoconservatives both constituted elite circles with a very small popular base. It remained for two other factions, the New Right and the Religious Right, to organize and mobilize a large popular constituency among nonelite segments of the population for the contemporary conservative movement. The *New Right* was formed by a series of activist conservative movement organizations, such as the Committee for the Survival of a Free Congress, founded by Paul Weyrich and Richard Viguerie, and the National Conservative Political Action Committee (NCPAC), founded by Terry Dolan. These organizations mobilized a vast base of popular support for conservative causes using new technologies of mobilization such as phone banking, computerized mailing lists, and direct mail appeals.

New Right organizations emphasized themes that were as much populist as conservative, such as resentment of the Eastern political establishment, defense of family and conventional morals, and popular control over schools and churches. New Right organizations raised money and mobilized voters for conservative causes. They supported conservative congressional candidates and orchestrated campaigns against the reelection of liberal legislators. In 1978 alone, the New Right made financial contributions to 200 conservative candidates and provided $440,000 worth of campaign services. In 1980, it reported raising $7.6 million and spending $3.3 million in trying to unseat liberal Democrats (Gottfried and Flemming, 1988:80).

Closely allied with these New Right activist organizations were *Religious Right* movement organizations, such as the Christian Voice, organized by Gary Jarmin, and most conspicuously the Moral Majority, organized by Reverend Jerry Falwell and others. Religious Right movement organizations recruited extensively from among the members of Protestant evangelical churches, especially nondenominational covenant churches, and also from among the followers of Christian televangelists. Using the same direct mail techniques as the New Right political organizations, they generated a vast popular constituency. Religious Right leaders supported economic and political conservatism, but their real interest was in social issues.

As part of a crusade to save the American family, the Religious Right opposed the feminist-sponsored Equal Rights Amendment, homosexual rights proposals, and legalized abortion. In their view, liberalized divorce laws and a general air of permissiveness had spawned a wide range of "alternative lifestyles" that resulted in spiraling rates of divorce, abortion, and adolescent suicide. They argued that the federal tax code offered massive disincentives for family life, that tax deductions for day care amounted to a subsidy for mothers who neglected their children, and that inflation eroded personal exemptions constituted an assault on traditional families burdened by the expense of rearing children on a single income. Some argued that the Social Security system was a scam for breaking up intergenerational family ties (Gottfried and Flemming, 1988:86).

By the 1980s, conservatism developed into a powerful countermovement with a large popular base well connected to conservative political elites and upper-class money. We have called it a countermovement because it was reacting to the successes of the status-equality movements of the 1960s and their inroads against the traditional bases of status privilege and power. Its popular appeal was amplified by growing economic insecurity, eroding living standards, and family pressures of the large middle classes, discussed in Chapters 3 and 4. In the 1980s, many were willing to chastise the poor and celebrate the rich. Haute couture, condominiums, yuppies, and "Beamers" (BMWs) symbolized the aspirations of the decade (but certainly not the reality for most). Large segments of the population rejected providing for the disadvantaged and expanding civic rights for all persons; they celebrated the ability of business, not government, to solve the country's problems (Rubin, 1996:137).

Conservatism, both cultural and economic, became a pervasive ideology shaping politics. The conservative movement defended the status order that had been under siege by reform movements of the 1960s. Traditional values were reasserted: religious fundamentalism, patriotism, family, sexual conventionalism (with antiabortion linked to these), free enterprise, and an ethical defense of laissez-faire capitalism. By the 1980s, *liberal* had become the derogatory "L-word" in American political discourse. Dominant status groups redefined public issues—men's rights, reverse discrimination, racial quotas, abortion, busing versus neighborhood schools—that all became passionate concerns (Walton, 1990:218). The movement was thus based on a mixture of *class grievances*—reasserting the rights of capitalist accumulation— and the *status grievances* of those defending traditional values and lifestyles.

These concerns and the mobilization of conservative voters transformed the political process to the benefit of conservative Republicans—who had a great deal to do with organizing the movement in the first place. The Reagan-Bush administrations were elected with overwhelming electoral majorities and a conservative reform agenda. Democratic President Clinton adapted by moving in a more conservative direction, and by 1994 Republicans controlled both houses of Congress with a conservative "agenda for change."

The conservative mood and political agendas for change had far-reaching consequences. Government became less active and interventionist; the tax code was made less progressive; and federal regulation of the economy, the environment, and consumer protection were weakened. Government support for organized labor evaporated, the "end of welfare as we know it" became a rhetorical slogan for both parties. The ERA, promoted in a decade-long struggle by feminists, and antidiscrimination laws protecting gay rights were apparently dead in the water by the mid-1980s. The most long-lasting residue of the conservative administrations and Congress was reconfiguring the U.S. Supreme Court with conservative justices. But conservative strategies of "reprivatization" bumped against powerful limits; the principle of government regulation and the safety nets of social programs were battered but not destroyed or dismantled (for some reasons we noted in Chapter 4). Similarly, the principle of full civil rights and social participation for all American status groups—established by the status-equality movements of the 1960s—was left unchallenged (although quota systems as a means of delivering this goal were!).

Economic conservatives were dismayed about what little headway powerful and committed administrations had made in actually reducing federal budgetary deficits and rolling back the "welfare state." Others (most notably Phillips, 1993; 1995) believed that growing government speculation and debt were part of capitalist heydays when government budgets were used as instruments of the rich and powerful. And more conservative politicians and judges failed to enact the social agenda so important to the New Right and Religious Right groups. In 2001, abortion was still legal (with many restrictions), but school prayer wasn't. And by 1996 doubts about the efficacy and social costs of minimal government and "privatizing everything" began to surface in the media (Levine, 1996; Palley, 1996).

What about the future? Perhaps we will see a continuation of pervasive conservative moods and movements, because they are supported by elite money and capture some durable American cultural themes (the election campaign of George W. Bush in 2000 focused on individualism, family, free enterprise, and hostility toward politics). Perhaps the social costs of vast and growing social inequality and ineffective minimal governments will produce its own reaction and create a new progressive movement, like the one generated in the 1890s. That movement produced a more activist government aimed at limiting social and economic conflict and producing a civil society and social peace. If so, it will certainly not be a precise replay of 1910, 1935, or even the 1960s, because the global and technological circumstances are vastly different. Perhaps—if cyclical theories of American political change are right—the end of a cycle of capitalist expansion and a resulting "turning of the wheel" is impending (see Chapter 5 and Phillips, 1990).

The main enduring legacy of the conservative agenda involves continued attacks on affirmative action programs. These attacks are products of real demographic changes in our most populous states (Texas, California, and Florida) but reflect the growing cultural indefensibility of affirmative action programs nationwide (see Leicht, 1999). We expect these attacks to continue. By the time you read this chapter, you should have a better idea how the story will unfold.

IN CONCLUSION: WHAT KINDS OF CHANGES DO REFORM MOVEMENTS PRODUCE?

We hope you recognize that the changes produced by reform movements are signifi-cant. Yet it is true that the change outcomes of even successful reform movements are complex and ambiguous, and always only partly successful. Reform movements are likely to wind up in a series of practical compromises with other interest groups and movements. *One reason* for this is that, to the extent that movements represent change from the bottom up, they wage an uphill battle to alter an established system, and there are usually more resources available to those seeking to perpetuate existing social arrangements than those seeking to transform them. Even when a reform movement succeeds in receiving considerable support from the top down, as those discussed here, it is capable of making significant—but limited—changes in the es-tablished social arrangements. A *second reason* for the limited impact of reform movements is that they operate in the context of powerful social forces. A movement may accelerate changes that are under way anyway for other reasons, as in the case of the feminist movement's push for expanded job opportunities for women in the context of a highly inflationary economy with pressures for dual income families. Or they can fail because they work against such trends, as in the case of the Religious Right's agitation to restore traditional families with single adult (male) wage earners.

Yet the impacts of reform movements are not trivial. All of the movements dis-cussed here left permanent impressions on the structure of American society and transformed the cultural assumptions that Americans argue about or take for granted. The agrarian reformers, workers, and Progressive reformers established the legiti-macy of social and political regulation of freewheeling capitalism. They established the rights of ordinary workers and farmers to organize on their own behalf and to ex-pect gainful employment and a modicum of economic security in "hard times." The status-equality movements of the 1950s and 1960s succeeded in breaking the caste-like barriers that prevented access to the social mainstream of American life and pro-duced significant gains in the social dignity of the lives of formerly disenfranchised categories of Americans. Even so, many African Americans, Native Americans, His-panics, and women found that when the formal barriers of discrimination were re-moved, they still remained trapped in urban ghettos, low-income work, migrant labor, or "pink-collar" jobs with little future. The status-equality revolts of the 1960s succeeded in delegitimizing status discrimination but bumped against harder realities of social class and produced more legal access than actual equality (see Wilson, 1987, 1996 for an elaboration of this point regarding African Americans). The con-servative movement redrew the boundaries between societal regulation and individ-ual life as it affects families, communities, and businesses. It reaffirmed and broadened some constitutive cultural assumptions of the American system: the pri-macy of private over public interests and the primacy of freedom over equality.

Let us summarize more concretely. Analysts of movements suggest that suc-cessful reform movements can produce four important kinds of change: (1) changing norms and public opinion and behavior, (2) specific legislation, (3) the creation of

new organizations or institutions, and (4) structural political or economic change
(Marks and McAdam, 1996):

1. *Changing norms, public opinion and behavior.* Successful reform movements can educate and resocialize people in ways that are felt throughout a society. For example, in
   the last twenty years the perspectives of the women's movement filtered into virtually
   every area of life in the United States. Childrearing practices, forms of address, television advertising, household labor, and occupational expectations all bear the imprint of
   the women's movement. It changed the way women viewed themselves. The environmental movement also reshaped the consciousness of Americans about recycling, consumer behavior, preserving biodiversity, and support for clean water and air legislation.
   The fact that these movements provoked strong resistance and countermovements indicates their impact. Whether they achieve particular goals or not, the discourses of successful reform movements dramatize issues for public attention (such as racial and
   sexual inequality, pollution, abortion, mental health, chemical abuse, domestic violence, or the safety of nuclear power). In that sense, they frame issues and create social
   problems and concerned publics.

2. *Specific legislation.* Some successful reform movements pass legislation that affects
   everyone. The Temperance movement passed the Eighteenth Amendment, which for a
   period of years made the manufacture, sale, or consumption of alcohol illegal. The Progressive movement produced laws that regulated the banking industry, the stock market,
   and the meatpacking industry. The labor movement passed laws guaranteeing the right
   of workers to strike and providing government arbitration of labor-management disputes. The environmental movement produced clean air and clean water acts and protection of endangered species. The women's movement failed to produce ratification of
   an Equal Rights Amendment to the Constitution after lobbying for its passage for more
   than a decade. Currently movements seek to limit access to handguns and to define term
   limits and reform the electoral system. And the pro-life and pro-choice movements seek
   laws that would prescribe reproductive behavior for all. The list could go on, but you get
   the idea. Obviously some laws are short lived (the Eighteenth Amendment), and the enforcement of some can be eroded by social change.

3. *The creation of new organizations.* Successful reform movements can give rise to
   durable SMOs that may become stable organizations in the cultural, social, and political landscape. Labor unions (AFL-CIO), the National Organization for Women (NOW),
   the NAACP, the Sierra Club, American Enterprise Institute, Boy Scouts, the YMCA,
   and the Church of Latter Day Saints are all examples. In a world historical sense, so are
   all the religious organizations deriving from the great world religions (e.g., Christianity,
   Judaism, Islam).

4. *Structural political or economic change.* Some successful movements provide new political or economic benefits to segments of the population. On rare occasions, the two go
   hand in hand. The civil rights movement granted southern blacks the vote, and ultimately a greater share of electoral power in the region. The movement economically
   benefited blacks—especially middle-class blacks—by ending some discriminatory employment practices and establishing affirmative action programs. Ironically, it broke the
   Democratic Party monopoly in the South and paved the way for Republican victories

regionally and nationally. In contrast, the women's movement in the United States appears to have had more of an impact economically than politically. On a smaller scale, the gay rights movement succeeded in establishing gays as a powerful interest group in San Francisco and several other cities, but attempts to produce legal nondiscrimination laws related to gays is sharply opposed by new right-wing movements and groups.

Structural change involves redistribution of power and economic benefits, and here the impacts of reform movements, even successful ones, are the most ambiguous. Whether the glass is half full or half empty is partly a matter of perspective. Reform movements invariably find themselves in conflict with other interests and groups for the distribution of power and economic resources. As controversial as it may be, changing culture and consciousness can be a variable sum game, with no real losers. Changing the distribution of resources, voting districts, the availability of jobs, housing, or education is often a zero sum game with real winners and losers. Yet purely symbolic change is rarely trivial and can delegitimate structural arrangements, making their transformation likely in the long run.

In this chapter we discussed some important American reform movements and how they have changed American society, the kinds of changes that reform movements typically produce, and the limits of such reform movements. Revolutionary movements accomplish more thorough transformations of social life, and we turn to these in the next chapter.

THINKING PERSONALLY ABOUT SOCIAL CHANGE

1. Talk with some older people about social movements that were active when they were younger. If you prompt them, everybody will remember some. Did they sympathize with any of them? Were they involved in any of them? How were they variously involved? Do they think any of these movements had any positive impact on conditions in society? Have some had negative impacts? For whom or what did people think they were positive or negative? Ask them to describe some. Have some of the movements they can remember just failed or withered away? Examples?

2. Think about impacts of earlier reform movements on your life today. How is it different because of earlier labor, feminist, civil rights, environmental, and educational or political reform movements? Consider some movements that are not too old as well, such as movements to reform drunk driving policies, to create an awareness of domestic violence as a problem, to provide access for handicapped persons, or to change laws to prevent discrimination against gay persons. When you start thinking about them, you should be able to think of quite a few. You probably experience these movement consequences in a mixture of positive and negative ways. Write a short essay, or organize a discussion with your peers about these consequences.

3. Think about the causes of success and failure for particular movements. What causes some to become widely appealing and have major impacts on change? What causes others (regardless of the validity of their concerns) to simply wither away in the dustbin of history? Can you think of some that have evolved into stable organizations without

much impact on social change? Can you identify others that have become stable enterprises of sorts, constantly selling T-shirts and other emblems without doing much?

NOTES

1. The terms *sex* and *gender* have different meanings, although they are often used interchangeably. Sex relates to differences between males and females that are rooted in biology (such as giving birth to and nurturing infants). Gender refers, on the other hand, to the social roles that come to be associated with sex differences in any given society. While the dividing line between sex and gender is blurry and debatable, it is quite clear that they are different things. While male and female are universal biological categories, gender is considerably more variable, both historically as well as cross-culturally. Gender relates to our learned notions about masculinity and femininity as well as behavior and rights thought appropriate for males and females in a given culture.

9

Revolutions

In contrast to reform movements, successful revolutionary movements are important elements of the dramatic and fundamental change processes that we call social revolutions. "A revolution," writes political scientist Samuel P. Huntington, "is a rapid, fundamental, and violent domestic change in the dominant values and myths of a society, in its political institutions, social structure, leadership, and government activities and policies." In a different but complementary view, communist theoretician V. I. Lenin said: "Revolutions are festivals of the oppressed and exploited. At no other time are the masses of the people in a position to come forward so actively as creators of a new social order" (both cited in Goldstone, 1986:69). These two statements define revolutions as rapid and fundamental transformations in socioeconomic, cultural, and political institutions, that are accompanied by class upheavals from below.

WHAT IS A SOCIAL REVOLUTION?

Sometimes we use the word *revolution* in a looser sense, as in the "sexual revolution" or the "computer revolution" as a metaphor for important cultural trends. But we are using the notion of revolution in a more specific sense here to mean a broader transformation that changes many areas of social life that must include a sudden collapse or overthrow of the state. It is also important to recognize that a sudden overthrow of the state in and of itself is not necessarily a revolution if it means only that one political elite has replaced another with no popular base or broader implications for social transformation.

So defined, successful revolutions are fairly rare and dramatic historical events. The most dramatic and clear-cut historic examples are the revolutions in France (1789), Russia (1917), and China (1949). Whether or not the American Revolution (1776) or the Puritan revolts in England (1640) qualify as real revolutions is debatable. But if successful revolutions are relatively rare, it does not follow that they have been historically unimportant. Revolutions have played an important role in social transformations that attended the creation of modern Japan (1868), Mexico (1910), Turkey (1923), Egypt (1952), and Iran (1906, 1979). In the 1950s and 1960s, revolutions transformed a host of developing societies, including Vietnam, Bolivia, and Cuba. And a revolution transformed Iran from a corrupt modernizing society into an Islamic fundamentalist one in 1979. In the 1980s, America found itself embroiled, as a third party, in domestic revolutionary struggles in Nicaragua, El Salvador, and Grenada. Finally—as we shall see—revolutionary struggles precipitated the collapse of state socialism in Eastern Europe and the former Soviet Union in the late 1980s.

THEORIES OF REVOLUTION

Four common ideas have shaped both popular and scholarly understanding of revolutions: (1) that increasing misery breeds revolt, (2) that revolutions result from the incompetence of the state to manage a variety of difficulties, (3) that they result from the circulation of subversive and radical ideas and ideologies, and (4) that they result from the difficulties of modernization (Goldstone, 1986:1–2). From Greek and Roman thinkers to Marx, many have argued that misery breeds revolt, but scholars of revolutions, beginning with Alexis De Tocqueville's analysis of the French Revolution, observed that, to the contrary, revolutions seem to occur after a long period of economic expansion and increasing standards of living.

Scholarly studies have suggested that state inability to manage, radical ideologies, and modernization difficulties *are* involved in revolutions, but none of these factors is adequate to explain why revolutions occur in some societies and not others. Why, for instance, did the French monarchy find the pressures of industrialization, urbanization, war, and so forth unmanageable while the English crown was able to manage similar problems without succumbing to a revolutionary collapse? Why did radical anticapitalist ideologies help stimulate revolutions in czarist Russia and imperial China, and not in industrial capitalist England and Germany (the real centers of socialist and radical Marxist thought and agitation)? Why did modernization result in revolutions in Mexico but not Costa Rica, or in Egypt but not Tunisia? These four ideas are not totally false, but, as you can see, neither are they adequate to understand much about revolutions without a great deal of qualification. If these are not very useful ideas, what are some? Let's briefly trace the development of social scientific thinking about the revolutions. You will recognize some of these ideas as specifications of the theories of social movements we discussed in Chapter 7.

The Natural History of Revolutions

In the 1920s and 1930s, a number of historians and sociologists began to study the classic Western revolutions (for example, in France, America, Russia) with the aim of discovering common patterns (Edwards, 1927; Pettee, 1938; Brinton, 1938/ 1965). They found, in fact, a remarkable configuration of common elements in the natural histories of these revolutions. We list seven:

The Desertion of Intellectuals. This phenomenon occurs for some time, even decades, prior to the revolution. Journalists, scholars, playwrights, poets, novelists, teachers, members of the clergy, and lawyers write condemnations of the regime and demand reforms. Even the natural supporters of the old order, such as aristocrats and landowners, become affected by the alienated tone of intellectual discourse, and there is a pervasive withdrawal of intellectual legitimation of the regime.

Attempted Reforms. Reforms are often undertaken by the regime shortly before its collapse, but these are typically "too little, too late." They are taken as a sign of weakness and encourage pressure for more radical reforms, which the regime is incapable of granting and still retaining control. Examples include the British crown's tax concessions to American colonists and the half-hearted economic and political reforms promulgated by the czarist Russian government in the years before the revolution.

A Political Crisis. Defeat in war, state bankruptcy, general economic collapse, famine, withdrawal of loyalty by the military and police, urban or rural riots and disorders (or some combination of these) precipitate a sudden collapse of the regime. The collapse occurs, not from pressure by revolutionary contenders for power, but rather from the inability of the state to manage or contain a multifaceted crisis. Thus revolutionaries find themselves with the upper hand not because they have grown stronger, but because of an incapacitating paralysis of the old regime.

A Period of Dual Rule Dominated by Moderates. This phase typically follows the fall of the old regime. Moderate reformers, who seek constitutional reforms using many of the old organizational forms left over from the old regime, rule in coalition with more radical factions. Thus the Kerensky government, which replaced the Czar, dealt with the more radical Bolsheviks, and the moderate American Continental Congress had to enter into coalition with the more radical Patriots' Societies. In more recent times, this effect could be seen when the parliamentary Bazargan government took power in Iran after the overthrow of the Shah's government and sought support from the more radical Islamic fundamentalist clergy. Radical factions mobilize, establish centers of control, and struggle with moderates to control the state.

The Triumph of the Radicals. This is the most likely outcome of the post-collapse power struggle. Moderates are likely to lose because, seeking to maintain continuity, they inherit many of the problems and inabilities to deal with them that caused the old regime to fail. Radicals are likely to succeed because, unlike the moderates, they are willing to take extreme measures both to deal with pressing problems and to secure their rule (Goldstone, 1986:4). However, as the American Revolution demonstrates, the triumph of the radicals is not inevitable. But it is only in revolts of national independence, where the old regime enemy is clearly external, that the moderates are likely to have a good chance of retaining control of the state.[1] Dramatic changes in social institutions and dominant ideology begin not shortly after the fall of the old regime, but later, when radicals succeed in wrenching control from the moderates.

A Reign of Terror.   An authoritarian period typically follows the triumph of the radicals, including the coercive suppression of competing political factions and movements, the reimposition of social order from the disorderly chaos of the revolution, and the implementation of the revolutionary "program." During this period previously obscure leaders may emerge with commanding, even absolute, control. Famous revolutionary leaders who emerged in this fashion include Cromwell, Napoleon, Stalin, Mao, Castro, and the Ayatollah Khomeini. The reign of terror may involve a variety of means to consolidate the new regime and to reimpose order, such as fear of the guillotine after the French Revolution, Stalin's secret police and the *gulag* of Siberian prison camps, or Mao's Cultural Revolution that gave radical youth gangs permission to terrorize and humiliate the rest of the population.

Moderation and Pragmatism.   This balancing out eventually follows the prolonged reign of terror because the radicals may have been defeated or died. Moderates who come to power condemn the excesses of the rule of terror and are less concerned with protecting the rule of the new regime—by now an established fact—and more concerned with promoting economic progress and stable institutions (Goldstone, 1986:5). Examples of this transition include the fall of Robespierre and the Jacobins in postrevolutionary France, Khrushchev's reforms and repudiation of Stalin in the Soviet Union, and the fall of Mao's allies, the "Gang of Four," in China.

These seven durable generalizations about the phases of development of revolutions have stood the test of time. While they provide valuable insights, however, they leave many questions unanswered. The main limitation of the life cycle approach is that it is descriptive and does not address questions about causation. What causes revolutions? What were the sources of opposition to the existing order? A second generation of scholars has addressed these issues.

Theories of Rebellion and Political Violence

In the 1950s and 1960s, many new or newly independent nations emerged in the Third World. While this phenomenon was part of the general process of modernization, it was often accompanied by various forms of political violence, such as coups, riots, rebellions, civil wars, and revolutions. Indeed, it was a common observation that revolutions are likely in societies undergoing rapid transition from traditional agrarian to modern urban industrial societies and most unlikely in truly modern industrial democracies, which spawn a multitude of reform movements (as documented in the last chapter). Scholars trying to understand the causes of revolution and its connection to the process of modernization developed general theories of revolts and political violence, all of which we have encountered before in Chapter 7 as more general perspectives about social movements. They include (1) relative deprivation theories, (2) system disequilibrium theories, and (3) resource mobilization theories.

Relative Deprivation Theories.   These theories improve on the notion that "misery breeds revolt." Gurr (1970) and Davies (1962, 1969) in particular argue that "people generally accept high levels of oppression and misery if they expect such discomforts to be their natural lot in life. Only when they expect a better life, and have their expectations frustrated are they likely to develop feelings of resentment that breed rebellion and political violence" (Goldstone, 1986:5). In other words, revolts are caused more by frustrated rising expectations than by increasing misery and oppression. In many emerging developing nations, generally rising expectations for material well-being are a consequence of cultural contact with developed societies. Davies argues that intense feelings of deprivation are produced when a prolonged period of prosperity that raises expectations for further improvement is followed by a sharp economic downturn that dashes those expectations (the *J-curve* of economic growth). Davies' research documents this social psychological configuration as a precursor to rebellion in a wide variety of historical cases.

System Disequilibrium Theories. These perspectives are specifications of functionalist theory (see Chapter 5) applied to understanding rebellion and political violence. They focus not on popular discontent, but on the changing relations between social institutions. Smelser (1962) and Johnson (1966) have argued that when the institutional subsystems of a society (its economy, political system, educational system, and so forth) change at similar rates, there is continuity, political stability, and the incremental processing of demands for social reform. But when the rate of change is very different among these institutional subsystems, the resulting disequilibrium and imbalance produces widespread disorientation, radical ideologies, and challenges to the legitimacy of the status quo. Under these conditions riot, rebellion, and revolutions flourish. This line of thinking would note, for example, that most of the classical revolutions in Western history (French, Russian, American) were preceded by dynamic and rapidly changing economic, educational, and demographic contexts coupled with relatively static political contexts, in which an old regime was trying to hang onto a political system appropriate for the past. In functionalist theory language, differing rates of institutional change result in the accumulation of stresses and tensions until the system can no longer contain them.

Huntington (1968) combined the relative deprivation and system-disequilibrium approaches to argue that *modernization* is the broadest cause of revolution in the contemporary world. This is because the economic and educational progress associated with modernization increases people's desire to participate in politics faster than political institutions can accommodate these desires. The gap between the desire for participation and the ability to do so results in widespread frustrations about political life (Goldstone, 1986:6). Yet as already mentioned, modernizing societies sometimes undergo revolutions and sometimes they do not. Scholars now recognize that not all societies undergo modernization in the same way or similarly experience the strains associated with modernizing change.

Resource Mobilization Theories. This perspective, which came to dominate the study of social movements in the 1960s, was applied to the study of revolutions. Tilly (1978) argued that neither discontent nor disequilibrium will lead to revolution if the discontented remain unorganized and lack resources. In other words, political violence and rebellion do not result in successful revolution unless the contenders for power have the resources and organization to engage in a sustained struggle with the authorities. This is why, Tilly explains, peasant revolts are usually short lived. Revolutions may start in the countryside, but they have a better chance of succeeding when moved to the city, with the geographic concentration and the abundance of resources to make mobilization for sustained struggle more likely.

In sum, social scientists by the 1960s had come to emphasize the conditions of widespread discontent, institutional change, and the possibility of resource mobilization by contenders for power as important causes of revolution. Yet the very generality of these arguments make it very difficult to understand with much precision where, when, and how revolutions succeed—as well as the circumstances under which they fail.

Another difficulty with these theories is that they tell us more about the outbreak of riots, revolts, and transitory political disorders than about the conditions under which revolts become successful social revolutions. The year 1848 is famous, for instance, as the year in which rebellions racked Western European nations. Widespread and simultaneous revolts of peasants and urban workers spread through Germany, France, Switzerland, Austro-Hungary, and Italy. All failed and were suppressed and destroyed by a powerful alliance of the urban middle classes, wealthy industrialists, and old royalists. To take another example, there have been many revolts in U.S. history, from the Whiskey Rebellion in the 1790s (a tax revolt among Pennsylvania farmers, suppressed by federal militia sent by President Washington), to the agrarian populists and radical unionists mentioned in the last chapter. All failed. History is replete with instances of riots, civil disorders, and organized revolts that failed, but successful social revolutions as defined here are relatively rare events. Why? The theories we mentioned are of little help in answering this question.

A final difficulty with the theories discussed here is that they view revolutions as primarily the work of purposive collective action by revolutionary social movements. While the pressures brought by such movements are part of the process, they are by no means all of the picture. Rather than being a prolonged struggle by insurgents to overthrow a massive powerful and repressive regime, revolutions typically involve a sudden and mysterious collapse of the regime, which is unable to manage normally routine affairs as well as extraordinary challenges. Some states are able to withstand such pressures and retain control, while others are incapable of doing so. In other words, social revolutions are the products of particular *system states,* or social configurations within the society and polity, as well as the work of contenders for power. The general theories of revolts and political violence described earlier tell us little about the set of social circumstances behind the sudden internal disintegration of states and social systems. But this question is addressed by the more recent analyses of social revolutions.

Structural Theories of Revolution

Scholars have turned from general theories of rebellion to a more careful examination of the comparative historical circumstances that are present when revolutions succeed. We rely in the following discussion largely on the work of Theda Skocpol, whose groundbreaking work has reshaped the social scientific understanding of revolutions (1976, 1994).

Skocpol's argument, based on comparative studies, is quite straightforward. A social revolution succeeds because the state has been weakened by a variety of simultaneously occurring external and internal pressures that it is unable to contain and manage. These include (1) international competition and conflict with other states, (2) disaffection and obstruction of state policies by important social elites that control important material and ideological support for the regime, (3) insufficient loyalty of the military and state police, and (4) pressure from a variety of popular uprisings (see Figure 9-1). We will discuss each of these in turn.

International Pressures.   States compete with each other for military strength, territory, and domination of trade. States that lose wars find themselves weakened in their capacity to resist pressures of revolution. Czarist Russia, the Ottoman Turks, and imperial China all suffered humiliating defeats by more powerful states, which weakened their legitimacy and ability to deal with internal opponents. But it is not just war: States are affected by how well their economies compete with other national economies. Those with relatively backward and unproductive economies relative to

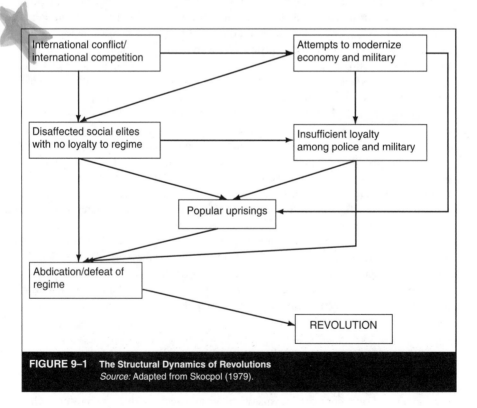

FIGURE 9–1   The Structural Dynamics of Revolutions
Source: Adapted from Skocpol (1979).

competing states may face overwhelming outside pressures. This is an important point because capitalism is really an expanding world system containing multiple political sovereignties. As France, Russia, China, Japan, and Ottoman Turkey came under competitive pressure in a capitalist market system, they each tried to mobilize national resources to stave off foreign economic domination. When they were unable to do so, the old regimes fell victim to elite revolutions from above in Japan and Turkey and collapsed entirely in France, Russia, and China, clearing the way for a popular revolution from below (more about these different types later).

   State-Elite Relations. Whether or not the state is able to mobilize economically and militarily to meet foreign competition depends upon internal relations. In order to gain or protect colonies or external markets, fight wars, or stimulate production for profitable world trade, the state must raise income and increase the scope of its authority. This means increasing tax levies, raising armies by conscription, and sponsoring capital development programs. Whether or not it is able to do so depends on the support of important social elites that control resources. Indeed, such central state projects may threaten traditional elite wealth, autonomy, or privileges.

   There are many examples of the importance of this state-elite relation. In competing with the English, the eighteenth-century French monarchy required the cooperation of noble-controlled parliaments, independent judicial bodies that could block and challenge the directives of the state. More recently, the Iranian clergy, because of their financial supporters in the bazaar economy, their role in the traditional courts, and their network of influence in the mosques and schools, retained control of resources to mount a challenge to the Shah. Thus when conflicts between the monarchy and elites arose—in France over the state bankruptcies arising from the Anglo-French wars of the eighteenth century and in Iran over the Shah's ambitious modernization plans—elite opposition was able to cripple and paralyze the central government (Goldstone, 1986:8). On the other hand, the English crown was able to elicit sufficient old aristocracy and new industrialist class support for the ambitious state projects of British economic and colonial expansion during the eighteenth and nineteenth centuries.

   Military Loyalty. The loyalty of the army and state police is also an important part of the stability of the state regime, particularly in times of state paralysis such as those mentioned or in times of widespread popular uprisings. The most well-known example of the importance of the loyalty of the military is in the case of the collapse of the Czarist regime in Russia. Returning home from World War I defeated, demoralized, and unpaid, elements of the Czarist army and navy refused to suppress urban riots (which began as food riots among the housewives of Petrograd). Not only did they mutiny and refuse to fire on rioters, but soldiers often joined in the disorders, which spread rapidly throughout the Russian cities and countryside. In the last instance, it was the undependability of the military and police that forced the czarist monarchy to abdicate. In another example, in the last days of imperial China the Manchu dynasty was unable to quell internal revolts (the Taiping and Boxer rebellions) and to limit foreign economic and military intrusions. The central government's projects to raise revenues and increase its control were hindered by resistance from local gentry and unreliable military units loyal to regional commanders rather than to the central government. Becoming completely paralyzed and bankrupt by 1911, coalitions between regional military commanders and the gentry-merchant leaders of provincial assemblies had enabled the provinces, one after another, to declare independence and withdraw support from the central government.

Under what conditions is the military loyal to the regime? Comparative research suggests that where recruits and officers are drawn from all classes, where there is a long training period for the rank and file, and where troops are isolated from civilians, the army is usually a reliable tool for the suppression of domestic disorders. Yet where army officers come primarily from a landed elite, they may sympathize with their own class in a conflict between elites and the central government. Where troops are recently recruited and fraternize with the populace, their sympathy for their civilian peers may weaken their allegiance to the state or officers. In either of these cases, the military is likely to be unreliable for the state and increase the vulnerability of the state to revolution (Trimberger, 1978).

Popular Uprisings.   The Marxian approaches to revolutions held that popular uprisings were the causes of revolutions. But in the absence of some of the conditions described earlier, popular uprisings are not sufficient to create revolution. Still, it is true that popular uprisings normally play a role in revolutionary processes. Most scholars distinguish between *rural uprisings* (of peasants, small farmers, sharecroppers, or Latin American *campesinos*) and *urban uprisings.*

Peasant revolts are common in traditional agrarian societies, yet they are usually short lived. Rural revolts are rarely caused by frustrated rising expectations, like those we discussed earlier, but rather to defend or restore their customary rights from the pressure of increasing rents and taxation (that enrich landlords or raise revenues for state projects such as those mentioned earlier). Peasant revolts are more about local issues than broad ideological concerns, and they dissipate when traditional rights and privileges are restored. Whether peasants can sustain continued rebellion depends on (1) whether they have communal traditions of solidarity and self government, (2) whether they have the economic or organizations resources to do so, and (3) whether landlords have the coercive power to control their behavior or suppress uprisings (Paige, 1975). Russian landlords during World War I and French landlords during the crown's bankruptcy in 1788–1789 had to face peasant uprisings without state protection or support and had no other means to defend themselves. Consequently peasant revolts spread rapidly through the countryside (Goldstone, 1986: 11). Still, it is usually true that for rural uprisings to have broader social significance, they either must be linked with the actions of groups outside the peasantry or must occur simultaneously with urban disorders.

Urban Uprisings.   Such civil disturbances are another matter and are potentially more explosive. In cities there are dense networks of workers, concentrated resources for rebellion, and obvious targets, such as state buildings, factories, and palaces. Research has demonstrated that urban rioters are not isolated, ignorant, newly arrived immigrants, but rather tend to be long-term residents who are better educated and more affluent that their peers (Rude, 1964). Two sorts of grievances stand out as causes of urban revolts: (1) *the cost of food,* and (2) *the availability of employment.* In the revolutions in France, Russia, and China, and throughout Europe in 1848, high unemployment and sharp jumps in food prices combined to create widespread antigovernment protests among workers (Goldstone, 1986: 11). Given the concentration of grievances and resources for rebellion in the cities and the fact that revolutionary ideologies normally circulate freely in cities, there is a great potential for urban disorders to evolve into sustained and systematic rebellion.

This is why many governments, both historically and in the contemporary world, have opted for cheap food policies for urban dwellers, even at the cost of levying considerable economic pain on farmers, or have subsidized food at levels that are unreasonably cheap in the context of world market prices. More recently, governments in communist Poland (in the 1960s) and Anwar Sadat's Egypt (in the 1970s) attempted to reduce state budgets by rescinding food subsidies and letting food prices rise to world market prices. They were faced with immediate and nationwide urban riots, and both regimes quickly reestablished food subsidies.

Urbanization per se is not a cause of rebellion. But combined with rapidly rising food prices and the inability of urban employment to provide jobs for waves of migrants from the countryside, it creates a great potential for outbreaks of political violence. Ominously, the rapid urbanization now under way in many developing nations is taking place under precisely these conditions.

Although they have a greater potential than rural uprisings to create a sustained rebellion, urban revolts alone do not make successful revolutions. Though urban revolts have featured prominently in virtually all of the revolutions we have discussed as examples, no revolution has succeeded solely on the basis of an urban uprising. The state can isolate and defeat urban rebels if it has the support of powerful elites and a loyal military and if urban rebels do not have the support, or at least the distraction, of simultaneous revolts in the countryside.

The Role of Marginal Elites.   We have discussed the role of traditional elites, such as nobles, landlords, merchants, financiers, and industrialists, in checking and paralyzing the state's capacity for effective action, but they are rarely the people who organize rebellion. Widespread disorders provide opportunities social movement leaders to mobilize, organize, and frame disturbances in abstract ideological contexts. But rather than falling to the traditional elites, this is typically the role of what Skocpol calls *marginal elites.* Who are they? They are civil servants, lawyers, bureaucrats, intellectuals, journalists, and military officers. They are, in short, highly educated new rather than old elites, who lack independent wealth or landholdings. Their livelihood depends rather on rational expertise and modern credentials. Whether or not they work for the state, their careers, identities, and outlooks are intertwined with state activities. Compared with traditional elites, marginal elites are likely to have a broad, modern cultural outlook, and in times of political crisis they are likely to call for democratization, the rationalization of the state, the extension of civil liberties, or the equalization of opportunity. They are likely to be the source of radical modernizing ideologies.

In the context of state paralysis and popular disorders, marginal elites are likely to be in the forefront in mobilizing revolutionary movements to overthrow the regime. As examples, organizing radicals of the French Revolution (among whom the Jacobins were the most extreme) were drawn primarily from the ranks of the non-noble, nonwealthy lawyers, professionals, and state functionaries. Russian Bolshevik and Chinese revolutionary leadership was drawn from university educated professionals and alienated intellectuals. Traditional elites and a disloyal military may weaken the state's capacity to act, and frustrated workers and peasants may create a climate of disorder, but it is the marginal elites who attempt to occupy the center stage and organize a new social order (Skocpol, 1976). They create the movement organizations that unify various dissident groups and provide an ideological master frame that unifies opposition to the regime.

Regime Disunity and Revolution. Even if there is no strong independent marginal elite that brings pressure on the regime, conflicts within the regime may cause the state to collapse. The state may be overthrown by the most modern segments within it. Trimberger (1978) has argued that military officials and bureaucrats without strong connections to the aristocracy or landowning class may be especially threatened by military or economic failures of the state. Such officials may initiate an *elite revolution* and seize control of the state. Lacking a stake in the traditional patterns of wealth and patronage, they are likely to advocate solving the problems of the state by radical modernizing strategies, including, for example, land reform, the eradication of aristocratic privileges, and rapid industrialization. Examples include the Meiji Restoration in Japan (1868), Attaturk's takeover of the moribund Ottoman regime by the Westernized Young Turks (1923), and Nasser's Young Officers' Revolt that overthrew King Farouk's government in Egypt (1952). Such elite revolutions are more than simple coups, because they bring with them ambitious programs of secularization, the rationalization of the state, and economic modernization.

Aside from the takeover of the state by frustrated modernizers, there is another pattern of state disunity that can lead to a collapse of the regime. Some states are what Eisenstadt (1978) has labeled *neopatrimonial systems.* That is, the top ruler maintains power not with the aid of a government bureaucracy, legal system, or even the traditional legitimacy of an aristocratic dynasty, but rather through an extensive but informal system of bribes and personal rewards to subordinates. Such systems involve a corrupt system of allocating the material rewards of the state in exchange for personal loyalties to the ruler. Since such systems are organized on the basis of the distribution of booty, they are particularly susceptible to disruption by international pressures or economic downturns that deprive the chief executives the spoils to distribute. Thus the patronage system crumbles and loyalties disappear. Goldstone (1986) has argued that the revolutions in Mexico, Cuba, and Nicaragua were of this variety, and to this list one could certainly add the collapse of the neopatrimonial system of Marcos and his cronies in the Philippines in 1989.

The structural perspective on revolutions developed here is an analytically powerful one. It provides the basis for understanding the conditions under which revolutions succeed, which is a more complex and theoretically interesting question than why rebellion occurs. So here's the important question: What would be the most likely combination of elements under which a revolution will almost certainly happen? It would be a society in which

- the state experiences powerful international pressures from its economic dealings with other nations, fortunes of war, and so forth.
- the state capacity for action is checked by resistance from traditional elites.
- there is significant unrest and uprisings in cities, the countryside, or both.
- an alienated but capable marginal elite seizes the opportunity to mobilize sustained resistance.
- the military is an unreliable tool of the state.
- the state itself is significantly divided into competing groups or factions.

Under this configuration of six conditions, it is almost impossible to think that a revolution would *not* occur. The point is that a state could manage one or several of these conditions, but not all of them simultaneously. In fact, a state with a reliable and efficient military can probably withstand quite a bit in terms of international pressure and popular uprisings. Exactly how many of these conditions have to be present for a revolution to happen? Well, the theory is good but not *that* predictive.

The theory also provides an understanding of why some societies, particularly industrial democracies, seem almost revolution-proof. Developed industrial democracies not only manage international pressures but exercise considerable control over the terms of competition and trade in the world economy (more about this in later chapters). Industrial democracies have consensus-making processes that constrain conflicts, both within the regime, and between the regime and powerful economic elites. Democratic rulers become adept at balancing the necessity to respect and reinforce elite privilege with the need to respond to popular grievances in ways that prevent the emergence of widespread disorders. There are adequate mechanisms of institutional incorporation and channels of mobility for opinion leaders (marginal elites without independent wealth) who are the potential organizers of rebellion. Popular grievances that become manifest in reform movements are not only accommodated, but, as we have seen the last chapter, become an important basis for mobilizing popular support for the regime or administration. And a loyal military and elite opposition is available to suppress more radical challenges to the system.

But not all revolution-proof states are modern parliamentary democracies. Historically, unified aristocracies were resistant to revolution, even in times of considerable crisis, such as in England during the seventeenth and eighteenth centuries. And in the modern world there are examples of thoroughly undemocratic systems that seem resistant to revolutionary collapse, such as South Korea, Singapore, and the (communist) People's Republic of China. Regime unity, support of critical elites, and a loyal military have enabled China to withstand considerable international pressure and popular unrest.

THE OUTCOMES OF REVOLUTION

Revolutions create dramatic social, cultural, economic, and political transformations. But probably no postrevolutionary society completely transcends the characteristics of the society that spawned it. And the extent to which the goals developed by revolutionary movements are in fact implemented after the revolution is an issue hotly debated by scholars (Goldstone, 1986:13). Were the goals of colonial revolutionaries converted into reality after the American Revolution? Well, sort of. Yes, but incompletely. In fact, some historians have argued that, other than the English crown being gone, postrevolutionary America strongly resembled colonial America in its ruling elites and in its economic and political arrangements. More significant transformations occurred some decades later under pressure from populist reform movements of the Western frontier during the Jacksonian era. Did the communist system that replaced the czarist Russia really create a "workers' paradise" of universal well-being, free from exploitation and alienation in which the state was withering away? Hardly. But beyond this question, which is often an ideologically loaded one anyway, scholars are beginning some careful comparative research about revolutionary outcomes. We'll mention only a few of these efforts here.

Most scholars agree that successful revolutions result in more centralized, bureaucratic, powerful, and often "modern" governments than existed under the old regime (Goldstone, 1986:13). Eckstein (1982) compared several Latin American countries that had revolutions with similar countries that did not. She concluded that after revolutions land reforms produced greater equality in land ownership, whereas in nonrevolutionary nations landed oligarchies succeeded in protecting their landholdings. In general, Eckstein found that peasants were the most immediate beneficiaries of revolution. In some countries, particularly socialist Cuba, there were significant gains in raising the general standards for health care and education—as compared to nations that did not undergo revolutions.

Kelly and Klein (1977) argue that after revolutions human factors in production (for example, education, skills, and entrepreneurialism) increase in importance to ownership of land as a basis of wealth and power. But countries that have experienced revolutions do not seem better off in terms of income equality or long-term economic growth than countries without revolutions. Kelly and Klein (1977) argue that while revolution may reduce inequality in the short run and may redefine the basis of inequality in more modern terms, in the long term there is a strong tendency for inequality to reemerge, and sometimes with it a new hereditary system of privilege.

A WORLD REVOLUTION: THE COLLAPSE OF THE COMMUNIST SYSTEM

From the 1940s to 1990, communist (or state socialist) societies in the Soviet Union, Eastern Europe, and China represented powerful and threatening alternatives to industrial capitalism. Consistent with the Marxist theory of history, communism sought to destroy and replace industrial capitalism. The Cold War struggle between the communist bloc and the free world became the overarching bipolar political conflict that defined the international political system. The Cold War threatened to become a "hot" war during the blockade of Berlin in the late 1940s and the Cuban missile crisis in the 1960s, and it did erupt into limited shooting wars in Korea and Vietnam. But though the Cold War always threatened to explode into a vast military conflict, it was mainly a constrained struggle for dominance between two systems—conducted in terms of a war of words between diplomats and geopolitical, ideological, and economic competition.

Yet the Cold War was a frightful period because the stability of the world political order was maintained by a balance of power, or—more appropriately—a balance of terror: At bottom global stability depended on the crude balance of thermonuclear weaponry possessed by the two systems. In the post–World War II era, people became acclimated to living in permanent "garrison states" with vast military establishments. The arms race consumed high proportions of national budgets in the creation and maintenance of instruments of mass destruction so vast that they had the potential to destroy the world many times over. Individuals learned to live, not easily, with the terrifying knowledge that the world could easily erupt into a global nuclear conflagration that would end human civilization, and perhaps even the basis of human life. American popular culture had a never-ending demand for genres of film and fiction organized around international conspiracy, nuclear holocaust, and "life after the bomb" themes.

If you lived in the 1980s, you lived through what historians of the future will surely view as one of the most momentous significant changes in modern times: the rapid transformation of the world political order because of the collapse of communism by 1991. As we have mentioned earlier, hardly anyone—scholars, politicians, or anyone else—would have predicted this outcome, particularly with the apparent suddenness and high drama with which it happened. In a span of six years (1985 to 1991), the world was unalterably changed. We have mentioned the significance of this change in earlier chapters, but only in passing, and now we want to return to it in some depth. In what follows we will discuss the changes leading up to the collapse and consider the usefulness of the ideas we have sketched here about social movements and revolutionary processes to understand what took place. We believe that they provide some powerful analytic tools for understanding how the communist system came to end as it did. We will finish by discussing several post-Soviet possibilities for change in this part of the world.

The Communist System

After the ouster of the moderates who governed briefly after the fall of the Russian czar, Lenin and the Bolsheviks gained control of the state and set about creating the communist society in 1917. But Lenin died in 1924 and was succeeded by Stalin, who not only continued the consolidation of the communist state, but by a reign of terror created a Soviet empire composed of many national groups (such as Georgians, Armenians, and Lithuanians) but dominated by Russians. From the 1920s to the 1950s, in spite of the world Depression and World War II, Stalin and the Communist Party succeeded in creating a *mono-organizational society*. This means it was a society wholly run by networks of official hierarchies, each of them enjoying a monopoly in a given field of activity and bound together and integrated by the Communist Party apparatus into a single, centralized organizational structure (Rigby, 1990:4).

The communist system was never completely unified or monolithic because of conflict among elites and factions, but it was as if all of the legal operating entities of society were taken over and run by a single giant firm. Stalin came to exercise dictatorial control over the party hierarchy, which in turn administered every aspect of economic, community, and cultural life. The power, status, and material rewards of persons were determined by formal position within the Party, state ministries, or their various subsidiary organizations rather than wealth, birth, or popularity. The system and its demands were legitimated by the goal of building a fully communist society and by the Marxist-Leninist worldview in which this goal was embedded. This worldview was protected from overt criticism and competition by close control over public communication and association, backed by powerful state police organizations (Rigby, 1990:6, 166).

In addition to too much centralized planning, a major dysfunction of the system was the disease of *departmentalism* (*vedomstvennost*). State ministries' planning and management systems were based on vertical hierarchical pyramids, centralized in Moscow, which directed enterprises and administrations throughout the Soviet Union. Each subordinate entity communicated only with the office above it in the same ministry and had no meaningful communication with neighboring enterprises that belonged to different ministries. This meant, for example, that in an urban area there was little communication or accountability among the various jurisdictions that controlled health, education, transportation, or the police, or among economic firms. This absence of horizontal linkages permeated the whole system and was a source of great inefficiency and incoherence (Lewin, 1988:105–106).

Change

The communist system under Stalin became a stable and rigid system partly because it retained a monopoly on assessing and praising itself and lacked the internal mechanisms of change that characterize more dynamic systems. In spite of these problems the system was relatively coherent and presided over large-scale upward mobility. It enjoyed a significant base of popular support. *But it did change.*

In the decades following World War II the urbanization and industrialization of Soviet society proceeded rapidly. During the 1930s, the Soviet Union was overwhelmingly rural, but by 1972 it had become predominantly urban. Accompanying urbanization and industrialization was the growth of a large "techno-scientific and intellectual class" (Lewin, 1988:31, 49). Living standards, though still far below those of the Western countries, increased significantly. Exact data are hard to come by, but Sovietologists agree that living standards improved in the 1950s and 1960s. The official claims that real incomes of workers increased by 55 percent in the 1950s are probably exaggerated but not wholly misleading (Rigby, 1990:121). The significant thing was that Soviet Union was "no longer a predominantly peasant society with a primitive work force comprised largely of unskilled manual laborers and commanded by primitively undereducated political leaders. It had become a predominantly urban society, still dominated by smokestack industry, but with a sizable middle class and a growing professional intelligentsia trained at the university level" (Smith, 1990:18).

Khrushchev's Reforms

After Stalin's death in 1953, Nikita Khrushchev became the Party leader and by 1958 had become Premier of the Soviet Union. Khrushchev denounced Stalin's dictatorial policies within the party, the "cult of personality," and attempted to restore "collective leadership" to the party: no more one-man rule, purges among party leaders, or arbitrary killing and imprisonment of "enemies of the people" by the state police; in short, an end to the rule of terror from top to bottom. A "cultural thaw" relaxed controls on the media and intellectual life. Actual political power became less concentrated in the top political leadership and slowly began to diffuse downward (Lewin, 1988:102-103). Khrushchev attempted to improve consumer life, with some success. He declared a policy of "peaceful co-existence" with the West but also boasted that the Soviet Union would quickly catch up with and overtake the West economically.

The part of the Soviet population most imbued with the spirit of reform was the "Khrushchev generation" of university-trained intellectuals and professionals. Now in their fifties and sixties, they were liberated from the heavy pall of Stalinism during their formative university years and were given hope for greater cultural freedom and personal autonomy (Smith, 1990:20-21). Dramatic Soviet technical achievements of the era—the successful launching of the Soviet Sputnik satellite in 1957 and Yuri Gagarin's manned space flight in 1961—made it indeed plausible that the communist world could indeed overtake the West. The Khrushchev cohort of intellectuals and party leaders has formed the backbone of reform efforts since that time, advocating the rule of law, freer expression, greater citizen participation, and a diminished role of the state and entrenched bureaucracy. Significantly, Mikhail Gorbachev was a member of that cohort.

Yet Khrushchev's reforms failed. The slow improvements in living standards, education, and health care could not offset the dramatic failure of Soviet agriculture—which no amount of tinkering with the state farm system seemed able to improve. Food shortages were chronic, and large amounts of grain were imported yearly to make up for shortfalls. And although crude indicators of productivity (the only measures that counted in the Soviet system of assessment) improved on many fronts, the inept system of bureaucratic misplanning and the ongoing disease of *vedommennost* (see earlier) guaranteed that Soviet goods and services were shoddy and not supplied in any real relation to consumer needs. Khrushchev's coexistence policy and his expensive and ultimately unsuccessful foreign "adventurism" in Africa, Cuba, and Latin America cost him the support of Party leaders.

The Brezhnev Years and the Deepening Crisis

Khrushchev was ousted in 1964 and Leonid Brezhnev, who represented Party conservatives, came to power and ruled until he died in 1982. Brezhnev attempted to "make the system work" by reintroducing order, discipline, and tightening up. Initially the system actually did improve and there were slow but steady improvements in the standard of living: Communal apartments were being replaced; better clothing, washing machines, and refrigerators became available. But Soviet efforts were concentrated in a few high-priority areas; steel and oil output actually surpassed that of the United States, and great resources were invested in the accumulation of an enormous nuclear arsenal. However it was viewed in the West, the invasion of Czechoslovakia in 1968 to suppress a heretical reform movement was widely popular among Russians, who were proud that their power had been asserted to keep the empire intact (Smith, 1990:21, 23). Brezhnev's greatest success was attaining superpower status with the Strategic Arms Limitation Treaty (SALT 1) that recognized the nuclear parity of the United States and the USSR.

But there were internal problems. The monopoly of power and tight controls over information gave the leaders of the upper, and even lower, echelons of the bureaucracy too many opportunities to abuse their offices, to misinform and lie, and to wallow in luxuries. A corrupt but implicit social pact had developed among the party elites, who were offered material opulence in exchange for silence and complicity (Przeworski, 1991:20). Neither rank-and-file Party members or the newly educated intelligentsia and professionals, of whom there were considerable numbers, had a chance to participate meaningfully in the political process or even to have reasonable control over their own careers. Widespread political apathy and cynicism ensued, with which the system had little ability to cope. It spilled over into low workplace morale and widespread alcoholism.

By the end of the 1970s, however, Soviet progress lost momentum and there began a long period of deterioration and retrogression in the quality of life.

[Bad harvests] . . . made food shortage endemic. There was rationing of meat and milk. . . . Industrial sectors went into decline; labor productivity went flat. The free health-care system, a much vaunted pride of Soviet socialism, had deteriorated so much that infant mortality rates rose while male life expectancy went down. The statistics were covered up, but people could experience for themselves the horrible inadequacies of the health system: shortages of medicine, unbearably long waits for treatment, serious infections picked up in hospitals, the bribery necessary to secure treatment. The press occasionally reported stories of corruption by middle-level officials. Moscow was full of unseemly rumors that reached into Brezhnev's own family and entourage . . . the army, Party officials, and the KGB were embarrassed and angered by the corruption and sloth of the Brezhnev era. The whole country was sliding into cynicism. (Smith, 1990:23)

As economic progress dwindled, the Soviets became bogged down in an unpopular and seemingly unwinnable war in Afghanistan. Contrary to Khrushchev's boasting in the 1960s, the Soviets did not overtake or even come close to catching up with the West. Industrial capitalism "did not falter and collapse as Marx and Lenin had predicted and scores of Soviet ideologists had dutifully echoed. Just the opposite had occurred. The West had leapfrogged ahead . . . so that by the 1980s the brightest people in the Soviet system could see the telling contrast between Soviet stagnation and Western progress. They could see that the world was passing them by" (Smith, 1990:7).

By the 1980s, cultural contact with the West was broad enough, especially between Party, professional, and scientific elites, so that Western Europe became the enviable standard of comparison and these comparisons became increasingly humiliating. Knowledge of this diffused throughout the Soviet system. Communism came to be seen not as a model for the future but an underdeveloped "something else" (Przeworski, 1991:20). At the same time, cultural controls were tightened and the ideological legitimacy declined even faster than the economy. The regime reverted to primitive propaganda, simplistic slogans, crude distortions of reality, and the heavy controls of culture and information—unmistakable signs of a worsening crisis of legitimacy (Lewin, 1990:113, 123). In every sphere reality fell short of people's expectations and public morale took a nosedive as cynicism and alienation became pandemic.

Finally, it is important for us to note what many in the West never recognized; *that the Communist Party was itself not monolithic but divided.* Throughout the Brezhnev period, and increasingly by the end of it, there were several "wings" or factions in the Communist Party. There were Old Guard conservatives like Brezhnev protecting the status quo, neo-Stalinists who wanted a return to a tougher line, and Khrushchevite reformers who wanted Stalinism explicitly rejected and favored a looser, freer system. In addition, there were legions of opportunists and careerists who would simply go with the flow, whatever it was. And, most important, many people rising through the Party hierarchy were as disenchanted by the system's failures and as disgusted by official corruption as non-Party intellectuals, although they dared not speak out (Smith, 1990:27–28). Brezhnev died in 1982, and after two transitional leaders (Cheminko and Andropov) it is in this context that Mikhail Gorbachev and a cohort of Nikita Khrushchev's political children came to power in 1985.

Gorbachev and Reform

Gorbachev's early years revealed little of the radical reformer he was to become. He promulgated campaigns for order and discipline and attempted to combat the widespread corruption of the Brezhnev era. Many high officials were dismissed or arrested, broad campaigns were mounted against alcoholism and slapdash performance in the workforce. Policies were aimed at increasing economic efficiency and acceleration (*uskorenie*). The only modest reforms, in fact, were to link rewards more closely with productivity and to authorize limited forms of individual and family enterprise, but the latter functioned mainly to legitimate (and tax) an extensive established "shadow" economy of blackmarketeers (Rigby, 1990:211–212).

In 1987, Gorbachev shifted from *revitalizing* the mono-organizational Soviet system to *changing* it. Whether he intended this all along and was using the first years as a period of consolidation or whether the difficulties of revitalization changed his mind is not clear. In any case, he began to publicly endorse the radical restructuring of the system, and particularly the Communist Party, as prerequisite for social and economic progress. "Restructuring" (*perestroika*) meant thorough liberalization in the political sphere and the development of "commodity–money relations" (that is, market mechanisms) in the economic sphere. Paralleling *perestroika* was the advocacy of "openness" (*glasnost*) in public communications, media, and intellectual life. Gorbachev did not advocate a multiparty system but did advocate the democratization of the Communist Party, with contested elections at all levels and the lifting of censorship and restrictions on freedom of speech and the press.

The seriousness of these sweeping reform ideas, which went far beyond any reform proposals of the Khrushchev era, was at first discounted by many Western leaders, including President Reagan, as representing nothing more than the latest version of Soviet ideological posturing and perhaps jockeying among the elite for control. But their effect on the people of the Soviet Union was electric; they unleashed and gave shape to a vast popular reservoir of popular grievances that had been pent up. In fact, by the time Gorbachev had come to power, social reform had hidden constituencies at every level in Soviet society:

> mineworkers and housewives incensed about the weary of chronic consumer shortages and the dismal quality of Soviet goods; farmers and teachers demoralized by rural decay; little people outraged by the arrogant, pervasive, Mafia-like corruption of ministers and high Party officials; others embittered by the rampant black market, and by underground millionaires profiting from the gaping inefficiency of Stalinist economics. . . . Scientists and engineers were worried about the Soviet Union's industrial stagnation and its growing technological inferiority to the West. Intellectuals and young military veterans were sickened by the futile war in Afghanistan. Army generals, intelligence chiefs, and civilian technocrats were alarmed by the Soviet inability to compete in the world market and by the prospect of becoming a fourth-rate power in the twenty-first century. . . . Cab drivers and poets alike were sick of the blatant hypocrisy of Soviet propaganda. There was a pervasive cynicism about the widening chasm between the pompous pretensions of Brezhnev and the bleak reality of a Russian's everyday life. (Smith, 1990:6)

The most natural and concentrated support for reform was among the growing university-educated middle class, who not only wanted a better material life—as did all Soviets—but also were eager for more personal and intellectual freedom, more respect for the individual, and more openness and honesty in Soviet life. Still, the desires for reform lay dormant until Gorbachev provided the liberal climate and political opportunity structure for them to emerge, which they did in an explosive mobilization in the late 1980s.

Probably the effect on freedom of the press was most dramatic. The press shifted overnight from being party cheerleader to the watchdog and critic of the regime. Magazines blossomed with exposes about crime, prostitution, and high-level corruption. Books formerly banned by censors (Solzenitzyn's *Gulag Archepelago,* Orwell's *1984,* Pasternak's *Dr. Zhivago*) were republished, widely read, and serialized on TV. Scientific sociology and public opinion polling about all manner of questions flourished. What was emerging was nothing short of a civil society, with important intermediary mechanisms of opinion formation and bodies of public opinion apart from the Party and the state.

An independent press not only helped create independent mechanisms of public opinion, but also accelerated the popular disillusionment with the communist system. By the late 1980s, the Soviet press had an endless flow of stories about how well things were for the people of the West:

> Television did admiring portraits of the McDonald's fast food chain . . . the efficiency of construction projects in Seattle, a well-run American family farm in Iowa, and even the way American political conventions operate. . . . Soviet viewers got an impressive look at the modem technology used by family farmers and . . . an incredible network of businesses serving the farmer. In a report on traffic congestion in New York City, Soviet TV also ran flattering shots of the interstate highway system—light-years ahead of the rutted, gutted Soviet roads. (Smith, 1990:164)

The conclusions people drew from such reports were inevitably unflattering to their own system.

Another important consequence of *glasnost* after 1987 was the emergence of a vast array of independent groups and social movement organizations (*neoformaly*). It is true that during the Brezhnev era there was a small but widely publicized "dissident" underground movement of intellectual protesters against the Soviet system. But that movement was suppressed and its leaders, such as Andrei Sakharov, were exiled. The dissident movement never numbered more than a few thousand activists at most. But after 1987 such groups blossomed in public with few attempts to suppress them. The most spectacular were the popular-front independence movements in the Baltic republics and other minority regions. Otherwise there were organized groups of *Afghansti,* Afghanistan war veterans lobbying for health care and preferred treatment as consumers; *Zelenni Svet* (Green World), a movement protesting pollution and nuclear-power stations; *Memorial,* a nationwide group dedicated to rehabilitating the victims of Stalinism; *Spaseniye* ("Salvation") a movement to preserve monuments of history and culture and to democratize public life; and, in Moscow, democratic interest groups such as Civic Dignity, the Club of Social Initiative, People's Action, and Democratic *Perestroika.* Later there were organizations of lawyers, peasant farmers, and even one for junior military officers, called "Shield" (Smith, 1990:431). Boris Yeltsin, then the Communist Party boss in Moscow, convened a meeting of over 100 such groups in 1989 to form the *Democratic Russia,* which openly declared itself an opposition movement, even though they were still technically illegal. More ominously, independent unions of coal miners in Siberia and the Ukraine declared a prolonged strike of 150,000 coal miners—the first truly large-scale labor strike since the Bolshevik Revolution in 1917.

Initially none of these movement organizations was a threat to the Party, even though Gorbachev used them as a populist force to challenge entrenched party bureaucrats. But as they began to merge into larger coalitions, such movement organizations began to challenge the Party openly. Change that was decreed from above became more insistent from below, outstripping anything that Gorbachev had imagined. "With the choke hold of fear broken and dissent now tolerated, Russians . . . plunged into election campaigns, mass demonstrations, environmental protests, miners' strikes . . . all evidence of a breathtaking growth of grass-roots activism" (Smith, 1990:556).

The Empire Crumbles

The most gripping news of the winter of 1989 was the dramatic collapse of state socialist regimes in Eastern Europe. The trouble began in Poland.

The contrast between Poland and the Soviet Union could not have been more striking. Poland had, for decades, a Catholic church that functioned as an ideological refuge and a countervailing force to the communist regime. Poland had a small private sector of farms and businesses that were never turned into state enterprises. Poland had an active academic and intellectual underground with its own publications that were never effectively controlled by the regime. But most importantly, Poland had an independent trade union, Solidarity, that became a protest movement within the communist system. There were, in fact, two Polish nationalisms: one a romantic popular conception of Polish nationhood, rooted in the church and popular culture, and another official Marxist nationalism, residing in the Party elite and the military.

Open rebellion began in 1976 but really flared in 1980, when Solidarity declared a crippling nationwide strike with wide support from the church, farmers, and the intelligentsia. Martial law was declared by the Polish military, an open admission that the Polish Communist Party could no longer rule without naked repression. Still, workers struck again in 1988 and a compromise with the popular workers' movement was imposed on the Party by the military (Prezworski, 1991:21). For a brief period a popularly elected government ruled in coalition with the military, but the military shortly bowed out. The Communist Party was gone, and the new regime quickly set about creating a market economy. The rest is history.

From Poland, the rest of the Eastern European regimes fell like dominoes. The Hungarian Communist Party split from the top, without pressure from below or being coerced by the military. Hungarians let East German refugees proceed to West Germany via Hungary, as did the Czechs. A vast crowd at Wenceslas Square in

Prague forced the Czech regime to abdicate and to remand the government to popular forces without a shot being fired. The Bulgarian and Romanian governments fell in turn, with the only real civil disorders being in Romania. Yugoslavia erupted into precommunist Balkan ethnic fratricide, and Albania imploded. The capstone of the "autumn of the people" in 1989 was the dramatic collapse of the repressive, neo-Stalinist East German Communist regime, with the destruction of the Berlin Wall, reported as high drama on international TV.

In an abstract sense the reason that all this happened was quite simple: The Soviets had let it be known that they would not send in Soviet troops and tanks to shore up Marxist regimes, as they had in Hungary in 1956 and again in Czechoslovakia in 1968. Left to their own devices, no Eastern European state was powerful enough to repress popular forces for change. The absence of the prospect of Soviet repression represented an expanded opportunity structure within which national communist regimes collapsed to contenders for power all over Eastern Europe (Tarrow, 1991:17–18). Eastern Europe was gone from the communist system in the blink of an eye, seemingly with Gorbachev's blessing, but to the great consternation of conservative party factions.

A more serious threat to the integrity of the communist system was the unraveling of the empire within the Soviet Union itself. In a popular election in 1989, Lithuanian communists were roundly defeated, and the Lithuanian parliament demanded complete independence from the Soviet Union, a move that quickly spread to the other Baltic Soviet Republics (Estonia, Latvia). Gorbachev could not tolerate this break but, in the limelight of world opinion as an international reformer and peacemaker, neither could he send in the tanks as Stalin or Brezhnev would have done. He stalled, alternately pleading and threatening a complete economic blockade, but ultimately conceded that Lithuania could secede, if they were willing to go slow through "proper channels" at considerable economic costs. But all of this became moot; by 1990 eleven of the fifteen Soviet Republics, including the Russian Republic, declared not independence but their sovereignty from the central government of the Soviet Union. The center was gradually losing power to the periphery at the base of the Soviet system.

This move to local autonomy took the shape of organized opposition as the "Interregional Group," organized by autocratic politicians at the local and republic levels. The Interregional Group was a coalition of nationalists in the republics seeking some form of self-determination and Russian radical democratic reformers in Moscow and Leningrad. It shared a hostility to central Party control as well as to the power of the military and the KGB and urged free assembly, the rule of law, and the democratic politics that Gorbachev had promised (Smith, 1990:476). All of this came to a head in 1989 and 1990 in the meetings of the Congress of People's Deputies and Supreme Soviets: the huge annual gatherings of political delegates from the far-flung Soviet empire. These meetings were historically ritual gatherings of elected delegates who gave their obedient stamp of approval to policies of the Party leaders. The 1989 and 1990 meetings were unprecedented, involving the clash of ideas, personalities, and interests, with arresting revelations, spontaneous outbursts, and passionate debate that galvanized the tens of millions of Soviet people watching on TV (Rigby,

1990:221). There was an open clash between two contending forces, the newly elected radicals bent on challenging the old system and forcing reform and the loyalist Old Guard determined to protect its power, with Gorbachev attempting retain control by playing off one side against the other.

The Limits of Reform

Cultural and political reforms had utterly transformed the Soviet Union in the span of a few years, so much that foreign observers were literally stunned. But economic reform was, by contrast, an abysmal failure. Gorbachev had several opportunities to dismantle the old system and move toward free market systems, but each time he pulled back from real change. He did not, as did the Chinese communist reformers, build a mass constituency for economic reform by giving peasants freedom to earn more votes by putting more food on the table in the cities (Smith, 1990:559). Genuine economic reforms were not attempted because of resistance from state planners and entrenched bureaucrats who would become superfluous in a free market system. The Russian people were fearful of reform because they had little knowledge of the workings of markets and a great fear of living under a different economic system. Reform was also unsuccessful because many reformers, including Gorbachev, feared the political backlash that would be the certain consequence of the economic hardships and chaos that would attend the dismantling of the old planned economy. Gorbachev wanted reform without pain, and while the old system was under attack everywhere, no new system was created in its place. The functioning of the Soviet economy deteriorated so rapidly that to many even the Brezhnev era looked good by comparison. Public opinion polls measured the steady deterioration of popular support for Gorbachev and his reforms. Without economic improvements, freedom of expression and political democracy had become hollow reforms.

Not only the masses of people, but virtually every elite in the USSR, except the intelligentsia and reformers themselves, found reason to oppose reforms. As mentioned, powerful government officials were faced with the possible loss of their key roles as managers of state enterprises. Regional and local party bosses were responsible for sorting out economic and other problems, despite their loss of powers and staff, and they were blamed—publicly now in the press and on talk shows—for things going wrong. By 1989, many were seething with anger and resentment about the whole idea of reforms. The military fared little better, suffering cuts in military budgets, and the careers of thousands were blighted by early retirement or nonpromotion. The state police found their power curtailed and lost their immunity to criticism. (Rigby, 1990:227–229). Party leaders were also frustrated and humiliated that Gorbachev's "new thinking" in international relations had resulted in a virtual capitulation to the West and the loss of Eastern Europe.

By 1990, Soviet politics had become a polarized conflict between left-wing democratic reformers and nationalists led by Boris Yeltsin, now the popularly elected president of the Russian Federation, and the conservative hardliner right wing of the Party, led by Valentin Pavlov and others. The democratic reformers had considerable strength in the regional governments of the republics, among rank-and-file members of the Communist Party, among urban intellectuals, and among the vast melange of democratic movement organizations mentioned earlier. They controlled the municipal governments of Moscow, Leningrad, and other cities with powerful and popular mayors. The hardliners had support from the high-level party officials and state planning bureaucrats (who still ran the economy), among the state police, and among some—but not all—factions of military officers.

Between these two sides there were bitter polemics that filled the pages of the Soviet press. The hardliners accused the democrats as selling out to the West and Zionism, of hating the Russian people, and of being prepared to create great upheaval by introducing alien ideas—pluralism and capitalism. Democrats, on the other hand, lumped all defenders of the system together and refused to differentiate among them. The notion of a moderate, responsible communist or Russian nationalist was not something that liberal cosmopolitan intellectuals were ready to entertain (Simes, 1991:48). Gorbachev attempted to hold the system together by first placating one side and then the other, but he was occupying a shrinking middle ground. He continued to appoint hardliners among his top advisors and as directors in state ministries at the same time that he acquiesced to democratic pressures for continuing reforms. After resisting for some time, Gorbachev finally gave in to demands by the reformers to alter the Soviet constitution by rescinding the legal monopoly of the Communist Party—thus creating the constitutional basis of a multiparty democracy. Striking at the heart of Communist Party control, this action sent the hardliners into orbit.

During the winter of 1990–1991, the Soviet Union and the international community were awash with rumors of coups d'etat, plots, and dark scenarios of various kinds. Liberal foreign minister Eduard Shevardnadze resigned dramatically with the prediction that "dictatorship is returning to the Soviet Union." The Interregional Group pressed Gorbachev to sign an "All Union Treaty" that would have loosened the Kremlin's control over republics, considerably weakened central Party organizations, and begun the devolution from a union to a confederation of republics. By the summer of 1991 he was prepared to sign. For hardliners, it was the last straw.

The Empire Strikes Back

On the morning of August 19, Soviet tank battalions left their barracks outside Moscow and began rolling toward the city. Gorbachev was placed under house arrest at his vacation home in the Crimea as military units moved toward the Russian government buildings to take over the "hotbed of democracy" of Yeltsin and his government. The coup was organized by a dozen or so leaders of the state police, state planning ministries, army, and high party officials, some of whom were Gorbachev's cabinet advisors. A Soviet general announced martial law in the rebellious Baltic republics. The coup plotters staged an international news conference at which they announced, incredulously, that Gorbachev was too ill to continue leadership and they, led by Vice President Gennady Yanayev, were assuming leadership of the Soviet Union. Soviet visitors in the United States tried to reassure journalists who interviewed them that the hardliners would never be able to hold power, even if they succeeded in taking it, but most Americans didn't believe them. To many Americans, it was the long-feared return of the dark forces that would restore the "Evil Empire."

From the beginning, however, the coup was botched: The borders were not sealed, nor were international telephones, fax machines, or most of the media under the control of the coup leaders. Military commanders had little knowledge about what they were being sent to do. Support from the non-Russian republics failed to materialize as most leaders and military commanders adopted a "wait and see" attitude before declaring their loyalty. From inside the government buildings, Yeltsin and others were busy on phones and fax machines soliciting the support of the international community, which unanimously condemned the coup and asked for the release of Gorbachev. The coup failed because it was incompletely executed, but also for lack of elite support and an outpouring of popular resistance, particularly among the educated classes.

Tens of thousands of Muscovites flocked to the Russian Parliament buildings and erected barricades to protect Yeltsin and his parliamentarians. They stayed for three days and nights, in violation of a curfew announced by the coup leaders, and implored soldiers and tank commanders, who were showered with food, flowers, and Russian flags, not to fire on them. There were huge anti-coup demonstrations in Leningrad, Kiev, and other cities, and coal miners struck again across Siberia. As the coup stalled, many leaders of the fifteen Republics finally joined world leaders in condemning the coup. In the final showdown, Soviet soldiers refused to fire on Russian citizens and some units switched sides to join in the defense of the parliament buildings. By the third day, the tanks and armored personnel vehicles had turned around and started back to their barracks. The coup was over and Yeltsin and the Russian political leaders had triumphed, but popular resistance by the people of the Soviet Union had made it possible. Coup leaders were jailed (but one committed suicide), and a dazed Gorbachev returned from the Crimea with little real comprehension of what had transpired.

The main problem was that the coup leaders, successful bureaucrats and apparatchiks, had lived too long inside the Kremlin and had failed to perceive the fundamental changes that had been taking place outside. Most of all they failed to understand the disappearance of the greatest legacy of Stalinism: fear (Sturua, 1991:65–66).

The Aftermath and the Future

Neither did Gorbachev understand the situation. He had so feared being ousted by the democratic reformers from the left that he was unprepared for a coup from the hardliners of the right, whom he thought he could control. He assumed that he could return in triumph to rebuild the Party and revitalize the state after dealing with his enemies who had plotted his overthrow. He was, of course, dead wrong. Power now lay with the reformers, the nationalists, and the Russian people, and they chose decisively. Statues of Lenin, Stalin, and the founder of the secret police were toppled all over the country, and the headquarters of the Central Committee of the Communist

Party and the state police were closed and their records impounded. The Russian government claimed control of all assets of the Party within the borders of the Russian Republic (other Republics followed suit). In Gorbachev's presence, Yeltsin signed a decree that suspended the Communist Party in Russia. Gorbachev tried to resist, but he subsequently resigned as General Secretary of the Communist Party of the Soviet Union and urged the Party to dissolve. By October, the republics had agreed to dissolve the Soviet Union. The Baltic Soviet Republics declared complete independence and the others were negotiating some form of confederation. After its more than seventy-year existence, the Soviet Union was no more.

In its place a Confederation of Sovereign Republics struggled to define autonomy and to negotiate some sort of relationship between the republics. By the mid-1990s, they had devolved into a huge Russian Republic ringed in the West and South by newly independent nations—homes of the national minorities the Soviet empire had absorbed (e.g., Estonia, Armenia, Lithuania, the Ukraine, Kyrgyzstan). Bad as it was, the old Soviet command economy went into a prolonged state of free fall, and living standards plummeted. Western-style markets and foreign investments slowly and incompletely emerged in a nation that had little experience or understanding of either, and many Russians found it impossible to distinguish between legitimate businesses and gangsters. This underscores the importance of institutionalized culture and law that legitimizes politics, business, and civil dispute. But in the throes of such a massive transition, that takes time to develop.

As with most such transitions, there are winners and losers, and some Russians benefit from the new order of things. Social inequality grows rapidly there, as in the rest of the contemporary world. The presidential election of 1996 exhibited noisy parties and factions from across the political spectrum (including liberal modernizers, Fascists, and old communists). Boris Yeltsin won again, not because he was "beloved" by the Russian people, but because the other alternatives were worse. Yeltsin resigned in January 2000 and was replaced by Vladimir Putin, who inherited a government still mired in power struggles and official corruption that makes corruption in the United States and Western Europe look benign by comparison. Stalled land reform measures, stalled investments in economic infrastructure, the continued unrest in Chechnya, and threats to civil liberties and political freedoms all remain significant and debilitating problems in the new Russia (*Economist,* 2001d).

Post-Soviet Possibilities

Now that state socialism as an economic system seems to be passing into the dustbin of history, writers and policy makers have asked: What happens next? We have labeled this section "post-Soviet possibilities" because it is not at all clear what types of political and economic systems will develop as a result of the collapse of the Soviet Union and the satellite states in Eastern Europe (the following discussion draws on Stokes, 1993; Tismineau, 1992; Przeworski, 1995; Stark and Bruszt, 1998).

There is one observation that virtually all writers agree on—"free market capitalism" (as we often call it) stands on the shoulders of a set of political and economic institutions that challenge the idea that free markets spontaneously erupt once government regulations and barriers are lifted. The economic and political institutions that make market capitalism work include:

1. A banking and credit system
2. Stable stock and securities markets
3. Institutionalized labor markets
4. A working public infrastructure (roads, sewers, power plants, transportation, and utilities)
5. A well-defined system of property rights
6. A judicial and legal system that monitors all of the above and sanctions those who break the rules

Most former state socialist nations also are interested in multiparty democracy, though what this means varies from one country to another (and from one citizen to another!). While most popular writers automatically link the development of multiparty democracy with market capitalism, the link is far from automatic. It may not be possible to have a democracy without a market economy of some sort, but it is certainly possible to have a market economy without multiparty democracy and the political freedoms that accompany it (as the experiences with dictatorships in South America in the 1970s and contemporary developments in Singapore and China have demonstrated).

Most obviously, the end of state socialism has meant the demise of the one-party state dominated by a communist party. Almost everywhere this has led to multiparty elections where a vast diversity of political interests competes for seats in national legislatures of all shapes and sizes. Most of these elections are governed by proportional representation rules in which all parties above a minimum voting threshold (usually around 5 percent of all votes cast) are granted seats in the legislature. Legislators then pick prime ministers from parties that receive the most votes or from the ranks of party coalitions that link multiple parties together in a ruling group.

But does the demise of the one-party state mean that all interested parties want multiparty democracy? Hardly! As Przeworski (1995) points out, most political factions will only accept multiparty democracy (1) if all political participants are committed to it, and (2) there are protections in place to shield losing parties and minority voters from retribution at the hands of the victors. The major problem in most former one-party states is that this requires an unusual amount of trust in the other parties in the system.

There are few coherent definitions of what a healthy democracy looks like, but most writers point to several basic characteristics that good democracies have. Most real democracies don't have all of these characteristics and others have some of these characteristics in limited amounts. In healthy democracies

1. *Losing is permissible.* Losers of elections and legislative fights accept the outcomes and resolve to "do better next time." In exchange for this agreement, the winners promise to protect the expressions of opinion and political activities of those who are out of office. If the victor in an election immediately abolishes all political opposition, there's a prob-

lem. If the losing parties immediately declare a civil war against the winners, that too is a problem.

2. *Stable sets of parties send clear signals to voters.* The number of parties that participate in each election doesn't fluctuate wildly, and specific parties represent a coherent set of policy choices from one election to the next. The differences between the parties are clear (the U.S. Republican and Democratic parties score poorly on this dimension), and voters have some idea what they are getting when they cast votes for specific parties.

3. *There is a strong functioning civil society.* Civil society refers to the myriad of connections that tie people to each other in groups that participate in a common life (cf. Etizioni, 1993). These connections occur mostly through independently organized groups: churches, schools, neighborhoods, clubs, and organizations that bring (mostly) adults together in a variety of settings to discuss their common interests and disagreements. While nobody is quite sure what the exact requirements for producing a functioning civil society are, one can sense when the bonds created by civil society are not present. A strong civil society does not mean that everyone likes each other; in fact, one of the signs of a functioning civil society is that conflicts are brought out in the open and discussed, often in heated but open exchanges. Democracies need functioning civil societies to build trust and to foster communication and participation.

4. *Actors focus on processes rather than outcomes.* Democracy is a *way* of making decisions. It doesn't guarantee that the best decision will be made. If democracy is only evaluated by the wisdom of the political decisions it produces, then it is in trouble. (Elshtain, 1995)

Dictatorships and other forms of government often justify themselves by promising concrete results. The process used to produce the results is viewed as the price that citizens have to pay for them. Healthy democracies place a great deal of faith in the belief that the specific processes associated with democracy will, in the long run, produce a favorable set of outcomes. But "favorable" is not the same as "best," nor does the burden of proof lie with evaluating the wisdom of any specific political choice.

From the standpoint of wedding new market economies to new multiparty democracies, however, the problems are more severe. Local populations often identify democracy with prosperity, looking to the United States and other developed nations as models. But the economic reforms required to convert a state socialist economy into a market economy usually will make large numbers of voters worse off before it makes them better off. Citizen who are impoverished by economic reforms become voters who vote for antireform politicians. If enough antireform politicians are elected, then the transition toward a market economy can grind to a halt.

Why is creating a market economy so hard? Because the political and economic institutions required to maintain it are so unique. Each of the institutions listed here plays a major role in making market economies work. Systems of *property rights* determine who gets access to resources and lays out the conditions for the use and sale of that access. Because most state socialist nations did not allow private citizens to own productive assets, these nations have had to figure out (1) how to create a market for productive assets apart from state ownership, and (2) how to sell state-owned assets to get them into private hands. Not surprisingly, there is no easy or fool-proof way to do this. To make matters worse, nations have to produce entirely new sets of laws regulating property rights that are completely different from those in state socialist societies and must produce court and legal systems to enforce them.

The problems are equally as serious when we turn to systems of banking. Market economies need financial institutions to provide loans at reasonable interest rates for entrepreneurs and businesses to engage in their activities. As Stark and Bruszt (1998) have shown, the ability of a bank to make good loans depends on the system of property rights. If the system of property rights is ambiguous, then people can secure loans without incurring any penalties for not repaying them or (worse still) can turn to the state to bail them out if business turns bad. Not surprisingly, a nation with a system of property rights that can't determine who owns what will not be able to assess taxes to maintain a public infrastructure, so tax dodging is rampant.

A functioning market economy also depends on a working infrastructure that makes economic transactions easier. In the United States and most developed nations, utilities and transportation systems are rarely an impediment to economic development except in extreme cases (California in 2001 being an example). We expect the lights to come on when we turn the switch, we expect our computers to work, and we expect clean water to come from the tap when we turn it on (at the temperature we desire, to boot!). We expect our trash to be picked up and our sewage to be treated in a way that won't damage the environment. We pick up the phone and expect to instantly find the person whose number we've dialed (from a cell phone no less). Citizens and businesses pay taxes to support these activities and usually pay private bills as well. The amount of money spent on these activities is a nontrivial portion of government expenditures each year and a significant portion of citizens' household budgets as well.

In state socialist societies, these services were not provided to promote economic efficiency. Consumer and business-oriented infrastructure was years behind where it was in the rest of the developed world and was not geared to dealing with a dynamic business environment. Systems of transportation and communications, in particular, have needed a serious overhall. It will be years before these systems are competitive with market economies in the rest of the developed world.

IN CONCLUSION: BUT WAS IT A REVOLUTION?

Let us end by returning to the notion of revolutions in general. How closely does the collapse of communism resemble what we said earlier about social revolution? Given that a government collapsed with profound political, economic, and social change, it is unavoidable to think that a revolution occurred. But scholars developed the notion of revolutions to describe kinds of movements and transformations that began in the 1700s and continued in developing regions of the contemporary world. Specialist scholars note many similarities between the collapse of communism and those processes, but also important differences.

Most conspicuously, we see what we described as revolutionary movements: a prolonged period preceding the collapse with high expectations for improvement, in conjunction with very modest actual improvement. These movements reached back to the Khrushchev period. The relative deprivation created by this dynamic was particularly pronounced after rapid actual deterioration of Soviet living standards in the mid-1970s and by the failure of Gorbachev's reforms to deliver any economic progress. Sufficient loosening of political and intellectual control created a political opportunity structure that enabled a vast mobilization of contenders for power, both within and without the regime. This effect is consistent with the resource mobilization perspectives discussed earlier.

Most of the elements of Skocpol's structural theory of revolution can be found in the collapse of communism. There is certainly ample evidence of strong international pressure on the Soviet state: the failure of the Soviets to keep up with the West economically, technologically, or militarily; the failure of Soviet schemes to gain influence among Third World nations; the military debacle in Afghanistan; and the ruinous financial consequences of the military arms race are all instances. The fact that the Soviet Union could provide little in the way of economic assistance to its allies and client states while routinely importing grain and other foodstuffs became an embarrassing international demonstration of the weakness of the Soviet economy for all to see. There was certainly an alienated class of marginal elites who illustrated the "desertion of the intellectuals" discovered so long ago by Crane Brinton, and others. There was no independent elite of wealthy persons or landlords to obstruct the regime, but there was certainly a high degree of factionalism and disunity within the regime and the party, so that intrigue and plots became pandemic. In this process power devolved from the central organs of the Party to include a much wider set of local, ideological, and opportunistic contenders for power. By the 1990s, the failure of reform had eroded Gorbachev's political base within the party. By the 1970s, public opinion in the USSR appeared to be apathetic but was really smoldering beneath the surface, ready to catch fire at the first sparks. Finally, as Skocpol theorized, the military proved an unreliable tool of the state, or in this case, a faction of the state seeking to exert its control.

The relative absence of popular uprisings and civil violence makes the transition out of communism different from other revolutions. States collapsed without a shot being fired, destruction of property, or loss of life in Poland, Hungary, Czechoslovakia, East Germany, and Bulgaria. True, in Romania there was a bloody revolt that resulted in the public lynching of dictator Ceausescu; Yugoslavia deteriorated into classic Balkan ethnic strife; and, as mentioned, there was periodic interethnic conflict in some non-Russian Soviet republics. But all told there was remarkably little violence or loss of life. During the abortive coup in Moscow three persons were killed in the confusion and maneuvering of military vehicles, but no shots were fired. All of this stands in stark contrast to the levels of violence and destruction that attended the American, French, and the (first) Russian revolutions. The most direct and obvious driving force in the collapse of the Soviet empire was disunity and conflict among elite factions within the government and Party, who in effect progressively dismantled themselves. As you might guess, a group of international scholars has studied this phenomenon intensely (see, for example, Rozman, 1992).

The transition from communism was unlike other revolutions because the regime did not resist reform but initiated it, and it could not contain this reform. It spilled out into political and social changes that could not be contained by the Communist Party–state system. When authoritarian regimes seek to liberalize, the result is uncertain democracy. When such states are under external pressure,

> elements of the ruling elite permit an airing of grievances to shore up their social base. Instead of demobilizing after their demands have been met, however, key groups in society mobilize broader followings around demands for wider and more meaningful participation in the political process. If the rulers open the political arena still more to admit new contenders for power; they lose control over . . . society and are ultimately forced to hand over power to . . . [others]. (O'Donnell and Schmitter, 1986)

The revolutionary collapse of the Soviet system had a different dynamic than historic revolutions and those that still occur in less modern nations. It has been conventional to see communist societies as variants of modern urban-industrial societies. But modernization was very uneven between cities and rural areas and between social classes. Perhaps as Polish scholar Adam Prezworski has suggested, communist societies were in truth neither traditional nor wholly modern, but types of an underdeveloped "something else" (1991:21). They will certainly connect with the world market economy. And, continuing to modernize, they will evolve societies that are not carbon copies of Western free market ones but that combine reforms with their own history, culture, and politics. Will revolutionary collapse occur in the remaining communist states (China, Cuba, North Korea)? Stay tuned.

THINKING PERSONALLY ABOUT SOCIAL CHANGE

In this chapter we use the word *revolution* in a more specific way than we do when talking about the sexual revolution, the computer revolution, or other pervasive long-term changes. Revolution here always involves a seemingly sudden change of a political regime (and other things as well), and it is a macro-level event. But we do talk about "rebellions" and "rebellious people" in smaller organizations and families.

1. Talk to some people of various ages who are old enough to have lived through the time when Soviet communism collapsed. Talk with them about how life in the United States was different before that collapse, and what it has become since. If you can, talk with someone who lived through or remembers the 1950s, when government officials in the United States engaged in a large-scale witch hunt to find communist subversives everywhere.

2. The United States has always had lots of reform movements (about everything imaginable!). It has had revolutionary movements but no successful ones since the first one (though it did fight a brutal civil war!). Why do you think this is true? How do people think about the American Revolution? How is it depicted in popular media and school

textbooks? If you can, talk to some British or Canadians about how it is understood there. If you know people from Mexico or Cuba, ask them about the revolutions in their national histories. Mexicans celebrate Cinco de Mayo like Americans do the Fourth of July. The Cuban revolution of 1959 had implications for the United States as well as Cuba (do you live South Florida?). Its consequences are still very obvious in American politics and foreign policy. In fact, the American relationship with Cuba remains a point of controversy among the United States and other Western Hemispheric nations, European allies, and trading partners. It has often shaped domestic politics as well. Find out something about revolutionary processes in all the Americas. In some places they continue.

3. The United States has not had successful revolutionary movements, but it has, and continues to have, revolutionaries. Read or talk with some people about radical militias, terrorist groups, "people's courts," the Klansmen and other Aryan Supremacist groups, and the so-called "Christian identity churches." At the end of the last chapter, one question asked what people you spoke with thought about the diversity of reform movements. What do they think of these groups?

CHAPTER

10

Technology, Innovation, and Networks

The last chapters were about social movements, human agency, and how large collections of people advocate or respond to change, sometimes in revolutionary ways. But change is often spurred by innovations and discoveries within a society, both scientific/technical and sociocultural ones. For instance, the invention of the internal combustion engine, television, silicon microchips, and effective birth control all significantly shaped the course of history in the twentieth century. Such innovations create new possibilities, but also problems and dilemmas. For instance, artificial insemination, surrogate motherhood, and medical innovations for sustaining life all created new health and reproductive potentials before society recognized or addressed the ethical, moral, and legal issues they raised (Newman, 1995: 479). This chapter focuses on (1) change from innovations (both technological and nontechnological), (2) how innovations spread within societies, and (3) their complex consequences for persons and social change.

INNOVATION AS A CHANGE PROCESS

Innovation can stimulate change by (1) the discovery or invention of novelty, (2) its communication to others, and (3) its adoption or rejection by people in a society. Yet exactly how innovations occur, which people adopt them, why they are adopted or not, and the complex mix of benefits or problems they create is not simple to understand. *Consider the following illustration.*

Right now we are using a computer to write this. We simply cannot imagine writing books the "old" way, with an old Olivetti-Underwood typewriter, cutting and pasting corrections and alterations. But some writers do, and some write books with pads of paper and pencils. Do you use a computer? Maybe so, maybe not. But unless you've been living under a rock somewhere, you know that new technologies for transmitting and storing information are transforming the world. *Information technology* includes *computers* with their incredible capability to transmit and store information (both words and numbers); the *Internet* that you may be "wired to," with which you might send or receive information about an incredible variety of subjects; the proliferation of *web pages* that advertise places, products, and services of all kinds; and *compact disks* that enable you to interact with what you are seeing. Information technology was not new to the 1990s, but the earliest computers were a few large ponderous contraptions that took up whole floors or buildings and were only owned and used by big organizations. Indeed, there is more computing power on our desks than the university had twenty-five years ago. Maybe you have a portable laptop computer you can take anywhere.

Computers and the flotsam and jetsam of information technology enabled humans to bring into being a new sense of reality, variously called *virtual reality, cyberspace,* or other pizzazzy terms. By changing technical capacities and our "sense of reality," information technologies changed the nature of work, creating new possibilities for companies but frustrating many employees' lives. They made the world market economy possible. (Recall the discussion of changing work and the U.S. economy in the first chapters?) Some argue that silicon microchips—the minute electric conductors at the physical heart of all computers—are the contemporary equivalents of the eighteenth-century steam power and are fueling a new "long-wave" economic cycle of global proportions. Human interaction mediated by technology is not new. Letters and phone calls are earlier forms. But electronic information technology has increased the possibility of finding people to collect bills, sell them products, or mobilize them for causes. It has radically altered the basis and customs of advertising oneself and finding, meeting, and carrying on relationships with other persons (both compatible and bothersome ones!).

Information technology transforms the various kinds of human interaction by *deterritorializing* interaction, meaning that the distance is increasingly less relevant for people doing things together—working, socializing, buying and selling, or joining networks devoted to causes (Phillips, 1996; Cornish, 1996:3; Castells, 1998). Harper has a great illustration of this. A sociologist from Washington State sent him an e-mail message to say that he met a person from China at a meeting in Brazil who was interested in a Chinese translation of a book he worked on in 1995. He gave Harper the e-mail address of that person at Beijing University. Harper sent a note about that to his Prentice Hall editor in New Jersey with a copy to the person in China—who happened to be in his office (around the world) and sent back a note within the day, as did Harper's editor in New Jersey. *When you think about that, it is remarkable.* From Nebraska, Harper got a note from Washington State, sent a reply to New Jersey and China, and heard back from both—all in about a day and a half. Such communication over vast spaces was unimaginable twenty years ago.

Deterritorialized interaction is remarkable. It raises the scale of human interaction with mixed consequences, not all of them experienced as good. It brings us into contact with a vast array of people, cultural styles, and organizations that are complex, dimly understood, and often outright destructive. It changes people's relationships and identification with local people, places, and nations by raising both the scope and complexity of social life. Among users of information technology there are "cybersavvies" and "cyberklutzes," the latter of whom often find computers and information technology overly complex, frustrating, and subject to seemingly whimsical malfunctions. While Internet access has spread worldwide (see Figure 10-1), large parts of the human population are left out in increasingly computerized postindustrial societies. They are left out because of complex interactions among their age cohort, social network connections, social class, experience, education, culture, and nationality—a complex reality with *profound* social implications.

In sum, this illustration should demonstrate (1) that innovation is a basis of social change; (2) that even technological innovations have sociocultural dimensions, with complex and often unpredictable consequences when widely adopted; and (3) that complex factors shape their spread, adoption, or rejection within human communities and societies. We will return to information technology throughout the chapter and will conclude by exploring some social implications of this revolution.

THE ACT OF INNOVATION

Innovative action involves "a linkage or fusion of two or more elements that have not been previously joined in just this fashion, so that the result is a qualitatively distinct whole. . . . It is a true synthesis in that the product is a unity which has properties entirely different from its individual antecedents" (Barnett, 1953:181). Innovative material gadgets or systems result in social change *if* they are incorporated in novel cultural patterns and human action. All innovation results from combinations of things and ideas that are qualitatively different from the status quo, but there are degrees of novelty:

- *Variation,* or a borderline innovation, involves the modification of something that already exists, like changing the shape of a tool or sail. There is no combination of diverse elements, but only a creative modification of "what exists."
- *Substitution,* where new materials or ideas are used. Examples include substituting metal for stone or feedback systems like thermostats to understand the workings of human societies.
- *Mutations* that involve novel combinations or reorganizations of elements rather than the substitution of one for another. An example is the innovation of printing in fifteenth-century Europe that combined block printing, first used to print playing cards and money; oil-based ink created by Flemish artists; metal casting with antimony that made lead hard enough to use; paper, imported to Europe through the Mongol empire; and a press, adapted from the wine and linen industry. Most basic of all, of course, was the alphabet, requiring the repetition of a few symbols—in contrast to the complex pictographic written languages of the Orient. (Ryan, 1969)

A distinction is sometimes made between *basic* (or strategic) and *improving* innovations. This distinction is based on the idea that some innovations are more important than others in that they involve greater novelty, and some are strategic in that they trigger other innovations. Thus the basic discovery of the facts about the circulation of the blood triggered other discoveries in medicine and physiology in rapid succes-

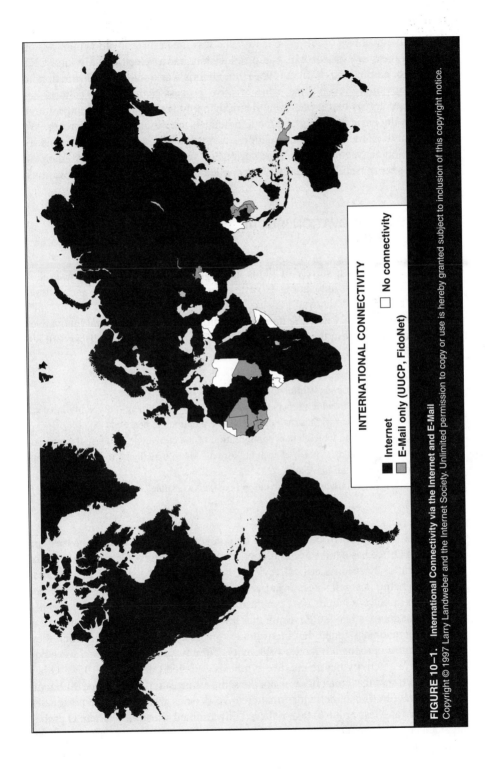

FIGURE 10–1. International Connectivity via the Internet and E-Mail
Copyright © 1997 Larry Landweber and the Internet Society. Unlimited permission to copy or use is hereby granted subject to inclusion of this copyright notice.

INTERNATIONAL CONNECTIVITY

■ Internet
▨ E-Mail only (UUCP, FidoNet)
□ No connectivity

sion. And the invention of the cathode ray tube was the basic innovation upon which a host of others are based (e.g., radio, television, radar, electric-eye doors, CRT terminals for computers). Barnett (1953) thought this was a subjective distinction, in that all innovations involve the same creative process and all have cultural antecedents. He argues that if one were to strictly apply the distinction, then primitive humans are the basic innovator and modern humans are the adapter or improver! We would grant to Barnett that the distinction is a relative one, yet if all that one means is a distinction between the more basic design and subsequent modifications then the distinction seems useful, especially when applied to a cluster of related innovations.

SOURCES OF INNOVATION: SOCIAL, AND CULTURAL

Scholarly research in a variety of fields about innovation and circumstances surrounding the spread of innovations is vast. Here we address the social and cultural conditions under which innovation is likely.

But first we briefly note the flurry of research interest in individual innovativeness or "creativity" from the 1950s and 1960s. One view from Gestalt psychology described innovation as a four-phase process:

1. *Perception of a problem,* stimulated by unfulfilled needs and wants.
2. *Setting the stage,* in which a person "assembles" all the elements of a solution (data, materials, notes, parts). This may or may not be a deliberate process.
3. *An act of insight,* in which a new configuration of meaning appears. Gestalt psychologists describe this as a "flash of insight," or an "Aha!" experience in which disparate elements seem to fall into place.
4. *Critical revision,* in which an innovation is made "workable" in some context. (Usher, 1954)

Innovations that are not widely adopted may never go through the last phase. The U.S. Patent Office has a huge accumulation of such innovations. Or, as in the case of solar-generated electricity, critical revision may be a long historical process that comes into being in small stages over years.

To these ideas scholars have emphasized the importance of an incubation period prior to creative insight. Research that reviewed reports of creativity among famous mathematicians found that innovators often described a period in which they were stuck in unproductive modes of activity. They typically engaged in some peripheral or rest activity before creative synthesis emerged (Hadamard, 1954). Other researchers found that creativity was not the same as measured intelligence (although it may be required in some fields), that creative persons were more interpersonally autonomous and less prone to take risks in "unwarranted situations." There is probably not a creative personality type (see Stein and Heinze, 1960; Getzels and Jackson, 1962; Wallach and Kogan, 1965).

Innovation and Society

Beyond individual attributes, *what social conditions make high rates of innovation likely?* Sociologists and others have identified six structural conditions in societies that make innovation more likely. We treat them here only in summary fashion.

    1. *Innovation is more likely when there are perceived internal inconsistencies (or "contradictions") that produce social tensions.* Note that this generalization emphasizes that inconsistencies must be perceived as inconsistencies. Any social condition can objectively exist for a long time without being perceived as stress producing. Poverty, racial discrimination, domestic violence, political corruption, and budget deficits are certainly not new or unique to the United States, but until such conditions are widely perceived by people and elites as problems deserving attention there will be few innovative institutional attempts to deal with these conditions. So perceived, they will generate innovation aimed at reducing social stress and more integrative conditions within society. This generalization could be viewed as a page torn from either neofunctionalist or conflict theories in sociology.

    2. *Innovation is likely in societies having difficulties with adaptations to the physical environment.* When that environmental adaptation is threatened, innovation becomes probable. Whether it is successful or not is another matter! In the United States, for instance, the dustbowl drought conditions of the 1930s stimulated a cascade of innovations in farming, land use, conservation, and tillage practices, as well as farm relief measures addressing this condition. Energy crises, a chronic source of innovation, are not new. The cutting of most trees in Western Europe (especially in England) forced attempts to find new energy sources (coal). There is an intriguing hypothesis here, though we know of no research that has studied it systematically: Every significant change in the mode of economic production was preceded by an innovation in the generation of energy, which was in turn stimulated by a near exhaustion of conventional energy sources. Early in American history, for instance, there was an energy crisis of sorts when whales were hunted to near extinction (whale oil was the major source of oil for lamps). This led to the development of kerosene as fuel for lamps. While today there seems not to be an immediate world shortage of the crude oil that powers most industrial economies (so long as the pipelines can be kept open by treaties, bribery, or war!), the accumulation of greenhouse gases that threaten to alter the climate may stimulate a cascade of innovative energy sources (Harper, 2001: chaps. 4, 6).

    3. *Innovation is more likely in societies that have broadly as opposed to narrowly defined social norms, rules, and role expectations.* The question is not the integration (or consistency) of social rule and norms, but the degree of latitude they provide. Evidence suggests that "ambiguity and latitude of structure and rules offers innovative opportunity through both tolerance for normative deviance and misunderstandings of both norms and expectations . . . loosely structured societies are more amenable to innovation" (Ryan, 1969:7).

    4. *Higher rates of innovation are more likely in societies, communities, or organizations that have higher rates of replacement and succession of people.* New people who replace older ones are carriers of innovation. The relationship between rates of

succession and the spread of change has long been noted for age cohorts (Mannheim, 1950; Ryder, 1965) and in organizations (Gouldner, 1954; Caplow, 1964; Scott, 1995). We discussed this effect in relation to American Baby Boomers and the flood of new immigrants in earlier chapters.

5. *Growth in population size and density is likely to stimulate innovation.* This is a forthrightly functionalist proposition (see Durkheim, 1983/1947; Mott, 1968). Growth in size and density produces integration problems of both *horizontal* and *vertical* integration that smaller systems don't have. What is likely to happen is the elaboration of coordinative structures or roles that address these stresses. Remember the discussion of bureaucracy in the first chapters?

6. *Innovations are stimulated by social catastrophes and disasters.* Wars, floods, economic depressions, and plagues are overwhelming events that societies cannot deal with by conventional means. Innovations, both technological and social, deriving from warfare would take a whole book to just catalog. But take another illustration: The devastation of frequent tornadoes in the American Midwest has produced an effective early warning system so that the loss of life from these is minimal today (though property damage is sometimes horrific). Innovations included not only meteorological warning systems, but the development of media response and disaster response procedures as well as state and national property insurance mechanisms that can apply. In general, such innovations aim at (1) dealing with the immediate effects of disaster, and (2) preventing or preparing for future occurrences. Indeed, you can view the United Nations and the World Bank as "institutional innovations" stimulated by "world" disasters (the Great Depression of the 1930s and World War II).

Innovation and "Necessity"

Implicit in these views of the innovation is that it happens as a problem-solving mechanism. But is this always so? *Is necessity really the mother of invention?* What is meant by "necessity," anyway? It obviously includes human physical and safety needs, but also perceived problems and needs about values and goals. The notion of needs involves some kind of felt tension, some source of dissatisfaction with the status quo. But there are many examples of innovations and inventions made without dissatisfaction being an obvious factor. Many innovations "look for a necessity," in a manner of speaking. For example, Teflon, a unique material that very few substances would stick to, was inadvertently discovered by DuPont chemists in 1938. Between 1939 and 1964, DuPont spent $100 million developing the manufacturing process and trying to find a marketable necessity until they came up with using it to coat frying pans in 1964 (Ryan, 1969:84).

Another accidental invention is the silicon microchip, the premiere innovation driving information technologies. Such miniature integrated circuit microchips were developed independently by Jack Kilbey and Robert Noyes six months apart in 1958 and 1959. The first models were about one-quarter inch square and capable of containing six to eight separate circuits. While in theory the uses of such small integrated circuits were obvious, there was no existing market for them and they were terribly expensive to produce. The impetus for their use and development came when NASA, at the urging of the Kennedy administration in the 1960s, decided to put a person on the moon. Microcircuitry had obvious advantages when space and payload were at a premium. Current microchips have undergone so much development (improving innovations) that now upwards of a million separate circuits can be contained in a quarter-inch microchip!

Even *experts* often do not understand the potential for an innovation to transform society and culture. Here are some striking and funny examples:

- "Radio has no future, heavier-than-air flying machines are impossible, X-rays will prove to be a hoax."—Lord Kelvin, English scientist (1824–1907)
- "Who the hell wants to hear actors talk?" Harry M. Warner, founder of Warner Bros. Studio (1927)
- "Rail travel at high speeds is not possible because passengers, unable to breathe, would die of asphyxia"—Dionysius Lardner, English scientist (1793–1859)
- "While theoretically and technically television may be feasible, commercially and financially I consider it to be an impossibility"—Lee DeForest, American inventor (1873–1960). (Hiller, 1996)

You can see that innovations are often made before their use is needed, obvious, or viewed as practical. But "necessities" can be created, particularly in consumer goods, through advertising, marketing, and the manipulation of perceived consumer needs. There are many cases of innovations that never become hooked to any human necessity and are never adopted on a wide scale. The archives of the U.S. Patent Office are literally full of such innovations, which are never needed and find no market. Necessity is often the mother of invention, but *an equally plausible* case can be made that invention is sometimes the mother of necessity! What you can conclude from all this is that for innovations to produce social change, they must be widely adopted and somehow become related to people's "needs and necessities" and to their capacities to adopt and use them.

Innovation and Culture

The probability of innovation is related to

- The size and complexity of the cultural base
- Whether many cultural rules and norms are viewed as practical or instrumental rather than as fixed moral or sacred rules
- The extent to which a culture normalizes innovation and change (Ogburn, 1938; White, 1949; Barnett, 1953)

The size and complexity of a cultural base is an interesting but abstract idea. The size and complexity of the cultural inventory available to innovators in a particular culture establishes limits within which they must function. The state of knowledge, range and kinds of artifacts, techniques, and instruments they can use make some new developments possible and others impossible. The mere accumulation of ideas and things provides more materials for innovators to work with (Barnett,

1950:40). This is obvious when you think about tools and materials available to craftsmen and inventors of material innovations, but scholars argue that it also applies to the realm of abstract knowledge, ideas, and social innovations.

A related idea is that *an innovation will not come into being until the cultural base is sufficiently developed to permit its occurrence.* At one level, this is a self-evident and not very interesting proposition. Medieval farmers, for example, could not have invented a modern tractor, even though they could have used one, because the cultural base was not ready. Such an invention would have required knowledge of the laws of gas expansion, the availability of refined petroleum distillates, and the mechanics of the internal combustion engine—all unavailable in European culture of the 1300s.

Another proposition is more interesting and contentious: *When the culture is ready for an invention, it will come into being, whether people want it or not* (White, cited in Cuzzort and King, 1980). If this is true, then culture is truly a self-generating force. This focus on cultural readiness is a perspective on innovation that contrasts sharply with the "great man" theory of innovation. As evidence, consider that large numbers of simultaneous inventions have been developed. Ogburn (1922) listed 150 such innovations. Here are just a few (cited in Cuzzort and King, 1980):

- Decimal fractions, by Rudolff (1530), Stevinus (1586), and Burgi (1592)
- Law of gases, by Boyle (1662) and Mariotte (1697)
- The telescope, by Della Porta (1558); Digges (1571); Johannides, Metius (1608); Lippershey (1608); Drebble, Fontana, Janssen (1608); Galileo (1609)
- The phonograph, by Edison (1877), Scott and Cros (1877)
- The skull is made of modified vertebrae, by Oaken (1776) and Goethe (1790)
- Theory of infection by microorganisms, by Fracastoro (1546) and Kircher (1546)
- Solution of the problem of respiration, by Priestley (1777), Scheele (1777), Lavoisier (1777), Spallanzani (1777), and Davy (1777)
- Theory of natural selection and variation, by Darwin (1858) and Wallace (1858)
- Theory of mutations, by Korschinsky (1899) and De Vries (1900)
- Use of gasoline engines in automobiles, by Otto (1876), Selden (1879), and Daimler (1885)

Concretely, of course, individuals are the *actual* innovators, but anthropologist Leslie White (1949) interprets such lists as evidence that culture is a self-generating force. When the cultural configuration of elements is ready for an innovation, it seems to appear simultaneously from several independent sources. This is an intriguing perspective: Any culture is "pregnant" at a given stage of development, that is, awaiting the development of innovations for which it is ready. An interesting project would be to try to forecast innovations (technological and social) that are just over the horizon, given the immense cultural inventories of contemporary societies. With global travel, communications, and electronic data storage, the cultural inventory available to twenty-first century inventors is enormous.

The rate of innovation is greater when more cultural rules and norms are viewed as pragmatic and instrumental rather than intrinsically legitimate, moral, or sacred rules. Most cultures have both types of rules: those that have intrinsic legitimation and those that have practical legitimation. In the United States, for instance, rules governing economic production and distribution tend to be pragmatic and utilitarian, and Americans are very willing to innovate in these realms. On the other hand, cultural rules governing sexuality and family relationships tend to be intrinsically legitimated, and Americans are much more reluctant to accept innovation in these realms, as the political controversies of the 1990s about family values illustrate. But in some cultures, intrinsically legitimated rules are very extensive, and even the most minute and mundane rules governing social interaction are imbued with sacred meaning. Such situations are not conducive to cultural innovation.

Perhaps even more important is *the extent to which a culture normalizes and expects innovation and change.* The more a culture's worldview sees the cosmos as being in a state of change, flux, and/or development, the more innovation will be encouraged. On the other hand, where the cosmos is viewed as a static closed system, innovation will be inhibited and change viewed as an aberration. Contemporary Americans tend to think of traditional and preliterate cultures as having a static picture of the universe and modern cultures as having an open-ended, evolutionary view. But the truth is a good deal more complicated than this. Anthropologists have observed that some preliterate societies do have worldviews that inhibit innovation. The Zuni Native Americans of New Mexico, for instance,

> were restrictive in their anticipations [for change]. . . . They neither hope for nor anticipate changes in any part of their culture, and they are resolute against any suggestion of the idea. They are extremely ethnocentric and are uninterested in the world around them; they, in fact, regard their village as the center of the world. (Barnett, 1953:56)

Other Native American and preliterates were different:

> The Navajo, who live close to the Zuni, take another view. They expect new developments in their culture; and their history, in so far as it is known, reveals that they have been receivers and adapters of alien customs throughout the period of their occupation of their present habitat. . . . They welcome change, accepting it as a realistic adjustment to the world around them. . . . The Samoans are also anticipators of change, but in a way different from that of the Navajo. They expect each individual among them to be unique in everything that he does. Imitation is deplored. Every woman has her own design for tapa cloth. . . . Every person is expected to improvise songs and dance steps for himself. Likewise for house builders, tattooers, and other specialists. The expectation of deviation even extends to religion and political organization, both for individuals and villages. Innovation is the rule, and in consequence the innovator receives only passing recognition. He is merely doing what is expected of him. (Barnett, 1953:56–57)

While there was variation among the more traditional cultures of the world (of which vestiges still exist), it is still probably true that historical development has everywhere promoted an open-ended worldview conducive to high rates of innovation. The Western Judeo-Christian notion of human beings having control over the environment; the idea of universal progress, deriving from Enlightenment thinking in the 1700s; and secularization, which gradually removed some cultural values and norms from sacred sanction, have all combined to produce a worldview that treats change as normal and legitimizes innovation in many spheres of social life. The sheer availability of information from different peoples and cultures makes the spread of cultural and technological innovations (or defenses against them) unavoidable in the modern world.

DIFFUSION: HOW INNOVATIONS SPREAD

The spread (or diffusion) of innovation was the subject of over 1500 studies dating back to the 1930s. Diffusion research was from such diverse intellectual fields as anthropology, rural sociology, medical sociology, educational research, and mass media studies. These studies produced some of the best empirical literature on social change processes, and their findings have been summarized and codified (see Rogers, 1962; Rogers and Shoemaker, 1971; Zaltman, 1973; Rothman, 1974; Zaltman and Duncan, 1977). While this research focuses on the diffusion by contact between different cultures, it also has a strong applied flavor and examines deliberate attempts to promote change. Researchers have studied, for instance, attempts to introduce new seed hybrids, drugs, and health projects in developing nations; innovations in media; educational reform; and the promotion of computers and information technologies. Research findings with diverse topics are remarkably consistent and cumulative.

Cross-Cultural Contact and Rates of Diffusion

Anthropologists who studied cultural change were interested in the spread of innovation between different cultures. It was an alternative to the nineteenth-century social evolution theories of change that were factually inadequate. Most research did not focus on finding some (mythical?) center of the diffusion of civilization, but on the spread of culture traits resulting from the contact between different cultures. Instead, they argued that culture contact, not indigenous maturation, is the source of most innovation and social change. This is debatable (it depends on what you are talking about). But it is certainly true that culture contact is a major factor in the spread of innovations. Besides the diffusion of discrete cultural items, anthropologists also studied *acculturation,* a more global term than diffusion—which means "the influence exercised by one culture on another, or the mutual influence of two cultures, that results in cultural change" (Lauer, 1977:294).

Anthropological research produced a number of useful generalizations about conditions of successful diffusion. Diffusion between cultures is *most likely*

- when the new item is perceived as being consistent with the structure and values of the host culture.
- when the culture item is material (versus nonmaterial).

- when there are a greater number of people in cross-cultural contact.
- when the quality of such contact is friendly rather than hostile.
- when the contact between two societies connects elites and central elements rather than peripheral or marginal elements of the two societies. (Spindler, 1977)

Sociologists also studied change by spreading innovation, and their early major contribution was to demonstrate that the *rate of adoption* for many innovations generally followed a sigmoid or S-shaped curve, starting out slowly, accelerating rapidly, and reaching a plateau when almost everyone who is going to adopt an innovation has done so (Chapin, 1928; Ogburn, 1922).

Later research found that the S-shaped diffusion curve *depends on the degree of social integration within a population.* In other words, where people in groups and organizations have many close relationships, the rate of adoption accelerates after a slow start, and plateaus or tapers off when almost everybody who is going to adopt it has done so. By contrast, where people are weakly connected, adoption of innovation spreads from person to person at the same (linear) rate and doesn't vary so much at different times. Studies have found this pattern, for instance, in rates of adoption of new drugs and medical techniques within different medical communities (Katz, 1960).

What Characteristics of Innovations Affect Diffusion?

In addition to conditions of contact between cultures and the degree of social integration within communities and populations, the characteristics of innovations themselves shape the extent to which they diffuse and are adopted. Scholars who examined evidence argued that five innovation characteristics do this:

1. The *relative advantage* of innovations over what exists at the time.
2. The *compatibility with existing cultural, social, and psychological characteristics* of potential adopters. For instance, forms of Christianity emphasizing separate congregations with no church hierarchy or bishops had the greatest missionary success in Samoa because that form was compatible with the autonomous village structure of Samoan society.
3. The *relative simplicity* of innovations. Other things being equal, simpler innovations are more likely to be adopted than complex ones.
4. The *divisibility* of innovations. If they can be tried out on a piecemeal basis, people will be most likely to adopt them. For instance, the remarkable spread of new seed hybrids among U.S. farmers occurred partly because they could be tried on small experimental plots. By contrast, new plans for governments or new school curriculums are often resisted because they are often not divisible and can't be "tried out" in small pieces.
5. Apart from simplicity, *the ease with which innovations can be communicated* shapes their likelihood of adoption. (Rogers, 1962; Thio, 1971)

The ease with which innovations can be communicated may result from their *observability,* or the extent to which they have *instrumental* versus *expressive* or esthetic effects (Ryan, 1969). Observability may be at the core of the finding by anthropologists that material culture items are more readily adopted than nonmaterial culture. It may also explain why the "disembodied techniques" of Eastern religions (like yoga and meditation) spread to the United States earlier and more easily than the complex metaphysical systems and worldviews within which they were imbedded.

Communication Channels for Innovation

Historically the diffusion of innovations required some kind of physical contact between people. Hence migrations and wars were always important sources of the diffusion of innovation, because immigrants and returning soldiers brought with them things that were regarded as innovations by their societies. The need for contact also meant that special categories of people (i.e., merchants, traders, explorers) have played a particular role in the historic diffusion of innovations.

The invention of the printing press in the fifteenth century provided a new possibility: the diffusion of innovation without physical contact between peoples. Literacy was historically in the hands of social elites or special categories of persons with supportive relations with them (e.g., scribes, monks). Thus the real impact of print media was dependent upon the development of mass education and literacy, a twentieth-century phenomenon that limits the effectiveness of print media because it has yet to happen on a larger scale in some developing nations. Electronic media created a new threshold. Radio and television had great potential for the mass diffusion of innovation because they do not require literacy. We noted earlier the "deterritorialized interaction" possible with proliferating forms of information technology, which gives them an enormous potential for the diffusion of all kinds of innovation. But like the limitations of print media, the absence of education, "computer literacy," and sufficient resources among parts of the human population limit the diffusion of information technologies.

Diffusion and the Mass Media

We are inundated with mass media messages trying to get us to do something, change something, or try some new product. And we worry a lot about the ability of the media to change people's behavior about things like violence and sexuality. But most research about the mass media suggests that they have limited *direct effects* for producing change. Mass communication is one-way communication with limited capacity for feedback from audiences who listen, read, or watch. Recipients of *mass communication* can't really ask questions, get clarification, or talk back in any meaningful way. Effective persuasion to adopt change usually requires *interactive communication* between an agent promoting change and potential adopters. Direct effects of mass media communication are limited because they are typically modified by interpersonal communication among persons who are tuned to the same media message. You are likely to discuss the significance of media messages with friends, family members, and co-workers, and they are critically reshaped and assessed by the perspectives of informal groups.

Other factors limit direct media effects. The *selective* exposure, perception, and retention that people bring to their media exposure also limit its ability to persuade people to change. People who initially feel more positively about a particular innovation and change are the ones most likely to be receptive to mass communication about it and most likely to interpret it in a favorable light. For example, television messages about voting Republican or using new contraceptive techniques are most likely to have positive impacts on people favorably inclined toward Republican politicians or contraception in the first place. People are, in other words, most likely to pay attention to, favorably interpret, and remember information about those things that they feel positive about to begin with. What people bring to the media is at least as important as what the media brings to people. Savvy advertisers have known this fact for a long time.

Mass communication has greater *direct effects* in persuading people under two conditions: One is when people are isolated, and a second is when social norms are not effective—in other words, when a condition of *anomie* (or normlessness) prevails (Larsen, 1964). Mass society theorists (e.g., Wirth, 1957) suggested that modernization produces higher levels of anomie and more social isolation so that greater proportions of people in contemporary societies are more susceptible to direct media persuasion. But many kinds of social research fail to support this *mass society thesis*. We don't think it is entirely wrong, but it is deeply flawed as a general theory to understand change in the contemporary world (see Chapters 2, 3, and 6).

The actual effects of mass media are quite complex. A summary of several decades of media research in the 1960s suggested the media can

- intensify existing attitudes and opinions.
- reduce the intensity of attitudes and opinions.
- create new attitudes and opinions.
- convert people to new attitudes and opinions contrary to prior ones. (Mapper, 1960)

Of these different possible effects, research suggests that *the last one is the least likely,* for reasons we noted earlier. In sum, the mass media appear to be more effective in disseminating new information than in changing established behavior or attitudes. They appear to have little persuasive effect without reinforcement by interpersonal communication in an informal group context. This is contrary to some of our worst fears about the ability of the media to directly seduce people to commit dangerous or antisocial behavior unless they were so inclined in the first place.

But the media can have important *long-term effects* for social change. They may not be able to get individuals to believe or try new things. They do, however, help socialize people and can shape the culture of knowledge, attitudes, and behavior that people bring to media exposure. For instance, the media may not cause violence but may help produce a culture where people are desensitized and less shocked by violence.

Communication, Diffusion, and Change

Many studies have discovered a "two-step flow of communication," meaning that communication originating within the mass media goes first to people termed opinion leaders before being transmitted to a segment of a population. We think that this should be termed a *two-step flow of influence,* since what these studies investigate is the flow of influence rather than merely communication (Katz and Lazarsfeld, 1955; Beal and Rogers, 1959; Wilkening, 1960).

Opinion leaders differ. *Cosmopolitan opinion leaders* are more oriented toward the mass media and more aware of specific innovations and their advantages than their local counterparts. Cosmopolitan opinion leaders are effective in discrete fields (art, science, music, politics, clothing styles, health, etc.). They are more likely than other people to belong to secondary groups such as special interest and professional organizations. Primary interpreters of specialized and mass media, they communicate information and channel information influence to people in local groups. In contrast, *local opinion leaders* hold central and strategic power positions in the local groups to which they belong. They are more likely than other group members to know and have working relationships with cosmopolitan leaders external to the local group or organization. They are gatekeepers who can effectively promote or bloc the adoption of innovations by members of local groups.

But this oversimplifies. Rather than two links, or stages, in many influence processes, there is typically a *multistep flow* (Menzel and Katz, 1955). Consider agricultural innovations such as new hybrids or genetically engineered crops. They typically begin with researchers (working in a college of agriculture or an agribusiness firm). Research is typically published in a specialty agricultural magazine or research bulletin and is likely to be picked up first by the county agricultural extension agents (cosmopolitan leaders), who in turn persuade locally prominent farmers or ranchers (local opinion leaders) to try out innovations. If the latter find it successful, other farmers will adopt the new practice.

Or consider information technologies, the illustration that began this chapter. A host of innovators developed computer and information technology ideas and hardware over several decades. Legions of specialists refined, adapted, and marketed these technologies for particular uses (like writing letters and constructing tables rather than keeping track of the trajectories of guided missiles). But none of these people was personally known to us. So how did we come to adopt some infotech in our work? Obviously because the university made it available. But also because over the years colleagues with special computer skills and an abiding infatuation with information technologies have promoted, advertised, helped, and ridiculed us into doing so. We can envision other chains of influence through which we acquire new sociological information or theory. They *are not* the same specific chains of opinion leaders (from most cosmopolitan to most local) that led us adopt some elements of information technology.

ADOPTION OF INNOVATION: SOCIAL SYSTEMS AND INDIVIDUALS

The *adopting units* of innovation can be either social systems (communities, organizations) or individuals. Individual adopters go through phases during adoption, where they (1) learn about innovations, (2) are persuaded to adopt them, (3) make a decision, and (4) try out a new thing or behavior. In social systems decisions to adopt may be authoritative, in which most individuals have little direct control over whether to adopt something or not (such as the adoption of a new city charter, a reformed system of welfare services, or school curriculum). Or adoption may be an optional collective decision that requires individual acquiescence (such as adopting new health behaviors or cable TV). The phases of adoption in social systems typically includes phases of

- *Stimulation* of interest within the system, typically by cosmopolitan opinion leaders removed from the actual organization or community
- *Initiation* of the new idea by local opinion leaders
- *Legitimation* of the innovation by locally prestigious and powerful persons
- *Decisions to adopt or reject* by some kind of decision-making body, democratic or otherwise (Rogers and Shoemaker, 1971)

Structurally, groups, organizations, and communities can effectively adopt new things or resist them when

- *They are cohesive,* where group "pressures to change or resist" will be more strongly felt by individuals
- *They have more concentrated power structures,* avoiding paralyzing conflict among powerful legitimizers of action
- *There is widespread participation in decisions to adopt or resist new ideas* (Eibler, 1965; Gamson, 1968; Davis, 1965; Zaltman, Duncan, and Holbeck, 1973)

Group cohesion and widespread participation are particularly important for the collective-optional innovations mentioned earlier. Participation can be of many sorts: surveys, petitions, referendums, and public hearings.

Most of the research about adoption of innovation focused on individuals, and most seek to contrast early and late adopters. Hundreds of such studies were conducted in the 1960s and 1970s, and most concluded that early adopters are higher in socioeconomic status (however measured) and are more likely to be active social participators than late adopters. By contrast, late adopters are depicted as semi-isolates, with low rates of social participation. We think it's interesting that late adopters knew about innovations at about the same time as early adopters, but there was a considerable time lag. Early adopters typically had (1) more resources for "risk" ventures, and (2) broad social contacts and more formal education enabling them to conceptualize the unfamiliar (see Rogers, 1962; Rogers and Shoemaker, 1971). If this is true, then change via innovation can be understood as a top-down process, organized and promoted by specialists and elites. The target population, or adopting units, is viewed as passive.

But wait. *Evidence for these generalizations is mixed*: Most research finds innovators and early adopters to be of higher status and central to the organization of groups and communities, but others consistently find them to be marginal and deviant (Rogers, 1962:183, 197). Rogers tried to unsnarl this mixed finding by arguing that in *top-down change* elites act as gatekeepers to prevent restructuring innovations from entering the system while favoring functioning innovations that do not immediately threaten to change the system (1973:81). Top-down change, according to Rogers, is more likely to succeed than *bottom-up change,* which involves a greater degree of social conflict and is most likely to succeed in times of perceived crisis.

But even this conclusion will not do. It assumes elites know (in advance) which innovations will reinforce existing hierarchies and power relations and which will really transform them. On the other hand, literatures about social movements and revolutionary processes discussed in the last chapters argue that much change is bottom up and genuinely restructuring. Furthermore, the anthropological literature is especially rich in finding large-scale unintended consequences of seemingly small innovations (e.g., Sharp, 1952). And consider the ultimate consequences of the seemingly modest political innovations (*perestroika* and *glasnost*) introduced by Mikhail Gorbachev in the 1980s to strengthen the Soviet system!

Retrospect: The Fate of Diffusion Research

We're sure it is not lost on you that much of the literature cited so far is now decades old. In spite of optimism after World War II that the mysteries of how change takes place were being unlocked, the research enterprise on diffusion of innovations ended in the mid-1970s, *for three reasons:* (1) because of the collapse of research funding by both private and public agencies, who came to recognize that improving the lot of humans by deliberate innovation was proving far more difficult and complex than imagined; (2) because its pervasive functionalist theoretical assumptions (often unacknowledged) were challenged by the renaissance of conflict and interpretive theories; and (3) because it stumbled into thorny questions that it did not have the intellectual capital to resolve (consider the "mixed evidence" noted earlier). But beginning in the 1970s, its agenda was incorporated within two new research areas spanning several social science disciplines: the study of institutional change and social networks.

INSTITUTIONAL CHANGE AND THE SPREAD OF INNOVATIONS

Innovations often spread through *institutional change* (Powell and DiMaggio 1996). Institutional change is the systematic change in the functioning of organizations brought about by attempts to respond to a changing world. Most discussions of modern bureaucracies from Weber onward have discussed the self-perpetuating nature of bureaucracies (see Chapter 2). The same forces affect most social groups of almost any size.

Think for a moment about some of the organizations and groups you belong to and have contact with: the university where you take classes, your employer, student government, fraternities and sororities, churches, support groups, and even families. In almost all of these groups, there are mechanisms for monitoring (1) how the organization or group is doing (Are members satisfied or dissatisfied? How is the organization or group performing relative to the goals they have set for themselves? etc.), and (2) how similar organizations or groups deal with common sets of problems that they face. Multiply these mechanisms over hundreds of thousands of groups and organizations, and an interesting process takes effect that Powell and DiMaggio refer to as *isomorphic change:* Organizations and groups that face common sets of problems develop similar solutions to them. But (and this is an important point) *these solutions may not actually solve the problem the group faces.* Instead, the adoption of the accepted solution makes the affected group or organization legitimate in the eyes of similar organizations and buffers the organization from further scrutiny regarding the problem.

What differs across groups and organizations is the source of the information and pressure that produces *isomorphic change. Coercive pressure* is pressure exerted by the law and oversight agencies. In these cases, changes are made because an external force mandates change and will punish the organization or group if the suggested changes aren't made. *Normative pressure* comes from professional networks of organizational and group actors. In these cases, networks of professionals decide among themselves the appropriate solution to a specific problem and that solution spreads through those networks. *Mimetic pressure* comes from simply observing what other, similarly situated organizations do.

Universities are good laboratories for studying isomorphic change and pressure. Virtually all universities (for example) have affirmative action offices, something that was rare as late as thirty years ago. The creation of affirmative action offices was a product of the general isomorphic change mechanisms we have been describing. The federal government exerted coercive pressure through the passage of the Civil Rights Act of 1964 and the creation of the Equal Employment Opportunity Commission (see Pedriana, 1999). Eventually, all universities that accepted federal funds had to show that they were in compliance with equal opportunity laws. Affirmative action offices were a logical response to the attempt to comply with this growing body of law. Professional groups (college professors, administrators, students, and alumni groups) also pressured universities to become more accountable for their treatment of traditionally underrepresented groups. The creation of affirmative action offices eventually created a network of equal opportunity professionals who discussed compliance issues among themselves and developed common sets of solutions. Finally, universities who otherwise might not have created affirmative action offices created them because other universities were doing it and it seemed to be necessary to remain a part of the in group.

Note that none of these changes necessarily means that civil rights enforcement on college campuses improved (though in many cases it did). But having an affirmative action office slowly became the measure of whether or not an institution was in compliance with federal laws. The burden of proof moved from those who had such offices to universities that did not. In this way, responses to common sets of challenges spread through systems of organizations and groups and produce innovation and change.

SOCIAL NETWORKS

Life is relational. *Social networks* are actual social interaction contacts among people, in terms of their frequency, duration, emotional intensity, or reciprocities. They might involve physical contact, communication, influence, power, exchanges, or interpersonal support. They may be long-lasting or transitory. Studying networks can change the way societies look. Much social research studies the characteristics of individuals such as age, education, gender, social class, ethnicity, and so on as if these were the fundamental building blocks of societies. But it is only because people participate in particular patterns of social networks that these things become salient. The same is true for entities like culture, groups, organizations, communities and institutions. Each is really a shorthand label that refers abstractly to a pattern of network relationships that existed at some time in history (Collins, 1988: 413).

Network analysis works like traffic engineers who use nighttime photography to estimate traffic flows. If you take long-exposure aerial photography of a city's traffic at night, you get a "pretty" pattern of thicker and thinner lines of light (from headlights). If you superimpose a series of photographs, the differences between thicker and thinner lines become increasingly clear, reflecting differences in traffic volume. Just as there are particular types of road junctions that may be generally associated with low or high accident rates, there may be different kinds of network contacts that produce recurrent patterned events and behavior (Wallace and Wolfe, 1995:361).

A *network conception* of the social world has many advantages: It begins not by assuming abstract or idealized structures like societies, cultures, organizations, or markets, but with actual patterns of who has contact with whom and with what regularity. Social networks are interconnected, open ended and seemingly infinite. Remarkably—when you think about it—they are the interpersonal mechanisms through which individuals are connected around the world, however directly or indirectly, and by which individuals, small groups, and big organizations are connected. Social networks exist among individuals (micro level), but also among groups, organizations, communities, and nations (macro level). Research moves from describing the structure of these connections to their implications (see Burt, 1982; Marsden and Lin, 1983).

However unique, particular nodes of social networks may be composed of

- *Dense and thick versus diffuse connections.* Individuals in denser networks are more affected by group standards than those in diffuse networks, and they are better able to adapt to stressful events.

- *Similar versus dissimilar actors.* Similar networks involve people of the same race, gender, or other social characteristics who communicate easily but share the same information. In dissimilar networks, communication is more difficult because people have very different information and experiences.
- *Strong ties versus weak ties.* In networks with strong ties, people are connected by powerful emotions and commitments. By comparison, strong ties are more likely to exist among relatively equal people; weaker ties are more likely between persons who are different, unequal, and have very different information, resources and experience. (Collins, 1988: 416–418; Granovetter, 1973)

Marc Granovetter's seminal work, entitled "The Strength of Weak Ties" (1973), found widespread evidence that *strong ties* provide effective interpersonal support but that *weak ties* more effectively brought people into contact with new ideas, resources, opportunities, and change. The implications for understanding the network structures through which innovations diffuse are obvious: Strong ties are more likely to connect people within groups who have the same information, resources, and problems. Weak ties, on the other hand, are more likely to connect people *between groups* who are very different. To find something really different or to get a good job, you are most likely to turn not to a close friend who is much like you, but to a distantly known person to whom you are referred. By the mid-1990s, network analysis had entered the popular culture with a whole new vocabulary of buzzwords. You can "network" (a verb), hire consultants, or turn to the whole new genre of self-help literature about networking (Lipnack, 1994).

Social scientists, on the other hand, have used network analysis to reconceptualize a wide variety of concerns. Economists, for instance, conceptualized the emerging world economy as *strategic networks* or *enterprise webs,* as we noted in Chapter 3. Sociologists have used network analysis to cast new light on interpersonal behavior, family and kinship systems, social cohesion, social mobility, power and political organization, and the covert control mechanisms that exist in free market economies (Bott, 1971; Granovetter, 1985; Marsden and Lin, 1983; Stack, 1974). Network analysis can help explain why the best products and ideas do not always succeed in the marketplace for ideas and things. Why, for instance, did a particular keyboard configuration dominate typewriters and PC keyboards, when other, possibly better ones, were available? Why did alternating current dominate the transmission of electric power, VHS format dominate videocassette formats, or light-water reactors dominate nuclear power designs? Why did Microsoft's Windows become the dominant PC software, even though Windows software was almost like the Apple decade-old "also-ran" Macintosh system? The major advantage for Microsoft's software was not its objective superiority. It became the industry standard because "everybody else was using it—inferior or not."

Economists now argue that network effects (or *path dependencies*) have a lot to do with the outcomes of competing technologies, ideas, and designs (Lohr, 1995). Network analysis can conceptualize questions about the spread of change about which the older diffusion research was ill equipped. How so?

Social Networks and the Spread of Change

We mentioned the intellectual impasse that ended the diffusion of innovation research tradition. Sometimes the instigation and early adoption of change was found among powerful elites who were normatively exemplary and centrally connected to the power and communication structure of groups, but other research found that change was promoted and adopted earliest by deviant persons of low socioeconomic status who were marginals or semi-isolated in terms of their network connections with the groups and communities through which diffusion flows.

Social network analysis clarified this confusion. For example, a study of kinds of communication within an Israeli kibbutz (gossip, general news, consumer information), separated *centrals* from *marginals* in terms of their location within the intragroup social networks (Weinmann, 1982). It found that the centrals tended to dominate the flow of communication within groups while the marginals dominated the flow of communication between groups. We need to underscore that Weinmann's findings apply to the flow of *information,* not influence. *Influence,* by contrast, was dominated by the network centrals, both within and between groups. Like Granovetter, Weinmann suggests that marginality plays an important role in the spread of innovation. It is associated with having extragroup ties and "serves as a crucial pathway for the flow of information between densely knit cliques or groups that would not be connected to each other at all were it not for the existence of weak ties (i.e., marginality)" (Granovetter, 1973:1363). While centrals apparently control the flow of influence, both within and between groups, marginals bridge groups and control the flow of information between groups. Weinmann suggests that marginals with their weak internal but many extragroup ties can be viewed as external scouts who import information and serve to "agglomerate micro-level behavior, attitudes, and opinions to large-scale patterns of macro-level processes" (Weinmann, 1982:766).

Macro Networks: Center-Periphery Models of Diffusion

The spread of change in macro networks (among cities, firms, or nations) benefited from network analysis that emphasizes not the *social locations* of actors (marginal vs. central) but rather the significance of *spatial locations* (central vs. peripheral) of actors in the spread of change.

Spatial center-periphery models describe how change flows among regions, cities, or nations rather than time-based (temporal) models like the linear, cyclical, and dialectical models of change described in Chapter 5. While anthropologists had given up the search for a mythical center of all civilization by the 1920s, the idea still informs some popular literature. (Take your pick: Where did it all start—Egypt, Mu, or Atlantis?) But the idea that culture traits flow from multiple centers of origin to peripheries remains a plausible one for scholars. Political philosopher and urban planner Donald Schon provided its most articulate statement (1971) when he argued that change typically spreads from centers of innovation to peripheral ultimate adopters and is often a centrally managed process of dissemination that involves training and the provision of resources and incentives for adoption (Schon, 1971:81). Historically such center-periphery diffusion depended on change agents (explorers, traders, soldiers, missionaries) who introduced innovative items in remote areas.

Schon described three variants of this center-periphery model of the spread of change (see Figure 10-2):

- *The Johnny Appleseed model.* Change agents are like evangelists roaming outlying territories spreading a message. Examples are traveling scholars, saints, and artisans of the Middle Ages; Voltaire and Thomas Paine; Thomas Edison spreading the gospel about electric lights; and the "bards" of activism of the 1960s in America, such as Ralph Nader or Saul Alinsky.
- *The magnet model.* Bright provincials go to the cultural center, learn the innovation, and then carry it home. Schon cites the nineteenth-century German universities, which attracted students from all over the world, as examples of the magnet model. As for more contemporary illustrations, consider that artists and fashion designers continue to study in Paris or that students from the Third World continue to go to the United States, Germany, or Japan to study and return home.
- *The proliferation of centers model.* A more complex model in which peripheral sites become subcenters with more remote peripheries of their own. Over time, these subcenters may become partly autonomous and differentiated from the original center or may even grow to eclipse its influence. (Schon, 1971)

Schon notes three factors that determine the effectiveness of a center-periphery system for the diffusion of change: (1) the amount of resources at the center and the "energy" it is able to invest in the process of diffusion; (2) the number of peripheral locations being served; and (3) the length of the spokes, or radii, over which persons,

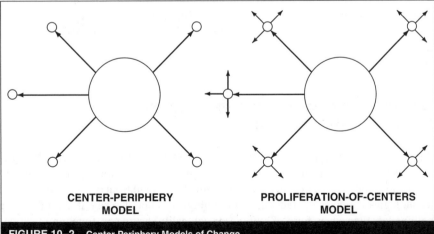

CENTER-PERIPHERY
MODEL

PROLIFERATION-OF-CENTERS
MODEL

FIGURE 10–2   **Center-Periphery Models of Change**
Source: From Donald A. Schon, *Beyond the Stable State: Public and Private Learning in a Changing Society,* copyright 1971 by Donald A. Schon and Random House, Inc. Used with permission of the author.

material, and information must flow. Ultimately, the effectiveness of a center-periphery system depends upon the maintenance of an effective logistical system; a center-periphery network may fail because the center lacks resources, overloads the spokes of transmission, or mishandles feedback from the periphery. Ancient world empires like Assyria or Rome, for example, often collapsed because they became overextended: Too few resources were used to supply too many remote sites over a far-flung geographical area. Center-periphery models can shed light on the spread of change in a variety of concrete contexts. They can, for instance, illuminate the growth, expansion, and perhaps the ultimate collapse of political empires, market systems, and a wide variety of cultural frameworks. Center-periphery models provide intriguing ways of understanding the growth and diffusion of diverse "cultural complexes" like Christianity, Coca-Cola, communism, and computers (Vago, 1980).

How would you describe the center-periphery diffusion of computers and information technology around the globe? Are potent cultural centers in California's Silicon Valley? In Bill Gates' office? Are Internet centers of diffusion the actual physical nodes—that is, the interconnected mainframes across the world to which the rest of us are peripherally connected in seemingly ethereal ways at our PC workstations? Posing the question as a middle-range rather than a macro one, how would you understand the spread of information technology at a company or university? Personally, we would begin with the dense agglomerations (social networks) of cybersavvy hackers who inhabit the mainframe computer centers and computer science departments that extend to proliferating satellite computer rooms and labs across the campus (to peripheries like the business and social science data labs, writing labs in the English and Journalism departments, and user-room pods in student dormitories). Experts and evangelists of information technology emerge in each of these subcenters. You can conceptualize center-periphery systems in either physical hardwiring networks or social networks through which news and influence travels. For social scientists, the latter is more interesting. This topic brings us full circle back to the information technology revolution where we began this chapter and promised to revisit.

IN CONCLUSION: BACK AT THE INFORMATION TECHNOLOGY REVOLUTION

Revolution? This is certainly a different way of using the word *revolution* than particular social and political events like the Cuban revolution or the collapse of the Soviet Union. But still, change deriving over time from the introduction of information technologies is pervasive, radical, and tumultuous. Some describe it as introducing nothing less than a new form of reality (virtual reality) having profound implications for both societies and persons. In our conclusion, we explore some social implications of this revolution.

Macro: Societies and Social Order

We noted these effects in discussing changes in work, economics, and politics in the first chapters, as well as early in this chapter. Increased capacities to store and transmit information as well as for deterritorialized interaction are the technological bases of emerging postindustrial economies and the world market economy, with all their tumultuous changes and mixed consequences. They make people's sense of national wealth, power, and identification more ambiguous than before. They vastly magnify the connections and opportunities among business people, investors, impassioned movement activists, and people of common interest as well as embezzlers, criminals, militias, and terrorists. Like every new technological development, information technologies will require new forms of social control, as did passenger airplanes. (Have you booked a flight at a big airport recently?) There is no central control of the Internet or web pages, and some argue that they will ultimately be self-policing without any political intervention. Well, maybe. But free markets don't work well without some regulation.

Information technologies made possible corporate profitability, along with massive layoffs and economies simultaneously composed of the gigantic corporate elephants and a multitude of tiny entrepreneurial ants. By some estimates, the United States generated 6 million new business ventures in 1998 alone (U.S. Department of Commerce, Bureau of the Census, 1999). Entrepreneurs abound, but four out of five small businesses fail in their first two years (Aldrich, 1999), and the reality of a stable and predictable career is vanishing for most people. But note that some people and nations are wired to the opportunities of information technologies and some are virtually left out (see Fig. 10.1). Information technologies provide stunning new capabilities but ironically may amplify and reproduce inequalities based on gender, education, and social class.

Micro: Relationships, Reality, and Self-Concepts

Will information technologies produce a genuinely new virtual reality that exists as images on computer consoles and mutates actual reality? Will it transform the social relationships and the self-concepts of persons? The essence of human understanding of yourself as an entity (who you are) is developed through interaction with others, beginning at birth and continuing through life (Mead, 1934; Berger and Luckmann, 1967). While historically mediated by technology (letters and phone calls), new technologies portend whole new possibilities for the extension and emersion of the self in the Internet, web pages, and computer games that connect people. There are new possibilities for role playing. The human self and identity emergent from face-to-face relations with real other persons is only partly manageable and has an objective character. By contrast information technologies make possible highly managed *virtual, hyper,* or *pseudo selves.* These venues enhance opportunities for creative self-mutation as well as for fraud and flim-flammery.

Online interaction with people has a detached character and is more ambiguous that face-to-face interaction because it lacks many verbal and nonverbal social context cues. One consequence is that Internet communicators can "flame" each other by sending ill-considered and intemperate responses. To compensate, a whole new culture of Internet etiquette has emerged, but the everyday life social cues that enable people to frame interaction and communication with meaning and significance is largely missing from Internet communication.

Couples can meet via e-mail, develop virtual intimacy and confidentiality, and construct romantic relationships (love on the Internet?). Such relationships may or may not be preludes to face-to-face meetings. The possibilities for new kinds of personal columns on web pages is enormous, and they raise new questions. Given that attraction and eroticism are largely in the human mind, how does cyberromance or virtual sex differ from the real thing? And how would you understand *infidelity?*

Problems in Infotopia?

As you can see, innovation as pervasive as these entail new possibilities but also problems. Human life can improve, but utopias are fictional. Here are some other downsides of the revolution.

- E-mail often has companies and employees overwhelmed and overmessaged. Secretaries used to be gatekeepers of mail, but e-mail and voice mail are so incessant that they often gum up the works; some people get 100 to 500 messages a day. Information technology generates its own junk mail. Some companies shut down their nets for periods during the day, and people are only more productive when technologies are used thoughtfully. It can be a powerful form of "information overload" (Dobrzynski, 1996).
- While consumers seem to be using the Internet more and more all the time, government statistics on e-commerce suggest that electronic transactions account for (at most) twelve percent of all consumer transactions, wholesale and retail (U.S. Department of Commerce, Bureau of the Census, 1999b). Internet and computer technology changes so rapidly that there is tremendous instability among e-commerce firms and dotcoms. This instability is one ingredient behind the crash of the NASDAQ stock market in 2000 and its continued difficulties. The NASDAQ stock market is where most U.S. technology stocks are traded, and the NASDAQ index has lost over half of its value since peaking in 1999 (*Economist,* 2001). Regardless of the other changes that infotopia brings, computers and information technology have not produced a short and easy road to riches for many who put their faith and money into them.
- For some, virtual reality and electronic relationships can be addictive and isolate people from real relationships. This is hardly a crisis, but many universities know about the problem when students spend hours per day online. Being plugged into virtual reality can compensate for social isolation and lead to neglect of real-world tasks. Some universities (e.g., the University of Maryland) have formed addiction support groups ("Caught in the Web") for students spending too much time on computers. Counselors at the University of California–Berkeley find some students so absorbed in electronic relationships that they neglect coursework, become socially isolated, and are likely to drop out. What is a wonderful tool for some becomes an addiction for others (Castells, 1996).

Thus, information technology has transformed the macroworld of large-scale relations around the globe in a multitude of ways. But we agree with Robert Hinze (1996) that interpersonally we're not in the revolution yet, and are still stuck in face-to-face relationships. Discussions of broad implications of pervasive technological change is useful. But we noted earlier that even experts don't have a very good track record for *concrete predictions* about the social implications of pervasive innovations. They are about as accurate as was movie producer Harry Warner's prognosis of talking pictures: "Who the hell wants to hear actors talk?" Little did he know!

In sum, this chapter has explored (1) both technological and non-technological change as innovation, (2) how those innovations spread within groups and societies, and (3) their complex consequences for people and social change.

THINKING PERSONALLY ABOUT SOCIAL CHANGE

1. Think of a time that you or somebody you know had a new idea or did something in a creative way. How was it a novel combination of things that existed to begin with?

2. How do you or people that you know accept new things or new ways of doing things? If this chapter is right, you usually don't only just learn about them, but are also influenced by social networks in which you participate. Think about your own social networks in different areas of life. How do you get advice about when to see a doctor? about what jobs to look for? about new things to buy? about new foods to try (or avoid!). When you get started doing this, it winds up being literally mindboggling. Think: Are the times that you get really "good deals" or "super new ideas" related to whether they are associated with strong or weak network ties? Examples?

3. Talk to people in different fields or professions (not just in universities) about their ideas of significant innovations or inventions that are not here yet but are just over the horizon. What are some of these? Think about future development in information technology. In biotechnology, agriculture, and food processing. In medicine and health care. In reproductive technology. In energy or transportation. What do you think are some of the social benefits and problems implied by future developments. (*Warning:* Treat all such speculations with a good deal of suspicion!)

4. Think about, or talk with a variety of people about, their reactions to new technology. There's a whole spectrum of reactions for different circumstances. Why do you think people react the way they do? How do their reactions relate to values, interests, education, social class, or social networks?

11

Creating Change

All of us have at times been so frustrated by our lives at work, as students, in families, or as citizens in the political community that we have wanted to change things. And we often have ideas, both large and small, about how things could be better or more effective than they are. Indeed, the issue—how one goes about trying to change things—is such an important nuts-and-bolts issue that it rarely needs any elaborate justification as an important topic to consider.

The problem, of course, is that understanding how and why change takes place is complicated enough, but trying to tell someone how to go about creating change is doubly difficult. While there was some optimism during the 1950s and 1960s that social scientists were beginning to learn a great deal about the planning of change, that confidence turned out to be partly an illusion. Instigating social change, particularly on a large scale, is a much more complex process than anyone realized. Partly this is because the social world is an interconnected system of things and it is rarely possible to change just one thing without ultimately implicating other things, people, and interests. In fact, some of our more cautious professional colleagues would argue that to try to extract any practical wisdom from the social science literature on change is something that only a fool would attempt.

Nonetheless, *we believe you are justified in asking—at some point—just what social scientists have learned about social change that is of any practical relevance.* It is also our judgment that there *are* some useful implications in the social science literature on social change that do have relevance for creating change, but you should not look for specific formulas. The most useful insights about creating change come from the literature about innovation and social movements, and we hope you will see the connections between this chapter and those earlier ones. This chapter is an attempt to spell out some of those implications.

The extent to which change is deliberately induced by human actors is itself a factor in the historical development of societies. Karl Mannheim (1940) suggested that early in human history most social change was the result of chance discovery through trial and error. Later, as the development of science produced systematic inquiry, came deliberate innovation in the form of what we would today term research and development. Thus systematic, deliberate innovation is now widely practiced, most obviously in technological matters, but also in organizational and social policy. Mannheim predicted that as systematic innovation becomes more pervasive, it will eventually result in more systematic social planning at the societal or total system level. The last part of Mannheim's career was spent grappling with how such pervasive social planning—which he saw as an inevitable evolutionary development in industrial societies—could be made consistent with the political norms of democracy. Mannheim is not, of course, the only scholar who grappled with the dilemmas of democratic planning. Etzioni's innovative work *The Active Society* (1968) is a more extensive argument that modern societies are becoming deliberately active and reflexive entities in terms of their ability to shape their own destinies. We mentioned his work in Chapter 6 when we discussed attempts of scholars to move beyond mechanistic theories of social change.

Whether or not you accept the desirability of such systemwide planning for change or the validity of these arguments, without question the interest in the planning of change is more pervasive in the contemporary world than in the past. Moore observed, "The proportion of contemporary change that is either planned or issues from the secondary consequences of deliberate innovations is much higher than in former times" (1974:2). Thus today corporations have a great interest in planning the expansion of their markets and promoting their products, such as cable TV or personal computers, and public agencies spend a great deal of time and energy in planning for full employment, economic growth, public health, and the like. Similarly, the plethora of social movements in contemporary America have an interest in deliberately promoting—if planning is too strong a term—their own vision of the "good society." One effect of the high level of interest in the deliberate creation of change is the burgeoning quasiscientific applied literature about the planning of change related to business (Zaltman, LeMasters, and Heffring, 1982; Bennis, Benne, and Chin, 1985), social services (Rothman, 1974), and community development (Warren, 1976). There is also much literature for social movement organizers based on social science insights as well as the accumulated wisdom of practice (Alinsky, 1972).

We will begin this chapter on creating change with (1) a discussion of two actual cases of attempts to introduce fairly complex and unpopular community change in the city we know, which took place during the mid-1970s, followed by discussions of (2) basic change strategies appropriate for different situations; (3) the role of violence as a strategy for the creation of change; (4) mixed-change strategies, which are more complex and involve the combination of several basic strategies; and (5) the role of the change agent, including some nuts-and-bolts strategies for reducing the resistance to change and a "cookbook" of issues that change agents need to consider. Finally, (6) we will address what we see as some important ethical and practical issues that surround the deliberate instigation of social change.

CREATING CHANGE IN OMAHA:
MUDDLING THROUGH AND PLANNING

In the mid-1970s, the Omaha city government applied for a $5 million community development grant from the federal Department of Housing and Urban Development (HUD). The grant money was to be used for a variety of community development projects, but probably the most important, from the city's standpoint, was the refurbishing and redevelopment of the downtown central business district. Over the previous two decades Omaha (with a metropolitan area population about 580,000) had, like most urban areas, witnessed the outmigration of people, business, and money from the older urban core to the outlying suburbs. And like most urban areas in the United States, the downtown business district was in danger of becoming a squalid zone of deserted office buildings and retail stores. The grant application was part of a larger ongoing effort to revitalize the downtown area as an attractive recreational area and to encourage businesses to stay or relocate in the downtown area. These efforts were enthusiastically endorsed by the Chamber of Commerce and the Omaha business community in general. Other provisions in the grant provided for refurbishing inner city residential neighborhoods judged to be in danger of becoming blighted. Every metropolitan area in the country has had to cope with similar trends and problems in recent years.

Scattered-Site Housing for the Poor

A provision in community development grants (required by HUD) was that the applicant community must provide funds for the development (construction or subsidization) of housing for low-income families. Such housing programs were to be located on scattered sites throughout the community to prevent the further ghettoization of the poor in isolated and dilapidated areas of the city. The city had to develop, in other words, a reasonable plan to locate publicly supported housing in otherwise rather affluent neighborhoods, in order to facilitate (in HUD's terms) the social integration of the poor and to prevent federal money from being used to further intensify housing patterns that reinforced economic class segregation. Furthermore, HUD specified that the city had to hold public hearings to ascertain the level of community support for such plans (not only the scattered-site provisions, as they came to be called). The city faithfully developed such scattered-site provisions (they planned to build multiple family dwellings for low-income families on vacant property in the middle of an affluent area in an outer northwestern suburb as well as in several other locations to be later announced). It also held public hearings. The city's community development plans were extensively reported in the local media prior to the scheduled hearings, but aside from the business community, whose support was deemed crucial, the city made only few and fragmentary efforts to sell the plan to the public at large prior to the actual publication of the plan in the local media.

At the first public hearing, the room was packed with residents of the northwestern suburb in question, who had begun to mobilize to oppose the plan to build low-income housing in their neighborhood. Fears and rumors had developed among the largely white upper-middle-class residents that the city was planning to build cheap tenements (soon to become dilapidated) that would be populated by unemployed black welfare mothers with large families. The residents alleged that the quality of the neighborhood and property values would be ruined by the program. Furthermore, they lobbied individual elected city council members with thinly veiled threats to lead campaigns to dump them at the next election and hired a lawyer to seek a court injunction preventing the city from implementing such a plan should the grant materialize. The press, of course, widely reported the high drama of the confrontation between the city and the neighborhood. In spite of the valiant attempts of the city's community development director to defend the plan and provide evidence that the objective consequences would not be as the residents feared, the city council directed the department to return to the drawing boards and develop a new scattered-site provision.

It did—which is to say that another neighborhood was targeted as the recipient of the city's multiple housing complex for the poor with precisely the same result: an angry and rancorous hearing, lurid press accounts, and the council's refusal to approve the plan. This was repeated several times with different neighborhoods targeted. The issue became a hot item of community discussion and dialogue. There were those who opposed the scattered-site provision on principle, as well as the larger effort of the community development program, and saw them as city and federal meddling in private local affairs. Most supported the city's larger effort and viewed the scattered-site provision as legitimate, at least in the abstract. But no one wanted a low-income housing complex in his or her particular backyard. In the final version of the grant proposal the city had chosen to locate such a complex on cheap and poorly drained land in an area of the city that was rapidly becoming a lower-income area anyway. HUD rejected that particular grant proposal but continued to subsidize funding for low-income persons in Omaha as it had in other cities since the 1950s.

In spite of this debacle, the city's housing authority (OHA) continued muddling through to promote the development of scattered-site housing for low-income households. By 1981, OHA had established 128 scattered-site apartments and single-family dwellings, and it had 777 of them by 1999. They are still concentrated in low-income areas, but exist in all areas of the city. In 1990, OHA began to demolish the old Depression-era housing projects, widely held to be breeding grounds for violence, gangs, drugs, and obstacles to the aspirations of poor households to improve. Residents of the new subsidized housing did indeed show signs of progress: They were more successful in finding jobs; their children did better in school; and the average stay of families in subsidized housing dropped from about seven years in 1986 to three years in 1991.

There is still opposition to scattered-site housing, but according to the OHA director, "public meetings and vocal opposition are largely a thing of the past." OHA was also sued by a group of residents for the "slow progress" that tacitly sanctioned the segregation of the poor. And poor families themselves, particularly the minority-group 60 percent who moved into middle-class neighborhoods, suffered incredible abuse—including ostracism and verbal insults, racist graffiti, and automobile vandalism. But there were also signs of greater acceptance over time. The person most responsible for ongoing change is the director of OHA, a long-term administrator who outlasted several mayors and had become a nationally respected but controversial leader in public housing. His efforts illustrate the power of human agency even in the most volatile and confining structural circumstances. There has been progress, but scattered-site housing remains a contentious community issue with little popular support.

School Desegregation

In the mid-seventies, school desegregation came to Omaha, as it did to many other American communities.[1] Such a program was mandated by the federal District Court in St. Louis, which, after hearing the plaintiff's arguments against the Omaha Public School District, agreed that the district had been negligent in promoting a racially integrated educational system. There was, of course, widespread opposition to court-mandated desegregation ("forced busing") in Omaha as well as across the country, and there were widespread fears that such a program would become as disastrous and disruptive in Omaha as had prior desegregation attempts in other cities (e.g., Boston and Pontiac, Michigan).

The school district—begrudgingly—began to develop a plan for the implementation of desegregation along guidelines specified by the court. The plan the district developed was complex but ingenious. First, there was an appeal to consensual values. The district did not publicly promote the virtues of integrated education (widely debated at the time), although it did not publicly deny them. The district urged citizens to "abide by the law"—a higher-order value about which there was little dissent. Second, the district formed—at the specification of the court—an independent voluntary association (Concerned Citizens for Omaha), which included a panoply of community notables from the educational, business, and religious communities as well as ordinary citizens, to promote "peaceful implementation of desegregation." Although the association cooperated with the district, it was legally independent of it. Third, the architects of the district's plan decided to pair white and nonwhite elementary schools and to bus students between the paired schools so that each school had a racial mix that approximated the court's ultimate target goal of a 40 to 60 percent racial balance. No school was exempted except those few that naturally met the court's racial balance guidelines.

At the junior high and high school levels, many of the schools naturally fell within the racial balance guidelines. There the district promoted a policy of voluntary "selective migration," that is, black students were encouraged to transfer to predominantly white schools, and curriculums were upgraded in several predominantly nonwhite schools to attract white students. A black high school that had had declining enrollments for some time was developed as a magnet school specializing in vocational and technical education (while such curricula were pruned back at other schools), and a predominantly black middle school was developed as a magnet center for science and math—and given some of the best teachers in the district, along with superior laboratory and computer facilities. The actual plan was not leaked to the press in bits and pieces but published all at once, taking up about three pages in the local newspaper.

During the summer before the plan was to be implemented, the Concerned Citizens operated bus tours for parents to visit the elementary schools their children would attend (complete with tea and cookies served by the principals and staffs of the schools). They operated a telephone hot line to provide information about the desegregation plan and to defuse rumors. They sponsored a speaker's bureau of community leaders and academicians to promote peaceful desegregation. They sponsored media ads promoting peaceful compliance with the plan, emphasizing again the virtues of compliance with the law and community harmony. Also during that summer there emerged a counterassociation, the Citizens for Educational Freedom, which sought to oppose desegregation and urged parents and students to boycott the schools if the plan was implemented in September. There were a few public demonstrations and vague threats of community disruption, but none that could be clearly linked to the counterassociation. The Archbishop of Omaha announced that the Catholic schools of Omaha would not accept new students from the public school system whose main motivation appeared to be to escape the desegregation plan.

By the 1990s, the Omaha Public School District had problems, like all central city school districts: gangs, drugs, and violence, and a concentration of students from low-income families. Vocal educational critics and the media focused more directly on other problems: performance issues (such as reading levels) and religion-related issues (such as prayer in schools and teaching about sexuality). Whether or not desegregation has achieved its goals is ambiguous: Schools are less racially segregated than they were in the mid-1970s, and educational outcomes and graduation rates for black students improved, though black-white gaps remain. But educational desegregation remains unpopular, and even its defenders argue that the original plan needs to be modified. But education desegregation remained unpopular, and by 1996 a diffuse community dialogue emerged about the general quality of public education that included the consequences of education.

A new school superintendent appointed a "desegregation task force" of educational and community leaders to evaluate the program. While one faction of the task force recommended a complete return to neighborhood schools, the task force recommended a more complex program of choice within four large geographic areas of the school district. Within each zone families could choose to send children to any neighborhood school, a magnet school with enhanced curricular resources (e.g., science and computers), or an academy. Academies were schools in predominantly low socioeconomic neighborhoods for which there were mandated lower class sizes, paraprofessionals (teachers aides), and incentives to attract veteran or master teachers. While the task force was deliberating, the federal circuit court announced the lifting of the court order that mandated desegregation in the first place. Faced with little public or legal opposition, the superintendent accepted the task force recommendation, and thus in 2000, the twenty-year history of the great social experiment of school desegregation in Omaha came to an end, to be replaced by a system of voluntary choice with zones.

The extent to which desegregation achieved its goals is ambiguous: schools are less racially segregated than they were in the mid-1970s, and educational outcomes (e.g., graduation rates) for African-American students improved, though "black-white" and socioeconomic gaps in standardized test scores remained wide. These gaps were richly documented by the publication of elementary reading achievement scores by schools and zones in the Omaha *World Herald* in the spring of 2001. Some argue that desegregation lifted the whole system by improving community dialogue, addressing the maldistribution of resources, and raising the educational "best practice" standard throughout the district, even though inequality remains. Others emphasize the failure of desegregation to address the gaps and inequalities that gave rise to the program in the first place.

Analysis

What accounts for the differences between the two change efforts? Perhaps they were so different that they should not be compared. Yet they had at least some similarities. Both were vastly unpopular with the majority of the population affected. Both threatened cherished values of the influential white middle classes—property values, educational quality, and welfare of their children—and both triggered latent racial prejudice that existed, although this was never openly admitted. Both were perceived as unwarranted meddling by Washington bureaucrats in local options and affairs. Beyond those similarities, there were some obvious differences between the two initiatives. Scattered-site housing was a required feature embedded in a larger grant proposal that was itself voluntary and optional. HUD provided no guidelines as to how communities would satisfy the scattered-site requirement, nor how the city should go about promoting its acceptance among the public. Desegregation was mandated by the court and was coming to Omaha, ready or not, under some conditions. The court, having the experience of desegregation programs in other cities, specified some things about the method of implementation and the plan to be developed by the school district.

Beyond these differences, though, there were some dramatic differences between the plan of implementation developed by the city government and that of the school district, and our argument is that the differences between these plans dramatically shaped the differing outcomes. *First,* the school district, and to some extent the voluntary association that it created, appealed to higher-order consensual values ("peacefully abide by the law and preserve community harmony") rather than the merits of integrated education. The local media overwhelmingly endorsed these values. The city, on the other hand, became drawn into a public controversy over the specific (and in the eyes of many, questionable) merits of scattered-site housing. The larger benefits of the community development grant became a vague background to the high drama of the near-weekly televised "shootouts" between the city planners and the targeted neighborhoods. And the terms of the debate were shaped by the opponents of the plan rather than by the city, which continually *responded* to the arguments of critics they were never able to effectively refute.

Second, the city's plan appeared to arbitrarily and unfairly place the costs of scattered-site housing on a few neighborhoods, while leaving most untouched. The school district's plan, on the other hand, equitably distributed the costs of desegregation. At the elementary level, none was exempted. No group of parents or neighborhoods could feel singled out to bear the "burdens" of desegregation. *Third,* the school district was able to close ranks and cohesively promote the plan, whereas there was a visible rift between the planning department and the elected city council, who came, as often as not, to be sympathetic to the neighborhood groups opposed to scattered-site housing. Indeed, the scattered-site proposals came to be identified more with the "bureaucratic planners" in the city planning department than with the city government as an undifferentiated entity, and many city officials sought to distance themselves—and their careers—from such plans.

Fourth, and perhaps most important, was the relatively effective mobilization of community support for the peaceful implementation of the desegregation plan using widely respected community opinion leaders and preexisting community organizational networks, contrasted with the relative absence of such efforts by the city planners. In retrospect, the school district and its civic allies developed a complex and ingenious campaign, lasting for several years, designed to mobilize public sentiments around the goals of peaceful implementation of court-mandated desegregation. By contrast, the efforts of the city and OHA seems the result of "muddling through" to the long-term goal of creating scattered-site housing by determined leaders and organizations operating in legal, media, and political circumstances that made effective planning impossible.

BASIC CHANGE STRATEGIES

Any effort to instigate change can be conceptualized as having three elements: (1) the change agent who seeks to promote change; (2) the change itself, which for practical purposes can be viewed as either changes in *behavior* (or relationships) or changes in *attitudes* (or norms and values); and (3) the target population or system that the change agent wants to convince to adopt the change. A target population or system can be individuals, groups and organizations, communities, or whole societies. Preliminary to any attempt to instigate change, the change agent should delineate (1) exactly *what* she wants to change, and (2) the precise boundaries and characteristics of the target population or system. Change agents can then select from among several broad strategies to promote change, depending on the nature of the target population and the change itself.[2]

Facilitative Strategies

Facilitative strategies should be used when the target group or system (1) recognizes a problem and the need for change, (2) is open to external assistance, and (3) is willing to engage in self-help. Within this strategy the change agent acts as a facilitator who provides resources, information, advice, and expertise. The change agent's task is often to make the target group (who are really clients in this case) aware of options and the existence of resources and to clarify issues. It is a *coopera-tive* strategy; the change agents and their clients collaborate in seeking solutions to problems already felt by the client. But though they perceive the need for *something,* clients may be only dimly aware of what kinds of changes are required, and the strat-egy may require a self-study or a needs-assessment study. When this is the case, the change agent's agenda must remain open-ended.

In other cases, the needs of clients may be fairly well defined and the problem is to convince clients that certain changes will work. For instance, efforts to introduce modern medicine in developing nations addressed fairly well-understood needs (sickness and health problems), but convincing local people that Western medicine was in any way superior to traditional folk medical practice often was a considerable task. This is a particularly acute problem when the discrepancy between the techni-cal knowledge and the worldview of the change agent and the client population is very great.

Facilitative strategies work best when (1) there are a multiplicity of broad goals (for example, community improvement), and (2) the change requires the active par-ticipation of a diversity of people. They are most inappropriate where (1) there is sig-nificant resistance to change among the client population, (2) the change is contrary to the values and interest of powerful segments of the client population, and, usually, (3) the change must occur quickly. Two additional things must be said:

First, the change agent must often be prepared to provide long-term support for *sustaining* the change after its initial adoption. To use again examples of induced change in developing societies, one can find many examples of schools, water sys-tems, and so forth that were enthusiastically built at the instigation of outside change agents who quickly departed after their construction and provided little long-term support or incentives for their long-term utilization.

Second, the facilitative strategy is often more effective if it provides benefits beyond the formal goals of the change itself (for example, interactional needs, status enhancement). Several years ago, Harper participated in a program evaluation study of a project sponsored by the U.S. Department of Agriculture called Project Green Thumb, the purpose of which was to employ retired farmers to refurbish small-town facilities (parks, fairgrounds) in southeast Nebraska. The program was designed not only as an economic benefit to the retired farmers, many of whom had no adequate pensions, but also to provide them with health, legal, and educational assistance. The program was largely successful in its formal goals, but that was not the major reason the retirees participated. They enjoyed the physical activity itself, but most of all, they enjoyed socializing with each other. They had fun. It is important for the change agent to try to construct the change process so that participating in the change process will be enjoyable and engaging for the client population.

Reeducative Strategies

Reeducative strategies are "relatively unbiased presentation(s) of facts . . . in-tended to provide a rational justification for action. . . . [they] assume that human be-ings are rational beings capable of discovering facts and adjusting their behavior accordingly when facts are presented" (Zaltman and Duncan, 1977:111). The strategy has been termed *reeducation* because it usually involves unlearning or overcoming prior learning. Reeducation takes time—to build new knowledge or skills—and hence is most important when time is not critical.

Reeducation is effective, and in fact necessary, when the target population or group does not possess the knowledge or skills to utilize an innovation or when there are fears, anxieties, and moral barriers to adoption. Reeducation can involve broad-based media campaigns that attempt to address moral issues and reduce fears about the consequences of adoption, or, when more specialized skills and competencies are involved, reeducation often means the creation of structured programs and workshops for specific groups of potential adopters. Thus both public and private agencies often create free (or nominally expensive) classes and workshops to develop skills related to the programs and products they seek to disseminate (for example, contraceptives, personal computers). Reeducation can be used both (1) to provide a *rationale* for adopting a change, and (2) to provide the target system with new knowledge and skills necessary to adopt a change. The former is usually easier than the latter, but the latter may often be necessary. When it is necessary to provide a rationale for change, reeducation becomes a campaign to promote change rather than a facilitative or cooperative strategy practiced among those already committed to some kind of change.

Segmentation of the total target population may also be necessary to make the message about the change understandable and appealing to different groups. Demographic characteristics (age groups, sex, education, socioeconomic class) are the most obvious categories for segmentation, but the change agent may also segment in terms of developing a different approach for opinion leaders versus rank-and-file members of the target population. Finally, it is important to say that reeducation is most effective when the advantages of and facts about the innovation are clear and unambiguous.

What are the limitations of reeducation as a change strategy? One limitation should be obvious to you from the last sentence of the previous paragraph. Facts surrounding the advantages and hazards of adoption are often ambiguous and unclear. Ironically, the major limitation of reeducation strategy is a function of its major characteristic: It appeals to the rationality of the actors in the target population, and so it is often an overly rationalistic approach to change. Reeducation is usually not effective—no matter how sensible the change is in the eyes of the change agent—when there are strong and conflicting emotions surrounding the change.

Similarly, reeducation is not likely to be effective *by itself* in promoting innovations that require dramatic alterations of behavior or group structure, because these are embedded in larger structures, values, and interests that may reinforce stability. Hence rational suggestions for social reform (for example, to decriminalize marijuana, legalize prostitution, prevent poverty by redistribution) often fail because they are contrary to established values and moral sentiments as well as to material vested interests. In this context, it is important to note that scientific studies and blue ribbon panels appointed to study social problems (e.g., pornography, crime, poverty) and make policy recommendations are often ignored in the absence of a larger political climate conducive to change.

There is a final difficulty with reeducation as a strategy of change: It is difficult for change agents to practice in a pure form. Is information really objective, neutral, and uncontestable? Rarely. And given an overwhelming interest in instigating change, does the change agent tend to stack the deck or strategically withhold certain information from the target population? Probably. In other words, the line between reeducation and persuasion is often fuzzy.

Persuasive Strategies

Persuasive strategies "attempt to bring about change partly through bias in the manner in which a message is structured and presented" (Zaltman and Duncan, 1977: 134). Persuasive strategies can be based on facts and rational appeals, or they can be totally false. Thus persuasion differs from reeducation by degree, in terms of the extent to which the change agent (1) arranges or selectively ignores facts, and (2) utilizes emotional and nonrational inducements (for example, hidden persuaders). Persuasion is most appropriate when the target population is unaware of the need for change or has a low commitment to change.

Unlike reeducation, persuasion is relatively effective when the facts are ambiguous and the costs and benefits of adoption are difficult to discern, which explains its widespread usage in advertising and political campaigns. When the relative advantage of adoption is in doubt, the change agent can easily combine persuasive efforts to change people's minds with material incentives. This means that persuasive strategies can sometimes short-circuit the need for long and extensive reeducation by media campaigns.

Persuasion does have another advantage in overcoming resistance to adoption since, in contrast to reeducation, the change agent is not required to present unbiased facts or the whole story. There are limits to the extent to which this is possible, however. Gross factual distortions may backfire and jeopardize the credibility of the change agent, particularly when the target population is sophisticated. As a rule of thumb, the more sophisticated and critical the target population, the more the change agent should rely on reeducation rather than persuasive strategies. There are other limits to the effectiveness of persuasion that are obvious: It is not effective when the target population has neither the skills nor the material resources to adopt. There are also obvious ethical problems with persuasion strategies, but we will deal with these separately.

Power Strategies

Power strategies use coercion or threats to obtain the compliance of the target population with some sort of change. The effective practice of power strategies requires that the change agent (1) possess resources to reward or punish the target system, and (2) be able to monopolize access to such rewards and resources by the target system. Power strategies are effective when the commitment to change is low, but they may be the *only* available strategy when change is perceived highly risky, irreversible, or undesirable. Furthermore, power strategies are most effective when (1) time is very short, and (2) the changes sought are behavioral rather than attitudinal. In other words, where the change sought requires mainly outward compliance rather than inward commitment.[3]

To speak of the use of power to induce change evokes very negative and unsavory images. Nonetheless, power strategies are quite commonly used and involve widely varying degrees of deprivation on the part of the target system. Moreover, we argue that they *can* be used within the framework of a democratic political process. The case of successful court-mandated desegregation analyzed earlier would be an example of such democratic coercion, as would attempts to regulate environmental pollution, promote auto safety, and civil rights. In each of those cases, the change to be promoted was instigated by the established democratic political process (either legislative or judicial) but the change, promulgated with legal penalties and sanctions, was not voluntarily accepted by portions of the target. There is probably a generalization here: Power strategies are most effective when supported by broadly accepted social values and the larger political community—that is, when they are used to coerce segments of a population to abide by widely accepted rules.

What are the costs and limitations of power strategies of inducing change? Unlike the previous strategies, power is almost always alienative in that it creates strains and estrangement in the relationship between the change agent and the target system, and it does not produce a stable commitment to the change itself. Power strategies may require ongoing surveillance by the change agent to ensure continuing compliance. The costs of such surveillance may be quite high, both in terms of its intrinsic costs to administer and in terms of its damage to the quality of relationships within the social system. Additionally, power is less effective for promoting changes that are highly complex so that they may require voluntary participation, or at least cooperation, on the part of the target population. Where this is the case, reeducation or persuasion is more appropriate.

We have outlined what are usually considered to be the basic types of strategies available to change agents. It remains to discuss how they can be combined into mixed forms. That discussion appears later in the chapter—but first a brief detour about the uses of violence in the creation of change.

THE ROLE OF VIOLENCE IN CREATING CHANGE

Power is often identified with violence. And while it is not always the case—violence is really a subform of power—it is a common observation that violence often accompanies significant social change in the forms of riots, guerrilla warfare, oppressive measures by the state, terrorism, and—the ultimate form—revolution (Vago, 1980:301). Violence is often advocated as a coercive power strategy to promote social change, and in fact it is so commonly associated with change that some analysts (Huntington, 1972:282) argue that in no society does significant social, economic, or political change take place without violence or the imminent likelihood of violence.

We don't necessarily agree with this thesis, but it is certainly true that violence is commonly associated with significant change. Violence is often advocated as a strategy by which disadvantaged groups call attention to their plight, and may be perceived by lower status groups as the only feasible strategy. Indeed, Emerson (1962) and others have argued that the only ultimate resources that lower participants hold is the power to disrupt the system, often violently. Wilson (1973) has written in a similar vein of the politics of disorder as a strategy to promote change.

As a deliberate strategy, the use of violence often involves two stages: (1) the disruption of the social system in a significant way to get attention and dramatize the seriousness of an issue, and (2) overtures to elites to come to the bargaining table to negotiate concessions. Such strategies have been commonly used by revolutionaries and terrorists (e.g., nationalists in the struggle for sovereignty in Northern Ireland) as well as by militant reformers. Indeed, the history of American reform movements cannot be understood without recognizing the frequent adoption of violent strategies to promote change by otherwise respectable citizens, ranging from the Whiskey Rebellion of the 1790s by the corn farmers of Pennsylvania (a tax revolt) to the bombing of abortion clinics by prolife activists in our time.

Do such strategies work to produce change? The evidence is that they often do. Looking again at major American reform movements—the abolitionists, the Populists, the labor movement, the civil rights movement, the antiwar movement, and the ecology movement—all were characterized by significant deliberate episodes of violence and other forms of the politics of disorder. Violence helped to trigger major changes in social policy and the direction of change. The civil rights movement, for example, did result in significant reforms (jobs, increased welfare benefits) that followed the outbursts of urban violence in the hot summers of the 1960s. Following the Birmingham riot in 1963, President Kennedy pressed Congress for the passage of his Civil Rights Bill to "get the struggle off the streets and into the courts." Failure to pass the bill, Kennedy warned, would lead to "continued if not increased racial strife—causing leadership on both sides to pass from the hands of reasonable and responsible men to the purveyors of hate and violence" (cited in Huntington, 1972). Hence the threat of continued civil disruptions by the lower participants galvanized the political elite to promulgate reforms.

Gamson (1975) conducted one of the rare systematic studies of violence in relation to change by examining the characteristics and circumstances of fifty-three "violence-prone" protest groups in American history in relation to the success and failure of their formal goals for change. Violence, Gamson found, was more likely to succeed when the goal sought by the group was narrow and concretely defined rather than broad and comprehensive, and particularly when the goals were defined in terms of gaining concessions and advantages rather than winning social acceptability.

Related to this effect, Gamson found that violence-prone groups were more likely to be successful when the group was more interested in removing others from power or displacing the privileged position of other groups rather than achieving power and privilege for themselves. Successful groups also were larger, more able to effectively and rapidly mobilize resources, and had a more centralized power structure—with power vested in an individual or an executive committee. Less successful violence-prone groups were found to be more decentralized, in that they allowed considerable leeway to local chapters to act on their own without approval from the top, and the protest organization exercised less discipline throughout its entire system of members and subgroups. Successful violence-prone groups were more successful when they chose unpopular targets (groups, leaders, or policies). Only one successful violence-prone group in Gamson's sample relied *exclusively* on violence (the Kentucky Night Riders, who coerced recalcitrant tobacco farmers into joining a trade association by whipping them and burning their barns and crops). Most used it as a supplement to other strategies, such as strikes, bargaining, and propaganda. Finally, Gamson found that successful use of violence was related to the larger societal context. Some groups, which had been having little success for a long time, were able to succeed during an intensified crisis. For example, the Steel Workers Organizing Committee was able to win concessions that steel companies had been effectively blocking for years from the National War Labor Board during World War II.

Having said all this, we must add that violence is a volatile strategy that doesn't always work and is particularly ambiguous as a strategy of change. Successful use of violent strategies requires a large base of public sympathy, if not outright support, for the broader goals of change. Even then, others may support the larger cause while distancing themselves from violent strategies to promote that cause. Furthermore, violent strategies may have a boomerang effect. They may erode public support for goals that would otherwise find significant public support. Thus at the 1968 Democratic convention, violence by the police against demonstrators ultimately eroded the credibility of the police and drew onlookers into the action on the side of the demonstrators. A more recent example is the effect of the bombing of the Federal Building in Oklahoma City on general sympathies for militia and other antigovernment, pro-gun social movements. While the leaders of many antigovernment pro-gun movements distanced themselves from Timothy McVeigh and the damage he perpetrated, the adverse publicity has done a lot to fuel calls for restricting the sales of certain types of weapons.

Another problem with the use of violence is the kind of society that develops when violence is commonly used to promote change. Oppenheimer (1969) argues that the use of violence prevents the emergence of a democratic and humane social order. People who are successful in the use of violence become habituated to its use in problem solving. Where this is the case, Oppenheimer argues, what is likely to develop is the antithesis of the Western vision of rule by law. Clearly, the deliberate encouragement of violence as a strategy for change is a grave choice, which may be justified only in extreme circumstances. Those circumstances do, however, exist.

Finally, it is important to note another thing about violence in the context of the social order. Most of the foregoing discussion is about violence from below by dissident groups and social movements (as indeed are most sociological writings about violence as a change strategy). But violence from above is a fact of life for many people in the world. It is impossible, for instance, to understand the violence-as-tactics of insurgent groups in the Philippines, South Korea, Central America, or South Africa without considering them in the context of state-sponsored terrorism that limits nonviolent responses and provokes violent ones. Such was also the case in the outbreaks of labor violence in the United States at the turn of the century.

MIXED AND COMPLEX STRATEGIES

While one strategy may predominate in any particular change effort, most efforts require a combination of strategies. *Complex* and *mixed strategies* are particularly required when the changes sought are themselves broad, complex changes operating at different structural levels and the target population is heterogeneous and diverse. There are a variety of ways of using complex strategies.

First, one might *segment* the target population into various subgroups, according to the appropriateness of different strategies. Thus for some subgroups reeducation may work, for others persuasion may work, while for others the use of various power strategies is best. This kind of differentiation depends upon the characteristics of the target population in relation to the change. Reeducation may be most appropriate, for instance, for very intellectually sophisticated sectors of the target population, who would be critical of the stacked deck implied in persuasive appeals. Facilitative strategies may work for those initially predisposed to adopt the change, while persuasion and/or power may be required to overcome the resistance of those not so predisposed. And different strategies and appeals may be required for cosmopolitan opinion leaders, local opinion leaders, and rank-and-file members of the target population (see Chapter 6 for an elaboration of this distinction).

A *second* way of combining strategies is to use different strategies in different stages of the adoption process: reeducation at the *awareness* stage, during which the target population is becoming aware of the possibilities of change; persuasion at the *evaluation* stage, where the target population is evaluating the relative advantages of the change; and facilitative strategies at the *adoption* stage, which make it easy for the target population to actually adopt the change. For example, attempts to introduce school desegregation (both in the Omaha instance cited earlier as well as in other communities) used reeducation, persuasion, and power strategies, both directed toward different subgroups in the target community as well as at different stages in the implementation process. A *third* way of combining different strategies is in a *freeze-and-thaw* combination—that is, alternating the use of power and persuasion. This is frequently done in labor management negotiations, when attempts to persuade the adversary of the justness of the cause are followed by attempts to impose sanctions. This strategy is also frequently employed in international diplomatic relations. Thus "in East-West relationships, both sides have tended to employ power to gain concessions and to follow that with overtures of peace and friendship" (Lauer, 1977:365).

It is very delicate and difficult to successfully practice this combined freeze-and-thaw strategy, however, and it may place contradictory demands on the role of the change agent. As we indicated earlier, power is typically *alienative,* since it implies at least the threat of coercion, while persuasion stresses trust between the change agent and the target system. And while power strategies encourage change agents to monopolize resources and information to deprive the target population of them, other strategies (facilitative, reeducative, and persuasive) press the change agent to at least *appear* to put resources in the hands of the target system and be open and honest regarding resources relevant to the change. Such contradictions implicit in the freeze-and-thaw strategy may hinder its effectiveness so much as to outweigh whatever advantages it has to offer. At the very least, the change agent who practices such a strategy will have to give considerable thought and effort to address such dilemmas and choose actions that minimize them.

A *fourth* way of mixing strategies is a mechanism referred to as *left flanking.* This is especially effective if social movements have moderate and radical factions committed to using different methods to produce change (see McAdam, McCarthy, and Zald, 1996). Left-flanked social movements are the moderates in the exchange, and they have at their disposal a powerful bargaining tactic to use with their opponents; "Deal with us, or you'll end up dealing with them!" In some change scenarios, the moderate and radical factions of a movement are actually coordinated, but in many cases they're not and the moderate faction has only limited control over the actions of their radical counterparts. However, regardless of whether moderates exercise any control over radicals or not, the *perception* that they might be able to makes them a powerful and appealing negotiating partner. Many descriptions of the relationships between different factions of the anti-abortion movement; the liberal and radical factions of the Palestinian movement in the Middle East; and the Irish Republican Army, the Real Irish Republican Army, and Sinn Fein in Northern Ireland fit this scenario.

Nonviolent Direct Action

No discussion of multiple strategies is complete without mention of the combination of strategies for change that grew out of the movement for national independence in India. These have since been widely developed, codified and practiced in other movements that represent the interests of the lower participants in society. Mohandas Gandhi, the creator of this strategy, called it *satyagraha,* which literally means "the force which is born of truth and love." *Satyagraha* includes both persuasion and power, but emphasizes nonviolent uses of power. It depends critically on the ability of change agents to mobilize a cadre of supporters capable of self-discipline, adherence to ethical principle, and—most of all—a willingness to endure deprivations. Bondurant (1972) has outlined nine steps in a *satyagraha* campaign:

1. Try to resolve the conflict or grievance by negotiation and arbitration (without compromising fundamentals).
2. Prepare the group for direct action (including preparations to suffer the consequences of the action).
3. Engage in propaganda and demonstrations.
4. Try once again to persuade the opponent to concede demands, explaining the further action to be taken if this is refused.
5. Begin various economic boycotts and various kinds of strikes.
6. Initiate a program of noncooperation with established authorities and institutions.
7. Engage in civil disobedience to selected laws.
8. Take over some of the functions of government.
9. Establish a parallel government to handle those functions.

As you can see, this is a progressive strategy that begins quite modestly but could continue to a radical social transformation (a political revolution or the departure of a colonial power). It is important to emphasize, however—as do its practitioners— that the strategy could stop at any point that concessions are made. Alternately, it could be abandoned at any point if the costs of the later stages are judged too high in relation to the benefits associated with the change.

Such nonviolent direction action has been widely influential among leaders of movements of the powerless directed toward gaining concessions from the powerful. Gandhi and the Congress party movement were able to finally force the powerful British colonial government to "quit India." It was adapted by Martin Luther King, Jr. and used in the early days of the civil rights movement, as well as (more recently) in Jesse Jackson's Operation Breadbasket and the student democracy occupation of Tienmen Square in Bejing. It has been used by community organizers such as Saul Alinsky on behalf of the poor and by Cesar Chavez, who spearheaded the drive among California farmworkers for better working conditions. Nonviolent direct action does not always succeed, but it has often been a powerful tool when used by lower participants who ordinarily have little influence on the course of social change. How so?

There are, we think, three keys to the success of nonviolent direct action. *First,* since it is a strategy often used by relatively powerless groups, its practitioners must think creatively and imaginatively about what tactics and resources they will use. According to Alinsky, a master tactician of community organization in the United States:

> I have emphasized . . . that tactics means you do what you can with what you've got, and that power has always gravitated towards those who have money and those whom people follow. The resources of the Have-Nots are (1) no money and (2) lots of people. . . . How can people use them? . . . Use the power of the law by making the establishment obey its rules. Go outside the experience of the enemy, stay inside the experience of your people. Emphasize tactics that your people will enjoy. (1972:138–139)

The practitioners of nonviolent direct action not only organized voters and created consumer boycotts, but also created a variety of imaginative tactics (such as sit-ins, swim-ins, and pray-ins) directed at the targets of change. Alinsky himself graphically and humorously illustrated the need for creativity by citing a suggestion he made during a campaign by African Americans in Rochester, New York, to gain concessions (jobs) from Eastman Kodak, a major employer in Rochester. He suggested a demonstration at the local concert hall, which had been donated to the city by the company.

> I suggested that we might buy one hundred seats for one of Rochester's symphony concerts. We would select a concert in which the music was relatively quiet. The hundred blacks who would be given the tickets would first be treated to a three-hour preconcert dinner in the community, in which they would be fed

nothing but baked beans, and lots of them; then the people would go to the symphony hall—with obvious consequences. Imagine the scene as the action began! The concert would be over before the first movement! (If this is a Freudian slip—so be it). (1972:139)

Second, and perhaps most obviously, the successful practice of nonviolent direct action requires the creation of a core of activists who are willing to suffer some deprivations in order to draw attention to an issue or embarrass the authorities. *Third,* such strategies succeed because they are likely to provoke the authorities into unprincipled violent reactions. This is the real core of successful nonviolent direct action strategies that progress beyond the initial polite negotiation stages. Thus the British bludgeoned demonstrators during the Indian independence movement, while Gandhi threatened to embarrass the British further by starving to death in their jails. During the 1950s white sheriffs unleashed their dogs on civil rights marchers in Alabama, and in the 1960s police and national guardsmen clubbed, teargassed, and shot student antiwar demonstrators. In the 1980s, South African police beat and jailed demonstrators of the black nationalist movement. These kinds of brutal responses are likely to be widely reported in the mass media. They draw distant onlookers and third parties into the controversy. While third-party sympathies may be polarized, nonviolent direct action strategies succeed to the extent that they are able to mobilize sympathetic public opinion and embarrass the authorities. The British ultimately quit India at the point where they could no longer suppress the independence movement without further erosion of the legitimacy of the British government policy in the eyes of world opinion, and of many Englishmen themselves.

What are some of the limitations of nonviolent direct action as a complex strategy? Some are obvious from the foregoing discussion. *First,* the issue must be one of enormous importance to the people seeking the change if they are to be willing to suffer the deprivations associated with such actions. *Second,* change agents must invest heavily in the creative use of resources and tactics and the maintenance of disciplined loyalty. These requirements may be unmanageable. *Third,* the strategy is likely to be ineffective when the grievances involve only conflicts of material interests with no moral or ethical basis. Not only must the grievance have a moral basis, but the insurgent group must be able to co-opt the moral high ground. *Fourth,* the strategy is not effective where there are no third-party onlookers or where the overwhelming sympathies of such third parties come to side with the authorities. This is always a possibility, particularly in complex social systems where onlookers are likely to be polarized. *Fifth,* nonviolent direct action is probably not effective in authoritarian systems that are so secure that favorable public opinion (either internal or external) is entirely irrelevant to the maintenance of control. Such systems may exist. The Russian dissident movement, for example, probably had a limited ability to affect major policy change in the Soviet Union. The Chinese government was so secure that they were able to violently suppress the Tienmen Square demonstration in front of a worldwide audience of television onlookers.

Even in such circumstances, however, adverse international publicity has some limited effect. Soviet emigres have suggested that to the extent that the Russian dissident movement or the condition of Soviet Jews have become objects of international attention and embarrassment to the regime, their behavior was often moderated. Similarly, Amnesty International has found that by publicizing the plight of political prisoners they have often—but not always—been able to secure their release from jails by authoritarian regimes of both the left and the right. And though the Chinese student democracy movement was crushed, the Chinese government has been answering pointed questions about human rights abuses from the international community ever since.

Let's pause now to review this discussion about creating change. We began by underlining the distinction between trends and deliberate attempts to instigate change, and then analyzed two cases of attempts to create change. Next, basic change strategies were discussed (facilitative, reeducative, persuasive, and power strategies). Following that was an extended aside about the role of violence in creating change, and finally, we have discussed the necessity for complex and mixed strategies, with a special emphasis on nonviolent direct action strategies. Now we will redirect the discussion toward more nuts-and-bolts issues and discuss some issues that we think are of practical value to would-be change agents (a category that probably includes all of us at some time or another).

BEING A CHANGE AGENT

We believe that the job of being a change agent should start with two kinds of questions. First is a *structural* question: How do you identify persons and subgroups who are the "strategic levers" of change in any particular target population? This means identifying the opinion leaders and community influentials (see Chapter 10) that can influence others in the system to adopt change. Second is a *social psychological* or an *interactional* question: How do you change the behaviors or the minds of the persons in question? The different strategies discussed earlier represent alternative ways of going about changing minds and/or behavior. But within any of these strategies there may be some things that change agents can do to reduce resistance to change. What are some of these things?

Drawing again on the materials of Chapter 10, one can reduce resistance to the adoption of a change by attempting to make the particular innovation (1) simple and easy to communicate, (2) divisible, and (3) maximally compatible with the status quo (values, needs). This is no easy task, particularly when dealing with broad-scale change, but change agents should attempt to think in these terms. The change agent may also be able to reduce resistance to change by shaping the climate in which such efforts take place in a number of ways. In general, resistance to change is less when

1. The clients feel that the change project is their own.
2. The change project is supported by top officials (unless the relations between the target population and top officials is itself a hostile and/or mistrustful one).
3. The clients see change as reducing their burdens.

4. The change involves new experiences that interest people.
5. There are no threats to the security or autonomy of people.
6. People join in diagnosing the problem.
7. The change project is supported by group consensus.
8. There are many similarities between the change agent and the clients in terms of background, outlook, and so forth.
9. There is a great deal of empathy between the change agents and others.
10. There is a high degree of trust between the people themselves.
11. The change program has built-in provisions for feedback from those affected.
12. The change program is open to ongoing revision.

Certainly, if all of these conditions were in place, chances of adoption would be maximized. But, alas, in an imperfect world, that may not be possible. We should emphasize, however, that change agents may be able to produce some of these conditions by their own efforts (e.g., facilitating a group consensus, securing the support of the top officials) where they do not naturally exist. Obviously, a great deal of ingenuity and inventiveness is required by change agents.

Planning and Grassroots Mobilizing

Planning for grassroots mobilizing is not as simple as it would first appear. Michael Lipsky (1968) explores the balancing act that faces groups of relatively powerless people as they attempt to create social change (see Figure 11-1).

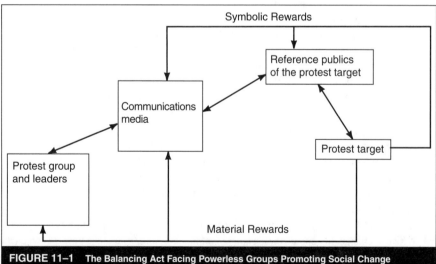

FIGURE 11–1 **The Balancing Act Facing Powerless Groups Promoting Social Change**
Source: Adapted from Lipsky (1968).

For the average citizen group, creating social change is a *balancing act* between the protest group (those who are committed to the change and willing to take action themselves to bring it about), the communications media, reference publics of potential sympathizers who won't join the protest group but may act in sympathy with their goals or at least not obstruct change, and the protest target, that group whose behavior the protest group seeks to change. Managing the interactions among members of the protest group, the media, and the reference public is especially difficult. Many of the activities that protest groups want to engage in disrupt the lives of the reference public. If protest groups are portrayed unsympathetically by the media and the media provides the only communication the public receives about the protest group, the reference public might resent the activities of the protest group and side with the protest target in resisting protestor's demands and repressing the group. But if protest groups only worry about communicating with the reference public, they risk alienating the activists who (usually) volunteer their time and effort to do the actual protest work! Very few organizations negotiate this balancing act successfully, which (in part) explains why change agents are often frustrated.

There is no cookbook for creating change. Why? As anyone who has attempted to cook a complex meal knows, exact specifications are always missing and recipes contain many vague instructions: "Add salt to taste." How much is that? "Cook until vegetables are crisp, but do not overcook." What does that mean? Like cooking, social change requires experience, making do with imperfect ingredients, and often muddling through (sorry!). Still, there *are* some issues we think change agents need to consider. We've divided them into issues about *plans* and about *grassroots mobilizing*.

Plans for social change involve a number of issues:

1. The first task of a good plan is to define the goals of the desired change. Goals are of two sorts. There are *conceptual* goals, which specify exactly what is to change (What's the problem? What do I want to change? How could the situation be improved?). Then there are *operational* goals that are more concrete than conceptual goals, and ask for specification of exactly the behaviors, attitudes, structures, or group processes that are to be changed. These operational goals also provide clues about how one might measure the extent to which the change has actually occurred.
2. Next, a good plan needs to specify as precisely as possible the target or client population: Who is to change? Target or client populations can be defined as individuals, populations, groups, organizations, or communities. A good plan will also identify the channels of communication or influence and "opinion leaders" within the target or client population.
3. A good plan will identify situations or times when the target population is most receptive to change. In general, these *change-conducive situations* include times (1) when the target group is experiencing stress about the present situation, (2) when there are cross-pressures from conflicting group affiliation that tug the individual in different directions,[4] and (3) when the target group has the time or resources to adopt change.

4. A good plan will develop an inventory of resources available. Resources can mean people (and the prestige of persons), money, and material resources as well as loyalties and commitments. As we noted, change agents should define resources creatively, looking for nonobvious resources or creative ways of using the obvious ones.

5. A good plan should consider appropriate strategies (e.g., facilitation, reeducation, persuasion, or power), how they might be combined, and how their contradictions might be addressed.

6. Finally, a good plan should include mechanisms for the ongoing monitoring of change so that it can be modified, fine-tuned, or abandoned. An assessment of relative success or failure is important. Change agents must decide whether to continue their efforts, provide ongoing support services for adoption, or abandon such efforts entirely. The last judgment should not be made prematurely, but at some point it is inevitable.

As for grassroots mobilizing, change requires more than good plans, and unless you are working in a big powerful bureaucracy it often requires organizing for action at the grassroots. Here are some guidelines by John Gardner, former cabinet officer and founder of one of America's largest citizens' organizations (Common Cause):

1. Create a full-time continuing organization.

2. Limit the number of targets and hit them hard. Most organizations dilute their efforts by taking on too many issues.

3. Form alliances with other organizations on particular issues.

4. Get professional advisers to provide you with accurate, effective information and arguments.

5. Communicate effectively and state your position in accurate, concise, and moving ways.

6. Persuade and use positive reinforcement—don't attack. Confine your remarks to the issue; don't make personal attacks on individuals. Try to find allies within social institutions, and compliment them when they do something you like.

7. Do your homework, and then privately approach public officials whose support you need. It's best not to bring up something at a public meeting unless you have the votes lined up ahead of time. Most political influence is carried on behind the scenes through one-on-one conversations.

8. Instead of fighting with your opponents, respect their beliefs and work with them to achieve your goals when possible.

9. Organize for action, not just for study, discussion, or education. Minimize meetings. Have a group coordinator, a series of task forces, a press and communications contact, legal and professional advisers, and a small group of dedicated workers. A small, well-organized group can accomplish more than a large, unwieldy one.

10. Work in groups, but keep in mind that people in groups can act collectively in ways that individuals know to be stupid.

11. Concentrate your efforts at the local and state levels. Stay on good terms with the press. (cited in Miller, 1992:688)

THE ETHICS OF INDUCING CHANGE

We promised to return to the ethical issues in creating change. If you have been bothered by the manipulative and deceptive overtones of some strategies described in the chapter, we admit that we are too. To speak of clients of change involved in collaborative enterprises is not a problem for us, but to speak of a *target population* is. Targets are, after all, things we shoot at.

Here are the various change strategies along a continuum in terms of the extent to which we believe that they involve ethical problems, as follows:

Facilitation	Reeducation	Persuasion	Power/Coercion

◄───►

Few ethical problems   Many ethical problems

Ethical problems in inducing change exist to the extent that change efforts do not respect the autonomy, rationality, and dignity of people to choose whether or not they wish to change or to be fully informed about the consequences of such choices. When there is lack of candor or full disclosure about such choices, there are ethical problems. In terms of these criteria, *facilitation* and *reeducation* (to the extent that the latter can be honestly practiced) do respect the autonomy, rationality, and dignity of persons who are the targets of change.

Persuasion, in comparison, respects the voluntary choice to adopt change but may overwhelm the person with distorted (or false) information, withheld information, and nonrational appeals to emotion. The target population is not aware of how information is arranged and loaded to persuade. It is, moreover, contrary to the accepted values of truth and full disclosure. By these standards, much contemporary advertising and political persuasion is unethical. *Power and coercive strategies* carry the greatest number of ethical problems because they deny voluntary adoption and rejection and maximally violate the autonomy and dignity of persons.

Regarding ethical problems, social psychologist Phillip Zimbardo and his colleagues suggested several criteria under which intervention is justified.

1. If there is informed consent.
2. If there is accessibility to one's usual sources of information and social support.
3. If there is the absence of threats of dire consequences of the failure to change.
4. If there are no "non-ordinary techniques" used that overwhelm reason (e.g., isolation, deprivation).
5. If there are no uses of special vulnerabilities, such as those associated with age, sex, education, or financial status. (1977: 189)

These are very strict standards that, if taken literally, would mean that facilitation and reeducation are the only permissible strategies for the ethical change agent. But we think this is an overly restrictive view.

Obviously, the ethical concerns surrounding manipulation and coercion are matters of degree. In everyday life when the degree of coercion is modest we are ordinarily willing to use it for socially sanctioned purposes (for example, to manipulate children to behave, get drivers to obey traffic laws, or prevent environmental pollution). Our willingness to use coercion depends not only upon the degree to which we perceive its side effects on the subjects to be moderate, but also upon how important we perceive the ultimate goal to be. Thus we may be willing to consider the use of capital punishment (the ultimate form of coercion) if we believe that it will achieve the important goal of lowering the rate of homicide.[5] Our argument is not that ethical issues are secondary or unimportant issues in the planning of change, but rather that they should be considered in the context of the importance and potential benefits of the change itself, either to the change agents or the target population (though these are very different criteria of judgment!).

This discussion of ethical problems is gradually devolving, as perhaps all do, into the age-old ethical conundrum: Do the ends justify the means? It is obvious that no single answer can be given. That is, *some* ends justify *some* means. But other than looking to the existing social values and norms for guidance, this is clearly a matter of judgment in each situation for which the agents promoting change must bear responsibility. Rather than attempting to discuss our reading of current social norms regarding what is permissible, let's pose a series of questions so that you can explore your own values.

Would *you* use manipulative persuasion or coercion to

1. Guarantee equal access to public facilities?
2. Gain the adoption of demonstrably superior techniques of food production in a less developed country?
3. Prevent people from having abortions?
4. Redistribute land in developing countries?
5. Redistribute vastly unequal wealth in industrial countries?
6. Gain the adoption of a form of government you believe to be significantly better than the existing one?
7. Get an individual to take a life-saving drug?
8. Get people to quit smoking cigarettes?
9. Promote family planning in less developed countries?
10. Promote the sale of a product that will make you rich?
11. Convert someone to a new system of religious beliefs (yours)?
12. Isolate a community to prevent the spread of a deadly plague?
13. Promote energy conservation in the United States?

Our answers to the above are yes on some and no on others. Clearly, the burden of ethical justification remains squarely on the shoulders of those seeking to induce change. Nor does it help to argue that you can use questionable strategies merely because others are doing so (you know . . . everybody's doing it . . .). Thus using the scientific literature about change does not remove one from the burdens of ethical choice. They are an inescapable part of social life.

IN CONCLUSION: SOME FINAL THOUGHTS
ABOUT THE FEASIBILITY OF CREATING CHANGE

With all of the difficulties we have raised about creating change, a would-be change instigator might say, "Why bother?" Considering the complexities and difficulties of any particular case, this may indeed be a rational response. To recapitulate, the difficulties are of two sorts: practical and ethical. After discussing the ethical difficulties, let us return briefly to the practical ones. They boil down to four types: (1) lack of clarity about the goals of change (what would be better than the present?), (2) lack of control over the resources necessary to bring about change, (3) unpredictability about the outcomes of one's efforts, and (4) unpredictability about the longer-range ramifications of change even when the short-run goals are successfully achieved. Although we alluded briefly to the fourth type of difficulty at the beginning of this chapter, we would like to expand on it by illustration.

The long-range ramifications of change are often unpredictable because it is impossible to change just one thing without ultimately implicating other things. This is because the social world is a *system* of elements (subgroups, levels, institutions) that are interconnected in subtle and complex ways. Consider the case of the Green Revolution, a good example of unintended, long-range, and sometimes bizarre ramifications of change. The Green Revolution was a worldwide effort to address the problem of world hunger by increasing agricultural productivity in developing countries. The problem was precisely that the change agents' concern with the immediate success of changing just one thing led them to be inattentive to the broader system context within which that one thing was embedded. Miracle seed varieties with extraordinarily high per-acre yields (primarily wheat and rice) were developed by Norman Borlag and others at Iowa State University, and their global distribution was sponsored by the Rockefeller and Ford Foundations in the 1950s and 1960s; by the 1970s, these efforts were labeled counterproductive in many nations (Lauer, 1977:213–214; Freeman, 1974:89–90). Why?

To begin with, the new seeds, while being marvelously more productive, required much heavier inputs of water, fertilizers, and pesticides. Thus, in spite of the sponsorship of governments and foundations, the new seeds were primarily beneficial to the more prosperous farmers and larger landowners, who could afford to invest in the support systems for the new seeds or who were deemed good credit risks by local banks. As these large producers raised larger crops and began to upgrade the technological level of production, they came to have an even greater market advantage over the small farmers. The large landowners began to buy up even more land from the smaller ones. The upshot of these trends was to increase unemployment among the small farmers, who sold out, and tenants, who were kicked out, as the large-scale producers consolidated their holdings and shifted to a higher level of commercialized production. The Green Revolution projects therefore benefited the small number of large landowners while marginalizing the (vast) majority of agriculturalists.[6]

The social, economic, and political implications of these changes were profound.

Urban economies became even more overburdened with displaced rural people. The efforts of governments to subsidize credit and price supports for the new seeds drained existing (inadequate) budgets for health, education, and social services. As the economic dominance of the large landowners increased, so did political unrest in the rural areas. National economies were increasingly penetrated by multinational corporations from the industrialized world who sold the fertilizers and pesticides. Governments subsidized the prices of the new crops, and producers shifted more to production for more lucrative external markets than for domestic consumption. This was the bitterest irony of all: In many areas the price of food actually increased so that many of the poor had worse diets than before. The Green Revolution was supported by most of the world's policy makers. In retrospect, it is not clear to us whether the promoters of the Green Revolution could have foreseen the tangled web of system interconnections that would result from the seemingly benign introduction of high yield seeds.

What are the implications of the practical difficulties mentioned and of the woeful tale of the Green Revolution? One possible implication is that since the difficulties of bringing about desirable change are so profound, one who attempts to do so is merely being foolish. This is the perennial wisdom of conservatives, who argue that one is best advised to "let nature take its course" and not exacerbate problems by well-intended but naive efforts to change things. Benign neglect, so the argument goes, is often the only prudent course. This is indeed often compelling advice. But it is not the only implication one could draw from considering the difficulties of deliberate change efforts. There are at least two others. First, it is not planning for change itself but the *absence* of an adequate plan that often causes change efforts to miscarry. Efforts to induce change are frequently driven by our passions in the absence of a well thought-out plan. And when we *do* plan, we often focus on the practical difficulties related to initial adoption rather than the longer-term systemic consequences. Elementary sociological wisdom suggests that the unintentional ramifications of intentional change are very important, and the planners of change should attempt to comprehend them. It is also true that this is often very difficult or, in some situations, impossible.

Setting aside the problems of the long-term systemic ramifications of change, the second implication we will draw here is that there is a virtue in thinking small about the goals of change. It is often intellectually more satisfying to think of making sweeping changes in the whole scheme of things, but it may be more feasible to strive to change smaller and more limited parts of the total scheme of things. We recognize that this is not popular counsel to those desiring to change the whole system, but if one wants at least some successes, it may be the only practical possibility. The wisdom of thinking small about change is supported by Gamson's research, mentioned earlier. He found that successful groups had more limited goals, pursued a single issue rather than multiple ones, and did not aim at displacement of their opponents (1975:38–54).

Etzioni (1968a) puts this idea of thinking small in a somewhat different way. He argues that we tend to think of society in terms of a medical model. That is, we view problems as symptoms of deeper causes, and we are always trying to get at the "root causes" and not merely the symptoms. But changing the root causes of problems is very difficult. Etzioni argues that it is often possible to find shortcuts that address problems by controlling the "symptoms" rather than changing the more intractable "underlying causes." Thus it is easier to provide more adequate street lighting and escort services than it is to address the underlying causes of street crime. And though effective affirmative action programs are difficult, they are not as difficult as trying to eradicate racism from American culture and society. Though the symptoms of underlying conditions may keep reoccurring, it may be more feasible and less costly to the society to address them than the deep causes. "True believers may insist on waiting for the needed revolution, but the victims will welcome the treatment of the symptoms" in the meantime (Lauer, 1977:357).

None of this should be taken to mean that we would urge people interested in change not to search for basic causes, or even to undertake to change them, if that is required and feasible. What we are urging is that if this becomes impossible or too scary, one need not give up entirely. In such cases significant improvements can often be made by creatively aiming low.

There is a bottom line here. Granted that creating social change is often costly and demanding. Granted that success, even partial success, is always uncertain. Granted that the long-term systemic consequences may be counterproductive to one's original intent. But even so, should one refuse to make efforts to change things if the issues are really important? The civil rights movement of the 1950s and 1960s was a long, costly, and difficult effort that only partly succeeded. Being aware of its high costs and limited successes, should its organizers have given up? We don't think so. The lives of millions of minority Americans are better today for those efforts, even though the goal of complete racial justice remains elusive. Or should Gandhi have given up the quixotic goal of organizing the world's poorest peasants to throw out one of the world's strongest colonial powers? Should one do nothing because the hope for improvement is small? To do so is to live fatalistically and without hope, unless one expects circumstances to improve naturally without human effort. Confronted by the realists of his day about the slim chances of success for the Indian independence movement, Gandhi responded, "To believe what has not occurred in history will not occur at all, is to argue disbelief in the dignity of man."

THINKING PERSONALLY ABOUT SOCIAL CHANGE

1. Think of an example, fairly recently, when some group, organization, or government official embarked on a broad campaign to change something in your neighborhood, community, city. It could be a campaign, for instance, to improve schools, improve or clean up neighborhoods, change traffic patterns, deal with homeless people, improve parks or recreational programs, clean up the environment, get public officials to be more responsive, reduce crime, or make public places safer. Who promoted the change? Did the change effort succeed, even partially? Why do you think it did or did not?

2. What strategies of stimulating change did those groups or people use? Did they use different strategies or combine them creatively for different people in the target population?

3. Imagine yourself as a change agent trying to change your neighborhood or community for the better. Pick some issue that you think would do that. Assume that you have some, but not unlimited, resources and money to use. How would you go about it? What things would you consider in order to change that particular issue?

NOTES

1. At that time Omaha's population was about 12 percent African American, and there was also a smaller but substantial Hispanic community.

2. The following conceptualization relies heavily on Zaltman and Duncan (1977).

3. There is, of course, a relationship between attitudes and behavior. Attitudinal change sometimes follows behavioral change. The converse is also often true. Decades of research by social psychologists have been unable to unsnarl the tangled web of causality between attitudes and behavior, and so the issue will not detain us here. Our argument is that in the long run attitudes and behaviors are often reinforcing, so they are roughly compatible. But in the short run, it may be possible to change behavior without affecting attitudes very much—or vice versa. It is important for the change agent to have sorted out which is the most important to change, because they imply different change strategies.

4. The concept of *cross-pressures* comes from political scientists, who developed the term to describe the behavior of a voter who is cross-pressured by membership in reference groups that pull his or her vote in different directions. The assumption, supported by much evidence, is that when group affiliations all consistently pull the individual to vote for particular parties or candidates, voter behavior is relatively unproblematic and can be understood as a direct function of those group affiliations. For instance, if one is white, wealthy, college educated, and a Presbyterian, one's vote for Republican candidates becomes rather predictable. This person is minimally open to political persuasion by Democratic candidates. When, on the other hand, such group affiliations pull politically in different directions—so to speak—the resultant voting behavior is more problematic. Consider the case of the African-American physician, whose professional affiliations and ethnic affiliations pull in politically different directions. The outcome not only becomes more unpredictable, but the individual in these circumstances is more amenable to political persuasion of various sorts. In the broader context of advocating change, the individual who is rooted in multiple and somewhat conflicting reference groups is more likely to be open to persuasion and adoption than one who is not so cross-pressured.

5. Personally, we find the evidence in support of that belief not convincing. But many do find it convincing.

6. Some nations avoided these effects by subsidizing credit for small producers. But many did not.

CHAPTER

12

The Emerging Global System: Development and Globalization

The first part of this book dealt with change in the United States, and the second part with more theoretical issues about change. Both parts alluded to change on a world scale, but in a fragmentary and offhand way. We now turn to global change in a more focused and coherent way. We argued in Chapter 1 that you cannot go very far in understanding the changing lives of people without considering how these are embedded in broader currents of societal change. Analogously, the same is true of nations; that is, understanding changes that occur in nations requires understanding how they are embedded in international contexts. That is what the rest of this book is about.

We're sure you are aware, at least abstractly, that the world is becoming a global system of some sort, in which everything ultimately affects everything else. This is common knowledge, but we still think and act in ways that do not always recognize the growing importance of our connections with people and nations in remote parts of the world. That is because we all experience *globalization* locally, and it is difficult to conceptualize the emerging and continuously changing web of social networks across the world. They are certainly not new to our times: Societies in diverse parts of the world have interacted economically and politically since the times of ancient civilizations, but global interaction is deeper and more extensive in the contemporary world. Today you really can't understand change in any particular society without situating it in a global context.

This chapter begins by discussing global development and *developmentalist* theories and policies that emerged when scholars became particularly concerned with world-scale change after World War II. It then moves to discuss criticisms of the 1960s of development and developmentalist perspectives, particularly those known as *dependency* and *world systems theory* perspectives. We conclude by examining newer perspectives about world-scale change or *globalization* that emerged in the 1990s.

TWO WORLDS

Consider the life circumstances of two different peanut farmers: one in the American state of Georgia and the other in the West African nation of Senegal, both internationally important regions for the commercial production of peanuts. The Georgia grower cultivates about 540 acres of peanuts and another 650 acres of corn. His fields are prepared by a large tractor, and he uses improved varieties of seed and fertilizers that have been developed by government-sponsored research. Pesticides are sprayed on his crops from an airplane, and the crops are harvested by a mechanical combine, which separates the peanuts for drying. They are stored in a modern warehouse. He sells his crop to a regional broker, who resells it to larger brokers in Atlanta, New York, or Chicago. The prices he gets are maintained well above the world market price by government price-support programs. The government also restricts imports and limits domestic acreage—all of which protect him from rapid price fluctuation. Research, mechanization, government support, and hard work enable him to net (after costs) as much as $100,000 in good years, and his family lives in comfort, enjoying the wide variety of basic and luxury goods and services available to affluent Americans.

The Senegalese grower cultivates a small farm near the village where he and his family live. Like the American farmer, he inherited his farm, which is the sole source of support for his family of five and three other relatives. Until recently his crop was hand planted and picked, but he has recently begun to mechanize. Fertilizers and pesticides are either too expensive or unavailable. His per-acre yield is about one-fifth that of the American grower. Storage facilities are rudimentary and there are losses because of insects and blight. The Senegalese grower sells his crop to a government corporation at well below the world market price; the corporation resells it on the world market at a higher price. The difference between what the farmer is paid and the government export price is a major source of government revenues.

Small farm size, poor yields, storage losses, and low prices keep the typical Senegalese farmer very poor. His net income is about $400 per year (by contrast, the field workers on a Georgia farm, who are poor by American standards, earn $100 per week when they work). In addition to the peanut crop, which he sells, the African farmer also grows food for his family, mainly millet that is made into gruel. His village has no electricity and is likely to have no school or health clinic. His wife draws water from a well near the village. One-fifth of the children born in the village do not survive to adulthood. While most of the Senegalese are poor small farmers, the minority who live in the capital city (Dakar) live much better. Government officials are likely to have nice homes, drive cars, and work in air-conditioned offices.

In both America and Senegal the political process affects and distorts the economic process. The Georgia farmer is represented in Washington by a member of Congress who is responsive to his need to maintain price supports. The poor Senegalese farmer has little or no political influence. The government is controlled by the minority of urban dwellers and is responsive primarily to their interests and needs (adapted from Honegger, 1987).

The lives of the American and Senegalese farmers sharply define two worlds—one *developed,* the other *developing*—that are vastly different in (1) geography, (2) standards of living, and (3) economic, social, and political structure. Of the two worlds, it is easier to define the developed world, which includes the modern industrialized nations of Europe and North America (as well as Japan, Australia, and New Zealand). The developing world includes most of the nations of South Asia, Latin and Central America, Africa, and the Middle East. Putting it another way, the developed world comprises the nations of the Northern Hemisphere, while the developing nations are concentrated in the Southern Hemisphere. The developing nations are also called Third World countries, which describes a historical sequence of development and modernization that began in northern Europe and America (the First World), continued in southern and eastern Europe (the Second World), and continues today in the rest of the world (the Third World).

Lumping all these countries into a single category called the Third World, or developing countries, obscures their diversity. They are economically similar because compared to the developed nations their economies are less productive, are more likely to be dependent upon a single or a few commodity exports, and have relatively large "subsistence" economic sectors. Beyond that, they differ significantly. Some have vast natural resources (Brazil, Zaire); others are virtually barren of usable natural resources (Chad, Central African Republic). They have diverse cultures and histories: Some have been politically independent for centuries (Ethiopia, Brazil, China), while others are former colonies of the Western nations (India, Nigeria). Some have a highly literate if not a highly skilled workforce (Sri Lanka, 90.7 percent; Paraguay, 92 percent), while in others literacy is rare (Somalia, 12 percent; Niger, 13 percent) (World Bank, 1991; U.N. Development Programme, 1996:135–137).

In spite of differences within the Third World, it is important for you to recognize that on a global basis many more people live like the Senegalese farmer than the American one. And even the Senegalese farmer is relatively well off by world standards, since about a fourth of the people in LDCs are residents of urban slums having neither land or other means of support, living lives of material destitution and despair. For them, development is a mirage. Their lives were described by a noted Indian economist/demographer as

> [having] . . . barely enough to eat and rarely have enough potable water. Health services are thinly spread. When work is available, pay is low and conditions are close to intolerable. Insecurity is permanent; there are no public systems of social security to condition the unemployment, sickness, or death of the family wage earner. Malnutrition, illiteracy, disease, high birth rate, underemployment and low income close off in turn each avenue to escape. (Dadzie, 1980:4)

But the peoples of the world are no longer content—if they ever were—to live in quiet desperation; "a passion for bread and freedom has swept over the world" (Lauer, 1977:299). Even in the poorest developing nations people are aware that abject misery is no longer the lot of all people. They do not want to surrender their cultural uniqueness to the forces of change, but they universally want development in terms of better material security, literacy, health, and life expectancy. They want freedom, self-determination and a better life. And they have come to believe that it is possible.

WHAT IS DEVELOPMENT?

It is difficult to precisely define development. It reminds us of the old joke about the man who couldn't define what a giraffe was but was sure that he knew one when he saw it. Furthermore, most definitions of development are *ethnocentric*—cast in terms of the cultural orientations of "the West."

To complicate matters further, we use some other terms as rough synonyms for development. Two of these are *modernization* and *industrialization.* At its root, *modernization* means Westernization, that is, the diffusion of Western or European social, economic, and cultural forms to the non-Western world. *Industrialization* is a narrower term than modernization, with four primary dimensions:

- Aggregate economic growth through transformation in the sources of energy used (from animate to inanimate)
- A shift from primary production (agriculture and mining) to secondary production (manufacturing)
- Growth in per capita incomes
- Diversification of occupations

Though modernization and industrialization are often linked, you can have modernization, for instance, of cultural and political forms, without much industrialization (more about this later).

Development typically means a general and less ethnocentric social change process. Like industrialization, it means growth in the material base of the society (in production, consumption, and per capita income), but not necessarily a shift to manufacturing as the dominant core of the economy. Mining, fishing, and agriculture can be highly developed. Development is the goal, and economic growth is an important means. So development means not only economic growth but also improvements in the quality of life and the gradual empowerment of people in societies. Thus development *has both objective and normative dimensions.* Like modernization, described in earlier chapters, development means a growth in social complexity and the scale of social life but does not necessarily mean the particular emulation of Western cultural and political institutions. Saudi Arabia is a society that is rapidly developing without becoming significantly Westernized, and there are vast differences between the ways that the United States and Japan have developed. Even so, most scholars admit that the notion of development is not entirely free of Western values and biases.

UNEVEN DEVELOPMENT

Since the idea of development is a complex one, it should not surprise you that the perceptions about the extent and success of development among the nations of the Third World is controversial.

More conservative social scientists emphasize development as economic growth. Reynolds, for instance, defined development as "intensive growth," in which the capacity to produce rises faster than population increases, as opposed to "extensive growth," where economic growth is absorbed by population growth and no per capita increase in incomes is possible. In his study of forty-one developing countries, Reynolds found that all except seven had reached the turning point to intensive growth by 1965 (the laggards were Afghanistan, Bangladesh, Ethiopia, Mozambique, Nepal, Sudan, and Zaire). Surprisingly, the majority had done so prior to 1910 (Reynolds, 1983). Conservative scholars and policy analysts applaud Brazil's rapid economic growth and expansion during the late 1960s and early 1970s as a model for successful development to be emulated.

But more liberal or progressive scholars emphasize that successful development involves growth with relative equity, so that the fruits of development are widely shared. They note, for instance, that the Brazilian "economic miracle" produced such unequal income distribution that its benefits were not shared by at least half of the population. While the Brazilian economy grew remarkably during this period, at an average rate of 7 percent a year, "the underprivileged half of the population has never been so underprivileged. The majority of those with relatively stable jobs earn less . . . (in the 1980s) . . . than they did twenty years ago" (Andrade, 1982:165). Brazil became a more authoritarian and repressive society during that period. In sharp contrast, conservative scholars saw growing economic and social inequality as *actually necessary* in the "early stages" of development (Handelman, 1996:235). We hope you recognize this is an important controversy, and not just an academic one, because it relates to the aspirations of people around the world for better lives. We will return to it later in this chapter.

In short, the United States, Canada, and most Western European nations experienced development earlier in history, and were successful in many ways. Among the vast and populous developing nations, some are buoyant successes and some are doing fairly well but with fragile development. But about 20 percent of the world's people live in nations that are developmental disasters where many children die young, people struggle for a calorie-adequate diet, and large parts of the population live at bare subsistence levels, hedged from disasters only by slim margins. These nations are plagued by chronic civil wars and political instability that produces large populations of uprooted refugees, both within and between nations (Clausen, 1985; Dadzie, 1980:24; U.N. Development Programme, 1996).

Development and Historical Periods

Development among nations of the world have fared better in some time periods and decades than in others (Reynolds, 1983). Between 1850 and 1914, there was a world economic boom that stimulated the economic growth in developed and developing nations alike. The rapid rise in world trade during this period produced growth in the developing countries, primarily as exporters of cash crops and commodities. Between 1914 and 1945, there were two world wars and a world depression that inhibited growth and development in all nations. This was followed by the greatest boom, from 1945 to 1970, in which there was an unprecedented growth of world trade, with national growth rates well above those of the earlier periods (Reynolds, 1983; Williamson, 1996).

Beginning about 1970, the world saw spectacular economic development progress for some countries and unprecedented decline for others. Among 15 countries representing 1.6 billion people (more than 25 percent of the world's population), incomes were rapidly rising. This was particularly true for China, India, and other Asian countries. But among 100 nations that represented another 25 percent of the world's people, economic decline or stagnation reduced living standards. For Latin America and sub-Saharan Africa, the 1980s is often called the "lost decade." In Latin America per capita income was lower in 1990 than in 1980, consumption fell by 6 percent, and investment fell by 4 percent. Inflation reached an average of 1500 percent a year, and by 1987 the region's total external debt was three times more than its exports! The situation was about as dismal in sub-Saharan Africa, and at the urging of international agencies many countries attempted to deal with the situation by policies of structural adjustment that often meant trying to balance the economy at the cost of unbalancing the lives of people.

But wait. If you consider noneconomic dimensions of development, *the decade was not totally lost,* even in Latin America and sub-Saharan Africa. In both regions life expectancy increased, as did adult literacy, and infant mortality decreased. Even under seriously adverse conditions, some human improvement was possible, though its progress lags far behind other regions. Politically, many countries in both Latin America and sub-Saharan Africa made a transition from military rule to democracy. In sub-Saharan Africa, for instance, nearly thirty multiparty presidential elections have been held (twenty-one of them for the first time ever). In fact, despite economic downturns and problems most developing nations made more progress in human and social dimensions of development (U.N. Development Programme, 1996:1–4,17). To summarize, three points are important.

- Rates of development vary historically and generally follow the economic conditions of the world economy.
- Widening disparities in economic performance are creating two worlds, ever more polarized. We illustrated this phenomenon earlier with the lives of Senegalese and American peanut farmers. Of the $23 trillion (GDP) in the whole world economy in 1993, only $5 trillion was in developing countries, even though they had 80 percent of the world's population, and the disparity has gotten worse since then.

- Some aspects of development (e.g., education, longevity, health conditions, political environments) don't vary precisely with economic conditions. Some richer countries are worse than they should be, and some poorer countries are better off than they should be at given levels of economic performance (U.N. Development Programme, 1996:1–5, 30).

Measuring Development: The Human Development Index

As you can see, *development* is a complex notion with many dimensions that can't really be captured by a single indicator or even a detailed set of statistical indicators. Even so, to compare nations around the world, analysts of the United Nations Development Programme invented the Human Development Index (HDI), a basic composite index of achievements in three fundamental dimensions of human development: (1) long and healthy life, (2) knowledge and education, and (3) a decent material standard of living. It is a more realistic measure of development than traditional measures, like dollars per capita, because it incorporates other important dimensions that purely economic measures miss.

The United Nations collects data about these dimensions from nations and its other agencies like UNESCO, and from private international agencies like the World Bank. The HDI for each of 174 nations is an average of the GNP per capita (in real $US), adult life expectancy (yrs), and the adult literacy rate. Dollars per capita is measured in real terms to control for inflation; because exchange rates with $US fluctuate rapidly, making comparisons difficult, the United Nations uses "purchasing power parity" (PPP, $US) conversion rates. Those rates estimate what a nation's currency would buy equivalent to what dollars would buy. HDI computation for each nation produces a single index number that is a proportion of the maximum possible value of 1. Finally, HDI indexes are ranked from 1 to 174 for the 174 nations included (United Nations, 1996:28–30, 131–132).

As you might guess, the European and North American nations rank at top, and the United Nations has divided developing countries into upper, middle, and lower tiers. Table 12–1 shows the HDI rank and indexes for selected nations with various other development indicators. It includes a measure of relative income inequality (a ratio of the national income shares going to the upper 20 percent of households compared to the lower 20 percent of households); an indicator of industrialization (percent of labor force employed in industry); annual population growth rates, in percent; and the social status of women (percent of women in the labor force; UN data reported only for developing countries).

Some highlights of the 1998 HDI rankings were:

- Of the 157 countries, 57 formed a higher human development tier, 69 formed a middle category, and 48 comprised a lowest human development category.
- Canada, the United States, and Japan had the highest HDI ranks. Among the developing countries, Hong Kong, Cyprus, South Korea, and Barbados lead. The Russian Federation ranked lowest in the upper tier of nations.

TABLE 12–1 LEVELS OF DEVELOPMENT, SELECTED INDICATORS AND HDI, 1998

	Real GDP per capita (US$ PPP)[a]	Life expect. at birth[b]	Adult literacy (percent)	Female prof/tech workers (percent of total)[c]	HDI index[d]	HDI rank[e] (1 to 174)
MDCs						
Canada	23,582	79	99	52	.935	1
United States	29,605	77	99	53	.929	3
Sweden	20,659	79	99	49	.926	6
Netherlands	22,176	78	99	46	.925	8
Austria	23,166	77	99	47	.908	16
LDCs						
Upper Tier						
South Korea	13,478	73	98	32	.854	31
Poland	7,619	73	99	60	.814	44
Mexico	7,704	72	91	40	.784	55
Malasia	8,137	72	86	44	.772	61
Russian Rep.	6,460	68	99	66	.771	62
Brazil	6,625	67	84	62	.747	74
Saudi Arabia	10,158	72	75	NA	.747	75
Middle Tier						
China	3,105	70	83	NA	.706	99
Indonesia	2,651	66	86	NA	.670	109
Bolivia	2,269	62	84	43	.643	114
Egypt	3,041	67	54	28	.623	119
Guatemala	3,505	64	67	NA	.619	120
Lower Tier						
India	2,077	63	56	21	.563	128
Bangladesh	1,361	59	40	35	.461	146
Haiti	1,383	54	48	NA	.440	150
Senegal	1,307	53	36	NA	.416	155
Mali	681	54	38	NA	.380	165
Ethiopia	574	43	36	NA	.309	171

Source: U.N. Development Programme (2000).

NA = Comparable data not available.

    a. Expressed in purchasing power parity terms (see text).

    b. Life expectancy at birth, expressed in years.

    c. The percentage of all professional and technical workers who are women.

    d. *Human development index:* Life expectancy (yrs.) + educational attainment (total school enrollment at all levels) + per capita real gross domestic product (in PPP terms, see text). Transformed into standard errors so that the maximum possible value is 1 and the minimum would be 0.

    e. Numerical rank of the HDI among 174 nations.

- Many East Asian and Pacific Rim nations combined high economic growth with relatively equitable income distributions; Latin American nations were concentrated at intermediate HDI levels; and sub-Saharan African nations were concentrated at low HDI levels.
- HDI ranking differs significantly than if ranked by income per capita alone. (U.N. Development Programme, 2000:30)

The HDI is a significant improvement to study rates of development and systematic comparisons between nations. But it does have the disadvantage that it is based on averages and can be misleading in nations where people differ significantly by gender, ethnic group, or region. Over several years, UN analysts have computed *disaggregated* HDIs within countries by region, race, or ethnicity. In the United States, the HDI for whites is significantly higher than for blacks or for any U.S. minority population. When the HDI is adjusted to reflect the status of women, the United States rank drops to fourth place, behind Sweden, Canada, and Norway, while that of China rises significantly. In India, for example, the HDI for the more developed region around Bhopal is four times that of more backward districts. In the Philippines, the HDI for the region around the national capital (Manila) is dramatically higher than in rural Mindanao, where 55 percent of the people live in poverty compared with 15 percent in the capital. And computing the Mexican HDI without its indigenous (Native American) population increases the HDI for the rest of the population by about 30 percent (U.N. Development Programme, 1996:31). Dissaggregating data in this way defines disparities within nations, and sometimes political flashpoints.

DEVELOPMENTALIST THINKING: PERSPECTIVES AND DIMENSIONS

In the decades after World War II, the idea of development dominated thinking about economic and social change in the Third World, and it held out the expectation that the economic prosperity and democratic political institutions found in the developed industrial nations would spread throughout the world (Johnson, 1986:679). *Developmentalist* scholars generally argued that the Western model of development (or modernization) had components and sequences that are of global relevance and can be replicated in other nations regardless of their history, culture, and geography (Lerner: 1958:46).

The study of development emerged in the 1950s as a loosely connected intellectual movement among prestigious social scientists from several disciplines. But developmentalism also had political and official support because

the United States suddenly found itself the leader of the Western world and the only defender of its economic and ideological interests against the Soviet Union and what then seemed to be a growing united world Communist revolutionary movement. The basic notion was that because it was the richest and the strongest of all nations, the United States must also be the most morally advanced of societies. It therefore became the model of how to be properly modern. The United States was bound by interest and duty to show the rest of the world how to follow in its path. (Chirot, 1981:259)

Developmentalism embodied not only a set of scholarly interests, but also idealism and humanitarian impulses—a desire to improve the human condition. It also embodied U.S. strategic and geopolitical interests as they were understood in the postwar decades. It functioned as an anticommunist ideology and a developmental strategy.

Economic Development

Not all development is economic, but economic change is at the heart of the development processes. Abstractly, it means the shift from a stable subsistence economy to a commercial one with self-sustaining economic growth. More concretely, economic development involves (1) the technological upgrading of economic production, (2) the development of an extensive money economy (as opposed to an exchange economy), and (3) the development of large-scale markets (Lerner, 1968; Levy, 1966).

Influential economist Walter Rostow conceptualized economic development as a takeoff *stage model,* analogous to an airplane moving down a runway—it gradually builds up enough momentum to take off into self-sustaining flight or, in the case of an economy, to self-sustaining growth. Here is how he described the stages of economic development.

1. *Traditional setting.* With traditional technology, the economy has a limited potential for production. There are large subsistence sectors and few or weakly developed markets.
2. *Preconditions for growth.* A widespread psychological desire for growth exists, with a degree of mass literacy and a central government. Importantly, infrastructures develop (communications, transportation, banking, investment, and credit systems).
3. *Takeoff.* Industrial technology rapidly grows in a few economic sectors (typically in agriculture or mining), and between 5 and 10 percent of the GNP is reinvested in economic growth.
4. *Drive to maturity.* The application of high technology across many sectors of the economy.
5. *A mature industrial economy.* The gradual emergence of a diverse, mass-consumption economy. (Rostow, 1962)

Rostow's model captures how Western economists understood industrialization in the 1960s; it remains suggestive and useful, but with many limitations and difficulties. Some stages seem arbitrarily separated, especially the preconditions and the takeoff. Does one really precede the other? But its biggest problem is that most developing countries long ago evolved beyond traditional subsistence economies, but many have somehow not managed to takeoff or develop "mature" industrial mass-consumption economies. Why? These questions are largely unanswered.

Social Development

Pervasive social change accompanies economic change. As sociologists depicted it, the typical bases of relationships between people began to change in developing societies:

1. The dominant pattern of social relationships begins to shift from those based on binding traditions to ones based on rational interests and exchanges.
2. Relationships based on loyalty to particular persons, such as kin and tribe, are replaced by relationships based on more universally applied standards and principles, such as competency and citizenship.
3. Relationships in traditional societies tend to be *functionally diffuse,* involving broad commitments between persons, but development signals an increase in more segmented relationships where people have limited rights and obligations, such as relationships between employers and employees or practitioners and clients.
4. Development (modernization) produces an increase in the avoidance of intimacy and growth of large-scale, secondary relationships. (Levy, 1966; Parsons, 1964, 1966)

At the level of *structures* (rather than relationships) social development was abstractly described as an increase in scale and specialization and a decrease in the self-sufficiency of "local units" such as families and villages (Levy, 1966). Stated in these abstract terms, we hope you note a strong similarity between how social development was described with both the discussion of modernity in Chapter 2 and functionalist perspectives on change discussed in Chapter 6. This is not accidental. Modernization theory was created at the same time that functionalism was the dominant mode of explanation in American social science.

Political Development

Development involves *nation building,* that is, the knitting together of diverse ethnic, linguistic, and tribal regions into integrated national administrative systems. In many former colonial developing countries, such as Nigeria and Malaysia, the only political common denominator among different peoples was their colonial history. Nation building had to start from scratch. In those developing countries that were long independent, such as Ethiopia and Siam (now Thailand), nation building meant transforming traditional kingdoms into "modern" bureaucratic administrative systems. Nation building is a process in which tribal or village loyalties and authority weaken as they coexist with systems of universal citizenship, national political parties, and a civil service bureaucracy (Smelser, 1966). Such structural changes in the polity involve the creation of new integrative ideologies and principles that combine with traditional culture (e.g., democracy). Political modernization involves an increase in popular participation in government, although whether democracy is required was long a controversial issue among development scholars.

All developing countries try to broaden the base of political mobilization and loyalty, yet it is common knowledge that many have been ruled by a single party or an outright authoritarian regime even when they have the superficial trappings of a parliamentary system. The only hint of democracy in some developing country has been conflict among factions within the dominant party (as has long been the case in Mexico until very recently). Political development requires (1) the creation of states that can integrate and command the loyalties of diverse regions and factions, and (2) a climate of long-term political stability. The consensus among development economists was that a degree of domestic order and political stability is necessary for economic development to take place. "The single most important explanatory variable . . . [regarding economic development] . . . is the political and administrative competence of government" (Reynolds, 1983:976). With the benefit of decades of hindsight we now know that *democracy* is required—that is, regular elections, respect for human fights, pluralism, and personal freedom (Wiarda, 1996:139).

Creative Fusions of Tradition and Modernity: Social Status and Authority

Development transforms the basic social statuses and authority patterns in important ways. In brief, there is a decline in the power of *ascribed statuses,* based on such "given" characteristics as age, sex, and family lineage, and an increase in the importance of *achieved statuses* based on characteristics such as education, skills, and so forth. This has profound implications because the latter are (in theory) open to change within the life span of an individual, while the former are not. Thus the movement from a castelike system of social stratification to a classlike one provides at least the basis for an increase in *social mobility.*

But you should not understand this model simplistically, as the wholesale replacement of a traditional pattern of social status and authority system with a modern one. A study of the attempts by the national government of Ghana to introduce better public health and sanitation practices in two Ghanian towns illustrates this point. In one town the changes were not widely adopted, partly because the persons responsible for promoting them were national civil servants who were perceived as a threat by the existing tribal chiefs and authorities. But in another town the changes were implemented more successfully because the traditional authorities had extensive roles in promoting the new programs, roles that reinforced rather than eroded their traditional bases of authority (Wunsch, 1977). A more familiar example is the role of Gandhi in the creation of modern India. He was the leader of a modern national independence movement and a mass-based national political party, but at the same time he was the epitome of the traditional Hindu ethical leader. The point is that while development involves the emergence of different bases of status and authority, this often works by a creative fusion of the traditional with the modern.

Development and Families

William Goode documented eight marital and family changes occurring on a global basis that are associated with development by the 1980s: (1) marital selection is taken from the hands of elders, (2) ethnic endogamy declines, but not class endogamy, (3) the proportion of the population that is unmarried increases, (4) age-discrepant marriages increase, (5) the dowry or bride price customs weaken, (6) concubinage and polygamy decline, (7) infanticide decreases, and (8) family size ultimately decreases (Goode, 1982:183–187).

There is a danger of seeing changing in family and kinship only as responses to more powerful changes, like industrialization and urbanization. For example, the family systems in China and Japan, while similar in some ways, have had a very different impact on the development process. In China, rules of inheritance specified that land be equally divided among the sons, which led to the fragmentation of land-holding and wealth. The ultimate loyalty was to the family elders, who often resisted modernization. In Japan, by contrast, inheritance rules specified that family wealth and land be passed on to the oldest son. This practice had the effect of preserving large pools of land and capital that were instrumental in the modernization process of Japan. Another significant difference was that in Japan the ultimate family loyalty was not to one's elders, but to the emperor. Thus when state-sponsored modernization began in Japan in the 1800s, the loyalties to the emperor and the existence of large pools of wealth greatly facilitated the process (Goode, 1982:191–192). In many developing countries traditional kinship networks sponsor people to migrate from rural to urban areas, and relatives help new immigrants in finding jobs. Likewise, urban dwellers, who often have higher incomes, send money and help back to relatives in rural areas. The point is that changes in family and kinship systems are not always effects of the development process. They can shape it as well.

But there is a deeper danger than seeing families only as dependent institutions in the developmental change process. It used to be believed by social scientists that modern forms of the family emerged with development quite recently—within the last several hundred years. Development was believed to cause a shift from primarily extended, consanguine families to nuclear, conjugal families like those in the contemporary West. Industrialization, urbanization, and (in some versions) capitalism transformed large self-sufficient rural households into small urban homes. Each man had to go out to find employment in factories or offices. No longer did each person contribute to the family economic resources, and older people were no longer sheltered by loved ones. Each person chose his or her own marriage partner. For better or worse, the modern family was born.

This was a powerful argument with both scholarly and popular appeal. But it had one main flaw. *It is not true.* Careful historical research finds that extended consanguine families were never a predominant pattern in rural America before the Industrial Revolution (or most urbanization), or in Western Europe during the late Middle Ages (Demos, 1970; Collins and Coltrane, 1995:102; Laslett, 1971). Nor were recognizably nuclear family systems absent in many cultures around the world. If by modern families we mean nuclear families with relatively close companionate ties between husbands and wives, this is certainly not a recent development. Why they appeared in Western Europe but not in other places in the world is not clear (Collins and Coltrane, 1995:106). But this is not to say that families and households are not being reinvented in the context of development, or for that matter in contemporary developed countries like the United States (see Chapter 3).

EXPLAINING FAILED DEVELOPMENT

There was a buoyant optimism among developmentalist thinkers in the 1950s. Stimulating development, modernization, and progress around the world seemed deceptively simple. All that was required was (1) enough capital investment from the developed nations, (2) the transfer of Western economic technology, (3) an international climate of free trade and low tariff barriers for the sale of the products of the developing countries, and (4) the widespread diffusion of Western ideas and the "revolution of rising expectations."

But something went badly awry. Instead of gradually diffusing human progress, a widening gap emerged, both within and between nations, among the world's rich and poor. In 1996, the world's 358 billionaires controlled assets greater than the combined incomes of nations where 45 percent of the world's people live. Eighty-nine countries were worse off economically than they were a decade ago. In seventy developing countries incomes are lower than they were in the 1960s. And in 1996, "more than half the people on the planet—at least 3 billion—have incomes of less than $2 a day, and live in a two-class world that is a breeding ground for hopelessness, anger, and frustration" (United Nations, 1996). "An emerging global elite, mostly urban-based and inter-connected in a variety of ways, is amassing great wealth and power, while more than half of humanity is left out" (Speth, 1996:9).

There is a more abstract way of understanding this world trend. In 1960, the richest 20 percent of the world's people absorbed 70 percent of all global income; by 1989, (the latest year for which comparable figures are available) their share of global wealth increased to nearly 83 percent. The poorest 20 percent, meanwhile, saw their share of global income drop from a meager 2.3 percent to a more meager 1.4 percent of global income. The ratio of the richest fifth's share to the poorest's thus grew from 30 to 1 in 1960 to 59 to 1 in 1989 (Harper, 1996:250; Postel, 1994:5). (See Table 12-2.)

What happened? There are explanations from within developmentalist theory:

1. Some argued that the capital investment and technology transfer from the industrial nations was simply not sufficient to stimulate development in the Third World.
2. Some argued that these inputs were sufficient and that many developing countries lacked the skilled labor and administrative resources—or human capital—to utilize them.
3. The most ethnocentric explanation was that the persistence of traditional culture in developing countries, particularly the lack of a cultural ethic valuing hard work and economic growth, sabotaged economic modernization.

TABLE 12–2 GLOBAL INCOME DISTRIBUTION, 1960–1998			
	Share (%) of Global Income Going to the		
Year	Richest 20%	Poorest 20%	Ratio of Richest to Poorest
1960	70.2	2.3	30 to 1
1970	73.9	2.3	32 to 1
1980	76.3	1.7	45 to 1
1989	82.7	1.4	59 to 1
1998	84.0	1.0	84 to 1

Source: U.N. Development Programme (2000).

4. Some argued that modernization was deflected by the existence of antiquated political and landholding structures and by the political dominance of those groups who profit not from improving the lot of the poor masses, but from exploiting them.
5. Others put the matter more simply: Modernization was deflected by rampant official corruption at all levels.
6. Some, particularly Western economists, maintained that modernization failed because governments of the developing countries were too attracted to socialist versus capitalist models of development.
7. Perhaps the most pervasive argument was that development failed because the *population growth* of many developing countries outstripped *economic growth*. This last argument is a complex one, and we will return to it in the next chapter. (See Thompson, 1978, for an elaboration of these arguments.)

Development may not have abjectly failed, but it certainly did not turn out as developmentalist perspectives anticipated. They are not useless but are surely deeply flawed. In the 1960s a powerful critique of developmentalism emerged, more devastating than these explanations of developmental failures. Among economists this critique was called *dependency theory* and among sociologists, *world systems theory.* The critique suggests that developmental change among nations is shaped by their position in emerging global political and economic systems. The critique argues that the fate of the Third World is shaped decisively by conditions external to any given nation.

DEPENDENCY AND WORLD SYSTEMS THEORY

Dependency and world systems theories (WST) are radical and fundamental critiques of developmentalism that have historical roots in Marxist-Leninist notions about neocolonialism and colonial expansion. They reject the most basic assumptions of development and modernization theories—that contact with Western developed countries stimulates successful development among developing countries. In contrast, dependency and WST thinkers believe that *underdevelopment* in the developing countries arose at the same time and by the same processes as did *development* in the richer developed countries. "There was, in other words, a simultaneous and intertwined development of some countries and underdevelopment of others" (Stokes, 1984:492).

Dependency theorists argue that the intrusion of Western capitalism destroys the self-sufficiency of Third World economies, loots them of resources, and blocks the ripening of diversified capitalist development. For example, American economist Paul Baran has argued:

> At the beginning of the eighteenth century, before Britain assumed control, India was a relatively prosperous country with a growing industrial system based largely on textiles. The countryside was organized into village communities that farmed communally and provided for themselves. Britain took conscious steps to destroy Indian industry so that the British could sell their own industrial products in India without competition. Furthermore Britain introduced cash-crop farming on a massive scale to secure raw materials and encouraged the development of large landholdings to facilitate this process. As a result, the village economy was destroyed, leaving millions of landless and destitute peasants at the mercy of landlords for their survival. (cited in Stokes, 1984:492)

Dependency thinkers argue that to blame development failures among many developing countries on the inadequate diffusion of Western values and technology or on the persistence of tradition (as did some developmentalists) misses the critical point of their domination by Western nations.

Among economists, dependency theory was developed by Argentinean economist Raul Prebisch as early as 1949. By the 1960s, the views of Latin American *dependencistas* were widely known among American economists and social scientists. University of Chicago economist Andre Gunder Frank (1969) summarized their argument this way:

1. The "underdeveloped" countries are in fact highly developed adjuncts to the capitalist countries of Europe and North America.
2. The rich countries could not have become that way without exploiting the poor ones, so that underdevelopment is simply the reverse side of development.
3. Development theories focus on factors internal to the poor nations and ignores their embeddedness in a world economy dominated by the rich ones.

Frank and others argue that developmentalist theories function as ideological justifications for continued capitalist domination of the Third World.

Sociopolitical Contexts of Dependency and World Systems Theory. We noted earlier that developmentalist thinking had political and ideological support for its growth after World War II. Likewise, there were sociopolitical circumstances surrounding the meteoric rise in popularity of dependency and WST as alternative perspectives. Its popularity grew in the 1960s, when the moral and political optimism of the postwar period began to erode and America entered a period of pessimism and uncertainty. This entailed the eruption of major racial troubles in the 1960s and the almost simultaneous start of the United States debacle in Vietnam, combined with chronic inflation, the devaluation of the American dollar, and a general loss of American self-confidence. Established assumptions and axioms were turned inside out: America became viewed as the very model of evil, and capitalism, which had been seen as the cause of social progress, became a sinister exploiter and the main agent of poverty in most of the world. Imperialism, not backwardness and lack of modernity, was the new enemy (Galtung, 1981:259–260).

STRUCTURE AND DYNAMICS OF THE WORLD SYSTEM

In sociology, the most comprehensive and systematic formulation of this alternative perspective was that of Immanuel Wallerstein and colleagues, who coined the term *world systems theory* (1974). Wallerstein begins with three assumptions about the evolution of the modern world.

1. Since about the year 1500 most of the world has been in contact with the modernizing nations of Europe, and by 1800 the scope of that contact had increased so that through their colonial empires the Europeans controlled most world trade.
2. Since 1900 the colonial empires broke up, to be replaced with economic control through a system of trade.
3. Thus, in the contemporary world there is a world economic system of trade and investment, that is, a global economic exchange network divided among competing national political entities. This contemporary *world system* is an international system of economic and political stratification, in which nations compete for control.

    Wallerstein thus takes the old Marxian notion of class conflict within society and broadens it to understand international economic and political conflict.

Structure

The world system has three tiers of nations. These turn out to be similar to empirical HDI levels as determined by the United Nations, but they are not identical. There are *core societies*. These are the Western industrial developing countries, which have highly diversified economies. They import raw materials, export both agricultural and manufactured goods, and through the control of prices and investments they control the terms of trade in the world system. At the other end of the spectrum are *peripheral societies*. According to WST, these are not merely underdeveloped societies, but societies that have historically been *differently developed*. They have a narrow economic base with little diversification. They are the commodity producers that are likely to depend upon the export of a few crops or mineral resources. They find it virtually impossible to transform their position in the world system. They are highly dependent on core nations for capital, technology, and markets for their products. Peripheral countries, precisely because they are so poor, are politically as well as economically weak and must generally accept the terms of trade they are confronted with as a set of givens over which they have little or no control (Lofchie and Commins, 1984:4).

Between the core and peripheral extremes of the world system are *semiperipheral* nations. These are intermediate in terms of their wealth, political autonomy, and degree of economic diversification. These are countries like Taiwan, Korea, Malaysia, Brazil, and Mexico, where development has been relatively successful compared to the poorest Third World nations. In relation to the most powerful core nations of Europe, Portugal, Ireland, and Greece could be considered semiperipheral nations. They are still dependent on investment and trade from the wealthy core, and they provide good places for investment when well-organized labor forces in the core nations bid up domestic labor costs.

Dynamics: The Roots of Underdevelopment

Developmentalists viewed "underdevelopment" as existing in nations with original premodern states and traditional social organization and culture. In contrast, WST views this phenomenon as resulting from the long interconnection between core and peripheral societies in an international division of labor. Development and underdevelopment arose simultaneously and were causally related. Historically, colonial administrators directly manipulated the periphery. But even in Third World countries that were politically independent for some time, there is a legacy of control. Thus in many parts of Asia and Latin America, semifeudal agricultural systems (major barriers to development) were consciously created to exploit natural resources more efficiently. The system of large agricultural estates owned by wealthy elites is not the remnant of some traditional period but a relatively modern offspring of the world system that was created to produce cash crops for a capitalist world economy (Griffin, 1969).

In the contemporary world, the dependent status of the developing countries is indirect and economic rather than direct and political. There are at least four sources of ongoing dependency: (1) the nature of world markets for the commodity products of the developing countries, (2) the debt trap, (3) the role of multinational corporations in the world economy, and (4) the inherent weakness of "extraverted" economies. We will address each of these.

The World Market for Tropical Commodity Products. Most developing countries earn money by exporting primary commodity products such as coffee, fruits, tobacco, peanuts, tin, or copper. Many are largely dependent upon a few commodity exports (e.g., coffee and tobacco in Kenya). But in the world market there are many producers for most of these products. For example, coffee is exported by Kenya, Tanzania, Ethiopia, Uganda, Brazil, Colombia, and all of the Central American nations. On the other side of the market, there are only a few significant buyers, increasingly multinational trading corporations (such as General Foods and Nestles). As a result, coffee tends to be a *buyer's market:* The few buyers can shop around, and the many producers compete with each other to bid down prices. In addition, these markets tend to have what economists call an *elastic demand,* which means that the demand for such goods fluctuates so that a decrease in supply does not increase price but simply lowers demand. Furthermore, many of the products of tropical countries (such as bananas) are not necessities, and when the price is high there are many substitutes for overseas buyers. By comparison, the commodity products of temperate-zone countries (e.g., grain, corn, beef) tend to be traded in robust *inelastic demand markets,* where demand remains relatively stable regardless of supply or price. They tend to be *sellers' markets.* Finally, there is a danger that some of the commodity products of developing countries will be replaced with synthetic products (as happened to rubber and hemp).

All this means that *producers* in developing countries have little price leverage in international markets, and the long-term trend is toward falling commodity prices. Since the mid-1970s, there has been a dramatic collapse in the world prices for Ghana's cocoa, Morocco's phosphates, and Chile's copper. Copper was a major component of electrical wiring. Think about the implications of the new "miniaturized circuitry" and fiber optics cable in communication for Chileans. In such narrow commodity-based economies, as the prices for their commodity products fall, so do national and per-capita incomes (Lowenthal, 1986).

To complicate matters, between 1974 and the early 1980s, inflation and interest rates for borrowing money soared, meaning that the "dollar reserves" that developing countries used to pay debts and buy imported goods declined in real value so they could not keep consuming imported manufactures from developed countries at the same rate. Export revenues from developed countries took a nose dive, while the share of world trade for developing countries declined from 28 to 19 percent in the 1980s (McMichael, 1996:126). The social consequences of such economic distress were disastrous. They translated into more refugees, hunger, crime, and less money in national budgets to improve health, education, and human services. The point is that such dependence and vulnerability is *structural.* It is built into the role of peripheral developing countries in the world economy.

The Debt Trap.   In these circumstances, developing countries sought (and were encouraged to seek) foreign loans to provide capital for development, to supplement export earnings, and to cushion the effects of fluctuating commodity prices. Most developing countries are now heavily in debt. Between 1970 and 1978, the average increase in external debt among the ninety poorest countries in the world was 400 percent. And even in the most successful tier of developing nations, debt has skyrocketed. Brazil, for example, had an external debt of $3.5 billion in 1970. By 1990 Brazil's foreign debt exceeded $111 billion. Collectively, the Third World owed at least $1.3 trillion to the core nations by 1990 (World Bank, 1991:24). About 60 percent of these loans came from private banks; developing countries became increasingly dependent on them; and significantly larger proportions of their national earnings go to service previous debts. Levels of indebtedness are so large that many nations are chronically on the verge of default, unable to pay even the interest to service the loans, much less payments on the loan principal. Hence, many countries are mired in a debt trap choking their economies (U.N. Development Programme, 2000).

By the mid-1980s, this debt crisis in the Third World was so general that the lending agencies were petitioned by developing countries to renegotiate the conditions of loans by (1) developing plans to declare temporary moratoriums on payments, (2) reducing interest rates, (3) stretching out payments, and (4) in some cases, entirely forgiving portions of loans. Private banks and international agencies (like the World Bank and International Monetary Fund) complied with what are known as structural adjustment loans (SALs). But there were strings attached. SALs required the petitioning countries to pursue programs of economic austerity that weakened restrictions on imports from the core, controlled wages, cut social development programs, removed price controls, and tightened internal credit systems. Governments of developing countries were obliged to cut food and petroleum subsidies to consumers, reduce wages, and eliminate public projects that provided employment. Governments were advised to apply their cash savings to debt payments. In 1982, Mexico and Brazil became the first countries to reschedule debts in this way, signaling the start of an international debt regime. International fiscal management of the world economy by the core really swung into high gear. And Mexico began debt swapping, in which foreign investors would buy Mexican debt in exchange for Mexican assets, increasing the penetration and control of periphery economies by the core (McMichael, 1996:128; Stokes, 1984:496).

The growing recognition of the debt problems faced by developing countries led to a push by some international and religious organizations (most notably the Catholic Church) to forgive the outstanding debts of developing countries during the year 2000. While this didn't happen, significant segments of the international development community that would have dismissed such proposals twenty years ago are now seriously entertaining them. Right now debt forgiveness is still on the table and is still (as of 2001) a major topic of discussion at international gatherings of all sorts.

Multinational Corporations.   Multinational corporations (MNCs) are often the agents of increasing economic penetration and control. Though MNCs operate on a global scale, they are typically headquartered in the core nations, with manufacturing plants, sales divisions, and raw material production facilities in the developing countries. You will recognize some of their names, which are household words: DuPont, Ford, Exxon, ITT, Procter and Gamble, Unilever, Volkswagen, Shell, and so forth (Stokes, 1984:496). Developmentalist economists often envisioned MNCs as the "engines of development." But in fact they often drain scarce capital from developing countries and wrench control of the economy from indigenous owners. In Latin America, for instance,

> for every dollar of net profit earned by a global corporation fifty-two cents left the country, even though 78 percent of the investment funds used to generate that dollar of profit came from local sources. [In mining, petroleum, and smelting] . . . the capital outflow resulting from the operations of global corporations

is even worse. Each dollar of profit is based on an investment that was 83 percent financed from local savings; yet only 21 percent of the profit remains in the local economy. (Barnet and Muller, 1974:153–154)

MNCs are not developmental agencies; they place their own profit and growth ahead of the needs of their host countries (Stokes, 1984:497). Economic resources are primarily allocated in ways profitable to the MNC and only secondarily in terms of the development needs of the host country.

Consider how the penetration of agribusiness firms misallocates national resources. While many developing countries have chronic food shortages, farmland is being converted to production of products other than food for more lucrative export markets. In Colombia, for instance, a hectare of land growing carnations sells for about a million pesos per year, while a hectare of land planted in wheat or corn brings only 12,500 pesos. MNCs, understandably, encourage the growing of carnations rather than wheat or corn. And most of the profits will be sent to the United States or Western Europe. That which remains in Colombia will be used to buy more land to grow more carnations. Such is the result of using MNC profit rather than domestic needs (calories and protein), to determine what will be grown (Barnet and Muller, 1974, cited in Stokes, 1984:498).

Extraverted Economies. In general terms, the weakness of the peripheral nations is that they have *extraverted economies,* that is,

- They function as appendages of the world economy.
- They lack internal integration. (Amin, 1976)

They function as appendages of the world economy because increasingly basic economic and social decisions are not made by nationals of a given developing country but by the corporate board of MNCs in Europe or North America, or by executives of the International Monetary Fund or the World Bank. And the economies lack integration because the enterprises in developing countries often have closer ties with economic firms and banks in the core nations than they have with economic entities in their own countries. A vivid example of the lack of integration can be found in the transportation systems in many developing countries. Railways and roads are likely to run "from the interior to the nearest seaport, rather than knitting the country together as is the case in developed countries. It is thus often easier to ship goods from the interior of many African countries, for example, to Europe than to elsewhere in the same country" (Stokes, 1984:494). This is a physical reflection of what Amin means by extroversion. The central weakness of extraverted economies is that they lack the capacity to generate autonomous economic growth. Thus they do not develop the economic dynamic for self-sustaining economic development, which development theorists describe as the takeoff.

In sum, the nature of tropical commodity markets, the debt trap, the intrusions of MNCs, and extroverted economies are the roots of stalled development and dependency among the peripheral nations and many semiperipheral nations of the world system. Even in those developing countries that seem to successfully develop, the human dimensions are often lacking. Consider the case of Brazil that we noted earlier, with its savage inequalities and deteriorating living standards for much of the population. As Brazilian president Emilio Medici put it in the 1970s, "Brazil is doing well, but its people are not" (cited in Barnet and Muller, 1974).

WST and Development

Dependency theory and WST are mainly explanations of developmental failures, but theorists did have suggestions about how successful development could take place. The earliest suggestion was that developing countries should strive for autonomy and self-reliance within the world market system. They urged policies of import substitution, for developing countries to substitute local manufactured goods for imports as a means of freeing them from dependent status as mere suppliers of raw materials. They argued that developing countries must engage in a process of import substitution and *delinking,* that is, withdrawing as much as is possible from the world market economy, which perpetuates dependence. That, it was argued, would stimulate diversified internal development, relying mainly on internal resources and producing primarily for domestic consumption.

Delinking implied working toward a more introverted economy with its implied protectionism and trade barriers, which contrasts dramatically with policies suggested by developmentalist thinking and also with the requirements of strategic adjustment loans for debt management by Western banks and international agencies. Some advocated nothing short of the breakup of the world capitalist market system, but of course it was the socialist system that collapsed in the 1980s and continues in highly compromised forms only in a few backwater outposts like North Korea and Cuba. Even the People's Republic of China, which has made the most disciplined and consistent effort at autonomous development, has, since the 1970s, sought to avoid continuing backwardness by establishing extensive trading connections with the world market system.

Most WST scholars argue that taking steps to create a juster world economy is the key to promoting genuine development in developing countries. One influential commission, called the Brandt Commission because it was convened by West German leader Willy Brandt, proposed the establishment of a "new international economic order." It recommended that the developed nations sponsor a large-scale transfer of resources to developing countries, the elimination of "foreign aid" that comes in the form of credits to do business with industrial nation firms, IMF reforms that respect the domestic and political objectives of developing nations, price supports for the commodity products of the Third World nations, and greater access to markets in the industrial nations. But since it is unlikely that the industrial nations or their multinational firms and banks would voluntarily give up their advantageous position in the world system by such a broad renegotiation of the terms of international trade, these reforms are not politically feasible.

WST and Developmentalist Perspectives

The two perspectives on development we have sketched here are dramatically different. We think each has pieces of development puzzles and are both right and wrong in different ways. Developmentalist perspectives assume that the development process in developing countries will take place roughly as it did in the original modernization of developed countries. They assume that close contact with the Western nations will produce self-sustaining economic growth, a reduction in material inequality, and an increase in social and individual welfare in the developing nations. WST was better at explaining why development often failed. Its central tenet (dogma?) is that close contact with the West has produced underdevelopment and dependency, growing inequality, and a decrease in social welfare.

Development perspectives had elaborate—if flawed—understandings of the *internal* social, political, and cultural changes that accompany development. These analyses are notably lacking in WST. The conflict between the two perspectives is not only about the consequences of contact between the core and the periphery but, more abstractly, about how much weight to give internal national factors (e.g., resources, population growth, political factors, literacy) and how much weight to give external ones (the nature and state of the world market system). Both models are loaded with different kinds of ideological baggage.

There are many excellent empirical cross-national research studies that compare these perspectives and they exhibit mixed findings, depending on how research hypotheses and measures are designed. For research supportive of WST, see Bradshaw and others (1993). For research critical of WST, see Firebaugh and Beck (1994), and for research supporting mixed and weak confirmation of WST ideas, see Van Rossem (1996). Evidence suggests that the most successful development has occurred among East Asian "newly industrialized nations" like Korea and Taiwan, and it has utilized production for export rather than production to substitute imports, contrary to WST and dependency perspectives. But evidence also strongly suggests that development occurs under conditions of relative income equality, unlike Mexico and Brazil, and contrary to much developmentalist thinking (Handelman, 1996:234–239).

GLOBALIZATION

By the 1980s, a *postdevelopment era,* entailing a different understanding of global change, had begun, stimulated by growing integration of nations around the world in the world market, the failure of many nations to manage development and the increasing global management of development by big international banks, multinational agencies like the World Bank, the International Monetary Fund, and the United Nations. This postdevelopmentalism involved the growing weakening of state authority and the growing influence of large world and macroregional groupings in which nations agree about common rules regarding trade, investment, and political stability and conditions. The development of the World Trade Organization, the

North American Free Trade Association, the coalition of nations that fought in the Gulf War or peacekeeping forces in Haiti and the Balkans, international election monitoring committees, and the emergence of global environmental accords all illustrate this trend. As a sociologist succinctly observed, "in circumstances of accelerating global integration, the nation-state has become too small for the big problems and too big for the small problems of life" (Giddens: 1990:65).

The heart of such *globalization,* however, was global economic managerialism that aimed to stabilize the world market system. It was not new; it has roots going back to the post–World War II economic and security treaties. But the new global managers included transnational political, banking, and corporate elites that have a shared interest in an expanding and stable global economy. What is evolving has been described as a "transnational political elite" (a ruling class?). In the 1990s, development was coming to mean *participation in the world market.*

Manuel Castells (1998) points to several developments that are reflective of postdevelopment globalization. The increasing economic polarization between those nations and regions that are integrated into the new information economy and those that are not has led to the rise of the *Fourth World,* places and peoples that are completely left behind in the economics of the twenty-first century and from whom the information economy asks nothing. Unlike the periphery nations of the world system that are exploited for their natural resources and trade with core nations on unfavorable terms, the Fourth World is completely ignored, culturally and economically excluded from the information economy. The major areas where this marginalization is occurring is in parts of sub-Saharan Africa and in inner cities in the United States. The global information economy also has produced a *global criminal economy* (especially severe in Russia and Latin America) the size and global reach of which rivals Fortune 500 corporations and the gross national product of all but the most prosporous nations.

Globalization and global management replaces older ideas and agendas about development that was organized separately by nations, *but the notion of development has not lost its currency.* Its frame of reference has shifted, particularly by emerging nongovernmental organizations (NGOs) that fill the vacuum as governments increasingly cannot assist groups and causes smaller than nations (such as women's groups, ethnic organizations, workers, and environmentalists). You can understand these groups as what the last several chapters called social movements. Thousands of regional and local development projects continue, designed to improve conditions or stabilize states. And at global levels, development focuses on improving and stabilizing the global market economy. At both micro and macro levels, the idea of *sustainable development* has gained currency. It is used both by grassroots movements and global managers (such as those of the World Bank) (McMichael, 1996: 147–150).

The Social Consequences of Globalization

The *dark side* of globalization has three long-term social manifestations, which we will briefly note:

- A growing global labor surplus that generates global migrations
- The intensification of informal economic activity
- The growing crisis of declining government legitimacy at national levels

Global Labor Surplus.   Labor is becoming redundant on a worldwide basis. In earlier chapters we discussed the causes and consequences of corporate downsizing in the U.S. economy, but you need to understand that the same process occurs in other MDCs. In France, for instance, the GNP grew by 80 percent between 1973 and 1993, but unemployment grew from roughly one-half million to 5.1 million (Goldsmith, 1994:18). But the trend is not limited to developed countries. Among developing countries, the process of *depeasantization* has been going on for a long time, but it accelerated in the 1980s as more and more subsistence farmland and forests were absorbed into the cash market economy. As displaced peasants lose markets to cheap imported foods (such as subsidized U.S. or French grain) and surrender their land to large scale agro-export operations, they flood the towns and cities looking for work. Such displaced rural migrants become attractive labor forces for foreign investment when national barriers to trade and investment fall (as may be required by structural adjustment loans, discussed earlier). Responding to the NAFTA accord, the Ford motor company moved assembly plants from Michigan to Chihuahua, Mexico, and replaced workers earning more than $17 per hour with those earning between $1.55 and $2.87 per hour. In the process Ford replaced a fully automated plant in Michigan with a semiautomated one in Chihuahua, requiring 700 Mexican workers to do what 400 Michigan workers used to do (Harper, 1994). The result of such free trade policies in a globally managed economy is sometimes called *harmonization,* or, more cynically, a "race to the bottom." Given the competitive pull of low-cost labor areas, harmonization has the effect of leveling existing wages, safety standards, and social safety nets (McMichael, 1996: 179–182).

Informalization.   Globalization is accompanied by the rapid growth of informal or marginal economic activity. More people work "off the books" on the fringes of markets, performing casual and unregulated labor, working in cooperative arrangements, street vending, or illegal occupations (such as prostitution or drug dealing). In the United States, for instance, an army of servants, child care workers, and housecleaners receive income that is neither reported nor taxed. In Latin America, where official employment rose about 3.2 percent annually during the 1980s, informal jobs rose at more than twice that rate. By the 1990s, about a third of urban jobs in Asia and Latin America, and more than half in Africa, are estimated as informal. Among the urban poor in Mexico, collective pooling of resources to acquire land, shelter, and basic public services like water and electricity led to the establishment of networks among friends and neighbors some describe as a new *culture of the commons.* Putting the best face on informalization, it often results in creative survival strategies and the formation of new cooperatives or *micro enterprises* among the poorest of the poor (McMichael, 1996:195).

Legitimacy Crisis.   A consequence of globalization is an erosion of governmental legitimacy. We discussed this effect in the United States in earlier chapters.

Given increasing global integration and management, the erosion of the capacities of nations expresses itself in a decline in truly representative politics. No one votes for a global management system. Yet as states and governments undertake housekeeping functions for the world market economy, they shed their own representative role and citizens lose faith. Citizens lose faith in national governments, and national policies often exacerbate social divisions and tensions between classes, ethnic groups, and regions.

The erosion of legitimacy takes many forms:

- Foreign ownership of important national resources (banking and energy systems)
- The unraveling of political coalitions important to national development projects
- The dismantling of social services to needy people
- The growth of a global criminal economy, with resources that rival many states

All of these factors mean that the government's legitimacy becomes more fragile (McMichael, 1996:197; Castells, 1998). Ironically, declining legitimacy is related to the wave of democratization that increased around the world in the 1980s. Developmentalist thinking was often uncomfortable in linking democracy with development, observing that throughout the Third World, many governments were authoritarian-bureaucratic and militaristic. Not only were Brazil and Chile in military hands, even model developing countries such as Singapore and South Korea were governed by authoritarian and militaristic regimes. But as globalization took place, declining state legitimacy and state capacity *also encouraged movements for democracy.*

Social Responses to Globalization

The consequences of globalization have elicited social responses among diverse nations around the world. Here we note five of them; democratization, fundamentalism, environmentalism, feminism, and cosmopolitan localism.

1. *Democracy* was spreading around the world by the 1990s, even in nations long governed by authoritarian regimes. Ironically, economic difficulties, growing inequality, and the shrinking of the state can offer opportunities for contenders for power, political activism, and the crumbling of traditional patronage systems. Political democracy grew in Africa and Latin America, long characterized by authoritarian (often military) regimes. Chapter 9 examined the collapse of the Soviet Union and the growth of hardship but also more democratic national governments. Another example is in Mexico, where regional revolutionary movements, growing demands for democracy, and the increasing difficulties of an authoritarian regime led to the first electoral defeat for the Permanent Revolutionary Party. Growing new democracies are often fragile, corrupt, and chaotic; they lack the protection and legitimacy provided by a deeply institutionalized legal culture and tradition. Elections are often observed by international election monitoring groups. But relative to the authoritarian past, they are democracies anyway (Diamond and Plattner, 1993; Markoff, 1996).

2. *Fundamentalism* expresses a desire to return to a simpler life and more traditional culture and behavior. Fundamentalist movements can take religious as well as nationalistic and secular forms (such as the call to restore traditional religion, government, culture and family life). The growth and political engagement of conservative religion is visible in the United States. Islamic fundamentalism has become a pervasive force in the Middle East. It may accept modern technology but opposes the inroads of Western culture into Islamic nations. It seeks to establish law, government, and family life based on the teachings of Islam. Fundamentalism articulates the uncertainties and distress brought about by the failure of development and growing globalism. It advocates alternative ways of organizing life on national, regional, and local levels (McMichael, 1996: 211–215; Giddens, 1994).

3. *Environmentalism* is a diverse global basket of social movements and non-governmental organizations that observe and protest the consequences of human activity that poisons or destroys the natural world, and they question whether nature and its bounties are infinite. They do this particularly in view of ever-growing human population and consumption levels. In the United States modern environmentalism began with the publication of *Silent Spring* by Rachel Carson in 1962, documenting the toxic effect of pesticides and agricultural chemicals on wildlife. But environmentalism has become truly global: Environmental "Green" movements and organizations have proliferated around the world in virtually every nation to promote sustainable development policies in different ways. One researcher counted 6000 of them in 1993, and the worldwide United Nations Environmental Programme was headquartered in Kenya (Harper, 1997:289–330). In developed countries, such movements and organizations attempt to control how the free market economy works to minimize environmental impacts. Among developing countries, environmental movements are more likely to question the benefits of unregulated market forces (Harper, 1997:289–330; McMichael, 1996:216).

4. *Feminism* has likewise emerged in the form of NGOs and movements around the world. Earlier feminist movements were primarily concerned with the integration of women into human societies and improvement in the status of women. But many more recently realized that the establishment of individual property rights in developed countries and development policy in the developing nations typically privileged men and disadvantaged women. In Mexico in 1975 and China in 1996, the United Nations sponsored global conferences about women's concerns that moved from "integrationist" approaches that address problems of equity for women to new approaches recognizing the important role of women in food and population problems, environmental protection, and sustainable development. No longer is patriarchy simply a women's problem. We will return to this issue in the next chapter (see Handelman, 1996:78–103; Sachs, 1996:94).

5. *Cosmopolitan localism* means that as globalism intensifies, multiculturalism and local differences proliferate and intensify. Ironically, the more integrated, connected world of nations and peoples is increasingly envisioned not as a homogenous world where differences and contrasts are leveled out, but as a discontinuous world where differences and uniqueness flourish in a multitude of places (McMichael, 1996:234). It is a world of huge multinational corporations, multilateral banks and political structures (like NATO and the UN), but also a world of small entrepreneurs and

local groups working for improved lives, recognition and liberty. Although often cultural, civic, and political as well as economic, cosmopolitan localism is analogous to the new U.S. dual economy (of elephants and ants) we described earlier. Such local groups and movements carry hopes of human progress, but also dangers, because they are often based on deadly hostility toward others—new "tribalisms," if you will. Consider the deadly civil strife in Bosnia Herzegovina, Azerbiajan, Somalia, Rwanda, Liberia, Mexico, Haiti, India, and other places.

IN CONCLUSION: DEVELOPMENT, GLOBALIZATION, AND HUMAN PROGRESS

We began this chapter by discussing *development* as scholarly perspectives and realities (*partly failed ones*) We then moved to a new perspective and reality, *globalization,* and explored its dimensions and social consequences. Let's conclude by turning briefly to the supremely important human and value-laden side of development and globalization: improving the quality of human life. In a word, *progress.* Put another way, what works in development and integrating global systems *to produce a better life for people?*

After thirty years of experience and research about development and globalization, a rough consensus exists about important elements for human progress. These are easy to list abstractly, but hard to produce everywhere. They include:

- Free and open economic markets, but lower income inequality
- Democracy and guarantees of human rights for all persons
- Effective legal systems, and internal stability and security
- Widespread literacy and good public education at all levels
- Effective social programs and safety nets for human hardship
- Attention to family planning and environmental problems
- Effective but *limited* government planning systems

With these features human progress is likely. Without them, it is unlikely (Wiarda, 1993:140).

In 1996, the United Nations Development Programme urged policy makers everywhere to promote human progress by linking economic growth with human concerns by working toward

1. *Greater income equality and economic opportunities,* making it more likely that economic growth will be translated into improved human well-being.
2. *Job opportunities and patterns of employment* that are well paid and labor intensive.
3. *Broad access to productive assets* such as land, banking, and financial credit. By doing this states can do much to level the playing field.
4. Use of *significant public revenues for social spending* providing basic social services for all (such as education, health, and hardship relief).

5. *Gender equity* that provides better access to education, child care, and social opportunities for women. (Allowing women to exercise choices has been demonstrated to be a certain way to promote economic growth with human improvement.)

6. A *population policy* that lowers fertility and promotes the survival and well-being of mothers and children.

7. *Good governance* that addresses the needs of the whole population and encourages participation in decision making at many levels. (Where that is the case, the connection between development/globalization and human well-being is likely to be strong and durable.)

8. An *active civil society* of nongovernmental organizations, movements, and civic groups that play a vital role in mobilizing public opinion and community action; and extending government services to those unserved (U.N. Development Programme, 1996:6–7).

Progress toward these goals is very difficult in poor developing countries as well as in wealthy developed countries like the United States. In a postindustrial world some trends move in the opposite directions.

There is a great divide in thinking about how to connect globalization with human progress and greater well-being. *Globalists* believe improvement will come through free trade, investment, and an open world economy, so long as there is a reasonably equal playing field between people and nations. They are the cheering squad for the emerging world economy. But we're sure you recognize that the playing field is now very unequal and getting more so, making this claim at best a fiction, or at worst justification for the small number of powerful people and organizations to dominate the world. By contrast, *localists* assume that human empowerment and improvement will come from the grassroots, as people participate and mobilize in multitudes of local groups, movements, and nongovernmental organizations that force elites to respond to their concerns. The obvious problem is that they envision a struggle between a multitude of groups of ants and the relatively few large elephants.

A *global civil society* needs to emerge that joins local groups into regional ones, and regional ones into national and international networks of concerned people, organizations, movements, and nongovernmental organizations. The growing vulnerability of workers in the world economic order requires the development of international networks of workers' organizations (unions) that can prevent corporate ability to abuse workers in one nation to the benefit of those in another. International networks of employees, feminists, indigenous peoples, environmentalists, scientists, and human rights advocates are now visible and have played a noisy, visible, and contentious but increasingly effective unofficial role at official world conferences, such as recent United Nations conferences about population, environment, development, cities, and women's issues. They are beginning to affect the policies of governments and entities such as the World Bank. This is a basis for hope, but though ideas about democracy, human rights, and sustainable development have wide currency, such a world civil society capable of providing real counterbalance to the economic and "techno-industrial" forces producing greater global integration is quite immature and embryonic (McMichael, 1996:255–257).

To conclude, we think that neither the world nor your life can work very well if you ignore either the people in your community or those around the world. Pursuing a lifeboat strategy of isolation in neighborhoods or nations where some prosper and others sink into misery is simply not workable in an interconnected world. As the English poet John Donne wrote upon hearing a church bell next to a cemetery, more than three centuries ago, "No man is an island. . . . Never send to know for whom the bell tolls. It tolls for thee."

THINKING PERSONALLY ABOUT SOCIAL CHANGE

1. Think about how you are personally connected with a variety of other people in developed nations and developing nations. Write an essay or organize a discussion among several people about this connection. Start with some obvious hints from the text. (Look carefully at the labels of the things that you buy or own. Did you fill a car with gas or drink a cola recently?) Then move to less obvious connections. (Do you, or does anyone you know, make or grow things that sell around the world? Do you know anyone who was a part of a military peacekeeping force anywhere recently? Did you ever make a charitable contribution that was to help people in other countries respond to hardship or disaster?)

2. Listen to people talk about those in other countries. How do they understand development, and why it seems so difficult? What do you think this says about their views of themselves and people around the world?

3. How do people understand and react to globalization? Do they find it fascinating? Puzzling or frightening? Do they feel enriched or threatened? Do they have a sense of new possibilities or that "something important is being lost," or a complex mixture of both? What are some reactions to globalization that are visible in your area or community?

4. Has growing globalization affected the student body, courses and curriculum, and the things that people argue about where you go to school? How so, or why not? If you can, find foreign students from both other developed countries and developing countries willing to talk with you about globalization and its problems for very different perspectives.

13

Society, Environment, and Change

The last chapter focused on global change and the emerging global system in terms of development in the Third World and the interconnections between nations in the world economic system. This chapter explores global change in a different way by examining the growing connections among population growth, energy, food resources and ecological consequences—in other words, on the changing relationship between human social activity and the resource base of the planet. But before doing this, we want to describe more explicitly an ecological perspective as it relates to understanding global change. This chapter explores some important environmental and resource dimensions of global change as they relate to the changing quality of human life now and in the future. The next chapter examines various speculations about the future of the world.

ECOLOGICAL PERSPECTIVES ON CHANGE AND PROBLEMS

In the last chapter we discussed growing global economic and political ties among the peoples and nations of the world. Underlying the growing global interconnectedness of human life is another obvious but often overlooked level of interdependency: that between humans and the natural environment. An *ecological perspective* focuses on the relationship between human social activity and the environmental capacity of the planet to support life. Humans share the life support system of nature with other species. Even though they are often understood separately, all human economic, technical, political, and cultural activities are in fact ultimately rooted in and dependent upon the resources of the biophysical environment of the planet. The relationships between living things and the planet form complex and delicately balanced webs of energy transformations and food chains that are called ecosystems by biologists. More formally, an *ecosystem* is an interdependent biotic community that depends in turn on the resources of the physical environment.

Put differently, the survival of all living things depends upon the *carrying capacity* of the earth to support life. The interaction between the resources on the earth's crust and living things is a vast recycling system, where living things make withdrawals from the natural environment as they use air, water, soil, and minerals, and return wastes to that environment, most of which are reabsorbed and recycled. In addition, you must recognize that all living things have the capacity to alter the carrying capacity of the physical environment. When their natural predators are eradicated, for instance, herbivore populations (e.g., deer) may multiply to the extent that they strip the environment of vegetation. And human societies have been known to overuse the environment (e.g., soil fertility and water resources) in such a way that the basis for economic production is altered. When that happens, the short-run consequences are disastrous. Deer begin to starve, as may humans, although human populations generally have migrated out of an ecologically devastated region before starving. As the demands of living things diminish because they starve or migrate, many aspects of the natural environment may gradually rebuild (vegetation, soil fertility).

But it is significant that many of the natural resources relevant to the maintenance of industrial societies are not recyclable in the same way that fresh water, vegetation, and soil minerals are. Using petroleum and natural gas for energy destroys them for good. Technological change can enable humans to find and use resources more efficiently. But they are finite. When they are gone, they are gone for good, Actually, it is unlikely that we will use up the last drop of any nonrenewable resource; but it is possible to use up the easily accessible and high-quality supplies, so that finding, transporting, and refining the remaining supplies is so expensive that its use is inherently uneconomical.

You might be wondering why we are reviewing these elementary concepts about ecology, because they are discussed (in considerably more depth!) in high school biology texts. The reason is that we often behave as if they were not true. Or, perhaps more accurately, we only see half of the picture. We are aware of how we use and exploit the environment for our consumption but seem unaware of the consequences of our enormously amplified capacity to modify that environment and of our ultimate dependence upon it. This lack of awareness has characterized the outlooks of most sociologists and other social scientists as well as ordinary people. Most social science literature gives minimal recognition to the ecological rootedness of human economic, cultural, and social systems and implicitly assumes that human technological inventiveness has enabled *Homo sapiens* to somehow transcend the limitations of nature.[1]

The fact that ecological myopia is so widespread is understandable. Historically, human populations were much smaller and less dense; human technological capacity to exploit the environment was more rudimentary; and human consumption (withdrawals) rarely reached the threshold of permanent damage to the environment. Throughout most of human history the ability of *Homo sapiens* to modify the biophysical environment was quite limited. The earth was an open system with seemingly limitless space and resources that could be freely used. Things are much different in the modern world. Human populations are much larger and denser (the world population doubled between 1950 and 1985); much of the world possesses high technology with a capacity to significantly alter the natural environment on a unprecedented scale; and most people today desire a level of material consumption that is historically unprecedented. Under these circumstances, an ecological perspective should become a much more important outlook for understanding human affairs, change, and problems. It is increasingly important that we view the earth as a closed system.

From this perspective, a number of disturbing questions flow. Do industrial societies have the ability to overwhelm the absorptive capacity of the earth to recycle pollutants and wastes? If development should succeed on a global basis, as people everywhere fervently desire, would the earth be able to produce the required amounts of food, energy, and creature comforts on a sustainable basis? Again, would such high consumption levels produce intolerable levels of pollution? Does the extensive reshaping of the natural world in modern times disrupt the food chains and energy transformations among species in ways that are subtle but critical for maintaining the equilibrium of the ecosystem? Is the scale of human material consumption now such that renewable resources (such as fertile soil and fresh water) cannot be regenerated rapidly enough? Also frightening is the possibility—raised since the 1970s—that the human consumption of many nonrenewable resources may be approaching absolute finite limits in the future. Is the potential of human ingenuity and technical inventiveness sufficient to transcend these finite limits (if there are any)? Are such technological fixes extravagantly expensive when their real ecological costs are accounted for? Are they so inordinately complex that they have built-in tendencies to break down?

The political implications of these problems are also ominous, if uncertain. A little-noted ecological dimension of the political instability and civil wars in El Salvador, Nicaragua, Somalia, Rwanda, and even in developing Brazil is the rapid doubling of the population combined with the overexploitation of the biotic environment. Goldstone (1986) documented a general relationship between revolution and rapid population growth. How do these demographic and environmental circumstances affect the prospect for the evolution of a peaceful, cooperative, and orderly world political order—as opposed to one racked by revolution, civil wars, or more general conflagrations?

These are indeed scary questions. But our intent is not to scare you because there is not sufficient evidence to say that any of these things are certainly going to happen. But there is enough evidence that they are at least possibilities. We raise them here not as predictions, but rather as important reasons for understanding global change and problems in an ecological perspective. This chapter explores (1) *related aspects of social change and environmental problems,* including population growth, urbanization, and world hunger; (2) *the human impact and global environmental change,* including energy, agricultural resources, and biodiversity. Its conclusion briefly discusses prospects for social and environmental stability and some differences between economic and ecological worldviews for understanding these problems.

ASPECTS OF ECOLOGICAL CHANGE
AND PROBLEMS

Population Growth

We are used to thinking of growth in linear terms. But world population has grown *exponentially*. This means that human population grew very slowly for centuries, but is now growing very rapidly. As long ago as the year 1 C.E., there were only about 250 million people on the entire planet. By the 1600s, that had doubled to about a half-billion. The second doubling occurred about 1850, and then again by about 1930. By 1970, the world's population had reached about 4 billion (Pirages, 1984:59). In 1994, it was 5.6 billion and was growing at a rate of about 1.8 percent annually. Using what they deemed the most likely fertility and mortality trends, the United Nations predicted that by 2025 world population would be somewhere between 7.6 billion and 9.4 billion (the middle projection was 8.5 billion) (United Nations, 1991; U.S. Population Reference Bureau, 1996). (See Figure 13–1.)

While these numbers are staggering, the consequences are even more so, for such growth increases the population pressure on food and economic resources of all sorts. A larger population eats more, consumes more, and pollutes more. According to a distinguished demographer, "In 1950 the world contained 2.5 billion people, and there was little evidence of damage to the biosphere. . . . [in the 1990s] . . . with over 5 billion there is a great deal of evidence. With another 2.5 billion and continuance of present trends of production and consumption, disaster faces us. The planet cannot over a long period support that many people" (Keyfitz, 1991:77).

Not all observers are as pessimistic, however, and many think that the world can indeed support a much larger population. How large is a matter of conjecture. Furthermore, there is some evidence that while population is growing, the rate of world population growth is declining. The crude birth rate has dropped from 37 per thousand in 1950 to 25 per thousand in 1990 and is expected to be about 18 per thousand in 2020 (United Nations, 1991). *There is a hazard here for interpretation*: Whoever wants to argue that the population growth problem is declining and self-correcting points to the diminishing percentage increase; whoever wants to argue the continued existence of danger points to the growing billions of people.

The Demographic Transition Model. The current gradual diminishing of the rate of world population growth can be understood in terms of what demographers have called the *demographic transition model,* which is a relatively simple conceptual model of population change (see Figure 13–2). It has three stages.

"Primitive" social organization (Stage I) where mortality [is] . . . relatively high . . . and fertility is correspondingly high; "transitional" social organization (Stage II) where mortality is declining, fertility remains high, and the population exhibits high rates of natural increase; and a "modern" stage (Stage III) . . . where mortality has stabilized at a relatively low mean value, fertility is

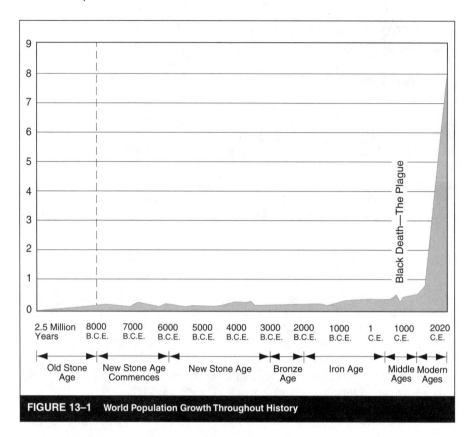

FIGURE 13–1 **World Population Growth Throughout History**

approaching the level of mortality, and a stationary population size is possible in the near future. (Humphrey and Buttel, 1982)

What caused this demographic transition to occur in the industrial world? *First,* industrialization upgraded both manufacturing and agricultural productivity so that the economic base could support much larger populations. *Second,* medical advances in the control of epidemic disease and improvements in public services (urban sewage and water systems, garbage collection, etc.) contributed to improved health and reduced mortality rates. *Third,* as populations became increasingly urbanized, family changes occurred. Children—their education and rearing—became more of an economic burden than an asset. Industrialization was coupled with opportunities for women to work outside the family and the establishment of national social security programs apart from kinship. Industrialization, therefore, produced a variety of incentives for smaller families. In other words, as economic incentives changed, cultural norms promoting large families began to weaken.

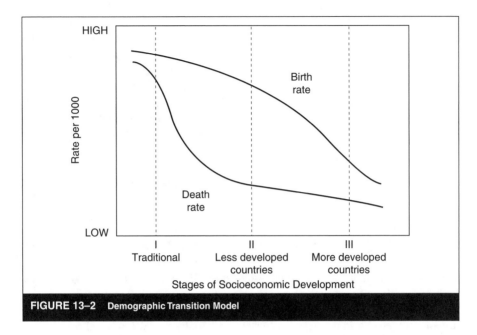

FIGURE 13–2   Demographic Transition Model

Finally, research shows that while industrialization is inversely related to fertility, another important consequence was the level of economic equality: "In the European nations the demographic and economic transitions led to a general improvement in living standards for all persons and a gradual reduction in income inequalities" (Birdsall, 1980). However it came about, birth rates in all industrialized countries began to decline as economic development proceeded. We should emphasize that though the rate of population growth of the industrial nations is declining, their consumption levels are high, and even their lower rates of growth add significantly to the absolute increases in world population.

The Uneven Distribution of Population Change.   So far, most of the reduction in the population growth rate has been accounted for by the declining birth rates in the industrial nations and parts of East Asia. For many developing countries it is still a very different story. Nine of ten babies born today live in the poorer regions of the globe. The reason that Third World populations are growing very rapidly compared to the First World nations is that since World War II there was very rapid introduction of enough improvements in nutrition and health care to dramatically reduce the death rate. Babies born in the poor nations today have a historically unprecedented chance of surviving to adulthood, and the average life spans of the developed and developing nations have converged.

But economic development—with its widespread improvement in living standards, changed economic incentives, and establishment of social security systems not tied to kinship—has not kept pace with the rapid decline in mortality rates. As we noted in the last chapter, many developing countries are still mired in stalled, dependent, or deformed development. Traditional cultural norms favoring large families still exist in much of the Third World. There may well be more Brazilians or Indians who are now vaguely middle class. But at the same time there are larger numbers of Brazilians and Indians than ever before in history who are landless peasants living in unprecedented squalor, chronic hunger, joblessness, and despair. In the terms of the demographic transition model, many Third World nations seem stuck in Stage II, with rapid decreases in mortality but no reductions in fertility in sight.

Urbanization in the Third World

In the Third World there are large masses of displaced farmers pushed off the land by the consolidation of small subsistence farms into large cash-crop estates. But they are also demographic refugees, pushed off the land by the less visible but powerful population pressure of high birth rates in rural areas. Some have migrated to other countries where economic conditions are better: There is a small but growing stream of international migration from the developing countries to the industrial nations. But more significant is the pattern of internal migration from the countryside to the cities of the Third World.

Migration from the country to the city is an ancient pattern, but the *urbanization* of the First World nations was caused not only by the push of rural poverty but also by the pull of exploding economic opportunities in the industrializing cities. Urbanization in the Third World is today largely a matter of the push of rural poverty without the simultaneous pull of dynamic economic growth in the cities. That is to say that the rapid growth of cities in the Third World today represents change from an agrarian society to a service society, without the intermediate stage of industrial urbanization with its vastly expanded urban economy. Thus the cities of the Third World, such as Calcutta, Cairo, Dakar, Jakarta, and Rio de Janeiro, are awash with displaced peasants with grim prospects for fruitful urban employment. Migration to the cities is fueled not only by poverty and population pressure from the countryside, but also by political policy that gives preferential treatment to city dwellers. That is where national governments concentrate schools, receive investments from multinational firms, and are concerned with regulating the price and supply of foodstuffs. By subsidizing the price of food (a policy practiced by most Third World nations), life is made easier for urbanites while farm incomes are depressed. So political policy also accelerates the migration to cities. As they accumulate, a high concentration of poor and frustrated displaced peasants provide a powerful base for political disorders in the form of riots, strikes, and the like, which makes national governments even more sensitive to their needs. (In Chapter 9 we noted the significance of urban uprisings in revolutionary processes.)

Between 1950 and 1990 the number of people around the world living in cities of 4 million or more leaped from 88 to 495 million, making such megacities the fastest-growing class of cities. Most of this urbanization was, in fact, in developing regions. In 1950, there were five such megacities among LDCs; by the mid-1990s, there were forty-three. In the year 2000, for instance, Mexico City's population surpassed that of New York City. Even so, more than 70 percent of the world's urban population still lives in cities of fewer than 2 million people. But people in these smaller cities suffer many of the same environmental and social ills as residents of the megacities. Studies of cities suggest that the overall wealth of a city, not its size, determines living conditions. Among developing countries pollution and resource scarcity affect residents directly, whereas wealthier cities are able to export water and solid waste and import resources (Wilken, 1995:100).

Population Growth as a Global Environmental Problem.   How important is population growth as a cause of global social and environmental problems? As you might guess, experts and policy makers disagree. There continue to be *neo-Malthusians*[2] who argue that population growth is creating a global disaster of the greatest magnitude, that it will lead only to widespread environmental despoliation, famine, disease, and war (Ehrlich and Ehrlich, 1992). Others take a more moderate position, arguing that world population growth is a component of the volatile world situation, but perhaps not the most important one. They argue that the culprits are not only the number of people, but also how much they consume and the degree to which their consumption damages the environment. At the other extreme some have taken a position dubbed *supply-side demography:* that population growth is not a problem at all, emphasizing that as the world has become more populous it has also become more prosperous.

To be fair, you need to know that this last position represents a tiny fringe of scholars (mostly economists) rather than the vast body of scholarly opinion (see Simon, 1995; Wattenberg, 1987). A study by the National Academy of Sciences (NAS) in the mid-1980s took the middle ground in this debate about the relationship of population growth to the well-being of people and environmental protection, reflected in this summation:

> One of the more important findings to come from a study of the relationship between population size and the environment is the misplaced importance given to world population size as a cause of natural resource scarcities and pollution. . . . [we do not] imply that world population growth should be . . . neglected as a cause of environmental problems, [but] a fixation on it as the major reason for pollution and energy crises would be sociologically misguided. (Humphrey and Buttel, 1982:60)

There are several reasons for this moderate position that represented the weight of scholarly opinion in the mid-1980s. *First,* demographers and policy makers observed that through the 1970s fertility reduction programs (emphasizing family planning and contraception) were smashing successes in some developing countries. They were particularly successful in parts of East Asia, including the Koreas (both), Taiwan, Malaysia, Indonesia, but also large and populous Brazil and Mexico. And the rapid decline of fertility in China, with its 1 billion people, was taken to be very significant for braking future world population growth. China was beginning to look more like a First World than a Third World country in terms of its demographic growth rate. *Second,* while such programs were dismal failures in the poorest developing countries, evidence from the 1980s suggested that such programs can be effective in nations that define development priorities primarily in terms of the alleviation of poverty rather than economic growth and high average income levels (Birdsall, 1980: 10). For such programs to work, it was no longer thought necessary to wait till the Bangladeshis became fully "developed" like the Danes or Dutch, but only necessary to address the most basic human health, hunger, and material security problems—a much more doable agenda. *Third,* others noted the accumulating evidence that family size declined everywhere that greater educational and economic opportunities were created for women. (Stay tuned for more about this.) Even stubbornly high fertility rates in most African and some Latin American nations only meant that different timetables were in operation. *Fourth,* upbeat assessments about progress in breaking world population growth were coupled with equally rosy assessments about how many people the earth could comfortably support. Experts predicted that the earth could comfortably support 15 and maybe even 20 billion people (McFals, 1991:35; National Academy of Science, 1969)!

To summarize, in the 1980s most scholars assumed (1) that developing countries would complete the demographic transition before irreversibly damaging the earth's carrying capacity for human life, and (2) that the much slower growth rates among developed countries were no problem. *But by the mid-1990s, that optimism had all but vanished,* and neither of these assumptions continued to represent the consensus of scholarly opinion. As we note in the next section, progress in braking world population growth stalled in the 1980s. In addition, overwhelming evidence continued to mount about the negative environmental impact of human societies and economies—for instance, in drastically altering the earth's climate, destroying the water tables and fertile soils that provide the capacity to feed the earth's growing billions, producing toxins that poison not only humans but other species, and destroying the habitats of those other creatures with which we cohabit on the planet.

Further, it was increasingly clear that the problem was not just rapid population growth of developing countries, but also unprecedented consumption levels among the more affluent classes everywhere—especially in the developed nations. And it was noted that the typical developed nation citizen costs the environment many times more than does the typical citizen of a developing country. By 1996, the developed nations, with about 20 percent of the world's population, accounted for a vastly overproportionate 60 to 80 percent of the earth's natural resource use, including 80 percent of its paper, iron, and steel; 75 percent of its timber and energy; 60 percent of its meat, fertilizer, and cement; and one half of its fish and grain. Inequalities in percapita consumption comparisons were more dramatic: Among European and North American nations, each person uses twenty times as much aluminum and seventeen times as much copper as a person in the developing nations. While dramatic inequalities exist, the developing countries share of global resources is slowly rising with population growth and will continue to do so given even moderately successful economic growth (Brown, J., 1996:368).

Consequently, the modest middle-ground position of the NAS changed dramatically, and their best reading of evidence had changed in a stunning way by the 1990s. The NAS and the British Royal Society of London, two of the world's most prestigious scientific organizations and neither known for taking extreme stands, issued an unprecedented joint statement. They said that unless rapacious population growth and mushrooming consumption levels were soon halted, "advances in science and technology no longer could be counted on to avoid either irreversible environmental degradation or continued poverty for much of humanity" (quoted in Miller, 1992). Does population growth cause serious social and environmental problems? *Yes.* Is it the only cause of those problems? *No.*

What to Do? Should Population Policy Address Fertility, Inequality, or Patriarchy?

Even when it is recognized as a significant problem, disagreement exists about the causes of population growth and what to do about it. Although the debate is an intellectual one about causes and policy, it has long embodied politically and emotionally charged issues. That was apparent at the UN conferences about population problems, which met in Bucharest, Romania (1974); Mexico City (1984); and Cairo, Egypt (1994). In the 1974 Bucharest conference, seven countries refused to send delegates even to discuss such problems, and the ones that did quickly separated into different factions. At that time the major divide was between the representatives of the developed nations against those of the developing and socialist bloc nations. Representatives of the developed nations argued that *the world is poor because it is becoming overpopulated.* They said that exponential population growth is a prime cause of global instability because it increases pressure on resources, creates scarcities, and undercuts economic development efforts in the Third World. They maintained that since the growth rates in the developed world were declining, the major responsibility for curbing world population growth was among developing countries. Most representatives of the latter countries argued, to the contrary, that *the world is becoming overpopulated because it is so poor.* They argued, consistent with the demographic transition model, that to expect exponential growth "to level off before economic growth and improvement is to put the cart before the horse . . . when people perceive no improvement in the living standards they will not change their behavior patterns for promises of future benefits" (Pirages, 1978:60).

There is evidence for such a view. In a study of the failure of India's family planning programs, Mamdani (1972) found that the poor in developing nations have compelling reasons to have large families: (1) children provide a form of old age support; (2) children provide economic support through their labor on the farm or the sale of their labor to others; and (3) children add little to household expenditures in a condition of deep poverty. Consistent with abundant evidence from demographic transitions, living in chronic poverty does not provide the incentives for reducing fertility, and population programs directed at this goal are likely to fail. This line of argument views the most powerful causes of poverty in the developing countries not as population growth per se, but as the economic constraints of developmental failure caused by their positions in the world market system (Mamdani, 1972). Representatives of the developing nations at the Bucharest conference were quick to point out that if concerns were over consumption of global resources and degradation of the environment, the real locus of the problem is with the developed nations. As we noted earlier, the 20 percent of the world's population living in developed countries use an overproportionate share of the earth's resources to satisfy the consumerism and nonessential wants of their lifestyles. But obtaining raw material to satisfy *minimum basic human needs* is often difficult among poor countries. Thus poverty *and* population growth are maintained by global inequality.

In rejoinder, representatives of the developed nations replied that it is simply not possible to support the world's population at a level like that of their countries without devastating the resource base and food stocks of the planet. Again, *there was evidence to support the rejoinder* (and there is now). For instance, if the Chinese, with a population of about 1 billion people (in the 1970s), were miraculously raised to U.S. consumption standards, it would increase the world's energy consumption by 100 percent, not to mention all the other resources and minerals it would take to develop the industrial infrastructure to do this (Pirages, 1978:62). In the 1990s, if the more than 1 billion Chinese were suddenly to have had an abundant and protein-rich diet as do North Americans, they would have needed to buy all of the grain for sale on international markets, and even that would probably not be enough (Brown, 1994).

As you might guess, the 1974 UN population conference ended in a state of inconclusiveness. At the next conference in Mexico City (1984), most nations recognized world population growth as a significant problem and sent delegates. But there opposition to reducing fertility through family planning programs came from a surprising source: the United States. Responding to powerful anti-abortion forces in domestic politics, twenty years of American leadership on world populations issues came to an end, and the United States withdrew aid and financial support for family planning programs and the UN Population Fund. As a consequence, progress in limiting population growth that occurred in the 1970s came to a halt, and the 1980s was known as the "lost decade" for lack of greater progress in limiting world population growth as well as for developmental failures, as in noted in the last chapter (Camp, 1993:132–133).

In the 1994 Cairo conference, the International Conference on Population and Development was different (note the significance of the name change). Because they were encouraged to attend, the official conference was surrounded by a diverse and cacophonous mélange of nongovernmental, civic, and social movement groups representing scientists and scholars, environmentalists, religious groups, feminists, and human rights activists from around the world, who sought to influence policy outcomes of the gathering.

The overwhelming consensus among delegates at Cairo in 1994 was that world population growth is a problem that exacerbates core social and environmental problems, whereas the notion that population growth is *the* cause of all human problems was rejected. To limit population growth, they emphasized creating conditions under which couples willingly lower the number of children they have. They affirmed (1) the traditional strategies of making family planning/contraception available to all people, and (2) addressing the issues of poverty and destitution, which amplify population growth. Powerful evidence suggested that everywhere these strategies made some difference. *But* they also emphasized something quite new: (3) empowering women. Many women, particularly in developing countries, where 90 percent of the world's population growth happens, have large families simply because they have no other way to achieve social and economic security for themselves. Women in strongly patriarchal (male-dominated) societies are often forced to marry young. They get paid much less than men when they are allowed to work, have little access to land or bank credit, and have hardly any opportunity to participate in political life.

In 1995, the Fourth World Conference on Women, held in Beijing, emphasized the same point. A pervasive consensus among women's organizations as well as scholars about development and population policy maintains that policies designed to improve the well-being of women, policies that expand their access to health care, education, and employment, would help. Giving women more social choices and making men more responsible for families would go far to limit population growth, address environmental problems, and promote human development (Harper, 1996:191; Sachs, 1995:94; 1996:88). But you can understand that those in power in patriarchal societies strongly resist such strategies for change. Returning to the question that began this section: Should strategies to limit population growth address changing fertility, inequality and poverty, or patriarchy? The obvious answer is *yes,* all, in combination. Effectively promoting these strategies in combination is important; we're sure you recognize it will not be easy.

Hunger as a Global Problem

At present the problems of world hunger do not result from the lack of resources or the technical capacity to feed the world's population. They are a *maldistribution* problem: Many of the world's most efficient food-producing regions have small or low-density populations, and many of the densely populated and rapidly growing regions are increasingly less self-sufficient. This maldistribution occurs not only because the high-output regions are superficially more efficient at producing food, though that is certainly true. Food productivity in most regions has increased (until recently), but also a major problem is that the development policies of the poorer regions have not (until recently) emphasized food production for domestic consumption as a priority. In many nations the production of food could be increased by simply shifting agricultural production away from cash market crops such as tobacco, coffee, or cotton.

Political authoritarianism and the absence of free markets and responsive governments are powerful forces that turn scarcity and hardships into famine. In the well-publicized famines of the 1980s and 1990s in Somalia, Ethiopia, Haiti, and Rwanda, the absence of democracy, civil war, and government reluctance to admit problems turned drought and hardship into mass starvation. (Maybe you remember the TV pictures.) But famine was averted in more democratic Zimbabwe. Furthermore, while many Indians routinely suffer malnourishment, the Indian government was democratic and responsive enough to prevent mass starvation. Not so neighboring Bangladesh. Evidence about the role of the absence of responsive governments in preventing famine in the contemporary world is overwhelming (Sen, 1991).

To put it another way, actual starvation, and to some extent chronic malnutrition, is not *directly* caused by population growth that outstrips our capacity to produce food, but more directly by inequality, poverty, and political conditions within and between nations. Because of the way development and globalization have occurred, the poor are simply not able to consume their share of the world's food. Currently the problem of world hunger is more a political and economic than a technical problem of producing food. At the turn of the twenty-first century, there is enough food in the world, *if redistributed,* to feed everybody in the world with enough calories to maintain health. *But you need to know what this means.* Redistributing food so that everyone has a calorie-adequate diet, your fair share as a North American means that you would eat a few cups of rice (or some other grain) daily, supplemented by a weekly banana or green vegetables, and rarely—if ever—animal protein.

So, *yes,* there is theoretically enough food to feed everybody in the world, and the most direct causes of famine have to do with maldistribution problems. But distribution problems are inherently political and hard to resolve. They exist even within the United States, where malnutrition and poverty exist alongside incredible affluence. The world situation is analogous. In other words, the actual outlook into the twenty-first century is bleaker than was thought in the 1980s, when research was more optimistic that improving agriculture and bringing more land into food production would support a considerably larger population (Norse, 1992; Oram, 1988; United Nations, FAO and IIASA, 1982).

These findings, as we have seen, are now widely regarded as overly optimistic and riddled with unrealistic assumptions. They assumed that rich and poor alike would be willing to share the same diet with no luxuries, that livestock would be banished to land incapable of growing crops, and that significantly more land could be put into food production. In fact, much of the assumed potential cropland is so marginal (dry and infertile) that few farmers would find it worth the effort. Compensating for those assumptions suggests that—using today's best agricultural technology—about half of the nations cannot feed their populations in the twenty-first century, and with high inputs of money, more irrigation, and expensive new agricultural technologies—unrealistic for many parts of the world—about a third of the nations will have difficulty (Harrison, 1993:47–48).

In sum, while quite a bit of uncertainty exists about the details of projections about population growth and food-producing capacity, there is a consensus that feeding a growing population with shrinking per capita food-producing capacity will be very difficult (Harper, 1996:187). Global per-capita food production has actually been shrinking since the early 1990s. (See Table 13–1.)

HUMAN IMPACTS AND GLOBAL ENVIRONMENTAL CHANGE

Before the modern age and the spread of industrialism around the world, human populations were so small and diffuse, and human technological capacities so embryonic, that it is doubtful that human social and economic activity was a major force in altering the global environment as a whole. Even so, archaeologists have recently

| TABLE 13–1 | PRODUCTION TRENDS PER PERSON, GRAIN, SEAFOOD, AND BEEF, 1950–1999 |

	Production Trends (percent change)			
Foodstuff	1950–1970	1970–1980	1980–1990	1990–1999
Grain	8	10	4	−8
Seafood	109	−4	24	1
Beef	51	14	11	10.3

Source: Brown et al. (2000).

marshaled compelling evidence that unsustainable agricultural practices and degraded environments in most early agricultural civilizations contributed significantly to their decline. There is evidence for such outcomes about the Mayan and Mesopotamian civilizations as well as the Western Roman empire (see Harper, 1996:41, 46). But compelling evidence exists that *since the beginning of the twentieth century, unprecedented large human populations and industrial technology have been major factors in global environmental and ecosystem change.* Here we address human environmental impacts related to (1) how we generate and use energy, (2) how we produce food, (3) how our activities affect the variety among species of plants and animals (biodiversity), and (4) different kinds of environmental impacts among MDCs and LDCs.

Generating and Using Energy

Most fuels that drive industrial economies (including their high-tech agricultural systems) are carbon-based fuels such as coal, natural gas, and petroleum products. At least 80 percent of the energy that fuels economies and human comforts and consumption depends on such fuels. Hydroelectric generators in large dams make most of the rest, with nuclear plants accounting for about 5 percent of the world's energy budget.

U.S. dependence on petroleum products was vividly demonstrated in 1973, when economic boycotts from the oil producers (OPEC) created oil shortages around the world. Petroleum prices soared, sending price increases cascading through the economies of most nations. If you are too young to remember this, ask your parents or an older person; we're sure they will have vivid memories of the winter of 1973 (Harper, 1996:200)! At about the same time, a prestigious futurist group called the "Club of Rome" produced a widely read report arguing that human economic activity and energy consumption was growing so rapaciously that the world was on the verge of running out of gas, as well as some other minerals essential for industrial economies (we will return to the Club of Rome report and reactions to it in the next chapter). Ordinary citizens, policy makers, and scientists had a hard time disentangling the effects of the boycott from an impending real shortage in energy supplies.

We now know that there was no impending oil (or natural gas) shortage. But there are very real environmental concerns about the health and environmental impacts of extracting, refining, transporting, and consuming petroleum products. It produces significant air pollution, and oil leaking from pipelines and oil spills have a damaging effect on land and ocean ecosystems. Further, if energy consumption continues to grow at existing rates, the consensus among energy experts (even those who work for oil companies) is that global oil supplies will become very tight by the middle of the twenty-first century. We will probably never absolutely run out of gas, but we will use up the cheap, accessible supplies so that what remains is hard to get and expensive. The costs of many of its present uses (like driving your private car) may become prohibitive. In any case, the fossil fuel age will very likely come to an end sometime in the next century (Flavin and Lensen, 1994).

But if the 1970s were dominated by the specter of supply shortages, the new century is haunted by the various consequences of using and burning oil (and other fuels) in such vast quantities. The world environment is literally splattered with oil from leaky pipes and tanker wrecks, and the consequent urban smog from the combustion of fossil fuels regularly produces pulmonary diseases in many cities like London, Los Angeles, Mexico City, and Beijing. As if this were not bad enough, burning fossil fuels spews at least 6 billion tons of carbon into the atmosphere each year, mainly in the form of carbon dioxide, which increases the atmosphere's ability to trap and hold heat from radiant solar energy—dubbed the *greenhouse effect.* Research shows that the global mean temperature has risen about 1 degree centigrade in the last 100 years and is expected to rise as much as by 4 to 8 degrees by 2050. *This is no joke.* Even such seemingly small global mean increases would make the world's climate warmer than at any time in human history, resembling that of the Eocene era 40 million years ago. Such rapid changes in temperature could outstrip the ability of many plant and animals species to migrate or adapt (Kraus et al.; 1992:28). Atmospheric and oceanic systems that regulate the weather would be disrupted. If so, polar ice caps could melt, flooding many of the world's most densely inhabited coastal regions. Some regions would become wetter while others become drier, but the tropics would be stricken with unprecedented heat waves. The prime agricultural areas in the temperate zones may shift northward and southward to where, in many instances, the topsoil is thinner than the present grain belt regions of the world. U.S. agriculture might be devastated.

When Harper wrote about the greenhouse effect in an earlier edition of this book, this was all scientific conjecture, but by 1995 the world's organized scientific bodies believed that the important evidence was in. How much and how quickly the earth's climate will warm, and its effects on particular regions, is not clear. But there is vast scientific consensus that the earth's climate is warming and that human economic activity (particularly burning fossil fuels) is the main culprit (Intergovernmental Panel on Climate Change, 1995; see also Wigley, 1995).

Further, the same thing is true of energy that is true of the consumption of most other natural resources: The developed nations consume a vastly overproportionate share. With about 20 percent of the world's people, developed nations consume 50 percent of the total fossil fuels that are central to development and the key to global warming. In per-capita terms, one U.S. or Canadian citizen consumes as much energy as do 3 Japanese, 6 Mexicans, 14 Chinese, 38 Indians, 168 Bangladeshis, 280 Nepalis, or 531 Ethiopians (Brown, J., 1996:368; Goodland et al., 1993:5)!

If fossil fuel energy systems are the chief culprits for global warming, are there any other alternatives? *Yes indeed.* In the short term, natural gas could replace most fossil fuels. It is also a carbon-based fossil fuel, but a cleaner-burning one that produces much less carbon dioxide per calorie of energy than either petroleum or coal (the dirtiest and most polluting fuel). Nuclear energy was long viewed as a nonpolluting alternative source of energy, but the frightful risks of nuclear disasters like Chernobyl, the difficulties of disposing of nuclear wastes, and the prodigious costs of nuclear plants all meant that the nuclear option looks like a failed one (Miller, 1992:500).

There are many other alternatives: wind power, solar power, biogas generators (which produce methane and other gases from decaying plant refuse), and improving the efficiency of our machines. The efficiency option has an enormous potential to make our present energy system less polluting and climate changing as well as to conserve supplies. But only relatively wealthy nations can afford it. Some of these alternatives are technically and economically ready now. Experts estimate, for example, the upper Great Plains states (where the wind always blows) could easily and economically produce enough electricity by quiet, nonpolluting wind generators to power the whole North American continent (Flavin and Lenssen, 1994). Other alternatives (e.g., photovoltaic solar power) are nearing technical feasibility and economic competitiveness and might become practical and competitive within several decades—assuming intense research and development. Even so, photovoltaic electricity grew rapidly in the 1990s among developing countries, to power sun-drenched but remote villages, where the costs of providing electricity via long power lines from big power plants was prohibitive.

The ultimate technological energy fantasy for environmentalists is to use hydrogen gas in much the way we use or envision uses for propane, butane, and natural gas. Hydrogen could be produced by electrolyzing water with electricity from photovoltaic cells, and the exhaust from the combustion of hydrogen is ordinary water vapor, not toxic byproducts or greenhouse gases. (If you have taken a high school chemistry course, you have probably seen water electrolysis.) The potential for energy-intensive industrial economies to develop environmentally benign *hydrogen-based* rather than *carbon-based* systems is vast. The technology has been sketched out, but it will be decades before it will be practical and economical.

You can probably recognize that the costs of reconfiguring all the world's economies in such a way are also vast. Which brings us to an important point: The main barriers to shifting to alternative and more environmentally benign energy systems are not technological, but economic and institutional. The biggest barrier to shifting to alternative and more environmentally benign energy systems is not even its costs. While these are substantial, they are manageable if introduced incrementally over several decades. The main barrier is political opposition from the existing gas, oil, and coal companies. They are making money just fine, thank you, from the existing fossil fuel system, and around the world they enjoy generous state monopoly status, tax writeoffs, and subsidies. But while formally defending the fossil fuel economy with all their political clout (which is considerable!), even the big oil and coal companies have read the handwriting on the wall and are quietly investing in the development of alternative energy sources.

Agricultural Resources: Soil and Water

As we noted before, the most concrete and pressing energy problem for most of the world's people is not about gas or electricity. It is, rather, "What's for lunch?" The reason food supplies are a growing problem, as we noted earlier, is that the mushrooming population, combined with the technologies we have used to increase food production, have everywhere put agricultural resources under stress. The most basic of these are *soil* and *water.* In 1992, a United Nations study of soils from 220 selected sites concluded that in the last forty-five years the earth's arable soil had been severely degraded, that globally at least 1 percent was damaged by erosion, chemicals, and overgrazing, and that much of this soil was so severely damaged that rebuilding or reclaiming the soil was so expensive that it was beyond the means of many nations and individual farmers (Harper, 1996:74).

Other research found that even the UN study understated the global degradation of soils. The World Resources Institute concluded that about 20 percent of the earth's arable soil has received some degree of degradation, including

- 35 percent from overgrazing, in which too many animals strip the plant cover and compact the soil, reducing its ability to hold moisture
- 30 percent from deforestation, prevalent in South America but in the 1990s occurring most rapidly in Asia
- 28 percent from harmful agricultural practices, such as overfertilization, poor drainage, or ignoring the need for fallow periods, which is responsible for much soil damage in North America
- 8 percent from urban and industrial pollution. (World Resources Institute, 1993: 324–325)

Among nations, the U.S. record in slowing soil degradation is outstanding, but nonetheless in 1992 the U.S. Soil Conservation Service estimated that 25 percent of U.S. croplands were eroding faster than they could be preserved, and in 1996 conservative congressional groups advocated budget-cutting measures that would abolish the Soil Conservation Service (see Stroh and Raloff, 1992:215). Commenting on the world soil situation in the 1990s, the normally optimistic James Speth, associated with both the World Resources Institute and the United Nations, said that "if topsoil erosion continues at post-World War 11 rates, feeding an exploding world population could prove extremely difficult" (cited in Stroh and Raloff, 1992:215).

Water resources are similarly under stress. Between 1950 and 1992, human water consumption tripled (70 percent used for agriculture). There is a staggering amount of water on the planet, but much of it (salty oceans, water vapor in the atmosphere) is unusable by humans. Of the usable fraction of global water, limits to its ever-expanding consumption were visible everywhere as shrinking rivers and lakes, falling water table, disappearing wetlands, and water polluted so severely that it is not fit for human consumption or even for industrial or agricultural uses (Postel, 1992).

As you might guess, water shortages are most severe in and tropical and low-latitude nations, particularly in Africa and the Mideast, where demand regularly exceeds supplies. But water supplies for agriculture and human consumption are critical in such diverse places as California, Mexico, Jordan, India, and Australia. Because irrigation became the cornerstone of modern agriculture, groundwater supplies are particularly critical in large areas of China, India, and the Middle East. Irrigation overdrafts are also common in the United States, where water is being pumped out of the ground on average 25 percent more rapidly than it is being replaced. Such irrigation overdrafts are particularly critical in America's salad bowl, in California's San Joaquin Valley, and in the Great Plains, where water from the vast Ogalalla Aquifer is being pumped from the ground at a rate about 140 percent faster than it is being replaced. At that rate the Great Plains, which supplies 40 percent of the nation's beef and much of the world's grain, will be a barren waste land in several decades (Harper, 1996:78; Postel, 1993). Water supplies are so tight that shortages routinely boil over into political conflicts—they contribute to perennial legal conflict between Nebraska and Colorado, and often contributed to shooting wars in the Middle East and parts of Africa (Falkenmark and Widstrand, 1992).

What about food from the ocean? The picture is equally dreary. By 1989, all of the ocean fisheries were being fished at or beyond capacity. The world has about fifteen major ocean fisheries, and thirteen of them are in visible decline. Although 1994 was a peak harvest year for ocean fish, marine biologists believe that harvest to be unsustainable as the seafood available per capita shrinks indefinitely, being divided among (at least) 90 million more people each year (Brown, 1996:4). Like the water wars we just discussed, fishing wars fueled conflict in the mid-1990s. In 1995, for instance, Canadian patrol boats seized Spanish trawlers off Newfoundland, while Iceland and Norway battled for fishing in the Arctic waters, and 7.5 million Indian fishers went on strike to protest joint ventures with foreign fishing fleets (Platt, 1996:30–31). In sum, not only actual food production, *but agricultural resources to produce food are all under assault and are currently declining when viewed in per-capita terms.* (See Table 13–2.)

Human Impacts on Other Species: Declining Biodiversity

Stanford University biologists estimate that humans and their chosen crop creatures use an astounding 40 percent of the earth's living things in one way or another. Aside from direct consumption of other species for such things as food or clothing, a major source of the extinction of wild species is loss of habitats when people cut forests or clear land for crops (Vitousek et al., 1986).

What is the scope of declining biodiversity? That is impossible to quantify (since many of the world's species of flora and fauna have not even been catalogued).

TABLE 13–2 POPULATION SIZE AND AVAILABILITY OF RENEWABLE RESOURCES,
Circa 1990, With Projections for 2010

	Circa 1990 (in millions)	2010 (in millions)	Total Change %	Per Capita Change %
Population	5,290	7,030	+33	—
Fish catch (tons)	85	102	+20	–12
Irrigated land (hectares)	237	277	+17	–12
Cropland (hectares)	1,444	1,516	+5	–21
Range and pasture (hectares)	3,402	3,540	+4	–22
Forests (hectares)	3,413	3,165	–7	–30

Source: From *State of the World 1994: A Worldwatch Institute Report on Progress toward a Sustainable Society* by Lester R. Brown et al., eds. © 1994 by Worldwatch Institute. Reprinted by permission of W. W. Norton & Company, Inc.

But aside from a tiny group of scientific doubters who get a lot of media attention, the vast consensus among the world's biologists and ecologists is that human activity in the contemporary world represents the greatest assault on nature since the curious waves of extinctions in the Cetaceous Age, when dinosaurs and many other species became extinct (see Wilson, 1990). The scope of current estimates of extinctions might amaze you.

- *Amphibians.* Worldwide decline observed in recent years. Wetland drainage and invading species are threats, as well as the capacity for amphibians to absorb toxins through their skins.
- *Birds.* Three-fourths of the world's bird species are declining in population or threatened with extinction.
- *Mammals.* Almost half of Australia's surviving mammals are threatened with extinction. France, Germany, the Netherlands, and Portugal all report more than 40 percent of their mammals as threatened.
- *Carnivores.* Virtually all species of wild cats and most bears are declining seriously in numbers.
- *Primates.* An order of mammals that includes monkeys, apes, and lemurs as well as humans. More than two-thirds of the world's 150 known species are threatened with extinction.
- *Reptiles.* Of the world's 270 turtle species, 42 percent are threatened with extinction.
- *Fish.* One-third of North America's freshwater fish stocks are rare, threatened, or endangered. One-third of America's coastal fish species have been in decline in population since 1975 (Brown, 1986:110).

Most people (including us) want to preserve the diversity of wild things for their beauty and intrinsic value as the earth's biological heritage. But there may be more practical reasons. How important are these other creatures of the wilderness for maintaining the ecosystems of the earth on which humans depend? That is an impossible question to answer with any certainty, but most ecologists think that as humans destroy, alter, or appropriate more natural systems for ourselves, the environmental services provided by other creatures are compromised. At some point scientists envision a chain reaction of environmental decline: widespread flooding and erosion brought on by deforestation, worsened drought and crop losses from desertification, pervasive aquatic pollution, and fisheries losses from wetlands destruction.

To put it another way: Is a simplified biotic world composed mainly of humans and our favorite fellow traveler species that have adapted to us (not only dogs, cats, pigs, and chickens, but also sparrows, crabgrass, and cockroaches!) a viable ecosystem in its own right—to say nothing about providing for large human populations? No one knows, but many ecologists doubt it.

IN CONCLUSION: SOCIETIES, ENVIRONMENT, AND GLOBAL STABILITY

Humans are in the process of simply overwhelming the dilutive and regenerative capacity of the ecosystems that sustain us. Although we deny it vigorously, when it is put in personal terms we actually like doing so. Most people everywhere like to have more money to be able to consume more. Did you ever hear of a successful elected politician who ran on a platform to slow real economic growth? Yet both rapid population growth and rapaciously growing consumption of natural resources contribute to serious degradation of the natural resources and ecosystems that support human life. We hope by now you recognize that the way both of these forces work is not simple. Not all consumption is equally damaging to the environment, and not all people damage the earth in the same way.

For example, not all consumption requires equal amounts of material resources. Some consumption (e.g., services and information) requires relatively little material. Postindustrial economies driven by information technologies do lower per-capita consumption of natural resources. But, given absolute increases in population and desires for higher living standards around the world, that is little comfort. Additionally, the growing gap between developed and developing countries noted in the last chapter means that hopes for new technologies that bring greater efficiency and substitutes for scarce raw materials are dim among developing countries, because those technologies are mostly owned by enterprises in developed nations.

Further, the world's rich and poor take their toll on the environment in different ways: the rich through high per-capita consumption and production of wastes and the poor through their pressure on fragile lands. In most developing countries, growing affluent classes consume on a level comparable to citizens of developed nations. The latter have had the greater global environmental impact—contributing mightily to global warming and pollution with heavy use of fossil fuels. Among developing countries, production of food, fiber, mining, and the disposal of wastes have had mostly local impacts on soils, forests, biodiversity and water. In the 1970s, environmentalists were mainly worried about the depletion of nonrenewable resources, such as fossil fuels, metals, and other minerals. But by the 1990s, it was clear that the so-called renewable resources—such as soil, forests, air, water, fisheries, and biodiversity—

are being exploited at unsustainable rates (Brown, J., 1996:386). *There are no technological substitutes for these resources.*

We have argued in this chapter that creating a sustainable world that manages population growth and human environmental impacts requires that consumption be increased among at least a fifth of the world's most destitute persons—not to mention that social justice requires it. Further, because they assault the natural world, population and consumption growth increase social unrest and political instability within and between nations. Neither population size nor environmentally driven scarcities directly cause unrest and instability, but they can amplify the deprivation, frustration, and outrage that more directly cause desperate migration and refugee streams, violence, and rebellion. Traditionally, policy makers thought of national and international security in terms of military balance and economic forces. That way of understanding national and international security will continue, but increasingly security issues will be understood in demographic and environmental terms as well (Homer-Dixon, 1996).

There is time left in the twenty-first century—but not a lot of it—to create a sustainable world. The greatest barriers to doing so are not technological but political and institutional. Collectively, nations know better ways of limiting population growth, halting destructive environmental change, and living humanely on the planet—if governments take the politically difficult steps to curve excessive consumption and manage resources. They can, particularly if the developed nations, and most particularly if the United States, takes the lead (Brown, J., 1996:366). Can the planet continue to sustain human societies after the massive assault on nature and the earth's carrying capacity since the beginning of the industrial era? This is, we think, the supremely important long-range question about social change for the twenty-first century, since it is about the maintenance of the biological and geophysical carrying capacity of the earth to support human societies as we know and desire them to be. We will return to this question in the next chapter.

The problems of collectively inventing a viable human future are enormous. But equally impressive are the possibilities of human inventiveness and the abilities of humans both to adapt to necessity and shape the directions of change. We turn more directly to human futures in the next chapter.

Postscript: Economic and Ecological Worldviews

This whole chapter is an extension of a theme of the last one: that there is an emerging world system and, consequently, a single world problem, that faces not only the dilemmas of human development and progress, but distinct and interpenetrating environmental dilemmas (population growth, food, energy resources, environmental degradation). We hope by now you can see that these factors affect the future quality of life (if not the survival) of individuals and nations. For the world problem there is no main or single cause: It is rather sustained by the ongoing interaction among them. And coping with the world problem requires that we somehow attend to all of these dimensions and the ways that they interact.

An important barrier to our ability to deal with these problems is that our view of human problems and our policies are normally driven by *economic* rather than *environmental* perspectives. These perspectives not only have different scholarly origins, but mostly disparate worldviews that underlie the working ideas of the two kinds of scholarly disciplines that seek to inform public policy. The *economic perspective* sees growth in productivity, resources, products, and human services as the solutions to most human problems. Social as well as economic well-being is associated with a growing GNP, the most common summary measure of human as well as economic progress. As human populations increased in modern times, food, energy, and material goods became more plentiful, the human life span became longer, and more people were healthier and better fed than ever before. Even in the most sluggish growth period since 1980, an economist would note (1) a global increase in the worth of goods and services by about $5 trillion, (2) a moderation of energy prices and inflation in general, (3) an expansion of international trade, (4) the creation of millions of new jobs, (5) the steady increase of the value of stocks and bonds, and (6) probably a diminution of world hunger and increases in material security in much of the world (Brown, 1991:6–7). All of these factors would be taken as indicators of human progress.

Economic theory and indicators see the future as more or less continuous with the past and emphasize technological creativity to deal with limits to economic growth. Environmental limits, when they are recognized at all, are rarely taken into account in economic costs accounting (they are described as *externalities* that do not show up at all on balance sheets). The economic view prevails in the worlds of industry, finance, and among national governments and international development agencies (Brown, 1991; Henderson, 1988). Economists do, of course, recognize problems—periodic recessions, budget deficits, Third World debt, the food crisis in Africa, the unsettling effect of energy price increases—but to an economist things appear manageable. The pages of the *Wall Street Journal* and the reports of the World Bank are bullish about the economic prospects for the new millenium.

From an *ecological (or environmental) perspective,* things look very different. Economic growth has been bought with considerable damage to natural systems and resources. Every major indicator of the earth's biophysical conditions shows this deterioration: Forests are shrinking, deserts are expanding, croplands are losing topsoil, fresh water is becoming scarce, the stratospheric ozone layer continues to thin, greenhouse gases are accumulating, the number of plant and animal species is diminishing, air pollution has reached health-threatening levels in hundreds of cities, and damage from acid rain can be seen on every continent. The measures of economic growth mentioned earlier are so optimistic because they miss entirely the environmental debts the world is incurring. In a form of deficit financing, we are consuming the earth's capital at an alarming rate, which is the opposite of an environmentally sustainable economy. Herman Daley, a rare environmentally conscious economist, says that "there is something fundamentally wrong in treating the earth as if it were a business in liquidation" (Brown, 1991:5, 9).

Economic arguments are often more persuasive than ecological arguments because economic costs are often tangible in the present, while environmental costs are often less concrete and operate in a highly diffuse way over a longer period of time.

As individuals, we live in the short run, but it is also important to realize that long-run human survival in any reasonably positive terms requires that we do not opt for short-run benefits that destroy the carrying capacity of the earth to support human life. Arriving at a reasonable balance between short-run needs versus long-term interests and between national versus global interests confronts humans with a complex and difficult range of choices.

Even so, ecological perspectives are coming to compete with economic ones in both popular thinking and public policy making. By the 1990s, environmental politics was an important part of national political debates (as witnessed by the attention paid to Al Gore's book, *Earth in the Balance*), although not yet competing on an equal footing with more traditional bread-and-butter economic issues of employment, inflation, taxation, and the like. Environmental issues are now routinely on the agendas of international meetings of the Group of Seven industrial nations that meet annually to discuss global problems. Environmental treaties are beginning to be important, such as the Montreal Accord of 1987. It called for the significant reduction of ozone gases by 1998 (a target only partially met), and most nations are now phasing out the production of CFC chemicals (cooling system chemicals that harm the ozone layer). The World Bank now takes into account environmental policies of Third World nations in extending loans or credit.

These efforts, however, are still embryonic in terms of what needs to be done. Reaching an international agreement on a plan to stabilize the world climate will be much more difficult, because it requires a wholesale restructuring of the world's energy system. That problem, as well as population stabilization and dampening consumption levels where necessary, are coming to be understood as necessary, but in the 1990s neither worldwide institutional machinery nor the requisite political will are in place to address these issues effectively. Our hunch is, however, that during the twenty-first century ecological issues (in their various dimensions) will come to compete with the more conventional economic ones that drive politics and policy around the world. Stay tuned.

THINKING PERSONALLY ABOUT SOCIAL CHANGE

1. Unlike other species, human reaction to population density is mediated by attitudes and cultural definitions about how many are too many. A dense population is one thing in a culturally homogenous city where few are poor, and there is a culture of civility (like Amsterdam). But a dense population is quite another thing where many are poor, culturally dissimilar, and there is a weak culture of civility. What do you think the American experience of growing populations will be? On a smaller scale, think of the times when you have lived in a dense environment with others (e.g., a shared apartment, college dormitory, or military base). How would you describe that experience? What kinds of special rules emerged to deal with problems of crowding? Not all rules deal with population density problems, but many do. In American cities, how do wealthy people deal with problems of urban crowding and congestion?

2. Consider the water you use. You might be interested in calculating approximately how much water you (with your family or roommates) use during a day. Here are some typical amounts:

   • washing a car with the hose running, 180 gallons
   • watering a lawn for 10 minutes, 75 gallons
   • running a washing machine at top level, 60 gallons
   • ten-minute shower, 25–50 gallons
   • average tub bath, 36 gallons
   • handwashing dishes, water running, 30 gallons
   • automatic dishwasher, 10 gallons
   • each toilet flush, 5–7 gallons
   • brushing teeth, water running, 2 gallons (Miller, 1992:356)

   You might be amazed! We were. Multiply that by the households in your community. What is the source of water in your community? What are some concerns about water supply or purity or how much water to allocate to agriculture, industrial, or household use? *Do another mental experiment:* Keep track of the trash you and your family or roommates create over a week. What is it, mainly? Suppose instead of having it hauled off, you let it pile up on the street or in your yard? How long would it take to fill your yard, or the streets?

3. Look at the newspapers or watch TV news in your community. What kinds of environmental problems are described? What are some varied reactions of people you know, when they hear about these?

NOTES

1. Environmental sociology (a subdiscipline that grew in the late 1960s) has described conventional social science as being implicitly done in a *human exemptionalism paradigm,* whereby humans alone among other species are treated as being more or less exempt from the limitations of the natural system. It has called for recasting social science theory in terms of a new *ecological paradigm,* which views human social life as ultimately rooted in nature (see, for instance, Catton and Dunlap, 1980:22–26).

2. So termed because they repeat, in a modified way, the arguments of the eighteenth-century thinker Thomas Malthus, who argued that there was an inherent tendency for population to grow faster than food supplies.

14

World Futures

The desire to look into the future is very ancient, and every society has probably had its seers, visionaries, and prophets who had a special role in envisioning the future. But in times when human populations were smaller and more isolated and the resources of the earth seemed limitless, it was probably less important to be concerned with the future except in times of widespread crisis. Today not adapting or even thinking about social change and the future is irresponsible. We often drift along in a resolute inertia that translates into a sort of death wish. But disconnecting from change does not recapture the past; it loses the future. More than ever today, we think you need to be concerned with how events shape the nature of the world you will live in and that your children and grandchildren will inherit. We know this is often difficult, because both as individuals and nations we tend to be more concerned with making do in the present, letting the future take care of itself. It is nonetheless true that how we behave now, in connection with other global actors, shapes the possibilities of what is to come.

While the visionary, prophet, or seer is a social role as ancient as human beings, in the 1960s a significant network of scholars emerged that has made serious intellectual attempts to envision the future. *Futurists* come from different areas of expertise, such as philosophy and literature as well as the social and physical sciences, and have used methods as diverse as literary scenarios, panels of experts, and computer simulations. The futurist enterprise has been sponsored by business and government agencies around the globe, and their writings have been immensely popular.[1] Such speculations always fascinate us. To be quite honest, their record for accurate and detailed prediction of the future has not been much better than that of traditional prophets and seers (given the pessimism of much of the thinking about the future, that is cause for hope!). In point of fact, it is impossible to predict the future in any accurate detail. There are simply too many variables that interact in unpredictable ways.

Yet to dismiss futurism because concrete predictions often go awry misses an important point. We agree with Edward Cornish, an influential futurist who argued that the primary goal of futurism is not to predict the future accurately but rather to help people make better decisions so that a better future can be created. Similarly, physicist Dennis Gabor argued that "We cannot predict the future; we can only invent it" (cited in Phol, 1981:7). In other words, the future is not some inexorable unfolding of trends that will inevitably come, regardless of what people think or do about them. People are not passive observers of trends. Once they become aware of trends that are underway, they often behave—both individually and collectively—in ways that modify the likelihood that the trends will continue without modification. And it is also true that our visions of the future are—in themselves—important factors that shape which futures do in fact come into being. In short, we think that it is important to understand trends and images of the future not because they inevitably come to pass, but because they contain *implications for possible alternative futures.* One can't know the future with any great certainty, but one can consider images of alternative futures. *That is what this chapter is about.*

The last chapters focused on development, globalization, and the impacts of human societies and populations on the world environment. Together they form a backdrop relevant to understanding possible world futures. This chapter extends and pulls together coherently some things mentioned in these and earlier chapters and is therefore a fitting conclusion to the book. *First,* we discuss some important U.S. and global forces and trends now underway that will continue to shape the next fifty years (until at least 2050). *Second,* we turn to two longer-term scenarios of the human future with very different visions and choices for the human future (extending to at least 2100). *Third,* we conclude by compactly describing the fundamental social transformation that we are now living through, which is only the third really fundamental such transformation in the history of humans on the earth. For lack of a better term, we call it the *Third Revolution.*

NEW WORLD ORDER OR NEW WORLD CHAOS?

The collapse of world communism by the early 1990s was truly a "hinge of history," in futurist visionary Gerald Platt's phrase: closing the door on one epoch and opening it on another. It was a world event that signaled the accumulation of decades of change, even though the actual collapse took place with such seeming suddenness that it took the world by surprise (as we noted in Chapter 9). Unlike the Soviet regime, the Chinese communist regime reasserted its political monopoly by force of arms in 1989, but it's fair to say that even the Chinese economy and foreign policy were transformed beyond all recognition. By the mid-1990s, similar changes were underway in the few backward and isolated outposts of communism (Vietnam, North Korea, Cuba). The significance of this world event for the persons who lived through it continues to be momentous. The larger significance for the human future of the world is that the old bipolar political system of the Cold War is suddenly moot. The Cold War affected the United States in many negative ways, but in retrospect fifty years of engagement with the Soviet threat was partly responsible for positive institutional innovation. In order to compete and provide a better model of human progress than the Soviets, American domestic policy produced

1. A strong and stable state
2. Advances in management of the economy
3. Progress in social equity and human welfare
4. A positive national identity

The long Cold War, rather than a national political consensus for American development and change, produced a domestic social bargain or contract in the United States. Given a weak national consensus, however, there is evidence that the domestic order forged by the Cold War is coming apart: The center is losing power, resulting in new challenges and political fault lines for political parties and presidents (Deudney and Ikenberry, 1995; Phillips, 1995; for illustration, see also Chapters 1–3). Internationally, the danger of a nuclear war is lower, but dangers from conventional conflict may be greater. If the world is a safer place—in thermonuclear terms—it is also true that the old structure that gave shape to the political stability of the world is also gone. The world is in a state of flux. American President George Bush, Sr. spoke of a "new world order," but by the middle of the 1990s others were referring to a deepening "new world chaos."

Is the world becoming more chaotic? We don't think so. The emerging new world of the twenty-first century is certainly infused with its share of randomness and chaos, but perhaps no more than earlier transformations (in the 1880s, for instance). Social change, particularly large-scale transformation, is always messy and confusing, but we think that there are some coherent forces and trends that will give shape to the next fifty years.

LOOKING AT THE NEXT FIFTY YEARS

Human societies have always had some systemlike connections among them, but societies are increasingly interdependent as we come closer to the modern world. A *system* is a network of interconnected parts that affect each other so that change in various parts affects all the others as well as (ultimately) the nature of the system as a whole. The opposite of a system is an *aggregate* of parts or pieces that may occupy adjacent space but are minimally interdependent. This is the abstract meaning of growing global interdependence. Historically, from the seventeenth to the twenty-first century, nation-states were the most important and powerful social units of the relationships between societies. But in the emerging new world, the power and sovereignty of nation-states is being compromised in several different ways. According to Anthony Giddens (cited earlier), "in circumstances of accelerating global integration the nation-state has become too small for the big problems and too big for the small problems of life" (1990:65). You can understand the emerging new world on at least three different levels: global, regional, and local.

Globalization

The effectiveness, power, and sovereignty of nation-states is being compromised because there are many things that nation-states cannot do well without money, control, and resources from many agents in different nations; and increasingly human life is being conducted and regulated by various supranational structures and agents of various kinds. The emerging global system has four kinds of dimensions: (1) a global marketplace, (2) a global resource base, (3) global flows of popular culture, and (4) global security problems driven by demography and environmental impacts. Since we have mentioned most of these dimensions earlier, we will note them here only in summary form.

The Global Marketplace. International trade, in terms of the flow of raw materials, manufactured goods, and technology, is increasingly important to the domestic economies of all nations. There is an increasingly important global financial system of investments, loans, and currency regulations by banks, international agencies, and governments that knit together the economic fates of nations in various parts of the world. The world's most prosperous cities are those oriented to a world economy (see Chapter 5), and in many senses money, goods, and immigrants flow between the globe's world-class cities in ways that circumvent the strictures of the national governments. These cities include New York, Tokyo, Mexico City, Miami, London, Hong Kong, Moscow, and Buenos Aires (see Sassen, 1994; Castells, 1998.) In all nations, the volume of world trade has grown faster than the volume of domestic trade.

Such economic interdependency should be obvious to you as you view the volume and variety of goods on the shelves in American stores that are manufactured by our trading partners in other industrial nations. Or look at the labels on the clothes in your closet for a sense of your involvement with workers in developing countries. Many critics bemoan this loss of national economy and urge the reassertion of national control over economic life by reestablishing tariffs and cutting the ties that bind the world market system. But consider the implications of doing so. Imagine that the United States is suddenly prevented from importing foreign goods or selling our products to other nations. There would be immediate shortages of petroleum, iron ore, copper, chromium, and dozens of other strategic minerals that drive the industrial economy. Prices of many goods (from Nike shoes to computers) would skyrocket. In the short run, some workers and industries would benefit from the absence of foreign competition, but others would be devastated in the absence of international customers or suppliers. In the longer run, there would be significant price increases and a general deterioration of the economy so that the wages and living standards of most Americans would decline. Undoubtedly other nations would retaliate with their own protectionist measures, perhaps stimulating exactly what the architects of the World Bank and less regulated trade at the Bretton Woods conference in 1944 sought to avoid: another global depression like that of the 1930s, possibly followed by another world war (Ikenberry, 1996).

But the implications of this thickening web of economic connections for the future are profound and perplexing: Within all nations the nature of social life will be transformed. The introduction of the mass media and fertilizers in developing countries, for example, carry with them not only changes in the organization of work, but also altered relations among communities, altered status relationships, altered family roles, and altered relationships among people generally. Technologies bring with them new sets of values and expectations. (Consider again the impact of the diffusion of information technologies that we noted in Chapter 10.) The economic sovereignty of all nations is reduced as they become more vulnerable to the inroads of larger, transnational markets within which labor, capital, and technology flow across national borders. The perplexing question is simply this: What is the meaning of citizenship as the economic life of all people becomes more shaped by the imperatives of the global market and less by nation-states?

The Global Resource Base.   Economic globalization is driven not simply by an expanding capitalist market system, but also by vast and deepening interdependencies in access to the natural resources of the world. We noted some examples of these linkages in the last chapter by discussing energy resources. Even the wealthiest nations are becoming resource dependent. In the United States, where in the nineteenth century natural resources seemed inexhaustible, there is now neither the crude oil nor the mineral resources to sustain economic functioning. Japan is virtually devoid of most natural resources. Few nations of the Middle East are self-sufficient for food. Every nation, it turns out, needs something another nation has; some nations have almost nothing they need (Barber, 1992:55).

Information and Technology.   The internationalization of economic activity in its myriad forms depends upon the global flow of information and technology. The hardware of this system is the new communications technology of integrated computer, television, cable, satellite, laser, and microchip technologies that combine into a vast interactive communications and information network. The software is the global diffusion of science, economic technology, and culture. English is becoming the language of science and business, and the whole world speaks in logarithms and binary mathematics.

The globalization of information and technology not only provides a common matrix for the global economy; it limits political control. Television, fax machines, and satellite surveillance have made it impossible to keep political dirty little secrets, as the Soviets, the Argentineans, the Chinese, and the Mexicans have all discovered. Fax transmissions provided, for example, a running account of the Chinese regime's massacre of student protesters in Tiananmen Square in 1989, and there was nothing that the regime could do to suppress the free flow of international news as that atrocity unfolded. All societies are becoming permeable to information, and it is really becoming more difficult for regimes to manage the news.

Popular Culture.   We mentioned these dimensions of globalization earlier, but here's a new one. As much as industrial technology and information, the diffusion of popular culture is creating a global cultural system. As young people we liked the Beatles (British), and like many enjoyed the meteoric rise to international prominence of ABBA (Swedish) in the 1970s. But the United States is the unquestioned exporter of popular culture. In the 1990s the Japanese bought Hollywood film studios faster than Americans buy Japanese VCRs (Barber, 1992:58). In the summer 2001, one of the most popular movies in France was *Pearl Harbor,* the multimillion-dollar dramatization of the December 7, 1941 bombing of Pearl Harbor by the Japanese. When Leicht was traveling through Germany, France, and the Netherlands in 2001, he searched the radio dial in vain for locally produced folk music. Except for the local languages used by the disc jockeys, most of the music could have been heard in Chicago or Kansas City; much of it was produced in the United States, and a majority of the lyrics were in English. On Harper's 1990 trip to Poland, Radio Poland treated him to two hours of John Philip Sousa marches on July 4. And on a trip to China, their tour guide in Beijing proudly pointed to a two-story building overlooking Mao's tomb at Tiananmen Square to announce that they were looking at the world's largest Kentucky Fried Chicken restaurant, with a seating capacity of 400! Local culture is by no means disappearing, but American music and film, as well as Kentucky Fried Chicken in Beijing, McDonald's in Moscow, and Coca-Cola in Indonesia are creating a common (sometimes too common!) cultural layer.

Demography and Environmental Problems.   As the last chapter makes clear, environmental problems are global. Radiation from the Chernobyl nuclear plant disaster poisoned the milk of Polish schoolchildren and killed the reindeer herds of Laplanders. Acid rain from Pittsburgh kills Canadian forests, as that produced by industries in the Czech Republic does to those in southwestern Poland. The greenhouse gases accelerate not only from burning hydrocarbon fuels, but also from the Brazilian farmers who cut down the rain forests to clear farmland and by Indonesians who make a living cutting their lush jungle for lumber. There is a growing awareness of environmental problems everywhere, but, as we noted in the last chapter, it often runs counter to the desire for economic growth and a better human material life that are almost universally shared.

Let us reemphasize the national and international security problems we also noted briefly in the last chapter. Rapid population growth and environmental scarcities do not cause wars between countries, but they do sometimes sharply aggravate stresses within countries, helping to stimulate ethnic clashes, urban unrest, and insurgencies. A case in point is the continual clashes between the government of Brazil, national and multinational logging interests, and the indigenous peoples of the Brazilian rainforest. This twenty-plus-year conflict has been marked by frequent violence, murder, and destruction of property as indigenous peoples are pushed further and further inland and demand for wood harvesting and economic development in the rainforest limits native access to fishing and other natural food sources. Such violence will not be limited to developing countries. They destabilize trade and economic relations, provoking migration, and generate complex humanitarian disasters that divert militaries and absorb huge amounts of aid (Homer-Dixon, 1996:359).

Each of these five dimensions is transnational, transideological, and transcultural. They are, as Neil Smelser said long ago about the Industrial Revolution, "once-to-a-system" changes that will not go away or be easily reversible in the near future.

Their interaction will produce new formations of global elites in all societies: capitalists, politicians, researchers, and bureaucrats as well as commercial pilots, computer programmers, international bankers, media specialists, oil riggers, entertainment celebrities, ecology experts, demographers, accountants, professors, and rock musicians and star athletes. They will increasingly compose a breed of men and women for whom the particulars of religion, ethnicity, and nationality will seem only marginal elements in a working identity (Barber, 1992:55; Galtung, 1981). Whether you see the creation of a true global "ruling class" depends on definitions. But there is undoubtedly a growing homogeneity of outlook and interests among the cultural, technocratic, and political elites who negotiate with each other and manage the global system.

This emerging global order that we have sketched will not be free of problems, tensions, or deep contradictions. *First,* despite elite pretensions, there is nothing about it that is necessarily very democratic. It lends itself to surveillance as well as liberty, to new forms of manipulation and covert control as well as new kinds of participation. Fragile democracies were everywhere resurgent in the 1990s, but during the 1970s globalization flourished in junta-led Chile, in military-governed Taiwan and Korea, and in autocratic Singapore and Indonesia as well as in the democracies of Europe and North America. As we noted earlier (Chapter 12), even the emergence of democracies may only signal mainly erosion of the power of national elites and may only transmit control upward to supranational elites. *Second,* the global system is obviously compatible with a rapaciously widening chasm of social inequity—both within and between nations—unprecedented in the twentieth century. It may produce a relatively small stratum of affluent elites around the globe, but it is doubtful whether globalization by itself can deliver for the majority of the world's people on near universal human desires for equity and human progress. Even if you ignore the deteriorating circumstances of the middle classes in many developed nations, consider the far-greater insecurities and indignities suffered by about one-fifth of the world's people in 1996:

- *Income.* 1.3 billion people in developing countries live in poverty, as do 200 million in the developed countries.
- *Clean water.* 1.3 billion people in developing countries do not have access to safe water.
- *Literacy.* 900 million adults are illiterate.
- *Food.* 800 million people in developing countries have inadequate food supplies, 500 million of these are chronically malnourished, and 175 million are under the age of five.
- *Housing.* 500 million urban dwellers worldwide are homeless or do not have adequate housing; 100 million young people are homeless.
- *Preventable death.* Between 15 and 20 million people die annually because of starvation or disease aggravated by malnutrition, substandard housing, unsafe water, or poor sanitation. Ten million of these are in densely populated cities. (Renner, 1996:81)

Such inequities and insecurities will produce dangerous fissures within and between nations (Klare, 1996). Swedish social scientist Johann Galtung's (1981) political-economic analysis of these fissures began with the commonplace observation that as hand labor as a mode of economic production declines on a worldwide basis, routine production and the assembly of things will continue to be transferred to developing countries, where labor is much cheaper. Some developing countries will prosper in this international niche as centers of routine production in the world system. Developed countries will continue to exercise overwhelming control in the world market system, but increasingly through the financing, creation, and export of innovation and new technologies. But in the developed nations there will not be enough good jobs for much of the population, whose employment is likely to become increasingly marginalized. (Remember downsizing and the growth of the low-wage service sector in Chapters 3 and 4?)

All people consume, however, and in developed countries they have high expectations for living standards. While some developing countries will be ignored by the world market, even those that are not will have deep cleavages and tensions. Many are dual societies, with a more modern economic sector as well as a large traditional (or subsistence) sector. Modern or Westernized elites will increasingly exploit the non-Western or traditional part by "depriving it systematically of production factors, buying its land or evicting the tenants, exhausting its raw materials, siphoning capital accumulated through banking systems . . . and so on" (Galtung, 1981:128). There are relatively large populations in this traditional economic sector, who are either left in neglect, exist as displaced migrants to cities in developing countries, or become refugees. *But tensions arise when large numbers of people are materially unproductive and stability can only be purchased at the expense of somebody or something.* Thus Galtung envisions increasing stress within developed and developing countries, and ongoing tensions between them in terms of trade and political interaction.

The export of these tensions is another global process. Even if Galtung's analysis is true, we don't think it is a formula for an inevitable future global apocalypse or collapse, but it does signal that the emerging global system is a volatile, unstable system, with deep and intractable economic and political fissures and potentials for conflict. Those fault lines, interacting with others generated by demography and human environmental impacts, will—to say the least—require astute management.

Reemergent Localism

Globalization and its stresses are powerful forces that will inevitably shape the future. Some of its parameters are relatively well understood, even if its implications for the future are debatable. The reemergence of vibrant *localism* is another, perhaps even more volatile, force. At the same time that globalization is producing economic and political integration, there is a persisting and perhaps revitalized sense of the local, particularistic, and subnational identities in social life. In earlier chapters we mentioned the persistence of diversity within the homogenizing tendencies of the mass society. Similarly, the emergence of homogenizing trends within the global society has not led to the erosion of the local differences and loyalties.

The news headlines feature these local attachments prominently. While the organizations of the world system, such as the United Nations, the World Bank, multinational corporations, or the World Court often appear as ghostly veneers of dubious reality, the localists often appear to be the real actors—or troublemakers—of the world, and their actions increasingly affect ordinary Americans. The World Trade Center disaster of September 11, 2001 represents many things, but from our standpoint it is the most recent example of the increasingly dramatic clash between globalism and reemerging localism. America is increasingly defined as the origin of all things global and as a target of those whose cultures and identities are threatened by the homogenizing trends in global society. In one of the more interesting ironies of the past few years, the very improvements in global communications and transportation that promoted globalization in the first place now allow dissenters to take their battles straight to those who they deem responsible, wherever they are in the world. Osama Bin Laden's group of Islamic militants is only the latest and most dramatic example of a far wider set of issues and problems.

In more general terms, who are we speaking about? Dissenting minorities, sometimes nations, but more often parts of nations, as ethnic, religious, and regional subcultures. They are the turbulent Kurds, Basques and Catalonians in Spain, Puerto Rican nationalists, Ossetians, Armenians, Azerbaijanis, East Timoreans, Quebecois, Catholics of Northern Ireland, Scotch Nationalists, Abkhasians, Zulus, Berbers of the Sahara, Tamils, Sikhs, Hutus, Tutsis, and, of course, Palestinians. In the United States, they are the Sioux, the Navaho, the Mohawks, as well as the Mexican Americans and Miami Cubans and others you can probably think of. They are people with a fierce and vibrant nationalist pride and culture who refuse to be absorbed and homogenized within nation states, and certainly not within a faceless globalism of technocrats and world managers. Their identity is rooted in history rather than modernity.

They are often people who are inhabitants of states not their own, who often want a state of their own. Such were the Lithuanians, Ukrainians, Armenians, and others until the collapse of the Soviet Union. That union collapsed partly because Soviet leaders underestimated the pent-up force of such subnational loyalties of their Soviet nationalities that would explode upon loosening the bonds of empire. Yugoslavia collapsed into a historic Balkan fratricidal war among the Serbs, Bosnians, Croatians, and others that was still ongoing in 2001. The Czechs and Slovaks obtained a political divorce after being hybridized since 1920. Emerging localism often reveals nationalist prejudices that are not only ugly and deep-seated but downright murderous (Barber, 1992:61). In the great multiethnic nations, communal conflict seems as intense as ever—for example, between the Hindus, Muslims, and Sikhs in India or between the dominant Han Chinese and Tibetans of the western regions of China. And the concept of race continues as a (the?) most divisive American domestic cleavage.

Around the world, powerful nation-states often proved incapable of dissolving subnational and tribal loyalties in a framework of national solidarity. The emerging global system does not appear to be any better as a universal solvent. The sovereignty of nation-states is being compromised simultaneously by (1) the evolution of global structures and elites, and (2) devolution via the increased vitality, visibility, and mobilization of groups with local or subnational loyalties that have grievances against nation-states.

Globalism is the product of the possibilities of profit making within an expanding system of world trade as well as of the deepening interdependencies linked to resources and environmental problems. It is the product of the penetration of modern technology, ideas, and culture. It will grow because it relates to how people make a living and who they depend upon to survive. Localism is growing not because of such functional interdependencies but because it serves the needs of people for identity; it provides a sense of history and selfhood in a way that the culture of globalism seems unable to do. Localism celebrates the richness, dignity, and diversity of peoples. Globalism may be the future, but localism is about roots and history.

On the positive side, globalism is the enemy of narrowness, parochialism, isolation, fractiousness, and war. It homogenizes the historic cleavages of race, nation, and religion into a universalistic system of values and techniques. On the negative side, globalism produces a bland culture without character or color. Localism, by contrast, reproduces color, character, and the richness of diversity and human selfhood. The dark side of localism is ethnocentrism and prejudice, anger rather than tolerance, antirationality, and often war. Indeed, the world's most dangerous and destructive wars are not purely about the struggle to control resources. They are between sectarian zealots seeking to conquer the infidel. They are holy wars or jihads about identity, nationhood, and true faith. These are all matters about which rational compromise is least likely. Ongoing intracommunal strife in India, Ireland, the Middle East, and sub-Saharan Africa are examples. The conflict between Palestinians and Israelis is another case in point. In these, conflict is only partly about resources like land. It is also a conflict about identity, history, religion, and human dignity—which makes it frightfully difficult to resolve.

In sum, globalism and localism are both important world trends that will shape our future. They are in some respects polar opposites that will perhaps serve to define an important source of contradictions and tensions in the present and near future. But there is a third force that may mediate them.

Regionalism and Confederation

The global system emerges not as an undifferentiated whole, but rather as nodes of trading centers and political-strategic alliances. As the Cold War ended, the nations of the world were moving into a political-economic tripolarity of three roughly equal blocs of nations. This is yet a third way that the sovereignty of their constituent nation-states are becoming compromised. There is one forming in Western Europe, one in North America, and one in East Asia (Bergsten, 1991; Garten, 1989).

Since the early 1990s the most dramatic regional developments were made by the Europeans. Since the formation of the European Common Market by the Treaty of Rome nearly forty years ago, the European nations have cooperated in many areas, but in 1992 they formally merged into a single organic European Union (EU) in which capital, labor, and most goods flow across borders without tariffs. The EU is working toward common welfare, labor, and environmental policies, and there are plans for a common currency (the euro in 2002) and the integration of military forces. Wealthier northern nations will invest in and subsidize the southern economies (Greece, Spain, and Portugal) for an interim period to equalize European standards of prosperity and productivity. The historic national conflict and economic protectionism among the Germans, French, and Italians is at an end; the small nations have been given a voice in economic management that exceeds anything they had under the old system, which was thoroughly dominated by larger nations.

Most nations that had for years resisted joining the Common market (the British and the Scandinavians) decided to enter the EU by 1996 (though the British have had second thoughts recently). German banks will be able to serve the needs of Belgian depositors, engineers from the Netherlands would be automatically licensed in Italy, construction crews from Britain will be able to work freely on French projects, and the Portuguese will have rights to freely fish in Danish waters. European firms will increasingly merge into huge continental conglomerates and will result in the world's largest single market, reaching from Iceland to Greece and Finland to Portugal. The creation of a "common European house" was a gigantic and complex political as well as economic achievement. National identities will remain, but the Europeans will participate in a single huge economic, social, and political order.

The United States is still the single largest *national* economy in the world, but the North American Free Trade Association (NAFTA) ratified by the United States, Canada, and Mexico in 1993 makes North America an even larger integrated economic zone than the EU, and in 1994 plans were to expand NAFTA to include first Chile and then other Latin American economies in a truly hemispheric free trade zone, extending from the north shore of Alaska to Tierra del Fuego at the tip of Latin America. It could fuse the economic lives of at least 850 million people. In many ways NAFTA only ratified globalizing trends that had been under way for some time. The Canadian and Mexican economies were becoming organically tied the United States for some time (one-third of U.S. overseas investments are in Canada, and more in the single province of Ontario than in all of Japan). Notwithstanding the historic fears of Canadians about becoming an economic colony of the United States, much of the New York skyline is owned by Canadians. Along the Rio Grande, a series of bimodal metropolitan areas have been evolving for decades, on different sides of the river, that have interconnected urban economies. There was considerable political resistance to the incorporation of Mexico in NAFTA. Mexico's cheap labor promised to benefit consumers but frightened labor leaders. Some investors worried about corruption and poor infrastructure, and environmentalists worried about lack of enforcement for environmental standards in Mexico.

NAFTA is an unprecedented arrangement between developed and developing countries; no one was quite sure how it would work. Compared to the EU, NAFTA is a more purely economic agreement, without the commitment to more organic social and political union. The so-called side agreements to NAFTA envisioned a more organic social contract and laid the framework for a commission on environmental cooperation, a North American development bank, and a border commission to address troublesome U.S.-Mexican border issues. Labor unions exhibited some signs of moving into closer relationships among nations. But even now powerful groups within each nation opposed these developments, which remained largely on paper. Our sense is that a common social contract will emerge but that it will take decades.

The rapid rise of the East Asian economies in the last forty years is the most astounding case. Japan, Korea, Taiwan, Singapore, and more recently Thailand, Malaysia, and Indonesia have led the world in meteoric economic growth rates. Between 1965 and 1988, these economies increased their share of the world gross domestic product from 5 to 20 percent and some have joined the ranks of the high-income nations (World Bank, 1991:21). From Melbourne to Seoul intraregional trade and investment expanded rapidly. There was dramatic growth in virtually every nation on the Pacific Rim, but the dynamo propelling economic integration was Japan. In 1991 Japan had half the population as the United States but invested more than the Americans, was the world's largest creditor nation, and was the second largest national economy in the world (Bergsten, 1991). The real acceleration of East Asian economic integration came in 1985, when the value of the Japanese yen soared (by 1995 it had experienced just as dramatic a deflation). The Japanese bought cheaper imports from Hong Kong, South Korea, and Thailand and began to invest heavily in those nations, where labor and raw materials were cheaper. From there it was a short step to the movement of labor-intensive industries from Japan to neighboring countries while the more technologically driven industries stayed in Tokyo and Osaka.

The East Asian division of labor that was being orchestrated by Japan was far from complete but well under way in the early 1990s (Garten, 1981:16). This integration has been derailed by a persistent and chronic recession in the Japanese economy starting in 1997 and the recent (2000) economic collapse of Malaysia and Indonesia. If these economies rebound and incorporate the People's Republic of China, the East Asian economies will be the world largest conglomeration of economies and people.

While the internal integration and trade within each of these three trading blocs has grown, they remain very much dependent upon external trade among themselves and in the world market system more generally. In fact, the percentage of economic assets accounted for by international trade is about the same in the United States, Europe, and Japan and has roughly doubled in all regions since 1970 (Bergsten, 1991). In the world of superblocs some nations such as Russia, China, Brazil, and India, remain nonaligned, and they could become future battlegrounds for economic incorporation. Further, multinationals continue to roam the mazelike structure of the world economy, irrespective of region. Hughes Aircraft builds satellites for Australia to mount on Chinese rockets, and Japanese banks were major investors in the much advertised tunnel under the English Channel linking motor transportation of Britain to the continent. Mergers and investments between firms in different blocs such as those between Bridgestone and Firestone (tires) and the First Boston Bank and Credit Suisse are too common for the regional blocs to be airtight.

There are some negative possibilities in the future development of the tripartite regional blocs. Triads are notoriously unstable. Any possible combination of two against one could be imagined. Many in Europe would like to gang up with the

United States against East Asia. Others fear that a unified Europe would become an inward-looking, discriminatory outfit that would shut us out and consider our more natural interest to be with the Pacific Rim nations. Finally, one could imagine Europe and the Asians ganging up on the United States (and others in the Western Hemisphere). They have been griping for years about the failure of Americans to come to grips with some fundamental internal problems—monetary policies, trade imbalances, and low savings rates, for instance. Any such two-against-one combination could destabilize the whole system (Bergsten, 1991).

On the other hand there are positive possibilities. The regional blocs could develop what Bergsten (1991) calls "competitive interdependence," a deliberate oxymoron meaning that each works to improve its own competitive position while at the same time working to develop new modes of managing and stabilizing the global system. This is difficult, unprecedented, but not inconceivable in the emerging scheme of things. Hegemony in the world system has always been the property, sometimes by default, of a single state. The British, with the power of the pound sterling and the Royal Navy, managed and dominated the old colonial system of the eighteenth and nineteenth centuries, a prerogative that they abdicated after World War I. After World War II American dollars and military might managed the postwar system and held together the alliance of "free world" industrial nations.

To some extent, the United States is still a critical linchpin binding regional confederations and still exercises the remnants of hegemonic power. The United States has an enormous number of trade and historic political ties with Europe. Some of these, like the North Atlantic Treaty Organization (NATO), date from World War II. Cross-region investment between the United States and Europe is large and dense. Which foreign nationals do you think in 2001 had the largest investment in American property and companies? Did you guess the Japanese? Wrong. It was the British. Further, the United States emphasized its role as a global power by hosting the 2001 World Trade Organization Conference in Seattle, Washington. The nations of the world in all regional confederations still see the United States as a critical broker of effective military security, humanitarian relief, peacekeeping, or election monitoring (as recent cases of Haiti, Bosnia, Rwanda, and the Middle East demonstrate).

Even if American hegemony continues a slow decline (as we think it will), collective leadership among three roughly equal confederations of nations is unprecedented. But its chances of working are, we think, better than fair. The constituent nations of the three blocs have been political and military allies for more than fifty years. They have a habit of cooperating, rather successfully, on economic matters. The core nations in each bloc are all stable democracies. Moreover, the best interests of the nations of the world overwhelmingly favor the development of outward-looking trading blocs working in a framework of cooperative allied relations. The other direction points to a contraction of world trade, recession, and perhaps war.

At the beginning of the section we argued that the rise of tripartite regionalism may offer the best hope of mediating between the dark sides of bland technocratic globalism and intolerant retribalization. Why? *First,* while the global system is rational, it is driven by the imperatives of efficiency and profits rather than any sense of civic obligation. The global market system and the multinational corporations that drive it are superb mechanisms for generating wealth, not for promoting civic well-being, human dignity, or social justice. Localism, on the other hand, is all about human dignity and identity and is little concerned with economic rationality or broader global stability. A world with powerful yet outward-looking regional trading blocs seems (to us) to be the best way of combining concerns for economic rationality, efficiency, and stability with commitments to the welfare of concrete persons in civil societies that only states can make.

Second, with the post-Cold War diminution of superpower hegemony, such tripartite economic blocs are inherently voluntaristic, broadly representative, and democratic—unlike the global system and localism. The form this would ideally take is that of a confederational union of semiautonomous nations (and perhaps smaller communities) tied together into regional economic associations and markets—participatory and self-determining in local matters at the bottom, but representative and accountable at the top.

Third, it seems to us that powerful regional economic blocs formed by democratic polities can best nourish effective multilateral organizations (such as the UN and the World Bank) and a global civil society of civic movements and nongovernmental organizations. We think these are both required to coordinate and manage the frightful problems and fractiousness of the combination of globalism and often lethal localism involved with such problems as international drug trafficking, malnutrition, terrorism, environmental degradation.

PROPHETIC VISIONS: SOME LONGER VIEWS

Let's shift the time frame from the next fifty years to well into the latter half of the twenty-first century. We deal with two scenarios that are a good deal fuzzier and more speculative, but they are very different. These are arguments mainly about the infinite sustainability of growth (in population and material consumption). One is very optimistic and the other is more pessimistic, but, as you will see, even the pessimistic one has a vision of a positive human future embedded within it. Each provides some hope for a better human future, but in very different terms, and they form the outer boundaries of speculation and debate about the future that has been going on for at least the last fifty years. Without tracing the whole history of that debate, we begin with the two most articulate scenarios.

Prophets of Boom

Since the 1960s, Herman Kahn (the late director of the Hudson Institute) and his colleagues have constantly articulated arguments in favor of a bright global future. In the words of Kahn and Phelps:

> We offer a generally optimistic view of the economic present and future, but with caution and qualifications. We believe that barring serious bad luck or bad management, the prospects for achieving eventually a high level of broadly

worldwide economic affluence and beneficent technology are bright, that this is a good and logical goal for mankind, and that our images of the economic future may substantially determine our progress toward that goal. (1979:202)[2]

How so? Kahn argued that global change now and in the future is part of a *great transition* that began with industrialization in the 1700s. He and his colleagues maintained that "in much the same way that the Agricultural Revolution spread round the world, the Industrial Revolution has been spreading and causing a permanent change in the quality of human life. However, instead of lasting 10,000 years, this second diffusion process is likely to be largely completed with a total span of about 400 years or roughly by the late twenty-second century" (Kahn, Brown, and Martel, 1976:20).

The great transition has three phases, encompassing (1) the Industrial Revolution and industrial societies of the early twentieth century; (2) the super-industrial economy—meaning the emerging global economy of high technologies, service industries, and multinational corporations; and (3) the future transition to a true postindustrial society. These phases overlap and complement each other in time in different parts of the world but, according to Kahn, the general pattern of evolution is clear. Kahn expects the general pattern of the great transition to follow an S-shaped curve. That is, from the 1800s there were exponential increases in world population, the gross world product (GWP), and per-capita incomes. Beginning in the mid-1970s there was, and will continue into the future, a leveling of world population growth and a decline in previously exponential rates of world economic growth, but a continuous spread of affluence so that world per-capita incomes will continue to increase. Kahn and his colleagues are at pains to stress that the slowing of economic growth will occur because with the spread of affluence, there will be a reduction in the growth of *demand,* rather than shortages of *supply.*

In the 1970s there began to be a gap, which will continue for some time, between the living standards of the poor and the rich nations, a gap that Kahn argues is inevitable as industrialism spreads and living standards are raised in some parts of the world relative to others. But he argues that this is analogous to the misery of the working and living conditions of early industrialism, which eventually spread better living conditions to all classes in industrial societies. In this position Kahn was reflecting a central proposition of developmentalist theory in the 1970s—that though development produced growing inequalities, those would diminish over time. We only note that by 2001 that has yet to happen. Maybe it's too soon. You can see Kahn's depiction of the great transition and his estimates of changes in population growth, the gross world product, and per-capita incomes in Figure 14–1.

By 2175 Kahn and his colleagues expect superindustrial societies to be everywhere and true postindustrial ones to be rapidly emerging in many places. The colonization and economic utilization of space will be substantial. They predict after this date a slowing down of both population and economic growth rates, not only in percentage terms but in absolute numbers. But the slowdown of economic growth rates does not mean a decline in standards of living because of (1) the economies of scale that accompany large-scale systems, and (2) intensive technological progress that

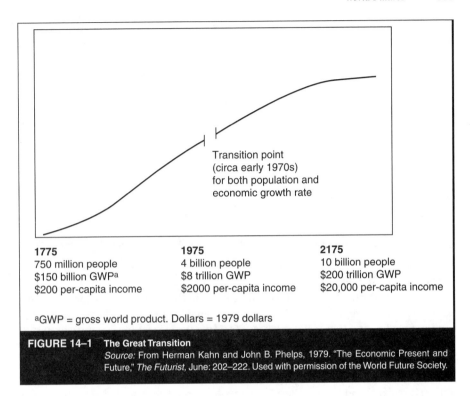

1775	1975	2175
750 million people	4 billion people	10 billion people
$150 billion GWP[a]	$8 trillion GWP	$200 trillion GWP
$200 per-capita income	$2000 per-capita income	$20,000 per-capita income

[a]GWP = gross world product. Dollars = 1979 dollars

FIGURE 14–1   **The Great Transition**
Source: From Herman Kahn and John B. Phelps, 1979. "The Economic Present and Future," *The Futurist,* June: 202–222. Used with permission of the World Future Society.

will provide energy savings and will substitute new resources for scarce ones. Thus in the context of growing economic efficiency, rapid advances in technology, and a stabilizing world population, unparalleled affluence can be sustained on a global basis.

What kind of social world does this vision of the future imply? Before the end of the twentieth century, Kahn and his colleagues expect to see a world of extremely large-scale, specialized, and complex economic and political systems with global interconnections. They envision "increasing worldwide unity in technology, private industry, commercial and financial institutions, but relatively little unity in international legal and political institutions. Despite much hostility [there will be] a continuing, even growing, importance of multinational corporations as innovators and diffusers of economic activity and rapid growth" (Kahn, Brown, and Martel, 1976, cited in Freeman and Jahoda, 1978:48).

Technological developments may provide some basis for flexibility and decentralization, but the need for large-scale coordination and management will mean that political and economic power will still be significantly centralized. Since the societies of the future will be technology intensive, they will be, according to Kahn, increasingly dominated by specialists, technocratic elites, and what they call the "knowledge industry." The "problem of production" will progressively be "solved," and most people will work in service and/or information industries. Culturally, it will be a world dominated by values that are secular, pragmatic, utilitarian, manipulative, and hedonistic. Affluence will gradually diffuse on a global basis, so that there will be an end to the more absolute forms of poverty, but much more attention will be paid to the disruptive ecological effects of economic activity than at present. While they recognize problems and dangers and do not think that progress will come smoothly or painlessly, Kahn and his colleagues "think that it is not very practical to adopt any deliberate alternative to growth, and it is probably safer to keep on growing than to try to stop. Attempting to change the historical trend would either have little effect or lead to disaster" (Kahn and Phelps, 1979:211).

In a nutshell, the "prophets of boom" accept the present trends of change as basically benign. It is a *cornucopian* view of the future. With faith in human good will and inventiveness, they would counsel full steam ahead!

Prophets of Gloom

There is, as you might guess, a more pessimistic vision of the future that stands in sharp contrast to the optimistic forecast of Kahn and his colleagues. The most influential view resulted from a 1960s futurist think tank called the Club of Rome, which was originally located in Italy and sponsored by a variety of industrialists and multinational corporations. Rather than relying on the mental and intuitive models of Kahn and his colleagues, the methodology of the Club of Rome used an elaborate computer simulation called a *world system dynamics (WSD) model,* developed by Massachusetts Institute of Technology scientists Jay Forrester, Donella Meadows, Jorgen Randers, and their colleagues. The MIT modelers started with what was known about current patterns and trends in population growth, economic growth, resource consumption, food supply, and pollution effects, each of which had been growing exponentially. They then developed an elaborate set of coefficients for how continued growth in each of these areas would impact the others. They ran the model backward in time to see if it reflected known history (it did) and then forward in time to project the sum of these interactions into the future for several hundred years.

The result, published in 1972 as *The Limits to Growth,* depicted a classic outbreak-crash pattern familiar to biological ecologists (Meadows et al., 1972). It is what happens when populations of animals (say, deer) grow at such a rate that they strip the environment of available food supplies. After doing so, their population declines precipitously. The human outbreak-crash pattern predicted by the WSD model argues that current exponential growth in population, resource consumption, and food production will produce such enormous stress on the carrying capacity of the planet by 2100 that the resource and capital inputs to support such consumption levels will not be sustainable. So much investment of wealth is required to obtain dwindling supplies of natural gas, silver, petroleum, nickel, zinc, and other resources to maintain world industrial development that capital investments can no longer keep up with the growing needs. This shortfall prevents increases in fertilizer production, heath care, education, and other vital activities. Without food and necessary services, world population and living standards will undergo a steady decline shortly after the

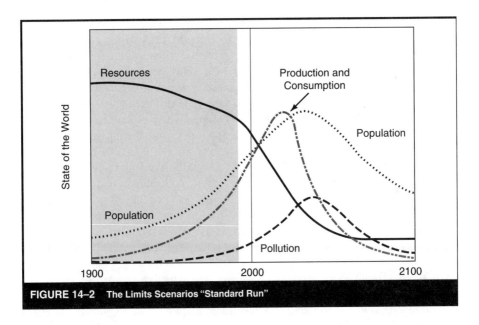

FIGURE 14–2   The Limits Scenarios "Standard Run"

beginning of the twenty-first century (Humphrey and Buttel, 1982:97–98). This is depicted in Figure 14–2, in what the MIT analysts called their "standard run," reflecting world conditions in the early 1990s. Though similar to their findings in 1972, Figure 14-2 is actually from newer data and a revised model published in 1992.

The MIT world systems modelers produced a large variety of computer runs of the simulation to reflect more optimistic assumptions (e.g., doubling resource supply estimates, controlling population growth and pollution effects), but the result was the same: At some time shortly after the turn of the century (2100), growth would be unsustainable. The problem was not any single dimension but the cumulative effects of the way that they interact. And the underlying problem is growth itself. Hence the MIT modelers emphasized the urgency of global efforts to dampen exponential economic growth itself (not just population growth and pollution side effects) and efforts to move toward a steady-state world. In this view, it is not enough to simply wait for markets to adjust to scarcity of food and nonrenewable resources; by that time irreversible declines in ecological equilibrium and resource availability may have already taken place, and a variety of points of no return may have been passed. Nor can technology save us. All that technological advances can do is delay the inevitable end, since dominant cultural patterns and institutional arrangements perpetuate conditions of profligate consumption and "problem solving by growth" that are in the end self-defeating and environmentally destructive. The specter raised by this vision is that if present trends continue, after 2100 a smaller human population will be eking out a more marginal existence on an exhausted and polluted planet.

Within a year of its publication in 1972, *The Limits to Growth* was attacked from all sides in a blizzard of commentary. It was sharply refuted by a group of British economists and physical scientists. Their report, titled *Models of Doom: Critiques of "The Limits to Growth,"* agreed in principle with techniques of mathematical model building but sharply disagreed with many particular assumptions and conclusions (Cole et al., 1973). Others criticized their use of aggregated world data, arguing that different regions are likely to fare quite differently. Another criticism was more ethical than scientific: Efforts to dampen world economic growth would have the most dire consequences for the poor nations of the south, particularly in the absence of global political initiatives to promote a more equitable distribution of global resources. These kinds of distributional questions are not addressed by the MIT modelers (see Oltmans, 1974 for an interesting collection of comments).

Subsequent publications addressed some but not all of these concerns (Mesarovic and Pestel, 1974; Tinbergen, 1976). The tone of these reports was more moderate, but still pessimistic. In fact, the newest by WSD modelers, entitled *Beyond the Limits* (1996), concludes that in some ways, the world population has already exceeded the earth's limits. Evidence, for instance, of declining per-capita food production is now quite widespread, as we documented in the last chapter. *Yet they argue that economic and ecological collapse is not inevitable and that there are ways of achieving sustainable development.* Given rapid and effective population stabilization measures, investment in technical efficiencies, and further controls on pollutants and soil erosion, the world could comfortably support a larger population (of, say, 8 billion persons) until at least 2100. But time grows short, and "delaying the transition to a sustainable world has already had its costs" (Meadows et al., 1992:201). In 2001 there were already 6.1 billion people in the world.

Appropriate Technology and Voluntary Simplicity. Other ideas about desirable futures coexisted with the limits scenario. As well as policy and technology, they emphasized culture and lifestyle changes. Their proponents maintained that learning to live with limits is not just a nasty necessity, but could be a basis for better lifestyles—though they would be ones in which material consumption and rapid growth are not primary values. They advocated the adoption of appropriate technologies, that is, "technologies that are best able to match the needs of all people in a society in a sustainable relationship with the environment" (Humphrey and Buttel, 1982:187). In contrast to complex high technologies, they are often (1) simpler (and can be understood and repaired by the people who use them), (2) less prone to failures (as are more complex technological systems), and (3) have less severe ecological side effects.

More appropriate technology includes the substitution of organic fertilizers for inorganic ones that have deleterious effects on soil and water and the substitution of wind-generated electricity for coal or nuclear electricity. Generating electricity by nuclear plants to watch TV or light rooms when wind power is practical, cheaper, and less environmentally intrusive is compared in this scenario to cutting butter with a chainsaw! The most articulate spokesperson for the use of appropriate technology was the late British economist E. F. Schumacher, whose book *Small Is Beautiful* was widely influential (1973; see also Lovins, 1977). The adoption of appropriate technologies would alleviate some environmental problems that go with complex high-tech solutions and systems. Furthermore, they tend to be *decentralized* strategies that would alleviate the problems of overcomplexity, alienation, and the powerlessness of people in large-scale, bureaucratic, and highly centralized economic and energy systems.

In the 1970s, a sort of intellectual and cultural movement developed around these themes. It encouraged people to change their lifestyles toward voluntary simplicity (Elgin, 1981). By living more frugally and simply, individuals (particularly in developed nations) could change patterns of consumption and reduce pollution and environmental disruption. How many people were experimenting with real voluntary simplicity is not known. Voluntary simplicity is less convenient than the average American lifestyle. It values simple rather than fancy habits and appliances (e.g., cooking from scratch rather than eating convenience foods, using clotheslines rather than clothes dryers, bicycling or using mass transportation). It requires planning and foresight. Its advocates argued that lowering material consumption need not deprive people of things that really matter, like conversation, family and community gatherings, theater, music, and spirituality (Durning, 1992:140–141).

It may not be lost on you that the concept of voluntary simplicity runs counter to the powerful consumerist culture (and the wishes of the advertising industry!) in the developed nations. Our assessment is that relatively few Americans have been willing to give up life in the fast lane for the virtues of a simpler, less hurried life. Furthermore, voluntary simplicity has little appeal to the world's poor, who already live in involuntary simplicity of a more malevolent kind.

The Two Visions: Analysis

Here are two strikingly different visions of the future. One is a cornucopian vision of the future in which human ingenuity and technological innovation provide the basis for the present trajectories of world population and growth in material consumption to continue indefinitely. The other envisions a world of limits, where present trends of population and consumption cannot continue indefinitely without dire human consequences. We noted earlier that these two views constituted a debate about human interactions with the planet that has been raging since the 1940s. In 1948, two scholars independently saw human populations degrading the planet disastrously unless we reversed the trends of human deterioration (Osborn, 1948; Voght, 1948). That was countered by the more optimistic projections of many business and political leaders, who foresaw a brilliant future with the end of poverty, the conquest of disease, and an abundant life (Sarnoff et al., 1956). Kahn and his colleagues, and then the world systems modelers, simply elaborated the ongoing debate. In 1982, a report was published by an advisory branch to the U.S. president, the Council of Environmental Quality, in collaboration with twelve federal agencies and more than 150 scientific experts.[3] The conclusions of this report, *The Global 2000 Report to the President,* were alarming and pessimistic. The report summarized: "If present trends continue, the world in 2000 will be more crowded, more polluted, less stable ecologically and more vulnerable to disruption. Serious stresses involving population, resources, and the environment are clearly visible ahead. Despite greater material output, the world's people will be poorer in many ways. . . . For the millions of desperately poor, the outlook for food and necessities will not be better than today, and for many it will be worse. Barring revolutionary technological advances, life on the earth will be more precarious in 2000 than it is now—unless the nations of the world act decisively to alter current trends" (Council on Environmental Quality, 1980: 1). The overall message of *The Global 2000 Report* was not one of despair but of great concern and pessimism if trends continued. It attempted to focus political concerns of the United States and other governments on these issues.

Predictably, critics responded immediately. Herman Kahn (then still living) and economist Julian Simon took up the debate and responded at a scientific meeting in 1983:

> If present trends continue, the world in 2000 will be less crowded (though more populous), less polluted, more stable ecologically, and less vulnerable to resource-supply disruption than the world we live in now. Stresses involving population, resources, and environment will be less in the future than now. . . . The world's people will be richer in most ways than they are today. . . . The outlook for food and other necessities of life will be better [and] life for most people on the earth will be less precarious economically than it is now. (Simon and Kahn, 1984)

Their optimistic view emphasized that

- Life expectancies have been rising in most of the world, indicating demographic, scientific, and economic progress.
- Food supplies have improved dramatically since World War II. Actual famine death rates have declined.
- The availability of cropland will not constrain agriculture in the future.
- Mineral resources are becoming more abundant rather than less, and world oil prices may fall below present levels.
- Threats of air and water pollution have been vastly exaggerated. (cited in Southwick, 1996: 86)

After the death of Herman Kahn, economist Julian Simon (2000) inherited his role as the chief articulator of the view that current trends are producing a positive, cornucopian future. Less optimistic WSD modelers published an update in 1992 (*Beyond the Limits*). By 1995, some environmental journalists were more optimistic, writing about the improvement of many U.S. environmental problems, if not worldwide ones (McKibben, 1995; Easterbrook, 1995). The controversy continues.

What is going on here? How can different analysts disagree so much about the future? How do they do so even when they look at the same world and sometimes use the same facts? Which view has the closest approximation to the actual future? The debate is often sterile and unproductive, with each side grasping a portion of the truth, but not the whole truth. Still, it is an important controversy to understand, and not just one for scholars, but for people around the world and their children (including you and us).

Part of the answer to these questions has to do with differences in the training and mindsets of the two groups of analysts, who by their training have learned to think about the world in different ways. They have different paradigms for the way the world works. Scenarios emphasizing future limits were created by persons from a variety of scientific backgrounds, including population experts, environmental scientists and ecologists, hydrologists, physical scientists and geologists, mathematics and computer modelers, soil scientists, biologists, climatologists, and some social scientists. Scenarios emphasizing more optimistic cornucopian futures were created by economists, business people, technical experts in management, and journalists. Clearly, the two groups of analysts look at the same situation from different points of view (Brown, 1991:5–9; Harper, 1996:48–58).

Another part of the answer to these questions has to do with the selectivity of people's view of the world and its future. No scholars or writers are completely exempt from this. For example, you can view the United States and see tremendous progress in science, education, economics, and well-being. Or you can see alarming problems of urban ghettos, homeless populations, toxic waste dumps, and social decline. What is the real truth? For whom? Selectivity is even more of a problem when viewing the world. It is perfectly possible to tour the world by jet aircraft and air-conditioned taxi, stay in luxury hotels, and come away with the impression of great progress and prosperity. Likewise, you can tour the world visiting urban slums, refugee camps, exhausted deserts, and areas of war and terrorism, and conclude that the visions of doom are here to haunt us today (Southwick, 1996:88).

Considering this, it is no wonder that different analysts can look at the world today, think about the future, and reach totally different conclusions. Between scenarios written by the overwhelming consensus within scientific communities and those written by business leaders, economists, and journalists, which do you trust the most to sort through facts and fancies, and to come to grips with objectivity and reality? In the last chapter we cited official statements by the world's most respected scientific communities. We have more trust in their assessment. But the optimists provide a key insight: We should focus on human ingenuity to increasing limits, as well as the limits themselves. Many societies adapt well to scarcities and problems and often wind up better than they were before. The limits the world faces are a product of both its physical context and the ingenuity it can bring to bear on that context. But we may face a widening *ingenuity gap,* and some parts of the world are locked into the rising need for ingenuity and the limited capacity to supply it (Homer-Dixon, 1996:365).

A better future for most of the world and its people? This is the really important question, but I'm sure you recognize it as an outrageously complex and difficult one. The most intellectually honest answer is, "Who knows?" But one can have hope for a better future and still accept a fairly pessimistic interpretation of the evidence, as we do. In thinking about adapting, inventing, and managing our way to positive futures, please remember that history provides some examples of massive social transformations and relatively successful management of problems. Earlier pessimists thought them unlikely. Examples? In the nineteenth century, feudalism was abandoned in Japan, as was slavery around the world. This century saw the retreat of imperialism and the creation of a united Europe. War provides obvious examples. Given the belief that national survival was at stake during World War II, the U.S. population mobilized and transformed itself in remarkable ways. The Marshall Plan for the reconstruction of Europe after the war was equally impressive. In 1947, America spent nearly 3 percent of its GNP on this huge set of projects (Ruckelshaus, 1990: 131–132). By 1990, similarly, the Soviet empire had collapsed, an event long thought unlikely by many realists of the time–even Sovietologists. Remarkably, in 1993 the Union of South Africa transformed itself peacefully and democratically from a country with a brutal, authoritarian government and racial caste system into a democratic, multiethnic society with a black man as its elected president.

For relatively successful global management, consider the creation of world weather forecasting, the control of electromagnetic wavelengths for communication with minimum chaos, progress in the eradication of infectious diseases, the regulation of international civil aviation, research for agricultural development, various efforts at UN peacekeeping and peacemaking and attempts to provide relief for refugees, cooperation in Antarctica and outer space, and, in spite of their weaknesses, agreement about a law of the sea, treaties about ozone production and biodiversity (Cleveland, 1993: 51–55). All of these examples of social change or global scale management efforts signaled progress. None brought complete success, and they do not guarantee a brighter future. But they do provide hope, and hope is essential for positive change.

IN CONCLUSION: THE THIRD REVOLUTION

From beginning to end, this book has referred to a fundamental human transformation we are now living through—but in piecemeal terms. We bring to a close looking at the future as well as the book by exploring this transformation more coherently. If the collapse of the Soviet Union was a hinge of history, closing a door on one epoch and opening a door on another one, this transformation is a much larger one. It is only the third great transformation in human history that fundamentally changed human livelihoods, culture and social life, and connections with nature. You know the earlier transformations: (1) the *Agricultural Revolution* of Neolithic times, and (2) the *Industrial Revolution* beginning in the 1600s (see Chapter 5). As major transformations, the first stretched thousands of years and the second started several hundred years ago. They were truly revolutionary in historic retrospect but probably did not seem so from the vantage point of people living them out one day at a time.[4]

During the *Agricultural Revolution* of Neolithic times, many humans transformed themselves from hunter-gatherers to horticulturists, or cultivators of grains. That change was based on the diffusion of certain discoveries and innovations, but also on the tendencies of hunter-gatherers to consume beyond the limits of their wild food supply. Agriculture amplified people's impact on the environment and changed their attitudes, as wilderness changed from a source of sustenance to areas of weeds, pests, and predators to be cleared for gardens and fields. Thus the Agricultural Revolution was both a fundamental transformation of society and of human-environment relations. By enabling populations to grow large and remain settled, it produced a fundamental change toward increased differentiation that transformed a simple system organized around kinship to complex systems of stratified social classes and specialized institutions.

The second great transformation, the *Industrial Revolution,* is a little more than two hundred years old. Like the Agricultural Revolution, the Industrial Revolution was stimulated by critical inventions and environmental shortages (e.g., the virtual clear-cutting of English timber by the late 1600s). Also like the Agricultural Revolution, it enabled human populations to grow much larger than previously. Like farming, industrialization transformed social forms. These included the *urban revolution,* as increasing proportions of the population lived in cities and engaged in nonagricultural occupations; a state revolution, as the loosely organized kingdoms of agricultural societies evolved into powerful national governments; and a *bureaucratic revolution,* as huge complex organizations came to organize and dominate many spheres of life. Like the Agricultural Revolution, the Industrial Revolution magnified the human impact on natural environments, separated people from the biophysical world, and led humans to believe that they were not dependent upon it. But in reaction, the industrial degradation of the land also led people to romanticize nature and produced environmental movements. Most developing countries are somewhere in transition between agricultural and industrial societies, which is why their potential for environmental destruction is truly massive if they repeat historic development trajectories (Olsen, 1991: 564–566; Harrison, 1993:300–301).

These first two human revolutions are still with us and have not yet run their course. But many observers believe that we are in the midst of another transformation that is a reworking of industrialism, even as it transformed agricultural societies. For want of a better terrain, we'll call it simply the *Third Revolution.* Intellectuals and scholars have been observing this phenomenon for several decades in terms of very different social and theoretical perspectives. Some describe the evolution of postindustrial societies. Some describe an emerging *information society.* Some have depicted the transmutation of the assumptions and social forms of modern societies (modernity) into postmodern ones. Some see an emerging world of New Age spirituality. And around the world, fundamentalists of all sorts, religious as well as cultural, recognize that their traditional world is under attack by currents of change. As you can see, with so many versions of this Third Revolution, it is hard to know now how label it. Our guess is that within this new century there will be a consensus about how to describe it. But all of these perspectives agree that massive pressures for social change are accumulating in societies, and that the result will be major, not minor, alterations (Olsen, 1991:568).

In spite of various descriptions, some emerging aspects of the Third Revolution are clear. First, it will be an *information revolution,* meaning that the creation, storage, transmission, and utilization of all kinds of information—especially scientific and technical knowledge—will become as primary a force in human societies as growing food and making things were in the past. We will still, of course, need food and things, but increasingly specialized information will drive the creation of wealth, the old productive forces will be increasingly controlled by information technology (as in computers), and a majority of workers will handle information, not plants, animals, or machines (Olsen, 1991:565). This is not a new argument (see Chapters 4 and 10), but information technology is not necessarily the gateway to utopia, as some enthusiasts have implied. In terms of human-environment relations, it may be neutral: It enhances our capacity to plunder the environment on a large scale and won't necessarily make us more environmentally frugal. But the correlation between economic growth and ecological destruction is weakening, and information technology may bring less per-capita—but not aggregate—resource consumption.

The *second* aspect of the Third Revolution that is increasingly clear is the *interdependence revolution*. We have said a lot about this trend in the last few chapters. We are being pulled together into integrated yet volatile webs of interdependencies that have many social and environmental dimensions. It used to be possible to study communities and cities, theoretically at least, as distinct entities with their own internal dynamics without paying much attention to the political, economic, demographic, and environmental forces that impinge upon them from other regions. No more. This does not mean that regional or local differences, concerns, and attachments will disappear. Far from it: we noted earlier that the postcommunist world is full of local groups struggling for autonomy. We can no longer behave as if other people around the world don't matter. As with the information revolution, growing human interdependence has mixed implications for reshaping the human future. The important point is that whatever else the Third Revolution is, these two dimensions will be so interwoven in it that it will be an informational-interdependence revolution (Olsen, 1991:566; Castells, 1998).

A *third* aspect of the Third Revolution may be a *sustainability revolution*. We say "may be," because this is not as certain to be a part of the forthcoming big transition as are the informational-interdependence revolutions. It now seems unavoidable that the world that you and your children live in will be warmer, more crowded, more interconnected, and more socially diverse, with less wilderness, fewer species, and a more constrained food-producing system. In an extraordinarily short period, a matter of decades, we will need to feed, house, nurture, educate and employ at least as many more people as already live on the earth. Still, people may succeed in creating a reasonably secure and sustainable world of global organizations, nations, communities, groups, and families. We know a lot about what is required, but doing it is something else, because doing it threatens established social practices and structures of power everywhere. We now know that both social and environmental sustainability require greater equity among the world's people. That a sustainability revolution is part of the coming Third Revolution is possible, but it is also a hope.

Human ingenuity, rational choice-making capacity, and growing awareness of our darkening social, political, and environmental predicaments of the next century all make a bright future more likely. But there is certainly enough evidence around to justify pessimism. Even so, as we argued earlier about the process of social change, outcomes are not predetermined but depend on contingencies and human agency.

The happy ending will not naturally evolve, nor are we trapped by powerful forces that will destroy us. Where we arrive in between these outcomes is up to you and your children, and their children. Hope is simply a necessity if we are to survive the incredible human journey.

THINKING PERSONALLY ABOUT SOCIAL CHANGE

1. The future is full of promise, but also uncertainty and threats. Consequently, writers and some scholars deal with both future utopias and dystopias. There seems to be more of a market for the latter these days! What kinds of problems do you foresee that are most likely to affect you personally? Your children? Conversely, what are some possibilities for a brighter future? Personally, what talents, skills, or attitudes can help you have a good future?

2. Talk to some people who are different from you. Do they envision the future very differently? What are the factors that you think make them either more, or less, optimistic than you?

3. It's easy to talk about societies that are sustainable both socially and environmentally. What are some things that you think need to be done to realize that vision? What are some important barriers? Personally, how might you arrange your own life to help that process? Why should you care?

4. Here's a quote from Gandhi, leader of the Indian independence movement, and inspirer of much of the thinking of the "small is beautiful" movement: "Civilization, in the real sense of the term, consists not in the multiplication of wants, but in their deliberate and voluntary reduction." Do you agree with him? Why or why not?

NOTES

1. Given the perennial fascination of writing about the future, it is hard to locate historically the beginning of contemporary futurism. We are talking about a social network of thinkers that emerged in the 1960s and included such widely popular writers as Alvin Toffler (*Future Shock,* 1970; *The Third Wave,* 1980) and John Naisbitt (*Megatrends,* 1982), as well as scholars from virtually all academic disciplines. Structurally, contemporary futurism has its own organizations (the largest of which is the World Future Society), conferences, and periodicals. Some futurists are freefloating intellectuals who have carved out for themselves unique careers as writers, speakers, and business consultants. At the other end of the movement are the highly structured and more academic think tanks concerned wholly or partly about the future. These would include the Hudson Institute (Herb London), the Worldwatch Institute (Lester Brown and his colleagues), The Club of Rome (Forrester, Meadows et al.), the Social Policy Research Unit at Sussex University in the United Kingdom (Freeman, Cole, and Jahoda), the Modrzhinskaya and Kosolapov groups in the Soviet Union, and the Bariloche Foundation in Argentina.

2. Kahn's writings are voluminous and we make no attempt to survey them here in any comprehensive way. The most elaborate early statement of his perspective is Kahn and Weiner (1967). We have relied here mainly on the short article by Kahn and Phelps (1979).

3. Besides the Council on Environmental Quality, there were the U.S. Departments of Agriculture, Energy, and the Interior; the Agency for International Development; the Environmental Protection Agency; the Central Intelligence Agency; the Federal Emergency Management Agency; the National Science Foundation; the National Aeronautics and Space Administration; the National Oceanic and Atmospheric Administration; and the Office of Science and Technology Policy.

4. Adapted from Harper, 1996:393–396, copyright by Prentice Hall; used with permission.

Epilogue:
Living in a Rapidly Changing World

We began this book by describing some important changes in the lives of individuals in our own families. But most of the book has been about large-scale structural and cultural change. We would like to end by returning briefly to the level of the changing lives of individuals. *What are some lessons that can be drawn from our exploration of social change about how individuals cope with change?* There are four major points that we would like to leave you with about living in a changing world, some drawn from the material of the book and some, admittedly, from our own personal philosophies.

1. *Expect change.* That may sound too obvious, but we think all of us have a longing for a world that is sheltered from the uncertainty of change. It is tempting to think that our lives will stop changing after we successfully conquer the next hurdle (whatever that may be—graduation, a new job, a new marriage). We want the world to settle down and stabilize. But alas, we think that is an illusion. Life is a continuous process of adapting to change. Life is not a safe harbor, but a hazardous journey on an open sea, and its final destination (short of death) is always uncertain, both individually and collectively. We think the important thing about expecting change is not only to attempt to understand its directions, but also to learn to live with a degree of ambiguity and uncertainty.

2. *Understand change.* While it is true that the outcomes of change are always uncertain, there are nonetheless some major trends and dimensions of change that one can understand. The more you understand about these trends and the mechanisms by which they take place, the easier it will be for you to live in a changing world. This book is, we hope, a modest contribution to your understanding of change and change processes in the contemporary world. It has emphasized the importance of understanding the relationship between macro and micro change and the idea that changes in the personal and family lives of people are embedded in macroscopic change (in institutions and large-scale structures). Such macro change conditions and limits the possibil-

ities we have as individuals, but seldom are we left without any maneuvering room or alternatives as to how we might adapt to such changes.

Another major emphasis of this book has been the importance of what might be called *system thinking* about change: understanding how change in one unit or dimension is connected to changes in other elements of a larger system. In some ways, system thinking is fundamentally at odds with how we are taught to think in the United States. We learn to isolate one aspect or dimension of life and focus on its development in a fragmented way without understanding its connections to other things or levels of change. Sometimes this is called tunnel vision. But we need to be able to think about change in a contextual way and understand how various dimensions and levels of social reality interact. That is admittedly not easy. Again, we hope that this book has contributed to your ability to see things in a systemic fashion.

In the introductory chapter we introduced some common distinctions about different kinds of change (linear versus cyclical, short term versus long term). One of those distinctions in particular we would like to return to: that between changes driven by deep structural causes and changes driven by changing rules of the game. From the standpoint of the individual person, changes driven by deep structural causes may be virtually irreversible. Change driven by technology is of this sort, as is the increasing scale of social life, the growth of the human population, and the likelihood of ecological constraints on human economic activity. The emergence of a global system, as described in the last few chapters, is such a permanent change. Never again, we think, will the fate of individuals, communities, and nations be independent of what is happening on the other side of the globe. It seems virtually unthinkable, in the absence of a global catastrophe, that in the future you will live your life with a small human population, in small isolated communities, with resources so abundant that their use is not in question. Don't look for the disappearance of computers or the return of blacksmiths!

But other kinds of change is caused by alterations of what we have called the "rules of the game," that is, by changing political, policy, and legal arrangements. These arrangements are important because they define who benefits, who wins, and who loses. In relationship to individual adaptations to change, our point is simply this: *Changes driven by deeply embedded technical, demographic, and structural causes are not likely to be altered suddenly or rapidly.* You may as well learn to adapt to them. But to the extent that your life is supported, benefited, or for that matter disadvantaged by existing laws and public policy, watch out, because those rules of the game can change suddenly and rapidly. Tax laws can be rewritten. New industries can be subsidized and old ones can lose their subsidies. Social welfare benefits—such as tuition scholarships, aid for dependent children, health insurance, Social Security, and the like—can change rapidly. Such public policy change, created by the actions of legislators and court decisions, can create new beneficiaries and new categories of losers.

3. *Change yourself.* To the extent that the directions of change in the world are not subject to your control, you must be able to adapt to change. That means that if you can't modify your environment, you need to be able to modify yourself. There are, for sure, limits to how much self-modification is possible; there are needs rooted in biology, and therefore the possibility of human characteristics not subject to self-modification. But beyond these biologically based requirements, other aspects of the human self and

its needs are constructed by the socialization process and culture, and are quite mutable. But since we learn many of these needs early in life and often inherit them from an older generation, they are highly susceptible to being frustrated by the changing conditions of the social world. A great amount of human unhappiness and frustration results from becoming locked into a certain set of learned expectations that cannot be satisfied in a world of change. To believe that to be happy we must realize any particular set of learned expectations is to live with illusion. People can live and thrive under all kinds of conditions. Fortunately, the self is quite mutable.

Let us illustrate this point by discussing what I think is a major impediment to happiness among contemporary Americans. We are, we believe, still quite bound by the American cultural dream of universal affluence. We would all like to be rich, and we believe that happiness is to be found in owning more things. This consumerist cultural ethic may have been appropriate in an expanding frontier society or in the post–World War II period of rapid and continuous economic expansion, but today it is becoming a central problem in American culture. That many can realize the consumerist dream is increasingly unlikely in a crowded world of limits and tradeoffs, where there are no open frontiers (except those of the human spirit), and in which there are possibly absolute limits for growth in material consumption.

Our point is that the need for high levels of material consumption is a culturally programmed need that one can simply define away (if, of course, one learns to resist the seductive appeals of the consumerist ethic, see Schor, 1998). You need not be unhappy because you are not rich and affluent. That is a self-imposed frustration. We need to learn to transcend the seemingly natural questions in the American scheme of things (such as, "How can I get more?") to be able to ask other sorts of questions, such as, "How much is enough?" (And whether or not more will be better.) These are actually not natural questions in the American scheme of things. But they are, we think, crucial questions to adapting positively to change in an age of seemingly stubborn limits to cornucopian material growth.

Self-change may demand breaking through the expectations others have for you, whether these are well intentioned or vicious. It may mean not accepting your place anymore. It may mean struggling to gain control of the self and to restore the unity of your mind and body. It certainly means putting aside cynicism and fatalism. The attitudes that people are basically rotten and that nothing can ever be changed are part of an ideology that encourages inaction and passivity (Ash Garner, 1977:412; Elshtain, 1996; Goldfarb, 1991) and are the antithesis of creative self-mutation. If you cannot change the world, you can change yourself and redefine the expectations that make you unhappy.

4. *Change society.* It is true that some things are, practically speaking, beyond our ability as individuals to control. In the short run, we must adapt to them to live. But in fact how people live as individuals and the choices they make do indeed shape the direction and pace of change. Although it is tempting to think of social change as some inexorable set of forces that proceeds willy-nilly, divorced from human action, in the final analysis this is not true. To paraphrase Marx, people do make history, though they do not always do so on their own terms. We think it is important that while you are busy

adapting and surviving in a changing world, you invest some time and energy working to bring about a better world for others. To live only for yourself is, we think, to live irresponsibly as a member of a human community. We think it is ethically irresponsible to knowingly profit from the misery of others or even to withdraw from any effort at social betterment and seek your own private salvation. That is our private opinion, but it is not only our own private opinion. It is also the ethical teaching of all of the great world religions, and of all of the purely secular ethical systems (such as secular humanism or Marxism). We think that being an ethically responsible person requires that you be engaged in some effort to shape social change in a positive direction.

It is true that most of us are not at the pinnacles of power in society, and it is tempting to throw up our hands and say, "Well, what can I do? I'm just one person." Our answer would be that it is important that you do something, however modest. Few of us are saints or martyrs, willing to devote our whole lives to the work of trying to create a better world for others. Most people do not want to be saints or martyrs; nor do the circumstances of their lives—their struggle to earn a living, to enjoy themselves a little, to live in peace with their family and friends—permit them to be (Ash Garner, 1977:412). But after satisfying such circumstances, each of us has some measure of discretionary time, talent, energy, and resources that can be invested in efforts to shape the outcomes of the human journey in a positive way. Do you expend them all on yourself and on self-gain? That, we think is ethically unconscionable.

How each of us pursues this ethical imperative to work for a better world will necessarily vary. It requires that you have some image of what a positive future would look like. And it requires that you have some knowledge about how to create change (we have devoted a whole chapter to this earlier, so we will not reiterate it here). One thing is certain. The task of creating a better world for others cannot be an individualistic effort; it must be a collective one. We cannot go it alone. We must unite in organizations that can help create a humane future or, to use Roberta Ash Garner's apt metaphor, "that can be the midwives for the birth of a new society. The birth pangs are inevitable. Our task is to ease the delivery, reduce the amount of suffering, and insure the life and health of the infant" (1977:412). You may not as yet have found an organization that is completely worthy of your efforts. But there are a large variety of organizations pursuing different goals and having different tactics. We urge you to learn more about them and to adopt a cause and a tribe that reflect your vision of the good society.

References

Adorno, Theodor
    1974 "Theses against Occultism." *Telos,* 19:7.

Aldrich, Howard
    1999 *Organizations Evolving.* Thousand Oaks, CA: Sage.

Alexander, C.
    1984 "Pulling the Nuclear Plug," *Time,* (Feb. 2).

Alexander, Jeffrey
    1985 *Neofunctionalism.* Beverly Hills, CA: Sage.

Alinsky, Saul
    1972 *Rules for Radicals.* New York: Vintage Press.

Amato, Paul R., and Alan Booth
    1997 *A Generation at Risk: Growing Up in an Era of Family Upheaval.* Cambridge, MA: Harvard University Press.

American Enterprise Institute
    1981 "Public Opinion Roundup." *Public Opinion* (Aug./Sept.). Washington, DC: American Enterprise Institute for Policy Research.

Amin, San-tir
    1976 *Unequal Development: An Essay on Social Formations of Peripheral Capitalism.* New York: Monthly Review Press.

Ammerman, Nancy T.
    1987 *Bible Believers: Fundamentalists in the Modern World.* New Brunswick, NJ: Rutgers University Press.

Andrade, R. de Castro
    1982 "Brazil: The Economics of Savage Capitalism," in Manfred Bienefeld and Martin Godfrey (eds.), *The Struggle for Development.* Chichester, UK: John Wiley and Sons.

Applebaum, Richard P.
    1970 *Theories of Social Change.* Chicago: Markham.

Aquilino, William S.
    1990 "The Likelihood of Parent-Adult Children Coresidence: Effects of Family Structure and Parental Characteristics." *Journal of Marriage and the Family,* 52:405–419.

Aron, Raymond
    1968 *Progress and Disillusion.* New York: Fredrick A. Praeger.

Armendariz, Virgil
    1995 "Immigration Facts." *Nebraska Rural Action.* Center for Rural Affairs. Walthill, NE (Sept.).

Ash Garner, Roberta
    1977 *Social Change.* Chicago: Rand McNally.

Associated Press
1986   "Economic Pie Sliced 'Thinner in Heartland.'" *Omaha World Herald* (July 10): 1.

Baca-Zinn, and D. Stanley Eitzen
1993   *Diversity in American Families.* New York: HarperCollins.

Baker, Bob
1991   "Shackles or Savior? Computerized Workplace Changes How Humans Relate." *Los Angeles Times,* cited in the *Omaha World Herald* (July 7): G1.

Bane, Mary Jo
1989   "One Fifth of the Nation's Children: Why Are They Poor?" *Science* (Sept.): 1047–1048.

Baran, Paul
1957   *The Political Economy of Growth.* New York: Monthly Review Press.

1969   *The Longer View: Essays toward a Critique of Political Economy.* New York: Monthly Review Press.

Barber, Benjamin R.
1992   "Jihad vs. McWorld." *Atlantic Monthly* (Mar.): 53–61.

Barber, Bernard
1971   "Function, Variability, and Change in Ideological Systems," in Bernard Barber and Alex Inkeles (eds.), *Stability and Social Change,* pp. 244–265. Boston: Little Brown.

Barnet, Richard J.
1980   *The Lean Years: Politics in the Age of Scarcity.* New York: Simon and Schuster.

Barnet, Richard J., and Ronald E. Muller
1974   *Global Reach: The Power of Multinational Corporations.* New York: Simon and Schuster.

Barnett, Homer G.
1953   *Innovation: The Basis of Cultural Change.* New York: McGraw Hill.

Bartos, Otomar J.
1996   "Postmodernism, Postindustrialism, and the Future," *Sociological Quarterly,* 37, 2:307–327.

Baudrillard, Jean
1975   *The Mirror of Production.* St Louis, MO: Telos Press.

Beal, George M., and Everett Rogers
1959   "The Scientist as Referent in the Communication of New Technology." *Public Opinion Quarterly,* 22:555–563.

Beck, Ulrich
1992   *Risk Society: Towards a New Modernity.* Newbury Park, CA: Sage.

Bell, Daniel
1969   *The Coming of Post-Industrial Society.* New York: Basic Books.

1992   "Modernism, Postmodernism, and the Decline of Moral Order," in Jeffrey C. Alexander and Steven Siedman (eds.), *Culture and Society,* pp. 319–329. Cambridge, MA: Cambridge University Press.

Bellah, Robert, Richard Masden, William Sullivan, Ann Swidler, and Steven Tipton
1985   *Habits of the Heart: Individualism and Commitment in American Life.* Berkeley, CA: University of California Press.

Benford, Robert
1993   "Frame Disputes within the Nuclear Disarmament Movement." *Social Forces,* 71:677–701.

Bennis, Warren G., Kenneth D. Benne, and Robert Chin
1985   *The Planning of Change.* New York: Holt, Rinehart and Winston.

Berger, Peter L., and Thomas Luckmann
1967   *The Social Construction of Reality.* New York: Doubleday.

Bergsten, C. Fred
1991   "The World Economy after the Cold War." Address to the Commonwealth Club of California (Nov. 4).

Berk, Richard A.
1974   *Collective Behavior.* Dubuque IA: Wm C. Brown Publishers.

Bernhard, Virginia, David Burner, and Elizabeth Fox Genovese
1991   *First Hand America: A History of the United States,* vol. 2. St. James, NY: Brandywine Press.

Bernstein, Michael
   1994   *Understanding America's Economic Decline.* Cambridge, UK: Cambridge University Press.
Birdsall, Nancy
   1980   "Population and Poverty in the Developing World." *Population Bulletin,* 35:1–48.
Blackburn, Mckinley, and David Bloom
   1987   *Family Income Inequality in the United States: 1967–1984,* monograph 1294. Cambridge, MA: Harvard Institute of Economic Research.
   1989   *Family Size and Family Achievement.* Berkeley: University of California Press.
Blackburn, McKinley, and David Bloom
   1985   "What Is Happening to the Middle Class?" *American Demographics* (Jan.): 18–25.
Blake, Judith
   1979   "Structural Differentiation and the Family: A Quiet Revolution," in Amos H. Hawley (ed.), *Societal Growth: Processes and Implications.* New York: Free Press.
   1989   *Family Size and Achievement.* Berkeley, CA: University of California Press.
Bluestone, Barry and Bennett Harrison
   1982   *The Deindustrialization of America: Plant Closings, Community Abandonment, and the Dismantling of Basic Industry.* New York: Basic Books.
Blumer, Herbert
   1962   "The Field of Collective Behavior." In Alfred McClung Lee (ed.), *Principles of Sociology.* New York: Barnes and Noble.
   1969   *Symbolic Interaction: Perspective and Method.* Englewood Cliffs, NJ: Prentice Hall.
Boli, John, and George M. Thomas
   1997   "World Culture in a World Policy: A Century of International Non-Governmental Organization." *American Sociological Review,* 62:171–190.
Bolton, Charles D.
   1972   "Alienation and Action: A Study of Peace Group Members." *American Journal of Sociology,* 78: 537–561.
Bott, Elizabeth
   1971   *Family and Social Networks.* London: Tavistock.
Bondurant, Joan V.
   1972   "Satyagraha as Applied Socio-political Action." In Gerald Zaltman, Philip Kotler, and Ira Kaufman (eds.), *Creating Social Change.* New York: Holt, Rinehart and Winston.
Boston Globe
   1986   "Ozone Is Simple Gas that Shields World from Harmful Radiation," *Omaha World Herald* (Nov. 23): 1K.
Boulding, Kenneth
   1970   *A Primer on Social Dynamics.* New York: Free Press.
Bradshaw, York W., Rita Noonan, Laura Gash, and Claudia Buchmann Sershen
   1993   "Borrowing against the Future: Children and Third World Indebtedness," *Social Forces* 71: 629–656.
Bradshaw, York, and Michael Wallace
   1996   *Global Inequalities.* Thousand Oaks, CA: Pine Forge Press.
Braverman, Harry
   1974   *Labor and Monopoly Capital: The Degradation of Work in the Twentieth Century.* New York: Monthly Review Press.
Brint, Steven
   1994   *In an Age of Experts: The Changing Role of Professionals in Public Life.* Princeton, NJ: Princeton University Press.
Brinton, Crane
   1938/
   1965   *The Anatomy of Revolution.* Englewood Cliffs, NJ: Prentice Hall.
Broder, David
   1991   "Speech Raises Question How Much Bush Knows about Real Life," *Omaha World Herald* (May 20).

Brown, Janet Welsh
1996 "Population, Consumption, and the Path to Sustainability," *Current History,* 95, 604: 366–371.

Brown, Lester
2000 *Vital Signs 2000.* New York: W. W. Norton.

Brown, Lester et al.
1976 *World Population Trends,* Paper 8. Washington, DC: Worldwatch.
1986 *The State of the World, 1986.* New York: W. W. Norton.
1991 *The State of the World, 1991.* New York: W. W. Norton.
1994 "Who Will Feed China?" *Worldwatch,* 7, 5:10–15.

Brown, Lester, Christopher Flavin, and Hal Kane
1996 *Vital Visions, 1996: The Trends that Are Shaping Our Future.* New York: W. W. Norton.
1982 *Mergers in Perspective.* Washington, DC: American Enterprise Institute.

Buechler, Steven
1995 "New Social Movement Theories," *Sociological Quarterly,* 36, 3:441–465.

Burnam, Walter Dean
1969 "The End of American Party Politics," in Henry Etzkowitz (ed.), 1974, *Is American Possible? Social Problems from Conservative, Liberal and Socialist Perspectives.* St Paul, MN: West.

Burns, T. R., and Thomas Dietz
1992 "Cultural Evolution: Social Rule Systems, Selection, and Human Agency," *International Sociology,* 7, 3:259–283.

Burns, Tom, and G. M. Stalker
1961 *The Management of Innovation.* London: Tavistock.

Burt, Ronald
1982 *Toward a Structural Theory of Action.* New York: Academic Press.

Burton, Michael G.
1984 "Elites and Collective Protest," *Sociological Quarterly,* 25:45–66.

Camp, Sharon L.
1993 "Population: The Critical Decade," *Foreign Policy,* 90 (Spring): 125–144.

Caplow, Theodore
1964 *Principles of Organization.* New York: Harcourt, Brace and World.

Caplow, Theodore et al.
1982 *Middletown Families: Fifty Years of Change and Continuity.* Minneapolis, MN: University of Minnesota Press.

Castells, Manuel
1996 *The Rise of the Network Society.* Oxford, UK: Blackwell.
1998 *The End of Millenium.* Oxford, UK: Blackwell.

Catton, William R., and Riley E. Dunlap
1980 "A New Ecological Paradigm for Post-Exuberant Sociology." *American Behavioral Scientist,* 23 (Sept./Oct.): 15–47.

Cetron, Marvin, and D. Davis
1989 *American Renaissance.* New York: St. Martin's Press.

Chalfant, H. Paul, Robert Beckley, and C. Eddie Palmer
1994 *Religion in Contemporary Society,* 3rd ed. Itasca, IL: F. E. Peacock.

Chapin, F. S.
1928 *Cultural Change.* New York: Century.

Cherlin, Andrew
1981 *Marriage, Divorce, and Remarriage.* Cambridge, MA: Harvard University Press.
1992 *Marriage, Divorce, Remarriage.* Cambridge: Harvard University Press.
1996 *Public and Private Families: An Introduction.* New York: McGraw Hill.

Chesshire, John, and Keith Pavitt
1978 "Some Energy Futures," in Christopher Freeman and Marie Jahoda (eds.), *World Futures,* London: Martin Robinson.

Chirot, Daniel

1981 "Changing Fashions in the Study of the Social Causes of Economic and Political Change, in James F. Short (ed.), *The State of Sociology*. Beverly Hills, CA: Sage.

1986 *Social Change in the Modern Era*. New York: Harcourt Brace Jovanovich.

Chodak, Szymon

1973 *Societal Development*. New York: Oxford University Press.

Church, George, J.

1994 "We're #1 and It Hurts: The U.S. Outruns the World, But Some Workers Are Left Behind," *Time*, (Oct. 24): 52–56.

Clausen, A. M.

1985 "Poverty in the Developing Countries—1985." Hunger Project Paper 3 (Mar.). New York: The Hunger Project.

Clawson, Dan, and Alan Neustadtl

1998 *Dollars and Votes: How Business Campaign Contributions Subvert Democracy*. Philadelphia, PA: Temple University Press.

Cleveland, Harlan

1993 *Birth of a New World: An Open Moment for International Leadership*. San Francisco, CA: Jossey-Bass.

Cole, H. S. D. et al.

1973 *Models of Doom: Critiques of* The Limits to Growth. New York: Universe Books.

Coleman, James

1982 *The Asymmetric Society*. Syracuse, NY: Syracuse University Press.

1957 "The Diffusion of an Innovation among Physicians." *Sociometry*, 20:253–270.

1990 *Foundations of Social Theory*. Cambridge, MA: Harvard University Press.

Coleman, James, and Donald R. Cressy

1984 *Social Problems*, 2nd ed. New York: Harper and Row.

1987 *Social Problems*, 3rd ed. New York: Harper and Row.

Collins, Randall

1975 *Conflict Sociology: Toward an Explanatory Science*. New York: Academic Press.

1988 *Theoretical Sociology*. New York: Harcourt Brace Jovanovich.

Collins, Randall, and Scott Coltrane

1995 *Sociology of Marriage and Family: Gender, Love, and Property*, 4th ed. Chicago: Nelson Hall.

Cook, Earl

1971 "The Flow of Energy in Industrial Society." *Scientific American*, 224, 3:134–147.

Coontz, Stephanie

1992 *The Way We Never Were: American Families and the Nostalgia Trap*. New York: Basic Books.

Cornish, Edward

1996 "The Cyber Future: 92 Ways Our Lives Will Change by the Year 2025," *The Futurist*, 30, 1 (Jan./Feb.):3.

Coser, Lewis

1977 *Masters of Sociological Thought*. New York: Harcourt Brace Jovanovich.

Council on Environmental Quality

1980 *The Global 2000 Report to the President*. Washington, DC: Government Printing Office.

Crotty, William J., and Gary C. Jacobson

1980 *American Parties in Decline*. Boston, MA: Little Brown.

Cuzzort, Ray and Edith King

1980 *Humanity and Sociological Thought*, 3rd ed. Hinsdale, EL: Dryden Press.

Dadzie, K. K. S.

1980 "Economic Development," *Scientific American*, 243, 3, (Sept.):1–7.

Dahrendorf, Ralph

1958 "Out of Utopia: Toward a Reorientation of Sociological Analysis," *American Journal of Sociology*, 64:115–127.

1959 *Class and Class Conflict in Industrial Society.* Stanford, CA: Stanford University Press.

1968 *Essays in the Theory of Society.* Stanford, CA: Stanford University Press.

Darmstadter J.
1971 *Energy in the World Economy.* Baltimore MD: The Johns Hopkins Press.

Davies, James C.
1962 "Toward a Theory of Revolution," *American Sociological Review,* 25:5–19.

1969 "The J-curve of Rising and Declining Satisfactions as a Cause of Some Great Revolutions and a Contained Rebellion," in Hugh Davis Graham and Ted Robert Gurr (eds.) *The History of Violence in America.* New York: Praeger.

Davis, Burl E.
1968 "System Variables and Agricultural Innovativeness in Eastern Nigeria." PhD. thesis, Michigan State University.

Davis, Richard H.
1965 "Personal and Organizational Variables Related to the Adoption of Educational Innovations in a Liberal Arts College." PhD. Thesis, University of Chicago.

De Man, Paul
1979 *Allegories of Reading.* New Haven, CT: Yale University Press.

Demerath, Nicholas J.
1984 "World Politics and Population," in Susan Strange (ed.), *Paths to International Political Economy.* London: George Allen and Unwin.

Demos, John
1970 *A Little Commonwealth: Family Life in Plymouth Colony.* New York: Oxford University Press.

DeParle, Jason
1991 "The Nation: Richer Rich, Poorer Poor; and a Fatter Green Book." *The New York Times* (May 26):E2.

Derber, Charles
1996 *The Wilding of America.* New York: St. Martin's Press.

Deudney, Daniel, and G. John Ikenberry
1995 "American after the Long War." *Current History,* 94, 595:364–369.

Diamond, Larry, and Marc Plattner
1993 *The Global Resurgence of Democracy.* Baltimore, MD: Johns Hopkins.

Dione, E. J.
1996 "The Return of Progressivism," *Morning Edition,* National Public Radio (Mar. 13).

Dobrzynski, Judith H.
1996 "E-Mail Has Companies Overwhelmed, Overmessaged." *The New York Times,* cited in the *Omaha World Herald* (May 12):G1.

Dolbeare, Kenneth, and Janette Hubbell
1996 *USA 2012: After the Middle Class Revolution.* Chatham, NJ: Chatham House.

Douglas, John H.
1976 "The Slowing Growth of World Population." *Science News,* 13 (Nov.):316–317.

Dubofsky, Melvyn
1975 *Industrialism and the American Worker, 1865–1920.* Arlington Heights, IL: Harlan Davidson.

Durkheim, Emile
1893/
1947 *The Division of Labor in Society.* New York: Free Press.

Durning, Alan
1991 "Asking How Much Is Enough." in Lester Brown et al., *The State of the World,* pp. 153–169. New York: W. W. Norton.

1992 *How Much Is Enough: The Consumer Society and the Future of the Earth.* New York: W. W. Norton.

Duvall, Evelyn M., and Brent C. Miller
1985 *Marriage and Family Development,* 6th ed. New York: Harper and Row.

Easterbrook, Greg
    1995   *A Moment on the Earth:* The Coming Age of Environmental Optimism. New York: Viking Press.

Eckersley, Richard
    1993   "The West's Deepening Cultural Crisis," *The Futurist,* 27, 6 (Nov./Dec.):8–12.

Eckstein, Susan
    1982   "The Impact of Revolution on Social Welfare in Latin America," *Theory and Society,* 11:43–94.

The Economist
    1999   "Two Sharks in a Fishbowl." www.economist.com (September 9).
    2000   "The Big Leap." www.economist.com (January 13).
    2001a "A Spanner in the Productivity Miracle." www.economist.com (August 9).
    2001b "Get a Parachute." www.economist.com (August 23).
    2001c "Economic Overview." www.economist.com (October 11).
    2001d "Putin's Choice." www.economist.com (July 19).
    2001e "NASDAQ Composite." www.economist.com (October 20).

Edsall, Thomas B., and Mary Edsall
    1996   *Chain Reaction: The Effects of Race, Rights, and Taxes on American Politics.* New York: W. W. Norton.

Edwards, Lyford P.
    1927   *The Natural History of Revolution.* Chicago: University of Chicago Press.

Edwards, Richard
    1993   *Rights at Work: Employment Relations in the Post-Union Era.* Washington, DC: Brookings Institution.

Edwards, Richard, Michael Reich, and Thomas E. Weisskopf
    1978   *The Capitalist System: A Radical Analysis of American Society.* Englewood Cliffs, NJ: Prentice Hall.

Ehrlich, Paul, and Anne Ehrlich
    1992   *The Population Bomb.* New York: Ballantine Books.

Eibler, Herbert J.
    1965   "A Comparison of the Relationship between Certain Aspects or Characteristics of the Structure of the High School Faculty and the Amount of Curriculum Innovation." PhD. thesis, University of Michigan.

Eisenstadt, S. N.
    1978   *Revolutions and the Transformation of Societies: A Comparative Study of Civilizations.* New York: Free Press.

Eisinger, Peter
    1973   "Conditions of Protest Behavior in American Cities." *American Political Science Review,* 67:11–28.

Eitzen, Stanley
    1974   *In Conflict and Order: Understanding Society.* Boston, MA: Allyn and Bacon.

Eldersveld, Samuel J.
    1964   *Political Parties: A Behavioral Analysis.* Chicago, IL: Rand McNally.

Elgin, Duane
    1981   *Voluntary Simplicity: Toward a Way of Life That Is Outwardly Simple, Inwardly Rich.* New York: Morrow.

Ellul, Jaques
    1964   *Technological Society.* New York: Vintage.

Elshtain, Jean Bethke
    1995   *Democracy on Trial.* New York: Basic Books.

Emerson, Richard M.
    1962   "Power-Dependence Relations." *American Sociological Review,* 27 (Feb.):31–41.

Etzioni, Amitai
    1968a   *The Active Society.* New York: Free Press.

1968b "Shortcuts to Social Change?" *Public Interest,* 12:40–51.

1993 *The Spirit of Community: Rights, Responsibilities, and the Communitarian Agenda.* New York: Crown.

Etzkowitz, Henry
1974 *Is America Possible? Social Problems from Conservative, Liberal, and Socialist Perspectives.* St. Paul, MN: West.

Etzkowitz, Henry, and Ronald M. Glassman
1991 *The Renascence of Sociological Theory.* Itasca, IL: F. E. Peacock.

Evans, Peter B., and John D. Stephens
1988 "Development and the World Economy," in Neil Smelser (ed.), *Handbook of Sociology.* Beverly Hills, CA: Sage.

Fairweather, George W.
1972 *Social Change: The Challenge to Survival.* Morristown, NJ: General Learning Press.

Falkenmark, M., and C. Widstrand
1992 "Population and Water Resources: A Delicate Balance," *Population Bulletin,* 47, 3:1–15.

Fanon, Franz
1967 *Black Skins and White Masks.* Charles Lam Markmann (trans.). New York: Grove Press.

1968 *The Wretched of the Earth.* Constance Farrington (trans.). New York: Grove Press.

Farley, John
1988 *Majority-Minority Relations.* Englewood Cliffs, NJ: Prentice-Hall.

Farrell, Christopher
1994 "The Triple Revolution," *Business Week* (Oct.):22–25.

Faux, Jeff
1983 "By Deficits Possessed," *The New Republic* (Feb. 14).

Federal Reserve System
1984 "Survey of Consumer Finances," *Federal Reserve Bulletin,* 70:689.

Ferguson, Marilyn
1980 *The Aquarian Conspiracy: Personal and Social Transformation in the 1980s.* Los Angeles: J. P. Tarcher.

Fickett, Arnold P., Clark W. Gellings, and Amory Lovins
1990 "Efficient Use of Energy," *Scientific American,* 263, 3 (Sept.).

Fineman, H.
1991 "The New Politics of Race," *Newsweek* (May 6).

Firebaugh, Glenn, and Frank D. Beck
1994 "Does Economic Growth Benefit the Masses? Growth, Dependence, and Welfare in the Third World." *American Sociological Review,* 59, 5 (Oct.):631–651.

Flavin, Christopher
1984 "Reassessing the Economics of Nuclear Power," in Lester Brown et al., *The State of the World.* New York: W. W. Norton.

1986 "Moving beyond Oil," in Lester Brown et al., *The State of the World.* New York: W. W. Norton.

Flavin, Christopher, and Nicholas Lenssen
1991 "Designing a Sustainable Energy System," in Lester Brown et al., *The State of the World.* New York: W. W. Norton.

1994 *Power Surge: Guide to the Coming Energy Revolution.* New York: W. W. Norton.

Ford, Ramona L.
1988 *Work, Organization, and Power: Introduction to Industrial Sociology.* Needham Heights, MA: Allyn and Bacon.

Forrester, Jay W.
1985 "Economic Conditions Ahead: Understanding the Kondratieff Wave," *The Futurist* (June): 16–20.

Foucault, Michael
1965 *Madness and Civilization.* New York: Random House.

Frank, Andre Gunder
1969   *Capitalism and Underdevelopment in Latin America: Historical Studies of Chile and Brazil.* New York: The Monthly Review Press.

1972   "Who Is the Immediate Enemy?" in James D. Crockcroft, Andre Gunder Frank, and Dale L. Johnson (eds.), *Dependence and Underdevelopment: Latin America's Political Economy.* Garden City, NY: Doubleday Anchor.

Freeman, David M.
1974   *Technology and Society: Issues in Assessment, Conflict, and Choice.* Chicago: Rand McNally.

Freeman, Christopher, and Marie Jahoda
1978   *World Futures: The Great Debate.* London: Martin Robertson.

Freeman, Jo
1979   *Women: A Feminist Perspective,* 2nd ed. Palo Alto, CA: Mayfield.

Freeman, Richard B.
1997   *Working under Different Rules.* New York: Russell Sage Foundation.

Freeman, Richard B., and James L. Medoff
1984   *What Do Unions Do?* New York: Basic Books.

French, J. P. R., et al.
1960   "An Experiment on Participation in a Norwegian Factory." *Human Relations,* 3:3–19.

Friedan, Betty
1963   *The Feminine Mystique.* New York: W. W. Norton.

Friedman, Debra
1983   "Why Workers Strike: Individual Decisions and Structural Constraints." In Michael Hechter (ed.), *The Microfoundations of Macrosociology.* Philadelphia: Temple University Press.

Friedman, John, and Wolf Goetz
1982   "World City Formation: An Agenda for Research and Action," *International Journal of Urban and Regional Research,* 6, 3:309–343.

Frisbie, W. Parker
1977   "The Scale and Growth of World Urbanization," in John Walton and Donald E. Carns (eds.), *Cities in Change.* Boston, MA: Allyn and Bacon.

Galbraith, James
1998   *Created Unequal: The Crisis in American Pay.* New York: Free Press.

Gale, Richard P.
1986   "Social Movements and the State: The Environmental Movement, Countermovement, and Government Agencies." *Sociological Perspectives,* 29:202–240.

Galtung, Johan
1981   "Global Processes and the World in the 1980s," in W. Ladd Hollis and James N. Rosenau (eds.), *World System Structure: Continuity and Change.* Beverly Hills, CA: Sage.

Galvin, Kevin
1995   "Americans Seeking More Leisure Time," Associated Press, cited in *Omaha World Herald* (Dec. 10):1, 4.

Gamson, William A.
1968   "Rancorous Conflict in Community Politics," in Terry N. Clark (ed.), *Community Structure and Decision-Making: A Comparative Analysis.* San Francisco: Chandler.

1974   "Violence and Political Power: The Meek Don't Make It." *Psychology Today,* 8:35–41.

1975   *The Strategy of Social Protest.* Homewood, IL: Dorsey Press.

Gannon, Thomas M.
1981   "The New Christian Right in America as a Social and Political Force." Paper presented to the 1981 meeting of the Association for the Sociology of Religion, Chicago.

Gans, Herbert
1974   "The Equality Revolution," in Herbert Gans (ed.), *More Equality.* New York: Vintage Books.

Garten, Jeffrey E.
1989   "Trading Blocs and the Evolving World Economy," *Current History,* 88, 534 (Jan.).

Gartner, William
1996 *Morning Edition,* National Public Radio, (Aug. 30).

Gelles, R. J., and O. P. Cornell
1990 *Intimate Violence in Families.* Newbury Park, CA: Sage.

Gerlach, Luther P., and Virginia H. Hine
1970 *People, Power, and Change: Movements of Social Transformation.* New York: Bobbs-Merrill.

Getzels, Jacob W., and Phillip W. Jackson
1962 *Creativity and Intelligence: Explorations with Gifted Students.* New York: John Wiley.

Giddens, Anthony
1990 *The Consequences of Modernity.* Stanford, CA.: Stanford University Press.

1995 *A Contemporary Critique of Historical Materialism,* 2nd ed. Stanford, CA: Stanford University Press.

Glock, Charles Y.
1987 "The Ways the World Works," *Sociological Analysis,* 49, 2:93–103.

Goldberg, Robert A.
1991 *Grassroots Resistance: Social Movements in Twentieth Century America.* Belmont, CA: Wadsworth.

Goldfarb, Jeffrey
1991 *The Cynical Society: The Culture of Politics and the Politics of Culture in American Life.* Chicago, IL: University of Chicago Press.

Goldsmith, James
1994 *The Trap.* New York: Carrol and Graf.

Goldstone, Jack A. (ed.)
1986 *Revolutions: Theoretical, Comparative, and Historical Studies.* New York: Harcourt Brace Jovanovich.

Goode, William J.
1971 "World Revolution and Family Patterns," *Journal of Marriage and Family,* 33:624–635.

1982 *The Family.* Englewood Cliffs, NJ: Prentice-Hall.

Goodland, R., H. Daly, and J. Kellenberg
1993 "Burdensharing in Transition to Environmental Sustainability." Paper presented to the seventh general assembly of the World Future Society, Washington, DC (June 27).

Gordon, David
1978 "Capitalist Development and the History of Cities," in William K. Tabb and Larry Sawers (eds.), *Marxism and the Metropolis: New Perspectives in Urban Political Economy,* pp. 25–63. New York: Oxford University Press.

Gottfried, Paul, and Thomas Flemming
1988 *The Conservative Movement.* Boston, MA: Twayne.

Gouldner, Alvin
1954 *Patterns of Industrial Bureaucracy.* New York: Free Press.

Granovetter, Mark S.
1973 "The Strength of Weak Ties." *American Journal of Sociology,* 73:1360–1380.

1984 "Small Is Beautiful: Labor Markets and Establishment Size." *American Sociological Review,* 49, 3 (June): 323–324.

1985 "Economic Action and Social Structure: The Problem of Embeddedness." *American Journal of Sociology,* 91, 3 (Nov.):481–510.

Gribben, John R.
1981 *Future Worlds.* New York: Plenum Press.

Griffin, William B.
1969 *Culture Change and Shifting Populations in Central Northern Mexico.* Tucson, AZ: University of Arizona Press.

Gross, D. M., and S. Scott
1990 "Proceeding with Caution," *Time* (July 16).

Gross, Neal, and Bryce Ryan
1943 "Diffusion of Hybrid Seed Corn in Two Iowa Communities." *Rural Sociology,* 8, 1:15–24.

Gurney, Joan N., and Kathleen J. Tierney
1982 "Relative Deprivation and Social Movements: A Critical Look at Twenty Years of Theory and Research," *Sociological Quarterly,* 23, 1:33–47.

Gurr, Ted
1970 *Why Men Rebel.* Princeton, NJ: Princeton University Press.

Habermas, Jürgen
1973 *Legitimation Crisis.* Thomas McCarthy (trans.). Boston, MA: Beacon Press.

Hadamard, Jaques
1954 *An Essay on the Psychology of Invention in the Mathematical Field.* Princeton, NJ: Princeton University Press.

Hagen, Everett C.
1962 *On the Theory of Social Change.* Homewood, IL: Dorsey Press.

Hall, Richard H.
1994 *Sociology of Work: Perspectives, Analyses, and Issues.* Thousand Oaks, CA: Pine Forge Press.

Hancock, Lyn Nell, Mark Miller, Pat Wingert, Ginny Carroll, and Vert Smith
1996 "Redrawing Color Lines," *Newsweek* (Apr. 29):34–35.

Handelman, Howard
1996 *The Challenge of Third World Development.* Upper Saddle River, NJ: Prentice Hall.

Handler, Douglas P.
1988 *Business Demographics.* New York: Dunn and Bradstreet, Economic Analysis Department.

Hannigan, John A.
1991 "Social Movement Theory and the Sociology of Religion: Toward a New Synthesis." *Sociological Analysis,* 52, 4:311–332.

1995 *Environmental Sociology: A Social Constructionist Perspective.* New York: Routledge.

Harper, Charles L.
1974 "Spirit Filled Catholics: Some Biographical Comparisons." *Social Compass,* 21, 3:311–324.

1981 "The Cult Controversy: Values in Conflict." *Proceedings of the Association for the Sociology of Religion–Southwest,* pp. 65–72.

1982 "Cults and Communities: The Community Interfaces of Three Marginal Religious Movements," *Journal for the Scientific Study of Religion,* 21, 1:26–38.

1996 *Environment and Society: Human Perspectives on Environmental Issues.* Upper Saddle River, NJ: Prentice Hall.

2001 *Environment and Society: Human Perspectives on Environmental Issues,* 2nd ed. Upper Saddle River, NJ: Prentice Hall.

Harper, Charles L., and Kevin Leicht
1984 "Religious Awakenings and Status Politics: Sources of Support for the New Religious Right." *Sociological Analysis,* 45, 4:339–353.

Harper, Doug
1994 "Auto Imports Jump in Mexico." *The New York Times* (July 7):D.

Harrington, Michael
1962 *The Other America.* New York: MacMillan.

Harris, Louis
1987 *Inside America.* New York: Vintage Books.

Harris, Marvin, and Eric B. Ross
1987 *Death, Sex, and Fertility: Population Regulation in Preindustrial and Developing Societies.* New York: Columbia University Press.

Harrison, G. A.
1993 *Human Adaptation.* New York: Oxford University Press.

Harrison, Paul
1993 *The Third Revolution: Population, Environment and a Sustainable World.* London: Penguin Books.

Hayes, Jeffry W., and Seymour Martin Lipset
1993/
1994 "Individualism: A Double-edged Sword." *The Responsive Community* (Winter):69–80.

Heilbroner, Robert L., and Lester C. Thurow
1987 *Economics Explained.* New York: Simon and Schuster.

Heller, Scott
1991 "Reeling from Harsh Attacks, Educators Weigh How to Respond to 'Politically Correct' Label." *Chronicle of Higher Education* (June 12): A1.

Henderson, Hazel
1988 *The Politics of the Solar Age: Alternatives to Economics,* rev. ed. Indianapolis, IN: Knowledge Systems.

Herberg, Will
1960 *Protestant, Catholic, Jew.* Garden City, NY: Doubleday Anchor.

Herskovitz, Melville J.
1936 *Man and His Works.* New York: Knopf.

Hiller, Richard A.
1996 TIAA-CREF Community Seminar, personal communication (April 25).

Hinze, Robert
1996 "Identity and the Internet." Session discussant, Midwest Sociological Society annual meeting, Chicago, IL.

Hodson, Randy, and Theresa Sullivan
1995 *The Social Organization of Work.* 2nd ed. Belmont, CA: Wadsworth.

Hoffer, Eric
1951 *The True Believer.* New York: New American Library.

Holdren, John
1975 "Energy Resources," in W. W. Murdock (ed.), *Environment: Resources, Pollution, and Society.* Sunderland, MA: Sinauer Associates.

1990 "Energy in Transition," *Scientific American,* 263, 3 (Sept.).

Homer-Dixon, Thomas
1996 "Environmental Scarcity, Mass Violence, and the Limits to Ingenuity." *Current History,* 95, 604:359–365.

Honnegger, Otto C.
1987 *The Nguba Connection.* Produced by WBGH Boston and Swiss TV, Zurich.

Horowitz, Irving Louis
1979 "Beyond Democracy: Interest Groups and the Patriotic Gore." *The Humanist* (Sept./Oct.): 4–10.

Horton, Paul, and Gerald Leslie
1974 *The Sociology of Social Problems.* Englewood Cliffs, NJ: Prentice-Hall.

Howe, Neil, and William Straus
2000 *Millenials Rising: The Next Great Generation.* New York: Vintage Books.

Humphrey, Craig R., and Fredrick R. Buttel
1982 *Environment, Energy, and Society.* Belmont CA: Wadsworth.

Huntington, Samuel P.
1968 *Political Order in Changing Societies.* New Haven, CT. Yale University Press.

1972 "Reform and Political Change," in Gerald Zaltman, Philip Kotler, and Ira Kaufman (eds.)., *Creating Social Change.* New York: Holt, Rinehart and Winston.

Hutter, Mark
1981 *The Changing Family: Comparative Perspectives.* New York: John Wiley.

Huyssen, Andreas
1990 "Mapping the Postmodern," in Jeffrey Alexander and Steven Seidman (eds.), *Culture and Society: Contemporary Debates.* New York: Cambridge University Press.

Ikenberry, G. John
1996 "The Myth of Post-War Chaos." *Foreign Affairs,* 5, 3 (May/June):79–92.

Inkeles, Alex
1979 "Continuity and Change in the American National Character." In Seymour Martin Lipset (ed.), *The Third Century.* Stanford, CA: Hoover Institution Press.

Institute for Social Research
1979   "Deepening Distrust of Political Leaders Is Jarring Public's Faith in Institutions," *Institute for Social Research Newsletter.* Ann Arbor, MI: Institute for Social Research, University of Michigan.

Intergovernmental Panel on Climate Change
1995   *The IPCC Assessment of Knowledge Relevant to the Interpretation of Article 2 of the UN Framework Convention on Climate Change: A Synthesis Report* (draft). Geneva, Switzerland (July 31).

International Energy Agency
1985   *Annual Oil Market Report, 1984.* Paris: Organization for Economic Cooperation and Development.

Janowitz, Morris
1978   *The Last Half Century.* Chicago: University of Chicago Press.

Jenkins, Craig J.
1983   "Resource Mobilization Theory and the Study of Social Movements." *Annual Review of Sociology,* 9:527–553.

Jenkins, J. Craig, and Charles Perrow
1977   "Insurgency of the Powerless: Farm Worker Movements (1946–1972)." *American Sociological Review,* 42,2:249–268.

Johnson, Allan G.
1986   *Human Arrangements: An Introduction to Sociology.* New York: Harcourt Brace Jovanovich.

Johnson, Chalmers
1966   *Revolutionary Change.* Boston, MA: Little Brown.

Kabada, Lini
1966   "Liberal Arts Majors Find Degrees of Success in the Job Market." *Philadelphia Inquirer,* cited in the *Omaha World Herald* (June 16):1, 3.

Kain, E.
1990   *The Myth of Family Decline.* Lexington, MA: Lexington Books.

Kahn, Herman, W. Brown, and L. Martel
1976   *The Next 200 Years.* New York: Morrow.

Kahn, Herman, and John B. Phelps
1979   "The Economic Present and Future." *The Futurist* (June).

Kahn, Herman, and Anthony I. Weiner
1967   *The Year 2000: A Framework for Speculation on the Next Thirty-Three Years.* New York: Macmillan.

Katz, Elihu
1960   "Communication Research and the Image of Society: Convergence of Two Traditions." *American Journal of Sociology,* 65:435–440.

Katz, Elihu, and Paul Lazarsfeld
1955   *Personal Influence: The Part Played by People in the Flow of Mass Communication.* New York: Free Press.

Kazin, Michael
1994   *The Populist Persuasion.* New York: Basic Books. Cited in the *Omaha World Herald,* "Is America's Anger in the 1990s Rooted in the Turbulent 1960s?" (May 14, 1995):6-A.

Kegan, Robert
1994   *In over Our Heads: The Mental Demands of Modern Life.* Cambridge, MA: Harvard University Press.

Kelly, Jonathan, and Herbert S. Klein
1977   "Revolution and the Rebirth of Inequality: A Theory of Stratification in Post-revolutionary Society," *American Journal of Sociology,* 83:78–99.

Kennedy, Robert E.
1989   *Life Chances: Applying Sociology,* 2nd ed. New York: Holt, Rinehart and Winston.

Kennedy, Paul
1987   *The Rise and Fall of Great Powers.* New York: Random House.

Kenney, Martin, W. Richard Goe, Oscar Contreras, Jairo Romero, and Mauricio Bustos
2001 "Learning Factories or Reproduction Factories? Labor-Management Relations in the Japanese Consumer Electronics Maquiladoras in Mexico." In Daniel B. Cornfield, Karen E. Campbell and Holly J. McCammon (eds.), *Working in Restructured Workplaces,* pp. 81–104. Thousand Oaks, CA: Sage.

Kent, Mary M.
1984 *World Population: Fundamentals of Growth.* Washington, DC: Population Reference Bureau.

Keyfitz, Nathan
1991 "Population Growth Can Prevent the Development That Would Slow Population Growth," in Jessica Tuchman Mathews (ed.), *Preserving the Global Environment: The Challenge of Shared Leadership.* New York: W. W. Norton.

Klandermans, Bert
1986 "New Social Movements and Resource Mobilization: The European and American Approach." *Journal of Mass Emergencies and Disasters,* 4:13–37.

Klandermans, Bert, and Sjoerd Goslinga
1996 "Media Discourse, Movement Publicity and the Generation of Collective Action Frames." In Doug McAdam, John D. McCarthy and Mayer N. Zald (eds.), *Comparative Perspectives on Social Movements: Political Opportunities, Mobilizing Structures and Cultural Framings,* pp. 312–337. Cambridge, UK: Cambridge University Press.

Klare, Michael T.
1996 "Redefining Security: The New Global Schisms." *Current History,* 94, 595:353–558.

Knoke, David, and Edward O. Laumann
1987 *The Organizational State: Social Choice in National Policy Domains.* Madison, WI: University of Wisconsin Press.

Kohl, Stephen J.
1985 *Images of Deviance and Control: A Sociological History.* New York: McGraw Hill.
1990 "Welcome to the PARASITE CAFE: Postmodernity as a Social Problem." *Problems,* 37, 4 (Nov.):421–442.

Kornhauser, William
1959 *The Politics of Mass Society.* Glencoe, IL: The Free Press.

Kouvitaris, George
1996 *Political Sociology.* Needham, MA: Allyn and Bacon.

Kraus, F., W. Bach, and J. Koomey
1992 *Energy Policy in the Greenhouse.* New York: Wiley.

Kriesbeg, Louis
1982 *Social Conflicts.* Englewood Cliffs, NJ: Prentice-Hall.

Kriesi, Hanspeter
1988 "The Interdependence of Structure and Action: Some Reflections on the State of the Art," in Bert Klandermans, Hanspeter Kriesi, and Sidney Tarrow (eds.), *From Structure to Action: Comparing Social Movement Research across Cultures.* Greenwich, CT: JAI Press.

Kubik, Jan
1994 *The Power of Symbols against the Symbols of Power.* University Park, PA: Penn State University Press.

Ladd, Everett C.
1979 "The American Party System Today." in Seymour Martin Lipset (ed.), *The Third Century.* Stanford, CA: The Hoover Institution Press.

Ladd, Everett C., and Charles D. Hadley
1975 *Party Systems: Political Coalitions from the New Deal to the 1970s.* New York: Norton.

Larson, Otto
1964 "Social Effects of Mass Communication," in Robert E. Faris (ed.), *Handbook of Modern Sociology.* Chicago: Rand McNally.

Lasch, Christopher
1979 *The Culture of Narcissism: American Life in an Age of Diminishing Expectations.* New York: The Free Press.

Laslett, Peter
  1970   *The World We Have Lost: England Before the Industrial Age.* New York: Scribners.
Lauer, Robert H.
  1977   *Perspectives on Social Change.* Boston, MA: Allyn and Bacon.
Law, Kim S., and Edward J. Walsh
  1983   "The Interaction of Grievances and Structures in Social Movement Analysis," *Sociological Quarterly,* 24,1:123–136.
LeBon, Gustav
  1896/
  1960   *The Crowd.* New York: Viking Press.
Leicht, Kevin T.
  1998   "Work (if you can get it) and Occupations (if there are any): What Social Scientists Can Learn from Predictions of the End of Work and Radical Workplace Change." *Work and Occupations* 25:36–48.
  1999   *The Future of Affirmative Action.* Stamford, CT: JAI Press.
  2001   "The Future of Work." In York Bradshaw, Joseph P. Healey, and Rebecca Smith (eds.), *Sociology for a New Century,* pp. 421–439. Thousand Oaks, CA: Pine Forge Press.
Leicht, Kevin T., and Mary L. Fennell
  2001   *Professional Work.* Oxford, UK: Blackwell.
Leik, Robert J., and Anita Sue Kolmann
  1977   "Isn't It More Rational to Be Wasteful?" Paper presented at the University of Houston Energy Symposium, Houston, TX.
Lenski, Gerhard, and Jean Lenski
  1982   *Human Societies: An Introduction to Macrosociology.* New York: McGraw Hill.
Lenssen, Nicholas, and Christopher Flavin
  1996   "Meltdown." *World Watch,* 9, 3 (May/June):23–31.
Lerner, Daniel
  1958   *The Passing of Traditional Society: Modernizing the Middle East.* New York: The Free Press.
  1968   "Modernization, Social Aspects," in *International Encyclopedia of the Social Sciences,* 10:387. New York: The Free Press.
Levine, Robert A.
  1996   "The Economic Consequences of Mr. Clinton." *Atlantic Monthly,* 27,1 (July):60–63.
Levitan, Sar A., Richard S. Belous, and Frank Gallo
  1988   *What's Happening to the American Family?* rev. ed. Baltimore, MD: The Johns Hopkins Press.
Levy, Frank
  1987   *Dollars and Dreams: The Changing American Income Distribution.* New York: Russell Sage Foundation.
Levy, Marion, Jr.
  1966   *Modernization and the Structure of Societies,* vol. 1. Princeton, NJ: Princeton University Press.
Lewin, Moshe
  1988   *The Gorbachev Phenomenon.* Berkeley, CA: University of California Press.
Lewy, Guenter
  1974   *Religion and Revolution.* New York: Oxford University Press.
Lichter, Daniel T., Diane K. McLaughlin, and David C. Ribar
  1998   "Welfare and the Rise of Female-Headed Families." *American Journal of Sociology,* 103:112–143.
Lindsey, Lawrence B.
  1992   "America's Growing Economic Lead." *Wall Street Journal* (Feb. 7).
Lipnack, Jessica
  1994   *The Age of the Network: Organizing Principles for the 21st Century.* New York: Omneo.
Lipset, Seymour Martin
  1989   *Continental Divide: The Values and Institutions of the United States and Canada.* Toronto, Ontario: C. D. Howe Institute and the National Planning Association (USA).

Lipset, Seymour M., and Earl Raab
1970   *The Politics of Unreason: Right-Wing Extremism in America.* New York: Harper and Row.

Lipset, Seymour M., and William Schneider
1983   *The Confidence Gap: Business, Labor, and Government in the Public Mind.* New York: The Free Press.

Lipsky, Michael
1968   "Protest as a Political Resource." *American Political Science Review,* 62:1144–1158.

Lofchie, Michael F., and Stephen K. Commins
1984   "Food Deficits and Agricultural Policies in Sub-Saharan Africa," The Hunger Project, Paper 2 (Sept.). San Francisco, CA: The Hunger Project.

Lohr, Steve
1995   "Business Often Goes to the Swift, Not the Best," *The New York Times* (Aug. 6):3.

Lovins, Amory
1976   "Energy Strategy: The Road Not Taken." *Foreign Affairs* (Fall): 65–96.

1977   *Soft Energy Paths.* Cambridge, MA: Ballinger.

Lowenthal, Abraham F.
1986   "Threat and Opportunity in the Americas," cited in *World Development Forum,* 4, 6 (Mar. 31).

Lowi, Theodore J. and Benjamin Ginsberg
1994   *American Government: Freedom and Power,* 3rd ed. New York: W. W. Norton.

Luhmann, Niklas
1982   *The Differentiation of Society.* New York: Columbia University Press.

Mack, Raymond, and Calvin P. Bradford
1979   *Transforming America,* 2nd ed. New York: Random House.

Makhijani, A. B., and A. J. Lichtenberg
1972   "Energy and Well Being." *Environment,* 14:10–18.

Malbin, Michael
1982   *Money and Politics in the United States.* Chatham, NJ: Chatham House.

Mamdani, Mahmood
1972   *The Myth of Population Control.* London: Reeves and Turner.

Mannheim, Karl
1940   *Man and Society in an Age of Reconstruction.* New York: Harcourt Brace.

1950   *Freedom, Power and Democratic Planning.* New York: Oxford University Press.

Mapper, Joseph
1960   *The Effects of Mass Communication.* New York: The Free Press.

Marcuse, Herbert
1964   *One Dimensional Man.* Boston MA: Beacon Press.

Markoff, John
1996   *Waves of Democracy: Social Movements and Political Change.* Thousand Oaks, CA: Pine Forge Press.

Marks, Gary, and Doug McAdam
1996   "Social Movements and the Changing Structure of Political Opportunity in the European Union." *Journal of West European Politics,* 19:249–278.

Marshall, T. H.
1950/
1964   *Citizenship, Class, and Social Development.* Garden City, New York: Doubleday.

Marsden, Peter V., and Nan Lin, eds.
1983   *Social Structure and Network Analysis.* Beverly Hills, CA: Sage.

Marwell, Gerald
1994   Cited in the *Omaha World Herald,* "Is America's Anger in the 1990s Rooted in the Turbulent 1960s?" (May 14, 1995):6-A.

Marx, Karl
1920   *The Poverty of Philosophy.* H. Quelch (trans.). Chicago: Charles H. Kerr.

Marx, Karl, and Fredrick Engles
   1968   *Karl Marx and Frederick Engles: Selected Works in One Volume.* New York: International Publishers.

Maslow, Abraham H.
   1971   *The Farther Reaches of Human Nature.* New York: Viking Press.

Massey, D.
   1990   "American Apartheid: Segregation and the Making of the American Underclass," *American Journal of Sociology,* 96:329–357.

Massey, Douglas S.
   1996   "The Age of Extremes: Concentrated Affluence and Poverty in the Twenty-First Century. *Demography,* 33:395–412.

Matras, Judah
   1975   *Social Inequality, Stratification, and Mobility.* Englewood Cliffs, NJ: Prentice-Hall.

Mayer, Susan
   1997   *What Money Can't Buy: Family Income and Children's Life Chances.* Cambridge, MA: Harvard University Press.

Mazur, Allan
   1991   *Global Social Problems.* Englewood Cliffs, NJ: Prentice-Hall.

McAdam, Doug
   1982   *Political Process and the Development of Black Insurgency, 1930–1970.* Chicago: University of Chicago Press.

   1986   "Recruitment to High Risk Activism: The Case of Freedom Summer." *American Journal of Sociology,* 92:64–90.

McAdam, Doug, John D. McCarthy, and Mayer N. Zald
   1988   "Social Movements," in Neil Smelser (ed.), *Handbook of Sociology.* Beverly Hills, CA: Sage.

   1996   *Comparative Perspectives on Social Movements: Political Opportunities, Mobilizing Structures, and Cultural Framings.* Cambridge, UK: Cambridge University Press.

McCarthy John D., and Mayer N. Zald
   1973   *The Trends of Social Movements in America: Professionalization and Resource Mobilization.* Morristown, NJ: General Learning Press.

McCormack, Thelma Herman
   1951   "The Motivation of Radicals," *American Journal of Sociology,* 56:17–24.

McFalls, Joseph A., Jr.
   1991   "Population: A Lively Introduction," *Population Bulletin,* 46,2 (Oct.). Washington, DC: Population Reference Bureau.

McKibben, Bill
   1995   "An Explosion of Green." *Atlantic Monthly,* 275, 4 (Apr.):61–83.

McLaughlin, Barry
   1969   *Studies in Social Movements: A Social Psychological Perspective.* New York: The Free Press.

McMichael, Phillip
   1996   *Development and Social Change: A Global Perspective.* Thousand Oaks, CA: Pine Forge Press.

McPhail, Clark
   1971   "Civil Disorder Participation: A Critical Examination of Recent Research," *American Sociological Review,* 36,6:1058–1072.

Mead, George Herbert
   1934   *Mind, Self, and Society: From the Standpoint of a Social Behaviorist.* Chicago: University of Chicago Press.

Meadows, Donella H., Dennis L. Meadows, and Jorgen Randers
   1992   *Beyond the Limits: Confronting Global Collapse, Envisioning a Sustainable Future.* Post Mills, VT: Chelsea Green.

Meadows, Donella H., Dennis L. Meadows, Jorgen Randers, and William W. Behrens HI
   1972   *The Limits to Growth: A Report for the Club of Rome's Project on the Predicament of Mankind.* New York: New American Library.

Melucci, Alberto
   1980   "The New Social Movements: A Theoretical Approach." *Social Science Information,* 19:199–226.

   1996   *Challenging Codes: Collective Action in the Information Age.* Cambridge, UK: Cambridge University Press.

Menzel, Herbert, and Elihu Katz
   1955   "Social Relations and Innovation in the Medical Profession: The Epidemiology of A New Drug." *Public Opinion Quarterly,* 19:337–352.

Menzel, Herbert, James Coleman, and Elihu Katz
   1957   "The Diffusion of Innovation among Physicians." *Sociometry,* 20:253–270.

Mesarovic, Mihajlo, and Eduard Pestel
   1974   *Mankind at the Turning Point: The Second Report to the Club of Rome.* New York: New American Library.

Mesenbourg, Thomas L.
   2002   "Measuring Electronic Business: Definitions, Underlying Concepts, and Measurement Plans." U.S. Bureau of the Census www.census.gov/epcd/www/ebusiness.htm

Miller, G. Taylor
   1992   *Living in the Environment,* 7th ed. Belmont, CA: Wadsworth.

Miller, Tom
   1996   Cited in "Lower Surfing Figures May Cool Internet Fever," *Omaha World Herald* (Jan. 12):1.

Mills, C. Wright
   1959   *The Sociological Imagination.* New York: Grove Press.

Moore, Barrington
   1966   *The Social Origins of Dictatorship and Democracy: Lord and Peasant in the Making of the Modern World.* Boston, MA: Beacon.

Moore, Wilbert E.
   1974   *Social Change,* 2nd ed. Englewood Cliffs, NJ: Prentice-Hall.

Morris, Aldon
   1984   *The Origins of the Civil Rights Movement.* New York: The Free Press.

Morse, Nancy C., and Everett Rierner
   1956   "The Experimental Change in a Major Organizational Variable." *Journal of Abnormal and Social Psychology,* 52:120–129.

Mott, Paul E.
   1968   *The Organization of Society.* Englewood Cliffs, NJ: Prentice-Hall.

Muller, Edward N.
   1980   "The Psychology of Political Protest and Violence." In Ted Robert Gurr (ed.), *Handbook of Political Conflict.* New York: Free Press.

Murphy, John W.
   1989   *Postmodern Social Analysis and Criticism.* Westport, CT: Greenwood Press.

Myers, Dowell
   1995   Cited in "Study Finds Immigrants do Join America Dream," *Omaha World Herald* (Nov 3):1–10.

Naisbett, John
   1994   *Global Paradox.* New York: Avon Books.

National Academy of Sciences
   1969   *Resources and Man.* San Francisco: Freeman, Cooper.

National Opinion Research Center
   2000   *General Social Survey, 2000.* Roper Center for Public Opinion Research, University of Connecticut.

National Public Radio
   1996   "Children and Poverty," *Morning Edition* (June 11).

The New York Times
   1996a   "Many Agree Generations Aren't at War," cited in the *Omaha World Herald,* (Feb. 25):12-A.

   1996b   "The Downsizing of America" (Mar. 3):A1, A26.

   1996c   "The Company as Family, No More" (Mar. 4):A1.

Newhouse News Service
1986   "The Year Is 2050, Earth Warmer, More Dangerous." *Omaha World Herald* (Nov. 23): 1K.

1986b   "Stormier Planet Seen as Ocean Temps Rise." *Omaha World Herald* (Nov. 23): 1K.

1990   "Fewer Jobs Expected to Offer Pensions." *Omaha World Herald* (Jan. 28): G1.

Newman, David M.
1996   *Sociology: Exploring the Architecture of Everyday Life.* Thousand Oaks, CA: Pine Force Press.

Nisbet, Robert A.
1966   *The Sociological Tradition.* New York: Basic Books.

1969   *Social Change and History.* London: Oxford University Press.

Norse, David
1992   "A New Strategy for Feeding a Crowded Planet." *Environment,* 35, 5:6–39.

Nunn, Clyde Z., Harry J. Crockett, and J. Allen Williams
1978   *Tolerance for Non-conformity.* San Francisco: Jossey-Bass.

Oberschall, Anthony
1973   *Social Conflict and Social Movements.* Englewood Cliffs, NJ: Prentice-Hall.

O'Connor, James
1973   *The Fiscal Crisis of the State.* New York: St. Martin's Press.

O'Donnell, Guillermo, and Philippe Schmitter
1986   "Political Life after Authoritarian Rule: Tentative Conclusions about Uncertain Transitions," in Guillermo O'Donnell, Phillipe C. Schmitter, and Laurence Whitehead (eds.), *Transitions from Authoritarian Rule: Latin America and Southern Europe,* vol. 4. Baltimore, MD: The Johns Hopkins University Press.

OECD (Organization for Economic Cooperation and Development)
1982   *Economic Outlook.* Paris (Dec.).

Ogburn, William F.
1922   *Social Change with Respect to Culture and Original Nature.* New York: B. W. Huebsch.

1938   *Social Change.* New York: Viking Press.

Olsen, Douglas E.
1995   "The Top 10 Technologies for the Next 10 Years." *The Futurist,* 29,1 (Sept.-Oct.):9–17.

Olsen, Marvin E.
1978   *The Process of Social Organization,* 2nd ed. New York: Holt, Rinehart, and Winston.

1991   *Societal Dynamics: Exploring Macrosociology.* Englewood Cliffs, NJ: Prentice Hall.

Olsen, Marvin E., Dora Lodwick, and Riley Dunlap
1992   *Viewing the World Ecologically.* Boulder, CO: Westview Press.

Olson, Mancur
1965   *The Logic of Collective Action.* Cambridge, MA: Harvard University Press.

Oltmans, Willem L. (ed.)
1974   *On Growth: The Crisis of Exploding Population and Resource Depletion.* New York: G. P. Putnam's Sons.

Oppenheimer, Martin
1969   *The Urban Guerrilla.* Chicago: Quadrangle Press.

Oran, P. A.
1988   "Building an Agroecological Framework." *Environment,* 14.

Orum, Anthony
1972   *Black Students in Protest.* Washington, DC: American Sociological Association.

Osborn, R.
1948   *Our Plundered Planet.* Boston: Little Brown.

Page, Ann L., and Donald A. Clelland
1978   "The Kanawha County Textbook Controversy: A Study of the Politics of Life Style Concern." *Social Forces,* 57,1:265–281.

Paige, J. M.
1975   *Agrarian Revolution: Social Movements and Export Agriculture in the Underdeveloped World.* New York: The Free Press.

Palley, Thomas I.
1996 The Forces Making for an Economic Collapse." *Atlantic Monthly,* 27,1 (July):43–59.

Palmore, Erdman
1969 "Predicting Longevity: A Follow-up Controlling for Age." *The Gerontologist,* 9 (Winter): 247–250.

Parrillo, Vincent N.
1996 *Diversity in America.* Thousand Oaks, CA: Pine Forge Press.

Parsons, Talcott
1951 *The Social System.* Glencoe, IL: The Free Press.

1964 "Evolutionary Universals in Society." *American Sociological Review,* 29:339–357.

1966 *Societies.* Englewood Cliffs, NJ: Prentice-Hall.

Parsons, Talcott, and Robert F. Bales
1955 *Family Socialization and Interaction Process.* Glencoe, IL: The Free Press.

Patterson, Orlando
1991 *Freedom in the Making of Western Culture.* New York: Basic Books.

Pavalko, Ronald M.
1988 *Sociology of Occupations and Professions.* Itasca, IL: F. E. Peacock.

Payer, Cheryl
1975 *The Debt Trap: The IMF and the Third World.* New York: Monthly Review Press.

Pedriana, Nicholas
1999 "The Historical Foundations of Affirmative Action, 1961–1971," *Research in Social Stratification and Mobility,* 17:36–81.

Pelto, Pertti J., and Ludger Muller-Willie
1972 "Snowmobiles: Technological Revolution in the Arctic," in H. Russell Bernard and Pertti J. Pelto (eds.), *Technology and Cultural Change.* New York: Macmillan.

Penner, Rudolph G., Isabel V. Sawhill, and Timothy Taylor
2000 *Updating America's Social Contract: Economic Growth and Opportunity in the New Century.* New York: W. W. Norton.

Perrow, Charles
1979 "Three Mile Island: A Normal Accident." Unpublished manuscript, cited in Michael S. Bassis and Richard S. Gelles, *Social Problems* (New York: Harcourt Brace and Jovanovich, 1982), p. 103.

Peters, Ted
1988 "Discerning the Spirits of the New Age." *Christian Century* (Aug. 31–Sept. 7):764–765.

Pettee, George S.
1938 *The Process of Revolution.* New York: Harper and Row.

Pettigrew, Thomas R.
1964 *A Profile of the Negro American.* Princeton, NJ: Van Nostrand.

Phillips, David J.
1996 "Defending Territorial Space." *The Information Society,* 12,1 (Jan.–Mar. 1966). http://www.ics.uci.edu/-kiing/tis.html

Phillips, Kevin
1982 *Post-Conservative America: People, Politics, and Ideology in a Time of Crisis.* New York: Random House.

1990 *The Politics of Rich and Poor: Wealth and the American Electorate in the Reagan Aftermath.* New York: Random House.

1993 *Boiling Point: Republicans, Democrats, and the Decline of Middle Class Prosperity.* New York: Random House.

1995 *Arrogant Capital: Washington, Wall Street, and the Frustration of American Politics.* Boston: Little Brown.

Phol, Frederick
1981 "Science Fiction and Science: A Sometimes Synergy." *National Forum,* 61, 3 (Summer):6–7.

Pion, Georgine M., and Mark W. Lipsey
1981 "Public Attitudes Toward Science and Technology: What Have the Surveys Told Us?" *Public Opinion Quarterly,* 45:303–316.

Pirages, Dennis
 1984 "An Ecological Approach," in Susan Strange (ed.), *Paths to International Political Economy,* pp. 53–69. London: George Allen and Unwin.

Platt, Anne E.
 1996 "World Fish Harvest Hits New High." *Vital Signs: The Trends That Are Shaping Our Future.* New York: W. W. Norton.

Popenoe, David
 1996 *Life without Father: Compelling New Evidence that Fatherhood and Marriage Are Indespensible for the Good of Children and Society.* New York: Martin Kessler Books.

Pornper, Gerald
 1984 "Party Politics." *Society,* 21, 6:61–68.

 1984b "The Decline of the Party in American Elections." *Political Science Quarterly,* 92:21–42.

Postel, Sandra
 1992 "Water Scarcity." *Environmental Science and Technology,* 26,12:2332–2333.

 1994 *Carrying Capacity: Earth's Bottom Line,* in Lester Brown et al. (eds.), *The State of the World,* pp. 3–21. New York: W. W. Norton.

Prechel, Harland
 2000 *Business and the State: Historical Transitions and Corporate Transformation, 1880s–1990s.* Albany, NY: SUNY Press.

Przeworski, Adam
 1991 "The 'East' Becomes the 'South'? The 'Autumn of the People' and the Future of Eastern Europe." *Political Science and Politics,* 24, I (Mar.):20–24.

 1994 *Democracy and the Market: Political and Economic Reforms in Eastern Europe and Latin America.* Cambridge, UK: Cambridge University Press.

Puddington, Arch
 1995 "What to do about Affirmative Action." *Commentary* (June).

Putnam, Robert D.
 2000 *Bowling Alone: The Collapse and Revival of American Community.* New York: Simon and Schuster.

Reich, Robert B.
 1991 *The Work of Nations: Preparing Ourselves for 21st Century Capitalism.* New York: Knopf.

Reichstul, Henri-Philippe, and Lidia Goldenstein
 1980 "Do Complexo Cafeciro a Industgrializacao." *Gazeta Mercantil,* Edicao Especial (19 Jan.).

Reiss, Ira L.
 1980 *Family Systems in America,* 3rd ed. New York: Holt, Rinehart and Winston.

Renner, Michael
 1996 *Fighting for Survival: Environmental Decline, Social Conflict, and the New Age of Insecurity.* New York: W. W. Norton.

Reynolds, Lloyd G.
 1983 "The Spread of Economic Growth to the Third World: 1850–1980." *Journal of Economic Literature,* 21 (Sept.):941–980.

Riesman, David
 1960 *The Lonely Crowd: A Study of the Changing American Character.* New Haven, CT: Yale University Press.

Rifkin, Jeremy
 1995 *The End of Work: The Decline of the Global Labor Force and the Dawn of the Post-Market Era.* New York: Putnam.

Rigby, T. H.
 1990 *The Changing Soviet System.* Brookfield, VT: Edward Elgar.

Rigney, Bernice
 1986 Personal communication.

Riley, Matilda W.
 1985 "Age Strata and Social Systems." In R. H. Binstock and E. Sharas (eds.), *Handbook of Aging and the Social Sciences,* 2nd ed., pp. 31–61. New York: Van Nostrand.

Ritzer, George E.
1983   *Sociological Theory.* New York: Random House.
1988   *Contemporary Sociological Theory,* 2nd ed. New York: Random House.
1993   *The McDonaldization of Society.* Newbury Park, CA: Pine Forge Press.
2000   *The McDonaldization of Society,* Millenium Edition. Thousand Oaks, CA: Pine Forge Press.

Robbins, Thomas, and Dick Anthony
1990   "Change and Conflict in American Religions," in Thomas Robbins and Dick Anthony, (eds.), *In Gods We Trust: New Patterns of Religious Pluralism in America,* 2nd ed. New Brunswick, NJ: Transaction Books.

Rodes, Robert I.
1970   *Imperialism and Underdevelopment: A Reader.* New York: Monthly Review Press.

Rogers, Everett M.
1962   *Diffusion of Innovations.* New York: The Free Press.

Rogers, Everett M., and Lawrence D. Kinkaid
1981   *Communication Networks.* New York: The Free Press.

Rogers, Everett M., and Floyd F. Shoemaker
1971   *Communication of Innovations: A Cross-Cultural Approach.* New York: The Free Press.

Rogers, Everett M.
1973   "What Are the Opportunities and Limitations in Linking Research with Use? Paper presented at the International Conference on Making Population/Family Research Useful, Honolulu, HI.

Rogers, Roy H.
1973   *Family Interaction and Transaction.* Englewood Cliffs, NJ: Prentice-Hall.

Roof, Wade Clark and William McKinney
1987   *American Mainline Religion: Its Changing Shape and Future.* New Brunswick, NJ: Rutgers University Press.

Rosenfeld, R., and A. L. Kallenberg
1990   "Cross-National Comparison of the Gender Gap in Income." *American Journal of Sociology,* 96:69–106.

Rosenthal, Donald B., and Robert L. Crain
1968   "Executive Leadership and Community Innovation: The Fluoridation Experience." *Urban Affairs Quarterly,* 1:39–57.

Ross, Catherine E., and John Mirowsky
1990   "Women, Work, and Family: Changing Gender Roles and Psychological Well-Being," in Maureen T. Hallinan, David M. Klein, and Jennifer Glass (eds.), *Change in Societal Institutions.* New York: Plenum Press.

Ross, Catherine E., John Mirowsky, and Joan Huber
1983   "Dividing Work, Sharing Work, and In-between: Marriage Patterns and Depression." *American Sociological Review,* 48,6:809–823.

Rostow, W. W.
1962   *The Process of Economic Growth.* New York: W. W. Norton.

Rothman, Jack
1974   *Planning and Organizing for Social Change: Action Principles from Social Science Research.* New York: The Free Press.

Rothman, Barbara Katz
1991   "Symbolic Interactionism," in Henry Etzkowitz and Ronald M. Glassman (eds.), *The Renaissance of Sociology Theory: Classical and Contemporary.* Itasca, IL: RE. Peacock.

Rozman, Gilbert
1992   "The Connection between Political and Economic Reform in Communist Regimes," in Gilbert Rozman, Seizaburo Sato, and Gerald Segal (eds.), *Dismantling Communism: Common Causes and Regional Variations.* Baltimore, MD: Johns Hopkins University Press.

Rubin, Beth
1996   *Shifts in the Social Contract.* Thousand Oaks, CA: Pine Forge Press.

Ruckelshaus, William D.
1990   "Toward a Sustainable World," in Editors of Scientific American, *Managing the Planet Earth: Readings from Scientific American,* pp. 126–136. New York: W. H. Freeman.

Rude, George
  1964   *The Crowd in History: A Study of Popular Disturbances in France and England 1730–1848.*
          New York: Wiley.

Ryan, Bryce
  1969   *Social and Cultural Change.* New York: Ronald Press.

Ryder, Norman
  1965   "The Cohort as a Concept in the Study of Social Change." *American Sociological Review,* 30,
          6:834–861.

Sanderson, Stephen K.
  1999   *Macrosociology.* New York: Longman.

Sarnoff, D.
  1956   *The Fabulous Future.* New York: Dutton.

Sachs, Aaron
  1995   "Population Growth Steady," in Lester Brown et al. (eds.), *Vital Signs 1995: The Trends That
          Are Shaping Our Future.* New York: W. W. Norton.
  1996   "Population Increase Slightly Down," in Lester Brown et al. (eds.), *Vital Signs 1996: The
          Trends That Are Shaping Our Future.* New York: W. W. Norton.

Sample, Tex
  1996   "Generation X: Media and the Church." Speech, St. Paul United Methodist Church, Omaha,
          Nebraska (Jan. 20).

Sassen, Saskia
  1994   *Cities in a World Economy.* Thousand Oaks, CA: Pine Forge Press.

Schaff, A.
  1970   "The Marxist Theory of Social Development," in Shmuel Noah Eisendtadt (ed.), *Readings in
          Social Evolution and Development.* Oxford: Pergamon Press.

Schattsneider, E. E.
  1960   *The Semi-Sovereign People.* New York: Holt, Rinehart and Winston.

Schlesinger, Arthur M.
  1986   *The Cycles of American History.* Boston: Houghton Mifflin.

Schnaiberg, Allan
  1980   *The Environment: From Surplus to Scarcity.* New York: Oxford University Press.

Schneider, Louis
  1976   *Classical Theories of Social Change.* Morristown, NJ: General Learning Press.

Schon, Donald
  1971   *Beyond the Stable State.* New York: W. W. Norton.

Schor, Juliet
  1993   *The Overworked American: The Unexpected Decline of Leisure.* New York: Basic Books.
  1998   *The Overspent American: Upscaling, Downshifting, and the American Consumer.* New York:
          Basic Books.

Schumacher, E. F.
  1973   *Small Is Beautiful.* New York: Perennial Library.

Schultz, Ted
  1989   "The New Age: The Need for Myth in an Age of Science." *Skeptical Inquirer,* 13:375–379.

Schutz, Alfred
  1932/
  1967   *The Phenomenology of the Social World.* Evanston, IL: Northwestern University Press.

Schwartz, Michael
  1976   *Radical Protest and Social Structure.* New York: Academic Press.

Scott, W. Richard
  1995   *Institutions and Organizations: Foundations for Organizational Science.* Thousand Oaks,
          CA: Sage.

Seashore, Stanley E., and David G. Bowers
  1963   *Changing the Structure and Functioning of an Organization: Report of a Field Experiment.*
          Monograph 33, University of Michigan Institute for Social Research, Survey Research Cen-
          ter, Ann Arbor, MI.

Sen, Amartya Kuman
1991   *Poverty and Famines.* New York: Oxford University Press.

Shapiro, Andrew L.
1992   *We're Number One.* New York: Vintage Books.

Sharp, Lauriston
1952   "Steel Axes for Stone Age Australians." *Human Organization,* 11, 1.

Sheak, Robert J.
1994   "The Chronic Jobs Problems in the United States: No End in Sight," *Free Inquiry in Creative Sociology,* 22, 1 (May):23–32.

Sheak, Robert, and David Dabelko
1990   "The Employment Picture Is Not So Rosy." *Free Inquiry in Creative Sociology.* 18, 2: 115–120.

Shepard, Jon M.
1984   *Sociology,* 2nd ed. St. Paul, MN: West.

Shibutani, Tamotsu
1955   "Reference Groups as Perspectives." *American Journal of Sociology,* 60:562–569. Chicago: University of Chicago Press.

1961   *Society and Personality: An Interactionist Approach to Social Psychology.* Englewood Cliffs, NJ: Prentice-Hall.

Shupe, Anson, and William Stacey
1982   *Born Again Politics and the Moral Majority: What Social Surveys Really Show.* New York: Edwin Mellon.

Sidel, Ruth
1986   *Women and Children Last.* New York: Penguin.

1989   *On Her Own: Growing Up in the Shadow of the American Dream.* New York: Penguin.

Silvestri, George T., and John M. Lukasiewicz
1985   "Occupational Employment Projections: The 1984–1995 Outlook," *Monthly Labor Review,* 108 (Nov.):42–57.

Simes, Dimitri
1991   "Russia Reborn," *Foreign Policy,* 85, (Winter 1991–92):41–62.

Simmel, George
1968   "The Conflict in Modern Culture," in Peter Etzkhorn (ed.), *George Simmel: The Conflict in Modern Culture and Other Essays.* New York: Teachers College, Columbia University.

Simon, Julian
1981   *The Ultimate Resource.* Princeton, NJ: Princeton University Press.

1995   *The State of Humanity.* Oxford, UK: Blackwell.

2000   *The Great Breakthrough and Its Causes.* Ann Arbor, MI: University of Michigan Press.

Simon, Julian, and Herman Kahn (eds.)
1984   *The Resourceful Earth: A Response to Global 2000.* New York: Oxford University Press.

Simpson, John H.
1983   "Moral Issues and Status Politics," in Robert C. Liebman and Robert Wuthnow (eds.), *The New Christian Right.* New York: Aldine.

Sjoberg, Gideon
1960   *Pre-Industrial City: Past and Present.* New York: The Free Press.

1963   "The Rise and Fall of Cities: A Theoretical Perspective." *International Journal of Comparative Sociology,* no. 4.

Skaggs, Bruce C., and Kevin T. Leicht
1997   "Management Paradigm Change in the United States: A Professional Autonomy Perspective." Unpublished ms, Department of Sociology, University of Iowa, Iowa City, IA.

Skocpol, Theda
1976   "France, Russia, China: A Structural Analysis of Social Revolutions," *Comparative Studies in Society and History,* 18:175–209.

1979   *States and Social Revolutions: A Comparative Analysis of France, Russia and China.* New York: Cambridge University Press.

1994   *Social Revolutions in the Modern World.* Cambridge, UK: Cambridge University Press.

Skolnick, Arlene S.
1991   *Embattled Paradise: The American Family in an Age of Uncertainty.* New York: Basic Books.

Skolnick, Arlene S., and Jerome Skolnick
1977   *Family in Transition: Rethinking Marriage, Sexuality, Child Rearing, and Family Organiza-tion,* 2nd ed. Glenview, IL: Scott Foresman.

Slater, Phillip
1976   *The Pursuit of Loneliness.* Boston, MA: Beacon Press.

Smelser, Neil
1962   *Theory of Collective Behavior.* New York: The Free Press.

1966   "The Modernization of Social Relations," in Myron Wiener (ed.), *Modernization: The Dy-namics of Growth,* pp. 110–121. New York: Basic Books.

Smith, Hedrick
1990   *The New Russians.* New York: Random House.

Smith, James P., and Finis Welch
1978   *Race Differences in Earnings: A Survey and New Evidence.* Santa Monica, CA: Rand Cor-poration.

Snow, David, and Robert Benford
1988   "Ideology, Frame Resonance, and Participant Mobilization." In Bert Klandermans, Hanspeter Kriesi, and Sidney Tarrow (eds.), *From Structure to Action: Comparing Social Movement Research across Cultures,* pp. 197–217. Greenwich, CT: JAI Press.

Snow, David, and Susan Marshall
1984   "Cultural Imperialism, Social Movements, and the Islamic Revival," in Louis Kriesberg (ed.), *Social Movements, Conflict, and Change,* pp. 131–152. Greenwich, CT: JAI Press.

Snow, David, and Burke Rocheford
1983   "Structural Availability, the Alignment Process and Movement Recruitment." Paper pre-sented at the annual meeting of the American Sociological Association, Detroit.

Snow, David, E. Burke Rochford, Steven F. Worden, and Robert D. Benford
1986   "Frame Alignment Processes, Micro-Mobilization, and Movement Participation." *American Sociological Review* 51:464–481.

Snow, David, Louis Zurcher, and Sheldon Ekland-Olson
1980   "Social Networks and Social Movements: A Microstructural Approach to Differential Re-cruitment," *American Sociological Review,* 45:787–801.

Snyder, David Pearce
1996   "The Revolution in the Workplace: What's Happening to our Jobs?" *The Futurist,* 30, 2, (Mar.–Apr.):8–13.

So, Alvin Y.
1990   *Social Change and Development: Modernization, Dependency, and World-System Theories.* Sage Library of Social Research, vol. 178. Newbury Park, CA: Sage.

Sorokin, Pitrim
1937/
1941   *Social and Cultural Dynamics.* New York: American Book.

Southwick, Charles H.
1996   *Global Ecology in Human Perspective.* New York: Oxford University Press.

Spector, Malcolm, and John Kitsuse
1977   *Constructing Social Problems.* Menlo Park, CA: Cummings.

Spengler, Oswald
1932   *The Decline of the West.* New York: Knopf.

Spenner, Kenneth I.
1990   "Skill: Meanings, Methods and Measures." *Work and Occupations* 17:399–421.

Speth, Gustave James
1996   Cited in "U.N. Reports Widening Gap Between World's Rich, Poor." *The New York Times,* cited in *Omaha World Herald,* (July 15):9.

Spindler, Louise S.
1977   *Cultural Change and Modernization.* New York: Holt, Rinehart and Winston.

Stack, Carol
1974 *All Our Kin: Strategies for Survival in a Black Community.* New York: HarperCollins.

Stanley, Harold, and Richard J. Niemi
1995 *Vital Statistics on American Politics,* 5th ed. Washington, DC: Congressional Quarterly Press.

Stark, David, and Laszlo Bruszt
1998 *Postsocialist Pathways: Transforming Politics and Property in East Central Europe.* Cambridge, UK: Cambridge University Press.

Stark, Rodney
1996 *The Rise of Christianity: A Sociologist Reconsiders History.* Princeton, NJ: Princeton University Press.

Steele, Shelby
1990 *The Content of Our Character: A New Vision of Race in America.* New York: HarperCollins.

Stein, Morris I.
1957 "Social and Psychological Factors Affecting the Creativity of Industrial Research Chemists." Unpublished manuscript presented at the Industrial Research Institute, Pittsburg, PA (Oct.).

Stein, Morris I., and Shirley J. Heinze
1960 *Creativity and the Individual.* New York: The Free Press.

Stern, Kenneth S.
1996 *A Force upon the Plain: The American Militia Movement and the Politics of Hate.* New York: Simon and Schuster.

Steward, Julian
1955 "Evolution and Progress," in Alfred Kroeber (ed.), *Anthropology Today.* Chicago: University of Chicago Press.

Stimson, Catharine R.
1990 "New 'Politically Correct' Metaphors Insult History and Our Campuses," *Chronicle of Higher Education* (May 29):A40.

Stockhausen, Gerald, L.
1995-
96 "Our Champagne Glass Economy: Income Distribution in the United States." *Window,* 12, 2: 10–13.

Stokes, Gale
1993 *The Walls Came Tumbling Down: The Collapse of Communism in Eastern Europe.* New York: Oxford University Press.

Stokes, Randall
1975 "Afrikaner Calvinism and Economic Action: The Weberian Thesis in South Africa," *American Journal of Sociology,* 81:62–81.

1984 *Introduction to Sociology.* Dubuque, IA: Woren C. Brown.

Strauss, Anselm L.
1978 *Negotiations: Varieties, Contexts, Processes, and Social Order.* San Francisco, CA: Jossey-Bass.

Straus, Murray A.
1980 "A Sociological Perspective on the Causes of Family Violence." In Maurice R. Green (ed.), *Violence and the Family.* Boulder, CO: Westview.

Straus, Murray A., and Richard Gelles
1986 "Societal Change and Changes in Family Violence from 1975 to 1985." *Journal of Marriage and Family* (Aug.).

Stroh, M, and J. Raloff
1992 "New U.N. Soil Survey: The Dirt on Erosion." *Science News* (Apr. 4):215.

Sturua, Melor
1991 "The Real Coup." *Foreign Policy,* 85 (Winter 1991–92):62–72.

Sullivan, Teresa
1990 "The Decline of Occupations: Redefining the Labor Force." In Maureen T. Hallinan, David M. Klein, and Jennifer Glass (eds.), *Change in Societal Institutions.* New York: Plenum Press.

Sullivan, Teresa A., Elizabeth Warren, and Jay Lawrence Westbrook
2000   *The Fragile Middle Class: Americans in Debt.* New Haven, CT: Yale University Press.
Swidler, Ann
1986   "Culture in Action: Symbols and Strategies." *American Sociological Review,* 51:273–286.
Swift, David W.
1971   *Ideology and Change in the Public Schools.* Columbus OH: Charles E. Merrill.
Sztompka, Piotr
1993   *The Sociology of Social Change.* Cambridge, MA: Blackwell.
Tarrow, Sidney
1991   "Aiming at a Moving Target: Social Science and the Recent Rebellions in Eastern Europe." *Political Science and Politics,* 24, 1: 12–20.
Tausky, Curt
1984   *Work and Society.* Itasca, IL: F. E. Peacock Publishers.
Thio, Alex O.
1971   "A Reconsideration of the Concept of Adopter-Innovator Compatibility in Diffusion Research." *Sociological Quarterly,* 12,1:56–68.
1994   *Sociology: A Brief Introduction,* 2nd ed. New York: HarperCollins.
Thompson, W. Scott (ed.)
1978   *The Third World: Premises of U.S. Policy.* San Francisco: Institute for Contemporary Studies.
Thornton, Arland
1989   "Changing Attitudes toward Family Issues in the United States." *Journal of Marriage and Family,* 51:873–893.
Thurow, Lester
1980   *The Zero Sum Society.* New York: Penguin.
1984   "Building a World-Class Economy." *Society,* 22, 1 (Nov./Dec.):16–29.
1992   *Head to Head: The Coming Economic Battle among Japan, Europe and America.* New York: Morrow.
Tilly, Charles
1978   *From Mobilization to Revolution.* Reading, MA: Addison-Wesley.
1984   *Big Structures, Large Processes, Huge Comparisons.* New York: Russell Sage Foundation.
1990   *Coercion, Capital, and the European States, 990–1990.* Oxford, UK: Blackwell.
Tilly, Chris
1986   "U-Turn on Equality: The Puzzle of Middle Class Decline." *Dollars and Sense,* 116:11–13.
Tinbergen, Jan (coordinator)
1976   *RIO: Reshaping the International Order.* New York: Dutton.
Tismaneanu, Vladimir
1992   *Reinventing Politics: Eastern Europe from Stalin to Havel.* New York: The Free Press.
Toch, Hans
1965   *The Social Psychology of Social Movements.* Indianapolis, IN: Bobbs-Merrill.
Toffler, Alvin
1970   *Future Shock.* New York: Random House.
1972   *The Futurists.* New York: Random House.
1980   *The Third Wave.* New York: Morrow.
Tolbert, Charles, Patrick M. Horan, and E. M. Beck
1980   "The Structure of Economic Segmentation: A Dual Economy Approach." *American Journal of Sociology* 85:1095–1116.
Tonnies, Ferdinand
1887/
1963   *Community and Society* [Gemeinshaft und Gesellshaft]. New York: Harper & Row.
Toynbee, Arnold
1962   *A Study of History.* New York: Oxford University Press.
Trimberger, Ellen Kay
1978   *Revolution from Above: Military Bureaucrats and Development in Japan, Turkey, Egypt, and Peru.* New Brunswick, NJ: Transaction Books.

Tugwell, Franklin
1973 *Search for Alternatives: Public Policy and the Study of the Future.* Cambridge, MA: Winthrop.

Turnbull, Colin M.
1962 *The Lonely African.* New York: Simon and Schuster.

Turner, Jonathan
1981 *The Structure of Social Theory.* Homewood, IL: Dorsey Press.

1982 *The Structure of Sociological Theory.* Homewood, IL: Dorsey Press.

Turner, Jonathan, and Leonard Beeghley
1981 *The Emergence of Sociological Theory.* Homewood: Dorsey Press.

United Nations
1991 *World Population Prospects 1990.* New York: United Nations.

United Nations Development Programme
1992 *Human Development Report.* New York: Oxford University Press.

1996 *Human Development Report.* New York: Oxford University Press.

2000 *Human Development Report.* New York: Oxford University Press.

United Nations, FAO (Food and Agriculture Association) and HASA
1977 *FAO Production Yearbook, 1976.* Rome.

1982 *Potential Population Supporting Capacities of Lands in the Developing World.* Rome: Food and Agriculture Organization.

United Nations Population Division
1987 *The Prospects of World Urbanization.* Population Studies no. 101. New York: United Nations.

U.S. Congressional Joint Economic Committee
1981 "Rx: Modification of U.S. Policies Needed to Encourage R&D." *World of Work Review,* 6, 11 (Nov.):84–85.

U.S. Bureau of Labor Statistics
1994 CPS Unpublished Table No. 16. (March) Bureau of Labor Statistics.

U.S. Department of Commerce, Bureau of the Census
1965 *Statistical Abstract of the United States.* Washington, DC: Government Printing Office.

1970 *Historical Statistics of the United States, Colonial Times to 1970,* Part 1. Washington, DC: Government Printing Office.

1977 *Survey of Current Business.* Washington, DC: Government Printing Office.

1980 *Statistical Abstract of the United States.* Washington, DC: Government Printing Office.

1981 "Concentration Ratios in Manufacturing, 1977," in *Census of Manufacturers.* Washington, DC: Government Printing Office.

1982 "Money Income of Households, Families, and Persons in the United States: 1980." *Current Population Reports.* Washington, DC: Government Printing Office.

1983 *Current Population Report,* Series P-60, no. 137. Washington, DC: Government Printing Office.

1983 *Statistical Abstract of the United States.* Washington, DC: Government Printing Office.

1984 *Statistical Abstract of the United States.* Washington, DC: Government Printing Office.

1985 *Statistical Abstract of the United States.* Washington, DC: Government Printing Office.

1986 *Statistical Abstract of the United States.* Washington, DC: Government Printing Office.

1987 *Statistical Abstract of the United States.* Washington, DC: Government Printing Office.

1987 *Survey of Current Business,* August. Washington, DC: Government Printing Office.

1988 "Households, Families, Marital Status and Living Arrangements: March 1988." *Current Population Reports,* Series P-20, no. 432 (Sept.). Washington, DC: Government Printing Office.

1990 *Statistical Abstract of the United States.* Washington, DC: Government Printing Office.

1994 *Statistical Abstract of the United States.* Washington, DC: Government Printing Office.

1999a *Statistical Abstract of the United States.* Washington, DC: Government Printing Office.

1999b *Annual Survey of Manufactures.* Washington, DC: Government Printing Office.

U.S. Department of Commerce, Bureau of Economic Analysis
    1990   *Foreign Direct Investment by U.S. Companies.* Washington, DC: Government Printing Office.

U.S. Department of Commerce, Population Reference Bureau
    1985   *World Population Data Sheet,* cited in "Population Mounts; Concerns Also Grow," *Omaha World Herald* (Aug. 7, 1986).

Urban Institute
    1994   Cited in "Report Says Immigrants Create Jobs," *Omaha World Herald* (May 25):14.

Useem, Michael
    1975   *Protest Movements in America.* Indianapolis, IN: Bobbs-Merrill.

Useem, Bert
    1980   "Solidarity Model, Breakdown Model, and the Boston Anti-busing Movement." *American Sociological Review* 45:357–369.

Usher, Abbott P.
    1954   *A History of Mechanical Inventions.* Cambridge, MA: Harvard University Press.

Vago, Steven
    1980   *Social Change.* New York: Holt, Rinehart and Winston.

Valdivieso, Rafael, and Carey Davis
    1988   *U.S. Hispanics: Challenging Issues for the 1990s.* Washington, DC: Population Reference Bureau.

Valelly, Richard
    1990   "Vanishing Voters." *The American Prospect,* 1 (Spring):140–150.

VanderLoo, Hans, Erik Snel, and Bart Van Steenbergen
    1984   *Een Wenkend Perspectief? Nieuwe Social Bewegingen ern Culturele Veranderingen.* Arnersfoort, Netherlands: De Horstink.

Van Rossem, Ronan
    1996   "The World System Paradigm as General Theory of Development: A Cross-National Test," *American Sociological Review,* 61 (June):508–527.

Vitousek, Peter M., et al.
    1986   "Human Appropriation of the Products of Photosynthesis." *BioScience,* 36:368.

Voght, W.
    1948   *Road to Survival.* New York: William Sloane Associates.

Wade, Alice
    1986   "Social Security Area Population Projections, 1986." Actuarial Study no. 97. Office of the Actuary, Social Security Administration (SSA Pub. No. 11 11544).

Wallace, Ruth A., and Alison Wolf
    1995   *Contemporary Sociological Theory: Continuing the Classical Tradition,* 4th ed. Englewood Cliffs, NJ: Prentice-Hall.

Wallach, Michael A., and Nathan Kogan
    1965   "Creativity and Intelligence in Children's Thinking." *Trans-Action* (Jan./Feb.):38–43.

Wallerstein, Immanuel
    1974   *The Modern World System.* New York: Academic Press.

Wallerstein, Judith
    1996   "What Makes Marriages Work," Interview with Elaine Corey on *Morning Edition,* National Public Radio (July 3).

Wallis, Roy
    1977   *The Road to Total Freedom.* New York: Columbia University Press.

Walsh, Edward J.
    1981   "Resource Mobilization and Citizen Protest in Communities around Three Mile Island," *Social Problems,* 29:1–21.

Walton, John
    1990   *Sociology and Critical Inquiry: The Work, Tradition, and Purpose,* 2nd ed. Belmont, CA: Wadsworth.

Warren, Ronald
    1976   *Social Change and Human Purpose: Toward Understanding and Action.* Chicago: Rand McNally.

Washington Spectator
1991 "A Look at Fuel Supply and Cost," *Washington Spectator,* 17, 22 (Dec.).

Wattenberg, Ben J.
1976 *The Real America.* New York: Capricorn.

1987 *The Birth Dearth.* New York: Paros Books.

Weber, Max
1905/
1958 *The Protestant Ethic and the Spirit of Capitalism.* New York: Scribners.

1921 *Economy and Society.* Totowa, NJ: Bedminister Press.

Weeks, John R.
1989 *Population: An Introduction to Concepts and Issues.* Belmont, CA: Wadsworth.

Weinmann, Gabriel
1982 "On the Importance of Marginality: One More Step into the Two-Step Flow of Communication," *American Sociological Review,* 47:764–773.

Weinstein, E. A., and P. Deutschberger
1963 "Some Dimensions of Altercasting," *Sociometry,* 26:454–466.

Weitzman, Lenore
1985 *The Divorce Revolution: Unexpected Social and Economic Consequences for Women and Children in America.* New York: The Free Press.

Welch, Susan, Robert Darcey, and Janet Clark
1994 *Women, Elections, and Representation.* Lincoln, NE: University of Nebraska Press.

White, Leslie
1949 *The Science of Culture.* New York: Farrar and Strauss.

Whyte, William H.
1956 *The Organization Man.* New York: Simon and Schuster.

Wiarda, Howard J.
1993 *Introduction to Comparative Politics: Concepts and Processes.* Belmont, CA: Wadsworth

Wigley, Tom
1995 "A Successful Prediction?" *Nature* (Aug. 10).

Wilken, Elena
1995 "Urbanization Spreading," in Lester Brown, Christopher Flavin, and Hal Kane (eds.), *Vital Signs 1995: Trends That Are Shaping Our Future.* New York: W. W. Norton.

Wilkening, Eugene A.
1960 "Why Farmers Quit Doing Things." *Better Farming Methods,* 32:22–25.

Wilkinson, Doris Y.
1995 "Gender and Social Inequality: The Prevailing Significance of Race," *Daedalus,* 124, 1 (Winter): 167–178.

Williams, Robin
1970 *American Society: A Sociological Interpretation,* 3rd ed. New York: Knopf.

Williamson, Jeffry G.
1996 "Globalization and Inequality Then and Now: The Late 19th and Late 20th Century Compared," *Economic and Business History Abstracts,* NEBR working paper 5491 (Mar.). Cambridge, MA: Harvard University.

Willis, Jim
1995 "The Age of Multimedia and Turbonews," *The Futurist,* 2, 5, (Sept.-Oct.):18–23.

Wilson, E. O.
1990 "Threats to Biodiversity," in *Managing Planet Earth: Readings from Scientific American,* pp. 49–59. New York: W. H. Freeman.

Wilson, John
1973 *Introduction to Social Movements.* New York: Basic Books.

Wilson, Kenneth, and Anthony Orum
1976 "Mobilizing People for Collective Political Action." *Journal of Political and Military Sociology,* 4:187–202.

Wilson, William Julius
    1987   *The Truly Disadvantaged: The Inner City, the Underclass, and Public Policy.* Chicago, IL:
            University of Chicago Press.
    1996   *When Work Disappears: The New World of the Urban Poor.* New York: Knopf.

Wirth, Louis
    1957   "Urbanism as a Way of Life," in Paul K. Hatt and Ira Reiss (eds.), Cities and Society. New
            York: Free Press.

Wittfogel, Karl
    1957   *Oriental Despotism.* New Haven: Yale University Press.

Wood, James L., and Maurice Jackson
    1982   *Social Movements: Development, Participation, and Dynamics.* Belmont, CA: Wadsworth.

Wood, James L.
    1975   *New Left Ideology: Its Dimensions and Development.* Sage Professional Paper in American
            Politics Series, no. 2, pp. 4–44. Beverly Hills, CA: Sage.

World Bank
    1982   *World Development Report.* New York: Oxford.
    1984   *World Development Report.* Washington, DC: The World Bank.
    1986   *World Development Report.* New York: Oxford University Press.
    1991   *World Development Report, 1991: The Challenge of Development, World Development Indi-
            cators.* New York: Oxford University Press.

World Resources Institute
    1993   *Environmental Almanac.* New York: Houghton Mifflin.

Wriggins, W. H.
    1978   "Third World Strategies for Change," in Wriggins and Gunnar Adler-Karlsson (eds.), *Reduc-
            ing Global Inequalities.* Project of the Council on Foreign Relations. New York: McGraw-
            Hill.

Wunsch, James S.
    1977   "Traditional Authorities, Innovation, and Development Policy," *Journal of Developing
            Areas,* 11,3:357–372.
    1991   Personal communication.

Wuthnow, Robert
    1983   "The Political Rebirth of American Evangelicals." In Robert C. Liebman and Robert Wuth-
            now (eds.), *The New Christian Right: Mobilization and Legitimation.* New York: Aldine.
    1994   *Sharing the Journey: Support Groups and America's New Quest for Community.* New York:
            Free Press.

Yankelovich, Daniel
    1981   *New Rules: Searching for Self-Fulfillment in a World Turned Upside Down.* New York: Ran-
            dom House.

Yergin, Daniel, and M. Hillenbrand
    1982   *Global Insecurity: A Strategy for Energy and Economic Renewal.* Boston: Houghton Mifflin.

Yinger, Milton, and Steven Cutler
    1982   "The Moral Majority Viewed Sociologically," *Sociological Focus,* 15, 4:289–306.

Zald, Mayer M. and Roberta Asch
    1966   "Social Movement Organizations: Growth, Decay, and Change," *Social Forces,* 44:327–341.

Zaltman, Gerald
    1973   *Processes and Phenomena of Social Change.* New York: John Wiley.

Zaltman, Gerald, and Robert Duncan
    1977   *Strategies for Planned Change.* New York: John Wiley

Zaltman, Gerald, Robert Duncan, and Jonny Holbeck
    1973   *Innovations and Organizations.* New York: Wiley Interscience.

Zaltman, Gerald, K. LeMasters, and M. Heffring
    1982   *Theory Construction in Marketing: Some Thoughts on Thinking.* New York: John Wiley.

Zimbardo, Phillip, Ebbe Ebbeson, and Christina Maslach
   1977   *Influencing Attitudes and Changing Behavior.* Reading, MA: Addison-Wesley.
Zukin, Sharon, and Paul DiMaggio (eds.)
   1990   *Structures of Capital: The Social Organization of the Economy.* Cambridge, England: Cambridge University Press.
Zurcher, Louis A., and Russell L. Curtis
   1973   "A Comparative Analysis of Propositions Describing Social Movement Organizations," *Sociological Quarterly,* 14, 2:175–188.

Author Index

Subject Index